W9-CAH-668

The symbol ('), as in **moth′er**, is used to mark primary stress; the syllable preceding it is pronounced with greater prominence than the other syllables in the word. The symbol (′), as in **grand′moth′-er**, is used to mark secondary stress; a syllable marked for secondary stress is pronounced with less prominence than one marked (') but with more prominence than those bearing no stress mark at all.

a	act, bat		**o͝o**	book, put
ā	able, cape		**o͞o**	ooze, rule
â	air, dare		**ou**	out, loud
ä	art, calm			
			p	page, stop
b	back, rub		**r**	read, cry
ch	chief, beach		**s**	see, miss
d	do, bed		**sh**	shoe, push
			t	ten, bit
e	ebb, set		**th**	thin, path
ē	equal, bee		**t͡h**	that, other
f	fit, puff		**u**	up, love
g	give, beg		**û**	urge, burn
h	hit, hear			
			v	voice, live
i	if, big		**w**	west, away
ī	ice, bite		**y**	yes, young
			z	zeal, lazy, those
j	just, edge		**zh**	vision, measure
k	kept, make			
l	low, all		**ə**	occurs only in unaccented syllables and indicates the sound of
				a *in* along
m	my, him			e *in* system
n	now, on			i *in* easily
ng	sing, England			o *in* gallop
				u *in* circus
o	box, hot			
ō	over, no			
ô	order, ball			
oi	oil, joy			

Abbreviations Commonly Used in This Book

adj.	adjective	*interj.*	interjection
adv.	adverb	*l.c.*	lower case
art.	article	*n.*	noun
aux.	auxiliary	*pl.*	plural
Brit.	British	*prep.*	preposition
cap.	capital	*pron.*	pronoun
conj.	conjunction	*pt.*	past tense
def.	definition	*sing.*	singular
esp.	especially	*usu.*	usually
fem.	feminine	*v.*	verb

Random House
American
Dictionary

Random House **American** Dictionary

Second Edition

RANDOM HOUSE
NEW YORK

A

a, *adj. or indef. art.* **1.** some. **2.** one. **3.** any.

aard'vark', *n.* African ant-eating mammal.

a·back', *adv.* by surprise.

ab'a·cus, *n.* **1.** calculating device using rows of movable beads. **2.** slab at top of column.

a·baft', *prep. Naut.* **1.** behind. —*adv.* **2.** at the stern.

ab'a·lo'ne (ab'ə lō'nē), *n.* edible mollusk with mother-of-pearl shell.

a·ban'don, *v.* **1.** leave completely; forsake. **2.** give up. —*n.* **3.** freedom from constraint. —**a·ban'doned,** *adj.* —**a·ban'don·ment,** *n.*

a·base', *v.,* abased, abasing. lower; degrade. —**a·base'ment,** *n.*

a·bash', *v.* embarrass or shame.

a·bate', *v.,* abated, abating. lessen or subside. —**a·bate'ment,** *n.*

ab·at·toir' ('-twär'), *n.* slaughterhouse.

ab·bé' (-ā), *n.* abbot; priest.

ab'bess (-ě), *n.* convent head.

ab'bey (-ě), *n.* monastery or convent.

ab'bot, *n.* monastery head.

ab·bre'vi·ate', *v.,* -ated, -ating. shorten. —**ab·bre'vi·a'tion,** *n.*

ABC, *n., pl.* ABC's, ABCs. **1.** alphabet. **2.** (*pl.*) fundamentals.

ab'di·cate', *v.,* -cated, -cating. give up (power, office, etc.). —**ab'di·ca'tion,** *n.*

ab'do·men (-də-), *n.* part of body between thorax and pelvis; belly. —**ab·dom'i·nal** (-dom'-), *adj.*

ab·dom'i·nals, *n. pl.* muscles of abdomen. Also, **abs.**

ab·duct', *v.* kidnap. —**ab·duc'tion,** *n.* —**ab·duc'tor,** *n.*

a·beam', *adv. Naut.* across a ship.

a·bed', *adv.* in bed.

ab·er·ra'tion, *n.* **1.** deviation from normal or right course. **2.** mental lapse.

a·bet', *v.,* abetted, abetting. encourage in wrongdoing. —**a·bet'tor,** **a·bet'ter,** *n.*

a·bey'ance, *n.* temporary inactivity.

ab·hor', *v.,* -horred, -horring. loathe; consider repugnant. —**ab·hor'rence,** *n.* —**ab·hor'rent,** *adj.*

a·bide', *v.,* abode or abided, abiding. **1.** remain; stay. **2.** dwell. **3.** wait for. **4.** agree; conform. **5.** *Informal.* tolerate; bear.

a·bid'ing, *adj.* steadfast; lasting.

a·bil'i·ty, *n., pl.* -ties. **1.** power or talent. **2.** competence.

ab'ject, *adj.* **1.** humiliating. **2.** despicable. —**ab·ject·ly,** *adv.* —**ab·jec'tion,** *n.*

ab·jure', *v.,* -jured, -juring. renounce or forswear. —**ab'ju·ra'tion,** *n.*

ab'la·tive, *adj. Gram.* denoting origin, means, etc.

a·blaze', *adv., adj.* burning; on fire.

a'ble, *adj.,* abler, ablest. **1.** having sufficient power or qualification. **2.** competent. —**a'bly,** *adv.*

ab·lu'tion, *n.* washing, esp. as ritual.

ab'ne·gate', *v.,* -gated, -gating. deny to oneself. —**ab'ne·ga'tion,** *n.*

ab·nor'mal, *adj.* not normal; not usual or typical. —**ab·nor·mal'i·ty,** *n.*

a·board', *adv.* **1.** on a ship, train, etc. —*prep.* **2.** on.

a·bode', *n.* **1.** home. **2.** stay.

a·bol'ish, *v.* end, annul, or make void.

ab'o·li'tion, *n.* **1.** act of abolishing. **2.** end of slavery in the U.S. —**ab'o·li'tion·ist,** *n.*

A'-bomb', *n.* atomic bomb.

a·bom'i·na·ble, *adj.* hateful; loathesome. —**a·bom'i·na·bly,** *adv.*

a·bom'i·nate', *v.,* -nated, -nating. abhor or hate. —**a·bom'i·na'tion,** *n.*

ab'o·rig'i·nal, *adj.* **1.** original; first. —*n.* **2.** aborigine.

ab'o·rig'i·ne· (-rij'ə nē'), *n.* original inhabitant of a land.

a·bort', *v.* **1.** have or cause abortion. **2.** end prematurely. —**a·bor'tive,** *adj.*

a·bor'tion, *n.* expulsion of fetus before it is viable. —**a·bor'tion·ist,** *n.*

a·bound', *v.* be or have plentifully; teem.

a·bout', *prep.* **1.** concerning. **2.** near, in, on, or around. **3.** ready. —*adv.* **4.** approximately. **5.** *Informal.* almost. **6.** on all sides. **7.** oppositely. —*adj.* **8.** active.

a·bout'-face', *n.* reversal of position.

a·bove', *adv.* **1.** higher. **2.** previously. **3.** in or to heaven. —*prep.* **4.** higher or greater than. —*adj.* **5.** foregoing.

a·bove'board', *adv., adj.* honest; fair.

ab'ra·ca·dab'ra, *n.* **1.** word used in magic. **2.** meaningless talk.

a·brade', *v.,* abraded, abrading. wear or scrape off. —**a·bra'sion,** *n.*

a·bra'sive, *adj.* **1.** abrading. **2.** annoying. —*n.* **3.** material or substance used to grind or smooth.

a·breast', *adv., adj.* side by side.

a·bridge', *v.*, **abridged, abridging.** shorten. —**a·bridg'ment**, *n.*

a·broad', *adv., adj.* **1.** out of one's own country. **2.** in circulation.

ab·ro·gate', *v.*, **-gated, -gating.** end, annul, or repeal. —**ab·ro·ga'tion**, *n.*

a·brupt', *adj.* **1.** sudden; unexpected. **2.** steep. —**a·brupt'ly**, *adv.* —**a·brupt'ness**, *n.*

abs, *n.pl.* abdominals.

ab'scess, *n.* infected, pus-filled place.

ab·scond', *v.* depart suddenly and secretly.

ab'sent, *adj.* **1.** not present. **2.** lacking. —*v.* (ab sent'). **3.** keep away. —**ab'sence**, *n.*

ab·sen·tee', *n.* absent person.

ab'sent-mind'ed, *adj.* forgetful or preoccupied.

ab'sinthe, *n.* bitter green liqueur.

ab'so·lute', *adj.* **1.** complete; perfect. **2.** pure. **3.** unrestricted. **4.** despotic. —**ab'so·lute'ly**, *adv.*

absolute pitch, ability to identify exact musical tones.

absolute zero, temperature ($-273.16°$ C or $-459.69°$ F) at which molecular activity ceases.

ab·solve' (-zolv'), *v.*, **-solved, -solving. 1.** release or free. **2.** remit sins of. **3.** forgive. —**ab·so·lu'tion**, *n.*

ab·sorb', *v.* **1.** take in. **2.** occupy completely; fascinate. —**ab·sor'bent**, *adj.*, *n.* —**ab·sorp'tion**, *n.* —**ab·sorp'tive**, *adj.*

ab·stain', *v.* refrain (from). —**ab·sten'tion**, *n.*

ab·ste'mi·ous, *adj.* moderate in eating, drinking, etc.

ab'sti·nence, *n.* forbearance; self-restraint. —**ab'sti·nent**, *adj.*

ab'stract, *adj.* **1.** apart from specific matter. **2.** theoretical. **3.** hard to understand. **4.** (of art) not representing natural objects or forms. —*n.* **5.** summary. **6.** essence. —*v.* (ab strakt'). **7.** remove or steal. **8.** summarize. —**ab·strac'tion**, *n.*

ab·stract'ed, *adj.* preoccupied and absent-minded.

ab·struse', *adj.* hard to understand.

ab·surd', *adj.* ridiculous. —**ab·surd'ly**, *adv.* —**ab·surd'i·ty, ab·surd'ness**, *n.*

a·bun'dance, *n.* plentiful supply. —**a·bun'dant**, *adj.* —**a·bun'dant·ly**, *adv.*

a·buse', *v.*, **abused, abusing.** —*n.* (-byōoz') **1.** use or treat wrongly. —*n.* (-byōos') **2.** wrong use or treatment. **3.** insult. —**a·bu'sive**, *adj.*

a·but', *v.*, **abutted, abutting.** be adjacent to.

a·but'ment, *n.* structural part sustaining pressure.

a·buzz', *adj.* full of activity or talk.

a·bys'mal (-biz'-), *adj.* deep; measureless.

a·byss', *n.* **1.** very deep chasm. **2.** hell. Also, **a·bysm'** (ə biz'əm).

Ab·ys·sin'i·an (ab'ə sin'ē ən), *adj.* **1.** from ancient Ethiopia. —*n.* **2.** type of cat.

a·ca'cia (-kā'shə), *n.* tropical tree or shrub.

ac·a·dem'ic, *adj.* Also, **ac'a·dem'i·cal. 1.** of a school, college, etc. **2.** theoretical. —*n.* **3.** college student or teacher.

a·cad'e·my, *n.*, *pl.* **-mies. 1.** school. **2.** cultural society.

a·can'thus, *n.* Mediterranean plant.

ac·cede', *v.*, **-ceded, -ceding. 1.** consent. **2.** reach.

ac·cel'er·ate', *v.*, **-ated, -ating.** speed up; hasten. —**ac·cel'er·a'tion**, *n.*

ac·cel'er·a'tor, *n.* pedal that controls the speed of a vehicle.

ac'cent, *n.* **1.** emphasis. **2.** characteristic pronunciation. **3.** mark showing stress, etc. —*v.* (ak sent') **4.** emphasize.

ac·cen'tu·ate', *v.*, **-ated, -ating.** stress or emphasize. —**ac·cen'tu·a'tion**, *n.*

ac·cept', *v.* **1.** take or receive. **2.** believe. —**ac·cept'a·ble**, *adj.* —**ac·cept'ed**, *adj.* —**ac·cept'a·bil'i·ty**, *n.* —**ac·cept'a·bly**, *adv.* —**ac·cept'ance**, *n.*

ac'cess, *n.* **1.** right or means of approach. **2.** attack.

ac·ces'si·ble, *adj.* easy to reach or influence. —**ac·ces'si·bil'i·ty**, *n.*

ac·ces'sion, *n.* **1.** attainment of an office, etc. **2.** increase.

ac·ces'so·ry, *n.*, *pl.* **-ries. 1.** something added for convenience, decoration, etc. **2.** one who abets a felony.

ac'ci·dence, *n.* part of grammar dealing with inflection.

ac'ci·dent, *n.* unexpected event, usually unfortunate. —**ac'ci·den'tal**, *adj.* —**ac'ci·den'tal·ly**, *adv.*

ac'ci·dent-prone', *adj.* inclined to have accidents.

ac·claim', *v.* **1.** salute with applause, cheers, etc. —*n.* **2.** applause, cheers, etc. —**ac·cla·ma'tion**, *n.*

ac·cli'mate, *v.*, **-ated, -ating.** accustom to new conditions. Also, **ac·cli'ma·tize'.**

ac·cliv'i·ty, *n.*, *pl.* **-ties.** upward slope.

ac'co·lade', *n.* award, honor, or applause.

ac·com'mo·date', v., -dated, -dat ing. 1. do a favor for. 2. supply. 3. provide with room, food, etc. 4. adjust.

ac·com'mo·dat'ing, adj. helpful; obliging.

ac·com'mo·da'tion, n. 1. act of accommodating. 2. (pl.) space for lodging or travel.

ac·com'pa·ni·ment, n. 1. something added as decoration, etc. 2. subsidiary music for performer.

ac·com'pa·ny, v., -nied, -nying. 1. go or be with. 2. provide musical accompaniment for. —**ac·com'pa·nist**, n.

ac·com'plice, n. partner in crime.

ac·com'plish, v. do or finish.

ac·com'plished, adj. 1. done; finished. 2. expert.

ac·com'plish·ment, n. 1. completion. 2. skill or learning.

ac·cord', v. 1. agree; be in harmony. 2. cause to agree. 3. grant; allow. —n. 4. agreement; harmony. —**ac·cord'ance**, n. —**ac·cord'ant**, adj.

ac·cord'ing·ly, adv. therefore.

according to, 1. in keeping or proportion to. 2. on authority of.

ac·cor'di·on, n. bellowslike musical instrument.

ac·cost', v. approach or confront.

ac·count', n. 1. story; report. 2. explanation. 3. reason. 4. importance. 5. consideration. 6. record of transactions. —v. 7. explain. 8. report. 9. consider.

ac·count'a·ble, adj. 1. responsible. 2. explainable. —**ac·count'a·bly**, adv.

ac·count'ing, n. maintenance of transaction records. —**ac·count'ant**, n. —**ac·count'an·cy**, n.

ac·cred'it, v. 1. attribute. 2. certify with credentials. —**ac·cred'i·ta'tion**, n.

ac·cre'tion (-krē'-), n. increase by growth or addition.

ac·crue', v., -crued, -cruing. be added (to). —**ac·cru'al**, n.

ac·cul'tur·ate', v., -at·ed, -at·ing. adopt cultural traits of another group. —**ac·cul'tur·a'tion**, n.

ac·cu'mu·late', v., -lated, -lating. gather; collect. —**ac·cu'mu·la'tion**, n. —**ac·cu'mu·la·tive**, adj. —**ac·cu'mu·la'tor**, n.

ac'cu·rate, adj. exact; correct. —**ac·cu·rate·ly**, adv. —**ac'cu·ra·cy**, n.

ac·curs'ed, adj. 1. cursed. 2. hateful. Also, **ac·curst'**.

ac·cu'sa·tive, adj. Gram. denoting direct object of a verb.

ac·cuse', v., -cused, -cusing. blame; charge. —**ac·cu·sa'tion**, n. —**ac·cus'er**, n. —**ac·cu'sa·to·ry**, adj.

ac·cus'tom, v. make used to.

ac·cus'tomed, adj. 1. usual; habitual. 2. habituated.

ace, n. 1. playing card with single spot. 2. expert, esp. military pilot. 3. Tennis. serve opponent cannot touch. —v. 4. score ace against. 5. do very well on.

a·cer'bic (ə sûr'bik), adj. 1. sour. 2. sharp or severe. —**a·cer'bi·ty**, n.

a·ce'ta·min'o·phen (ə sē'tə min'ə fən), n. crystalline substance used to reduce pain or fever.

ac'e·tate', n. salt or ester of acetic acid.

a·ce'tic (-sē'-), adj. of or producing vinegar.

ac'e·tone' (as'i tōn'), n. flammable liquid used as solvent.

ac'et'y·lene', n. gas used in welding, etc.

ache, v., ached, aching, n. —v. 1. suffer dull pain. —n. 2. dull pain.

a·chieve', v., achieved, achieving. accomplish; bring about. —**a·chieve'ment**, n.

A·chil'les heel (ə kil'ēz), vulnerable spot.

ach'ro·mat'ic (ak'-), adj. colorless.

ac'id, n. 1. chemical compound containing hydrogen replaceable by a metal to form a salt. 2. sour substance. —adj. 3. of acids. 4. sour or sharp. —**a·cid'i·ty**, n.

ac·i·do'sis, n. poisoning by acids.

acid rain, rain containing chemicals from industrial pollution.

a·cid'u·lous, (-sij'-), adj. sour or sharp.

ack'-ack', n. Slang. anti-aircraft fire.

ac·knowl'edge, v., -edged, -edging. 1. recognize; admit. 2. show appreciation for. —**ac·knowl'edg·ment**, n.

ac'me, n. highest point.

ac'ne, n. skin eruption.

ac'o·lyte', n. altar attendant.

ac'o·nite', n. plant yielding medicine and poison.

a'corn, n. fruit of the oak.

a·cous'tic, adj. of sound or hearing. —**a·cous'ti·cal·ly**, adv.

a·cous'tics, n. 1. science of sound. 2. sound qualities.

ac·quaint', v. make known or familiar.

ac·quaint'ance, n. 1. someone personally known. 2. general knowledge.

ac'qui·esce', v., -esced, -escing. agree or comply. —**ac'qui·es'cence**, n. —**ac'qui·es'cent**, adj.

ac·quire', v., -quired, -quiring. get; obtain. —**ac·quire'ment**, n.

ac'qui·si'tion, n. 1. acquiring. 2. something acquired.

ac·quis'i·tive, *adj.* eager to acquire. —**ac·quis'i·tive·ness,** *n.*

ac·quit', *v.* —quitted, -quitting. 1. free of blame or guilt. 2. behave or conduct. —**ac·quit'tal,** *n.*

a'cre, *n.* unit of land area (1/640 sq. mi. or 43,560 sq. ft.). —**a'cre·age,** *n.*

ac'rid, *adj.* sharp; biting.

ac'ri·mo·ny, *n.* harshness of manner or speech. —**ac·ri·mo'ni·ous,** *adj.*

ac'ro·bat', *n.* performer on trapeze, etc. —**ac·ro·bat'ic,** *adj.*

ac'ro·nym, *n.* word formed from successive initials or groups of letters, as NATO, UNICEF.

a·cross', *prep.* 1. from side to side of. 2. on the other side of. —*adv.* 3. from one side to another.

ac·ryl'ic, *n.* synthetic fiber.

act, *n.* 1. something done. 2. law or decree. 3. part of a play, opera, etc. —*v.* 4. do something. 5. behave. 6. pretend. 7. perform, as on stage.

act'ing, *adj.* substitute.

ac·tin'ism, *n.* action of radiant energy in causing chemical changes. —**ac·tin'ic,** *adj.*

ac·tin'i·um, *n.* radioactive metallic element.

ac'tion, *n.* 1. process or state of being active. 2. something done. 3. behavior. 4. combat. 5. lawsuit.

ac'tion·a·ble, *adj.* providing grounds for a lawsuit.

ac'ti·vate', *v.* -vated, -vating. make active. —**ac·ti·va'tion,** *n.*

ac'tive, *adj.* 1. in action; busy, nimble, or lively. 2. *Gram.* indicating that the subject performs the action of the verb. —**ac'tive·ly,** *adv.* —**ac·tiv'i·ty,** *n.*

ac'tor, *n.* performer in play. —**ac'tress,** *n.fem.*

ac'tu·al (-choo-), *adj.* real. —**ac'tu·al·ly,** *adv.* —**ac'tu·al'i·ty,** *n.*

ac'tu·ar·y, *n., pl.* -aries. calculator of insurance rates etc. —**ac·tu·ar'i·al,** *adj.*

ac'tu·ate', *v.* -ated, -ating. cause to act; effect.

a·cu'i·ty (a kyōō'i tē), *n.* sharpness of perception.

a·cu'men (-kyōō'-), *n.* mental keenness.

ac'u·punc'ture, *n.* Chinese art of healing by inserting needles into the skin.

a·cute', *adj.* 1. sharp; pointed. 2. severe. 3. crucial. 4. keen, clever. 5. high-pitched. 6. (of an angle) less than 90 degrees. —**a·cute'ly,** *adv.* —**a·cute'ness,** *n.*

ad, *n. Informal.* advertisement.

A.D., anno Domini: in the year of our Lord.

ad'age, *n.* proverb.

a·da'gio (a dā' jō), *adj., adv. Music.* slow.

ad'a·mant, *n.* 1. hard substance. —*adj.* 2. Also, **ad'a·man'tine.** unyielding.

Ad'am's ap'ple, projection of thyroid cartilage in front of neck.

a·dapt', *v.* adjust to requirements. —**a·dapt'a·ble,** *adj.* —**a·dapt'a·bil'i·ty,** *n.* —**ad·ap·ta'tion,** *n.*

add, *v.* 1. unite or join. 2. find the sum (of). 3. increase.

ad·den'dum, *n., pl.* -da. something to be added.

ad'der, *n.* small venomous snake.

ad·dict', *n.* 1. person habituated to a drug, etc. —*v.* 2. (a dikt') habituate (to). —**ad·dic'tion,** *n.* —**ad·dic'tive,** *adj.*

ad·di'tion, *n.* 1. adding. 2. anything added. 3. **in addition to,** besides. —**ad·di'tion·al,** *adj.* —**ad·di'tion·al·ly,** *adv.*

ad'di·tive, *n.* added ingredient.

ad'dle, *v.* -dled, -dling. 1. confuse. 2. spoil.

ad·dress', *n.* 1. formal speech. 2. place of residence. 3. manner of speaking. 4. skill. —*v.* 5. speak or write (to). 6. send. 7. apply (oneself). —**ad·dress·ee',** *n.*

ad·duce', *v.* -duced, -ducing. present; cite.

ad'e·noid', *n.* mass of tissue in upper pharynx.

a·dept', *adj.* 1. skilled. —*n.* (ad' ept). 2. expert.

ad'e·quate, *adj.* sufficient; fit. —**ad'e·quate·ly,** *adv.* —**ad'e·qua·cy,** *n.*

ad·here', *v.* -hered, -hering. 1. stick or cling. 2. be faithful or loyal. —**ad·her'ence,** *n.* —**ad·her'ent,** *n., adj.* —**ad·he'sion,** *n.*

ad·he'sive, *adj.* 1. coated with a sticky substance. 2. sticky. —*n.* adhesive substance or material.

ad hoc, for a specified purpose.

ad ho'mi·nem, attacking an opponent personally instead of answering an argument.

a·dieu' (a dyōō', a dōō'), *interj. French.* good-by.

ad in·fi·ni'tum, to infinity; without end.

ad'i·os' (-ōs'), *interj. Spanish.* good-by!

ad'i·pose', *adj.* fatty.

ad·ja'cent, *adj.* near; adjoining.

ad'jec·tive, *n.* word describing a noun. —**ad·jec·ti'val,** *adj.*

ad·join', *v.* be next to.

ad·journ′, v. suspend (meeting) till another time. **—ad·journ′ment,** n.

ad·judge′, v., **-judged, -judging.** 1. decree or decide. 2. award.

ad·ju′di·cate′, v., **-cated, -cating.** decide on as a judge. **—ad·ju′di·ca′-tion,** n.

ad′junct, n. something added.

ad·jure′, v., **-jured, -juring.** request or command, esp. under oath.

ad·just′, v. 1. fit; adapt. 2. regulate. 3. settle. **—ad·just′a·ble,** adj. **—ad·just′er, ad·jus′tor,** n. **—ad·just′-ment,** n.

ad′ju·tant, n. military assistant to commandant.

ad-lib′, v., **-libbed, -libbing.** Informal. improvise.

ad·min·is·ter, v. 1. manage; direct. 2. dispense or give.

ad·min·is·tra′tion, n. 1. management. 2. dispensing. 3. executive officials. **—ad·min′is·tra′tive,** adj.

ad·min′is·tra′tor, n. manager.

ad′mi·ral, n. 1. high-ranking navy officer. 2. brightly colored type of butterfly.

ad′mi·ral·ty, n., pl. **-ties.** navy department.

ad·mire′, v., **-mired, -miring.** regard with pleasure, approval, etc. **—ad·mir′er,** n. **—ad·mi·ra′tion,** n. **—ad′-mi·ra·ble,** adj.

ad·mis′si·ble, adj. allowable.

ad·mis′sion, n. 1. act of admitting. 2. entrance price. 3. confession or acknowledgment.

ad·mit′, v., **-mitted, -mitting.** 1. allow to enter. 2. permit. 3. confess or acknowledge. **—ad·mit′tance,** n.

ad·mit′ted·ly, adv. without evasion or doubt.

ad·mix′ture, n. thing added.

ad·mon′ish, v. 1. warn. 2. reprove. **—ad′mo·ni′tion,** n. **—ad·mon′i·to′ry,** adj.

ad nau′se·am (ad nô′zē əm), to a sickening or disgusting degree.

a·do′, n. activity; fuss.

a·do′be (-bē), n. sun-dried brick.

ad′o·les′cence, n. period between childhood and adulthood. **—ad′o·les′cent,** adj., n.

a·dopt′, v. take or accept as one's own. **—a·dop′tion,** n. **—a·dopt′ive,** adj.

a·dore′, v., **adored, adoring.** regard highly; worship. **—a·dor′a·ble,** adj. **—ad′o·ra′tion,** n.

a·dorn′, v. decorate. **—a·dorn′ment,** n.

ad·re′nal (ə drēn′l), adj. of a pair of glands near the kidneys.

ad·ren′al·in, n. glandular secretion that speeds heart, etc.

a·drift′, adv., adj. floating about, esp. helplessly.

a·droit′, adj. expert; deft. **—a·droit′-ly,** adv. **—a·droit′ness,** n.

ad·sorb′, v. hold on a surface in a condensed layer.

ad′u·late′ (aj′ə lāt′), v., **-lated, -lating.** flatter excessively. **—ad′u·la′tion,** n. **—ad′u·la·to′ry** (-lə tôr′ē), adj.

a·dult′, adj. 1. full-grown; mature. **—n.** 2. full-grown person. **—a·dult′-hood,** n.

a·dul′ter·ate′, v., **-ated, -ating.** make impure. **—a·dul′ter·a′tion,** n. **—a·dul′ter·ant,** n.

a·dul′ter·y, n., pl. **-teries.** marital infidelity. **—a·dul′ter·er,** n. **—a·dul′ter·ess,** n.fem. **—a·dul′ter·ous,** adj.

ad·vance′, v., **-vanced, -vancing.** 1. move forward. 2. propose. 3. raise in rank, price, etc. 4. supply beforehand; lend. **—n.** 5. forward move. 6. promotion. 7. increase. 8. loan. 9. friendly gesture. **—adj.** 10. early. **—ad·vance′ment,** n.

ad·vanced′, adj. 1. progressive. 2. relatively learned, old, etc.

ad·van′tage, n. 1. more favorable condition. 2. benefit. **—ad′van·ta′geous,** adj.

ad′vent, n. 1. arrival. 2. coming of Christ. 3. (cap.) month before Christmas.

ad·ven·ti′tious, adj. accidentally added.

ad·ven′ture, n., v., **-tured, -turing.** **—n.** 1. risky undertaking. 2. exciting event. **—v.** 3. risk or dare. **—ad·ven′tur·er,** n. **—ad·ven′tur·ous,** adj.

ad′verb, n. Gram. word modifying a verb, verbal noun, or other adverb. **—ad·ver′bi·al,** adj.

ad′ver·sar′y, n., pl. **-saries.** opponent.

ad·verse′, adj. opposing; antagonistic. **—ad·verse′ly,** adv.

ad·ver′si·ty, n., pl. **-ties.** misfortune.

ad·vert′, v. refer.

ad′ver·tise′, v., **-tised, -tising.** bring to public notice. **—ad′ver·tis′er,** n. **—ad′ver·tise′ment,** n. **—ad′ver·tis′ing,** n.

ad·vice′, n. 1. opinion offered. 2. news.

ad·vis′a·ble, adj. wise; desirable. **—ad·vis′a·bil′i·ty,** n.

ad·vise′, v., **-vised, -vising.** 1. offer an opinion to. 2. recommend. 3. consult (with). 4. give news. **—ad·vis′er, ad·vi′sor,** n. **—ad·vise′ment,** n.

ad·vis′ed·ly, adv. after consideration; deliberately.

ad·vi′so·ry, adj. 1. giving advice. —n. 2. report on conditions.

ad′vo·cate, v., **-cated, -cating,** n. —v. (-kāt′). 1. urge; recommend. —n. (-kit). 2. supporter of cause. 3. lawyer. —**ad′vo·ca·cy,** n.

adz, n. axlike tool.

ae′gis (ē′jis) n. sponsorship.

ae′on (ē′ən), n. eon.

aer·ate, v., **-ated, -ating,** expose to air.

aer′i·al, adj. 1. of or in air. 2. lofty. —n. 3. radio antenna.

aer·o′bic (â rō′bik), adj. 1. needing oxygen to live. 2. of aerobics.

aer·o′bics, n.pl. exercises designed to strengthen the heart and lungs.

aer′o·dy·nam′ics, n. science of action of air against solids. —**aer′o·dy·nam′ic,** adj.

aer′o·naut′, n. pilot.

aer′o·nau′tics, n. science of flight in aircraft. —**aer′o·naut′i·cal,** adj.

aer′o·plane′, n. Brit. airplane.

aer′o·space′, n. 1. earth's atmosphere and the space beyond. —adj. 2. operating in aerospace.

aer′o·sol′, n. 1. liquid distributed through a gas. 2. spray of such liquid.

aer′o·space′, n. 1. the earth's atmosphere and space beyond. —adj. of missiles, aircraft, and spacecraft.

aes·thet′ic (es-), adj. 1. of beauty. 2. appreciating beauty. —**aes′thete** (-thēt), n.

aes·thet′ics, n. study of beauty.

a·far′, adv. at a distance.

af·fa·ble, adj. friendly; cordial. —**af′fa·bil′i·ty,** n.

af·fair′, n. 1. matter of business. 2. event. 3. amorous relationship.

af·fect′, v. 1. act on. 2. impress (feelings). 3. pretend to possess or feel.

af′fec·ta′tion, n. pretense.

af·fect′ed, adj. 1. vain; haughty. 2. diseased; infected. —**af·fect′ed·ly,** adv.

af·fec′tion, n. 1. love. 2. disease.

af·fec′tion·ate, adj. loving; fond. —**af·fec′tion·ate·ly,** adv.

af·fi′ance (ə fī′-), v. **-anced, -ancing.** become engaged to.

af′fi·da′vit, n. written statement under oath.

af·fil′i·ate′, v., **-ated, -ating,** n. —v. 1. join; connect. —n. (-ē it). 2. associate. —**af·fil′i·a′tion,** n.

af·fin′i·ty, n., pl. **-ties.** 1. attraction. 2. similarity.

af·firm′, v. 1. state; assert. 2. ratify. —**af′fir·ma′tion,** n.

af·firm′a·tive, adj. saying yes; affirming.

af·fix′, v. 1. attach. —n. (af′iks). 2. added part.

af·flict′, v. distress; trouble. —**af·flic′tion,** n.

af′flu·ent, adj. rich; abundant. —**af′flu·ence,** n.

af·ford′, v. 1. have resources enough. 2. provide.

af·fray′, n. fight.

af·front′, n., v. insult.

af′ghan, n. woolen blanket.

a·field′, adv. astray.

a·fire′, adv., adj. on fire.

a·flame′, adv., adj. in flames.

a·float′, adv., adj. 1. floating. 2. in circulation. 3. out of debt.

a·foot′, adv., adj. 1. on foot. 2. in existence.

a·fore′said′, adj. said before. Also, **a·fore′men′tioned.**

a·foul′, adv., adj. colliding; entangled; in conflict.

a·fraid′, adj. full of fear.

a·fresh′, adj. again.

Af′ri·can, n. native of Africa. —**Af′ri·can,** adj.

African-American, n., adj. black American.

Af′ri·kaans′ (af′ri käns′, -känz′), n. language of South Africa, derived from Dutch.

Af′ri·kan′er, n. white South African who speaks Afrikaans.

Af′ro, n. full, bushy hairstyle.

Af′ro-A·mer′i·can, n., adj. African-American.

aft, adv. Naut. at or toward the stern.

af′ter, prep. 1. behind. 2. about. 3. later than. 4. next to. 5. in imitation of. —adv. 6. behind. 7. later.

af′ter·birth′, n. placenta and other matter expelled from uterus after childbirth.

af′ter·ef·fect′, n. reaction.

af′ter·glow′, n. 1. glow in sky after sunset. 2. pleasant memory.

af′ter·life′, n. life after death.

af′ter·math′, n. results.

af′ter·noon′, n. period between noon and evening.

af′ter·thought′, n. later thought.

af′ter·ward, adv. later. Also, **af′ter·wards.**

a·gain′, adv. 1. once more. 2. besides.

a·gainst′, prep. 1. opposed to. 2. in or into contact with.

a·gape′, adv., adj. wide open.

ag′ate, n. 1. kind of quartz. 2. child's marble.

age, n., v., **aged, aging.** —n. 1. length of time in existence. 2. stage; period.

3. legal maturity. —v. 4. make or become older.

ag'ed, adj. 1. having lived long. 2. matured. —n.pl. 3. elderly persons.

age'ism, n. discrimination against elderly persons. —**age'ist,** n.

age'less, adj. 1. apparently not aging. 2. not outdated.

a'gen·cy (ā'jən sē), n., pl. -**cies.** 1. office. 2. action. 3. means.

a·gen'da, n. matters to be dealt with.

a'gent, n. 1. person acting for another. 2. cause; means. 3. official.

ag·glom'er·ate', v., -**ated,** -**ating,** adj., n. —v. 1. collect into a mass. —adj. (-ər it). 2. collected in a mass. —n. (-ər it). 3. such a mass. —**ag'-glom'er·a'tion,** n.

ag'gran·dize', v., -**dized,** -**dizing.** increase in size, rank, etc. —**ag·gran'-dize·ment** (-dəz-), n.

ag'gra·vate', v., -**vated,** -**vating.** 1. make worse. 2. anger. —**ag'gra·va'-tion,** n.

ag'gre·gate', adj., n., v., -**gated,** -**gating.** —adj. 1. combined. —n. 2. whole amount. —v. (-gāt'). 3. collect; gather. —**ag'gre·ga'tion,** n.

ag·gres'sion, n. hostile act; encroachment. —**ag·gres'sor,** n.

ag·gres'sive, adj. 1. boldly energetic. 2. hostile.

ag·grieve', v., -**grieved,** -**grieving.** wrong severely.

a·ghast' (ə gast'), adj. struck with fear or horror.

ag'ile (aj'əl), adj. quick; nimble. —**a·gil'i·ty,** n.

ag'i·tate', v., -**tated,** -**tating.** 1. shake. 2. disturb; excite. 3. discuss. —**ag'i·ta'tion,** n. —**ag'i·ta'tor,** n.

a·glow', adj., adv. glowing.

ag·nos'tic, n. one who believes God is beyond human knowledge. —**ag·nos'ti·cism,** n.

a·go', adj., adv. in the past.

a·gog', adj. eagerly excited.

ag'o·nize', v., -**nized,** -**nizing.** 1. torture. 2. suffer anxiety.

ag'o·ny, n., pl. -**nies.** intense pain or suffering.

ag'o·ra·pho'bi·a (ag'ər ə fō'bē ə), n. fear of open spaces.

a·grar'i·an, adj. of the land.

a·gree', v., -**greed,** -**greeing.** 1. consent or promise. 2. be in harmony. 3. be similar. 4. be pleasing. —**a·gree'ment,** n.

a·gree'a·ble, adj. 1. pleasant. 2. willing. —**a·gree'a·bly,** adv.

ag'ri·cul'ture, n. science of farming. —**ag'ri·cul'tur·al,** adj.

a·ground', adv., adj. Naut. onto the bottom.

a'gue (ā'gyōō), n. fever, usu. malarial.

ah (ä), interj. (exclamation of pain, surprise, joy, satisfaction, etc.)

a·head', adv. 1. in front; forward. 2. winning.

a·hoy', interj. Naut. hey there!

aid, v., n. help.

aide, n. assistant.

aide-de-camp', n., pl. **aides-de-camp.** military assistant.

AIDS (ādz), n. acquired immunity deficiency syndrome, a disease making one increasingly susceptible to infections and other diseases.

ail, v. 1. trouble; distress. 2. be sick.

ai'ler·on', n. flap on airplane wing.

ail'ment, n. illness.

aim, v. 1. point or direct. 2. intend. —n. 3. act of aiming. 4. target. 5. purpose. —**aim'less,** adj.

ain't, v. Illiterate or Dial. am, is, or are not.

air, n. 1. mixture of gases forming atmosphere of earth. 2. appearance; manner. 3. tune. —v. 4. expose to air. 5. broadcast.

air bag, bag that inflates automatically to protect passengers in a car collision.

air'borne', adj. carried by air; flying.

air'brush', n. 1. atomizer for spraying paint. —v. 2. paint with an airbrush.

air conditioning, control of interior air for temperature, humidity, etc. —**air-conditioned,** adj.

air'craft', n. vehicle or vehicles for flight.

air'field', n. ground area for airplanes to land on and take off from.

air' force', military branch that carries out operations in the air.

air'lift', n. 1. major transport by air. —v. 2. move by airlift.

air'line', n. air transport company.

air'man, n., pl. -**men.** aviator.

air'plane', n. powered heavier-than-air craft with wings.

air'port', n. airfield for loading, repairs, etc.

air raid, attack by aircraft.

air'ship', n. lighter-than-air aircraft.

air'sick'ness, n. nausea from motion in air travel. —**air'sick',** adj.

air'space', n. space above a nation, city, etc., over which it has jurisdiction or control.

air'tight', adj. 1. impermeable to air. 2. perfect; free of error.

air'waves', n.pl. medium of radio and television broadcasting.

air'y, adj., **air·i·er,** **air·i·est.** 1. of or like air. 2. delicate. 3. unrealistic. 4. well ventilated. 5. light; gay. —**air'i·ly,** adv. —**air'i·ness,** n.

aisle, n. partly enclosed passageway.

a·jar', adj., adv. partly opened.

a·kim'bo, adj., adv. with hands at hips.

a·kin', adj. 1. related. 2. alike.

al'a·bas'ter, n. translucent gypsum.

à la carte, with each dish separately priced.

a·lac'ri·ty, n. quickness; readiness.

à la mode, 1. in the fashion. 2. with ice cream.

a·larm', n. 1. fear of danger. 2. sudden warning. 3. call to arms. —v. 4. fill with fear.

alarm clock, clock with device to awaken sleeper.

a·larm'ist, n. spreader of needless fear.

a·las', interj. (cry of sorrow.)

al'ba·core', n. type of tuna.

al'ba·tross', n. large white sea bird.

al·be'it (ôl-), conj. though.

al·bi'no (-bī'-), n., pl. -nos. one lacking in pigmentation.

al'bum, n. 1. blank book for pictures, stamps, etc. 2. container with recordings.

al·bu'men (-byōō'-), n. egg white.

al·bu'min (-byōō'-), n. protein found in egg white, milk, blood, etc.

al'che·my (-kə mē), n. medieval chemistry. —**al'che·mist,** n.

al'co·hol', n. colorless intoxicating liquid formed by fermentation.

al'co·hol'ic, adj. 1. of alcohol. —n. 2. one addicted to alcohol.

al'co·hol·ism, n. addiction to alcohol.

al'cove, n. recessed space.

al'der, n. small tree, usually growing in moist places.

al'der·man, n., pl. -men. representative on city council.

ale, n. dark, bitter beer.

a·lert', adj. 1. vigilant. —n. 2. air-raid alarm. —v. 3. warn. —**a·lert'ly,** adv. —**a·lert'ness,** n.

al·fal'fa, n. forage plant.

al·fres'co (al fres'kō), adv., adj. in the open air. Also, **al fres'co.**

al'ga, n., pl. -gae (-jē). water plant; seaweed.

al'ge·bra, n. branch of mathematics using symbols rather than specific numbers. —**al'ge·bra'ic,** adj.

al'go·rithm (al'gə rith əm), n. set of rules or steps to solve mathematical problem, program computer, etc. —**al'go·rith'mic,** adj.

a·li'as, n. 1. otherwise known as. —n. 2. assumed name.

al'i·bi' (-bī'), n. 1. defense of accused one as being elsewhere. 2. excuse.

al'ien (āl'yən), n. 1. foreigner. —adj. 2. foreign.

al'ien·ate', v., -ated, -ating. lose friendship of; repel. —**al'ien·a'tion,** n.

a·light', v. 1. dismount after travel. 2. descend to perch or sit. —adv., adj. 3. lighted up.

a·lign' (ə līn'), v. bring into line. —**a·lign'ment,** n.

a·like', adj. 1. similarly. —adj. 2. similar.

al'i·men'ta·ry, adj. of or for food.

al'i·mo'ny, n. money for support of a wife after separation or divorce.

a·live', adj. 1. living. 2. active. 3. lively. 4. teeming; swarming.

al'ka·li' (-lī'), n. chemical that neutralizes acids to form salts. —**al'ka·line',** adj.

al'ka·loid', n. organic compound in plants, as morphine.

all, adj. 1. the whole of. 2. every. —n. 3. the whole; everything. —adv. 4. entirely.

Al'lah, n. Muslim name for God.

al·lay', v. quiet or lessen.

al·lege' (ə lej'), v., -leged, -leging. declare; state, often without proof. —**al'le·ga'tion,** n. —**al·leg'ed·ly,** adv.

al·le'giance, n. loyalty.

al'le·go'ry, n., pl. -ries. symbolic story. —**al'le·gor'i·cal,** adj.

al·le'gro, adv. Music. fast.

al'ler·gen, n. substance that causes allergic reaction. —**al'ler·gen'ic,** adj.

al'ler·gist, n. doctor who treats allergies.

al'ler·gy, n., pl. -gies. bodily sensitiveness to certain pollens, foods, etc. —**al·ler'gic,** adj.

al·le'vi·ate', v., -ated, -ating. lessen; relieve. —**al·le'vi·a'tion,** n.

al'ley, n. narrow street or path.

al·li'ance, n. 1. union; joining. 2. marriage. 3. treaty. 4. parties to treaty.

al·lied', adj. 1. joined by treaty. 2. related.

al'li·ga'tor, n. broad-snouted type of crocodile.

all'-im·por'tant, adj. supremely necessary.

all'-in·clu'sive, adj. comprehensive.

al·lit'er·a'tion, n. beginning of several words with same sound.

al'lo·cate', v., -cated, -cating. allot. —**al'lo·ca'tion,** n.

al·lot', v., -lotted, -lotting. 1. divide; distribute. 2. assign. —**al·lot'ment,** n.

all·out', *adj.* total; unrestricted.

al·low', *v.* **1.** permit. **2.** give. **3.** admit. —**al·low'a·ble**, *adj.* —**al·low'ance**, *n.*

al'loy, *n.* **1.** mixture of metals. —*v.* **1.** (a loi'). **2.** mix (metals). **3.** adulterate.

all right, **1.** yes; I agree. **2.** in a satisfactory way. **3.** safe; sound. **4.** acceptable; satisfactory.

all'spice', *n.* sharp, fragrant spice.

all'-star', *adj.* **1.** consisting of star performers. —*n.* **2.** member of all-star team or group.

all'-time', *adj.* never equaled or surpassed.

al·lude', *v.*, **-luded, -luding.** refer (to) in words. —**al·lu'sion**, *n.*

al·lure', *v.*, **-lured, -luring.** attract; tempt. —**al·lure'ment**, *n.*

al·lu'vi·um, *n.* earth deposited by rivers, etc. —**al·lu'vi·al**, *adj.*

al·ly', *v.*, **-lied, -lying,** *n., pl.* **-lies.** —*v.* **1.** unite in an alliance. —*n.* (al'ī). **2.** person, nation, etc., bound to another, as by treaty.

al'ma ma'ter, one's school.

al'ma·nac', *n.* calendar showing special events, etc.

al·might'y, *adj.* **1.** having all power. —*n.* **2.** (*cap.*) God.

al'mond (ä'mənd), *n.* edible nut of the almond tree.

al'most, *adv.* nearly.

alms (ämz), *n.pl.* charity.

al'oe, *n.* plant with fleshy leaves.

a·loft', *adv., adj.* high up.

a·lone', *adj., adv.* **1.** apart. **2.** by oneself.

a·long', *prep.* **1.** through length of. —*adv.* **2.** onward. **3.** together; with one.

a·long'side', *adv.* **1.** to one's side. —*prep.* **2.** beside.

a·loof', *adv.* **1.** at a distance. —*adj.* **2.** reserved; indifferent. —**a·loof'ness**, *n.*

a·loud', *adv.* loudly.

al·pac'a, *n.* South American sheep with soft, silky wool.

al'pha, *n.* first letter of Greek alphabet.

al'pha·bet', *n.* letters of a language in order. —**al'pha·bet'i·cal**, *adj.* —**al'pha·bet·ize'**, *v.*

al'pine (al'pīn, -pin), *adj.* **1.** of or like a high mountain. **2.** growing or found above the timberline.

al·read'y, *adv.* before this time.

al'so, *adv.* in addition.

al'tar, *n.* platform for religious rites. **2.** communion table.

al'ter, *v.* change. —**al·ter·a'tion**, *n.*

al'ter·ca'tion, *n.* dispute.

al'ter e'go, **1.** intimate friend. **2.** perfect substitute for oneself. **3.** other side of one's personality.

al'ter·nate, *v.*, **-nated, -nating,** *adj.*, *n.* —*v.* (-nāt'). **1.** occur or do in turns. —*adj.* (-nit). **2.** being by turns. —*n.* (-nit). **3.** substitute. —**al'ter·na'tion**, *n.*

al·ter'na·tive, *n.* **1.** other choice. —*adj.* **2.** offering a choice.

al·though', *conj.* even though.

al·tim'e·ter, *n.* device for measuring altitude.

al'ti·tude', *n.* height.

al'to, *n., pl.* **-tos.** lowest female voice.

al·to·geth'er, *adv.* entirely.

al'tru·ism', *n.* devotion to others. —**al'tru·ist**, *n.* —**al'tru·is'tic**, *adj.*

al'um, *n.* astringent substance, used in medicine, etc.

a·lu'mi·num, *n.* light, silvery metal. Also, *Brit.,* **al'u·min'i·um.**

a·lum'nus, *n., pl.* **-ni** (-nī). graduate. —**a·lum'na**, *n.fem., pl.* **-nae** (-nē).

al'ways, *adv.* **1.** all the time. **2.** every time.

Alz'hei·mer's disease (älts'hī marz, ölts'-), disease marked by increasing memory loss and mental deterioration, usually in old age.

am, *v.* 1st pers. sing. pres. indic. of **be.**

a.m., the period before noon. Also, **A.M.**

a·mal'gam, *n.* mixture, esp. one with mercury.

a·mal'gam·ate', *v.*, **-ated, -ating.** combine. —**a·mal'gam·a'tion**, *n.*

a·man'u·en'sis, *n., pl.* **-ses.** secretary.

am'a·ranth', *n.* plant grown as food and for its showy flowers.

am'a·ryl'lis, *n.* plant with large, lily-like flowers.

a·mass', *v.* collect.

am'a·teur' (-chöor'), *n.* nonprofessional artist, athlete, etc.

am'a·to'ry, *adj.* of love.

a·maze', *v.* **amazed, amazing.** surprise greatly. —**a·maze'ment**, *n.*

Am'a·zon', *n.* **1.** female warrior of Greek legend. **2.** tall, powerful woman.

am·bas'sa·dor, *n.* diplomat of highest rank.

am'ber, *n.* **1.** yellowish fossil resin. —*adj.* **2.** yellowish.

am'ber·gris' (-grēs'), *n.* gray secretion of sperm whale, used in perfumes.

am·bi·dex'trous, *adj.* using both hands equally well.

am'bi·ence (-bē-), *n.* surroundings; atmosphere. Also, **am'bi·ance.** —**am'bi·ent**, *adj.*

am·big'u·ous, *adj.* unclear in meaning. **—am·bi·gu'i·ty,** *n.*

am·bi'tion, *n.* **1.** desire for success, power, etc. **2.** object so desired. **—am·bi'tious,** *adj.*

am·biv'a·lent, *adj.* with conflicting emotions. **—am·biv'a·lence,** *n.*

am'ble (a mē'bla), *n., pl.* **-bas** or **-bae** (-bē). **1.** to go at an easy gait. **—n. 2.** easy gait.

am·bro'sia (-zha), *n.* food of classical gods.

am'bu·lance, *n.* vehicle for sick or wounded.

am'bu·la·to·ry, *adj.* able to walk.

am'bus·cade', *n.* ambush. **—v. 4.** attack thus.

am'bush, *n.* **1.** concealment for a surprise attack. **2.** surprise attack. **3.** place of such concealment. **—v. 4.** attack thus.

a·me'ba (a mē'ba), *n., pl.* **-bas** or **-bae** (-bē). microscopic one-celled animal. Also, **a·moe'ba.**

a·mel'io·rate', *v.,* **-rated, -rating.** improve. **—a·mel'io·ra'tion,** *n.*

a'men', *interj.* so be it!

a·me'na·ble, *adj.* willing; submissive.

a·mend', *v.* **1.** change or correct. **2.** improve. **—a·mend'ment,** *n.*

a·mends', *n.pl.* reparation.

a·men'i·ty, *n., pl.* **-ties.** pleasant feature, etc.

A·mer'i·can, *n.* **1.** citizen of the U.S. **2.** native of N. or S. America. **—adj. 3.** of the U.S. or its inhabitants. **4.** of N. or S. America.

American Indian, member of the aboriginal peoples of N. or S. America.

A·mer'i·can·ism, *n.* **1.** devotion to the U.S. **2.** custom, etc., of the U.S.

A·mer'i·can·ize', *v.,* make or become American in character.

am'e·thyst, *n.* violet quartz, used in jewelry.

a'mi·a·ble, *adj.* pleasantly kind or friendly. **—a'mi·a·bil'i·ty,** *n.* **—a'mi·a·bly,** *adv.*

am'i·ca·ble, *adj.* not hostile. **—am'i·ca·bly,** *adv.*

a·mid', *prep.* among. Also, **a·midst'.**

a·mid'ships' or **-ship',** *adv.* in or toward the middle part of a ship or aircraft.

a·mi'go (-mē'-), *n., pl.* **-gos.** *Spanish.* friend.

a·mi'no ac'id, type of organic compound from which proteins are made.

a·miss', *adv.* **1.** wrongly. **—adj. 2.** wrong.

am'i·ty, *n.* friendship.

am·mo (am'ō), *n.* *Slang.* ammunition.

am·mo'ni·a, *n.* colorless, pungent, water-soluble gas.

am·mu·ni'tion, *n.* bullets, shot, etc., for weapons.

am·ne'sia, *n.* loss of memory.

am'nes·ty, *n.* pardon for political crimes.

am·ni·o·cen·te'sis (am'nē ō sen tē'sis) *n., pl.* **-ses** (-sēz). surgical procedure of withdrawing fluid from pregnant woman for genetic diagnosis of fetus.

a·mok', *adv.* amuck.

a·mong', *prep.* **1.** in the midst of. **2.** in the group of. Also, **a·mongst'.**

a·mor'al (ā-), *adj.* indifferent to moral standards. **—a'mo·ral'i·ty,** *n.*

am'o·rous, *adj.* inclined to, or showing, love.

a·mor'phous, *adj.* formless.

am'or·tize', *v.,* **-tized, -tizing.** pay off. **—am'or·ti·za'tion,** *n.*

a·mount', *n.* **1.** sum total. **2.** quantity. **—v. 3.** add up (to); equal.

a·mour', *n.* love affair.

am'pere (-pēr), *n.* unit measuring electric current.

am'per·sand', *n.* sign (&) meaning "and."

am·phet'a·mine (-mēn), *n.* drug stimulating nervous system.

am·phib'i·an, *n.* animal living both in water and on land. **—adj. 2.** Also, **am·phib'i·ous.** operating on land or water.

am'phi·the·a'ter, *n.* theater with seats around a central area.

am'ple, *adj.,* **-pler, -plest.** **1.** sufficient. **2.** abundant. **—am'ply,** *adv.*

am'pli·fy', *v.,* **-fied, -fying.** make larger or louder. **—am'pli·fi'er,** *n.* **—am'pli·fi·ca'tion,** *n.*

am'pli·tude', *n.* **1.** extent. **2.** abundance.

am'pule (am'pyōōl, -pōōl), *n.* sealed glass or plastic vial containing solution for hypodermic injection. Also, **am'pul, am'poule.**

am'pu·tate', *v.,* **-tated, -tating.** cut off (a limb). **—am'pu·ta'tion,** *n.* **—am'pu·tee',** *n.*

a·muck', *adv.* murderously insane.

am'u·let, *n.* magical charm.

a·muse', *v.,* amused, amusing. **1.** entertain. **2.** cause mirth in. **—a·muse'ment,** *n.*

amusement park, park with various rides and other recreational devices.

an, *adj.* or *indef. art.* before initial vowel sounds. See **a.**

a·nach'ro·nism, *n.* chronological discrepancy. **—a·nach'ro·nis'tic,** *adj.*

an'a·con'da, *n.* large South American snake.

an'a·gram', n. word formed from letters of another.

a'nal, adj. of the anus.

an'al·ge'sic (an'al jē'zik), n. drug for relieving pain.

analog computer, computer that solves problems by using voltages as analogies of numerical variables.

an'a·logue' (an'l ôg', -og'), n. something analogous to something else. Also, an'a·log'.

a·nal'o·gy (-jē), n., pl. -gies. similarity in some respects. —a·nal'o·gous (-gas), adj.

a·nal'y·sis, n., pl. -ses. 1. separation into constituent parts. 2. summary. 3. psychoanalysis. —an'a·lyst, n. —an'a·lyt'ic, an'a·lyt'i·cal, adj. —an'a·lyze', v.

an'ar·chy (-kē), n. lawless society. —an'ar·chism, n. —an'ar·chist, n.

a·nath'e·ma, n. 1. solemn curse. 2. thing or person detested.

a·nat'o·my, n., pl. -mies. 1. structure of an animal or plant. 2. science dealing with such structure. —an'a·tom'i·cal, adj.

an'ces·tor, n. person from whom one is descended. —an'ces·try, n. —an·ces'tral, adj.

an'chor, n. 1. heavy device for keeping boats, etc., in place. 2. main broadcaster who coordinates TV or radio newscast. —v. 3. fasten by an anchor. 4. serve as anchor for (newscast). —an'chor·age, n.

an'chor·man', n. main. person who anchors a newscast. Also, an'chor·wom'an; masc. or fem., an'chor·per'son.

an·cho·vy (-chō vē), n., pl. -vies. small herringlike fish.

an'cient, adj. 1. of long ago. 2. very old. —n. 3. person who lived long ago.

an'cil·lar·y (an'sə ler'ē), adj. subordinate; auxiliary.

and, conj. 1. with; also. 2. Informal. (used in place of to in infinitive): Try and stop me.

an·dan'te (-tā), adv. Music. at moderate speed.

and'i'rons, n.pl. metal supports for logs in fireplace.

an·drog'y·nous (an droj'ə nəs), adj. having both masculine and feminine characteristics.

an'droid, n. automation in human form.

an'ec·dote', n. short story.

a·ne'mi·a, n. inadequate supply of hemoglobin and red blood cells. —a·ne'mic, adj.

a·nem'o·ne', n. buttercuplike plant with flowers in a variety of colors.

an'es·the'si·a (-zha), n. insensibility to pain, usually induced by a drug (an'es·thet'ic). —an'es·the·tize', v.

a·new', adv. again.

an'gel, n. spirit that attends God. —an·gel'ic, adj.

an'ger, n. 1. strong displeasure. —v. 2. cause anger in.

an·gi'na pec'to·ris (an ji'nə pek'tə ris), painful attack, usually caused by coronary artery disease.

an'gle, n., v., -gled, -gling. —n. 1. spread between converging lines or surfaces. —v. 2. fish with a hook on a line. 3. try for something by artful means. 4. bend in angles. —an'gler, n.

an'gle·worm', n. worm used in fishing.

An'gli·can, adj. 1. of the Church of England. —n. 2. member of this church.

An'gli·cize', v., -cized, -ciz·ing. make or become English in form or character.

An'glo-Sax'on, n. 1. person of English descent. 2. inhabitant of England before 1066. —adj. 3. of Anglo-Saxons.

An·go'ra, n. 1. cat, goat, or rabbit with long, silky hair. 2. (l.c.) yarn or fabric from Angora goat or rabbit.

an'gry, adj., -grier, -griest. 1. full of anger. 2. inflamed. —an'gri·ly, adv.

angst (ängkst), n. feeling of dread, anxiety, or anguish.

an'guish, n. intense pain or grief.

an·gu·lar, adj. having angles. —an·gu·lar'i·ty, n.

an'i·line (-lin), n. oily liquid used in dyes, plastics, etc.

an'i·mad·vert', v. criticize. —an'i·mad·ver'sion, n.

an'i·mal, n. 1. living thing that is not a plant. 2. beast. —adj. 3. of animals.

an'i·mate', v., -mated, -mating, adj. —v. (-māt'). 1. make alive or lively. —adj. (-mit). 2. alive. —an'i·ma'tion, n.

an'i·mism, n. belief that animals and natural objects have souls.

an'i·mos'i·ty, n., pl. -ties. strong ill will or enmity.

an'i·mus, n. strong dislike; animosity.

an'ise (an'is), n. plant yielding aromatic seed (an'i·seed').

an'kle, n. joint between foot and leg.

an'nals, n.pl. historical records.

an·neal', v. toughen or temper.

an·nex', v. 1. add; join. —n. (an' eks). 2. part, etc., attached. —an·nex·a'tion, n.

an·ni'hi·late', v., -lated, -lating. destroy completely. —**an·ni'hi·la'tion,** n.

an·ni·ver·sa·ry, n., pl. -ries. annual recurrence of the date of a past event.

an'no·tate', v., -tated, -tating. supply with notes. —**an'no·ta'tion,** n.

an·nounce', v., -nounced, -nouncing. make known. —**an·nounce'ment,** n. —**an·nounc'er,** n.

an·noy', v. irritate or trouble. —**an·noy'ance,** n.

an'nu·al, adj. 1. yearly. 2. living only one season. —n. 3. annual plant. 4. yearbook. —**an'nu·al·ly,** adv.

an·nu'i·ty, n., pl. -ties. annual income in return for earlier payments.

an·nul', v., -nulled, -nulling. make void. —**an·nul'ment,** n.

an'nu·lar, adj. in the shape of a ring.

An·nun'ci·a'tion, n. announcement to Virgin Mary of incarnation of Christ (March 25).

an'o·dyne' (-dīn'), n. medication that relieves pain.

a·noint', v. put oil, etc., on, as in consecration.

a·nom'a·ly, n., pl. -lies. something irregular or abnormal. —**a·nom'a·lous,** adj.

a·non', adv. Archaic. soon.

a·non'y·mous, adj. by someone unnamed. —**an'o·nym'i·ty,** n.

an'o·rak, n. hooded jacket; parka.

an'o·rex'i·a (an'ə rek'sē ə), n. 1. loss of appetite. 2. Also, **anorexia ner·vo'sa** (nûr vō'sa). eating disorder marked by excessive dieting.

an·oth'er, adj. 1. additional. 2. different. —n. 3. one more. 4. different one.

an'swer, n. 1. reply. 2. solution. —v. 3. reply to. 4. suit. 5. be responsible. 6. correspond.

an'swer·a·ble, adj. 1. able to be answered. 2. responsible.

ant, n. common small insect.

ant·ac'id, n. medicine to counteract acids.

an·tag'o·nism', n. hostility. —**an·tag'o·nist,** n. —**an·tag'o·nis'tic,** adj. —**an·tag'o·nize',** v.

ant·arc'tic, adj. (often cap.) of or at the South Pole.

an'te (an'tē), n. 1. (in poker) stake put in pot before cards are dealt. 2. price or cost of something. —v. 3. (in poker) put (one's ante) into the pot. 4. produce or pay (one's share).

ant'eat'er, n. tropical American mammal having long snout and feeding on ants and termites.

an'te·ced'ent (-sēd'-), adj. 1. prior. —n. 2. anything that precedes.

an'te·date', v., -dated, -dating. 1. happen earlier than. 2. date earlier than true time.

an'te·di·lu'vi·an, adj. before the Flood.

an'te·lope', n. deerlike animal.

an·ten'na, n., pl. -nae (-nē), for 1. feeler on the head of an insect, etc. 2. wires for transmitting radio waves, TV pictures, etc.

an·te'ri·or, adj. 1. earlier. 2. frontward.

an'te·room', n. room before the main room.

an'them, n. patriotic or sacred hymn.

an'ther, n. pollen-bearing part of stamen.

an·thol'o·gy, n., pl. -gies. collection of writings.

an'thra·cite', n. hard coal.

an'thrax, n. malignant disease of cattle, etc.

an'thro·poid', adj. resembling man.

an'thro·pol'o·gy, n. science of humankind. —**an'thro·pol'o·gist,** n.

an'ti·bi·ot'ic, n. substance (such as penicillin) derived from mold, etc., and used to destroy certain organisms.

an'ti·bod'y, n., pl. -bodies. substance in the blood that destroys bacteria.

an'tic, n. 1. odd behavior. —adj. 2. playful.

an·tic'i·pate', v., -pated, -pating. 1. expect and prepare for. 2. foresee. —**an·tic'i·pa'tion,** n.

an'ti·cli'max, n. disappointing or undramatic outcome.

an'ti·dote', n. medicine counteracting poison, etc.

an'ti·freeze', n. liquid used in radiator of automobile engine to prevent freezing of its cooling fluid.

an'ti·gen (an'ti jan, -jen'), n. substance that stimulates production of antibodies.

an'ti·his'ta·mine (-mēn'), n. substance used esp. against allergic reactions.

an'ti·mat'ter, n. matter whose particles have charges opposite to those of common particles.

an'ti·mo'ny, n. brittle white metallic element.

an'ti·pas'to, n., pl. -pas'tos, -pas'ti. appetizer in an Italian meal.

an'ti·pa'thy, n., pl. -thies. dislike; aversion.

an'ti·quar'i·an, adj. 1. of the study of antiquities. —n. 2. antiquary.

an'ti·quar'y (-kwer'ē), n., pl. -ries. collector of antiquities.

an'ti·quat'ed, adj. old or obsolete.

an·tique′ (-tēk′), *adj.* **1.** old or old-fashioned. —*n.* **2.** valuable old object.

an·tiq′ui·ty, *n., pl.* **-ties. 1.** ancient times. **2.** something ancient.

an′ti-Sem′ite (an′tē sem′īt, an′tī-), *n.* person hostile to Jews. —**an′ti-Se·mit′ic,** *adj.* —**an′ti-Sem′i·tism,** *n.*

an′ti·sep′tic, *adj.* **1.** destroying certain germs. —*n.* **2.** antiseptic substance.

an′ti·so′cial, *adj.* **1.** hostile to society. **2.** not sociable.

an·tith′e·sis, *n., pl.* **-ses.** direct opposite.

an′ti·tox′in, *n.* substance counteracting germ-produced poisons in the body.

an′ti·trust′, *adj.* opposing or intended to restrain business trusts or monopolies.

ant′ler, *n.* horn on deer, etc.

an′to·nym, *n.* word of opposite meaning.

a′nus, *n.* opening at lower end of alimentary canal.

an′vil, *n.* iron block on which hot metals are hammered into shape.

anx·i′e·ty (ang zī′-), *n., pl.* **-ties. 1.** worried distress. **2.** eagerness. —**anx′ious** (angk′shas), *adj.* —**anx′ious·ly,** *adv.*

an′y, *adj.* **1.** one; some. **2.** every. —*pron.* **3.** any person, etc. —**an′y·body, an′y·one,** *pron.* —**an′y·thing,** *pron.*

an′y·how, *adv.* in any way, case, etc. Also, **an′y·way.**

an′y·where, *adv.* in, at, or to any place.

A′-OK′ (ā′ō kā′), *adj., adv.* OK; perfect. Also, **A′-O·kay′.**

A′ one′ (ā′wun′), *adj.* excellent. Also, **A′ 1′, A′-1′.**

a·or′ta, *n., pl.* **-tas, -tae** (-tē). main blood vessel from heart.

a·pace (ə pās′), *adv.* with speed; quickly.

A·pache′ (ə pach′ē), *n., pl.* **A·pach′e, A·pach′es.** member of a group of American Indian peoples of the U.S. Southwest.

a·pache′ (ə päsh′), *n.* Parisian tough.

a·part′, *adv.* **1.** into pieces. **2.** separately.

a·part′heid (ə pärt′hīt), *n.* (formerly, in South Africa) separation of and discrimination against blacks.

a·part′ment, *n.* set of rooms in a dwelling.

ap′a·thy, *n., pl.* **-thies.** lack of emotion or interest. —**ap′a·thet′ic,** *adj.*

ape, *n., v.,* **aped, aping.** —*n.* **1.** large, tailless, monkeylike animal. —*v.* **2.** imitate stupidly.

a·pé·ri·tif (ə per′i tēf′), *n.* liquor served before meal to stimulate appetite.

ap′er·ture (-char), *n.* opening.

a′pex, *n.* tip; summit.

a′phid, *n.* plant-sucking insect.

aph′o·rism′, *n.* brief maxim.

aph·ro·dis′i·ac′, *adj.* **1.** sexually exciting. —*n.* **2.** aphrodisiac food, drug, etc.

a′pi·ar·y, *n., pl.* **-ries.** place where bees are kept.

a·piece′, *adv.* for each.

a·plomb (ə plom′, ə plum′), *n.* poise; self-possession.

A·poc′a·lypse, *n.* **1.** revelation of the apostle John. **2.** (*l.c.*) prophetic revelation. —**a·poc′a·lyp′tic,** *adj.*

A·poc′ry·pha, *n.* uncanonical parts of the Bible.

a·poc′ry·phal, *adj.* not verified; dubious

ap′o·gee, *n.* remotest point of satellite orbit.

a·pol′o·gist (-jist), *n.* advocate; defender.

a·pol′o·gize′, *v.* **-gized, -gizing.** offer apology.

a·pol′o·gy, *n., pl.* **-gies. 1.** statement of regret for one's act. **2.** stated defense. —**a·pol′o·get′ic,** *adj.*

ap′o·plex′y, *n.* sudden loss of bodily function due to bursting of blood vessel. —**ap′o·plec′tic,** *adj.*

a·pos′tate, *n.* deserter of one's faith, cause, etc. —**a·pos′ta·sy,** *n.*

a·pos′tle, *n.* **1.** disciple sent by Jesus to preach gospel. **2.** moral reformer. —**ap′os·tol′ic,** *adj.*

a·pos′tro·phe, *n.* **1.** sign (′) indicating an omitted letter, the possessive, or certain plurals. **2.** words in passing to one person or group. —**a·pos′tro·phize′,** *v.*

a·poth′e·car′y, *n., pl.* **-ries.** druggist.

a·poth′e·o′sis (ə poth′ē ō′sis), *n., pl.* **-ses** (-sēz). **1.** elevation to the rank of a god. **2.** ideal example; epitome.

ap·pall′, *v.* fill with fear and dismay. Also, **ap·pal′.** —**ap·pall′ing,** *adj.*

ap′pa·ra′tus, *n.* **1.** instruments and machines for some task. **2.** organization.

ap·par′el, *n.* **1.** clothes. —*v.* **2.** dress.

ap·par′ent, *adj.* **1.** obvious. **2.** seeming. —**ap·par′ent·ly,** *adv.*

ap·pa·ri′tion, *n.* specter.

ap·peal′, *n.* **1.** call for aid, mercy, etc. **2.** request for corroboration or review. **3.** attractiveness. —*v.* **4.** make an appeal.

ap·pear′, *v.* **1.** come into sight. **2.** seem.

ap·pear'ance, *n.* 1. act of appearing. 2. outward look.

ap·pease', *v.*, -peased, -peasing. 1. placate. 2. satisfy. —ap·pease'ment, *n.*

ap·pel'lant, *n.* one who appeals.

ap·pel'late, *adj.* dealing with appeals.

ap·pel·la'tion, *n.* name or title.

ap·pend', *v.* add; join.

ap·pend'age, *n.* subordinate attached part.

ap·pen·dec'to·my, *n.*, *pl.* -mies. surgical removal of the appendix.

ap·pen·di·ci'tis (-sī'-), *n.* inflammation of appendix.

ap·pen'dix, *n.*, *pl.* -dixes, -dices. 1. supplement. 2. closed tube from the large intestine.

ap·per·tain', *v.* belong or pertain.

ap'pe·tite', *n.* desire, esp. for food.

ap'pe·tiz'er, *n.* portion of food or drink served before meal to stimulate appetite. —ap·pe·tiz'ing, *adj.*

ap·plaud', *v.* praise by clapping, cheers, etc. —ap·plause', *n.*

ap'ple, *n.* common edible fruit.

ap'ple·jack', *n.* brandy made from fermented cider.

ap·pli'ance, *n.* special device or instrument.

ap'pli·ca·ble, *adj.* that can be applied.

ap'pli·cant, *n.* one who applies.

ap·pli·ca'tion, *n.* 1. act of applying. 2. use to which something is put. 3. relevance. 4. petition; request. 5. form filled out by applicant. 6. persistent attention.

ap·pli·qué' (ap'li kā'), *n.*, *v.*, -quéd, -quéing. —*n.* 1. cutout design of one material applied to another. —*v.* 2. decorate with appliqué.

ap·ply', *v.*, -plied, -plying. 1. put on. 2. put into practice. 3. use or devote. 4. be relevant. 5. make request.

ap·point', *v.* 1. choose; name. 2. furnish. —ap·point·ee', *n.* —ap·point'ive, *adj.*

ap·point'ment, *n.* 1. act of choosing or naming. 2. prearranged meeting. 3. equipment.

ap·por'tion, *v.* divide into shares. —ap·por'tion·ment, *n.*

ap'po·site, *adj.* suitable.

ap·praise', *v.*, -praised, -praising. estimate the value of. —ap·prais'al, *n.* —ap·prais'er, *n.*

ap·pre'ci·a·ble (-shē-), *adj.* noticeable; significant.

ap·pre'ci·ate' (-shē-), *v.*, -ated, -ating. 1. value at true worth. 2. increase in value. —ap·pre'ci·a'tion, *n.* —ap·pre'ci·a'tive (-sha-), *adj.*

ap·pre·hend', *v.* 1. take into custody. 2. understand.

ap·pre·hen'sion, *n.* 1. anxiety. 2. comprehension. 3. arrest.

ap·pre·hen'sive, *adj.* worried; anxious.

ap·pren'tice, *n.*, *v.*, -ticed, -ticing. —*n.* 1. assistant learning a trade. —*v.* 2. bind as such an assistant. —ap·pren'tice·ship', *n.*

ap·prise', *v.*, -prised, -prising. notify. Also, ap·prize'.

ap·proach', *v.* 1. come near to. 2. make a proposal to. —*n.* 3. coming near. 4. access. 5. method.

ap'pro·ba'tion, *n.* approval.

ap·pro'pri·ate', *adj.*, *v.*, -ated, -ating. —*adj.* (-prē it). 1. suitable; proper. —*v.* (-prē āt'). 2. designate for use. 3. take possession of. —ap·pro'pri·ate·ly, *adv.* —ap·pro'pri·ate·ness, *n.* —ap·pro'pri·a'tion, *n.*

ap·prove', *v.*, -proved, -proving. 1. think or speak well of. 2. confirm. —ap·prov'al, *n.*

ap·prox'i·mate, *adj.*, *v.*, -mated, -mating. —*adj.* (-mit). 1. near; similar. —*v.* (-māt'). 2. come near to. —ap·prox'i·mate·ly, *adv.* —ap·prox·i·ma'tion, *n.*

ap·pur'te·nance, *n.* accessory.

ap·pur'te·nant, *adj.* pertaining.

a'pri·cot', *n.* peachlike fruit.

A'pril, *n.* fourth month of year.

a'pron, *n.* protective garment for the front of one's clothes.

ap·ro·pos' (ap'rə pō'), *adv.* 1. opportunely. 2. with reference. —*adj.* 3. opportune.

apse, *n.* vaulted recess in a building, as in a church.

apt, *adj.* 1. prone. 2. likely. 3. skilled; able. —apt'ly, *adv.* —apt'ness, *n.*

ap'ti·tude', *n.* skill; talent.

Aq'ua·lung', *n.* *Trademark.* underwater breathing device using compressed air.

aq'ua·ma·rine', *n.* 1. light greenish blue. 2. beryl of this color.

a·quar'i·um, *n.*, *pl.* -iums, -ia. place for exhibiting aquatic animals and plants.

a·quat'ic, *adj.* of, or living in, water.

aq'ue·duct', *n.* artificial channel for conducting water.

a'que·ous, *adj.* of or like water.

aq'ui·line', *adj.* (of a nose) curved upward.

Ar'ab, *n.* 1. member of a people living or originating in Arabia, a peninsula in SW Asia. —*adj.* 2. of the Arabs. Also, A·ra'bi·an.

Ar'a·bic, *n.* 1. Semitic language spoken chiefly in SW Asia and N Africa.

—*adj.* 2. of Arabic, Arabia, or the Arabs.

Arabic numeral, any of the numerals 0, 1, 2, 3, 4, 5, 6, 7, 8, or 9.

ar·a·ble, *adj.* suitable for plowing.

ar·bit·er, *n.* judge.

ar·bit·ra·ment, *n.* judgment by an arbiter.

ar·bi·trar·y, *adj.* 1. subject to personal judgment. 2. capricious. 3. abusing powers; despotic. —**ar'bi·trar'i·ly,** *adv.*

ar·bi·trate, *v.,* **-trated, -trating.** adjudicate as, or submit to, an arbiter. —**ar'bi·tra'tion,** *n.* —**ar'bi·tra'tor,** *n.*

ar·bor, *n.* tree-shaded walk or garden.

ar·bo're·al, *adj.* of, or living in, trees.

ar·bor·vi'tae (är'bər vī'tē), *n.* evergreen tree related to cypress, with scaly bark.

ar·bu'tus (-byōō'-), *n.* 1. variety of evergreen shrub. 2. creeping flowering plant.

arc, *n.* 1. part of circle. 2. luminous current between two electric conductors.

ar·cade', *n.* 1. row of archways. 2. covered passage with stores.

ar·cane', *adj.* known only to those with special knowledge; secret.

arch, *n.* 1. upwardly curved structure. —*v.* 2. cover with an arch. —*adj.* 3. chief. 4. roguish.

ar·chae·ol'o·gy (-kē-), *n.* study of past cultures from artifacts. Also, **ar'che·ol'o·gy.** —**ar'chae·o·log'i·cal,** *adj.* —**ar'chae·ol'o·gist,** *n.*

ar·cha'ic, *adj.* 1. no longer used. 2. ancient.

arch·an'gel (ärk'-), *n.* chief angel.

arch·bish'op, *n.* bishop of highest rank.

arch·duke', *n.* royal prince.

arch'er, *n.* one who shoots a bow and arrow. —**arch'er·y,** *n.*

ar·chi·pel'a·go' (är'kəs-), *n., pl.* **-gos, -goes.** 1. body of water with many islands. 2. the islands.

ar'chi·tect, (är'kə-), *n.* designer of buildings. —**ar'chi·tec'ture,** *n.* —**ar'chi·tec'tur·al,** *adj.*

ar'chives (är'kīvz), *n.pl.* 1. documents. 2. place for documents.

arch'way', *n.* entrance covered by arch.

arc'tic, *adj. (often cap.)* of or at the North Pole.

ar'dent, *adj.* earnest; zealous. —**ar'dent·ly,** *adv.*

ar'dor, *n.* zeal.

ar'du·ous (-jōō-), *adj.* 1. difficult. 2. steep. 3. severe.

are, *v.* pres. indic. pl. of **be.**

ar'e·a, *n.* 1. extent of surface; region. 2. scope.

area code, three-digit number for direct long-distance telephone dialing.

a·re'na, *n.* open space for contests, etc.

aren't, contraction of **are not.**

ar'go·sy, *n., pl.* **-sies.** *Poetic.* large merchant ship or fleet.

ar'got (är'gō, -gət), *n.* special vocabulary used by particular group of people.

ar'gue, *v.,* **-gued, -guing.** 1. present reasons for or against something. 2. dispute. 3. persuade. —**ar'gu·ment,** *n.* —**ar'gu·men·ta'tion,** *n.*

ar'gu·men'ta·tive, *adj.* tending to dispute.

a'ri·a, *n.* operatic solo.

ar'id, *adj.* dry. —**a·rid'i·ty,** *n.*

a·rise', *v.,* **arose, arisen, arising.** 1. move or get up. 2. occur.

ar·is·toc'ra·cy, *n., pl.* **-cies.** 1. state governed by nobility. 2. nobility. —**a·ris'to·crat,** *n.* —**a·ris'to·crat'ic,** *adj.*

a·rith'me·tic, *n.* computation with figures. —**ar·ith·met'i·cal,** *adj.* —**ar·ith·met'i·cal·ly,** *adv.*

ark, *n. Archaic.* large ship.

arm, *n.* 1. upper limb from hand to shoulder. 2. weapon. 3. combat branch. 4. armlike part. —*v.* 5. equip with weapons.

ar·ma'da (-mä'-), *n.* fleet of warships.

ar'ma·dil'lo (är'mə dil'ō), *n.* burrowing mammal covered with plates of bone and horn.

ar'ma·ged'don (-ged'-), *n.* crucial or final conflict.

ar'ma·ment, *n.* 1. military weapons. 2. arming for war.

arm'chair', *n.* chair with supports for the arms.

arm'ful, *n., pl.* **-fuls.** capacity of both arms.

ar'mi·stice, *n.* truce.

ar'mor, *n.* protective covering against weapons.

ar'mor·y, *n., pl.* **-ries.** 1. storage place for weapons. 2. military drill hall.

arm'pit', *n.* hollow part under arm at shoulder.

ar'my, *n., pl.* **-mies.** 1. military force for land combat. 2. large group.

a·ro'ma, *n.* odor. —**ar'o·mat'ic,** *adj.*

a·round', *adv.; prep.* 1. on every side of. 2. somewhere in or near. 3. about.

a·rouse', *v.,* **aroused, arousing.** 1. awaken. 2. stir to act.

ar·peg'gi·o' (är pej'ē ō', -pej'ō), *n.* sounding of notes in a chord in succession instead of together.

ar·raign′ (ə rān′), v. 1. call to court. 2. accuse. **—ar·raign′ment,** n.

ar·range′, v., **-ranged, -ranging.** 1. place in order. 2. plan or prepare. **—ar·range′ment,** n.

ar′rant, adj. downright.

ar·ray′, v. 1. arrange. clothe. —n. 3. arrangement, as for battle. 4. clothes.

ar·rears′, n.pl. overdue debt.

ar·rest′, v. 1. seize (person) by law. 2. stop. —n. 3. seizure. 4. stoppage.

ar·rive′, v., **-rived, -riving.** reach a certain place. **—ar·riv′al,** n.

ar′ro·gant, adj. insolently proud. **—ar′ro·gance,** n. or **ar′ro·gant·ly,** adv.

ar′ro·gate′, v., **-gated, -gating.** claim presumptuously. **—ar′ro·ga′tion,** n.

ar′row, n. pointed stick shot by a bow.

ar·roy′o (ə roi′ō), n., pl. **-os.** steep, dry gulch.

ar′se·nal, n. military storehouse or factory.

ar′se·nic, n. 1. metallic element. 2. poisonous powder.

ar′son, n. malicious burning of a building.

art, n. 1. production of something beautiful or extraordinary. 2. skill; ability. 3. cunning. —v. 4. Archaic. are. **—art′ful,** adj.

ar·te′ri·o·scle·ro′sis, n. hardening of arteries.

ar′ter·y, n., pl. **-ries.** 1. blood vessel from the heart. 2. main channel. **—ar·te′ri·al,** adj.

ar·te′sian (-zhən) **well,** deep well whose water rises under its own pressure.

ar·thri′tis, n. inflammation of a joint. **—ar·thrit′ic,** adj.

ar′ti·choke′, n. plant with an edible flower head.

ar′ti·cle, n. 1. literary composition. 2. thing; item. 3. the words a, an, or the.

ar·tic′u·late, adj., v., **-lated, -lating.** —adj. (-lit). 1. clear. 2. able to speak. 3. jointed. —v. (-lāt′). 4. speak, esp. distinctly. 5. joint. **—ar·tic′u·la′tion,** n.

ar′ti·fact′, n. object made by human being or beings.

ar′ti·fice, n. trick.

ar·tif′i·cer, n. craftsperson.

ar·ti·fi′cial (-shəl), adj. 1. manufactured, esp. as an imitation. 2. affected. **—ar·ti·fi′cial·ly,** adv. **—ar·ti·fi′ci·al′i·ty** (-fish′ē-), n.

ar·til′ler·y, n. mounted, large guns.

ar′ti·san (är′tə zən), n. person skilled in a practical art.

art′ist, n. practitioner of fine art. **—ar·tis′tic,** adj. **—art′ist·ry,** n.

art′less, adj. natural.

art′y, adj., **artier, artiest.** Informal. self-consciously artistic.

as, adv. 1. to such an extent. —conj. 2. in the manner, etc., that. 3. while. 4. because. —pron. 5. that.

as·bes′tos, n. fibrous material formerly used in fireproofing.

as·cend′, v. 1. climb. **—as·cent′,** n.

as·cend′an·cy, n. domination; power. **—as·cend′ant,** adj., n.

As·cen′sion, n. bodily passing of Christ to heaven.

as·cer·tain′ (as′ər-), v. find out.

as·cet′ic (ə set′ik), n. 1. one who lives austerely. —adj. 2. austere or abstemious. **—as·cet′i·cism′,** n.

as·cor′bic ac′id, vitamin C.

as′cot (as′kat, -kot), n. tie or scarf with broad ends.

as·cribe′, v., **-cribed, -cribing.** attribute. **—as·crip′tion,** n.

a·sep′sis, n. absence of certain harmful bacteria. **—a·sep′tic,** adj.

a·sex′u·al (ā-), adj. without sex.

ash, n. 1. (pl. ashes) residue of burned matter. 2. a common tree. **—ash′y,** adj.

a·shamed′, adj. feeling shame.

ash′en, adj. pale gray.

a·shore′, adv., adj. on or to shore.

ash′tray′, n. container for tobacco ashes.

A′sian (ā′zhən), n. native of Asia. **—Asian,** adj.

A′si·at′ic, adj. n. Offensive. Asian.

a·side′, adv. 1. on or to one side. 2. separate.

as′i·nine, adj. stupid.

ask, v. 1. put a question to. 2. request. 3. invite. 4. inquire.

a·skance′, adv. with doubt or disapproval.

a·skew′, adv., adj. twisted.

a·sleep′, adj., adv. sleeping.

a·so′cial (ā sō′shəl), adj. 1. not sociable or gregarious. 2. selfish.

asp, n. poisonous snake.

as·par′a·gus, n. plant with edible shoots.

as·pect′, n. 1. appearance. 2. phase; condition. 3. direction faced.

as′pen, n. variety of poplar.

as·per′i·ty, n., pl. **-ties.** roughness.

as·per′sion, n. derogatory criticism.

as′phalt, n. hard, black material used for pavements, etc.

as·phyx′i·ate′, v., **-ated, -ating.** affect by a lack of oxygen; choke or smother. **—as·phyx′i·a′tion,** n.

as′pic, n. jelly made from meat or fish stock or vegetable juice.

as·pire′, v., **-pired, -piring.** long, aim, or seek for. **—as·pir′ant,** n. **—as′pi·ra′tion,** n.

as•pi•rin, n. crystalline derivative of salicylic acid, used for relief of headaches, etc.

ass, n. 1. donkey. 2. fool.

as•sail', v. attack. —**as•sail'ant**, n.

as•sas'sin, n. murderer, esp. of an important person. —**as•sas'si•nate'**, v. —**as•sas'si•na'tion**, n.

as•sault', n., v. attack.

as•say', v. analyze or evaluate. —**as•say'**, n.

as•sem'blage (ə sem'blij), n. 1. group; assembly. 2. act of assembling.

as•sem'ble, v., -bled, -bling. come or bring together.

as•sem'bly, n., pl. -blies. 1. group gathered together. 2. legislative body. 3. putting together of parts.

as•sem'bly•man, n., pl. -men. member of legislative assembly. Also, fem., **as•sem'bly•wom'an**; masc. or fem., **as•sem'bly•per'son**.

as•sent', v. 1. agree. —n. 2. agreement.

as•sert', v. 1. state; declare. 2. claim. 3. present (oneself) boldly. —**as•ser'tion**, n. —**as•ser'tive**, adj.

as•sess', v. evaluate, as for taxes. —**as•sess'ment**, n. —**as•ses'sor**, n.

as'set, n. 1. item of property. 2. quality.

as•sid'u•ous (ə sij'-), adj. persistent; devoted. —**as•sid'u•ous•ly**, adv.

as•sign' (ə sīn'), v. 1. give. 2. appoint. 3. transfer. —n. 4. one to whom something is transferred. —**as•sign'a•ble**, adj. —**as•sign•ee'**, n. —**as•sign'ment**, n.

as•sig•na'tion (-sig-), n. appointment; rendezvous.

as•sim'i•late', v., -lated, -lating. absorb or become absorbed; merge. —**as•sim'i•la'tion**, n.

as•sist', v., n. help; aid. —**as•sist'ant**, n., adj. —**as•sist'ance**, n.

as•so'ci•ate', v., -ated, -ating, n., adj. —v. (-āt'-) 1. connect or join. 2. keep company. —n. (-it). 3. partner; colleague. —adj. (-it). 4. allied. —**as•so'ci•a'tion**, n.

as'so•nance (as'ə nəns), n. similarity of sound in words or syllables. —**as'so•nant**, adj.

as•sort', v. 1. classify. 2. vary. —**as•sort'ed**, adj. —**as•sort'ment**, n.

as•suage' (ə swāj'), v., -suaged, -suaging. lessen (pain, grief, etc.).

as•sume', v., -sumed, -suming. 1. take without proof. 2. undertake. 3. pretend. 4. take upon oneself.

as•sump'tion, n. 1. unverified belief. 2. undertaking. 3. (cap.) ascent to heaven of Virgin Mary.

as•sure', v., -sured, -suring. 1. affirm to. 2. convince; make sure. 3. encourage. 4. insure. —**as•sur'ance**, n. —**as•sured'**, adj.

as'ter, n. plant with many petals around a center disk.

as'ter•isk, n. star (*) used in writing, etc.

a•stern', adv., adj. Naut. toward or at the rear.

as'ter•oid', n. planetlike body beyond Mars.

asth'ma (az'mə), n. painful respiratory disorder. —**asth•mat'ic**, adj., n.

a•stig'ma•tism, n. eye defect resulting in imperfect images. —**a•stig•mat'ic**, adj.

a•stir', adj., adv. active.

as•ton'ish, v. surprise greatly; amaze. —**as•ton'ish•ment**, n.

as•tound', v. amaze greatly.

as'tral, adj. of, from, or like the stars.

a•stray', adj., adv. straying.

a•stride', adj., adv., prep. straddling.

as•trin'gent, adj. contracting; styptic.

as•trol'o•gy, n. study of stars to determine their influence on human affairs. —**as•tro•log'i•cal**, adj. —**as•trol'o•ger**, n.

as'tro•naut', n. traveler outside earth's atmosphere.

as•tro•nom'i•cal, adj. 1. of astronomy. 2. extremely great, high, expensive, etc.

as•tron'o•my, n. science of all the celestial bodies. —**as•tron'o•mer**, n.

as'tro•phys'ics, n. branch of astronomy dealing with physical properties of celestial bodies. —**as'tro•phys'i•cist**, n.

as•tute', adj. shrewd; clever. —**as•tute'ness**, n.

a•sun'der, adv., adj. apart.

a•sy'lum, n. home for persons needing care.

a•sym'me•try (ā sim'i trē), n. lack of symmetry. —**a'sym•met'ric**, **a'sym•met'ri•cal**, adj.

at, prep. (word used in indicating place, time, etc.).

at'a•vism, n. reappearance in an individual of the characteristics of a remote ancestor. —**at'a•vis'tic**, adj.

ate, v. pt. of **eat**.

at'el•ier' (at'l yā'), n. workshop or studio, esp. of an artist.

a'the•ism, n. belief that there is no God. —**a'the•ist**, n. —**a'the•is'tic**, adj.

a•thirst', adj. 1. Archaic. thirsty. 2. eager.

ath'lete, n. expert in exercises, sports, etc. —**ath•let'ic**, adj.

athlete's foot, ringworm of the feet.

a·thwart', adv., prep. from side to side of.

at'las, n. book of maps.

ATM, automated teller machine, which provides certain bank services when an electronic card is inserted.

at'mos·phere', n. 1. air surrounding earth. 2. pervading mood. —**at'mos·pher'ic**, adj.

at·oll', n. ring-shaped coral island.

at'om, n. smallest unit making up chemical element. —**a·tom'ic**, adj.

atomic bomb, bomb whose force is derived from nuclear fission of certain atoms, causing the conversion of some mass to energy (**atomic energy**). Also, **atom bomb**.

at'om·iz'er, n. device for making a fine spray.

a·ton'al (ā tōn'l), adj. lacking tonality. —**a·to·nal'i·ty**, n.

a·tone', v., **atoned, atoning**. make amends (for). —**a·tone'ment**, n.

a·top', adj., adv., prep. on or at the top of.

a·tri'um (ā'trē əm), n. pl. -**a**, -**ums**. 1. enclosed court in public building. 2. either of two upper chambers of the heart.

a·tro'cious, adj. 1. wicked. 2. very bad. —**a·troc'i·ty**, n.

at'ro·phy, n., v. **-phied, -phying**. —n. 1. wasting away of the body. —v. 2. cause or undergo atrophy.

at·tach', v. 1. fasten, join, or associate. 2. take by legal authority.

at·ta·ché' (at'ə shā'), n. embassy official.

at·tach'ment, n. 1. an attaching. 2. something fastened on. 3. affectionate tie.

at·tack', v. 1. act against with sudden force 2. do vigorously. —n. 3. an attacking; onset.

at·tain', v. 1. reach; arrive at. 2. accomplish; fulfill. —**at·tain'a·ble**, adj. —**at·tain'ment**, n.

at'tar, n. perfume from flowers.

at·tempt', v., n. try.

at·tend', v. 1. be present at. 2. go with. 3. take care of. 4. give heed to. —**at·tend'ance**, n. —**at·tend'ant**, n., adj.

at·ten'tion, n. 1. act of attending. 2. careful notice. —**at·ten'tive**, adj. —**at·ten'tive·ly**, adv.

at·ten'u·ate', v., **-ated, -ating**. 1. make thin. 2. lessen; abate. —**at·ten·u·a'tion**, n.

at·test', v. declare or certify as true, genuine, etc. —**at·tes·ta'tion**, n.

at'tic, n. room right under the roof.

at·tire', v., **-tired, -tiring**. —v. 1. dress; adorn. —n. 2. clothes.

at'ti·tude', n. 1. feeling or opinion, esp. as expressed. 2. posture.

at·tor'ney, n. lawyer.

attorney general, pl. **attorneys general, attorney generals**. chief law officer of a country or state.

at·tract', v. 1. draw toward. 2. invite; allure. —**at·trac'tion**, n. —**at·trac'tive**, adj. —**at·trac'tive·ly**, adv. —**at·trac'tive·ness**, n.

at·trib'ute, v., **-uted, -uting**. —v. (ə trib'yōot). 1. ascribe; credit; impute. —n. (at'rə byōot'). 2. special quality, aspect, etc. —**at·tri·bu'tion**, n.

at·tri'tion (ə trish'ən), n. wearing down.

at·tune', v., **-tuned, -tuning**. harmonize.

a·typ'i·cal (ā tip'i kal), adj. not typical; irregular. —**a·typ'i·cal·ly**, adv.

au'burn, adj. reddish brown.

auc'tion, n. 1. sale of goods to highest bidders. —v. 2. sell by auction. —**auc'tion·eer'**, n., v.

au·da'cious, adj. bold; daring. —**au·dac'i·ty** (-das'-), n.

au'di·ble, adj. that can be heard. —**au·di·bil'i·ty**, n. —**au'di·bly**, adv.

au'di·ence, n. 1. group of hearers or spectators. 2. formal hearing or interview.

au'di·o', adj. 1. of sound reception or reproduction. —n. 2. audible part of TV.

au'di·o·vis'u·al, adj. using films, TV, and recordings, as for education.

au'dit, n. official examination of accounts. —**au'dit**, v. —**au'di·tor**, n.

au·di'tion, n. 1. hearing. —v. 2. give a hearing to.

au'di·to'ri·um, n. large meeting room.

au'di·to'ry, adj. of hearing.

au'ger, n. drill.

aught, n. 1. anything. 2. zero (0). —adv. 3. at all.

aug·ment', v. increase. —**aug'men·ta'tion**, n.

au'gur (ô'gar), v. predict; bode. —**au'gu·ry** (-gyə-), n.

Au'gust, n. eighth month of year.

au·gust', adj. majestic.

auk, n. northern diving bird.

aunt, n. 1. sister of one's mother or father. 2. wife of an uncle.

au pair (ō pâr'), person, usu. young foreign visitor, who does household tasks in exchange for room and board.

au'ra, n. atmosphere, quality, etc.

au'ral, adj. of or by hearing.

au're·ole', n. halo.

Au·re·o·my·cin (ô'rē ō mī'sin), *n.* Trademark. antibiotic drug effective against some diseases.

au' re·voir' (ō' rə vwär'), *French.* good-by.

au'ri·cle, *n.* 1. outer part of ear. 2. chamber in heart. —**au·ric'u·lar,** *adj.*

au·rif'er·ous *adj.* containing gold.

au·ro'ra (ə rôr'ə), *n.* display of bands of light in the night sky.

aus'pice (ô'spis), *n. (usually pl.)* patronage.

aus·pi'cious, *adj.* favorable.

aus·tere', *adj.* 1. harsh; stern. 2. severely simple. —**aus·ter'i·ty,** *n.*

Aus·tral'ian (-trāl'-), *n.* native or citizen of Australia. —**Australian,** *adj.*

Aus'tri·an, *n.* native of Austria. —**Austrian,** *adj.*

au·then'tic *adj.* reliable; genuine. —**au·then'ti·cal·ly,** *adv.* —**au·then·tic'i·ty,** *n.* —**au·then'ti·cate',** *v.*

au'thor, *n.* writer or creator. —**au'thor·ship',** *n.*

au·thor·i·tar'i·an, *adj.* favoring subjection to authority.

au·thor'i·ta·tive, *adj.* to be accepted as true.

au·thor'i·ty, *n., pl.* **-ties.** 1. right to order or decide. 2. one with such right. 3. recognized source of information, etc.

au'thor·ize', *v.*, **-ized, -izing.** permit officially. —**au·thor·i·za'tion,** *n.*

au'tism (ô'tiz əm), *n.* disorder characterized by extreme self-absorption and detachment from reality. —**au·tis'tic,** *adj.*

au'to, *n.* automobile.

au·to·bi·og'ra·phy, *n., pl.* **-phies.** story of one's own life.

au·toc'ra·cy, *n., pl.* **-cies.** absolute political power. —**au'to·crat',** *n.* —**au·to·crat'ic,** *adj.*

au'to·graph', *n.* signature.

au·to·im·mune', *adj.* of or relating to the body's immune response to its own components.

au'to·mat', *n.* restaurant with coin-operated service.

au'to·mate', *v.*, **-mated, -mating.** make or become automatic.

au·to·mat'ic, *adj.* 1. self-acting. 2. inevitably following. —**au·to·mat'i·cal·ly,** *adv.*

au·to·ma'tion, *n.* automatically controlled machinery.

au·tom'a·ton, *n.* mechanical device or figure; robot.

au'to·mo·bile', *n.* motor-driven passenger vehicle.

au·ton'o·my, *n.* self-government. —**au·ton'o·mous,** *adj.*

au'top·sy, *n., pl.* **-sies.** examination of body for causes of death.

au'tumn, *n.* season before winter; fall. —**au·tum'nal,** *adj.*

aux·il'ia·ry (ôg zil'yə rē), *adj., n., pl.* **-ries.** —*adj.* 1. assisting. 2. subsidiary. —*n.* 3. aid. 4. noncombat naval vessel. 5. verb preceding other verbs to express tense, etc.

a·vail', *v.* 1. be of use, value, etc. 2. take to (oneself) advantageously. —*n.* 3. benefit; advantage.

a·vail'a·ble, *adj.* present for use. —**a·vail·a·bil'i·ty,** *n.*

av'a·lanche', *n.* mass of snow, ice, etc., falling down mountain.

a·vant'-garde', *adj.* progressive, esp. in art.

av'a·rice, *n.* greed. —**av'a·ri'cious,** *adj.*

a·venge', *v.,* avenged, avenging. take vengeance for. —**a·veng'er,** *n.*

av'e·nue', *n.* 1. broad street. 2. approach.

a·ver', *v.,* averred, averring. affirm; declare.

av'er·age (-ij), *n., adj. v.,* **-aged, -aging.** —*n.* 1. sum of a series of numbers divided by the number of terms in the series. —*adj.* 2. of or like an average. 3. typical. —*v.* 4. find average of.

a·verse', *adj.* unwilling. —**a·verse'ly,** *adv.* —**a·verse'ness,** *n.*

a·ver'sion, *n.* dislike.

a·vert', *v.* 1. turn away. 2. prevent.

a'vi·ar'y (ā'-), *n., pl.* **-aries.** place in which birds are kept.

a'vi·a'tion, *n.* science of flying aircraft. —**a'vi·a'tor,** *n.* —**a'vi·a'trix,** *n.fem.*

av'id, *adj.* eager. —**a·vid'i·ty,** *n.*

av·o·ca'do (-kä'-), *n., pl.* **-dos.** tropical pear-shaped fruit.

av·o·ca'tion, *n.* hobby.

a·void', *v.* shun; evade. —**a·void'a·ble,** *adj.* —**a·void'ance,** *n.*

av·oir·du·pois' (av'ar də poiz'), *n.* system of weights with 16-ounce pounds.

a·vow', *v.* declare; confess. —**a·vow'al,** *n.*

a·wait', *v.* wait for.

a·wake', *v.,* awoke or awaked, awaking, *adj.* —*v.* 1. Also, **a·wak'en.** rouse from sleep. —*adj.* 2. not asleep.

a·wak'en, *v.* awake.

a·ward', *v.* 1. bestow; grant. —*n.* 2. thing bestowed.

a·ware', *adj.* conscious (of). —**a·ware'ness,** *n.*

a·wash', *adj.* overflowing with water.

a·way, *adv.* 1. from this or that place. 2. apart. 3. aside. —*adj.* 4. absent. 5. distant.

awe, *n., v.,* **awed, awing.** —*n.* 1. respectful fear. —*v.* 2. fill with awe. —**awe'some,** *adj.*

aw'ful, *adj.* 1. fearful. 2. very bad. 3. *Informal.* very.

aw'ful·ly, *adv.* 1. very badly. 2. *Informal.* very.

a·while, *adv.* for a short time.

awk'ward, *adj.* 1. clumsy. 2. embarrassing. 3. difficult; risky. —**awk'ward·ly,** *adv.* —**awk'ward·ness,** *n.*

awl, *n.* small drill.

awn, *n.* bristlelike part of a plant.

awn'ing, *n.* rooflike shelter, esp. of canvas.

AWOL (ā'wôl, -wol) *adj., adv.* absent without leave.

a·wry (ə rī'), *adv., adj.* 1. twisted. 2. wrong.

ax, *n.* small chopping tool. Also, **axe.**

ax'i·om, *n.* accepted truth. —**ax'i·o·mat'ic,** *adj.*

ax'is, *n., pl.* **axes** (ak'sēz). line about which something turns. —**ax'i·al,** *adj.*

ax'le, *n.* bar on which a wheel turns.

ay (ā), *adv.* always. Also, **aye.**

a·ya·tol'lah, *n.* chief Muslim leader.

aye (ī), *adv., n.* yes.

a·za'lea, *n.* flowering evergreen shrub.

az'ure (azh'-), *adj., n.* sky-blue.

B

B, b, *n.* second letter of English alphabet.

bab'ble, *v.,* **-bled, -bling.** 1. talk distinctly or foolishly. 2. make a murmuring sound. —**bab'ble,** *n.*

babe, *n.* 1. baby. 2. innocent person.

ba·boon', *n.* large monkey of Africa and Arabia.

ba·bush'ka, *n.* woman's head scarf.

ba'by, *n., pl.* **-bies,** *v.,* **-bied, -bying.** —*n.* 1. infant. 2. childish person. —*v.* 3. pamper. —**ba'by·hood',** *n.* —**ba'by·ish,** *adj.*

baby boom, period of increase in the rate of births.

ba'by-sit', *v.,* **-sat, -sitting.** tend another's baby for a few hours. —**ba'by-sit'ter,** *n.*

bac'ca·lau're·ate (-lôr'ē it), *n.* bachelor's degree.

bach'e·lor (bach'-), *n.* 1. unmarried man. 2. person holding first degree at a college. —**bach'e·lor·hood',** *n.* —**bach'e·lor·ship',** *n.*

ba·cil'lus (-sil'əs), *n., pl.* **-cilli** (-sil'ī). type of bacteria.

back, *n.* 1. hinder part of human body. 2. corresponding part of animal body. 3. rear. 4. spine. —*v.* 5. sponsor. 6. move backward. 7. bet in favor of. 8. furnish or form a back. —*adj.* 9. being behind. 10. in the past. 11. overdue. —*adv.* 12. at or toward the rear. 13. toward original point or condition. 14. in return. —**back'er,** *n.* —**back'ing,** *n.*

back'bite', *v.,* **-bit, -bitten, -biting.** discuss (someone) maliciously.

back'bone', *n.* 1. spine. 2. strength of character. —**back'boned',** *adj.*

back'break'ing, *adj.* fatiguing.

back'drop', *n.* 1. curtain at the back of a stage. 2. background of an event; setting.

back'fire', *v.,* **-fired, firing.** 1. (of an engine) ignite prematurely. 2. bring results opposite to those planned. —**back'fire',** *n.*

back'gam'mon, *n.* board game for two persons.

back'ground', *n.* 1. parts in the rear. 2. distant portions in a picture. 3. origins; antecedents.

back'hand', *n.* 1. in tennis and other sports, stroke made with back of hand facing direction of movement. —*adj.* 2. backhanded. —*adv.* 3. in a backhanded way. —*v.* 4. hit with a backhand.

back'hand'ed, *adj.* 1. with upper part of hand forward. 2. ambiguous.

back'lash', *n.* sudden, retaliatory reaction.

back'log', *n.* reserve or accumulation, as of work.

back'pack', *n.* 1. knapsack for hiking. —*v.* 2. hike using backpack.

back'-ped'al, *v.,* **-aled, -aling.** 1. slow a bicycle by pressing backward on pedals. 2. retreat from or reverse a previous stand or opinion.

back'side', *n.* 1. rear. 2. rump.

back'slide', *v.,* **-slid, -slidden** or **-slid, -sliding.** relapse into sin. —**back'slid'er,** *n.*

back'stroke', *n.* swimming stroke performed while lying on back.

back talk, impertinent talk.

back'track', *v.* retreat slowly.

back'up', *n.* 1. person or thing that

supports or reinforces another. 2. accumulation caused by a stopping, as of traffic. 3. alternate kept in reserve.

back'ward, *adv.* Also, **back'wards.** 1. toward the back or rear. 2. back foremost. 3. toward or in the past. 4. toward the back or past. 5. behind in time or progress. 6. bashful. —**back'ward·ly,** *adv.* —**back'ward·ness,** *n.*

back'wa'ter, *n.* place that is backward or stagnant.

back'woods', *n.pl.* wooded or unsettled districts. —**back'woods'man,** *n.*

ba'con, *n.* cured back and sides of a hog.

bac·te'ri·a (-tēr'ē ə), *n., pl. of* **bacterium.** simplest type of vegetable organism, involved in fermentation, production of disease, etc. —**bac·te'ri·al,** *adj.* —**bac·te'ri·al·ly,** *adv.* —**bac·te'ri·ol'o·gy,** *n.* science dealing with bacteria. —**bac·te'ri·o·log'i·cal,** *adj.* —**bac·te'ri·ol'o·gist,** *n.*

bad, *adj.,* **worse, worst,** *n.* —*adj.* 1. not good. 2. bad thing, condition, or quality. —*v.* 3. bad. 4. bad. pt. of **bid.** —**bad'ly,** *adv.* —**bad'ness,** *n.*

badge, *n.* emblem or decoration.

badg'er, *n.* 1. burrowing carnivorous mammal. —*v.* 2. harass.

bad'min·ton, *n.* game similar to lawn tennis.

baf'fle, *v.,* **-fled, -fling,** *n.* —*v.* 1. thwart; confuse. —*n.* 2. obstacle; obstruction. —**baf'fle·ment,** *n.*

bag, *n., v.,* **bagged, bagging.** —*n.* 1. sack or receptacle of flexible material. 2. purse. —*v.* 3. bulge. 4. put into a bag. 5. kill or catch. —**bag'gy,** *adj.* —**bag'gi·ness,** *n.*

ba'gel, *n.* hard ringlike roll.

bag'gage, *n.* trunks, suitcases, etc.

bag'pipe', *n.* (*often pl.*) musical instrument with windbag and two or more pipes. —**bag'pip'er,** *n.*

bail, *Law* (1, 2, 4). —*n.* 1. security for the return of a prisoner to custody. 2. person giving bail. 3. handle of kettle or pail. —*v.* 4. give or obtain liberty by bail. 5. dip water out of boat. 6. **bail out,** make a parachute jump. —**bail'a·ble,** *adj.* —**bail'ee',** *n.* —**bail'ment,** *n.* —**bail'or, bail'er,** *n.*

bail'iff, *n.* public officer similar to sheriff or deputy.

bail'i·wick, *n.* 1. district under bailiff's jurisdiction. 2. person's area of authority, skill, etc.

bait, *n.* 1. food used as lure in angling or trapping. —*v.* 2. prepare with bait. 3. set dogs upon for sport.

bake, *v.,* **baked, baking.** 1. cook by dry heat, as in an oven. 2. harden by heat. —**bak'er,** *n.*

bak'er·y, *n., pl.* **-eries.** place for baking; baker's shop.

ba·la·lai'ka (-lī'-), *n.* musical instrument similar to guitar and mandolin.

bal'ance, *n., v.,* **-anced, -ancing.** —*n.* 1. instrument for weighing. 2. equilibrium. 3. harmonious arrangement. 4. act of balancing. 5. remainder, as of money due. —*v.* 6. weigh. 7. set or hold in equilibrium. 8. be equivalent to. 9. reckon or adjust accounts. —**bal'anc·er,** *n.*

bal'co·ny, *n., pl.* **-nies.** 1. platform projecting from wall of building. 2. theater gallery.

bald, *adj.* 1. lacking hair on scalp. 2. plain; undisguised. —**bald'ly,** *adv.* —**bald'ness,** *n.*

bale, *n., v.,* **baled, baling.** —*n.* 1. large bundle or package. —*v.* 2. make into bales. —**bal'er,** *n.*

bale'ful, *adj.* evil; menacing. —**bale'ful·ly,** *adv.* —**bale'ful·ness,** *n.*

balk (bôk), *v.* 1. stop; stop short. 2. hinder; thwart. —*n.* 3. obstacle; hindrance. 4. in baseball, illegal stop in pitcher's motion. —**balk'y,** *adj.*

ball, *n.* 1. round or roundish body. 2. game played with ball. 3. social assembly for dancing. 4. *Informal.* good time. —*v.* 5. make or form into ball.

bal'lad, *n.* 1. narrative folk song or poem. 2. sentimental popular song.

bal'last, *n.* 1. heavy material carried to ensure stability. —*v.* 2. furnish with ballast.

ball bearing, 1. bearing in which a moving part turns on steel balls. 2. ball so used.

bal·le·ri'na (-rē'-), *n.* leading woman ballet dancer.

bal·let' (ba lā'), *n.* 1. theatrical entertainment by dancers.

ballistic missile, guided missile completing its trajectory in free fall.

bal·lis'tics, *n.* study of the motion of projectiles. —**bal·lis'tic,** *adj.*

bal·loon', *n.* 1. bag filled with a gas lighter than air, designed to float in atmosphere. —*v.* 2. go up in balloon. —**bal·loon'ist,** *n.*

bal'lot, *n., v.,* **-loted, -loting.** —*n.* 1. ticket or paper used in voting. 2. vote; voting. —*v.* 3. vote by ballot.

ball'park', *n.* baseball grounds.

ball'point' pen, pen laying down ink with small ball bearing.

ball'room', *n.* room for balls or dancing.

bal'ly·hoo', *n.* 1. *Informal.* exaggerated publicity. —*v.* 2. tout.

balm (bäm), *n.* **1.** fragrant, oily substance obtained from tropical trees. **2.** aromatic ointment or fragrance.

balm'y, *adj.* **balmier, balmiest. 1.** mild; refreshing. **2.** fragrant. —**balm'i•ly,** *adv.* —**balm'i•ness,** *n.*

ba•lo'ney, *n. Informal.* **1.** bologna. **2.** false or foolish talk.

bal'sa (bôl'-), *n.* tropical American tree with very light wood.

bal'sam, *n.* **1.** fragrant substance exuded from certain trees. **2.** any of these trees. —**bal•sam'ic,** *adj.*

bal'us•ter, *n.* pillarlike support for railing.

bal'us•trade', *n.* series of balusters supporting a railing.

bam•boo', *n., pl.* **-boos.** treelike tropical grass having a hollow woody stem.

bam•boo'zle, *v.,* **-zled, -zling.** *Informal.* confuse or trick.

ban, *v.,* **banned, banning.** —*v.* **1.** prohibit. —*n.* **2.** prohibition.

ba'nal, *adj.* trite. —**ba•nal'i•ty,** *n.*

ba•nan'a, *n.* **1.** tropical plant. **2.** fruit of this plant.

band, *n.* **1.** strip of material for binding. **2.** stripe. **3.** company of persons. **4.** group of musicians. —*v.* **5.** mark with bands. **6.** unite. —**band'mas'ter,** *n.* —**bands'man,** *n.*

band'age, *n., v.,* **-aged, -aging.** —*n.* **1.** strip of cloth for binding wound. —*v.* **2.** bind with bandage. —**band'ag•er,** *n.*

ban•dan'na, *n.* colored handkerchief with figures. Also, **ban•dan'a.**

ban'dit, *n., pl.* **-dits, -dit'ti.** robber; outlaw. —**ban'dit•ry,** *n.*

band'stand', *n.* platform on which band or orchestra performs.

band'wag'on, *n.* **1.** large, ornate wagon for carrying band in parade. **2.** cause or movement that appears popular and headed for success.

ban'dy, *v.,* **-died, -dying,** *adj.* —*v.* **1.** strike to and fro. **2.** exchange (words) back and forth. —*adj.* **3.** bent outward. —**ban'dy-leg'ged,** *adj.*

bane, *n.* thing causing death or destruction.

bane'ful, *adj.* destructive. —**bane'ful•ly,** *adv.* —**bane'ful•ness,** *n.*

bang, *n.* **1.** loud, sudden noise. **2.** (*often pl.*) fringe of hair across forehead. —*v.* **3.** make loud noise. **4.** strike noisily.

ban'gle, *n.* bracelet.

ban'ish, *v.* **1.** exile. **2.** drive or put away. —**ban'ish•ment,** *n.*

ban'is•ter, *n.* **1.** baluster. **2.** (*pl.*) balustrade.

ban'jo, *n., pl.* **-jos, -joes.** musical instrument similar to guitar, with circular body. —**ban'jo•ist,** *n.*

bank, *n.* **1.** pile; heap. **2.** slope bordering stream. **3.** place or institution for receiving and lending money. **4.** store of something, such as blood, for future use. —*v.* **5.** border with or make into bank. **6.** cover fire to make burn slowly. **7.** act as bank. **8.** deposit or keep money in bank. **9.** rely (on). —**bank'er,** *n.* —**bank'ing,** *n.*

bank'roll', *n.* **1.** money possessed. —*v.* **2.** pay for; fund.

bank'rupt, *n.* **1.** insolvent person. —*adj.* **2.** insolvent. **3.** lacking. —*v.* **4.** make bankrupt. —**bank'rupt•cy,** *n.*

ban'ner, *n.* flag.

banns, *n.pl.* notice of intended marriage. Also, **bans.**

ban'quet, *n.* **1.** feast. —*v.* **2.** dine or entertain at banquet. —**ban'quet•er,** *n.*

ban'shee, *n.* female spirit of Irish folklore whose wailing means a loved one is about to die.

ban'tam, *n.* **1.** breed of small domestic fowl. —*adj.* **2.** tiny.

ban'ter, *n.* **1.** teasing; raillery. —*v.* **2.** address with or use banter. —**ban'ter•er,** *n.*

ban'yan, *n.* East Indian fig tree.

bap'tism, *n.* immersion in or application of water, esp. as initiatory rite in Christian church. —**bap•tis'mal,** *adj.*

Bap'tist, *n.* Christian who undergoes baptism only after profession of faith.

bap•tize', *v.,* **-tized, -tizing. 1.** administer baptism. **2.** christen. —**bap•tiz'er,** *n.*

bar, *n., v.,* **barred, barring,** *prep.* —*n.* **1.** long, evenly shaped piece of wood or metal. **2.** band; stripe. **3.** long ridge in shallow waters. **4.** obstruction; hindrance. **5.** line marking division between two measures of music. **6.** place where liquors are served. **7.** legal profession or its members. **8.** railing in courtroom between public and court officers. **9.** place in courtroom where prisoners are stationed. —*v.* **10.** provide or fasten with a bar. **11.** block; hinder. —*prep.* **12.** except for. —**barred,** *adj.*

barb, *n.* **1.** point projecting backward. —*v.* **2.** furnish with barb. —**barbed,** *adj.*

bar•bar'i•an, *n.* **1.** savage or uncivilized person. —*adj.* **2.** uncivilized. —**bar•bar'i•an•ism,** *n.* —**bar•bar'ic,** *adj.* —**bar•bar'i•cal•ly,** *adv.*

bar'ba•rism, *n.* barbarian state or act.

bar·bar·i·ty, n., pl. **-ties. 1.** cruelty. **2.** crudity.

bar·ba·rous, adj. **1.** barbarian. **2.** harsh; harsh-sounding. —**bar·ba·rous·ly**, adv. —**bar·ba·rous·ness**, n.

bar·be·cue′, n., v., **-cued, -cuing.** —n. **1.** outdoor meal at which foods are roasted over an open fire. **2.** animal roasted whole. —v. **3.** broil or roast over an open fire. Also, **bar′be·que′.**

bar·ber, n. **1.** one who gives haircuts, shaves, etc. —v. **2.** shave or cut the hair.

bar·bi·tu·rate′ (bär bich′ə rāt′), n. sedative drug.

bar code, series of lines of different widths placed on item for identification by computer scanner.

bard, n. **1.** ancient Celtic poet. **2.** poet. —**bard′ic**, adj.

bare, adj., **barer, barest**, v., **bared, baring.** —adj. **1.** uncovered; unclothed. **2.** unfurnished. **3.** unconcealed. **4.** mere. —v. **5.** make bare. —**bare′ness**, n. —**bare′foot′**, adj., adv.

bare′back′, adv., adj. without saddle.

bare′faced′, adj. **1.** undisguised. **2.** impudent.

bare′ly, adv. **1.** no more than; only. **2.** nakedly.

bar′gain, n. **1.** agreement. **2.** advantageous purchase. —v. **3.** discuss or arrive at agreement. —**bar′gain·er**, n.

barge, n., v., **barged, barging.** —n. **1.** unpowered vessel for freight. —v. **2.** carry by barge. **3.** move clumsily. **4.** Informal. intrude. —**barge′man**, n.

bar′i·tone′, n. **1.** male voice or part between tenor and bass. **2.** baritone singer, instrument, etc.

bar′i·um (bâr′ē əm, bar′-), n. metallic element.

bark, n. **1.** cry of a dog. **2.** external covering of woody plants. **3.** Also, **barque.** three-masted vessel. —v. **4.** sound a bark. **5.** utter with barking sound. **6.** strip off bark of. **7.** rub off the skin of.

bark′er, n. person who stands at the entrance to a show, shouting out its attractions.

bar′ley, n. edible cereal plant.

bar mitz′vah (bär), Jewish religious ceremony recognizing manhood.

barn, n. farm building for storage and stabling. —**barn′yard′**, n.

bar′na·cle, n. type of shellfish that clings to ship bottoms, floating timber, etc. —**bar′na·cled**, adj.

ba·rom′e·ter, n. instrument for measuring atmospheric pressure. —**bar′o·met′ric, bar′o·met′ri·cal**, adj.

bar′on, n. member of lowest nobility. Also, n.fem. **bar′on·ess.** —**ba·ro′ni·al**, adj.

bar′on·et, n. member of hereditary British commoner ranks, ranking below baron. —**bar′on·et·cy**, n.

Ba·roque′ (-rōk′), n. artistic style marked by exuberant decoration and grotesque effects.

bar′rack, n. (usually pl.) **1.** building for lodging soldiers. —v. **2.** lodge in barracks.

bar′ra·cu′da-(-kōō′-), n. edible eellike fish inhabiting warm waters.

bar′rage′, n. barrier of concentrated artillery fire.

bar′rel, n., v., **-reled, -reling.** —n. **1.** wooden cylindrical vessel with bulging sides. **2.** quantity held in such vessel. —v. **3.** put in barrel or barrels.

bar′ren, adj. **1.** sterile; unfruitful. **2.** dull. —**bar′ren·ness**, n.

bar′ri·cade′, n., v., **-caded, -cading.** —n. **1.** defensive barrier. —v. **2.** block or defend with barricade.

bar′ri·er, n. obstacle; obstruction.

bar′row, n. **1.** flat frame for carrying load. **2.** artificial mound, as over a grade.

bar′ter, v. **1.** trade by exchange. —n. **2.** act of bartering.

ba·salt′ (-sôlt′), n. dark, hard rock. —**ba·sal′tic**, adj.

base, n., v., **based, basing**, adj., **baser, basest.** —n. **1.** bottom or foundation of something. **2.** fundamental principle. **3.** starting point. **4.** Mil. **a.** protected place from which operations proceed. **b.** supply installation. **5.** chemical compound which unites with an acid to form a salt. —v. **6.** make foundation for. —adj. **7.** despicable. **8.** inferior. **9.** counterfeit. —**base′ly**, adv. —**base′ness**, n.

base′ball′, n. game of ball played by two teams of nine players on diamond-shaped field. **2.** ball used.

base′board′, n. board or molding at the base of a room's walls.

base′line′, n. **1.** line between bases on baseball diamond. **2.** line at each end of tennis court. **3.** basic standard or level; guideline. Also, **base line.**

base′ment, n. story of building below the ground floor.

bash′ful, adj. shy; timid. —**bash′ful·ly**, adv. —**bash′ful·ness**, n.

ba′sic, adj. **1.** rudimentary. **2.** essential. —n. **3.** (pl.) rudiments. —**ba′si·cal·ly**, adv.

bas′il (baz′-), n. plant of mint family.

ba·sil'i·ca, *n.* **1.** ancient church. **2.** Roman Catholic church.

ba'sin, *n.* **1.** circular vessel for liquids. **2.** area drained by river. **3.** area of lower land, not drained to outside.

ba'sis, *n., pl.* **-ses. 1.** base (defs. 1, 2). **2.** principal ingredient.

bask, *v.* lie in or expose to warmth.

bas'ket, *n.* receptacle woven of twigs, strips of wood, etc.

bas'ket·ball', *n.* **1.** game of ball played by two teams of five players on rectangular court. **2.** ball used.

bas'-re·lief' (bä'ri lēf'), *n.* sculpture in which figures project slightly from the background.

bass, *adj., n., pl.* (for 3) **basses, bass.** —*adj.* **1.** (bās). of the lowest musical part or range. —*n.* **2.** (bās). bass part, voice, instrument, etc. **3.** (bas). various edible, spiny fishes.

bas'si·net', *n.* basket with hood, used as cradle.

bas·soon', *n.* baritone woodwind instrument.

bas'tard, *n.* **1.** illegitimate child. **2.** *Informal.* mean person. —*adj.* **3.** illegitimate in birth. **4.** not pure or authentic.

baste, *v.,* **basted, basting. 1.** sew with temporary stitches. **2.** moisten meat, etc., while cooking.

bas'tion (bas'chan), *n.* **1.** projecting part of fortification. **2.** fortified place. **3.** something that preserves or protects.

bat, *n., v.,* **batted, batting.** —*n.* **1.** club, esp. as used in ball games. **2.** nocturnal flying mammal. —*v.* **3.** strike with bat. **4.** take turn in batting. **5.** blink; flutter.

batch, *n.* material, esp. bread, prepared in one operation.

bat'ed, *adj.* (of breath) held back in suspense.

bath, *n., pl.* **baths. 1.** washing of entire body. **2.** water used. **3.** **bathroom',** *n.* —**bath'tub',** *n.*

bathe, *v.,* **bathed, bathing. 1.** take a bath. **2.** immerse in liquid; moisten. —**bath'er,** *n.*

ba'thos (bā'thos, -thōs), *n.* **1.** ludicrous change in tone from lofty to commonplace. **2.** false pathos; trite sentiment. —**ba·thet'ic,** *adj.*

bath'robe', *n.* robe worn going to and from bath.

ba·tik' (-tēk'), *n.* cloth partly waxed to resist dye.

bat mitz'vah (bät), Jewish religious ceremony for a girl, paralleling the bar mitzvah.

ba·ton', *n.* staff or rod, esp. one used by orchestral conductor.

bat·tal'ion, *n.* military unit of three or more companies.

bat'ten, *n.* **1.** strip of wood. —*v.* **2.** fasten or furnish with battens. **3.** fatten or grow fat.

bat'ter, *v.* **1.** beat persistently. **2.** damage by hard usage. —*n.* **3.** semiliquid cooking mixture. **4.** one who bats.

bat'ter·y, *n., pl.* **-teries. 1.** device for producing electricity. **2.** combination of artillery pieces. **3.** illegal attack by beating or wounding.

bat'tle, *n., v.,* **-tled, -tling. 1.** hostile encounter. —*v.* **2.** fight. —**bat'tle·field',** *n.* —**bat'tle·ground',** *n.* —**bat'tler,** *n.*

bat'tle·ment, *n.* indented parapet.

bat'tle·ship', *n.* heavily armed warship.

bat'ty, *adj.,* **-tier, -tiest.** *Slang.* crazy or eccentric.

baud (bôd), *n.* unit used to measure speed of a signal or data transfer, as in computers.

baux'ite (bôk'sīt), *n.* principal ore of aluminum.

bawd'y, *adj.,* **bawdier, bawdiest.** obscene. —**bawd'i·ness,** *n.*

bawl, *v.* **1.** shout out. —*n.* **2.** shout.

bay, *n.* **1.** inlet of sea or lake. **2.** vertical section of window. **3.** compartment or recess in a building. **4.** deep, prolonged bark. **5.** stand made by hunted animal or person. **6.** reddish brown. **7.** laurel tree. **8.** bark. **9.** bring to bay (def. 5). —*adj.* **10.** of the color bay.

bay'o·net, *n., v.,* **-neted, -neting.** —*n.* **1.** daggerlike instrument attached to rifle muzzle. —*v.* **2.** kill or wound with bayonet.

bay'ou (bī'ōō), *n., pl.* **bayous.** arm of river, etc.

ba·zaar', *n.* market place. Also, **ba·zar'.**

ba·zoo'ka, *n.* hand-held rocket launcher used esp. against tanks.

BB, *n., pl.* **BB's.** small metal shot fired from an air rifle (**BB gun**).

B.C., before Christ.

be, *v.* **1.** exist. **2.** occur.

beach, *n.* **1.** sand or pebbles of seashore. —*v.* **2.** run or pull a ship onto beach.

beach'head', *n.* part of beach landed on and seized by military force.

bea'con, *n.* **1.** signal, esp. a fire. —*v.* **2.** serve as beacon.

bead, *n.* **1.** small ball of glass, pearl, etc., designed to be strung. **2.** (*pl.*) necklace. —*v.* **3.** ornament with beads. —**bead'ing,** *n.* —**bead'y,** *adj.*

bea'gle, *n.* short-legged hunting dog.

beak, n. 1. bill of bird. 2. beaklike object.

beak'er, n. large glass.

beam, n. 1. horizontal support secured at both ends. 2. breadth of ship. 3. ray of light or other radiation. —v. 4. emit beams. 5. smile radiantly. —**beam'ing,** adj.

bean, n. 1. edible seed of certain plants. 2. plant producing such seed.

bear, v., **bore** (for 1–5) or **beared** (for 6), **bearing,** n. —v. 1. support. 2. carry. 3. undergo; endure. 4. move; go. 5. give birth. 6. act as bear (def. 9). —n. 7. large shaggy mammal. 8. clumsy or rude person. 9. speculator who counts on falling prices. —**bear'er,** n. —**bear'a·ble,** adj. —**bear'ish,** adj. —**bear'ish·ly,** adv.

beard, n. 1. hair on face of man. 2. similar growth or part. —v. 3. defy. —**beard'ed,** adj. —**beard'less,** adj.

bear'ing, n. 1. manner. 2. reference; relation. 3. Mach. part in which another part moves. 4. (often pl.) position; direction. 5. **bearings,** orientation.

beast, n. 1. animal. 2. coarse or inhuman person.

beast'ly, adj., -**lier, -liest.** 1. brutish. 2. nasty. —**beast'li·ness,** n.

beat, v., **beat, beaten** or **beat, beating,** n. —v. 1. strike repeatedly. 2. dash against. 3. mark time in music. 4. defeat. 5. throb. —n. 6. blow. 7. sound of a blow. 8. habitual rounds. 9. musical time. —**beat'en,** adj. —**beat'er,** n.

be·a·tif'ic, adj. blissful. —**be·a·tif'i·cal·ly,** adv.

be·at'i·tude, n. 1. blessedness. 2. (often cap.) declaration of blessedness made by Christ (Matthew 5).

beau (bō), n., pl. **beaus, beaux.** 1. lover. 2. fop.

beau'te·ous (byōō'-), adj. beautiful. —**beau'te·ous·ly,** adv. —**beau'te·ous·ness,** n.

beau'ti·ful, adj. having beauty. —**beau'ti·ful·ly,** adv.

beau'ti·fy, v., -**fied, -fying.** make beautiful. —**beau'ti·fi·ca'tion,** n.

beau'ty, n., pl. -**ties.** 1. quality that excites admiring pleasure. 2. beautiful thing or person.

bea'ver, n. 1. amphibious rodent, valued for its fur. 2. the fur.

be·cause', conj. 1. for the reason that. —adv. 2. by reason (of).

beck, n. beckoning gesture.

beck'on, v. signal by gesture. —**beck'on·er,** n.

be·come', v., **became, become, becoming.** 1. come to be. 2. suit.

—**be·com'ing,** adj. —**be·com'ing·ly,** adv.

bed, n., v., **bedded, bedding.** —n. 1. piece of furniture on or in which a person sleeps. 2. sleep. 3. piece of ground for planting. 4. foundation. —v. 5. plant in bed. —**bed'time',** n.

bed'bug', n. bloodsucking insect.

bed'ding, n. blankets, sheets, etc., for a bed. Also, **bed'clothes'.**

be·dev'il, v., -**iled, -il·ing.** 1. torment maliciously. 2. confuse; confound.

bed'fast', adj. unable to leave bed.

bed'fel·low, n. 1. sharer of bed. 2. ally.

bed'lam, n. 1. scene of loud confusion. 2. lunatic asylum.

Bed'ou·in (-ōō in), n. 1. desert Arab. 2. nomad.

bed'pan', n. shallow pan used as toilet for person confined to bed.

be·drag'gled, adj. dirty and wet.

bed'rid·den', adj. confined to bed.

bed'rock', n. 1. continuous solid rock under soil. 2. firm foundation or basis.

bed'room', n. sleeping room.

bed'sore', n. skin ulcer caused by long confinement in bed.

bed'spread', n. cover for bed.

bed'stead', n. frame for bed.

bee, n. 1. four-winged, nectar-gathering insect. 2. local gathering. —**bee'hive',** n. —**bee'keep'er,** n.

beech, n. tree bearing small edible nuts (**beech'nuts'**). —**beech'en,** adj.

beef, n., pl. **beeves.** 1. bull, cow, or steer. 2. edible flesh of such an animal. 3. brawn. —**beef'y,** adj. —**beef'i·ness,** n. —**beef'steak',** n.

bee'line', n. direct course.

beep, n. 1. short tone, usu. high in pitch, as from automobile horn or electronic device. —v. 2. make or cause to make a beep.

beep'er, n. small electronic device whose signal notifies person carrying it of telephone message.

beer, n. beverage brewed and fermented from cereals.

beet, n. biennial edible plant.

bee'tle, n., v., -**tled, -tling,** n. —v. 1. project. —n. 2. insect with hard, horny forewings.

be·fall', v., -**fell, -fallen, -falling.** happen; happen to.

be·fit', v., -**fitted, -fitting.** be fitting for. —**be·fit'ting,** adj.

be·fore', adv. 1. in front. 2. earlier. —prep. 3. in front of. 4. previously to. 5. in future of. 6. in preference to. 7. in precedence of. 8. in presence of. —conj. 9. previously to time when.

be·fore'hand', adv. in advance.

be·friend', v. act as friend toward.

be·fud'dle, v., **-dled**, **-dling**. confuse thoroughly. —**be·fud'dle·ment**, n.

beg, v., **begged**, **begging**. 1. ask for charity. 2. ask humbly.

be·get', v., **begot**, **begotten** or **begot**, **begetting**. procreate. —**be·get'ter**, n.

beg'gar, n. 1. one who begs alms. 2. penniless person. —v. 3. reduce to poverty. —**beg'gar·y**, n.

beg'gar·ly, adj. meager; penurious.

be·gin', v., **began**, **begun**, **beginning**. 1. start. 2. originate. —**be·gin'ner**, n. —**be·gin'ning**, n.

be·gone', interj. depart!

be·gon'ia (bi gōn'ya), n. tropical flowering plant.

be·grudge', v., **-grudged**, **-grudging**. 1. be discontented at (another's possessions or standing). 2. give or allow reluctantly.

be·guile' (-gīl'), v., **-guiled**, **-guiling**. 1. delude. 2. charm; divert. —**be·guile'ment**, n. —**be·guil'er**, n.

be·half', n. 1. side; part. 2. interest; favor.

be·have', v., **-haved**, **-having**. 1. conduct oneself. 2. act properly.

be·hav'ior, n. manner of behaving.

be·head', v. cut off the head of.

be·he'moth (bi hē'məth), n. any huge or extremely powerful creature or thing.

be·hest', n. urgent request.

be·hind', prep. 1. at the back of. 2. later than. —adv. 3. at the back. 4. in arrears. —n. 5. Informal. buttocks.

be·hold', v., **beheld**, **beholding**, interj. —v. 1. look at; see. —interj. 2. look! —**be·hold'er**, n.

be·hold'en, adj. obliged.

be·hoove', v., **-hooved**, **-hooving**. be necessary for (someone).

beige (bāzh), n. light brown.

be'ing, n. 1. existence. 2. something that exists.

be·la'bor, v. 1. discuss, etc., excessively. 2. beat.

be·lat'ed, adj. late. —**be·lat'ed·ly**, adv.

belch, v. 1. eject gas from stomach. 2. emit violently. —n. 3. act of belching.

be·lea'guer (bi lē'gər), v. beset; surround, as with difficulties.

bel'fry, n., pl. **-fries**. bell tower.

be·lie', v., **-lied**, **-lying**. 1. misrepresent. 2. show to be false. 3. lie about. —**be·li'er**, n.

be·lief', n. 1. thing believed. 2. conviction. 3. faith.

be·lieve', v., **-lieved**, **-lieving**. 1. trust. 2. accept as true. 3. regard as likely.

—**be·liev'a·ble**, adj. —**be·liev'er**, n.

be·lit'tle, v., **-littled**, **-littling**. disparage.

bell, n. 1. metal instrument producing ringing sound. —v. 2. put bell on. 3. flare outward. —**bell'-like'**, adj.

belle, n. beautiful woman.

bel·lig'er·ent (-lij'-), adj. 1. warlike. 2. engaged in war. —n. 3. nation at war. —**bel·lig'er·ence**, **bel·lig'er·en·cy**, n. —**bel·lig'er·ent·ly**, adv.

bel'low, v. 1. roar, as a bull. 2. utter in deep, loud voice. —n. 3. act or sound of bellowing.

bel'lows, n.sing. and pl. collapsing device producing strong current of air.

bel'ly, n., pl. **-lies**, v., **-lied**, **-lying**. —n. 1. abdomen. 2. inside. 3. protuberant surface. —v. 4. swell out.

bel'ly·ache', n., v., **-ached**, **-aching**. —n. 1. pain in the abdomen. —v. 2. Informal. complain.

be·long', v. 1. be a member of. 2. belong to, be the property of.

be·long'ing, n. possession.

be·lov'ed, adj. 1. greatly loved. —n. 2. one who is loved.

be·low', adv. 1. beneath. 2. in lower rank. —prep. 3. lower than.

belt, n. 1. band for encircling waist. 2. any flexible band. —v. 3. gird or furnish with belt. —**belt'ing**, n.

be·moan', v. lament.

be·mused', adj. lost in thought.

bench, n. 1. long seat. 2. judge's seat. 3. body of judges. 4. work table.

bench'mark', n. standard against which others can be measured or judged. Also, **bench' mark'**.

bend, v., **bent**, **bending**, n. —v. 1. curve. 2. become curved. 3. cause to submit. 4. turn or incline. —n. 5. a bending. 6. something bent.

be·neath', adj. 1. in a lower place, state, etc. —prep. 2. under. 3. lower than. 4. unworthy of.

ben·e·dic'tion, n. blessing.

ben·e·fac'tion, n. 1. doing of good. 2. benefit conferred. —**ben·e·fac'tor**, n. —**ben'e·fac'tress**, n.fem.

be·nef'i·cent, adj. doing good. —**benef'i·cence**, n. —**be·nef'i·cent·ly**, adv.

ben·e·fi'cial, adj. helpful. —**ben·e·fi'cial·ly**, adv.

ben·e·fi'ci·ar·y, n., pl. **-aries**. one who receives benefits.

ben'e·fit, n., v., **-fited**, **-fiting**. —n. 1. act of kindness. 2. entertainment for worthy cause. —v. 3. do good to. 4. gain advantage.

be·nev·o·lent, adj. desiring to do good. —be·nev·o·lence, n.

be·night·ed, adj. ignorant; in the dark.

be·nign (bi nīn'), adj. 1. kind. 2. favorable. —be·nign'ly, adv.

be·nig·nant (-nig'-), adj. 1. kind. 2. beneficial. —be·nig'nan·cy, n. —be·nig'nant·ly, adv. —be·nig'ni·ty, n.

bent, adj. 1. curved. 2. determined. —n. 3. curve. 4. inclination.

be·numb' (bi num'), v. 1. make numb. 2. make inactive; stupefy.

ben'zene (-zēn), n. colorless inflammable liquid, used as solvent.

ben'zine (-zēn), n. colorless inflammable liquid, used in cleaning, dyeing, etc.

be·queath', v. dispose of by will. —be·queath'al, n.

be·quest', n. legacy.

be·rate', v., -rated, -rating. scold.

be·reave', v., -reaved or -reft, -reaving. 1. deprive of. 2. make desolate. —be·reave'ment, n.

be·ret' (-rā'), n. cloth cap.

ber·i·ber'i, n. disease caused by vitamin deficiency.

ber'ry, n., pl. -ries, v., -ried, -rying. —n. 1. small juicy fruit. —v. 2. produce or gather berries.

ber·serk', adj. raging violently.

berth, n. 1. sleeping place for traveler. 2. mooring space for vessel. —v. 3. assign berth (def. 2) to.

ber'yl, n. green mineral.

be·seech', v., -sought, -seeching. implore; beg. —be·seech'ing·ly, adv.

be·set', v., -set, -setting. 1. attack on all sides. 2. surround.

be·side', prep. 1. at the side of. 2. compared with. 3. in addition to. —adv. 4. in addition.

be·sides', adv. 1. moreover. 2. otherwise. —prep. 3. in addition to. 4. other than.

be·siege', v., -sieged, -sieging. lay siege to. —be·sieg'er, n.

be·smirch', v. defile.

be·sot'ted (bi sot'id), adj. 1. drunk. 2. infatuated.

be·speak', v., -spoke, -spoken or -spoke, -speaking. 1. ask for in advance. 2. imply.

best, adj. 1. of highest quality. 2. most suitable. —adv. 3. most excellently. 4. most fully. —n. 5. best thing. —v. 6. defeat.

bes'tial (-chəl), adj. 1. beastlike. 2. brutal. —bes·ti·al'i·ty, n. —bes'tial·ly, adv.

be·stir', v., -stirred, -stirring. stir up.

best man, chief attendant of the bridegroom at a wedding.

be·stow', v. 1. present. 2. apply.

be·strew', v., -strewed, -strewed or -strewn, -strewing. 1. cover. 2. scatter.

bet, v., bet or betted, betting. —v. 1. risk on a chance result. —n. 2. thing or amount bet. —bet'ter, bet'tor, n.

be·take', v., -took, -taken, -taking. betake oneself, 1. go. 2. resort (to).

be'tel nut (bēt'l), seed of a palm, often chewed in tropics.

bête' noire' (bet' nwär'), most dreaded person or thing.

be·tide', v., -tided, -tiding. happen.

be·times', adv. Archaic. 1. early. 2. soon.

be·to'ken, v. 1. indicate.

be·tray', v. 1. deliver or expose by treachery. 2. be unfaithful to. 3. reveal. 4. deceive. 5. seduce. —be·tray'al, n. —be·tray'er, n.

be·troth' (bi trōth'), v. promise to marry. —be·troth'al, n.

bet'ter, adj. 1. of superior quality. 2. healthier. —adv. 3. in a more excellent way. 4. more. —n. 5. something better. 6. one's superior. —v. 7. improve on. —bet'ter·ment, n.

be·tween', prep. 1. in the space separating. 2. intermediate to. 3. connecting. —adv. 4. in the intervening space or time.

be·twixt', prep., adv. between.

bev'el, v., -eled, -eling. —n. 1. surface cutting off a corner. 2. instrument for drawing angles. —v. 3. cut or slant at a bevel.

bev'er·age, n. drink.

bev'y, n., pl. bevies. 1. flock of birds. 2. group.

be·wail', v. lament.

be·ware', v., -wared, -waring. be wary (of).

be·wil'der, v. confuse. —be·wil'dered, adj. —be·wil'der·ing, adj. —be·wil'der·ing·ly, adv. —be·wil'der·ment, n.

be·witch', v. enchant. —be·witch'ing, adj. —be·witch'ing·ly, adv.

be·yond', prep. 1. on the farther side of. 2. farther, more, or later on. —adv. 3. farther on. —n. 4. life after death.

bi·an'nu·al, adj. occurring twice a year. —bi·an'nu·al·ly, adv.

bi'as, n. 1. slant. 2. prejudice. —v. 3. prejudice.

bi·ath'lon (bī ath'lon), n. sports event combining cross-country skiing and rifle shooting.

bib, n. cloth to protect dress.

Bi'ble, n. Old and New Testaments.
—**Bib'li·cal,** adj. —**Bib'li·cal·ly,**
adv.

bib'li·og'ra·phy, n., pl. **-phies.** list of
associated writings.

bib'u·lous (bib'ya las), adj. fond of or
addicted to drink.

bi·cam'er·al, adj. composed of two
legislative bodies.

bi·cen·ten'ni·al, n. two-hundredth
anniversary. Also, **bi'cen·ten'a·ry.**

bi'ceps (-seps), n. muscle of upper
arm.

bick'er, v. squabble.

bi'cy·cle (-si-), n., v., **-cled, -cling.**
—n. 1. two-wheeled vehicle. —v. 2.
ride a bicycle. —**bi'cy·cler, bi'cy·**
clist, n.

bid, v., **bade** (for 1, 2) or **bid**
(for 3), **bidden** or **bid, bidding,** n.
—v. 1. command. 2. say. 3. offer. —n.
4. offer. —**bid'der,** n. —**bid'ding,** n.

bid'da·ble, adj. 1. worth bidding. 2.
Archaic. obedient.

bide, v., **bided, biding.** —**bide one's**
time, await opportunity.

bi·det' (bē dā'), n. tub for bathing
private parts.

bi·en'ni·al, adj. occurring every two
years. —**bi·en'ni·al·ly,** adv.

bier, n. stand for a corpse or coffin.

bi·fo'cal, adj. 1. having two focuses.
2. (of eyeglass lens) having separate
portions for near and far vision. —n.
3. (pl.) eyeglasses with bifocal lenses.

big, adj., **bigger, biggest.** 1. large. 2.
important. —**big'ness,** n.

big'a·my, n., pl. **-mies.** crime of mar-
rying again while legally married.
—**big'a·mist,** n. —**big'a·mous,** adj.

Big'foot', n. Sasquatch. Also, **Big'**
Foot'.

big'horn', n. wild sheep of western
U.S.

bight (bīt), n. 1. loop of rope. 2. deep
bend in seashore.

big'ot, n. bigoted person. —**big'ot·**
ry, n.

big'ot·ed, adj. intolerant. —**big'ot·**
ed·ly, adv.

bi·ki'ni (-kē'-), n. woman's brief
bathing suit.

bi·lat'er·al, adj. on or affecting two
sides.

bile, n. 1. digestive secretion of the
liver. 2. ill nature.

bilge, n., v., **bilged, bilging.** —n. 1.
outer part of ship bottom. 2. water in
a bilge. 3. wide part of cask. —v. 4.
Naut. cause to leak at the bilge.

bi·lin'gual, adj. speaking or expressed in
two languages. —**bi·lin'gual·ly,**
adv.

bil'ious (-yəs), adj. 1. pertaining to
bile or excess bile. 2. peevish.

bilk, v. cheat; defraud.

bill, n. 1. account of money owed. 2.
piece of paper money. 3. draft of proposed statute. 4. written list. 5. horny
part of bird's jaw. 6. poster. —v. 7.
charge.

bill'board', n. large outdoor advertising display panel.

bil'let, n., v., **-leted, -leting.** —n. 1.
lodging for a soldier. —v. 2. provide
with lodging.

bill'fold', n. wallet.

bil·let-doux' (bil'ā dōō'), n., pl. **bil-**
lets-doux (-dōōz'), love letter.

bil'liards, n. game played with hard
balls **(billiard balls)** on a table.
—**bil'liard,** adj. —**bil'liard·ist,** n.

bil'lion, n. thousand million. —**bil'**
lionth, adj., n.

bil·lion·aire', n. owner of billion dollars or more.

bil'low, n. 1. great wave. —v. 2. surge.
—**bil'low·y,** adj. —**bil'low·i·ness,**
n.

bi·month'ly, adv., adj. every two
months.

bin, n., v., **binned, binning.** —n. 1. box
for storing grain, coal, etc. —v. 2.
store in bin.

bi'na·ry (bī'-), adj. 1. involving two
parts, elements, choices, etc. 2. of a
numerical system in which each place
of a number is expressed as 0 or 1.

bind, v., **bound, binding.** 1. tie or encircle with band. 2. unite. 3. oblige. 4.
attach cover to book. —**bind'er,** n.

bind'ing, n. 1. something that binds.
—adj. 2. obligatory.

binge, n., v., **binged, binging.** —n. 1.
bout of excessive indulgence, as in
eating or drinking. —v. 2. go on
binge.

bin'go, n. game of chance using squares
with numbered spaces.

bin'na·cle, n. stand for ship's compass.

bin·oc'u·lars, n.pl. field glasses.

bi'o·chem'is·try, n. chemistry of living matter. —**bi'o·chem'i·cal,** adj.
—**bi'o·chem'i·cal·ly,** adv. —**bi'o·**
chem'ist, n.

bi'o·de·grad'a·ble, adj. decaying
and being absorbed into environment.

bi'o·en·gi·neer'ing, n. 1. application
of engineering principles to problems
in medicine and biology. 2. application of biological principles to manufacturing or engineering processes.

bi'o·eth'ics, n. study of ethical implications of medical or biological pro-
cedures.

bi•o•feed´back, n. method for achieving physical and emotional self-control through observation of one's waves, blood pressure, etc.

bi•og´ra•phy, n., pl. -phies. written account of person's life. —**bi•og´ra•pher,** n. —**bi´o•graph´i•cal, bi´o•graph´ic,** adj. —**bi´o•graph´i•cal•ly,** adv.

bi´o•haz´ard, n. 1. anything used in or produced by biological research that poses a health hazard. 2. risk posed by a biohazard.

biological warfare, use in war of deadly or disease-producing organisms.

bi•ol´o•gy, n. science of living matter. —**bi´o•log´i•cal, bi´o•log´i•cal•ly,** adv. —**bi•ol´o•gist,** n.

bi•on´ics, n. use of electronic devices to increase human strength or ability. —**bi•on´ic,** adj.

bi•op´sy, n., pl. -sies. examination of specimen of living tissue.

bi´o•sphere´ (bī´ə-), n. the part of the earth's surface and atmosphere that supports life.

bi´o•tech•nol´o•gy (bī´ō-), n. use of living organisms in making drugs or other products or to manage the environment.

bi•par´ti•san, adj. representing two parties or factions.

bi´ped, n. 1. two-footed animal. —adj. 2. having two feet.

birch, n. tree with smooth bark and dense wood. —**birch´en,** adj.

bird, n. vertebrate with feathers and wings.

bird´ie, n. score of one under par on a golf hole.

bird's´-eye´, adj. seen from above.

birth, n. 1. fact of being born. 2. lineage. 3. origin. —**birth´day´,** n. —**birth´place´,** n.

birth control, planned contraception.

birth´mark´, n. mark on skin from birth.

birth´rate´, n. number of births in a given place in a given time.

birth´right´, n. hereditary right.

bis´cuit, n. bread in small, soft cakes. —**bis´cuit•like´,** adj.

bi•sect´, v. cut into two parts. —**bi•sec´tion,** n. —**bi•sec´tion•al,** adj. —**bi•sec´tor,** n.

bi•sex´u•al, adj. 1. being both heterosexual and homosexual. —n. 2. bisexual person. —**bi•sex´u•al´i•ty,** n.

bish´op, n. 1. overseer of a diocese. 2. piece in chess.

bish´op•ric, n. diocese or office of bishop.

bi´son, n., pl. **bisons, bison.** oxlike North American mammal.

bisque (bisk), n. creamy soup.

bis´tro (bis´trō, bē´strō), n. small, modest café.

bit, n., v., **bitted, bitting.** —n. 1. mouthpiece of bridle. 2. restraint. 3. small amount. 4. drill. 5. unit of computer information. —v. 6. restrain with a bit.

bitch, n. 1. female dog. 2. Slang. mean or lewd woman. —v. 3. Slang. complain.

bite, v., **bit, bitten or bit, biting,** n. —v. 1. cut or grip with teeth. 2. sting. 3. corrode. —n. 4. act of biting. 5. wound made by biting. 6. sting. 7. piece bitten off. —**bit´er,** n.

bit´ing, adj. 1. harsh to the senses. 2. severely critical. —**bit´ing•ly,** adv.

bit´ter, adj. 1. of harsh taste. 2. hard to receive or bear. 3. intensely hostile. 4. something bitter. —**bit´ter•ish,** adj. —**bit´ter•ly,** adv. —**bit´ter•ness,** n.

bit´tern, n. type of heron.

bit´ters, n.pl. liquor with bitter vegetable ingredients.

bi•tu´men (-tōō´-), n. asphalt or asphaltlike substance. —**bi•tu´mi•nous,** adj.

bi´valve´, n. mollusk with two shells hinged together. —**bi´valve´, bi´val´vu•lar,** adj.

biv•ou•ac´ (biv´ōō ak´), n., v., -acked, -acking. —n. 1. temporary resting or assembly place for troops. —v. 2. dispose or meet in bivouac.

bi•week´ly, adv., adj. 1. every two weeks. 2. twice a week.

bi•zarre´ (-zär´), adj. strange.

blab, v., **blabbed, blabbing.** 1. talk idly. 2. reveal secrets.

black, adj. 1. without brightness or color. 2. having dark skin color. 3. without light. 4. gloomy. 5. wicked. —n. 6. member of a dark-skinned people, esp. of Africa or African ancestry. 7. black clothing. 8. something black. —v. 9. make or become black. —**black´ness,** n. —**black´ly,** adv. —**black´ish,** adj.

black´ball´, n. 1. adverse vote. —v. 2. vote against. 3. ostracize.

black´ber´ry, n., pl. -ries. 1. dark-purple fruit. 2. plant bearing it.

black´bird´, n. black-feathered American bird.

black´board´, n. dark board for writing on with chalk.

black´en, v. 1. black (def. 9). 2. defame.

black´guard (blag´ärd), n. 1. despicable person. —v. 2. revile. —**black′-guard•ly,** adv., adj.

black′head′, n. small fatty mass in a skin follicle, esp. on the face.

black hole, area in outer space whose great density prevents radiation of light.

black′jack′, n. 1. short flexible club. 2. game of cards; twenty-one. —v. 3. strike with a blackjack.

black′list′, n. list of persons in disfavor. —**black′list′,** v.

black′mail′, n. 1. extortion by intimidation. 2. payment extorted. —v. 3. extort by blackmail. —**black′mail′-er,** n.

black market, illegal buying and selling of goods in violation of government controls.

black′out′, n. 1. extinction of lights. 2. loss of consciousness.

black′smith′, n. 1. person who shoes horses. 2. worker in iron.

black sheep, person who causes embarrassment or shame to his or her family.

black′thorn′, n. thorny shrub with plumlike fruit.

black widow, poisonous spider.

blad′der, n. sac in body.

blade, n. 1. cutting part of knife, sword, etc. 2. leaf. 3. thin, flat part. 4. dashing young man. —**blad′ed,** adj. —**blade′like′,** adj.

blame, v., **blamed, blaming,** n. —v. 1. hold responsible for fault. 2. find fault with. —n. 3. censure. 4. responsibility for censure. —**blam′a•ble, blame′ful, blame′wor′thy,** adj. —**blame′less,** adj.

blanch, v. whiten.

bland, adj. 1. not harsh. 2. not interesting or flavorful. —**bland′ly,** adv. —**bland′ness,** n.

blan′dish, v. coax. —**blan′dish-ment,** n.

blank, adj. 1. not written or printed on. 2. without interest, emotion, etc. 3. white. 4. unrhymed. —n. 5. place lacking something. 6. space to be filled in. 7. paper containing such space. —v. 8. make blank. —**blank′-ly,** adv. —**blank′ness,** n.

blan′ket, n. 1. warm bed covering. —v. 2. cover.

blare, v., **blared, blaring,** n. —v. 1. sound loudly. —n. 2. loud, raucous noise.

blar′ney, n. 1. wheedling talk. —v. 2. wheedle.

bla•sé′ (blä zā′), adj. bored; unimpressed.

blas•pheme′ (-fēm′), v. speak impiously or evilly. —**blas•phem′er,** n.

—**blas′phe•mous,** adj. —**blas′phe-my,** n.

blast, n. 1. gust of wind. 2. loud trumpet tone. 3. stream of air. 4. explosion. 5. charge of explosive. —v. 6. blow. 7. blight; destroy. 8. explode. —**blast′er,** n.

blast′off′, n. rocket launching.

bla′tant, adj. brazenly obvious. —**bla′tan•cy,** n. —**bla′tant•ly,** adv.

blaze, n., v., **blazed, blazing.** —n. 1. bright flame. 2. bright glow. 3. brightness. 4. mark cut on tree. 5. white spot on animal's face. —v. 6. burn or shine brightly. 7. mark with blazes (def. 4).

blaz′er, n. sports jacket.

bla′zon (blā′zən), v. depict or proclaim.

bleach, v. 1. whiten. —n. 2. bleaching agent.

bleach′ers, n.pl. tiers of spectators' seats, usu. roofless.

bleak, adj. 1. bare; desolate. 2. cold. 3. dreary; depressing. —**bleak′ly,** adv. —**bleak′ness,** n.

blear, v. 1. dim, esp. with tears. —n. 2. bleared state. —**blear′y,** adj.

bleat, v. 1. cry, as sheep, goat, etc. —n. 2. such a cry. —**bleat′er,** n.

bleed, v., **bled, bleeding.** lose or cause to lose blood.

bleep, v. delete or block (sound, esp. speech) from a recording or broadcast.

blem′ish, v. 1. mar. —n. 2. defect. —**blem′ish•er,** n.

blend, v. 1. mix. —n. 2. mixture.

bless, v., **blessed** or **blest, blessing.** 1. consecrate. 2. request divine favor on. 3. make happy. 4. extol as holy. —**bless′ed,** adj. —**bless′ing,** n.

blight, n. 1. plant disease. 2. ruin. —v. 3. wither; decay. 4. ruin.

blimp, n. small airship or dirigible.

blind, adj. 1. sightless. 2. uncomprehending; unreasonable. 3. hidden. 4. without an outlet. 5. without advance knowledge. —v. 6. make blind. —n. 7. something that blinds. 8. ruse or disguise. —**blind′ly,** adv. —**blind′-ness,** n.

blind′fold′, v. 1. cover eyes. —n. 2. covering over eyes. —adj. 3. with covered eyes.

blink, v. 1. wink. 2. ignore. —n. 3. act of blinking. 4. gleam.

blip, n. 1. point of light on radar screen, indicating an object. 2. brief interruption or upward turn in a straight line or continuity.

bliss, n. 1. gladness. 2. supreme happiness. —**bliss′ful,** adj.

blis′ter, n. 1. vesicle on the skin. —v. 2. raise blisters on. **—blis′ter•y,** adj.

blithe, adj. joyous; cheerful. **—blithe′ly,** adv.

blithe′some, adj. cheerful.

blitz, n. Also, **blitz′krieg′** (-krēg′). 1. swift, violent war, waged by surprise. —v. 2. attack by blitz.

bliz′zard, n. violent snowstorm.

bloat, v. swell.

blob, n. 1. small lump or drop. 2. shapeless mass.

bloc, n. political or economic confederation.

block, n. 1. solid mass. 2. platform. 3. obstacle. 4. single quantity. 5. unit of city street pattern. —v. 6. obstruct. 7. outline roughly. **—block′er,** n.

block•ade′, n., v., **-aded, -ading.** —n. 1. shutting-up of place by armed force. 2. obstruction. —v. 3. subject to blockade.

block′bust′er, n. highly successful motion picture, novel, etc.

block′head′, n. stupid person.

block′house′, n. fortified structure.

blond, adj. 1. light-colored. 2. having light-colored hair, skin, etc. —n. 3. blond person. **—blonde,** adj., n.fem.

blood, n. 1. red fluid in arteries and veins. 2. life. 3. bloodshed. 4. extraction. **—blood′y,** adj. **—blood′i•ness,** n. **—blood′less,** adj.

blood′cur′dling, adj. causing terror or horror.

blood′hound′, n. large dog with acute sense of smell.

blood′mo•bile′, n. truck for receiving blood donations.

blood pressure, pressure of blood against inner walls of blood vessels.

blood′shed′, n. slaughter.

blood′shot′, adj. with eye veins conspicuous.

blood′stream′, n. blood flowing through the body's circulatory system.

blood′suck′er, n. 1. leech. 2. extortionist.

blood′thirst′y, adj. murderous.

bloom, n. 1. flower. 2. health. 3. healthy glow. —v. 4. blossom. 5. flourish. **—bloom′ing,** adj.

bloom′ers, n.pl. loose trousers formerly worn by women.

blos′som, n. 1. flower. —v. 2. produce blossoms. 3. develop.

blot, n., v. **blotted, blotting.** —n. 1. spot; stain. —v. 2. stain; spot. 3. dry with absorbent material. 4. destroy.

blotch, n. 1. large spot or stain. —v. 2. blot (def. 2). **—blotch′y,** adj.

blot′ter, n. 1. piece of paper for blot-

ting. 2. book in which events are recorded.

blouse, n. loosely fitting upper garment.

blow, v., **blew, blown, blowing,** n. —v. 1. (of air) move. 2. drive by current of air. 3. sound a wind instrument. 4. go bad. 5. explode. 6. blossom. —n. 7. blast of air. 8. sudden stroke. 9. sudden shock of calamity. 10. blossoming. **—blow′er,** n. **—blow′y,** adj.

blow′out′, n. rupture of an automobile tire.

blow′pipe′, n. pipe used to concentrate stream of air or gas.

blow′torch′, n. device producing hot flame.

blow′up′, n. 1. explosion. 2. Informal. emotional outburst. 3. photographic enlargement.

blub′ber, n. 1. fat of whales. —v. 2. weep.

bludg′eon (bluj′ən), n. 1. heavy club. —v. 2. strike with a bludgeon.

blue, n., adj. **bluer, bluest,** v., **blued, bluing** or **blueing.** —n. 1. color of sky. —adj. 2. (of skin) discolored by cold, etc. 3. melancholy. —v. 4. make blue. **—blue′ness,** n. **—blu′ish,** adj.

blue′ber′ry, n., pl. **-ries.** edible berry, usually bluish.

blue′bird′, n. small, blue North American bird.

blue′-col′lar, adj. of or designating factory workers or other manual laborers.

blue′jay′, n. crested North American jay.

blue′print′, n. white-on-blue photocopy of line drawing. **—blue′print′,** v.

blue ribbon, highest distinction or award, as first prize in a competition.

blues, n.pl. 1. melancholy. 2. melancholy jazz song.

bluff, v. 1. mislead by show of boldness. —n. 2. act of bluffing. 3. one who bluffs. 4. steep cliff or hill. —adj. 5. vigorously frank. 6. steep. **—bluff′ly,** adv. **—bluff′ness,** n. **—bluff′er,** n.

blu′ing, n. bleaching substance. Also, **blue′ing.**

blun′der, n. 1. mistake. —v. 2. make an error. 3. move blindly. **—blun′der•er,** n.

blunt, adj. 1. having a dull edge or point. 2. abrupt in manner. —v. 3. make blunt. **—blunt′ly,** adv. **—blunt′ness,** n.

blur, v., **blurred, blurring,** n. —v. 1. obscure. 2. make or become indistinct. —n. 3. smudge. **—blur′ry,** adj.

blurb, n. brief advertisement.

blurt, v. utter suddenly.

blush, v. 1. redden. 2. feel shame. —n. 3. reddening. 4. reddish tinge. —**blush'ful**, adj. —**blush'ing•ly**, adv.

blus'ter, v. 1. be tumultuous. 2. be noisy or swaggering. —n. 3. tumult. 4. noisy talk. —**blus'ter•er**, n.

bo'a, n. 1. nonpoisonous snake of tropical America. 2. long scarf of silk, feathers, etc.

boar, n. male of swine.

board, n. 1. thin flat piece of timber. 2. table, esp. for food. 3. daily meals. 4. official controlling body. —v. 5. cover or close with boards. 6. furnish with food. 7. take meals. 8. enter (a ship, train, etc.). —**board'er**, n.

boast, v. 1. speak with pride; be proud of. 2. speak with excessive pride. —n. 3. thing boasted. —**boast'er**, n. —**boast'ful**, adj.

boat, n. 1. vessel. —v. 2. go or move in boat. —**boat'house'**, n. —**boat'man**, n. —**boat'ing**, n.

boat'swain (bō'sən), n. petty officer on ship.

bob, n., v., **bobbed**, **bobbing**. —n. 1. short jerky motion. 2. short haircut. —v. 3. move jerkily. 4. cut short. —**bob'ber**, n.

bob'by pin, flat metal hairpin that opens like a spring.

bob'bin, n. reel; spool.

bob'cat', n., pl. **-cats, -cat**. North American lynx.

bob'o•link', n. North American songbird.

bob'sled', n., v., **-sledded, -sledding**. —n. 1. long sled with two pairs of runners and a steering mechanism. —v. 2. ride on a bobsled.

bob'tail', n. 1. short tail. —v. 2. cut short.

bob'white', n. North American quail.

bode, v., **boded, boding**. portend.

bo•de'ga (bō dā'gə), n. grocery store.

bod'ice, n. fitted waist.

bod'y, n., pl. **bodies**, v., **bodied, bodying**. —n. 1. animal's physical structure. 2. corpse. 3. main mass. 4. collective group. —v. 5. invest with body. —**bod'i•ly**, adj., adv.

bod'y•guard', n. guard for personal safety.

body language, conscious or unconscious communication through gestures or attitudes.

bog, n., v., **bogged, bogging**. —n. 1. swampy ground. —v. 2. sink or catch in a bog. —**bog'gy**, adj.

bo'gle, v., **-gled, -gling**. 1. refuse to act. 2. overwhelm with surprise.

bo'gus, adj. counterfeit; fake.

bo'gy, n., pl. **-gies**. hobgoblin. Also, **bo'gey, bo'gie**.

bo•he'mi•an (bō hē'mē ən), n. 1. person who leads an unconventional life. —adj. 2. of or characteristic of a bohemian.

boil, v. 1. heat to bubbling point. 2. be agitated. 3. cook by boiling. —n. 4. act or state of boiling. 5. inflamed sore. —**boil'er**, n.

bois'ter•ous, adj. rough; noisy. —**bois'ter•ous•ly**, adv. —**bois'ter•ous•ness**, n.

bok' choy' (bok' choy'), Asian plant whose leaves are used as a vegetable. Also, **bok'-choy'**.

bold, adj. 1. fearless. 2. conspicuous. —**bold'ly**, adv. —**bold'ness**, n.

boll (bōl), n. rounded seed vessel.

bo•lo'gna (bə lō'nē), n. beef and pork sausage.

Bol'she•vik, n., pl. **-viks, -viki**. Russian communist. Also, **Bol'she•vist**. —**Bol'she•vism'**, n. —**Bol'she•vik, Bol'she•vis'tic**, adj.

bol'ster, n. 1. long pillow. —v. 2. support. —**bol'ster•er**, n.

bolt, n. 1. bar fastening a door. 2. similar part in a lock. 3. threaded metal pin. 4. sudden flight. 5. roll of cloth. 6. thunderbolt. —v. 7. fasten. 8. swallow hurriedly. 9. move or leave suddenly. 10. sift. —**bolt'er**, n.

bomb, n. 1. projectile with explosive charge. 2. Slang. total failure. —v. 3. attack with bombs. 4. Slang. fail totally. —**bomb'proof'**, adj.

bom•bard', v. attack with artillery or bombs. —**bom•bar'dier'**, n. —**bom•bard'ment**, n.

bom'bast, n. high-sounding words. —**bom•bas'tic, bom•bas'ti•cal•ly**, adj.

bomb'er, n. 1. airplane that drops bombs. 2. one who plants bombs.

bomb'shell', n. something or someone having a sensational effect.

bo'na fide' (bō'nə fīd', -fī'dē), genuine.

bo•nan'za, n. 1. rich mass of ore. 2. good luck.

bon'bon', n. piece of candy.

bond, n. 1. something that binds or unites. 2. bondsman. 3. written contractual obligation. 4. certificate held by creditor. —v. 5. put on or under bond. 6. mortgage.

bond'age, n. slavery.

bond'man, n., pl. **-men**. man in bondage; male slave. Also, **bond'wom'an**, n.fem.

bonds'man, n., pl. **-men**. person who gives surety for another by bond.

bone, n., v., **boned, boning**. —n. 1.

piece of the skeleton. 2. hard substance composing it. —v. 3. remove bones of. —**bon'y,** adj.

bon'er, n. Slang. stupid mistake.

bon'fire', n. outdoor fire.

bon'go, n. pl. **-gos, -goes.** small hand drum played as one of pair.

bon'net, n. woman's or child's head covering.

bon'sai (-sī), n., pl. bonsai. dwarf tree or shrub.

bo'nus, n. extra payment.

boo, interj. (exclamation used to frighten or express contempt.)

boo'-boo', n. Slang. 1. stupid mistake. 2. minor injury.

boo'by, n., pl. **-bies.** Informal. fool. Also, **boob.**

booby prize, prize given to worst player in contest.

booby trap, hidden trap set for any person who happens on it.

book, n. 1. printed or blank sheets bound together. 2. (pl.) accounts. 3. division of literary work. —v. 4. enter in book. 5. engage beforehand.
—**book'bind'er,** n. —**book'case',** n. —**book'keep'er,** n. —**book'let,** n. —**book'sell'er,** n. —**book'store',** **book'shop',** n.

book'end', n. prop for books.

book'ie, n. bookmaker.

book'ish, adj. fond of reading. —**book'ish ness,** n.

book'mak'er, n. professional bettor.

book'worm', n. bookish person.

boom, v. 1. make a loud hollow sound. 2. flourish vigorously. —n. 3. loud hollow sound. 4. rapid development. 5. spar extending sail. 6. beam on derrick.

boom'er ang', n. 1. Australian throwing stick that returns in flight. —v. 2. make trouble for plotter rather than intended victim.

boon, n. benefit.

boon'docks', n.pl. 1. backwoods. 2. remote rural area.

boon'dog'gle, n. Informal. useless work paid for with public money.

boor, n. clownish, rude person. —**boor'ish,** adj.

boost, v. 1. lift by pushing. 2. praise; advocate. 3. increase. —n. 4. upward push. 5. assistance. —**boost'er,** n.

boot, n. 1. covering for foot and leg. 2. kick. —v. 3. kick. 4. dismiss or discharge.

booth, n. 1. light structure for exhibiting goods, etc. 2. small compartment.

boot'leg', n., v., **-legged, -legging,** adj. —n. 1. illicit liquor. —v. 2. deal in illicit goods. —adj. 3. illicit. —**boot'leg'ger,** n.

boo'ty, n. pl. **-ties.** plunder.

booze (booz) n., v., **boozed, boozing.** Informal. —n. 1. liquor. —v. 2. drink liquor excessively. —**booz'er,** n.

bor'der, n. 1. edge; margin. 2. frontier. —v. 3. make a border. 4. adjoin. —**bor'der land',** n. —**bor'der line',** n.

bore, v., **bored, boring,** n. —v. 1. drill into. 2. be uninteresting to. —n. 3. bored hole. 4. inside diameter. 5. dull person. —**bore'dom,** n. —**bor'er,** n.

bo'ric acid, antiseptic acid.

born, adj. brought from the womb.

born'-a gain', adj. having experienced Christian spiritual revival.

bor'ough, n. 1. small incorporated municipality. 2. division of city.

bor'row, v. 1. obtain on loan. 2. adopt.

bos'om, n. breast. —**bos'om y,** adj.

boss, n. 1. employer; superintendent. 2. powerful politician. —v. 3. control; manage. 4. be domineering. —**boss'y,** adj.

bot'a ny, n. science of plant life. —**bo tan'i cal, bo tan'ic,** adj. —**bot'a nist,** n.

botch, v. 1. bungle. 2. do clumsily. —n. 3. botched work. —**botch'y,** adj. —**botch'er,** n. —**botch'er y,** n.

both, adj., pron. 1. the two. —conj. 2. adv. 2. alike.

both'er, v. 1. annoy. 2. bewilder. —n. 3. annoying or disturbing thing. —**both'er some,** adj.

bot'tle, n., v., **-tled, -tling.** —n. 1. sealed container for liquids. —v. 2. put into bottle. —**bot'tler,** n.

bot'tle-neck', n. 1. narrow entrance or passage. 2. place or stage where progress is impeded.

bot'tom, n. 1. lowest or deepest part. 2. underside. 3. lowest rank. —v. 4. reach or furnish with bottom.

bot'tom less, adj. 1. without bottom. 2. without limit.

bottom line, basic or decisive point.

bot'u lism' (boch'a-), n. disease caused by spoiled foods.

bou'doir (boo'dwär, -dwôr), n. woman's bedroom or private sitting room.

bough (bou), n. branch of tree.

bouil'lon (bool'yon, -yan, boo'-), n. clear broth.

boul'der, n. large rounded rock.

boul'e vard', n. broad avenue.

bounce, v., **bounced, bouncing.** —v. 1. spring back. —n. 2. act of bouncing.

bound, adj. 1. in bonds. 2. made into book. 3. obligated. 4. going toward. —v. 5. jump. 6. limit. 7. adjoin. 8.

name boundaries of. —n. 9. jump. 10. (usually pl.) boundary.

bound'a•ry, n., pl. **-ries.** borderline; limit.

bound'less, adj. unlimited.

boun•te•ous, adj. 1. generous. 2. plentiful. Also, **boun'ti•ful.** —**boun•te•ous•ly,** adv. —**boun'te•ous•ness,** n.

boun'ty, n., pl. **-ties.** 1. generosity. 2. gift.

bou•quet' (bō kā′, bōō-), n. 1. bunch of flowers. 2. aroma.

bour'bon (bûr′bən), n. corn whiskey.

bour•geois' (bōōr zhwä′), n., pl. **-geois.** 1. one of the middle class. —adj. 2. of the middle class.

bour•geoi•sie' (-zē′), n. middle class.

bout, n. 1. contest. 2. attack; onset.

bou•tique' (bōō tēk′), n. small shop that sells fashionable items.

bo'vine, adj. oxlike.

bow (bou, for 1, 2, 3, 5, 9; bō, for 4, 6, 7, 8), v. 1. bend down. 2. bend in worship, respect, etc. 3. subdue. 4. curve. —n. 5. inclination of head or body. 6. strip of bent wood for shooting arrow. 7. looped knot. 8. rod for playing violin. 9. front of ship. —**bow'man,** n.

bow'el, n. 1. intestine. 2. inner parts. Also, **bow'els.**

bow'er, n. leafy shelter.

bowl, n. 1. deep round dish. 2. rounded hollow part. 3. ball rolled at pins in various games. —v. 4. roll a ball underhand. 5. play bowling games. —**bowl'ing,** n.

bow'leg'ged (bō leg′id), adj. having legs curved outward.

box, n. 1. receptacle of wood, metal, etc. 2. compartment. 3. blow, as of the hand or fist. 4. Also, **box'wood'.** evergreen tree or shrub. —v. 5. put into box. 6. fight with fists. —**box'er,** n. —**box'ing,** n. —**box'like',** adj.

box'car', n. completely enclosed railroad freight car.

box office, office at which tickets are sold, as for theater or sports events.

boy, n. male child. —**boy'hood,** n. —**boy'ish,** adj.

boy'cott, v. 1. abstain from dealing with or using. —n. 2. practice or instance of boycotting.

boy'friend', n. 1. male sweetheart or lover. 2. male friend.

bra, n. brassiere.

brace, n., v., **braced, bracing.** —n. 1. stiffening thing or device. 2. pair. 3. character, { or }, for connecting lines. —v. 4. fasten with brace. 5. make steady. 6. stimulate. —**brac'er,** n.

brace'let, n. ornamental wristband.

brack'et, n. 1. armlike support for ledge. 2. mark, [or], for enclosing parenthetical words. —v. 3. furnish with or place within brackets.

brack'ish, adj. salty.

brad, n. small wire nail.

brag, v., **bragged, bragging,** n. boast. —**brag'ger,** n.

brag'gart, n. boastful person.

braid, v. 1. weave together. —n. 2. something braided.

braille, n. alphabet for blind.

brain, n. 1. soft mass of nerves in cranium. 2. intelligence. —v. 3. dash out the brains. —**brain'y,** adj. —**brain'less,** adj.

brain death, complete ending of brain function, used as legal definition of death. —**brain'-dead',** adj.

brain'storm', n. sudden idea or impulse.

brain'wash', v. indoctrinate under stress.

braise (brāz), v., **braised, braising.** cook slowly in moisture.

brake, n., v., **braked, braking.** —n. 1. device for arresting motion. 2. thicket. 3. large fern. —v. 4. slow or stop with a brake. —**brake'man,** n.

bram'ble, n. 1. rose plant. 2. prickly shrub. —**bram'bly,** adj.

bran, n. husk of grain.

branch, n. 1. division of plant's stem or trunk. 2. limb; offshoot. 3. local office, store, etc. 4. division of body, system, family, etc. —v. 5. put forth or divide into branches.

brand, n. 1. trademark. 2. kind; make. 3. burned mark. 4. burning piece of wood. —v. 5. mark with a brand.

brand'ish, v. shake; wave.

brand'-new', adj. extremely new.

bran'dy, n., pl. **-dies.** spirit from fermented grapes.

brash, adj. 1. impudent; tactless. 2. rash; impetuous.

brass, n. 1. alloy of copper and zinc. 2. musical instrument such as trumpet or horn. 3. Informal. high-ranking officials. 4. impudence. —**brass'y,** adj.

bras•siere' (-zēr′), n. undergarment supporting the breasts.

brat, n. spoiled or rude child.

bra•va'do, n., pl. **-does, -dos.** boasting; swaggering.

brave, adj., **braver, bravest,** n., v., **braved, braving.** —adj. 1. courageous. —n. 2. North American Indian warrior. —v. 3. meet courageously. 4. defy. —**brave'ly,** adv. —**brave'ness, brav'er•y,** n.

bra'vo, interj. well done!

brawl, n. 1. quarrel. —v. 2. quarrel noisily. —**brawl'er,** n.

brawn, n. 1. muscles. 2. muscular strength. —**brawn'y,** adj.

bray, n. 1. cry of a donkey. 2. similar sound. —v. 3. sound a bray. —**bray'er,** n.

braze, v. **brazed, brazing.** work in brass. —**bra'zier** (-zhər), n.

bra'zen, adj. 1. of or like brass. 2. shameless; impudent. —v. 3. face boldly. —**bra'zen·ly,** adv. —**bra'zen·ness,** n.

bra'zier (-zhər), n. receptacle for burning charcoal.

breach, n. 1. a breaking. 2. gap in barrier. 3. infraction; violation. 4. break in friendship. 5. make breach.

bread, n. 1. food of baked dough. 2. livelihood. 3. Slang. money. —v. 4. cover with bread crumbs. —**bread'stuff',** n.

breadth, n. extent from side to side.

bread'win'ner, n. person who earns money to support a family or dependents.

break, v. **broke, broken, breaking,** —v. 1. separate into parts. 2. violate; dissolve. 3. fracture. 4. lacerate. 5. interrupt. 6. disclose. 7. fail; disable. 8. (pp. **broke**) ruin financially. 9. weaken. 10. tame. —n. 11. forcible disruption or separation. 12. gap. 13. attempt to escape. 14. marked change. 15. brief rest. 16. Informal. opportunity. —**break'a·ble,** adj. —**break'age,** n.

break'down', n. 1. failure to operate. 2. nervous crisis. 3. analysis of figures.

break'er, n. wave breaking on land.

break'fast, n. 1. first meal of day. —v. 2. eat or supply with breakfast.

break'neck', adj. reckless or dangerous, esp. because of excessive speed.

break'through', n. fundamental discovery.

break'wa'ter, n. barrier that protects against the force of waves.

breast, n. 1. chest. 2. milk gland. 3. seat of thoughts and feelings. —v. 4. oppose boldly.

breast'bone', n. sternum.

breast'stroke', n. swimming stroke in which the arms move forward, outward, and rearward while the legs kick outward.

breath, n. 1. air inhaled and exhaled. 2. ability to breathe. 3. light breeze. —**breath'less,** adj.

breathe, v. **breathed, breathing.** 1. inhale and exhale. 2. blow lightly. 3. live. 4. whisper.

breath'er (brē'thər), n. Informal. short rest.

breath'tak'ing (breth'-), adj. awesome or exciting.

breech'es, n.pl. trousers.

breed, v. **bred, breeding,** —v. 1. produce. 2. raise. —n. 3. related animals. 4. lineage. 5. sort. —**breed'er,** n.

breed'ing, n. 1. ancestry. 2. training. 3. manners.

breeze, n. light current of air. —**breez'y,** adj.

breth'ren, n a pl. of **brother.**

bre'vet', n. 1. promotion without increase of pay. —v. 2. appoint by brevet.

bre'vi·ar'y, n., pl. -aries. book of daily prayers and readings.

brev'i·ty, n. shortness.

brew, v. 1. prepare beverage such as beer or ale. 2. concoct. —n. 3. quantity brewed. 4. act or instance of brewing. —**brew'er,** n. —**brew'er·y,** n.

bri'ar (brī'ər), n. brier.

bribe, n., v. **bribed, bribing.** —n. 1. gift made for corrupt performance of duty. —v. 2. give or influence by bribe. —**brib'er,** n. —**brib'er·y,** n.

bric'-a-brac', n. small pieces of art, curios, etc.

brick, n. 1. building block of baked clay. —v. 2. fill or build with brick. —**brick'lay'er,** n.

brick'bat', n. 1. fragment of brick. 2. caustic criticism.

bride, n. woman newly married or about to be married. —**brid'al,** adj.

bride'groom', n. man newly married or about to be married.

brides'maid', n. bride's wedding attendant.

bridge, n., v. **bridged, bridging.** —n. 1. structure spanning river, road, etc. 2. card game for four players. 3. artificial replacement for tooth or teeth. —v. 4. span.

bridge'head', n. military position held on hostile river shore.

bri'dle, n., v. **-dled, -dling.** —n. 1. harness at horse's head. 2. restraining thing. —v. 3. put bridle on. 4. restrain.

brief, adj. 1. short. 2. concise. —n. 3. concise statement. 4. outline of arguments and facts. —v. 5. instruct in advance. —**brief'ly,** adv. —**brief'ness,** n.

brief'case', n. flat carrier for business papers, etc.

bri'er, n. 1. prickly plant. 2. plant with woody root.

brig, n. 1. two-masted square-rigged ship. 2. ship's jail.

bri•gade', n., v. **-gaded, -gading.** —n. 1. large military unit or body of troops. 2. form into brigade.

brig•a•dier', n. military officer between colonel and major general. Also, **brigadier general.**

brig'and, n. bandit.

bright, adj. 1. shining. 2. filled with light. 3. brilliant. 4. clever. —**bright'en**, v. —**bright'ly**, adv. —**bright'ness**, n.

bril'liant, adj. 1. sparkling. 2. illustrious. 3. highly intelligent. —n. 4. brilliant diamond. —**bril'liant•ly**, adv. —**bril'liance, bril'lian•cy, bril'liant•ness**, n.

brim, n., v., **brimmed, brimming.** —n. 1. upper edge; rim. —v. 2. fill or be full to brim.

brim'stone, n. sulfur.

brin'dle, n. brindled coloring or animal.

brin'dled, adj. having dark streaks or spots.

brine, n., v., **brined, brining.** —n. 1. salt water. 2. sea. —v. 3. treat with brine. —**briny**, adj.

bring, v., **brought, bringing.** 1. fetch. 2. cause to come. 3. lead.

brink, n. edge.

bri•quette' (bri ket'), n. small block of compressed coal dust or charcoal used as fuel. Also, **bri•quet'.**

brisk, adj. 1. lively. 2. stimulating. —**brisk'ly**, adv. —**brisk'ness**, n.

bris'ket, n. animal's breast.

bris'tle, n., v., **-tled, -tling.** —n. 1. short, stiff, coarse hair. —v. 2. rise stiffly. 3. show indignation. —**bris'tly**, adv.

Brit'ish, adj. of Great Britain or its inhabitants. —**Brit'ish•er**, n.

Brit'on, n. native of Great Britain.

brit'tle, adj. breaking readily. —**brit'tle•ness**, n.

broach (brōch), n. 1. tool for enlarging hole. —v. 2. use broach. 3. pierce. 4. mention for first time.

broad, adj. 1. wide. 2. main. 3. liberal. —**broad'ly**, adv.

broad'cast', v., **-cast** or **-casted, -casting**, n., adj. —v. 1. send by radio or television. 2. scatter widely. —n. 3. something broadcast. 4. radio or television program. —adj. 5. sent by broadcasting. —**broad'cast'er**, n.

broad'cloth', n. fine cotton material.

broad'en, v. widen.

broad'-mind'ed, adj. tolerant.

broad'side', n., adv., v., **-sided, -siding.** —n. 1. simultaneous firing of all guns on one side of warship. 2. concerted verbal attack. —adv. 3. directly on the side. —v. 4. hit broadside.

bro•cade', n., v., **-caded, -cading.** —n. 1. figured woven fabric. —v. 2. weave with figure.

broc'co•li, n. green edible plant.

bro•chure' (-shōōr'), n. pamphlet; booklet.

brogue, n. Irish accent.

broil, v. cook by direct heat. —**broil'er**, n.

broke, adj. 1. without money. 2. bankrupt.

bro'ken, v. 1. pp. of **break.** —adj. 2. in fragments. 3. fractured. 4. incomplete. 5. weakened. 6. imperfectly spoken.

bro'ker, n. commercial agent. —**bro'ker•age**, n.

bro'mide, n. 1. soothing compound; sedative. 2. trite saying.

bron'chi•al (brong'kē al), adj. of the bronchi, two branches of the trachea.

bron•chi'tis, n. inflammation in windpipe and chest. —**bron•chit'ic**, adj.

bron'co, n., pl. **-cos.** pony or small horse of western U.S. Also, **bron'cho.**

bronze, n., v., **bronzed, bronzing.** —n. 1. alloy of copper and tin. 2. brownish color. —v. 3. make bronzelike.

brooch (brōch), n. clasp or ornament.

brood, n. 1. group of animals born at one time. —v. 2. hatch. 3. think moodily. —**brood'y**, adj.

brook, n. 1. small stream. —v. 2. tolerate.

broom, n. 1. sweeping implement. 2. shrubby plant.

broom'stick', n. handle of a broom.

broth, n. thin soup.

broth'el (broth'al), n. house of prostitution.

broth'er, n., pl. **brothers, brethren.** male child of same parents. 2. member of same group. —**broth'er•hood'**, n. —**broth'er•ly**, adj.

broth'er-in-law', n., pl. **brothers-in-law.** 1. husband's or wife's brother. 2. sister's husband.

brow, n. 1. eyebrow. 2. forehead. 3. edge of a height.

brow'beat', v., **-beat, -beaten, -beating.** bully.

brown, n. 1. dark reddish or yellowish color. —adj. 2. of this color. —v. 3. make or become brown.

brown'ie, n. 1. elf who secretly helps with chores. 2. small, chewy chocolate cake. 3. girl scout aged 6 to 8.

browse, v., **browsed, browsing.** 1.

graze; feed. 2. examine books, etc., at leisure.—**brows'er,** *n.*

bruise, *v.,* **bruised, bruising,** *n.*—*v.* 1. injure without breaking.—*n.* 2. bruised injury.

brunch, *n.* 1. meal that serves as both breakfast and lunch.—*v.* 2. eat brunch.

bru·net', *adj.* dark brown, esp. of skin or hair.

bru·nette', *n.* brunet woman or girl.

brunt, *n.* main force.

brush, *n.* 1. instrument with bristles. 2. bushy tail. 3. brief encounter. 4. dense bushes, shrubs, etc.—*v.* 5. use brush. 6. touch lightly.

brusque, *adj.* abrupt; blunt. Also, **brusk.**—**brusque'ly,** *adv.* —**brusque'ness,** *n.*

Brus'sels sprouts, plant with small, cabbagelike, edible heads along its stalk.

brute, *n.* 1. beast. 2. beastlike person. —*adj.* 3. not human. 4. irrational. 5. like animals. 6. savage.—**bru'tal,** *adj.*—**bru·tal'i·ty,** *n.*—**bru'tal·ly,** *adv.*—**brut'ish,** *adj.*

bub'ble, *n., v.,* **-bled, -bling.**—*n.* 1. globule of gas, esp. in liquid. 2. something infirm or unsubstantial.—*v.* 3. make or give off bubbles.—**bub'bly,** *adj.*

buc·ca·neer', *n.* pirate.

buck, *v.* 1. leap to unseat a rider. 2. resist.—*n.* 3. male of the deer, rabbit, goat, etc.

buck'et, *n.* deep, open-topped container; pail.

buck'le, *n., v.,* **-led, -ling.**—*n.* 1. clasp for two loose ends.—*v.* 2. fasten with buckle. 3. bend. 4. set to work.

buck'ler, *n.* shield.

buck'ram, *n.* stiff cotton fabric.

buck'shot', *n.* large lead shot.

buck'skin', *n.* skin of buck.

buck'tooth', *n., pl.* **-teeth.** projecting tooth.

buck'wheat', *n.* plant with edible triangular seeds.

bu·col'ic (byoo kol'ik), *adj.* rustic; rural.—**bu·col'i·cal·ly,** *adv.*

bud, *n., v.,* **budded, budding.**—*n.* 1. small protuberance on plant. 2. small rounded part.—*v.* 3. produce buds. 4. begin to grow.

Bud'dhism (bood'iz əm), *n.* Eastern religion.—**Bud'dhist,** *n.*

bud'dy, *n., pl.* **-dies.** *Informal.* friend; comrade.

budge, *v.,* **budged, budging.** move slightly with effort.

budg'et, *n.* estimate of income and expense. 2. itemized allotment of funds.

—*v.* 3. plan allotment of. 4. allot.—**budg'et·ar'y,** *adv.*

buff, *n.* 1. thick light-yellow leather. 2. yellowish brown.—*adj.* 3. made or colored like buff.—*v.* 4. polish brightly.

buf'fa·lo', *n., pl.* **-loes, -los, -lo.** large bovine mammal.

buff'er, *n.* 1. cushioning device. 2. polishing device.

buf'fet, *n.* 1. blow. 2. (bə fā'). cabinet for china, etc. 3. (bə fā'). food counter.—*v.* 4. strike. 5. struggle.

buf·foon', *n.* clown.—**buf·foon'er·y,** *n.*—**buf·foon'ish,** *adj.*

bug, *n., v.,* **bugged, bugging.**—*n.* 1. insect, esp. a beetle. 2. microorganism. 3. defect or imperfection. 4. enthusiast. 5. hidden electronic eavesdropping device.—*v.* 6. install secret listening device in. 7. *Informal.* annoy or pester.

bug'bear', *n.* any source, real or imaginary, of fright or fear. Also, **bug'a·boo'.**

bug'gy, *n., pl.* **-gies.** light carriage.

bu'gle, *n., v.,* **-gled, -gling.**—*n.* 1. cornetlike wind instrument.—*v.* 2. sound a bugle.—**bu'gler,** *n.*

build, *v.,* **built, building,** *n.*—*v.* 1. construct. 2. form. 3. develop.—*n.* 4. manner or form of construction.—**build'er,** *n.*

build'ing, *n.* constructed shelter.

build'up', *n. Informal.* 1. steady increase. 2. publicity campaign.

bulb, *n.* 1. fleshy leaved, usually subterranean, bud. 2. rounded enlarged part. 3. electric lamp.—**bulb'ar,** *adj.*—**bulb'ous,** *adj.*

bulge, *n., v.,* **bulged, bulging.**—*n.* 1. rounded projection.—*v.* 2. swell out.—**bulg'y,** *adj.*

bul'gur (bool'gər), *n.* wheat used in parboiled, cracked, and dried form.

bu·lim'i·a (byoo lim'ē ə, -lē'mē ə, boo-), *n.* disorder marked by eating binges followed by self-induced vomiting.

bulk, *n.* 1. magnitude. 2. main mass. —*v.* 3. be of or increase in magnitude.

bulk'head', *n.* wall-like partition in a ship.

bulk'y, *adj.,* **bulkier, bulkiest.** of great bulk.—**bulkiness,** *n.*

bull, *n.* 1. male bovine. 2. bull-like person. 3. speculator who depends on rise in prices. 4. papal document. 5. *Slang.* lying talk.—*adj.* 6. male. 7. marked by rise in prices.—**bull'ish,** *adj.*

bull'dog', *n.* large, heavily built dog.

bull'doz'er, *n.* powerful earth-moving tractor.

bul'let, *n.* projectile for rifle or hand-gun.

bul'le•tin, *n.* brief account; news item.

bull'fight', *n.* combat between man and a bull. —**bull'fight'er,** *n.*

bull'finch', *n.* European songbird.

bull'frog', *n.* large deep-voiced frog.

bull'head'ed, *adj.* stubborn.

bul'lion (bool'yan) *n.* uncoined gold or silver.

bull'ock, *n.* castrated bull.

bull's'-eye', *n.* center of target.

bull terrier, dog breed from bulldog and terrier.

bul'ly, *n., pl.* **-lies,** *v.,* **-lied, -lying.** —*n.* 1. blustering, overbearing person. —*v.* 2. intimidate.

bul'rush', *n.* large rush or rushlike plant.

bul'wark, *n.* 1. rampart. 2. protection.

bum, *n. Informal.* 1. tramp or hobo. 2. loafer; idler. —*v.* 3. *Informal.* beg. —*adj.* 4. of poor quality. 5. false or misleading. 6. lame.

bum'ble, *v.,* **-bled, -bling.** 1. blunder. 2. bungle; botch.

bum'ble•bee', *n.* large hairy bee.

bum'mer, *n. Slang.* frustrating or bad experience.

bump, *v.* 1. strike; collide. —*n.* 2. act or shock of bumping. 3. swelling. —**bump'y,** *adj.*

bump'er, *n.* 1. device for protection in collisions. 2. glass filled to brim. —*adj.* 3. abundant.

bun, *n.* kind of bread roll.

bunch, *n.* 1. cluster. 2. group. —*v.* 3. group; gather.

bun'dle, *n., v.,* **-dled, -dling.** —*n.* 1. group bound together. 2. package. —*v.* 3. wrap in bundle. 4. dress warmly.

bun'ga•low, *n.* one-story cottage.

bun'gle, *v.,* **-gled, -gling,** *n.* —*v.* 1. fail to do properly. —*n.* 2. something bungled. —**bun'gler,** *n.*

bun'ion (-yan), *n.* swelling on foot.

bunk, *n.* 1. built-in bed. 2. bunkum.

bunk'er, *n.* 1. bin. 2. underground refuge.

bun'kum (bung'kam), *n.* nonsense. Also, **bunk.**

bun'ny, *n., pl.* **-nies.** *Informal.* rabbit.

bunt, *v.* push or tap forward.

bun'ting, *n.* 1. fabric for flags, etc. 2. flags. 3. finchlike bird.

buoy (boi), *n.* 1. float used as support or navagational marker. —*v.* 2. support by or as by buoy. 3. mark with buoy.

buoy'ant, *adj.* 1. tending to float. 2. cheerful. —**buoy•an•cy,** *n.* —**buoy'ant•ly,** *adv.*

bur, *n.* prickly seed case.

bur'den, *n.* 1. load. —*v.* 2. load heavily. —**bur'den•some,** *adj.*

bur'dock, *n.* coarse, prickly plant.

bu'reau (byŏŏr'ō), *n., pl.* **-eaus, -eaux.** 1. chest of drawers. 2. government department.

bu•reauc'ra•cy (byŏŏ rok'ra sē), *n., pl.* **-cies.** 1. government by bureaus. 2. bureau officials.

bu'reau•crat', *n.* official of a bureaucracy. —**bu'reau•crat'ic,** *adj.*

bur'geon (bûr'jan), *v.* 1. grow or develop quickly. 2. begin to grow.

bur'glar, *n.* thief who breaks and enters. —**bur'glar•ize',** *v.* —**bur'gla•ry,** *n.*

Bur'gun•dy, *n., pl.* **-dies.** dry red wine. Also, **bur'gun•dy.**

bur'i•al, *n.* act of burying.

bur'lap, *n.* coarse fabric of jute, etc.

bur•lesque', *n., v.,* **-lesqued, -lesquing.** —*n.* 1. artistic travesty. 2. sexually suggestive entertainment. —*v.* 3. make a burlesque of.

bur'ly, *adj.* **-lier, -liest.** 1. of great size. 2. brusque.

burn, *v.,* **burned** or **burnt, burning,** *n.* —*v.* 1. be on fire. 2. consume with fire; be afire. 3. heat; feel heat. 4. glow. 5. feel passion. —*n.* 6. burned place or condition. —**burn'er,** *n.*

bur'nish, *v.* 1. polish. —*n.* 2. gloss.

burn'out', *n.* 1. point at which rocket engine stops because it runs out of fuel. 2. fatigue and frustration from too much work and stress.

burp, *n.* light belch. —**burp,** *v.*

burr, *n.* 1. cutting or drilling tool. 2. rough protuberance. 3. bur.

bur'ro, *n., pl.* **-ros.** donkey.

bur'row, *n.* 1. animal's hole in ground. —*v.* 2. make or lodge in burrow. —**bur'row•er,** *n.*

bur•si'tis (bar sī'tis), *n.* condition in which a bursa (sac containing fluid) becomes inflamed, as in the shoulder or elbow.

burst, *v.,* **burst, bursting,** *n.* —*v.* 1. break open or issue forth violently. 2. rupture. —*n.* 3. act or result of bursting. 4. sudden display.

bur'y, *v.,* **buried, burying.** 1. put into ground and cover. 2. conceal. —**bur'i•er,** *n.*

bus, *n., pl.* **buses, busses,** *v.,* **bused** or **bussed, busing** or **bussing.** —*n.* 1. large passenger motor vehicle. —*v.* 2. move by bus.

bush, *n.* 1. low, shrubby plant. 2. land covered with bushes. —**bush'y,** *adj.* —**bush'i•ness,** *n.*

bushed, *adj. Informal.* exhausted; tired.

bush'el, n. unit of 4 pecks.

busi'ness (biz'nis), n. 1. occupation; profession. 2. trade. 3. trading enterprise. 4. affair; matter. —**busi'ness•man', busi'ness•wom•an,** n.

bus'ing, n. moving of pupils by bus to achieve racially balanced classes. Also, **bus'sing.**

bust, n. 1. sculpture of head and shoulders. 2. bosom. —v. Informal. 3. burst. 4. become or make bankrupt. 5. arrest. 6. hit.

bus'tle, v., -tled, -tling. 1. move or act energetically. —n. 2. energetic activity.

bus'y, adj., busier, busiest, v., busied, busying. —adj. 1. actively employed. 2. full of activity. 3. make or keep busy. —**bus'i•ly,** adv. —**bus'y•ness,** n.

bus'y•bod'y, n., pl. -bodies. meddler.

but, conj. 1. on the contrary. 2. except. 3. except that. —prep. 4. except. —adv. 5. only.

bu'tane (byoo'tān), n. colorless gas used as fuel.

butch (booch), adj. Slang. 1. (of a woman) having traits usu. associated with men. 2. (of a man) having exaggerated masculine traits.

butch'er, n. 1. dealer in meat. 2. slaughterer. —v. 3. kill for food. 4. bungle. —**butch'er•y,** n.

but'ler, n. chief male servant.

butt, n. 1. thick or blunt end. 2. object of ridicule. 3. large cask. 4. cigarette end. 5. Slang. buttocks. —v. 6. push with head or horns. 7. be adjacent; join. 8. strike with head or horns.

but'ter, n. 1. Also, **but'ter•fat'.** solid fatty part of milk. —v. 2. put butter on. —**but'ter•y,** adj.

but'ter•cup', n. plant with yellow cup-shaped flowers.

but'ter•fly', n., pl. -flies. insect with broad colorful wings.

but'ter•milk', n. milk with its butter extracted.

but'ter•nut', n. nut of walnutlike tree.

but'ter•scotch', n. kind of taffy.

but'tock, n. protuberance of rump.

but'ton, n. 1. disk or knob for fastening. 2. buttonlike object. —v. 3. fasten with button.

but'ton•hole', n., v., -holed, -holing. —n. 1. slit through which a button is passed. —v. 2. accost and detain in conversation.

but'tress, n. 1. structure steadying wall. —v. 2. support.

bux'om, adj. (of a woman) attractively plump. —**bux'om•ness,** n.

buy, v., bought, buying. 1. acquire by payment. 2. bribe. —**buy'er,** n.

buzz, n. 1. low humming sound. —v. 2. make or speak with buzz. —**buz'zer,** n.

buz'zard, n. carnivorous bird.

buzz'word', n. Informal. fashionable cliché used to give specious weight to argument.

by, prep. 1. near to. 2. through. 3. not later than 4. past. 5. using as means or method. —adv. 6. near. 7. past.

bye (bī), n. (in a tournament) automatic advancement to the next round.

by'gone', adj. 1. past. —n. 2. something past.

by'law', n. standing rule.

by'line', n. line, as in a newspaper, giving the writer or reporter's name.

by'pass', n. 1. detour. 2. surgical procedure in which diseased or blocked organ is circumvented. —v. 3. avoid through bypass.

by'play', n. action or speech aside from the main action.

by'-prod'uct, n. secondary product.

by'stand'er, n. chance looker-on.

byte (bīt), n. unit of computer information, larger than bit.

by'way', n. road that is little used.

by'word', n. 1. catchword. 2. proverb.

C

C, c, n. third letter of English alphabet.

cab, n. 1. taxicab. 2. (formerly) one-horse carriage. 3. part of locomotive, truck, etc., where operator sits.

ca•bal', n. group of plotters.

cab•a•ret' (-rā'), n. restaurant providing entertainment.

cab'bage, n. plant with edible head of leaves.

cab'in, n. 1. small house. 2. room in a ship or plane.

cab'i•net, n. 1. advisory council. 2. piece of furniture with drawers, etc. —**cab'i•net•mak'er,** n.

ca'ble, n., v., -bled, -bling. —n. 1. thick, strong rope. 2. cablegram. —v. 3. send cablegram (to).

ca'ble•gram', n. telegram sent by underwater wires.

cable TV, system of distributing television programs to subscribers over coaxial cables.

ca·boose' (kə bōōs'), *n.* car for the crew at the end of a train.

cab'ri·o·let' (kab'rē ə lā'), *n.* 1. type of one-horse carriage. 2. automobile with folding top.

ca·ca'o (kə kā'ō), *n., pl.* **-caos.** tropical tree whose seeds yield cocoa, etc.

cache (kash), *n., v.,* **cached, caching.** —*n.* 1. hiding place for treasure, etc. —*v.* 2. hide.

ca·chet' (ka shā'), *n.* 1. official seal or sign. 2. superior status; prestige.

cack'le, *v.,* **-led, -ling,** *n.* —*v.* 1. utter shrill, broken cry. —*n.* 2. act or sound of cackling.

cac'tus, *n., pl.* **-tuses, -ti.** leafless, spiny American plant.

cad, *n.* ungentlemanly person.

ca·dav'er, *n.* corpse. —**ca·dav'er·ous,** *adj.*

cad'die, *n., v.,* **-died, -dying.** —*n.* 1. person who carries one's golf clubs. —*v.* 2. work as caddie. Also, **cad'dy.**

ca'dence, *n.* rhythmic flow or beat.

ca·det', *n.* military or naval student.

cadge, *v.,* **cadged, cadging.** obtain by begging.

ca'dre (kad'rē, kä'drā), *n.* highly trained group around which an organization is built.

Cae·sar'e·an (si zâr'ē ən), *n.* Cesarean.

ca·fé' (ka fā'), *n.* restaurant.

caf·e·te'ri·a, *n.* self-service restaurant.

caf'feine (kaf'ēn), *n.* chemical in coffee, etc., used as stimulant. Also, **caf'fein.**

cage, *n., v.,* **caged, caging.** —*n.* 1. barred box or room. —*v.* 2. put in cage.

cag'ey, *adj.* **-ier, -iest.** shrewd; cautious. Also, **cag'y.** —**cag'i·ly,** *adv.* —**cag'i·ness,** *n.*

cais'son (kā'son), *n.* 1. ammunition wagon. 2. airtight underwater chamber.

ca·jole', *v.,* **-joled, -joling.** coax; wheedle. —**ca·jol'er·y,** *n.*

Ca'jun (kā'jən), *n.* Louisianan of Nova Scotia-French origin.

cake, *n., v.,* **caked, caking.** —*n.* 1. sweet baked dough. 2. compact mass. —*v.* 3. form into compact mass.

cal'a·bash', *n.* kind of gourd.

ca·lam'i·ty, *n., pl.* **-ties.** disaster. —**ca·lam'i·tous,** *adj.*

cal'ci·mine (kal'sə mīn'), *n., v.,* **-mined, -mining.** —*n.* 1. type of paint for ceilings, etc. —*v.* 2. cover with calcimine.

cal'ci·um, *n.* white metallic chemical element.

cal'cu·late', *v.,* **-lated, -lating.** compute or estimate by mathematics. —**cal'cu·la'tor,** *n.* —**cal'cu·la'tion,** *n.*

cal'cu·la'ting, *adj.* shrewd; scheming.

cal'cu·lus, *n.* branch of mathematics.

cal'dron (kôl-), *n.* cauldron.

cal'en·dar, *n.* 1. list of days, weeks, and months of year. 2. list of events.

cal'en·der, *n.* 1. press for paper, cloth, etc. —*v.* 2. press in such a machine.

calf, *n., pl.* **calves.** 1. young of cow, etc. 2. fleshy part of leg below knee.

cal'i·ber, *n.* 1. diameter of bullet or gun bore. 2. quality. Also **cal'i·bre.**

cal'i·brate', *v.,* **-brated, -brating.** mark for measuring purposes. —**cal'i·bra'tion,** *n.*

cal'i·co', *n., pl.* **-coes, -cos.** printed cotton cloth.

cal'i·per, *n. (usu. pl.)* compass for measuring.

ca'liph, *n.* head of a Muslim state.

cal·is·then'ics, *n.pl.* physical exercises.

calk (kôk), *v.* caulk.

call, *v.* 1. cry out loudly. 2. announce. 3. summon. 4. telephone. 5. name. 6. visit briefly. 7. cry or shout. 8. summons. 9. brief visit. 10. need; demand. —**call'er,** *n.*

cal·lig'ra·phy, *n.* fancy penmanship; art of beautiful writing. —**cal·lig'ra·pher,** *n.*

call'ing, *n.* 1. trade. 2. summons.

cal'lous (kal'əs), *adj.* 1. unsympathetic. —*v.* 2. harden.

cal'low, *adj.* immature.

cal'lus, *n.* hardened part of the skin.

calm, *adj.* 1. undisturbed. 2. not windy. —*n.* 3. calm state. —*v.* 4. make calm. —**calm'ly,** *adv.* —**calm'ness,** *n.*

cal'o·mel', *n.* white powder used as cathartic.

ca·lor'ic, *adj.* of heat.

cal'o·rie, *n.* measured unit of heat, esp. of fuel or energy value of food.

ca·lum'ni·ate', *v.,* **-ated, -ating.** slander. —**ca·lum'ni·a'tor,** *n.* —**cal'um·ny,** *n.*

ca·lyp'so (kə lip'sō), *n.* 1. musical style of the West Indies. 2. song in this style.

ca'lyx (kā'liks), *n.* small leaflets around flower petals.

cam, *n.* device for changing circular movement to straight.

ca·ma·ra·de·rie (kä'mə rä'də rē, kam'ə-), *n.* comradeship; fellowship.

cam'bric, *n.* close-woven fabric.

cam'cord'er, *n.* hand-held television camera with an incorporated VCR.

cam'el, *n.* Asian or African animal with one or two humps.

ca•mel'ia (kə mēl'yə, -mē'lē ə), *n.* shrub with glossy evergreen leaves and roselike flowers.

cam'e•o', *n., pl.* **-eos.** carved stone with layers in contrasting colors.

cam'er•a, *n.* device for making photographs.

cam'ou•flage' (kam'ə fläzh'), *n., v.,* **-flaged, -flaging.** —*n.* 1. protective, deceptive covering or construction. —*v.* 2. hide by camouflage.

camp, *n.* 1. place of temporary lodging, esp. in tents. 2. faction. 3. something that amuses by being overdone or tasteless. —*adj.* 4. Also, **camp'y.** amusing as camp. —*v.* 5. form, or live in, camp. —**camp'er,** *n.*

cam•paign' (-pān'), *n.* 1. military operation. 2. competition for political office. —*v.* 3. engage in campaign. —**cam•paign'er,** *n.*

cam'phor, *n.* white crystalline substance used as moth repellent, medicine, etc.

cam'pus, *n.* school grounds.

can, *v.,* **canned** (**could** for def. 1), **canning** (for def. 2), *n.* —*v.* 1. be able or qualified to. 2. put in airtight container. —*n.* 3. cylindrical metal container. —**can'ner,** *n.*

Ca•na'di•an, *n.* citizen of Canada. —**Canadian,** *adj.*

ca•nal', *n.* 1. artificial waterway. 2. tubular passage. —**can'al•ize',** *v.*

can'a•pé (kan'ə pē), *n.* morsel of food served as appetizer.

ca•nard', *n.* rumor.

ca•nar'y, *n., pl.* **-ries.** yellow cage bird.

ca•nas'ta, *n. Cards.* type of rummy whose main object is to establish sets of seven or more cards.

can'cel, *v.,* **-celed, -celing.** 1. cross out. 2. make void. —**can'cel•la'tion,** *n.*

can'cer, *n.* malignant growth. —**can'cer•ous,** *adj.*

can•de•la'brum (-lä'-), *n., pl.* **-bra.** branched candlestick.

can'did, *adj.* frank or honest. —**can'did•ly,** *adv.* —**can'did•ness,** *n.*

can'di•date', *n.* one seeking to be elected or chosen. —**can'di•da•cy,** *n.*

can'dle, *n.* waxy cylinder with wick for burning. —**can'dle•stick',** *n.*

can'dor, *n.* frankness.

can'dy, *n., pl.* **-dies,** *v.,* **-died, -dying.** —*n.* 1. sweet confection. —*v.* 2. cook in or cover with sugar.

cane, *n., v.,* **caned, caning.** —*n.* 1. stick used in walking. 2. long, woody stem. —*v.* 3. beat with a cane.

ca'nine (kā'nīn), *adj.* 1. of dogs. —*n.* 2. animal of dog family.

can'is•ter, *n.* small box.

can'ker, *n.* ulcerous sore. —**can'ker•ous,** *adj.*

can'na•bis (kan'ə bis), *n.* 1. hemp plant; marijuana. 2. parts of the hemp plant used as a drug.

canned, *adj.* 1. put into cans or sealed jars. 2. *Informal.* recorded.

can'ni•bal, *n.* person who eats human flesh. —**can'ni•bal•ism,** *n.* —**can'ni•bal•ize',** *v.,* **-ized, -izing.** strip of reusable parts.

can•nol'i (kə nō'lē), *n.* Italian pastry filled with sweet cheese, etc.

can'non, *n.* large mounted gun. —**can'non•eer',** *n.*

can'non•ade', *n.* long burst of cannon fire.

can'not, *v.* am, are, or is unable to.

can'ny, *adj.,* **-nier, -niest.** 1. careful. 2. shrewd. —**can'ni•ness,** *n.*

ca•noe', *n.* light boat propelled by paddles. —**canoe',** *v.*

can'on, *n.* 1. rule or law. 2. recognized books of Bible. 3. church official. —**ca•non'i•cal,** *adj.*

can'on•ize', *v.,* **-ized, -izing.** declare as saint. —**can'on•i•za'tion,** *n.*

can'o•py, *n., pl.* **-pies.** overhead covering.

cant, *n.* 1. insincerely virtuous talk. 2. special jargon.

can't, *v. Informal.* cannot.

can•ta•loupe' (-lōp'), *n.* small melon.

can•tan'ker•ous, *adj.* ill-natured.

can•ta'ta (-tä'-), *n.* dramatic choral composition.

can•teen', *n.* 1. container for water, etc. 2. military supply store. 3. entertainment place for soldiers, etc.

can'ter, *n.* easy gallop. —*v.* 2. go at easy gallop.

can'ti•cle, *n.* hymn.

can'ti•le'ver, *n.* structure secured at one end only.

can'to, *n., pl.* **-tos.** section of a long poem.

can'tor, *n.* synagogue or church singer.

can'vas, *n.* 1. cloth used for sails, tents, etc. 2. sails.

can'vass, *v.* 1. investigate. 2. solicit votes, etc.

can'yon, *n.* narrow valley. Also, **cañon.**

cap, *n., v.,* **capped, capping.** —*n.* 1. brimless hat. 2. cover. —*v.* 3. cover. 4. surpass.

ca•pa•ble, *adj.* able; qualified. —**ca'pa•bly,** *adv.* —**ca'pa•bil'i•ty,** *n.*

ca•pa'cious, *adj.* holding much.

ca•pac'i•ty, *n., pl.* **-ties.** 1. amount that can be contained. 2. capability. 3. position; role.

cape, *n.* 1. sleeveless coat. 2. projecting point of land.

ca'per, *v.* 1. leap playfully. —*n.* 2. playful leap. 3. pickled flower bud of Mediterranean shrub, used as seasoning.

cap'il•lar'y, *adj., n., pl.* **-laries.** —*adj.* 1. of or in a thin tube. —*n.* 2. tiny blood vessel.

cap'i•tal, *n.* 1. city in which government is located. 2. large letter. 3. money and property available for business use. 4. decorative head of structural support. —*adj.* 5. important or chief. 6. excellent. 7. (of letters) large. 8. punishable by death.

capital gain, profit from the sale of an asset, such as bonds or real estate.

cap'i•tal•ism', *n.* system of private investment in and ownership of business. —**cap'i•tal•ist,** *n.* —**cap'i•tal•is'tic,** *adj.*

cap'i•tal•ize', *v.,* **-ized, -izing.** 1. put in large letters. 2. use as capital in business. 3. take advantage. —**cap'i•tal•i•za'tion,** *n.*

cap'i•tol, *n.* building used by legislature, esp. (*cap.*) Congress.

ca•pit'u•late', *v.,* **-lated, -lating.** surrender. —**ca•pit'u•la'tion,** *n.*

ca'pon, *n.* castrated rooster.

cap•puc•ci'no (kap'ə chē'nō, kä'pə-), *n.* espresso coffee mixed with steamed milk.

ca•price' (kə prēs'), *n.* whim. —**ca•pri'cious,** *adj.*

cap'size, *v.,* **-sized, -sizing.** overturn; upset.

cap'stan, *n.* device turned to pull cables.

cap'sule, *n.* small sealed container. —**cap'su•lar,** *adj.*

cap'tain, *n.* 1. officer below major or rear admiral. 2. ship master. —**cap'tain•cy,** *n.*

cap'tion, *n.* heading.

cap'tious, *adj.* noting trivial faults. —**cap'tious•ly,** *adv.* —**cap'tious•ness,** *n.*

cap'ti•vate', *v.,* **-vated, -vating.** charm. —**cap'ti•va'tion,** *n.* —**cap'ti•va'tor,** *n.*

cap'tive, *n.* prisoner. —**cap•tiv'i•ty,** *n.*

cap'ture, *v.,* **-tured, -turing.** —*v.* 1. take prisoner. —*n.* 2. act or instance of capturing. —**cap'tor,** *n.*

car, *n.* vehicle, esp. automobile.

ca•rafe' (kə raf'), *n.* broad-mouthed bottle for wine, water, etc.

car'a•mel, *n.* confection made of burnt sugar.

car'at, *n.* 1. unit of weight for gems. 2. karat.

car'a•van', *n.* group traveling together, esp. over deserts.

car'a•way', *n.* herb bearing aromatic seeds.

car'bide, *n.* carbon compound.

car'bine (kär'bīn), *n.* short rifle.

car'bo•hy'drate, *n.* organic compound group including starches and sugars.

car•bol'ic acid, brown germicidal liquid.

car'bon, *n.* chemical element occurring as diamonds, charcoal, etc. —**car•bon•if'er•ous,** *adj.*

car'bon•ate', *v.,* **-ated, -ating.** charge or impregnate with carbon dioxide. —**car'bon•a'tion,** *n.*

carbon dioxide, chemical compound of carbon and oxygen: a gas produced esp. by animal respiration.

carbon monoxide, chemical compound of carbon and oxygen: a poisonous gas produced esp. by automobile engines.

Car'bo•run'dum, *n. Trademark.* abrasive material.

car'bun•cle, *n.* painful inflammation under skin.

car'bu•re'tor, *n.* mechanism that mixes gasoline and air in motor.

car'cass, *n.* dead body. Also, **car'case.**

car•cin'o•gen (kär sin'ə jən), *n.* cancer-producing substance. —**car'cin•o•gen'ic,** *adj.*

car•ci•no'ma (kär sə nō'mə), *n.* malignant tumor.

card, *n.* 1. piece of stiff paper, with one's name (**calling card**) or for game purposes (**playing card**) etc. 2. comb for wool, flax, etc. —*v.* 3. dress (wool, etc.) with card.

card'board, *n.* 1. thin, stiff pasteboard. —*adj.* 2. flimsy. 3. seeming too flimsy or stiff to be real.

car'di•ac', *adj.* of the heart.

car'di•gan, *n.* knitted jacket or sweater with buttons down the front.

car'di•nal, *n.* 1. main; chief. 2. (of numbers) used to express quantities or positions in series, e.g., 3, 15, 45. 3. deep red. —*n.* 4. red bird. 5. high official of Roman Catholic Church.

car'di•o•graph', *n.* instrument for recording movements of heart. —**car'di•o•gram',** *n.*

car•di•ol'o•gy, *n.* study of the heart

and its functions. —**car'di•ol'o•gist,** n.

car'di•o•vas'cu•lar, adj. of the heart and blood vessels.

care, n., v., **cared, caring.** —n. 1. worry. 2. caution. —v. 3. be concerned or watchful. —**care'free',** adj. —**care'ful,** adj. —**care'less,** adj.

ca•reen', v. tip; sway.

ca•reer', n. 1. course through life. 2. life work. 3. speed. —v. 4. speed.

ca•ress', v., n. touch in expressing affection.

car'et, n. mark (∧) indicating insertion.

care'worn', adj. haggard from worry.

car'fare', n. cost of ride by bus, subway, etc.

car'go, n., pl. **-goes, -gos.** goods carried by ship or plane.

car'i•bou' (-bōō'), n. North American reindeer.

car'i•ca•ture, n. mocking portrait. —**car'i•ca•ture,** v.

car'ies (kâr'ēz), n., pl. **-ies.** tooth decay.

car'il•lon', n. musical bells.

car'jack'ing, n. theft of car by force or threat. —**car'jack'er,** n.

car'mine (-min), n., adj. crimson or purplish red.

car'nage, n. massacre.

car'nal, adj. of the body.

car•na'tion, n. common fragrant flower.

car'ni•val, n. 1. amusement fair. 2. festival before Lent.

car'ni•vore' (-vōr'), n. flesh-eating mammal. —**car•niv'o•rous,** adj.

car'ob (kar'ab), n. 1. Mediterranean tree bearing long pods. 2. pulp from the pods, used as chocolate substitute.

car'ol, n., v., **-oled, -oling.** —n. 1. Christmas song. —v. 2. sing joyously. —**car'ol•er,** n.

car'om (kar'əm), v. 1. hit and rebound. —n. 2. rebound.

ca•rouse' (kə rouz'), n., v., **-roused, -rousing.** —n. 1. noisy or drunken feast. —v. 2. engage in a carouse. —**ca•rous'al,** n.

carp, v. 1. find fault. —n. 2. large fresh-water fish.

car'pel, n. seed-bearing leaf.

car'pen•ter, n. builder in wood. —**car'pen•try,** n.

car'pet, n. 1. fabric covering for floors. —v. 2. cover with carpet. —**car'pet•ing,** n.

car'pool', n. 1. group of automobile owners each of whom in turn drives the others along a given route, as in

commuting. —v. 2. participate in a carpool.

car'riage, n. 1. wheeled vehicle. 2. posture. 3. conveyance.

car'ri•on, n. dead flesh.

car'rot, n. plant with orange edible root.

car'rou•sel', n. merry-go-round.

car'ry, v., **-ried, -rying.** 1. convey; transport. 2. support; bear. 3. behave. 4. win. 5. extend. 6. have in stock. 7. carry out. accomplish. —**car'ri•er,** n.

cart, n. small wagon. —**cart'age,** n.

carte blanche (kärt' blänch', blänsh'), complete freedom to choose.

car•tel', n. syndicate controlling prices and production.

car'ti•lage, n. flexible connective body tissue. —**car'ti•lag'i•nous,** adj.

car•tog'ra•phy, n. production of maps. —**car•tog'ra•pher,** n.

car'ton, n. cardboard box.

car•toon', n. 1. comic or satirical drawing. 2. design for large art work. —**car•toon'ist,** n.

car'tridge, n. 1. cylindrical case containing bullet and explosive. 2. container with frequently replaced machine parts or supplies.

carve, v., **carved, carving.** cut into desired form. —**carv'er,** n.

cas•cade', n. waterfall.

case, n., v., **cased, casing.** —n. 1. instance; example. 2. situation; state. 3. event. 4. statement of arguments. 5. medical patient. 6. lawsuit. 7. category in inflection of nouns, adjectives, and pronouns. 8. **in case,** if. 9. container. —v. 10. put in case.

ca'sein (kā'sēn), n. protein derived from milk, used in making cheese.

case'ment, n. hinged window.

cash, n. 1. money. —v. 2. give or get cash for.

cash'ew, n. small curved nut.

cash•ier', n. 1. person in charge of money. —v. 2. dismiss in disgrace.

cash'mere (-mēr), n. soft wool fabric.

ca•si'no, n., pl. **-nos.** amusement or gambling hall.

cask, n. barrel for liquids.

cas'ket, n. coffin.

cas'se•role', n. covered baking dish.

cas•sette', n. compact case that holds film or recording tape.

cas'sock, n. long ecclesiastical vestment.

cast, v., **cast, casting,** n. —v. 1. throw. 2. deposit (vote). 3. pour and mold. 4. compute. —n. 5. act of casting. 6. thing cast. 7. actors in play. 8. form;

mold. 9. rigid surgical dressing. 10. tinge. 11. tinsel. —**cast'ing**, *n.*

cas·ta·net', *n.* pieces of bone shell, etc., held in the palm and struck together as musical accompaniment.

cast'a·way', *n.* shipwrecked person.

caste (kast), *n.* distinct social level.

cast'er, *n.* small swivel-mounted wheel. Also, **cast'or.**

cas'ti·gate', *v.*, **-gated, -gating.** scold severely. —**cas·ti·ga'tion**, *n.* —**cas'ti·ga'tor**, *n.*

cas'tle, *n.*, *v.*, **-tled, -tling.** —*n.* 1. royal or noble residence, usually fortified. 2. chess piece; rook. —*v.* 3. *Chess.* transpose rook and king.

cas'tor oil, vegetable oil used as cathartic.

cas'trate', *v.*, **-trated, -trating.** remove testicles of. —**cas·tra'tion**, *n.*

cas'u·al, *adj.* 1. accidental; not planned. 2. not caring.

cas'u·al·ty, *n.*, *pl.* **-ties.** 1. accident injurious to person. 2. soldier missing in action, killed, wounded, or captured.

cas'u·ist·ry (kazh'ōō-), *n.*, *pl.* **-ries.** adroit, specious argument. —**cas'u·ist**, *n.*

cat, *n.* common domestic animal.

cat'a·clysm', *n.* sudden upheaval. —**cat'a·clys'mic**, *adj.*

cat'a·comb', *n.* underground cemetery.

cat'a·logue', *n.*, *v.*, **-logued, -loguing.** —*n.* 1. organized list. —*v.* 2. enter in catalogue. Also, **cat'a·log'.**

ca·tal'pa, *n.* tree with bell-shaped white flowers.

cat'a·lyst, *n.* 1. substance that causes or speeds a chemical reaction without itself being affected. 2. anything that precipitates an event.

cat'a·ma·ran', *n.* two-hulled boat.

cat'a·mount', *n.* wild cat, as the cougar.

cat'a·pult', *n.* 1. device for hurling or launching. —*v.* 2. hurl.

cat'a·ract', *n.* 1. waterfall. 2. opacity of eye lens.

ca·tarrh' (-tär'), *n.* inflammation of respiratory mucous membranes.

ca·tas'tro·phe (-fē), *n.* great disaster. —**cat'a·stroph'ic**, *adj.*

catch, *v.*, **caught, catching**, *n.* —*v.* 1. capture. 2. trap or detect. 3. hit. 4. seize and hold. 5. be in time for. 6. get or contract. 7. be entangled. —*n.* 8. act of catching. 9. thing that catches. 10. thing caught. 11. tricky aspect. —**catch'er**, *n.*

catch'ing, *adj.* contagious.

catch'up, *n.* type of tomato sauce.

catch'word', *n.* slogan.

catch'y, *adj.* **catchier, catchiest.** memorable and pleasing.

cat'e·chism' (-kiz'am), *n.* set of questions and answers on religious principles. —**cat'e·chize'**, *v.*

cat'e·gor'i·cal, *adj.* unconditional. —**cat'e·gor'i·cal·ly**, *adv.*

cat'e·go'ry, *n.*, *pl.* **-ries.** division; class. —**cat'e·go·rize'**, *v.*

ca'ter, *v.* 1. provide food, amusement, etc. 2. be too accommodating. —**ca'ter·er**, *n.*

cat'er-cor'nered (kat'i-, kat'ē-, kat'ar-), *adj.* 1. diagonal. —*adv.* 2. diagonally.

cat'er·pil'lar, *n.* 1. wormlike larva of butterfly. 2. type of tractor.

cat'er·waul' (kat'ar wôl'), *v.* 1. utter long wails, as cats in rut. —*n.* 2. such a wail.

cat'fish', *n.* American fresh-water fish.

cat'gut', *n.* string made from animal intestine.

ca·thar'sis, *n.* 1. purging of emotions, as through art. 2. evacuation of bowels.

ca·thar'tic, *adj.* 1. effecting a catharsis. 2. evacuating the bowels. —*n.* 3. medicine doing this.

ca·the'dral, *n.* main church of diocese.

cath'e·ter, *n.* tube inserted into a body passage, as to provide or drain fluids.

Cath'o·lic, *adj.* 1. of or belonging to Roman Catholic Church. 2. (*l.c.*) universal. —*n.* 3. member of Roman Catholic Church. —**Ca·thol'i·cism'**, *n.*

cat'nip, *n.* plant with scented leaves.

CAT scan, 1. examination using x-rays at various angles to show cross section of body. 2. image produced by CAT scan.

cat's-paw', *n.* dupe used by another.

cat'sup, *n.* catchup.

cat'tail', *n.* tall spinelike marsh plant.

cat'tle, *n.* livestock, esp. cows. —**cat'tle·man**, *n.*

cat'ty, *adj.* **-tier, -tiest.** maliciously gossiping.

cat'walk', *n.* narrow access walk.

Cau·ca'sian, *adj.* 1. of the so-called "white race." —*n.* 2. Caucasian person. Also, **Cau·ca·soid.**

cau'cus, *n.* political conference.

cau'dal, *adj.* of the tail.

caul'dron (kôl'dran), *n.* large kettle.

cau'li·flow'er, *n.* plant with an edible head.

caulk (kôk), *v.* 1. fill or close seams of

to keep water or air out. —n. 2. Also,
caulk'ing. material used to caulk.

cause, n., v., **caused, causing.** —n. 1.
person or thing producing an effect.
2. reason. 3. aim; purpose. —v. 4.
bring about; produce. —**caus'al,** adj.
—**cau·sa'tion,** n.

cause'way, n. raised road.

caus'tic (kôs'-) adj. 1. burning or
corroding. 2. sharply critical.
—**caus'ti·cal·ly,** adv.

cau'ter·ize, v., **-ized, -izing.** burn.
—**cau'ter·y, cau'ter·i·za'tion,** n.

cau'tion, n. 1. carefulness. 2. warning.
—v. 3. warn. —**cau'tious,** adj.

cav'al·cade', n. procession, esp. on
horseback.

cav·a·lier', n. 1. knight or horseman.
2. courtly gentleman. —adj. 3.
haughty; indifferent. 4. offhand.

cav'al·ry, n., pl. **-ries.** troops on
horseback or in armored vehicles.
—**cav'al·ry·man,** n.

cave, n., v., **caved, caving.** —n. 1. hollow space in the earth. —v. 2. fall or
sink.

cav'ern, n. large cave.

cav'i·ar', n. roe of sturgeon, etc.,
eaten as a delicacy.

cav'il, v., **-iled, -iling.** n. —v. 1. find
trivial faults. —n. 2. trivial objection.

cav'i·ty, n., pl. **-ties.** hollow space.

ca·vort', v. prance about.

cay·enne' (kī en'), n. sharp condiment.

cay·use' (kī yōos'), n. Indian pony.

CB, citizens band: private two-way
radio.

CD, compact disc.

cease, v., **ceased, ceasing.** v. stop;
end. —**cease'less,** adj.

cease'-fire', n. temporary halt to
fighting; truce.

ce'dar, n. common coniferous tree.

cede, v., **ceded, ceding.** yield or give
up.

ceil'ing, n. 1. upper surface of room.
2. maximum altitude.

cel'e·brate', v., **-brated, -brating.** 1.
observe or commemorate. 2. act re-
joicingly. 3. perform ritually. 4. extol.
—**cel'e·bra'tion,** n. —**cel'e·bra'-
tor,** n.

ce·leb'ri·ty, n., pl. **-ties.** 1. famous
person. 2. fame.

ce·ler'i·ty (sə ler'-), n. speed.

cel'er·y, n. plant with edible leaf
stalks.

ce·les'tial, adj. of heaven or the sky.

cel'i·ba·cy (sel'ə bə sē), n. 1. unmarried state. 2. sexual abstinence.
—**cel'i·bate,** n., adj.

cell, n. 1. a small room or compartment. 2. microscopic biological struc-

ture. 3. electric battery. 4. organizational unit. —**cel'lu·lar,** adj.

cel'lar, n. room under building.

cel'lo (chel'ō), n. pl. **-los.** large violin-
like instrument held vertically on
floor.

cel'lo·phane', n. flexible, transparent
wrapping material.

cellular phone, mobile telephone
using radio transmission to complete
calls.

cel'lu·lite' (sel'yə līt', -lēt), n. lumpy
fat deposits, esp. in the thighs and
buttocks.

cel'lu·loid', n. hard, flammable substance.

cel'lu·lose', n. carbohydrate of plant
origin, used in making paper, etc.

Cel'si·us, n. temperature scale in
which water freezes at 0° and boils at
100°.

ce·ment', n. 1. clay-lime mixture that
hardens into stonelike mass. 2. binding material. —v. 3. treat with cement. 4. unite.

cem'e·ter·y, n., pl. **-teries.** burial
ground.

cen'o·taph' (sen'ə taf'), n. monument for one buried elsewhere.

cen'ser, n. incense burner.

cen'sor, n. 1. person eliminating undesirable words, pictures, etc. 2. official deprecation for reforms. —v. 3.
deal with as a censor. —**cen'sor-
ship,** n.

cen·so'ri·ous, adj. severely critical.

cen'sure (-shər), n., v. —**sured,
-suring.** —n. 1. disapproval. —v. 2.
rebuke.

cen'sus, n. count of inhabitants, etc.

cent, n. 1/100 of a dollar; penny.

cen'taur (-tôr), n. mythological creature, half horse and half man.

cen·te'nar·y, n. pl. **-naries.** 100th anniversary.

cen·ten'ni·al, n. 1. 100th anniversary. —adj. 2. of 100 years.

cen'ter, n. 1. middle point, part, or
person. —v. 2. place or gather at center. 3. concentrate. Also, **cen'tre.**

cen'ti·grade', adj. Celsius.

cen'ti·gram', n. 1/100 of gram.

cen'ti·li'ter (-lē'tər), n. 1/100 of liter.

cen'ti·me'ter, n. 1/100 of meter.

cen'ti·pede', n. insect with many
legs.

cen'tral, adj. 1. of or at center. 2.
main. —**cen'tral·ly,** adv.

cen'tral·ize', v., **-ized, -izing.** 1.
gather at a center. 2. concentrate control of. —**cen'tral·i·za'tion,** n.

cen·trif'u·gal (sen trif'ya gal), adj.
moving away from center.

cen•trip•e•tal, *adj.* moving toward center.

cen'trist (sen'trist), *n.* **1.** person with political views that are not extreme. —*adj.* **2.** of views that are not extreme.

cen'tu•ry, *n., pl.* **-ries.** period of one hundred years.

ce•ram'ics, *adj.* of clay and similar materials. —**ce•ram'ic**, *n.*

ce're•al, *n.* **1.** plant yielding edible grain. **2.** food from such grain.

cer•e•bel'lum (ser'ə-), *n.* rear part of brain.

cer'e•bral (ser'ə brəl, sə rē'-), *adj.* **1.** of brain. **2.** intellectual.

cerebral palsy, paralysis due to brain injury.

cer'e•brum, *n., pl.* **-brums, -bra.** front, upper part of brain.

cer'e•mo'ny, *n., pl.* **-nies.** formal act or ritual. —**cer•e•mo'ni•al**, *adj., n.* —**cer•e•mo'ni•ous**, *adj.*

ce•rise' (sə rēs', -rēz'), *adj., n.* medium to deep red.

cer'tain, *adj.* **1.** without doubt; sure. **2.** agreed upon. **3.** definite but unspecified. —**cer'tain•ly**, *adv.* —**cer'tain•ty**, *n.*

cer•tif'i•cate, *n.* document of proof.

cer'ti•fy', *v.* **-fied, -fying. 1.** guarantee as certain. **2.** vouch for in writing. —**cer'ti•fi•ca'tion**, *n.*

cer'ti•tude', *n.* sureness.

cer'vix (sûr'viks), *n., pl.* **cer•vix•es, cer•vi•ces** (sûr'və sēz', sər vī'sēz) necklike part, esp. lower end of uterus. —**cer'vi•cal**, *adj.*

Ce•sar'e•an (si zâr'ē ən), *n.* delivery of baby by cutting through abdomen and uterus. Also, **Cesarean section, C-section, Cae•sar'e•an.**

ces•sa'tion, *n.* stop.

ces'sion, *n.* ceding.

cess'pool', *n.* receptacle for waste, etc., from house.

Cha•blis' (shà blē'), *n.* dry white wine. Also, **cha•blis'.**

chafe, *v.,* **chafed, chafing.** make sore or warm by rubbing.

chaff, *n.* **1.** husks of grain, etc. **2.** worthless matter. —*v.* **3.** tease.

chaf'fer, *v.* bargain.

chafing dish, device for cooking food at table.

cha•grin' (shə grin'), *n.* **1.** shame or disappointment. —*v.* **2.** cause chagrin to.

chain, *n.* **1.** connected series of links. **2.** any series. **3.** mountain range. —*v.* **4.** fasten with chain.

chain reaction, process which automatically continues and spreads.

chain saw, portable power saw with teeth set on endless chain.

chair, *n.* **1.** seat with a back and legs. **2.** place of official or professor. **3.** chairman or chairwoman; chairperson. —*v.* **4.** preside over.

chair'man, *n.* **-men.** presiding officer. Also, *fem.,* **chair'wom'an;** *masc.* or *fem.,* **chair'per'son.**

chaise (shāz), *n.* light, open carriage.

chaise longue (shāz' lông'), type of couch.

chalet' (sha lā'), *n.* mountain house.

chal'ice (chôk), *n.* cup for ritual wine.

chalk (chôk), *n.* **1.** soft limestone, used in stick form to write on chalkboards. —*v.* **2.** mark with chalk. —**chalk'board',** *n.*

chal'lenge, *n., v.,* **-lenged, -lenging. 1.** call to fight, contest, etc. **2.** demand for identification. **3.** objection to juror. —*v.* **4.** make challenge to. —**chal'leng•er**, *n.*

cham'ber, *n.* **1.** room, esp. bedroom. **2.** assembly hall. **3.** legislative body. **4.** space in gun for ammunition.

cham'ber•maid', *n.* maid who cleans bedrooms.

chamber music, music for performance by a small ensemble in a room or small concert hall.

cha•me'le•on (kə mē'lē ən), *n.* lizard that can change its color.

cham'ois (sham'ē), *n.* **1.** European antelope. **2.** soft leather from its skin.

champ, *n.* **1.** *Informal.* champion. —*v.* **2.** bite.

Cham•pagne' (sham pān'), *n.* effervescent white wine. Also, **cham•pagne'.**

cham'pi•on, *n.* **1.** best competitor. **2.** supporter. —*v.* **3.** advocate. —*adj.* **4.** best. —**cham'pi•on•ship',** *n.*

chance, *n., v.,* **chanced, chancing,** *adj.* —*n.* **1.** fate; luck. **2.** possibility. **3.** opportunity. **4.** risk. —*v.* **5.** occur by chance. **6.** risk. —*adj.* **7.** accidental.

chan'cel, *n.* space around church altar.

chan'cel•ler•y, *n., pl.* **-leries.** position, department, or offices of chancellor.

chan'cel•lor, *n.* **1.** high government official. **2.** university head.

chan'cer•y, *n., pl.* **-ceries. 1.** high law court. **2.** helpless position.

chan'cre (shang'kər), *n.* lesion, as of syphilis.

chanc'y, *adj.,* **chancier, chanciest.** risky; uncertain.

chan'de•lier', *n.* hanging lighting fixture.

chan'dler, *n.* **1.** dealer in candles. **2.** grocer.

change, v., **changed, changing,** n. —v. 1. alter in condition, etc. 2. substitute for. 3. put on other clothes. —n. 4. alteration. 5. substitution. 6. novelty. 7. coins of low value. —**chang'er,** n. —**change'a·ble,** adj. —**change'a·bil'i·ty,** n.

change'o'ver, n. change from one condition or system to another.

chan'nel, n., v., **-neled, -neling.** —n. 1. bed of stream. 2. wide strait. 3. access; route. 4. specific frequency band, as in television. 5. convey or direct in channel.

chant, n. 1. song; psalm. —v. 2. sing, esp. slowly. —**chant'er,** n.

chant'ey (shan'-), n., pl. **-eys, -ies.** sailors' song. Also, **chant'y.**

chan'ti·cleer', n. rooster.

Cha'nu·kah (hä'nə kə), n. Hanukkah.

cha'os, n. utter disorder. —**cha·ot'ic,** adj.

chap, v., **chapped, chapping,** n. —v. 1. roughen and redden. —n. 2. Informal. fellow.

chap'el, n. small church.

chap'er·on' (shap'ə rōn'), n. 1. escort of young unmarried woman for propriety. —v. 2. accompany thus.

chap'lain, n. institutional clergyman.

chap'let, n. garland.

chaps, n.pl. leather leg protectors worn by cowboys.

chap'ter, n. 1. division of book, etc. 2. branch of society.

char, v., **charred, charring,** burn.

char'ac·ter, n. 1. personal nature. 2. reputation. 3. person in fiction. 4. written or printed symbol.

char'ac·ter·is'tic, adj. 1. typical. —n. 2. distinguishing feature.

char'ac·ter·ize', v., **-ized, -izing.** 1. distinguish. 2. describe. —**char'ac·ter·i·za'tion,** n.

cha·rade' (shə rād'), n. riddle in pantomime.

char'coal', n. carbonized wood.

charge, v., **charged, charging,** n. —v. 1. load or fill. 2. put electricity through or into. 3. command or instruct. 4. accuse. 5. ask payment of. 6. attack. —n. 7. load or contents. 8. unit of explosive. 9. care; custody. 10. command or instruction. 11. accusation. 12. expense. 13. price. 14. attack. —**charge'a·ble,** adj.

charg'er, n. battle horse.

char'i·ot, n. ancient two-wheeled carriage. —**char'i·ot·eer',** n.

cha·ris'ma (kə-), n. power to charm and inspire people. —**char'is·mat'ic,** adj.

char'i·ty, n., pl. **-ties.** 1. aid to needy persons. 2. benevolent institution. —**char'i·ta·ble,** adj.

char'la·tan (shär'-), n. pretender; fraud.

char'ley horse', cramp or sore muscle, esp. in the leg.

charm, n. 1. power to attract and please. 2. magical object, verse, etc. —v. 3. attract; enchant. —**charm'er,** n.

char'nel house, place for dead bodies.

chart, n. 1. sheet exhibiting data. 2. map. —v. 3. make a chart of.

char'ter, n. 1. document authorizing new corporation. —v. 2. establish by charter. 3. hire; lease.

char·treuse' (shär trōōz'), adj., n. yellowish green.

char'wom·an, n. woman who cleans offices, houses, etc.

char'y, adj., **charier, chariest.** careful.

chase, v., **chased, chasing,** n. —v. 1. go after with hostility. 2. drive away. 3. ornament (metal) by engraving. —n. 4. act or instance of chasing. —**chas'er,** n.

chasm, (kaz'əm), n. deep cleft in earth.

chas'sis (shas'ē), n. frame, wheels, and motor of vehicle.

chaste, adj., **chaster, chastest.** 1. virtuous. 2. simple. —**chas'ti·ty,** n.

chas'ten (chā'sən), v. punish to improve.

chas·tise', v., **-tised, -tising.** punish; beat.

chat, v., **chatted, chatting,** n. —v. 1. talk informally. —n. 2. informal talk.

cha·teau' (sha tō'), n., pl. **-teaux.** stately residence, esp. in France.

chat'tel, n. article of property other than real estate.

chat'ter, v. 1. talk rapidly or foolishly. 2. click or rattle rapidly. —n. 3. rapid or foolish talk.

chat'ter·box', n. talkative person.

chat'ty, adj., **-tier, -tiest.** loquacious.

chauf'feur (shō'fər), n. hired driver.

chau·vin·ism' (shō'-), n. blind patriotism. —**chau'vin·ist,** n., adj.

cheap, adj. of low price or value. —**cheap'ly,** adv. —**cheap'ness,** n. —**cheap'en,** v.

cheat, v. 1. defraud; deceive. —n. 2. fraud. 3. one who defrauds. —**cheat'er,** n.

check, v. 1. stop or restrain. 2. investigate; verify. 3. note with a mark. 4. leave or receive for temporary custody. —n. 5. stop; restraint. 6. written order for bank to pay money. 7. bill. 8. identification tag. 9. square pattern. 10. Chess. direct attack on king. —**check'er,** n. 1. piece used in checkers. —v. 2. diversify.

check'er•board', *n.* board with 64 squares on which the game of **checkers** is played.

check'list', *n.* list of items for comparison, verification, etc.

check'mate', *n., v.* **-mated, -mating.** *Chess.* —*n.* 1. inescapable check. —*v.* 2. subject to inescapable check.

check'out', *n.* 1. act of leaving and paying for hotel room. 2. counter where customers pay for purchases.

check'point', *n.* place, as at a border, where travelers are stopped for inspection.

ched'dar, *n.* sharp cheese.

cheek, *n.* 1. soft side of face. 2. *Informal.* impudence.

cheer, *n.* 1. shout of encouragement, etc. 2. gladness. —*v.* 3. shout encouragement to. 4. gladden. —**cheer'ful,** *adj.* —**cheer'less,** *adj.* —**cheer'y,** *adj.*

cheese, *n.* solid, edible product from milk.

cheese'burg'er, *n.* hamburger with melted cheese.

cheese'cloth', *n.* open cotton fabric.

chee'tah, *n.* wild cat resembling leopard.

chef (shef) *n.* chief cook.

chem'i•cal, *adj.* 1. of chemistry. —*n.* 2. substance in chemistry. —**chem'i•cal•ly**, *adv.*

chemical warfare, warfare with the use of chemicals to asphyxiate, poison, burn, etc.

che•mise' (shə mēz'), *n.* woman's undershirt.

chem'is•try, *n.* science of composition of substances. —**chem'ist**, *n.*

che'mo•ther'a•py, *n.* treatment of disease, esp. cancer, with chemicals.

chem'ur•gy, *n.* chemistry of industrial use of organic substances, as soybeans.

cheque (chek), *n. Brit.* bank check.

cher'ish, *v.* treat as dear.

cher'ry, *n., pl.* **-ries.** small red fruit of certain trees.

cher'ub, *n.* 1. (*pl.* **-ubim**) celestial being. 2. (*pl.* **-ubs**) angelic child.

chess, *n.* game for two people, each using 16 pieces on checkerboard.

chest, *n.* 1. part of body between neck and abdomen. 2. large box.

chest'nut', *n.* 1. edible nut of certain trees. 2. reddish brown. 3. *Informal.* stale joke.

chev'i•ot, *n.* sturdy worsted fabric.

chev'ron (shev'-), *n.* set of stripes indicating military rank.

chew, *v.* crush repeatedly with teeth. —**chew'er,** *n.*

chewing gum, flavored preparation for chewing, usu. made of chicle.

chew'y, *adj.* chewier, chewiest. not easily chewed.

Chi•an'ti (kē än'tē), *n.* dry red wine. Also, **chi•an'ti.**

chic (shēk), *adj.* cleverly attractive.

chi•can'er•y (shi kā'nə rē, chi-), *n., pl.* **-ies.** 1. deception; trickery. 2. trick.

Chi•ca'no (chi kä'nō), *n., pl.* **-nos.** Mexican-American. Also, *n.fem.* **Chi•ca'na.**

chick, *n.* 1. young chicken. 2. *Slang.* woman, esp. young one.

chick'a•dee', *n.* small gray North American bird.

chick'en, *n.* common domestic fowl.

chicken pox, contagious eruptive disease.

chick'pea', *n.* 1. plant, a legume, with pealike seeds. 2. its seed.

chic'le, *n.* substance from tropical tree, used in making chewing gum.

chic'o•ry, *n., pl.* **-ries.** plant with edible leaves and root used in coffee.

chide, *v.*, chided, chiding. scold. —**chid'er,** *n.*

chief, *n.* 1. head; leader. —*adj.* 2. main; principal. —**chief'ly,** *adv.*

chief'tain, *n.* leader.

chif•fon' (shi fon'), *n.* sheer silk or rayon fabric.

chif•fo•nier' (shif'ə nēr'), *n.* tall chest of drawers.

chig'ger, *n.* parasitic larva of certain mites.

chil'blains', *n.pl.* inflammation caused by overexposure to cold, etc.

child, *n., pl.* **children.** 1. baby. 2. son or daughter. —**child'hood**, *n.* —**child'ish**, *adj.* —**child'less**, *adj.* —**child'like**, *adj.*

child'bed', *n.* condition of giving birth.

chil'i (chil'ē), *n., pl.* **-ies.** 1. pungent pod of a red pepper, used in cooking. 2. dish made with these peppers. Also, **chile.**

chill, *n.* 1. coldness. —*adj.* 2. cold. 3. shivering. 4. not cordial. —*v.* 5. make or become cool. —**chill'y,** *adv.*

chill factor, chill to skin from low temperature of moving air.

chime, *n., v.*, **chimed, chiming.** —*n.* 1. set of musical tubes, bells, etc. —*v.* 2. sound harmoniously.

chim'ney, *n.* passage for smoke, gases, etc.

chim•pan•zee', *n.* large, intelligent African ape.

chin, *n.* part of face below mouth.

chi'na, *n.* ceramic ware.

chin·chil'la, n. small rodent valued for its fur.

Chi·nese', n., pl. -nese. native or language of China.

chink, n. 1. crack. 2. short ringing sound. —v. 3. make such a sound.

chintz, n. printed cotton fabric.

chintz'y, adj. chintzier, chintziest. gaudy; cheap-looking.

chip, n., v. chipped, chipping. —n. 1. small flat piece, slice, etc. 2. broken place. 3. small plate carrying electric circuit. —v. 4. cut or break off (bits). 5. dent; mark. 6. chip in, contribute.

chip'munk, n. small striped rodent resembling squirrel.

chip'per, adj. Informal. lively.

chi·rop'o·dy (kī-), n. treatment of foot ailments. —chi·rop'o·dist, n.

chi'ro·prac·tor (kī'-), n. one who practices therapy based upon adjusting body structures, esp. the spine. —chi'ro·prac'tic, n.

chirp, n. 1. short, sharp sound of birds, etc. —v. 2. make such sound. Also, **chir'rup.**

chis'el, n. 1. tool with broad cutting tip. —v. 2. cut with such tool. 3. Informal. cheat. —chis'el·er, n.

chit'chat', n. light talk.

chiv'al·ry (shiv'-), n., pl. -ries. 1. ideal qualities, such as courtesy and courage. 2. environment or way of life of a knight. —chiv'al·ric, chiv'al·rous, adj.

chive, n. onionlike plant with slender leaves.

chlo'rine, n. green gaseous element. —chlor'ic, adj. —chlor'in·ate', v.

chlo'ro·form', n. liquid used as anesthetic.

chlo'ro·phyll, n. green coloring matter of plants.

chock, n. wedge; block.

choc'o·late, n. 1. beverage, candy, etc., made from preparation of cacao seeds. 2. dark brown.

choice, n. 1. act or right of choosing. 2. person or thing chosen. —adj. 3. excellent. —choice'ness, n.

choir, n. group of singers, esp. in church.

choke, v. choked, choking, n. —v. 1. stop breath of. 2. obstruct. 3. be unable to breathe. —n. 4. act or sound of choking.

chol·er·a (kol'ər ə), n. acute, often deadly disease.

cho·les'te·rol (kə les'tə rōl'), n. biochemical in many bodily fluids and tissues, sometimes blocking arteries.

choose, v. chose, chosen, choosing. take as one thinks best. —choos'er, n.

choos'y, adj. choosier, choosiest. hard to please; particular.

chop, v. chopped, chopping, n. —v. 1. cut with blows. 2. cut in pieces. —n. 3. act of chopping. 4. slice of meat with rib. 5. jaw.

chop'per, n. 1. person or thing that chops. 2. Informal. helicopter.

chop'py, adj. -pier, -piest. forming short waves.

chop'sticks', n.pl. sticks used by Chinese and Japanese in eating.

chop su'ey, Chinese-style vegetable dish.

cho'ral, adj. of or for chorus or choir.

cho·rale' (kə ral', -räl'), n. 1. type of hymn. 2. group singing church music.

chord (kôrd), n. 1. combination of harmonious tones. 2. straight line across circle.

chore, n. routine job.

cho·re·og'ra·phy, n. art of composing dances. —cho're·og'ra·pher, n.

chor'is·ter, n. choir singer.

chor'tle, v. -tled, -tling, n. chuckle.

cho'rus (kō'-), n. 1. group of singers. 2. recurring melody.

chow, n. Slang. food.

chow'der, n. vegetable soup containing clams or fish.

chow mein, Chinese-style dish served on fried noodles.

Christ, n. Jesus Christ; (in Christian belief) the Messiah.

chris'ten, v. baptize; name.

Chris'ten·dom (-ən-), n. all Christians.

Chris'tian, adj. 1. of Jesus Christ, his teachings, etc. —n. 2. believer in Christianity. —Chris'tian·ize', v.

Chris·ti·an'i·ty, n. religion based on teachings of Jesus Christ.

Christ'mas, n. festival in honor of birth of Jesus (Dec. 25).

chro·mat'ic, adj. 1. of color. 2. Music. progressing by semitones.

chro'mi·um, n. lustrous metallic element. Also, **chrome.**

chron'ic, adj. constant; long-lasting; habitual. Also, **chron'i·cal.**

chron'i·cle, n., v. -cled, -cling. —n. 1. record of events in order. —v. 2. record in chronicle. —chron'i·cler, n.

chro·nol'o·gy, n., pl. -gies. summary of events in historical order. —chron·o·log'i·cal, adj.

chro·nom'e·ter, n. very exact clock.

chrys'a·lis (kris'ə-), n. pupa of butterfly, etc.

chrys·an'the·mum, n. large, colorful flower of aster family.

chub, n. thick-bodied fresh-water fish.

chub'by, adj., -bier, -biest. plump.

chuck, v. 1. pat lightly. —n. 2. light pat. 3. cut of beef.

chuck·le, v., **-led, -ling,** n. —v. 1. laugh softly. —n. 2. soft laugh.

chum, n. close friend. **—chum'my,** adj.

chump, n. Informal. fool.

chunk, n. big lump.

chunk'y, adj., **chunkier, chunkiest.** 1. thick or stout; stocky. 2. full of chunks.

church, n. 1. place of Christian worship. 2. sect.

churl, n. 1. peasant. 2. boor. **—churl'ish,** adj.

churn, n. 1. agitator for making butter. —v. 2. agitate.

chute (shōōt), n. 1. sloping slide.

chut'ney, n. East Indian relish.

chutz'pa (кнŏŏt'spə, hŏŏt'-), n. Slang. nerve; impudence; gall. Also, **chutz'pah.**

ci·ca·da (si kā'də), n. large insect with shrill call.

ci'der, n. apple juice.

ci·gar', n. roll of tobacco for smoking.

cig·a·rette', n. roll of smoking tobacco in paper tube.

cinch, n. 1. firm hold. 2. Informal. sure or easy thing.

cin'der, n. burned piece; ash.

cin·e·ma (sin'-), n. 1. motion pictures. 2. movie theater.

cin·e·ma·tog'ra·phy, n. art or technique of motion-picture photography. **—cin·e·ma·tog'ra·pher,** n.

cin'na·mon, n. brown spice from bark of certain Asian trees.

ci'pher (sī'-), n. 1. the symbol (0) for zero. 2. secret writing, using code. —v. 3. calculate.

cir'ca (sûr'kə), prep. approximately.

cir'cle, n., v., **-cled, -cling.** —n. 1. closed curve of uniform distance from its center. 2. range; scope. 3. group of friends or associates. —v. 4. enclose or go in circle.

cir'cuit, n. 1. set of rounds, esp. in connection with duties. 2. electrical path or arrangement. **—cir'cuit·ry,** n.

circuit breaker, device that interrupts electrical circuit to prevent excessive current.

cir·cu'i·tous (sər kyōō'ə-), adj. roundabout. **—cir·cu'i·tous·ly,** adv.

cir'cu·lar, adj. 1. of or in circle. —n. 2. advertisement distributed widely. **—cir'cu·lar·ize',** v.

cir'cu·late', v., **-lated, -lating.** move or pass around. **—cir'cu·la'tion,** n. **—cir'cu·la·to'ry,** adj.

cir·cum·cise', v., **-cised, -cising.** remove foreskin of. **—cir·cum·ci'sion,** n.

cir·cum'fer·ence (sər kum'fər əns), n. 1. outer boundary of a circle. 2. length of such a boundary. **—cir·cum·fer·en'tial,** adj.

cir'cum·flex', n. diacritical mark (ˆ).

cir·cum·lo·cu'tion, n. roundabout expression.

cir·cum·nav'i·gate', v., **-gated, -gating.** sail around.

cir·cum·scribe', v., **-scribed, -scribing.** 1. encircle. 2. confine.

cir·cum·spect', adj. cautious; prudent. **—cir·cum·spec'tion,** n.

cir'cum·stance', n. 1. condition accompanying or affecting event. 2. detail. 3. wealth or condition. 4. ceremony.

cir·cum·stan'tial, adj. 1. of or from circumstances. 2. detailed. 3. with definite implications.

cir·cum·vent', v., outwit or evade. **—cir·cum·ven'tion,** n.

cir'cus, n. show with animals, acrobats, etc.

cir·rho'sis (si rō'sis), n. chronic liver disease.

cir'rus (sir'-), n. high, fleecy cloud.

cis'tern (sis'-), n. reservoir.

cit'a·del, n. fortress.

cite, v., **cited, citing.** 1. mention in proof, etc. 2. summon. 3. commend. **—ci·ta'tion,** n.

cit'i·zen, n. 1. subject of a country. 2. inhabitant. 3. civilian. **—cit'i·zen·ship',** n.

citizens band, CB.

cit'ron (sit'rən), n. lemonlike Asian fruit.

cit'rus, adj. of the genus including the orange, lemon, etc.

cit'y, n., pl. **cities.** large town.

civ'ic, adj. 1. of cities. 2. of citizens.

civ'ics, n. study of civil affairs and rights and responsibilities of citizens.

civ'il, adj. 1. of citizens. 2. civilized. 3. polite. **—civ'il·ly,** adv. **—ci·vil'i·ty,** n.

ci·vil'ian, n. 1. nonmilitary or nonpolice person. —adj. 2. of such persons.

civ'i·li·za'tion, n. 1. act of civilizing. 2. civilized territory or condition.

civ'i·lize', v., **-lized, -lizing.** convert from barbaric or primitive state.

civil service, branches of governmental administration outside the armed forces.

civil war, war between parts of same state.

claim, v. 1. demand as one's right, property, etc. 2. assert. —n. 3. demand. 4. assertion. 5. something claimed. —**claim′ant,** n.

clair·voy′ant (klâr voi′ənt), adj. seeing things beyond physical vision. —**clair·voy′ant,** n. —**clair·voy′ance,** n.

clam, n. common mollusk, usually edible.

clam′ber, v. climb.

clam′my, adj., -mier, -miest. cold and moist. —**clam′mi·ness,** n.

clam′or, n. 1. loud outcry or noise. —v. 2. raise clamor. —**clam′or·ous,** adj.

clamp, n. 1. device for holding firmly. —v. 2. fasten with clamp.

clan, n. 1. related families. 2. clique. —**clan′nish,** adj.

clan·des′tine (-des′tin), adj. done in secret.

clang, v. 1. ring harshly. —n. 2. Also, **clang′or.** harsh ring.

clank, v. 1. ring dully. —n. 2. dull ringing.

clap, v., **clapped, clapping,** n. —v. 1. strike together, as hands in applause. 2. apply suddenly. —n. 3. act or sound of clapping. —**clap′per,** n.

clap′board (klab′ərd), n. horizontal overlapping boards on exterior walls.

clap′trap′, n. language not sincere but intended to win applause.

claque (klak), n. hired applauders.

clar′et, n. dry red wine.

clar·i·fy, v., -fied, -fying. make or become clear. —**clar′i·fi·ca′tion,** n.

clar·i·net′, n. musical wind instrument.

clar′i·on, adj. clear and loud.

clar′i·ty, n. clearness.

clash, v. 1. conflict. 2. collide. —n. 3. conflict. 4. collision.

clasp, n. 1. fastening device. 2. hug. —v. 3. fasten with clasp. 4. hug.

class, n. 1. group of similar persons or things. 2. social rank. 3. group of students ranked together. 4. division. 5. Slang. excellence. —v. 6. place in classes. —**class′mate′,** n. —**class′room′,** n.

class action, lawsuit on behalf of persons with complaint in common.

clas′sic, adj. Also, **clas′si·cal.** 1. of finest or fundamental type. 2. in Greek or Roman manner. —n. 3. author, book, etc., of acknowledged superiority. —**clas′si·cal·ly,** adv. —**clas′si·cism′,** n.

clas′si·fied, adj. (of information) limited to authorized persons.

clas′si·fy, v., -fied, -fying. arrange in classes. —**clas′si·fi·ca′tion,** n.

class·y, adj., classier, classiest.

Slang. stylish; elegant. —**class′i·ness,** n.

clat′ter, v., n. rattle.

clause, n. part of sentence with its own subject and predicate.

claus·tro·pho′bi·a, n. dread of closed places.

clav′i·chord (klav′i kôrd′), n. early keyboard instrument.

clav′i·cle (klav′i kəl), n. collarbone.

claw, n. 1. sharp, curved nail on animal's foot. —v. 2. tear or scratch roughly.

clay, n. soft earth, used in making bricks, pottery, etc. —**clay′ey,** adj.

clean, adj. 1. free from dirt, blemish, etc. 2. trim. 3. complete. —adv. 4. in clean manner. —v. 5. make clean. —**clean′er,** n.

clean′-cut′, adj. 1. neat. 2. clear-cut.

clean·ly (klen′lē), adj. keeping or kept clean. —**clean′li·ness,** n.

cleanse, v., **cleansed, cleansing.** make clean. —**cleans′er,** n.

clear, adj. 1. free from darkness or obscurity. 2. easily perceived. 3. evident. 4. unobstructed. 5. free of obligations or encumbrances. 6. blameless. —adv. 7. in a clear manner. —v. 8. make or become clear. 9. pay in full. 10. pass beyond. —**clear′ly,** adv. —**clear′ness,** n.

clear′ance, n. 1. space between objects. 2. authorization.

clear′-cut′, adj. apparent; obvious.

clear′ing, n. treeless space.

cleat, n. metal piece to which ropes, etc., are fastened.

cleave, v., **cleft** or **cleaved, cleaving.** split. —**cleav′er,** n. —**cleav′age,** n.

clef, n. musical symbol indicating pitch.

cleft palate, birth defect involving fissure in the roof of the mouth.

clem′a·tis, n. flowering vine.

clem′ent, adj. 1. lenient. 2. mild. —**clem′en·cy,** n.

clench, v. close tightly.

cler′gy, n., pl. -gies. religious officials. —**cler′gy·man,** n. —**cler′gy·wom·an,** n.fem.

cler′ic, n. member of the clergy.

cler′i·cal, adj. 1. of clerks. 2. of clergy.

clerk, n. 1. employee who keeps records, etc. 2. retail sales person.

clev′er, adj. nimble of mind. —**clev′er·ly,** adv. —**clev′er·ness,** n.

clew, n. 1. ball of yarn, etc. 2. Brit. clue.

cli·ché′ (klē shā′), n. trite expression.

click, n. 1. slight, sharp noise. —v. 2. make a click. 3. Slang. succeed.

cli'ent, *n.* one who hires a professional.

cli'en·tele' (-tel'), *n.* patrons.

cliff, *n.* steep bank.

cliff'-hang'er, *n.* **1.** melodramatic serial in which each part ends in suspense. **2.** suspenseful situation.

cli'mate, *n.* weather conditions. —**cli·mat'ic,** *adj.*

cli'max, *n.* high point; culmination. —**cli·mac'tic,** *adj.*

climb, *v.* **1.** ascend; rise. **2. climb down. a.** descend. **b.** *Informal.* retreat; compromise. —*n.* **3.** ascent. —**climb'er,** *n.*

clinch, *v.* **1.** fasten (a nail) by bending the point. **2.** hold tightly. —*n.* **3.** act of clinching. —**clinch'er,** *n.*

cling, *v.,* clung, clinging. hold firmly to.

clin'ic, *n.* hospital for nonresident or charity patients. —**clin'i·cal,** *adj.*

clink, *v.* **1.** make light, ringing sound. —*n.* **2.** such a sound.

clink'er, *n.* fused mass of incombustible residue.

clip, *v.,* clipped, clipping, *n.* —*v.* **1.** cut with short snips or blow. **2.** hit sharply. —*n.* **3.** act of clipping. **4.** metal clasp. **5.** cartridge holder. —**clip'ping,** *n.*

clip'per, *n.* **1.** cutting device. **2.** fast sailing vessel.

clique (klēk), *n.* small exclusive group.

clit'o·ris (klit'ər is), *n., pl.* **clitorises** or **clitorides** (kli tôr'i dēz'). erectile organ of vulva.

cloak, *n.* **1.** loose outer garment. —*v.* **2.** cover with cloak. **3.** hide.

clob'ber, *v. Informal.* maul.

clock, *n.* device for measuring time.

clock'wise', *adv., adj.* in direction of turning clock hands.

clock'work', *n.* **1.** mechanism of a clock. **2.** perfectly regular function, like that of a clock.

clod, *n.* piece of earth.

clog, *v.,* clogged, clogging, *n.* —*v.* **1.** hamper; obstruct. —*n.* **2.** obstruction, etc. **3.** heavy wooden shoe.

clois'ter, *n.* **1.** covered walk. **2.** monastery or nunnery.

clone, *n., v.,* cloned, cloning. —*n.* **1.** organism created by asexual reproduction. **2.** *Informal.* duplicate. —*v.* **3.** grow as clone.

close, *v.,* closed, closing, *adj.,* closer, closest, *adv., n.* —*v.* (klōz) **1.** shut, obstruct, or end. **2.** come to terms. —*adj.* (klōs) **3.** shut. **4.** confined. **5.** lacking fresh air. **6.** secretive. **7.** stingy. **8.** compact. **9.** near. **10.** intimate. —*adv.* (klōs) **11.** in a close man-

ner. —*n.* (klōz) **12.** end. —**close'ly,** *adv.* —**close'ness,** *n.* —**clo'sure,** *n.*

closed shop, place of work where workers must belong to union.

clos'et, *n.* **1.** small room or cabinet for clothes, etc. —*adj.* **2.** *Slang.* clandestine.

close'up' (klōs'-), *n.* **1.** photograph taken at close range. **2.** intimate view.

clot, *n., v.,* clotted, clotting. —*n.* **1.** mass, esp. of dried blood. —*v.* **2.** form clot.

cloth, *n.* fabric of threads.

clothe, *v.,* clothed or clad, clothing. dress.

clothes, *n.pl.* garments; apparel. Also, **cloth'ing.**

cloud, *n.* **1.** mass of water particles, etc., high in the air. —*v.* **2.** grow dark or gloomy. **3.** lose or deprive of transparency. —**cloud'y,** *adj.* —**cloud'i·ness,** *n.*

clout, *n.* **1.** blow from hand. **2.** *Informal.* political or similar influence. —*v.* **3.** strike with hand.

clove, *n.* **1.** tropical spice. **2.** section of plant bulb.

clo'ver, *n.* three-leaved plant, esp. for forage.

clown (kloun), *n.* **1.** comic performer, esp. in a circus. **2.** prankster. **3.** boor; fool. —*v.* **4.** act like a clown. —**clown'ish,** *adj.*

cloy, *v.* weary by excess sweetness.

club, *n., v.,* clubbed, clubbing. —*n.* **1.** heavy stick or bat. **2.** organized group. **3.** playing-card figure (♣). —*v.* **4.** beat with club.

club'foot', *n.* deformed foot.

cluck, *n.* **1.** call of hen. —*v.* **2.** utter such call.

clue, *n.* hint in solving mystery, etc.

clump, *n.* cluster.

clum'sy, *adj.,* -sier, -siest. awkward. —**clum'si·ly,** *adv.* —**clum'si·ness,** *n.*

clus'ter, *n.* **1.** group; bunch. —*v.* **2.** gather into cluster.

clutch, *v.* **1.** seize; snatch. **2.** hold tightly. —*n.* **3.** grasp. **4.** (*pl.*) capture or mastery. **5.** device for engaging or disengaging machinery.

clut'ter, *v., n.* heap or litter.

coach, *n.* **1.** enclosed carriage, bus, etc. **2.** adviser, esp. in athletics. —*v.* **3.** advise.

co·ag'u·late', *v.,* -lated, -lating. thicken, clot, or congeal. —**co·ag'u·la'tion,** *n.*

coal, *n.* **1.** black mineral burned as fuel. —*v.* **2.** take or get coal.

co·a·lesce' (-les'), *v.,* -lesced, -lescing. unite or ally. —**co·a·les'cence,** *n.*

co·a·li·tion, n. alliance.

coarse, adj.. **coarser, coarsest. 1.** rough or harsh. **2.** vulgar. **—coarse'ly,** adv. **—coarse'ness,** n. **—coars'en,** v.

coast, n. **1.** seashore. **—v. 2.** drift easily, esp. downhill. **3.** sail along coast. **—coast'al,** adj.

coast'er, n. **1.** something that coasts. **2.** object protecting surfaces from moisture.

coast guard, military service that enforces maritime laws, saves lives and property at sea, etc.

coat, n. **1.** outer garment. **2.** covering, as fur or bark. **—v. 3.** cover or enclose.

coat of arms, emblems, motto, etc., of one's family.

coax, v. influence by persuasion, flattery, etc. **—coax'er,** n.

co·ax'i·al (-ak'sē əl), adj. having a common axis, as **coaxial cables** for simultaneous transmission of radio or television signals.

cob, n. corncob.

co'balt, n. **1.** silvery metallic element. **2.** deep blue-green.

cob'ble, v., **-bled, -bling,** n. **—v. 1.** mend (shoes). **—n. 2.** Also, **cob'ble·stone'.** round stone for paving, etc. **—cob'bler,** n.

co'bra, n. venomous Asian snake.

cob'web', n. silky web made by spiders.

co·caine', n. narcotic drug used as local anesthetic and drug of abuse.

cock, n. **1.** male bird, esp. rooster. **2.** valve. **3.** hammer in lock of a gun. **4.** pile of hay. **—v. 5.** set cock of (a gun). **6.** set aslant.

cock·ade', n. hat ornament.

cock'a·too', n. colorful crested parrot.

cock'er, n. small spaniel.

cock'eyed', adj. **1.** having an eye that squints or cannot look straight. **2.** tilted or slanted to one side. **3.** foolish; absurd. **4.** drunk.

cock'le, n. **1.** mollusk with radially ribbed valves. **2.** inmost part.

cock'ney, n. **1.** resident of London, esp. East End. **2.** pronunciation of such persons.

cock'pit', n. **1.** space for pilot or helmsman. **2.** pit where cocks fight.

cock'roach', n. common crawling insect.

cock'tail', n. **1.** drink containing mixture of liquors. **2.** mixed appetizer.

cock'y, adj., **cockier, cockiest.** saucy and arrogant; too sure of oneself.

co'coa, n. **1.** powdered seeds of cacao,

used esp. in making a beverage. **—adj. 2.** brown.

co'co·nut', n. large, hard-shelled seed of the tropical **co'co palm.**

co·coon', n. silky covering spun by certain larvae.

cod, n. edible Atlantic fish. Also, **cod'fish'.**

co'da (kō'də), n. final passage of a musical movement, following the last formal section.

cod'dle, v., **-dled, -dling. 1.** pamper. **2.** cook in almost boiling water.

code, n., v., **coded, coding. —n. 1.** collection of laws or rules. **2.** system of signals or secret words. **—v. 3.** put in code.

co'deine (-dēn), n. drug derived from opium.

codg'er (koj'ər), n. eccentric man, esp. an old one.

cod'i·cil (kod'ə səl), n. supplement, esp. to a will.

cod'i·fy', v., **-fied, -fying.** organize into legal or formal code. **—cod'i·fi·ca'tion,** n.

co·ed', n. female student, esp. in co-educational school.

co·ed·u·ca'tion, n. education in classes of both sexes. **—co·ed·u·ca'tion·al,** adj.

co·ef·fi'cient, n. number by which another is multiplied.

co·erce', v., **-erced, -ercing.** force; compel. **—co·er'cion,** n.

co·e'val, adj. of same age or date.

co·ex·ist', v. **1.** exist simultaneously. **2.** exist together peacefully. **—co·ex·ist'ence,** n. **—co·ex·ist'ent,** adj.

cof'fee, n. powdered brown seeds of certain tropical trees, used in making a beverage.

cof'fer, n. chest.

cof'fin, n. box in which body is buried.

cog, n. tooth on wheel (**cog'wheel'**), connecting with another such wheel.

co'gent (kō'jənt), adj. convincing. **—co'gen·cy,** n. **—co'gent·ly,** adv.

cog'i·tate' (koj'-), v., **-tated, -tating.** ponder. **—cog·i·ta'tion,** n. **—cog'i·ta'tor,** n.

co'gnac (kōn'yak), n. brandy.

cog'nate, adj. related.

cog·ni'tion, n. knowing.

cog'ni·zance, n. notice, esp. official. **—cog'ni·zant,** adj.

cog·no'men, n. surname.

co·hab'it, v. live together, esp. as husband and wife without being married. **—co·hab·i·ta'tion,** n.

co·here', v.v., **-hered, -hering.** stick together. **—co·he'sion,** n. **—co·he'sive,** adj.

co·her'ent, adj. making sense. —**co·her'ence,** n.

co'hort, n. 1. associate; companion. 2. group, esp. of soldiers.

coif·fure' (kwä fyŏŏr'), n. arrangement of hair.

coil, v. 1. wind spirally in rings. —n. 2. ring. 3. series of spirals or rings.

coin, n. 1. piece of metal issued as money. —v. 2. make metal into money. 3. invent. —**coin'age,** n. —**coin'er,** n.

co·in·cide', v. -cided, -ciding. 1. occur at same time, place, etc. 2. match. —**co·in'ci·dence,** n. —**co·in'ci·den'tal,** adj. —**co·in'ci·den'tal·ly,** adv.

co'i·tus (kō'i təs), n. sexual intercourse. —**co'i·tal,** adj.

coke, n., v., coked, coking. —n. 1. solid carbon produced from coal. 2. Slang. cocaine. —v. 3. convert into coke.

co'la, n. soft drink containing extract from kola nuts.

col'an·der (kul'-), n. large strainer.

cold, adj. 1. giving or feeling no warmth. 2. not cordial. —n. 3. absence of heat. 4. illness marked by runny nose, etc. —**cold'ly,** adv. —**cold'ness,** n.

cold'-blood'ed, adj. 1. callous; unemotional. 2. with blood at same temperature as environment. —**cold'-blood'ed·ly,** adv. —**cold'-blood'ed·ness,** n.

cold cream, preparation for cleansing or soothing the skin.

cold war, rivalry between nations just short of armed conflict.

cole'slaw', n. sliced raw cabbage.

col'ic, n. sharp pain in abdomen or bowels.

col·i·se'um, n. large stadium.

col·lab'o·rate', v., -rated, -rating. work together. —**col·lab'o·ra'tion,** n. —**col·lab'o·ra'tor,** n.

col·lage' (kə läzh'), n. work of art made with various materials pasted on a surface.

col·lapse', v., -lapsed, -lapsing. —v. 1. fall in or together. 2. fail abruptly. —n. 3. a falling-in. 4. sudden failure. —**col·laps'i·ble,** adj.

col'lar, n. 1. part of garment around neck. —v. 2. seize by collar.

col'lar·bone', n. slender bone connecting sternum and scapula; clavicle.

col·lat'er·al, n. 1. security pledged on loan. —adj. 2. additional. 3. on side.

col'league, n. associate in work, etc.

col·lect', v. 1. gather together. 2. take

payment of. —adj., adv. 3. payable on delivery. —**col·lec'tion,** n. —**col·lec'tor,** n.

col·lect'i·ble, n. 1. object collected. —adj. 2. able to be collected.

col·lec'tive, adj. 1. joint; by a group. —n. 2. socialist productive group. —**col·lec'tiv·ist,** n.

col·lec'tiv·ism', n. principle of communal control of means of production, etc. —**col·lec'tiv·ist,** n.

col'lege, n. school of higher learning. —**col·le'giate,** adj.

col·lide', v., -lided, -liding. come together violently.

col'lie, n. large, long-haired dog.

col'lier (-yər), n. 1. ship for carrying coal. 2. coal miner.

col·li'sion, n. 1. crash. 2. conflict.

col·lo'qui·al, adj. appropriate to casual rather than formal speech or writing. —**col·lo'qui·al·ism',** n. —**col·lo'qui·al·ly,** adv.

col'lo·quy (-kwē), n., pl. -quies. conversation.

col·lu'sion, n. illicit agreement.

co·logne' (kə lōn'), n. perfumed toilet water.

co'lon, n. 1. mark of punctuation (:). 2. part of large intestine. —**co·lon'ic,** adj.

colo'nel (kûr'nəl), n. military officer below general. —**colo'nel·cy,** n.

co·lo'ni·al·ism', n. policy of extending national authority over foreign territories. —**co·lo'ni·al·ist,** n., adj.

col'on·nade' (-nād'), n. series of columns.

col'o·ny, n., pl. -nies. 1. group of people settling in another land. 2. territory subject to outside ruling power. 3. community. —**co·lo'ni·al,** adj., n. —**col'o·nist,** n. —**col'o·nize',** v.

col'or, n. 1. quality of light perceived by human eye. 2. pigment; dye. 3. complexion. 4. vivid description. 5. (pl.) flag. 6. pace. —v. 7. give or apply color to. 8. distort in telling. Also, Brit., **col'our.** —**col'or·a'tion,** n.

col·o·ra·tu·ra (tyŏŏr'ə), n. lyric soprano specializing in music containing ornamental trills.

col'or·blind', adj. 1. unable to distinguish certain colors. 2. without racial bias.

col'ored, adj. Often Offensive. of a race other than Caucasian.

col'or·ful, adj. 1. full of color. 2. vivid; interesting.

col'or·less, adj. 1. without color. 2. uninteresting. —**col'or·less·ly,** adv.

co·los'sal, adj. huge; vast.

co·los'sus, n. anything colossal.

colt, n. young male horse.

col•um•bine', n. branching plant with bright flowers.

col•umn, n. 1. upright shaft or support. 2. long area of print. 3. regular journalistic piece. 4. long group of troops, ships, etc. —co•lum'nar, adj. —col'umn•ist, n.

co'ma, n. prolonged unconscious state.

comb, n. 1. toothed object, for straightening hair or fiber. 2. growth on a cock's head. 3. crest. 4. honeycomb. —v. 5. dress with comb. 6. search.

com•bat, v. -bated, -bating, n. fight; battle. —com•bat'ant, n. —com•bat'ive, adj.

com•bi•na'tion, n. 1. act of combining. 2. things combined. 3. alliance. 4. sets of figures dialed to operate a lock.

com•bine', v. -bined, -bining, n. —v. 1. unite; join. —n. (kom'bīn). 2. combination. 3. machine that cuts and threshes grain.

com'bo, n. Informal. small jazz or dance band. 2. combination.

com•bus'ti•ble, adj. 1. inflammable. —n. 2. inflammable substance.

com•bus'tion, n. burning.

come, v. came, come, coming. 1. approach or arrive. 2. happen. 3. emerge.

come'back', n. 1. return to former status, prosperity, etc. 2. clever retort.

co•me'di•an, n. humorous actor. —co•me'di•enne', n.fem.

com'e•dy, n., pl. -dies. 1. humorous drama. 2. drama with happy ending.

come'ly (kum'lē), adj. -lier, -liest. attractive. —come'li•ness, n.

com'er, n. Informal. one likely to have great success.

com'et, n. celestial body orbiting around and lighted by sun, often with misty tail.

com'fort, v. 1. console or cheer. —n. 2. consolation. 3. ease. —com'fort•a•ble, adj. —com'fort•a•bly, adv.

com'fort•er, n. 1. one who comforts. 2. warm quilt.

com'ic, adj. 1. of comedy. 2. Also, com'i•cal. funny. —n. 3. comedian. —com'i•cal•ly, adv.

comic strip, sequence of drawings relating comic incident or story, often appearing serially in newspaper.

com'ma, n. mark of punctuation (,).

com•mand', v. 1. order. 2. be in control of. 3. overlook. —n. 4. order. 5. control. 6. troops, etc., under commander.

com•man•dant', n. (-dant', -dänt'), n. 1. local commanding officer. 2. director of Marine Corps.

com•man•deer', v. seize for official use.

com•mand'er, n. 1. chief officer. 2. Navy. officer below captain.

com•mand'ment, n. 1. command. 2. precept of God.

com•man'do, n., pl. -dos, -does. soldier making brief raids against enemy.

com•mem'o•rate', v. -rated, -rating. honor memory of. —com•mem•o•ra'tion, n. —com•mem'o•ra'tive, adj.

com•mence', v. -menced, -mencing. start.

com•mence'ment, n. 1. beginning. 2. graduation day or ceremonies.

com•mend', v. 1. praise. 2. entrust. —com•mend'a•ble, adj. —com'men•da'tion, n. —com•mend'a•to'ry, adj.

com•men'su•rate (-shə rit, -sə-), adj. equal or corresponding. —com•men'su•rate•ly, adv.

com'ment, n. 1. remark or criticism. —v. 2. make remarks.

com'men•ta•ry, n., pl. -taries. 1. comment. 2. explanatory essay.

com'men•ta•tor, n. one who discusses news events, etc.

com'merce, n. sale or barter.

com•mer'cial, adj. 1. of or in commerce. —n. 2. Radio & TV. advertisement.

com•mer'cial•ize', v. -ized, -izing. treat as matter of profit.

com•min'gle, v., -gled, -gling. blend.

com•mis'er•ate', v., -ated, -ating. feel sympathetic sorrow. —com•mis•er•a'tion, n.

com'mis•sar', n. Soviet government official.

com'mis•sar'y, n., pl. -saries. store selling food and equipment.

com•mis'sion, n. 1. act of committing. 2. document giving authority. 3. group of persons with special task. 4. usable condition. 5. fee for agent's services. —v. 6. give commission to. 7. authorize. 8. put into service.

com•mis'sion•er, n. government official.

com•mit', v., -mitted, -mitting. 1. give in trust or custody. 2. refer to committee. 3. do. 4. obligate. —com•mit'ment, n.

com•mit'tee, n. group assigned to special duties.

com•mode', n. washstand or small cabinet.

com•mo'di•ous, adj. roomy.

com•mod'i•ty, *n., pl.* **-ties.** article of commerce.

com'mo•dore', *n.* officer below rear admiral.

com'mon, *adj.* 1. shared by all; joint. 2. ordinary; usual. 3. vulgar. —*n.* 4. area of public land. —**com'mon•ly,** *adv.*

com'mon•er, *n.* one of common people.

common law, system of law based on custom and court decisions.

com'mon•place', *adj.* 1. ordinary; trite. —*n.* 2. commonplace remark.

com'mons, *n.* 1. (*cap.*) elective house of certain legislatures. 2. large dining room.

com'mon•weal', *n.* public welfare.

com'mon•wealth', *n.* 1. democratic state. 2. people of a state.

com•mo'tion, *n.* disturbance.

com•mu'nal, *adj.* of or belonging to a community.

com•mune' (kə myōōn'), *v.,* **-muned, -muning,** *n.* —*v.* 1. talk together. —*n.* (kom'yōōn). 2. small community with shared property. 3. district.

com•mu'ni•cate', *v.,* **-cated, -cating.** 1. make known. 2. transmit. 3. exchange news, etc. —**com•mu'ni•ca•ble,** *adj.* —**com•mu'ni•ca'tion,** *n.* —**com•mu'ni•ca'tive,** *adj.* —**com•mu'ni•cant,** *n.*

com•mun'ion, *n.* 1. act of sharing. 2. group with same religion. 3. sacrament commemorating Jesus' last supper; Eucharist.

com•mu'ni•qué' (-kā'), *n.* official bulletin.

com'mu•nism, *n.* 1. social system based on collective ownership of all productive property. 2. (*cap.*) political doctrine advocating this. —**com'mu•nist,** *n., adj.* —**com'mu•nis'tic,** *adj.*

com•mu'ni•ty, *n., pl.* **-ties.** 1. people with common culture living in one locality. 2. public.

com•mute', *v.,* **-muted, -muting.** 1. exchange. 2. reduce (punishment). 3. travel between home and work. —**com'mu•ta'tion,** *n.* —**com•mut'er,** *n.*

com•pact', *adj.* 1. packed together. 2. pithy. —*v.* 3. pack together. —*n.* (kom'pakt). 4. small cosmetic case. 5. agreement. —**com•pact'ly,** *adv.* —**com•pact'ness,** *n.*

compact disc, optical disc on which music, data, or images are digitally recorded. Also, **CD.**

com•pac'tor, (kəm pak'tər, kom'pak-), *n.* appliance that compresses trash into small bundles.

com•pan'ion, *n.* 1. associate. 2. mate. —**com•pan'ion•a•ble,** *adj.* —**com•pan'ion•ate,** *adj.* —**com•pan'ion•ship',** *n.*

com•pa'ny, *n., pl.* **-nies.** 1. persons associated for business or social purposes, etc. 2. companionship. 3. guests. 4. military unit.

com•par'a•tive, *adj.* 1. of or based on comparison. —*n.* 2. *Gram.* intermediate degree of comparison. —**com•par'a•tive•ly,** *adv.*

com•pare', *v.,* **-pared, -paring.** 1. consider for similarities. 2. *Gram.* inflect to show intensity, etc. —**com'pa•ra•ble,** *adj.* —**com•par'i•son,** *n.*

com•part'ment, *n.* separate room, space, etc.

com'pass, *n.* 1. instrument for finding direction. 2. extent. 3. tool for making circles.

com•pas'sion, *n.* pity or sympathy. —**com•pas'sion•ate,** *adj.*

com•pat'i•ble, *adj.* congenial. —**com•pat'i•bil'i•ty,** *n.*

com•pa'tri•ot, *n.* person from one's own country.

com•pel', *v.,* **-pelled, -pelling.** force.

com•pen'di•ous, *adj.* concise.

com•pen'di•um, *n., pl.* **-diums, -dia.** full list or summary.

com'pen•sate', *v.,* **-sated, -sating.** 1. make up for. 2. pay. —**com•pen•sa'tion,** *n.* —**com•pen'sa•to'ry,** *adj.*

com•pete', *v.,* **-peted, -peting.** contend; rival.

com'pe•tent, *adj.* 1. able enough. 2. legally qualified. 3. sufficient. —**com'pe•tence, com'pe•ten•cy,** *n.* —**com'pe•tent•ly,** *adv.*

com'pe•ti'tion, *n.* 1. contest. 2. rivalry. —**com•pet'i•tive,** *adj.* —**com•pet'i•tor,** *n.*

com•pile', *v.,* **-piled, -piling.** put together; assemble. —**com•pil'er,** *n.* —**com'pi•la'tion,** *n.*

com•pla'cen•cy, *n., pl.* **-cies.** satisfaction, esp. with self. Also, **com•pla'cence.** —**compla•cent',** *adj.* —**com•pla'cent•ly,** *adv.*

com•plain', *v.* 1. express pain, dissatisfaction, etc. 2. accuse. —**com•plain'er, com•plain'ant,** *n.* —**com•plaint',** *n.*

com•plai'sant, *adj.* agreeable; obliging.

com'ple•ment, *n.* 1. that which completes. 2. full amount. —*v.* (-ment'). 3. complete. —**com•ple•men'ta•ry,** *adj.*

com•plete', *adj.,* **-pleted, -pleting.** —*adj.* 1. entire; perfect. —*v.* 2. make complete. —**com•plete'ly,** *adv.*

—com•plete′ness, n. —com•ple′tion, n.

com•plex′, adj. 1. having many parts; intricate. —n. (kom′pleks). 2. complex whole. 3. obsession. —com•plex′i•ty, n.

com•plex′ion, n. color of skin.

com′pli•cate′, v.. -cated, -cating. make complex or difficult. —com′pli•ca′tion, n.

com•plic′i•ty (-plis′ə-), n., pl. -ties. partnership in crime.

com′pli•ment, n. (-mənt). 1. expression of praise. —v. (-ment′). 2. express praise.

com′pli•men•ta•ry, adj. 1. of or being a compliment. 2. free.

com•ply′, v., -plied, -plying. act in accordance. —com•pli′ance, n. —com•pli′ant, adj. —com•pli′a•ble, adj.

com•po′nent, adj. 1. composing. —n. 2. part of whole.

com•port′, v. 1. conduct (oneself). 2. suit. —com•port′ment, n.

com•pose′, v., -posed, -posing. 1. make by uniting parts. 2. constitute. 3. put in order; calm. 4. create and write. 5. set printing type.

com•posed′, adj. calm.

com•pos′er, n. writer, esp. of music.

com•pos′ite, adj. made of many parts.

com′post, n. decaying mixture of leaves, etc.

com•po′sure, n. calm.

com•pote (kom′pōt), n. stewed fruit.

com′pound, adj. 1. having two or more parts, functions, etc. —n. 2. something made by combining parts. 3. enclosure with buildings. —v. (kəm pound′). 4. combine. 5. condone (crime) for a price.

com′pre•hend′, v. 1. understand. 2. include. —com′pre•hen′si•ble, adj. —com′pre•hen′sion, n.

com′pre•hen′sive, adj. inclusive. —com′pre•hen′sive•ly, adv. —com′pre•hen′sive•ness, n.

com•press′, v. 1. press together. —n. (kom′pres). 2. pad applied to affected part of body. —com•pres′sion, n. —com•pres′sor, n.

com•prise′, v., -prised, -prising. consist of. Also, com•prize′. —com•pris′al, n.

com′pro•mise′, n., v., -mised, -mising. —n. 1. agreement to mutual concessions. 2. something intermediate. —v. 3. settle by compromise. 4. endanger.

comp•trol′ler (kən-), n. controller.

com•pul′sion, n. compelling force. —com•pul′so•ry, adj.

com•pul′sive, adj. due to or acting on inner compulsion.

com•punc′tion, n. remorse.

com•pute′, v., -puted, -puting. calculate; figure. —com′pu•ta′tion, n.

com•put′er, n. electronic apparatus for storing and retrieving data, making calculations, etc.

com•put′er•ize′, v.. -ized, -izing. do by computer.

com′rade, n. close companion. —com′rade•ship′, n.

con, adv., n., v., conned, conning. —adv. 1. opposed to a plan, etc. —n. 2. argument against. —v. 3. study. 4. Informal. deceive; swindle.

con•cave′, adj. curved inward. —con•cave′ly, adv. —con•cav′i•ty, n.

con•ceal′, v. hide. —con•ceal′ment, n.

con•cede′, v., -ceded, -ceding. 1. admit. 2. yield.

con•ceit′, n. 1. excess self-esteem. 2. fanciful idea. —con•ceit′ed, adj.

con•ceive′, v., -ceived, -ceiving. 1. form (plan or idea). 2. understand. 3. become pregnant. —con•ceiv′a•ble, adj. —con•ceiv′a•bly, adv.

con′cen•trate′, v., -trated, -trating. n. —v. 1. bring to one point. 2. intensify. 3. give full attention. —n. 4. product of concentration. —con′cen•tra′tion, n.

concentration camp, guarded compound where political prisoners, minorities, etc., are confined.

con•cen′tric, adj. having common center.

con′cept, n. general notion.

con•cep′tion, n. 1. act of conceiving. 2. idea.

con•cep′tu•a•lize′ (-chōō ə līz′), v., -lized, -lizing. 1. form a concept of. 2. think in concepts. —con•cep′tu•al•i•za′tion, n.

con•cern′, v. 1. relate to. 2. involve. 3. worry. —n. 4. matter that concerns. 5. business firm.

con•cern′ing, prep. about.

con•cert′, n. 1. musical performance. 2. accord.

con•cert′ed, adj. 1. planned together. 2. performed together or in cooperation. —con•cert′ed•ly, adv.

con′cer•ti′na (-tē′-), n. small accordion.

con•cer′to (kən cher′tō), n., pl. -tos or -ti (-tē). musical piece for one or more principal instruments and orchestra.

con•ces′sion, n. 1. act of conceding. 2. what is conceded. 3. grant or franchise conceded by government or controlling authority.

conch (kongk), *n.* spiral sea shell.

con·cil·i·ate', *v.*, **-ated, -ating.** win over; reconcile. **—con·cil·i·a'tion,** *n.* **—con·cil'i·a·to'ry,** *adj.*

con·cise', *adj.* brief; succinct. **—con·cise'ly,** *adv.* **—con·cise'ness,** *n.*

con'clave, *n.* private meeting.

con·clude', *v.*, **-cluded, -cluding.** 1. finish; settle. 2. infer. **—con·clu'sion,** *n.* **—con·clu'sive,** *adj.*

con·coct', *v.* make by combining. **—con·coc'tion,** *n.*

con·com'i·tant, *adj.* 1. accompanying. **—** *n.* 2. anything concomitant. **—con·com'i·tant·ly,** *adv.*

con'cord, *n.* agreement.

con·cord'ance, *n.* 1. concord. 2. index of principal words of book.

con·cor'dat, *n.* agreement, esp. between Pope and a government.

con'course, *n.* 1. assemblage. 2. place for crowds in motion.

con·crete', *adj., n., v.* **-creted, -creting.** **—** *adj.* 1. real; objective. 2. made of concrete. **—** *n.* 3. material of cement and hard matter. **—** *v.* 4. (kon krēt') become solid. **—con·crete'ly,** *adv.* **—con·crete'ness,** *n.* **—con·cre'tion,** *n.*

con'cu·bine', *n.* woman living with but not married to man.

con·cu'pis·cent (-pi sant), *adj.* lustful. **—con·cu'pis·cence,** *n.*

con·cur', *v.*, **-curred, -curring.** 1. agree. 2. coincide. 3. cooperate. **—con·cur'rence,** *n.* **—con·cur'rent,** *adj.* **—con·cur'rent·ly,** *adv.*

con·cus'sion, *n.* shock or jarring from blow.

con·demn', *v.* 1. denounce. 2. pronounce guilty. 3. judge unfit. 4. acquire for public purpose. **—con'dem·na'tion,** *n.*

con·dense', *v.*, **-densed, -densing.** 1. reduce to denser form. 2. make or become compact. **—con'den·sa'tion,** *n.* **—con·dens'er,** *n.*

con'de·scend', *v.* 1. pretend equality with an inferior. 2. deign. **—con'de·scen'sion,** *n.*

con'di·ment, *n.* seasoning.

con·di'tion, *n.* 1. state of being or health. 2. fit state. 3. requirement. **—** *v.* 4. put in condition. **—con·di'tion·al,** *adj.* **—con·di'tion·al·ly,** *adv.*

con·dole', *v.*, **-doled, -doling.** sympathize in sorrow. **—con·do'lence,** *n.*

con'dom (kon'dam, kun'-), *n.* thin sheath worn over the penis during intercourse to prevent conception or infection; prophylactic.

con'do·min'i·um, *n.* apartment house in which units are individually owned. Also, *Informal,* **con'do.**

con·done', *v.*, **-doned, -doning.** excuse.

con'dor, *n.* vulture.

con·duce', *v.*, **-duced, -ducing.** contribute; lead. **—con·du'cive,** *adj.*

con'duct, *n.* 1. behavior. 2. management. **—** *v.* (kon dukt'). 3. behave. 4. manage. 5. lead or carry.

con·duc'tor, *n.* 1. guide. 2. director of an orchestra. 3. official on trains. 4. anything that conveys electricity, heat, etc.

con'duit (-dwit), *n.* pipe for water, other fluid.

cone, *n.* 1. form tapering from round base to single point. 2. fruit of fir, pine, etc.

con·fec'tion, *n.* candy or other sweet preparation. **—con·fec'tion·er,** *n.* **—con·fec'tion·er'y,** *n.*

con·fed'er·a·cy, *n., pl.* **-cies.** 1. league. 2. (*cap.*) Confederate States of America.

con·fed'er·ate, *adj., n., v.* **-ated, -ating.** **—** *adj.* (-ar it). 1. in league. 2. (*cap.*) of **Confederate States of America,** separated from U.S. during Civil War. **—** *n.* (-ar it). 3. ally. 4. accomplice. 5. (*cap.*) citizen of Confederate States of America. **—** *v.* (-ə rāt'). 6. be allied. **—con·fed·er·a'tion,** *n.*

con·fer', *v.*, **-ferred, -ferring.** 1. bestow. 2. consult. **—con·fer'ment,** *n.*

con'fer·ence, *n.* 1. meeting. 2. discussion.

con·fess', *v.* 1. admit. 2. declare one's sins, as to priest. **—con·fes'sion,** *n.*

con·fes'sion·al, *adj.* 1. characteristic of confession. **—** *n.* 2. place in church set apart for confession.

con·fes'sor, *n.* 1. one who confesses. 2. one who hears confessions.

con·fet'ti, *n.* bits of colored paper.

con'fi·dant', *n.* one to whom secrets are told. **—con'fi·dante',** *n.fem.*

con·fide', *v.*, **-fided, -fiding.** 1. trust with secret. 2. entrust.

con'fi·dence, *n.* 1. full trust. 2. assurance. **—con'fi·dent,** *adj.* **—con'fi·dent·ly,** *adv.*

confidence game, swindle in which the swindler first gains the victim's confidence.

con'fi·den'tial, *adj.* 1. entrusted as secret. 2. private. **—con'fi·den'tial·ly,** *adv.*

con'fig·u·ra'tion, *n.* external form.

con·fine', *v.*, **-fined, -fining.** **—** *v.* 1. keep within bounds. 2. shut or lock up. **—** *n.* (pl.) (kon'finz). 3. boundary. **—con·fined',** *adj.* 1. in childbed. 2. stuffy.

con·fine'ment, n. 1. imprisonment. 2. childbirth. 3. period of being confined.

con·firm', v. 1. make sure. 2. make valid. 3. strengthen. 4. admit to full church membership. —con'fir·ma'tion, n.

con'fis·cate' (kon'fis kāt'), v., -cated, -cating. seize by public authority. —con'fis·ca'tion, n.

con·fla·gra'tion, n. fierce fire.

con·flict', v. 1. oppose; clash. —n. (kon'flikt). 2. battle. 3. antagonism.

con·flu'ence, n. act or place of flowing together. —con'flu·ent, adj.

con·form', v. 1. accord; adapt. 2. make similar. —con·form'a·ble, adj. —con·form'ist, n. —con·form'i·ty, n.

con'for·ma'tion, n. form.

con·found', v. 1. confuse. 2. perplex.

con·found'ed, adj. 1. bewildered. 2. damned.

con·front', v. 1. meet or set facing. 2. challenge openly. —con'fron·ta'tion, n.

con·fuse', v. 1. throw into disorder. 2. associate wrongly. 3. disconcert. —con·fu'sion, n.

con·fute', v. -futed, -futing. prove to be wrong. —con'fu·ta'tion, n.

con·geal', v. make solid or thick. —con·geal'ment, n.

con·gen'ial, adj. agreeable; suited. —con·ge'ni·al'i·ty, n.

con·gen'i·tal, adj. from birth. —con·gen'i·tal·ly, adv.

con·gest', v. fill to excess. —con·ges'tion, n.

con·glom'er·ate, n. adj. v., -ated, -ating. —n. (-ər it). 1. mixture. 2. rock formed of pebbles, etc. 3. company owning variety of other companies. —adj. (-ər it). 4. gathered into a ball. 5. mixed. —v. (-ə rāt'). 6. gather into round mass. —con·glom'er·a'tion, n.

con·grat'u·late', v., -lated, -lating. express sympathetic joy. —con·grat'u·la'tion, n. —con·grat'u·la·to'ry, adj.

con'gre·gate', v., -gated, -gating. assemble. —con'gre·ga'tion, n.

con'gre·ga'tion·al, adj. 1. of congregations. 2. (cap.) denoting church denomination wherein each church acts independently. —con'gre·ga'tion·al·ism, n. —con'gre·ga'tion·al·ist, n.

con'gress, n. 1. national legislative body, esp. (cap.) of the U.S. 2. formal meeting. —con·gres'sion·al, adj.

—con'gress·man, n. —con'gress·wom·an, n. fem.

con·gru'ent, adj. agreeing or coinciding. —con·gru'ence, n.

con·gru'i·ty, n., pl. -ties. agreement. —con·gru'ous, adj.

con'ic, adj. of like cone. Also, con'i·cal.

co'ni·fer, n. tree bearing cones. —co·nif'er·ous, adj.

con·jec'ture, n., v., -tured, -turing. guess. —con·jec'tur·al, adj.

con·join', v. join together.

con·ju'gal, adj. of marriage. —con'ju·gal·ly, adv.

con'ju·gate', v., -gated, -gating, adj. —v. (-gāt'). 1. Gram. give in other forms of (verb). —adj. (-git). 2. coupled. —con'ju·ga'tion, n.

con·junc'tion, n. 1. combination. 2. Gram. word that links words, phrases, clauses, or sentences. —con·junc'tive, adj.

con·junc'ti·vi'tis (kən jungk'tə vī'tis), n. inflammation of the conjunctiva, a mucous membrane of the eye.

con·jure', v., -jured, -juring. invoke or produce by magic. —con'jur·er, n.

conk (kongk, kôngk), v. Slang. 1. strike on the head. 2. conk out. a. break down. b. go to sleep. —n. 3. blow on the head.

con·nect', v. 1. join; link. —con·nec'tion; Brit. con·nex'ion, n. —con·nec'tive, adj. n.

con·nive', v., -nived, -niving. conspire. —con·niv'ance, n. —con·niv'er, n.

con'nois·seur' (kon'ə sûr'), n. skilled judge.

con·note', v., -noted, -noting. signify in addition; imply. —con'no·ta'tion, n.

con·nu'bi·al, adj. matrimonial. —con·nu'bi·al·ly, adv.

con'quer, v. 1. acquire by force. 2. defeat. —con'quer·or, n. —con'quest, n.

con·san·guin'e·ous, adj. related by birth. —con·san·guin'i·ty, n.

con'science, n. recognition of right or wrong in oneself. —con'sci·en'tious, adj.

conscientious objector, person who refuses to serve in armed forces for moral or religious reasons.

con'sci·on·a·ble (-shən-), adj. approved by conscience.

con'scious, adj. 1. in possession of one's senses. 2. aware. 3. deliberate. —con'scious·ly, adv. —con'scious·ness, n.

con'script, adj. 1. drafted. —n. 2. one

drafted. —v. (kən skript') 3. draft for military service. —con•scrip'tion, n.

con'se•crate', v., -crated, -crating. 1. make sacred. 2. devote. —con'se•cra'tion, n.

con•sec'u•tive, adj. 1. successive. 2. logical. —con•sec'u•tive•ly, adv.

con•sen'sus, n. agreement.

con•sent', v. 1. agree; comply. —n. 2. assent.

con'se•quence', n. 1. effect. 2. importance.

con'se•quent', adj. following; resulting. —con'se•quen'tial, adj. —con'se•quent•ly, adv.

con'ser•va'tion, n. preservation, esp. of natural resources. —con'ser•va'tion•ism, n. —con'ser•va'tion•ist, n.

con•serv'a•tive, adj. 1. favoring existing conditions. 2. cautious. —n. 3. conservative person. —con•serv'a•tive•ly, adv. —con•serv'a•tive•ness, n.

con•serv'a•to'ry, n., pl. -ries. 1. school of music or drama. 2. hothouse.

con•serve', v., -served, -serving. —v. 1. keep intact. —n. (kon'sûrv). 2. kind of jam.

con•sid'er, v. 1. think over. 2. deem. 3. respect. —con•sid'er•ate, adj.

con•sid'er•a•ble, adj. important or sizable. —con•sid'er•a•bly, adv.

con•sid'er•a'tion, n. 1. thought. 2. regard. 3. fee.

con•sid'er•ing, prep. in view of.

con•sign', v. 1. deliver. 2. entrust. 3. ship. —con•sign'ment, n.

con•sist', v. be composed.

con•sist'en•cy, n., pl. -cies. 1. firmness. 2. density. 3. adherence to principles, behavior, etc. —con•sist'ent, adj. —con•sist'ent•ly, adv.

con•sis'to•ry, n., pl. -ries. church council.

con•sole', v., -soled, -soling, n. —v. 1. cheer in sorrow. —n. (kon'sōl). 2. control panel of organ or electrical system. —con•so•la'tion, n. —con•sol'a•ble, adj. —con•sol'er, n.

con•sol'i•date', v., -dated, -dating. 1. make or become firm. 2. unite. —con•sol'i•da'tion, n.

con'som•mé' (kon'sə mā'), n. clear soup.

con'so•nant, n. 1. letter for a sound made by obstructing breath passage. —adj. 2. in agreement. —con'so•nance, n.

con'sort, n. 1. spouse. —v. (kən sôrt'). 2. associate.

con•sor'ti•um (kən sôr'shē əm, -tē-

-shəm,), n., pl. -tia. 1. combination for business purposes. 2. association.

con•spic'u•ous, adj. 1. easily seen. 2. notable. —con•spic'u•ous•ly, adv. —con•spic'u•ous•ness, n.

con•spire', v., -spired, -spiring. plot together. —con•spir'a•cy, n. —con•spir'a•tor, n.

con'sta•ble, n. police officer.

con•stab'u•lar'y, n., pl. -laries. police.

con'stant, adj. 1. uniform. 2. uninterrupted. 3. faithful. —n. 4. something unchanging. —con'stan•cy, n. —con'stant•ly, adv.

con'stel•la'tion, n. group of stars.

con'ster•na'tion, n. utter dismay.

con'sti•pate', v., -pated, -pating. cause difficult evacuation of bowels. —con'sti•pa'tion, n.

con•stit'u•ent, adj. 1. being part; composing. —n. 2. ingredient. 3. represented voter. —con•stit'u•en•cy, n.

con'sti•tute', v., -tuted, -tuting. 1. compose. 2. make.

con'sti•tu'tion, n. 1. make-up. 2. physical condition. 3. system of governmental principles. —con'sti•tu'tion•al, adj.

con•strain', v. 1. force or oblige. 2. confine. —con•straint', n.

con•strict', v. draw together; shrink. —con•stric'tion, n. —con•stric'tor, n.

con•struct', v. build or devise. —con•struc'tion, n.

con•struc'tive, adj. 1. of construction. 2. helpful. —con•struc'tive•ly, adv.

con•strue', v., -strued, -struing. interpret.

con'sul, n. local diplomatic official. —con'su•lar, adj. —con'su•late, n.

con•sult', v. 1. ask advice of. 2. refer to. 3. confer. —con•sult'ant, n. —con'sul•ta'tion, n.

con•sume', v., -sumed, -suming. 1. use up. 2. devour. 3. engross.

con•sum'er, n. 1. one that consumes. 2. purchaser of goods for personal use.

con•sum'er•ism, n. movement to defend consumer interests.

con•sum'mate, v., -mated, -mating. adj. (kən sum'it for adj.) 1. complete or perfect. —con•sum•ma'tion, n.

con•sump'tion, n. 1. act of consuming. 2. amount consumed. 3. wasting disease, esp. tuberculosis of lungs. —con•sump'tive, adj., n.

con'tact, n. 1. a touching. 2. association. 3. business acquaintance. —v. 4.

put or bring into contact. **5.** communicate with.

contact lens, lens for correcting vision, put directly on eye.

con·ta′gion, n. spread of disease by contact. —**con·ta′gious,** adj.

con·tain′, v. **1.** have within itself. **2.** have space for. —**con·tain′er,** n.

con·tam′i·nate′, v., -nated, -nating. make impure. —**con·tam′i·na′tion,** n.

con·temn′, v. scorn.

con′tem·plate′, v., -plated, -plating. **1.** consider. **2.** observe. **3.** intend. —**con′tem·pla′tion,** n.

con·tem′po·rar′y, adj., n., pl. -raries. —adj. **1.** Also, **con′tem·po·ra′ne·ous.** of same age or period. —n. **2.** contemporary person.

con·tempt′, n. **1.** scorn. **2.** disgrace. **3.** disobedience or disrespect of court or legislature. —**con·tempt′i·ble,** adj. —**con·temp′tu·ous,** adj.

con·tend′, v. **1.** be in struggle. **2.** assert. —**con·tend′er,** n.

con·tent′, adj. **1.** Also, **con·tent′ed.** satisfied. **2.** willing. —v. **3.** make content. —n. **4.** Also, **con·tent′ment.** ease of mind. **5.** (kon′tent) (often pl.). what is contained. **6.** (kon′tent) capacity. —**con·tent′ed·ly,** adv.

con·ten′tion, n. **1.** controversy. **2.** assertion. —**con·ten′tious,** adj.

con·test′, n. **1.** struggle; competition. —v. (kən test′) **2.** fight for. **3.** dispute. —**con·test′ant,** n.

con′text, n. surrounding words or circumstances.

con·tig′u·ous, adj. **1.** touching. **2.** near.

con′ti·nent, n. **1.** major land mass. —adj. **2.** temperate. —**con′ti·nen′tal,** adj. —**con′ti·nence,** n.

con·tin′gen·cy, n., pl. -cies. chance; event.

con·tin′gent, adj. **1.** conditional; possible. —n. **2.** quota or group. **3.** contingency.

con·tin′ue, v., -tinued, -tinuing. **1.** go or carry on. **2.** stay. **3.** extend. **4.** carry over. —**con·tin′u·al,** adj. —**con·tin′u·al·ly,** adv. —**con·tin′u·ance,** n. —**con·tin′u·a′tion,** n.

con′ti·nu′i·ty, n., pl. -ties. **1.** continuous whole. **2.** script.

con·tin′u·ous, adj. unbroken. —**con·tin′u·ous·ly,** adv.

con·tin′u·um (-yōō əm), n., pl. -ua. continuous extent, series, or whole.

con·tort′, v. twist; distort. —**con·tor′tion,** n.

con′tour (-tŏŏr), n. outline.

con′tra·band′, n. goods prohibited

from shipment. —**con′tra·band′,** adj.

con′tra·cep′tion, n. prevention of pregnancy. —**con′tra·cep′tive,** adj., n.

con′tract, n. **1.** written agreement. —v. (kən trakt′) **2.** draw together; shorten. **3.** acquire. **4.** agree. —**con·trac′tion,** n.

con′trac·tor, n. one who supplies work by contract.

con′tra·dict′, v. deny as being true or correct. —**con′tra·dic′tion,** n. —**con′tra·dic′to·ry,** adj.

con·tral′to, n., pl. -tos. lowest female voice.

con·trap′tion, n. strange machine; gadget.

con′tra·pun′tal, adj. of or relating to counterpoint.

con′tra·ry, adj., n., pl. -ries. —adj. **1.** opposite. **2.** (kən trâr′ē). perverse. —n. **3.** something contrary. —**con′tra·ri·ness,** n. —**con′tra·ri·ly,** —**con′tra·ri·wise′,** adv.

con·trast′, v. **1.** show unlikeness. **2.** compare. —n. (kon′trast) **3.** show of unlikeness. **4.** something unlike.

con′tra·vene′, v., -vened, -vening. **1.** oppose. **2.** violate. —**con′tra·ven′tion,** n.

con·trib′ute, v., -uted, -uting. give in part; donate. —**con′tri·bu′tion,** n. —**con·trib′u·tor,** n. —**con·trib′u·to′ry,** adj.

con·trite′, adj. penitent. —**con·tri′tion,** n.

con·trive′, v., -trived, -triving. **1.** plan; devise. **2.** plot. —**con·triv′ance,** n.

con·trol′, v., -trolled, -trolling. —v. **1.** have direction over. **2.** restrain. —n. **3.** power of controlling. **4.** restraint. **5.** regulating device. —**con·trol′la·ble,** adj.

con·trol′ler, n. **1.** government or corporate officer who superintends finances. **2.** person or device that regulates.

con′tro·ver′sy, n., pl. -sies. dispute or debate. —**con′tro·ver′sial,** adj.

con′tro·vert′, v. **1.** dispute. **2.** discuss. —**con′tro·vert′i·ble,** adj.

con·tu·ma′cious (-tōo-), adj. stubbornly disobedient. —**con′tu·ma·cy,** n.

con′tu·me·ly, n., pl. -lies. contemptuous treatment.

con·tu′sion, n. bruise.

co·nun′drum, n. riddle involving pun.

con′ur·ba′tion, n. continuous mass of urban settlements.

con′va·lesce′, v., -lesced, -lescing.

recover from illness. —con·va·les'·cence, n. —con·va·les'·cent, adj. n.

con·vec'tion, n. transference of heat by movement of heated matter.

con·vene', v., -vened, -vening. assemble.

con·ven'ient, adj. handy or favorable. —con·ven'ience, n.

con'vent, n. community of nuns.

con·ven'tion, n. 1. meeting. 2. accepted usage. —con·ven'tion·al, adj.

con·verge', v., -verged, -verging. meet in a point. —con·ver'gence, n. —con·ver'gent, adj.

con·ver'sant, adj. acquainted.

con·ver·sa'tion, n. informal discussion. —con·ver·sa'tion·al, adj. —con·ver·sa'tion·al·ist, n.

con·verse', v., -versed, -versing. n. —v. 1. talk informally. —adj. n. (adj. kan vûrs', n. kon'vûrs). 2. opposite. —con·verse'ly, adv.

con·vert', v. 1. change. 2. persuade to different beliefs. 3. exchange for something of equivalent value. —n. (kon'vûrt). 4. converted person. —con·ver'sion, n. —con·vert'er, n.

con·vert'i·ble, adj. 1. able to be converted. —n. 2. automobile with folding top.

con·vex', adj. curved outward. —con·vex'i·ty, n.

con·vey', v. 1. transport. 2. transmit. —con·vey'or, n.

con·vey'ance, n. 1. act of conveying. 2. vehicle. 3. transfer of property.

con·vict', v. 1. find guilty. —n. (kon'vikt). 2. convicted person.

con·vic'tion, n. 1. a convicting. 2. firm belief.

con·vince', v., -vinced, -vincing. cause to believe.

con·viv'i·al, adj. sociable.

con·voke', v., -voked, -voking. call together. —con·vo·ca'tion, n.

con'vo·lu'tion, n. coil. —con'vo·lut'ed, adj.

con·voy', v. 1. escort for protection. —n. (kon'voi). 2. ship, etc., that convoys. 3. group of ships with convoy.

con·vulse', v., -vulsed, -vulsing. shake violently. —con·vul'sion, n. —con·vul'sive, adj.

co'ny, n., pl. -nies. rabbit fur.

coo, v., cooed, cooing. murmur softly. —coo, n.

cook, v. 1. prepare by heating. —n. 2. person who cooks. —cook'book', n. —cook'er·y, n.

cook'ie, n. small sweet cake. Also, cook'y.

cool, adj. 1. moderately cold. 2. calm. 3. not enthusiastic. —v. 4. make or

become cool. —cool'ant, n. —cool'er, n. —cool'ly, adv. —cool'ness, n.

coo'lie, n. Asian laborer.

coop, n. 1. cage for fowls. —v. 2. keep in coop.

coop'er, n. person who makes barrels.

co·op'er·ate', v., -ated, -ating. work or act together. Also, co-op'er·ate'. —co·op'er·a'tion, n.

co·op'er·a·tive (-a tiv), adj. 1. involving cooperation. 2. willing to act with others. —n. 3. Also, co-op. jointly owned apartment house or business.

co·opt' (kō opt'), v. 1. choose as fellow member. 2. win over into larger group.

co·or'di·nate', v., -nated, -nating. adj., n. —v. (-nāt'). 1. put in same or due order. 2. adjust. —adj., n. (-nit). 3. equal. Also, co·or'di·nate. —co·or'di·na'tion, n. —co·or'di·na'tor, n.

coot, n. aquatic bird.

cop, n. Slang. police officer.

cope, v., coped, coping, n. —v. 1. struggle successfully. —n. 2. cloak worn by priests.

cop'i·er, n. machine for making copies.

cop'ing, n. top course of wall.

co'pi·ous, adj. abundant.

cop'per, n. soft reddish metallic element.

cop'per·head', n. venomous snake.

co'pra, n. dried coconut meat.

copse (kops), n. thicket. Also, cop'pice.

cop'u·late', v., -lated, -lating. have sexual intercourse. —cop'u·la'tion, n.

cop'y, n., pl. copies, v., copied, copying. —n. 1. reproduction or imitation. 2. material to be reproduced. —v. 3. make copy of. —cop'y·ist, n.

cop'y·cat', n. one who imitates another.

cop'y·right', n. 1. exclusive control of book, picture, etc. —v. 2. secure copyright on. —adj. 3. covered by copyright.

co·quette' (-ket'), n. female flirt.

cor'al, n. 1. hard substance formed of skeletons of a marine animal. 2. reddish yellow.

cord, n. 1. small rope. 2. Elect. small insulated cable. 3. unit of measurement of wood.

cor'dial, adj. 1. hearty; friendly. —n. 2. liqueur. —cor·dial'i·ty, n. —cor'dial·ly, adv.

cor'don, n. 1. honorary cord, ribbon, etc. 2. line of sentinels.

cor'do·van, n. soft, smooth leather.

cor'du·roy, n. ribbed cotton fabric.

core, n. v., **cored, coring.** —n. 1. central part. —v. 2. remove core of.

co'ri·an·der, n. pungent herb whose leaves and seeds are used in cooking.

cork, n. 1. outer bark of a Mediterranean oak tree. 2. stopper of cork, rubber, etc. —v. 3. stop with a cork.

cork'screw', n. spiral, pointed instrument for pulling corks.

cor'mo·rant, n. voracious water bird.

corn, n. 1. maize. 2. any edible grain. 3. single seed. 4. horny callus, esp. on toe. —v. 5. preserve, esp. in brine.

corn'cob', n. woody core of an ear of corn, in which grains are embedded.

cor'ne·a, n. transparent part of coat of the eye.

cor'ner, n. 1. place where two lines or surfaces meet. 2. exclusive control. —v. 3. put in corner. 4. acquire exclusive control of (stock or commodity).

cor'ner·stone', n. 1. stone representing start of construction of a building. 2. something basic or essential; starting point.

cor'net', n. musical wind instrument resembling trumpet.

cor'nice, n. horizontal projection at top of a wall.

corn'starch', n. starchy flour made from corn.

cor·nu·co'pi·a, n. horn-shaped container, symbol of plenty.

corn'y, adj., **cornier, corniest.** trite, sentimental, or old-fashioned.

co·rol'la, n. petals of a flower.

cor'ol·lar'y, n., pl. **-laries.** proposition proved in proving another.

co·ro'na, n., pl. **-nas, -nae.** circle of light, esp. around sun or moon.

cor'o·nar'y, adj., n., pl. **-naries.** —adj. 1. of arteries supplying heart tissues. —n. 2. heart attack.

cor'o·na'tion, n. crowning.

cor'o·ner, n. official who investigates deaths not clearly natural.

cor'o·net, n. small crown.

cor'po·ral, adj. 1. physical. 2. Mil. lowest noncommissioned officer.

cor·po·ra'tion, n. legally formed association for business, etc. —**cor'po·rate,** adj.

cor·po're·al, adj. tangible.

corps (kôr), n., pl. **corps.** 1. military unit. 2. any group.

corpse, n. dead body.

cor'pu·lent, adj. fat. —**cor'pu·lence,** n.

cor'pus (kôr'pəs), n., pl. **-pora.** 1. large or complete collection of writings. 2. body, esp. when dead.

cor'pus·cle (-pə səl), n. minute body in blood.

cor·ral', n., v., **-ralled, -ralling.** —n. 1. pen for stock. —v. 2. keep in corral. 3. corner or capture.

cor·rect', v. 1. mark or remove errors. 2. rebuke or punish. 3. counteract. —adj. 4. right. —**cor·rec'tion,** n. —**cor·rec'tion·al,** adj. —**cor·rec'tive,** adj., n. —**cor·rect'ly,** adv.

cor·re·late', v., **-lated, -lating.** bring into mutual relation. —**cor·re·la'tion,** n. —**cor·rel'a·tive,** adj., n.

cor·re·spond', v. 1. conform or be similar. 2. communicate by letters. —**cor·re·spond'ence,** n.

cor·re·spond'ent, n. 1. writer of letters. 2. reporter in distant place. —adj. 3. corresponding.

cor'ri·dor, n. passageway.

cor·rob'o·rate', v., **-rated, -rating.** confirm. —**cor·rob·o·ra'tion,** n. —**cor·rob'o·ra'tive,** adj.

cor·rode', v., **-roded, -roding.** 1. eat away gradually. 2. be eaten away. —**cor·ro'sion,** n. —**cor·ro'sive,** adj., n.

cor'ru·gate', v., **-gated, -gating.** bend into folds. —**cor·ru·ga'tion,** n.

cor·rupt', adj. 1. dishonest; evil. 2. tainted. —v. 3. make or become corrupt. —**cor·rupt'i·ble,** adj. —**cor·rup'tion, cor·rupt'ness,** n.

cor·sage' (kôr säzh'), n. small bouquet to be worn.

cor'sair, n. pirate.

cor'set, n. undergarment for confining figure.

cor·tege' (kôr tezh'), n. procession.

cor'tex, n. 1. bark. 2. outer covering of brain or other organ.

cor'ti·sone (-sōn', -zōn'), n. hormone used esp. in treating arthritis.

cor·vette', n. small fast vessel.

cos·met'ic, n. 1. preparation for beautifying skin, hair, etc. —adj. 2. of cosmetics. 3. superficial.

cos'mic, adj. 1. of the cosmos. 2. vast.

cos'mo·pol'i·tan, adj. worldly.

cos'mos, n. ordered universe.

cost, n. 1. price paid. 2. loss or penalty. —v. 3. require as payment. —**cost'ly,** adj.

cos'tume, n., v., **-tumed, -tuming.** —n. 1. historical dress, stage garb, etc. —v. 2. dress or supply with costume.

co'sy, adj., **-sier, -siest.** cozy.

cot, n. light bed.

cote, n. shelter for pigeons, sheep, etc.

co'te·rie, n. group of social acquaintances.

co·til'lion (-til'yən), n. 1. elaborate dance. 2. ball, esp. for debutantes.

cot'tage, n. small house.

cottage cheese, soft, mild cheese made from skim milk.

cot'ter, n. pin fitting into machinery opening.

cot'ton, n. downy plant substance made into fabric.

cot'ton•mouth', n. venomous snake of swamps of southeastern U.S. Also, **water moccasin.**

cot'ton•seed', n. oily seed of cotton plant.

cot'ton•wood', n. species of poplar.

couch, n. 1. bed. —v. 2. express.

couch potato, person who watches much television.

cou'gar (kōō'-), n. large American feline.

cough, v. 1. expel air from lungs suddenly and loudly. —n. 2. act or sound of coughing.

cough drop, lozenge for relieving cough, sore throat, etc.

could, v. pt. of **can.**

coun'cil, n. deliberative or advisory body. —**coun'cil•man**, n. —**coun'cil•wo•man**, n.fem. —**coun'cil•or**, **coun'cil•lor**, n.

coun'sel, n. v. -seled, -seling. —n. 1. advice. 2. consultation. 3. lawyer. —v. 4. advise. —**coun'se•lor**, **coun'sel•lor**, n.

count, v. 1. find total number. 2. name numbers to. 3. esteem. 4. rely. 5. be important. —n. 6. a counting. 7. total number. 8. item in indictment. 9. European nobleman.

count'down', n. 1. backward counting in time units to scheduled event.

coun'te•nance, n., v. -nanced, -nancing. —n. 1. appearance; face. 2. encouragement. —v. 3. tolerate.

coun'ter, n. 1. table, display case, etc., in store. 2. one that counts. 3. anything opposite. —v. 4. oppose. 5. return (blow). —adv., adj. 6. contrary.

coun'ter•act', v. act against; neutralize. —**coun'ter•ac'tion**, n.

coun'ter•bal'ance, n., v. -anced, -ancing. —n. 1. anything that balances another. —v. 2. weigh against equally. (koun'tar bal'-əns).

coun'ter•clock'wise', adv., adj. opposite to direction of turning clock hands.

coun'ter•cul'ture, n. culture of those who reject established values.

coun'ter•feit, adj. 1. fraudulently imitative. —n. 2. fraudulent imitation. —v. 3. make counterfeits. 4. feign. —**coun'ter•feit'er**, n.

coun'ter•mand', v. revoke (command).

coun'ter•part', n. match or complement.

coun'ter•point', n. combining of melodies.

coun'ter•pro•duc'tive, adj. giving results opposite to those intended.

coun'ter•sign', n. 1. secret signal. —v. 2. sign to confirm another signature.

count'ess, n. woman spouse or equal of count or earl.

count'less, adj. innumerable.

coun'try, n., pl. -tries. 1. region. 2. nation. 3. rural districts. —**coun'try•man**, n. —**coun'try•wom'an**, n.fem. —**coun'try•side'**, n.

coun'ty, n., pl. -ties. political unit within state.

coup (kōō), n., pl. **coups**. daring and successful stroke.

coup d'é•tat' (-dä tä'), pl. **coups d'é•tat** (-dä täz', -tä'). overthrow of a government by force.

coupe (kōōp), n. closed automobile with large rear compartment. Also, **cou•pé'** (kōō pā').

cou'ple, n., v. -pled, -pling. —n. 1. pair. —v. 2. fasten or unite. —**cou'pler**, n. —**cou'pling**, n.

cou'plet, n. pair of rhyming lines.

cou'pon (kōō'pon, kyōō'-), n. certificate or ticket entitling holder to a gift or discount, or for use as an order or entry form, etc.

cour'age, n. bravery. —**cou•ra'geous**, adj.

cour'i•er, n. messenger.

course, n., v. coursed, coursing. —n. 1. continuous passage. 2. route. 3. manner. 4. series of studies. 5. one part of meal. —v. 6. run.

court, n. 1. enclosed space. 2. level area for certain games. 3. palace. 4. assembly held by sovereign. 5. homage or attention. 6. place where justice is dealt. 7. judge or judges. —v. 8. woo. —**court'house'**, n. —**court'ship**, n. —**court'yard'**, n.

court'e•san (kôr'tə zən, kûr'-), n. prostitute associating with noble or wealthy men.

cour'te•sy, n., pl. -sies. 1. good manners. 2. indulgence. —**cour'te•ous**, adj.

cour'ti•er, n. person in attendance at court.

court'ly, adj. elegant.

court'-mar'tial, n., pl. **courts-mar'tial**, v. -tialed, -tialing. —n. 1. military court. —v. 2. try by court-martial.

cous'in, n. child of uncle or aunt.

cove, n. deep recess in shoreline.

cov'en (kuv'ən, kō'vən), n. assembly of witches.

cov'e•nant, n. solemn agreement.

cov'er, v. 1. be or put something over. 2. include. 3. have in range. 4. meet or offset. —n. 5. something that covers. 6. concealment. —**cov'er•ing,** n.

cov'er•age, n. 1. protection by insurance. 2. awareness and reporting of news.

cov•er•let, n. quilt.

cov'er•up', n. concealing of illegal activity, a blunder, etc.

cov'et, v. desire greatly or wrongfully. —**cov'et•ous,** adj.

cov'ey, n. small flock.

cow, n. 1. female of bovine or other large animal. —v. 2. intimidate.

cow'ard, n. person who lacks courage. —**cow'ard•ice,** n. —**cow'ard•ly,** adj., adv.

cow'boy', n. Western U.S. cattle herder. Also, **cow'hand'; cow'girl',** n. fem.

cow'er, v. crouch in fear.

cowl, n. 1. hooded garment. 2. hood-like part.

cow'slip', n. plant with yellow flowers.

cox'comb', n. dandy.

cox'swain (kok'sən), n. person who steers boat or racing shell. Also, **cox.**

coy, adj. affectedly shy. —**coy'ly,** adv. —**coy'ness,** n.

coy•o•te (kī ō'tē), n. animal related to wolf.

co'zy, adj. -zier, -ziest. intimately comfortable. —**co'zi•ly,** adv. —**co'zi•ness,** n.

CPR, cardiopulmonary resuscitation, a form of lifesaving designed to restart the action of heart and lungs, as after a heart attack.

CPU, central processing unit, the key component of a computer system.

crab, n. crustacean with broad flat body.

crab apple, small tart apple.

crab'by, adj. -bier, biest. grouchy. —**crab'bi•ness,** n.

crack, v. 1. make sudden, sharp sound. 2. break without separating. —n. 3. sudden, sharp sound. 4. break without separation. 5. smokable form of cocaine.

crack'down', n. stern enforcement of laws or regulations.

crack'er, n. 1. crisp biscuit. 2. firecracker. 3. Disparaging and Offensive. yokel.

crack'le, v. -led, -ling, n. —v. 1. crack repeatedly. —n. 2. crackling sound.

crack'pot', n. person with irrational theories.

crack'up', n. nervous breakdown.

cra'dle, n., v., -dled, -dling. —n. 1. bed on rockers for baby. —v. 2. place in a cradle.

craft, n. 1. skill; skilled trade. 2. cunning. 3. vessels or aircraft. —**crafts'man,** n. —**crafts'wom•an,** n. fem.

craft'y, adj. craftier, craftiest. sly. —**craft'i•ly,** adv.

crag, n. steep rough rock. —**crag'gy,** adj.

cram, v., crammed, cramming. fill tightly.

cramp, n. 1. involuntary muscular contraction. —v. 2. affect with a cramp. 3. hamper.

cran'ber'ry, n., pl. -ries. red acid edible berry.

crane, n. 1. tall wading bird. 2. lifting device or machine.

cra'ni•um, n., pl. -niums, -nia. skull. —**cra'ni•al,** adj.

crank, n. 1. right-angled arm for communicating motion. 2. Informal. grouchy or eccentric person. —v. 3. turn with a crank.

crank'y, adj. crankier, crankiest. ill-tempered. —**crank'i•ness,** n.

cran'ny, n., pl. -nies. cleft.

crap, n. Slang. 1. worthless material. 2. false or meaningless statements.

crape, n. crepe (defs. 1, 2).

crap'pie, n. small fish.

craps, n. dice game.

crash, v. 1. strike noisily. 2. land or fall with damage. —n. 3. noise or act of crashing. 4. collapse. 5. act or instance of crashing. 6. rough fabric.

crass, adj. gross; stupid. —**crass'ly,** adv. —**crass'ness,** n.

crate, n., v., crated, crating. —n. 1. box or frame for packing. —v. 2. put in crate.

cra'ter, n. cup-shaped hole, esp. in volcano or on moon.

cra•vat', n. necktie.

crave, v., craved, craving. yearn or beg for.

cra'ven, adj. 1. cowardly. —n. 2. coward.

craw, n. crop of bird.

crawl, v. 1. move slowly, as on stomach. —n. 2. act of crawling. 3. swimming stroke. —**crawl'er,** n.

cray'fish', n. fresh-water crustacean resembling a lobster. Also, **craw'fish'.**

cray'on, n. stick of colored clay or chalk.

craze, v., crazed, crazing, n. —v. 1. make insane. 2. mark with fine cracks, as glaze. —n. 3. mania.

cra'zy, adj., -zier, -ziest. insane. —**cra'zi•ly,** adv. —**cra'zi•ness,** n.

creak, v. **1.** squeak sharply. —n. **2.** creaking sound. —**creak'y,** adj.

cream, n. **1.** fatty part of milk. —v. **2.** make with cream. **3.** work to a creamy state. **4.** Informal. defeat utterly. —**cream'er'y,** n. —**cream'y,** adj.

cream'er'y, n., pl. **-eries.** place dealing in milk products.

crease, n., v., **creased, creasing.** —n. **1.** mark from folding. —v. **2.** make creases in.

cre'ate', v., **-ated, -ating.** cause to exist. —**cre'a'tion,** n. —**cre'a'tive,** adj. —**cre'a'tor,** n.

crea'ture, n. **1.** animate being. **2.** anything created.

cre'dence, n. belief.

cre'den'tial, n. verifying document.

cred'i'ble, adj. believable. —**cred'i'bil'i'ty,** n. —**cred'i'bly,** adv.

cred'it, n. **1.** belief. **2.** trustworthiness. **3.** honor. **4.** time allowed for payment. —v. **5.** believe. **6.** ascribe to.

cred'it'a'ble, adj. praiseworthy. —**cred'it'a'bly,** adv.

credit card, card entitling holder to charge purchases.

cred'i'tor, n. person owed.

credit union, cooperative group that makes loans to its members at low interest rates.

cred'u'lous, adj. overwilling to believe. —**cre'du'li'ty,** n.

creed, n. formula of belief. Also, **cre'do** (krē'dō).

creek (krēk, krik), n. brook.

creep, v., **crept** or **creeped, creeping,** n. —v. **1.** move stealthily; crawl. —n. **2.** Slang. disagreeable person.

creep'y, adj., **creepier, creepiest.** causing uneasiness or fear.

cre'mate', v., **-mated, -mating.** burn (corpse) to ashes. —**cre'ma'tion,** n. —**cre'ma'to'ry,** adj., n.

Cre'ole, n. **1.** one of French and Spanish blood born in Louisiana. **2.** (l.c.) pidgin that has become native language of a group.

cre'o'sote', n. oily liquid from tar.

crepe (krāp), n. **1.** light crinkled fabric. **2.** Also, **crepe paper.** thin, wrinkled paper used for decorating. **3.** thin, light pancake.

cre'scen'do (krə shen'dō), n., pl. **-dos.** Music. gradual increase in loudness.

cres'cent (kres'ənt), n. **1.** moon in its first or last quarter. **2.** object having this shape.

cress, n. plant with pungent leaves.

crest, n. **1.** tuft or plume. **2.** figure above coat of arms.

crest'fal'len, adj. abruptly discouraged or depressed.

cre'tin (krēt'n), n. **1.** person affected with cretinism, congenital thyroid deficiency. **2.** stupid, obtuse, or boorish person.

cre'tonne (kri ton'), n. heavily printed cotton.

cre'vasse' (krə vas'), n. fissure, esp. in glacier.

crev'ice, n. fissure.

crew, n. **1.** group of persons working together, as on ship. —v. **2.** form crew of.

crew cut, haircut in which the hair is cut close to the head.

crib, n., v., **cribbed, cribbing.** —n. **1.** child's bed. **2.** rack or bin. —v. **3.** put in a crib. **4.** plagiarize.

crib'bage, n. card game using scoreboard with pegs.

crick, n. muscular spasm.

crick'et, n. **1.** leaping, noisy insect. **2.** British open-air ball game with bats.

cri'er, n. one who cries or announces.

crime, n. **1.** unlawful act. **2.** sin. —**crim'i'nal,** adj., n. —**crim'i'nol'o'gy,** n.

crimp, v. **1.** make wavy. **2.** n. crimped form.

crim'son, adj. deep red.

cringe, v., **cringed, cringing.** shrink in fear or servility.

crin'kle, v., **-kled, -kling,** n. wrinkle or rustle. —**crin'kly,** adj.

crin'o'line (krin'l in), n. **1.** stiff, coarse fabric used as lining. **2.** petticoat.

crip'ple, n., v., **-pled, -pling.** —n. **1.** Sometimes Offensive. lame person. —v. **2.** make lame.

cri'sis, n., pl. **-ses.** decisive stage or point.

crisp, adj. **1.** brittle. **2.** fresh. **3.** brisk. **4.** curly. —v. **5.** make or become crisp.

criss'cross', adj. **1.** marked with crossed lines. —n. **2.** crisscross pattern. —v. **3.** mark with crossed lines.

cri'te'ri'on, n., pl. **-teria.** standard for judgment.

crit'ic, n. **1.** skilled judge. **2.** person arguing against something.

crit'i'cal, adj. **1.** severe in judgment. **2.** involving criticism. **3.** crucial. —**crit'i'cal'ly,** adv.

crit'i'cize', v., **-cized, -cizing. 1.** discuss as a critic. **2.** find fault with. —**crit'i'cism,** n.

cri'tique' (-tēk'), n. critical article.

croak, v. utter a low, hoarse cry.

cro'chet' (krō shā'), v. form thread into designs with hooked needle.

crock, n. earthen jar. —**crock'er'y,** n.

croc'o'dile', n. large aquatic legged reptile with long, powerful jaws and tail.

cro·cus, *n.* small bulbous plant blooming in early spring.

crois·sant (kwä sän'; krə sänt'). crescent-shaped roll of flaky pastry.

crone, *n.* witchlike old woman.

cro·ny, *n.* close friend.

crook, *n.* 1. tight curve. 2. bend. 3. *Informal.* dishonest person. —*v.* 4. bend. —**crook'ed,** *adj.*

croon, *v.* 1. sing softly. —*n.* 2. such singing. —**croon'er,** *n.*

crop, *n., v.,* **cropped, cropping.** —*n.* 1. produce from the soil. 2. short whip. 3. pouch in gullet of bird. —*v.* 4. remove ends. 5. cut short. 6. reap. 7. **crop up,** appear. —**crop'per,** *n.*

cro·quet' (-kā'), *n.* game with wooden balls and mallets.

cro·quette', *n.* fried or baked piece of chopped food.

cro·sier (krō'zhər), *n.* staff of bishop.

cross, *n.* 1. structure whose basic form has an upright with transverse piece. 2. emblem of Christianity. 3. figure resembling cross. 4. trouble. 5. mixture of breeds. —*v.* 6. make sign of cross over. 7. put, lie, or pass across. 8. oppose or frustrate. 9. mark (out). 10. mix (breeds). —*adj.* 11. transverse. 12. ill-humored. —**cross'ly,** *adv.* —**cross'ness,** *n.*

cross'bow', *n.* weapon consisting of a bow fixed on a stock like that of a rifle.

cross'-coun'try, *adj.* 1. proceeding over fields, through woods, etc., rather than on a road or track. 2. from one end of a country to the other. —*n.* 3. sport of cross-country racing.

cross'-ex·am'ine, *v.,* **-ined, -ining.** examine closely, as opposing witness. Also, **cross'-ques'tion.**

cross'-eye', *n.* visual disorder. —**cross'-eyed',** *adj.*

cross reference, reference from one part of a book, index, etc., to another.

cross'road', *n.* 1. road that crosses another. 2. (*pl.*) **a.** intersection. **b.** decisive point.

cross section, 1. section made by cutting across something. 2. picture representing such a section. 3. representative sample of a whole.

cross'word puz'zle, puzzle in which words determined from numbered clues are fitted into pattern of horizontal and vertical squares.

crotch, *n.* forked part.

crotch'et (kroch'it), *n.* 1. small hook. 2. whim.

crotch·et·y, *adj.* grumpy. —**crotch'et·i·ness,** *n.*

crouch, *v.* 1. stoop or bend low. —*n.* 2. act or instance of crouching.

croup (krōōp), *n.* inflammation of throat.

crou·pier (krōō'pē ar, -pē ā'), *n.* attendant who handles bets and money at gambling table.

crou·ton (krōō'ton), *n.* small cube of toasted bread.

crow, *v.* 1. cry, as cock. 2. boast. —*n.* 3. cry of cock. 4. black, harsh-voiced bird.

crow'bar', *n.* iron bar for prying.

crowd, *n.* 1. large group of people. —*v.* 2. throng. 3. press or push.

crown, *n.* 1. cover for head, esp. of a sovereign. 2. power of a sovereign. 3. top. —*v.* 4. put crown on. 5. reward or complete.

cru'cial, *adj.* 1. decisive. 2. severe. —**cru'cial·ly,** *adv.*

cru'ci·ble, *n.* vessel for melting metals, etc.

cru'ci·fix, *n.* cross with figure of Jesus crucified.

cru'ci·fy', *v.,* **-fied, -fying.** put to death on cross. —**cru'ci·fix'ion,** *n.*

crude, *adj.,* **cruder, crudest,** *n.* —*adj.* 1. unrefined. 2. unfinished. —*n.* 3. *Informal.* unrefined petroleum. —**crude'ly,** *adv.* —**crude'ness, cru'di·ty,** *n.*

cru'el, *adj.* 1. disposed to inflict pain. 2. causing pain. —**cru'el·ly,** *adv.* —**cru'el·ness, cru'el·ty,** *n.*

cru'et, *n.* stoppered bottle for vinegar, etc.

cruise, *v.,* **cruised, cruising,** *n.* —*v.* 1. sail or fly at moderate speed. 2. travel for pleasure. —*n.* 3. cruising trip.

cruis'er, *n.* 1. kind of warship. 2. small pleasure boat.

crul'ler, *n.* sweet doughnutlike cake.

crumb, *n.* small bit of bread, etc.

crum'ble, *v.,* **-bled, -bling.** break into fragments; decay.

crum'my, *adj.,* **-mier, -miest.** *Informal.* 1. run-down; shabby. 2. cheap; worthless. 3. wretched; miserable.

crum'ple, *v.,* **-pled, -pling,** *n.* wrinkle; rumple.

crunch, *v.* 1. chew or crush noisily. —*n.* 2. *Informal.* reduction of resources, esp. economic.

cru·sade', *n., v.,* **-saded, -sading.** —*n.* 1. expedition to recover Holy Land from the Muslims. 2. campaign for good cause. —*v.* 3. engage in crusade. —**cru·sad'er,** *n.*

crush, *v.* 1. bruise or break by pressing. 2. subdue. —*n.* 3. dense crowd.

crust, *n.* 1. hard outer part or covering. 2. *Informal.* impertinence. —*v.* 3. cover with crust.

crus·ta·cean (-shən), n. sea animal having hard shell. — **crus·ta·cean,** adj.

crutch, n. 1. staff fitting under the armpit for support in walking. 2. Informal. temporary aid or expedient.

crux, n., pl. **cruxes, cruces.** vital point.

cry, v., **cried, crying,** n., pl. **cries.** —v. 1. make sounds of grief, etc. 2. utter characteristic sounds. 3. shout. —n. 4. act or sound of crying.

cry·o·gen·ics (krī′ə jen′iks), n. study or use of extremely low temperatures. —**cry·o·gen′ic,** adj.

crypt, n. underground chamber.

cryp·tic, adj. mysterious.

cryp·tog·ra·phy (krip tog′rə fē), n. study or use of code and cipher systems. —**cryp·tog′ra·pher,** n.

crys·tal, n. 1. clear transparent mineral. 2. body with symmetrical plane faces. 3. fine glass. 4. cover of watch face. —**crys′tal·line,** adj.

crys·tal·lize, v., **-lized, -lizing.** 1. form or cause to form into crystals. 2. assume or cause to assume definite form.

C′-sec·tion, n. Cesarean.

cub, n. young fox, bear, etc.

cub·by·hole, n. small enclosed space.

cube, n., v., **cubed, cubing.** —n. 1. solid bounded by six squares. 2. Math. third power of a quantity. —v. 3. make into cubes. 4. Math. raise to third power. —**cu′bic, cu′bi·cal,** adj.

cu·bi·cle, n. small room.

cub·ism, n. style of painting and sculpture marked by reduction of natural forms to geometric shapes. —**cub′ist,** adj., n.

cuck·old, n. husband of unfaithful wife.

cuck·oo, n. small bird.

cu·cum·ber, n. common long edible fruit.

cud, n. food that cow, etc., returns to mouth for further chewing.

cud·dle, v., **-dled, -dling.** hold tenderly; nestle.

cudg·el, n., v., **-eled, -eling.** —n. 1. short thick stick. —v. 2. beat with cudgel.

cue, n. 1. (esp. on stage) something that signals speech or action. 2. rod for billiards.

cuff, n. 1. fold or band at end of sleeve or trouser leg. 2. slap. —v. 3. slap.

cui·sine (kwi zēn′), n. cookery.

cu′li·nar′y (kyōō′-), adj. of cooking.

cull, v. select best parts of.

cul·mi·nate, v., **-nated, -nating.**

reach highest point. —**cul′mi·na′tion,** n.

cul·pa·ble, adj. deserving blame. —**cul′pa·bil′i·ty,** n.

cul·prit, n. person arraigned for or guilty of an offense.

cult, n. religious sect or system.

cul·ti·vate, v., **-vated, -vating.** 1. prepare and care for (land). 2. develop possibilities of. —**cul′ti·va′tion,** n. —**cul′ti·va′tor,** n.

cul·ti·vat·ed, adj. educated and well-mannered.

cul·ture, n. 1. raising of plants or animals. 2. development of mind. 3. state or form of civilization.

cul·vert, n. channel under road, etc.

cum·ber·some, adj. clumsy.

cu·mu·la·tive, adj. increasing by accumulation.

cu·mu·lus (kyōō′myə ləs), n., pl. **-li.** cloud in form of rounded heaps on flat base. —**cu′mu·lous,** adj.

cu·ne·i·form (kyōō nē′ə fôrm′), adj. 1. composed of slim wedge-shaped elements, as the writing of some ancient peoples. —n. 2. cuneiform writing.

cun·ning, n. 1. skill. 2. guile. —adj. 3. clever. 4. sly.

cup, n. small open drinking vessel.

cup·board (kub′ərd), n. closet for dishes, etc.

Cu′pid (kyōō′pid), n. Roman god of carnal love, usu. represented as a winged, naked infant with a bow and arrows.

cu·pid′i·ty, n. greed.

cu·po·la (kyōō′-), n. rounded dome.

cu′prous, adj. containing copper.

cur, n. worthless dog.

cu·rate, n. clergyman assisting rector or vicar.

cu·ra·tor, n. person in charge of museum collection.

curb, n. 1. strap for restraining horse. 2. restraint. 3. edge of sidewalk. —v. 4. control.

curd, n. substance formed when milk coagulates. —v. 2. change into curd.

cur·dle, v., **-dled, -dling.** congeal.

cure, n., v., **cured, curing.** —n. 1. treatment of disease. 2. restoration to health. —v. 3. restore to health. 4. prepare for use. —**cur′a·ble,** adj. —**cur′a·tive,** adj., n.

cure′-all, n. cure for anything; panacea.

cur′few, n. evening signal to leave streets.

cu′ri·o′, n., pl. **-rios.** odd valuable article.

cu•ri•os•i•ty, n., pl. -ties. 1. desire to know. 2. odd thing.

cu•ri•ous, adj. 1. wanting to know. 2. prying. 3. strange. —cu•ri•ous•ly, adv.

curl, v. 1. form in ringlets. 2. coil. —n. 3. ringlet.

cur•lew, n. shore bird.

curl•i•cue, n. fancy curl.

cur•mud•geon (kər muj′ən), n. bad-tempered, difficult person.

cur•rant, n. 1. small seedless raisin. 2. edible acid berry.

cur•ren•cy, n., pl. -cies. 1. money in use in a country. 2. prevalence. 3. circulation.

cur•rent, adj. 1. present. 2. generally known or believed. —n. 3. stream; flow. 4. water, air, etc., moving in one direction. 5. movement of electricity. —cur•rent•ly, adv.

cur•ric•u•lum, n., pl. -lums, -la. course of study.

cur•ry, n., pl. -ries, v. -ried, -rying. —n. 1. East Indian hot sauce or powder. —v. 2. prepare with curry. 3. rub and comb (horse, etc.). 4. seek (favor) with servility. —cur•ry•comb′, n.

curse, v., cursed or curst, cursing. —n. 1. wish that evil befall another. 2. evil so invoked. 3. profane oath. 4. cause of evil. —v. 5. wish evil upon. 6. swear. 7. afflict.

cur•sor (kûr′sər), n. movable symbol on computer screen to indicate where data may be input.

cur•so•ry, adj. superficial.

curt, adj. brief, esp. rudely so. —curt′ly, adv.

cur•tail′, v. cut short. —cur•tail′-ment, n.

cur•tain, n. 1. piece of fabric hung to adorn, conceal, etc. —v. 2. provide or cover with curtains.

curt′sy, n., pl. -sies, v. -sied, -sying. —n. 1. bow by women. —v. 2. make curtsy.

cur•va•ture, n. 1. a curving. 2. degree of curving.

curve, n., v., curved, curving. —n. 1. bending line. —v. 2. bend or move in a curve.

cush•ion, n. soft bag of feathers, air, etc.

cusp, n. pointed end.

cus′pid, n. canine tooth.

cus•pi•dor, n. receptacle for spit, cigar ash, etc.

cuss, v. Informal. curse.

cus•tard, n. cooked dish of eggs and milk.

cus•to•dy, n., pl. -dies. 1. keeping; care. 2. imprisonment. —cus•to′di•an, n.

cus′tom, n. 1. usual practice. 2. set of such practices. 3. (pl.) a. duties on imports. b. agency collecting these. —adj. 4. made for the individual. —cus′tom•ar•y, adj. —cus′tom•ar′i•ly, adv.

cus′tom•er, n. 1. purchaser or prospective purchaser. 2. Informal. person.

cut, v., cut, cutting. —v. 1. sever, as with knife. 2. wound feelings of. 3. reap or trim. 4. shorten by omitting part. 5. dilute. 6. move or cross. 7. be absent from. —n. 8. a cutting. 9. result of cutting. 10. straight passage. 11. engraved plate for printing.

cu•ta′ne•ous, adj. of the skin.

cut′back′, n. reduction in rate, quantity, etc.

cute, adj., cuter, cutest. Informal. pretty or pleasing.

cu′ti•cle, n. epidermis, esp. around nails.

cut′lass, n. short curved sword.

cut′ler•y, n. knives, etc., collectively.

cut′let, n. slice of meat for frying or broiling.

cut′off′, n. 1. point beyond which something is no longer effective or possible. 2. road that leaves another to make a shortcut.

cut′-rate′, adj. offered or selling at reduced prices.

cut′ter, n. 1. one that cuts. 2. small fast vessel. 3. light sleigh.

cy′a•nide′ (sī′ə nīd′), n. poisonous salt of hydrocyanic acid.

cy•ber•net′ics (sī′bər net′iks), n. study of organic control and communications systems and mechanical or electronic systems analogous to them, such as robots.

cy•cla•mate′, n. artificial sweetening agent.

cy•cle, n., v., -cled, -cling. —n. 1. recurring time or process. 2. complete set. 3. bicycle, etc. —v. 4. ride bicycle. —cy′clic, cyc′li•cal, adj. —cy′clist, n.

cy′clone, n. 1. rotary weather system. 2. tornado. —cy•clon′ic, adj.

cy•clo•pe′di•a, n. encyclopedia.

cy′clo•tron′, n. device used in splitting atoms.

cyl•in•der, n. 1. round elongated solid with ends that are equal parallel circles. 2. machine part or opening in this form. —cy•lin′dri•cal, adj.

cym′bal, n. brass plate used in orchestras.

cyn′ic, n. person who doubts or lacks goodness of motive. —cyn′i•cal, adj. —cyn′i•cism, n.

cy′no•sure (sī′na-), n. object that attracts by its brilliance.

cy′press, n. evergreen tree of pine family.

cyst (sist), n. sac containing morbid matter formed in live tissue.

cys′tic fi•bro′sis (sis′tik fī brō′sis), hereditary disease marked by breathing difficulties, infection, and growth of excess fibrous tissue.

czar (zär), n. former emperor of Russia. Also, **tsar.**

D

D, d, n. fourth letter of English alphabet.

dab, v., **dabbed, dabbing. 1.** strike or apply lightly. —n. **2.** small moist lump. —**dab′ber,** n.

dab′ble, v., **-bled, -bling. 1.** splatter. **2.** play in water. **3.** be active or interested superficially. —**dab′bler,** n.

dachs′hund (däks′hŏŏnd′), n. long, short-legged dog.

Da′cron, n. Trademark. strong synthetic fabric resembling nylon.

dad′dy, n., pl. **-dies.** Informal. father.

daf′fo•dil, n. plant with yellow flowers.

daft, adj. **1.** insane. **2.** foolish. Also, **daf′fy.** —**daft′ly,** adv.

dag′ger, n. short knifelike weapon.

dahl′ia (dal′ya). showy cultivated flowering plant.

dai′ly, adj. **1.** of or occurring each day. —n. **2.** daily newspaper.

dain′ty, adj., **-tier, -tiest,** n., pl. **-ties.** —adj. **1.** delicate. —n. **2.** delicacy. —**dain′ti•ly,** adv. —**dain′ti•ness,** n.

dair′y, n., pl. **dairies.** place for making or selling milk, butter, etc. —**dair′y•man,** n. —**dair′y•wom•an,** n. fem.

da′is (dā′is), n. raised platform, as for seats of honor.

dai′sy, n., pl. **-sies.** yellow-and-white flower.

dale, n. valley.

dal′ly, v., **-lied, -lying. 1.** sport; flirt. **2.** delay. —**dal′li•ance,** n.

Dal•ma′tian, n. large black-and-white dog.

dam, n., v., **dammed, damming.** —n. **1.** barrier to obstruct water. **2.** female quadruped parent. —v. **3.** obstruct with dam.

dam′age, n., v., **-aged, -aging.** —n. **1.** injury. **2.** (pl.) payment for injury. —v. **3.** injure. —**dam′age•a•ble,** adj.

dam′ask, n. woven figured fabric. —adj. **2.** pink.

dame, n. **1.** woman of rank. **2.** Slang (sometimes offensive). any woman.

damn, v. **1.** declare bad. **2.** condemn to hell. —**dam′na•ble,** adj. —**dam•na′tion,** n.

damp, adj. **1.** moist. —n. **2.** moisture.

3. noxious vapor. —v. Also, **damp′en. 4.** moisten. **5.** depress. **6.** deaden. —**damp′ness,** n.

damp′er, n. **1.** control for air or smoke currents. **2.** discouraging influence.

dam′sel, n. maiden.

dance, v., **danced, dancing,** n. —v. **1.** move rhythmically. —n. **2.** act of dancing. **3.** gathering or music for dancing. —**danc′er,** n. —**dance′a•ble,** adj.

dan•de•li′on, n. plant with yellow flowers.

dan′der, n. **1.** loose skin scales from various animals. **2.** Informal. anger; temper.

dan′druff, n. scales on scalp.

dan′dy, n., pl. **-dies,** adj., **-dier, -diest.** —n. **1.** fashionable dresser. —adj. **2.** fine.

Dane, n. native of Denmark.

dan′ger, n. exposure to harm. —**dan′ger•ous,** adj.

dan′gle, v., **-gled, -gling.** hang loosely.

Dan′ish, adj. **1.** of Denmark, the Danes, or their language. —n. **2.** the language of the Danes. **3.** (sometimes l.c.) pastry filled with cheese or fruit.

dank, adj. unpleasantly damp. —**dank′ness,** n.

dap′per, adj. neat.

dap′ple, n., adj., v., **-pled, -pling.** —n. **1.** mottled marking. —adj. **2.** mottled. —v. **3.** mottle.

dare, v., **dared** or **durst, dared, daring,** n. —v. **1.** be bold enough. **2.** challenge. —n. **3.** challenge. —**dar′ing,** adj., n.

dare′dev′il, n. **1.** recklessly daring person. —adj. **2.** recklessly daring.

dark, adj. **1.** lacking light. **2.** blackish. **3.** ignorant. —n. **4.** absence of light. —**dark′en,** v. —**dark′ness,** n.

dark′room′, n. place for developing and printing films.

dar′ling, n. loved one.

darn, v. mend with rows of stitches. —**darn′ing,** n.

dart, n. **1.** slender pointed missile. —v. **2.** move swiftly.

dash, v. **1.** strike or throw violently. **2.**

frustrate. —*n.* 3. violent blow. 4. small quantity. 5. punctuation mark (—) noting abrupt break. 6. rush.

dash'board', *n.* instrument board on motor vehicle.

dash'ing, *adj.* 1. lively. 2. stylish. —**dash'ing·ly**, *adv.*

das'tard, *n.* coward. —**das'tard·ly**, *adj.*

da'ta, *n.pl.* (*sing.* **datum**) facts or other information.

da'ta·base', *n.* collection of data, esp. one accessible by computer.

data processing, high-speed handling of information by computer.

date, *n., v.*, **dated, dating.** —*n.* 1. particular time. 2. fleshy, edible fruit of **date palm.** 3. appointment. 4. social engagement arranged beforehand, esp. one of a romantic nature. 5. person with whom one shares such an engagement. —*v.* 6. exist from particular time. 7. fix date for or with.

daub, *v.* 1. cover with mud, etc. 2. paint clumsily. —*n.* 3. something daubed. —**daub'er**, *n.*

daugh'ter, *n.* female child. —**daugh'ter·ly**, *adj.*

daugh'ter-in-law', *n., pl.* **daughters-in-law.** son's wife.

daunt, *v.* 1. frighten. 2. dishearten.

daunt'less, *adj.* bold; fearless.

dav'en·port', *n.* large sofa.

dav'it, *n.* crane for boat, etc.

daw'dle, *v.*, **-dled, -dling.** waste time. —**daw'dler**, *n.*

dawn, *n.* 1. break of day. —*v.* 2. begin to grow light. 3. become apparent.

day, *n.* 1. period between two nights. 2. period (24 hours) of earth's rotation on its axis.

day'break', *n.* first appearance of light; dawn.

day care, supervised care for young children or the elderly, usu. in daytime and at a center outside the home.

day'dream', *n.* 1. reverie; fancy. —*v.* 2. indulge in reveries. —**day'dream'er**, *n.*

day'light', *n.* 1. light of day. 2. openness.

daylight-saving time, time one hour later than standard time, usu. used in the summer. Also, **daylight saving time.**

day'time', *n.* time from sunrise to sunset.

daze, *v.*, **dazed, dazing**, *n.* —*v.* 1. stun. —*n.* 2. dazed condition.

daz'zle, *v.*, **-zled, -zling.** overwhelm with light.

DDT, strong insecticide.

de-, prefix indicating: 1. reverse, as

deactivate. 2. remove, as *decaffeinate.* 3. reduce, as *degrade.*

dea'con, *n.* 1. cleric inferior to priest. 2. lay church officer. —**dea'con·ess**, *n.fem.* —**dea'con·ry**, *n.*

dead, *adj.* 1. no longer alive or active. 2. infertile. 3. complete; absolute —*n.* 4. dead person or persons. —**dead'en**, *v.*

dead end, 1. street, corridor, etc., that has no exit. 2. position with no hope of progress. —**dead'-end'**, *adj.*

dead'beat', *n.* 1. person who avoids paying debts. 2. sponger.

dead heat, race in which two or more competitors finish in a tie.

dead'line', *n.* last allowable time.

dead'lock', *n.* standstill.

dead'ly, *adj.*, **-lier, -liest.** 1. fatal. 2. dreary. 3. extremely accurate.

dead'pan', *adj.* without expression; appearing serious and detached.

dead'wood', *n.* useless or extraneous persons or things.

deaf, *adj.* unable to hear. —**deaf'en**, *v.* —**deaf'ness**, *n.*

deal, *v.*, **dealt, dealing.** —*v.* 1. conduct oneself toward. 2. do business. 3. distribute. —*n.* 4. transaction. 5. quantity. —**deal'er**, *n.*

dean, *n.* 1. head of academic faculty. 2. head of cathedral organization.

dear, *adj.* 1. loved. 2. expensive. —*n.* 3. dear one. —**dear'ly**, *adv.*

dearth, *n.* scarcity.

death, *n.* end of life. —**death'ly**, *adj. adv.* —**death'bed'**, *n.*

death'less, *adj.* enduring.

de·ba'cle (dā bā'kəl), *n.* 1. breakup; rout. 2. utter failure.

de·bar', *v.*, **-barred, -barring.** exclude.

de·base', *v.*, **-based, -basing.** reduce in quality. —**de·base'ment**, *n.*

de·bate', *v.*, **-bated, -bating.** —*n.* 1. controversial discussion. —*v.* 2. argue; discuss. —**de·bat'a·ble**, *adj.* —**de·bat'er**, *n.*

de·bauch' (-bôch'), *v.* 1. corrupt; pervert. —*n.* 2. period of corrupt indulgence. —**de·bauch'er·y**, *n.*

de·ben'ture (di ben'chər), *n.* short-term, negotiable, interest-producing note representing debt.

de·bil'i·tate', *v.*, **-tated, -tating.** weaken. —**de·bil'i·ta'tion**, *n.*

de·bil'i·ty, *n., pl.* **-ties.** weakness.

deb'it, *n.* 1. recorded debt. 2. account of debts. —*v.* 3. charge as debt.

deb'o·nair', *adj.* relaxed and cheerful.

de·bris' (də brē', dā'brē), *n.* rubbish; ruins.

debt, *n.* 1. something owed. 2. obligation to pay. —**debt'or**, *n.*

de·bunk', v. expose as false or exaggerated.

de·but' (-byōō'), n. first public appearance. —**deb·u·tante'**, n.fem.

dec·ade, n. 10-year period.

dec·a·dence, n. decline in quality of power. —**dec·a·dent**, adj.

de·caf·fein·at·ed (dē kaf'ə nā'təd), adj. having the caffeine removed.

dec·a·gon', n. polygon with 10 angles and 10 sides.

dec·a·he'dron, n., pl. **-drons, -dra**. solid figure with 10 faces.

de'cal (dē'kal, di kal'), n. picture or design on specially prepared paper for transfer to wood, metal, etc.

Dec·a·logue', n. Ten Commandments.

de·camp', v. depart, esp. secretly.

de·cant', v. pour off.

de·cant'er, n. bottle.

de·cap'i·tate', v., **-tated, -tating**. behead. —**de·cap·i·ta'tion**, n.

dec·ath'lon, n. contest of 10 events.

de·cay', v., n. decline in quality, health, etc.

de·cease', n., v., **-ceased, -ceasing**. —n. 1. death. —v. 2. die. —**de·ceased'**, adj., n.

de·ceit', n. 1. fraud. 2. trick. —**de·ceit'ful**, adj.

de·ceive', v., **-ceived, -ceiving**. mislead.

de·cel'er·ate' (dē sel'ə rāt'), v. slow down.

De·cem'ber, n. 12th month of year.

de·cen·cy, n., pl. **-cies**. 1. conformity to standards of morality or behavior. 2. respectability. 3. adequacy. 4. kindness or willingness to help. —**de'cent**, adj. —**de'cent·ly**, adv.

de·cen'tral·ize', v., **-ized, -izing**. end central control of. —**de·cen'tral·i·za'tion**, n.

de·cep'tion, n. 1. act of deceiving; fraud. —**de·cep'tive**, adj.

dec'i·bel', n. unit of intensity of sound.

de·cide', v., **-cided, -ciding**. settle; resolve.

de·cid'ed, adj. unambiguous; emphatic. —**de·cid'ed·ly**, adv.

de·cid'u·ous (di sij'ōō əs), adj. shedding leaves annually.

dec'i·mal, adj. 1. of tenths. 2. proceeding by tens. —n. 3. fraction in tenths, hundredths, etc., indicated by dot (**decimal point**) before numerator.

dec'i·mate' (des'ə māt'), v. **-mated, -mating**. kill or destroy large part of.

de·ci'pher (-sī'-), v. find meaning of. —**de·ci'pher·a·ble**, adj.

de·ci'sion, n. 1. something decided. 2. firmness of mind.

de·ci'sive, adj. 1. determining. 2. resolute. —**de·ci'sive·ly**, adv.

deck, n. 1. level on ship. 2. pack of playing cards. —v. 3. array.

de·claim', v. speak rhetorically. —**de·claim'er**, n.

dec'la·ma'tion, n. oratorical speech. —**de·clam'a·to'ry**, adj.

de·clare', v., **-clared, -claring**. 1. make known; proclaim. 2. affirm. —**dec·la·ra'tion**, n. —**de·clar'a·tive, de·clar'a·to'ry**, adj.

de·clen'sion, n. grammatical inflection or set of inflections.

dec'li·na'tion, n. 1. slope. 2. angular height of heavenly body.

de·cline', v., **-clined, -clining**, n. —v. 1. refuse. 2. slant down. 3. give grammatical inflections. 4. fail; diminish. —n. 5. downward slope. 6. deterioration.

de·cliv'i·ty, n. pl. **-ties**. downward slope.

de·code', v., **-coded, -coding**. decipher from code.

de·com·pose', v., **-posed, -posing**. 1. separate into constituent parts. 2. rot. —**de·com·po·si'tion**, n.

de·con·ges'tant, n. 1. relieving mucus congestion of the upper respiratory tract, esp. the sinuses. —n. 2. decongestant agent.

dé·cor' (dā kôr', di-), n. style of decoration, as of a room. Also, **de·cor'**.

dec'o·rate', v., **-rated, -rating**. furnish with ornament. —**dec'o·ra'tion**, n. —**dec'o·ra'tive**, adj.

dec'o·rous, adj. proper; dignified.

de·co'rum, n. propriety. —**dec'o·rous**, adj.

de·coy', n., v. lure.

de·crease', v., **-creased, -creasing**, —v. 1. lessen. —n. 2. (dē'krēs). 2. lessening.

de·cree', n., v., **-creed, -creeing**. —n. 1. published command. —v. 2. proclaim or command.

de·crep'it, adj. feeble with age. —**de·crep'i·tude'**, n.

de·crim'i·nal·ize', v., **-ized, -izing**. cease to treat as crime. —**de·crim'i·nal·i·za'tion**, n.

de·cry', v., **-cried, -crying**. disparage.

ded'i·cate', v., **-cated, -cating**. 1. set apart. 2. devote. 3. inscribe (book) in honor of person or thing. —**ded·i·ca'tion**, n.

de·duce', v., **-duced, -ducing**. derive logically; infer. —**de·duc'i·ble**, adj.

de·duct', v. subtract. —**de·duct'i·ble**, adj.

de·duc'tion, n. act or result of deducting or deducing. —de·duc'tive, adj.

deed, n. 1. act. 2. written conveyance of property. —v. 3. transfer by deed.

dee'jay', n. disc jockey.

deem, v. think; estimate.

deep, adj. 1. extending far down or in. 2. difficult to understand. 3. profound. 4. low in pitch. —n. 5. deep part or space. —adv. 6. at great depth. —deep'en, v. —deep'ly, adv.

deep'-freeze', v., -froze, -frozen, -freezing. —n. 1. freeze rapidly for preservation. —n. 2. refrigerator that deep-freezes.

deep'-fry', v., -fried, -frying. cook in boiling fat. —deep'-fry'er, n.

deep'-seat'ed, adj. firmly implanted.

deer, n., pl. deer. ruminant animal, usually horned.

de·face', v., -faced, -facing. mar. —de·face'ment, n.

de fac'to (dē fak'tō, dā-), 1. in fact; in reality. 2. actually existing, esp. without legal authority.

de·fame', v., -famed, -faming. attack reputation of. —def·a·ma'tion, n.

de·fault', n. 1. failure; neglect. —v. 2. fail to meet obligation.

de·feat', v. 1. overthrow.

de·feat'ism, n. readiness to accept defeat. —de·feat'ist, n.

def'e·cate (def'i kāt'), v., -cated, -cating. void feces from bowels. —def'e·ca'tion, n.

de·fect', n. 1. fault; imperfection. —v. (di fekt'). 2. desert a cause, country, etc. —de·fec'tive, adj.

de·fec'tion, n. default in duty, loyalty, etc.

de·fend', v. 1. protect against attack. 2. uphold. —de·fend'er, n.

de·fend'ant, n. party accused of a crime or sued in court.

de·fense', n. 1. resistance to attack. 2. defending argument. —de·fense'less, adj. —de·fen'sive, adj., n.

de·fer', v., -ferred, -ferring. 1. postpone. 2. yield in opinion. 3. show respect. —de·fer'ment, n.

def'er·ence, n. act of showing respect. —def'er·en'tial, adj.

de·fi'ance, n. 1. bold resistance. 2. disregard. —de·fi'ant, adj. —de·fi'ant·ly, adv.

de·fi'cien·cy, n., pl. -cies. lack; insufficiency. —de·fi'cient, adj.

def'i·cit, n. deficiency of funds.

de·file', v., -filed, -filing. 1. befoul. 2. desecrate. 3. march in file. —n. 4. narrow pass. —de·file'ment, n.

de·fine', v., -fined, -fining. 1. state

meaning of. 2. determine or outline precisely. —def'i·ni'tion, n.

def'i·nite, adj. 1. exact. 2. with fixed limits. —def'i·nite·ly, adv.

de·fin'i·tive, adj. conclusive. —de·fin'i·tive·ly, adv.

de·flate', v., -flated, -flating. release gas from.

de·fla'tion, n. abnormal fall in prices. —de·fla'tion·ar'y, adj.

de·flect', v. turn from true course. —de·flec'tion, n.

de·fo'li·ate', v., -ated, -ating. 1. strip of leaves. 2. clear of vegetation, as to expose hidden enemy forces. —de·fo'li·a'tion, n. —de·fo'li·ant, n.

de·form', v. mar form of. —de·form'i·ty, n.

de·fraud', v. cheat.

de·fray', v. pay (expenses).

de·frost', v. 1. remove frost or ice from. 2. thaw.

deft, adj. skillful. —deft'ly, adv. —deft'ness, n.

de·funct', adj. dead.

de·fuse', v. 1. remove detonating fuse from. 2. make less dangerous or tense.

de·fy', v., -fied, -fying. challenge; resist.

de·gen'er·ate', v., adj. adj., n. —v. (-a rāt'). 1. decline; deteriorate. —adj. (-ar it). 2. having declined. 3. corrupt. —n. (-ar it). 4. degenerate person. —de·gen'er·a'tion, n. —de·gen'er·a·cy, n.

de·grade', v., -graded, -grading. reduce in status. —deg'ra·da'tion, n.

de·gree', n. 1. stage or extent. 2. 360th part of a complete revolution. 3. unit of temperature. 4. title conferred by college.

de·hu'man·ize', v., -ized, -izing. treat as lacking human qualities or requirements.

de·hy'drate', v., -drated, -drating. deprive of moisture. —de·hy·dra'tion, n.

de'i·fy', v., -fied, -fying. make a god of. —de'i·fi·ca'tion, n.

deign (dān), v. condescend; haughtily consent.

de'ism (dē'iz əm), n. belief in the existence of a God based on reason and evidence in nature, rather than on divine revelation. —de'ist, n. —de·is'tic, adj.

de'i·ty, n., pl. -ties. god or goddess.

dé·jà vu' (dā'zhä vōō'), feeling of having lived through same moment before.

de·ject'ed, adj. disheartened. —de·jec'tion, n.

de ju•re (di jŏŏr′ē, dā jŏŏr′ā), by right or according to law.

de•lay′, v. 1. postpone. 2. hinder. —**de•lay′**, n. —**de•lay′er**, n.

de•lec′ta•ble, adj. delightful. —**de•lec′ta•bly**, adv. —**de•lec′ta′tion**, n.

del′e•gate, v., **-gated, -gating.** —n. 1. deputy. 2. legislator. —v. (-gāt′) 3. send as deputy. 4. commit to another. —**del′e•ga′tion**, n.

de•lete′, v., **-leted, -leting.** cancel; erase. —**de•le′tion**, n.

del•e•te′ri•ous, adj. harmful.

del′i (del′ē), n. delicatessen.

de•lib′er•ate, v., **-ated, -ating.** —adj. (-ər it). 1. intentional. 2. unhurried. —v. (-ə rāt′). 3. consider. 4. confer. —**de•lib′er•a′tion**, n. —**de•lib′er•ate•ly**, adv. —**de•lib′er•ate•ness**, n. —**de•lib′er•a•tive**, adj. —**de•lib′er•a′tor**, n.

del′i•ca•cy, n., pl. **-cies.** 1. fineness. 2. nicety. 3. choice food.

del′i•cate, adj. 1. fine. 2. dainty. 3. fragile. 4. tactful. —**del′i•cate•ly**, adv.

del•i•ca•tes′sen, n. store that sells cooked or prepared food.

de•li′cious, adj. pleasing, esp. to taste. —**de•li′cious•ly**, adv. —**de•li′cious•ness**, n.

de•light′, n. 1. joy. —v. 2. please highly. 3. take joy. —**de•light′ed**, adj. —**de•light′ful**, adj.

de•lin′e•ate, v., **-ated, -ating.** sketch; outline. —**de•lin′e•a′tion**, n.

de•lin′quent, adj. neglectful; guilty. —n. 2. delinquent one. —**de•lin′quen•cy**, n.

de•lir′i•um, n. mental disorder marked by excitement, visions, etc. —**de•lir′i•ous**, adj.

de•liv′er, v. 1. give up. 2. carry and turn over. 3. utter. 4. direct. 5. save. —**de•liv′er•ance**, n. —**de•liv′er•y**, n.

del•phin′i•um, n., pl. **-iums, -ia.** blue garden flower.

del′ta, n. 1. 4th letter of Greek alphabet. 2. triangular area between branches of river mouth.

de•lude′, v., **-luded, -luding.** mislead.

del′uge, n., v., **-uged, -uging.** —n. 1. great flood. —v. 2. flood. 3. overwhelm.

de•lu′sion, n. false opinion or conception. —**de•lu′sive**, adj.

de•luxe′ (-luks′). adj. of finest quality.

delve, v., **delved, delving.** dig. —**delv′er**, n.

dem′a•gogue (-gôg′), n. unscrupulous popular leader. Also, **dem′a•gog′.** —**dem′a•gog′uer•y**, n.

de•mand′, v. 1. claim. 2. require. 3. ask for in urgent or peremptory manner. —n. 4. claim. 5. requirement.

de•mean′, v. 1. conduct (oneself). 2. lower in dignity. —**de•mean′or**, n.

de•mean′or, n. conduct; behavior; deportment.

de•ment′ed, adj. crazed.

de•mer′it, n. 1. fault. 2. rating for misconduct.

demi•god′, n. one partly divine and partly human.

de•mil′i•ta•rize′, v., **-rized, -rizing.** free from military influence. —**de•mil′i•ta•ri•za′tion**, n.

de•mise′ (di mīz′), n., v., **-mised, -mising.** —n. 1. death. 2. transfer of estate. —v. 3. transfer.

dem′i•tasse′, n. small coffee cup.

dem′o (dem′ō), n. product, as a recording or automobile, distributed, displayed, or offered for trial, to attract buyers.

de•mo′bi•lize′, v., **-lized, -lizing.** disband (army). —**de•mo′bi•li•za′tion**, n.

de•moc′ra•cy, n., pl. **-cies.** 1. government in which the people hold supreme power. 2. social equality. —**dem′o•crat′**, n. —**dem′o•crat′ic**, adj. —**dem′o•crat′i•cal•ly**, adv.

dem′o•graph′ic, of statistics on population. —**dem′o•graph′i•cal•ly**, adv. —**de•mog′ra•phy**, n.

de•mol′ish, v. destroy. —**dem•o•li′tion**, n.

de′mon, n. evil spirit.

de•mon′ic, adj. inspired. 2. like a demon. Also, **de′mo•ni′a•cal.**

dem′on•strate′, v., **-strated, -strating.** 1. prove. 2. describe and explain. 3. manifest. 4. parade in support of or opposition. —**de•mon′stra•ble**, adj. —**dem′on•stra′tion**, n. —**dem′on•stra′tor**, n.

de•mon′stra•tive, adj. 1. expressive. 2. explanatory. 3. conclusive.

de•mor′al•ize′, v., **-ized, -izing.** corrupt morals, courage, etc., of. —**de•mor′al•i•za′tion**, n.

de•mote′, v., **-moted, -moting.** reduce in rank.

de•mur′, v., **-murred, -murring.** n. —v. 1. object. —n. 2. objection.

de•mure′, adj. modest. —**de•mure′ly**, adv.

den, n. 1. cave of wild beast. 2. squalid place. 3. comfortable room in a home for conversation, reading, etc.

de•ni′al, n. 1. contradiction. 2. refusal to agree or give.

den′i•grate′, v., **-grated, -grating.** speak badly of; defame or disparage.

den'im, n. 1. heavy cotton fabric. 2. (pl.) trousers of this.

den'i·zen, n. inhabitant.

de·nom'i·nate', v., -nated, -nating. name specifically.

de·nom'i·na'tion, n. 1. name or designation. 2. sect. 3. value of piece of money. —**de·nom'i·na'tion·al,** adj.

de·nom'i·na'tor, n. lower term in fraction.

de·note', v., -noted, -noting. 1. indicate. 2. mean. —**de·no·ta'tion,** n.

de·noue·ment' (dā'noō män'), n. 1. final resolution of plot or story. 2. outcome of series of events. Also, **dé·noue·ment'.**

de·nounce', v., -nounced, -nouncing. 1. condemn. 2. inform against.

dense, adj., denser, densest. 1. compact. 2. stupid. —**dens'ly,** n. —**dense'ly,** adv. —**dense'ness,** n.

dent, n. 1. hollow. —v. 2. make a dent.

den'tal, adj. of teeth.

den'ti·frice, n. teeth-cleaning substance.

den'tin, n. hard tissue that forms most of a tooth. Also, **den'tine** (-tēn).

den'tist, n. person who prevents and treats oral disease. —**den'tist·ry,** n.

den'ture, n. artificial tooth or teeth.

de·nude', v., -nuded, -nuding. make bare. —**de·nu·da'tion,** n.

de·nun'ci·a'tion, n. 1. condemnation. 2. accusation.

de·ny', v., -nied, -nying. 1. declare not to be true. 2. refuse to agree or give.

de·o'dor·ant, n. agent for destroying odors.

de·part', v. 1. go away. 2. die. —**de·par'ture,** n.

de·part'ment, n. 1. part; section. 2. branch. —**de·part'men'tal,** adj.

de·pend', v. 1. rely. 2. be contingent. —**de·pend'ence,** n. —**de·pend'ent,** adj., n.

de·pend'a·ble, adj. reliable. —**de·pend'a·bil'i·ty,** n. —**de·pend'a·bly,** adv.

de·pict', v. 1. portray. 2. describe. —**de·pic'tion,** n.

de·pil'a·to'ry (di pil'ə tôr'ē), adj., n., pl. -ries. —adj. 1. capable of removing hair. —n. 2. depilatory agent.

de·plete', v., -pleted, -pleting. reduce in amount. —**de·ple'tion,** n.

de·plore', v., -plored, -ploring. lament. —**de·plor'a·ble,** adj.

de·ploy', v. spread out strategically. —**de·ploy'ment,** n.

de·pop'u·late', v., -lated, -lating. deprive of inhabitants. —**de·pop'u·la'tion,** n.

de·port', v. 1. banish. 2. conduct (oneself). —**de·por·ta'tion,** n.

de·port'ment, n. conduct.

de·pose', v., -posed, -posing. 1. remove from office. 2. testify. —**de·po·si'tion,** n.

de·pos'it, v. 1. place. 2. place for safekeeping. —n. 3. sediment. 4. something deposited. —**de·pos'i·tor,** n.

de·pot (dē'pō), n. 1. station. 2. storage base.

de·prave', v., -praved, -praving. corrupt. —**de·prav'i·ty,** n.

dep're·cate', v., -cated, -cating. disapprove of. —**dep're·ca'tion,** n. —**dep're·ca·to'ry,** adj.

de·pre'ci·ate' (-shi āt'), v., -ated, -ating. 1. reduce or decline in value. 2. belittle. —**de·pre'ci·a'tion,** n.

dep're·da'tion, n. robbery or destruction.

de·press', v. 1. deject. 2. weaken. 3. press down. —**de·pres'sant,** adj., n.

de·pres'sion, n. 1. act of depressing. 2. depressed state. 3. depressed place. 4. decline in business. —**de·pres'sive,** adj.

de·prive', v., -prived, -priving. 1. divest. 2. withhold from. —**dep'ri·va'tion,** n.

depth, n. 1. distance down. 2. profundity. 3. lowness of pitch. 4. deep part.

dep'u·ta'tion, n. delegation.

dep'u·ty, n., pl. -ties. agent; substitute. —**dep'u·tize',** v.

de·rail', v. cause to run off rails.

de·range', v., -ranged, -ranging. 1. disarrange. 2. make insane. —**de·range'ment,** n.

der'by, n., pl. -bies. 1. stiff, rounded hat. 2. race or contest.

de·reg'u·late', v., -lated, -lating. free of regulation. —**de·reg'u·la'tion,** n.

der'e·lict, adj. 1. abandoned. 2. neglectful. —n. 3. something abandoned. 4. vagabond; vagrant.

der'e·lic'tion, n. neglect; abandonment.

de·ride', v., -rided, -riding. mock. —**de·ri'sion,** n. —**de·ri'sive,** adj.

de·rive', v., -rived, -riving. 1. get from source. 2. trace. 3. deduce. 4. originate. —**der'i·va'tion,** n. —**de·riv'a·tive,** n., adj.

der·ma·ti'tis (dûr'mə tī'tis), n. inflammation of the skin.

der·ma·tol'o·gy, n. medical study and treatment of the skin. —**der·ma·tol'o·gist,** n.

der'o·gate', v., -gated, -gating. detract. —**der'o·ga'tion,** n. —**de·rog'a·to'ry,** adj.

der′rick, *n.* crane with boom pivoted at one end.

de•scend′ (di send′), *v.* 1. move down. 2. be descendant. —**de•scent′**, *n.*

de•scend′ant, *n.* person descended from specific ancestor; offspring.

de•scribe′, *v.,* -scribed, -scribing. 1. set forth in words. 2. trace. —**de•scrib′a•ble**, *adj.* —**de•scrip′tion**, *n.* —**de•scrip′tive**, *adj.*

de•scry′ (de skrī′), *v.,* -scried, -scrying. happen to see.

des′e•crate′, *v.,* -crated, -crating. divest of sacredness. —**des•e•cra′tion**, *n.*

de•seg′re•gate′, *v.,* -gated, -gating. eliminate racial segregation in —**de•seg•re•ga′tion**, *n.*

des′ert, *n.* 1. arid region. 2. (dizûrt′) due reward or punishment. —*adj.* 3. desolate; barren. —*v.* 4. (di zûrt′) abandon. —**de•sert′er**, *n.* —**de•ser′tion**, *n.*

de•serve′, *v.,* -served, -serving. have due one by right.

des′ic•cate′, *v.,* -cated, -cating. dry up. —**des•ic•ca′tion**, *n.*

de•sign′, *v.* 1. plan. 2. conceive form of. —*n.* 3. sketch or plan. 4. art of designing. 5. scheme. 6. purpose. —**de•sign′er**, *n.*

des′ig•nate′, *v.,* -nated, -nating. 1. indicate. 2. name. —**des•ig•na′tion**, *n.*

de•sign′ing, *adj.* scheming.

de•sire′, *v.,* -sired, -siring. —*v.* 1. wish for. 2. request. —*n.* 3. longing. 4. request. 5. thing desired. 6. lust. —**de•sir′a•ble**, *adj.* —**de•sir′ous**, *adj.* —**de•sir′a•bil′i•ty**, *n.*

de•sist′, *v.* stop.

desk, *n.* 1. table for writing. 2. specialized section of an organization, as in a newspaper office.

desk′top′ publishing, design and production of publications using a microcomputer.

des′o•late, *adj.,* *v.,* -lated, -lating. —*adj.* (-lit). 1. barren. 2. lonely. 3. dismal. —*v.* (-a lāt′) 4. lay waste. 5. make hopeless. —**des•o•la′tion**, *n.*

de•spair′, *n.* 1. hopelessness. —*v.* 2. lose hope.

des′per•a′do (-rä′-, -rā′-), *n.,* *pl.* -does, -dos. desperate criminal.

des′per•ate, *adj.* 1. reckless from despair. 2. despairing. —**des′per•a′tion**, *n.*

des′pi•ca•ble, *adj.* contemptible. —**des′pi•ca•bly**, *adv.*

de•spise′, *v.,* -spised, -spising. scorn.

de•spite′, *prep.* 1. in spite of. —*n.* 2. insult.

de•spoil′, *v.* plunder. —**de•spoil′ent**, *adj.*

de•spond′, *v.* lose courage or hope. —**de•spond′ent**, *adj.*

des′pot′, *n.* tyrant. —**des•pot′ic**, *adj.* —**des′pot•ism′**, *n.*

des•sert′, *n.* sweet course of meal.

des′ti•na′tion, *n.* goal of journey.

des′tine (-tin), *v.,* -tined, -tining. 1. set apart. 2. predetermine by fate.

des′ti•ny, *n.,* *pl.* -nies. 1. future, esp. as predetermined. 2. fate.

des′ti•tute′, *adj.* 1. without means of support. 2. deprived. —**des′ti•tu′tion**, *n.*

de•stroy′, *v.* 1. ruin. 2. end. 3. kill.

de•stroy′er, *n.* 1. one that destroys. 2. fast, light naval vessel.

de•struct′, *v.* be destroyed automatically.

de•struc′tion, *n.* 1. act or means of destroying. 2. fact of being destroyed. —**de•struct′i•ble**, *adj.* —**de•struc′tive**, *adj.*

de•sul′to•ry, *adj.* not methodical. —**des′ul•to′ri•ly**, *adv.*

de•tach′, *v.* take off or away. —**de•tach′a•ble**, *adj.*

de•tached′, *adj.* 1. separate. 2. uninterested.

de•tach′ment, *n.* 1. act of detaching. 2. unconcern. 3. impartiality. 4. troops for special duty.

de•tail′, *n.* 1. individual or minute part. 2. **in detail**, with all details specified. 3. troops for special duty. —*v.* 4. relate in detail. 5. assign.

de•tain′, *v.* 1. delay. 2. keep in custody. —**de•ten′tion**, *n.*

de•tect′, *v.* 1. discover, esp. in or after some act. 2. perceive. —**de•tec′tion**, *n.* —**de•tec′tor**, *n.*

de•tec′tive, *n.* professional investigator of crimes, etc.

dé•tente′ (dā tänt′), *n.* relaxation of international tension.

de•ter′, *v.,* -terred, -terring. discourage or restrain.

de•ter′gent, *adj.* 1. cleansing. —*n.* 2. cleansing agent.

de•te′ri•o•rate′, *v.,* -rated, -rating. make or become worse. —**de•te′ri•o•ra′tion**, *n.*

de•ter′mi•nate, *adj.* able to be specified.

de•ter′mi•na′tion, *n.* 1. act of determining. 2. firmness of purpose.

de•ter′mine, *v.,* -mined, -mining. 1. settle; decide. 2. ascertain. 3. limit. —**de•ter′mi•na•ble**, *adj.*

de•ter′mined, *adj.* firmly resolved.

de•ter′rence, *n.* discouragement, as of crime or military aggression. —**de•ter′rent**, *adj.,* *n.*

de•test′, *v.* hate or despise. —**de•**

test'a·ble, *adj.* —**de·test'a·bly,** *adv.* —**de·tes·ta'tion,** *n.*

de·throne', *v.,* **-throned, -throning.** remove from a throne.

det'o·nate', *v.,* **-nated, -nating.** explode. —**det'o·na'tion,** *n.*

de'tour, *n.* 1. roundabout course. —*v.* 2. make detour.

de·tox'i·fy, *v.,* **-fied, -fying.** rid of poison or effects of alcohol or drug use. —**de·tox'i·fi·ca'tion,** *n.*

de·tract', *v.* take away quality or reputation. —**de·trac'tion,** *n.*

det'ri·ment, *n.* loss or damage. —**det'ri·men'tal,** *adj.*

de·val'u·ate', *v.,* **-ated, -ating.** reduce in value. Also, **de·val'ue.** —**de·val'u·a'tion,** *n.*

dev·as·tate', *v.,* **-tated, -tating.** lay waste. —**dev·as·ta'tion,** *n.*

de·vel'op, *v.* 1. mature; perfect. 2. elaborate. 3. bring into being. 4. make (images on film) visible. 5. acquire; gain gradually. —**de·vel'op·ment,** *n.* —**de·vel'op·er,** *n.*

de·vi·ate', *v.,* **-ated, -ating.** 1. digress. 2. depart from normal. —**de'vi·a'tion,** *n.* —**de'vi·ant,** *adj.*

de·vice', *n.* 1. contrivance. 2. plan. 3. slogan or emblem.

dev'il, *n.* 1. Satan. 2. evil spirit. 3. wicked person.

devil's advocate, person who takes opposing view for the sake of argument.

de·vi'ous, *adj.* 1. circuitous. 2. with low cunning. —**de·vi'ous·ly,** *adv.*

de·vise', *v.,* **-vised, -vising.** 1. plan; contrive. 2. bequeath. —**de·vis'er,** *n.*

de·vi'tal·ize', *v.,* **-ized, -izing.** remove vitality of. —**de·vi'tal·i·za'-tion,** *n.*

de·void', *adj.* destitute.

de·volve', *v.,* **-volved, -volving.** 1. transfer or delegate. 2. fall as a duty.

de·vote', *v.,* **-voted, -voting.** appropriate to something.

de·vot'ed, *adj.* 1. zealous. 2. dedicated.

dev·o·tee' (dev'ə tē'), *n.* devoted one.

de·vo'tion, *n.* 1. consecration. 2. attachment or dedication. 3. (*pl.*) worship. —**de·vo'tion·al,** *adj.*

de·vour', *v.* consume ravenously.

de·vout', *adj.* pious.

dew, *n.* atmospheric moisture condensed in droplets. —**dew'y,** *adj.*

dex·ter'i·ty, *n.* 1. physical skill. 2. cleverness. —**dex'ter·ous,** *adj.*

dex'trose, *n.* type of sugar.

di·a·be'tes, *n.* disease causing body's inability to use sugar. —**di·a·bet'ic,** *adj., n.*

di·a·bol'ic, *adj.* fiendish. Also, **di·a·bol'i·cal.**

di'a·dem', *n.* crown.

di·ag·nose', *v.,* **-nosed, -nosing.** determine nature of (disease). —**di'ag·no'sis,** *n.* —**di'ag·nos'tic,** *adj.*

di·ag'o·nal, *adj.* 1. connecting two angles. 2. oblique.

di'a·gram', *n.,* *v.,* **-gramed, -graming.** chart or plan. —**di'a·gram·mat'ic,** *adj.*

di'al, *n.,* *v.,* **-aled, -aling.** —*n.* 1. numbered face, as on watch, telephone, or radio. —*v.* 2. select or contact with use of dial.

di'a·lect, *n.* language of district or class. —**di'a·lec'tal,** *adj.*

di'a·lec'tic, *n.* art or practice of debate or conversation by which truth of theory or opinion is arrived at logically. Also, **di'a·lec'tics,** *n.* —**di'a·lec'ti·cal,** *adj.*

di'a·logue', *n.* conversation between two or more people. Also, **di'a·log'.**

di·al'y·sis (dī al'ə sis), *n.* process of removing waste products from blood of someone with kidney disease.

di·am'e·ter, *n.* straight line through center of a circle.

di'a·met'ri·cal, *adj.* 1. of diameters. 2. completely in contrast.

di'a·mond, *n.* 1. hard, brilliant precious stone. 2. rhombus or square. 3. (*pl.*) suit of playing cards. 4. baseball field.

di'a·per, *n.* infant's underpants. —*v.* 2. put diaper on.

di'a·phragm' (-fram'), *n.* 1. wall in body, as between thorax and abdomen. 2. vibrating membrane. 3. dome-shaped contraceptive device.

di'ar·rhe'a (dī'ə rē'ə), *n.* intestinal disorder. Also, **di'ar·rhoe'a.**

di'a·ry, *n., pl.* **-ries.** personal daily record. —**di'a·rist,** *n.*

di'a·ther'my, *n.* therapeutic heating of body by electric currents.

di·a·ton'ic (dī'ə ton'ik), *adj. Music.* made up of the eight notes of the major or minor scale.

di'a·tribe', *n.* denunciation.

dice, *n.pl., sing. die, v.,* **diced, dicing.** —*n.* 1. small cubes, used in games. —*v.* 2. cut into small cubes.

dic'ey, *adj.* **-ier, -iest.** not certain; risky.

di·chot'o·my, *n., pl.* **-mies.** division into two irreconcilable groups.

dick'er, *v.* bargain.

dic'tate', *v.,* **-tated, -tating.** —*v.* 1. say something to be written down. 2. command. —*n.* 3. command. —**dic·ta'tion,** *n.*

dic·ta'tor, *n.* nonhereditary absolute

ruler. —**dic'ta•to'ri•al**, *adj.* —**dic'-ta•tor•ship'**, *n.*

dic'tion, *n.* style of speaking or writing.

dic'tion•ar'y, *n., pl.* **-aries.** book on meaning, pronunciation, spelling, etc., of words.

di•dac'tic, *adj.* instructive. —**di•dac'ti•cism**, *n.*

did'n't, *n. Informal.* did not.

die, *v.*, **died, dying**, *n., pl.* (for 3) **dies.** —*v.* 1. cease to be. 2. lose force; fade. —*n.* 3. shaping device. 4. sing. of **dice.**

die'hard', *n.* defender of lost cause.

di•er'e•sis (dī er'ə sis), *n., pl.* **-ses.** sign (¨) over a vowel indicating separate pronunciation, as in Noël.

die'sel (dē'-), *n.* 1. engine using air compression for ignition. 2. machine or vehicle powered by such an engine. 3. fuel consumed by a diesel engine.

di'et, *n.* 1. food. 2. food specially chosen for health, slimness, etc. 3. formal assembly. —*v.* 4. adhere to diet. —**di'e•tar'y**, *adj.* —**di'e•tet'ic**, *adj.* —**di'e•tet'ics**, *n.*

di'e•ti'tian (dī'i tish'ən), *n.* person who is an expert in nutrition and dietary requirements. Also, **di•eti'cian.**

dif'fer, *v.* 1. be unlike. 2. disagree.

dif'fer•ence, *n.* 1. unlikeness. 2. disagreement; quarrel. 3. amount separating two quantities. —**dif'fer•ent**, *adj.* —**dif'fer•ent•ly**, *adv.*

dif•fer•en'ti•ate', *v.*, **-ated, -ating.** 1. alter. 2. distinguish between.

dif'fi•cult', *adj.* 1. hard to do or understand. 2. unfriendly or unmanageable.

dif'fi•cul'ty, *n., pl.* **-ties.** 1. condition of being difficult. 2. embarrassing or difficult situation. 3. trouble; struggle. 4. disagreement or dispute.

dif'fi•dent, *adj.* timid; shy. —**dif'fi•dence**, *n.*

dif•frac'tion, *n.* breaking up of rays of light to produce spectrum.

dif•fuse', *v.*, **-fused, -fusing**, *adj.* —*v.* (-fyōōz') 1. spread or scatter. —*adj.* (-fyōōs') 2. not to the point. 3. spread or scattered. —**dif•fu'sion**, *n.*

dig, *v.*, **dug** or **digged, digging**, *n.* —*v.* 1. thrust down. 2. lift to extract. 3. form by extraction. 4. *Slang.* understand or appreciate. —*n.* 5. sarcastic remark.

di•gest', *v.* 1. prepare (food) for assimilation. 2. assimilate mentally. —*n.* (dī'jest) 3. collection or summary, esp. of laws. —**di•ges'tion**, *n.* —**di•ges'tive**, *adj.* —**di•gest'i•ble**, *adj.* —**di•gest'i•bil'i•ty**, *n.*

dig'it, *n.* 1. finger or toe. 2. any Arabic numeral, as 0, 1, 2, etc.

dig'it•al, *adj.* of, using, or expressing data in numerals.

dig'i•tal'is (dij'i tal'is, -tā'lis), *n.* medicine derived from the leaves of the foxglove, used to stimulate the heart.

dig'ni•fied', *adj.* marked by dignity; stately.

dig'ni•fy', *v.*, **-fied, -fying.** 1. honor. 2. honor more than is deserved.

dig'ni•tar'y, *n., pl.* **-ries.** eminent or high-ranking person.

dig'ni•ty, *n., pl.* **-ties.** 1. nobility. 2. worthiness. 3. high rank, office, or title.

di•gress', *v.* wander from main purpose, theme, etc. —**di•gres'sion**, *n.*

dike, *n.* 1. bank for restraining waters. 2. ditch.

di•lap'i•dat'ed, *adj.* decayed.

di•lap'i•da'tion, *n.* ruin; decay.

di•late', *v.*, **-lated, -lating.** expand. —**di•la'tion**, *n.*

dil'a•to'ry, *adj.* delaying; tardy. —**dil'a•to'ri•ness**, *n.*

di•lem'ma, *n.* predicament.

dil'et•tante' (-tänt'), *n.* superficial practitioner.

dil'i•gence, *n.* earnest effort. —**dil'i•gent**, *adj.*

dill, *n.* plant with aromatic seeds and leaves.

di•lute', *v.*, **-luted, -luting.** thin, as with water; weaken. —**di•lu'tion**, *n.*

dim, *adj.*, **dimmer, dimmest**, *v.*, **dimmed, dimming.** —*adj.* 1. not bright. 2. indistinct. —*v.* 3. make or become dim. —**dim'ly**, *adv.*

dime, *n.* coin worth 10 cents.

di•men'sion, *n.* 1. property of space; extension in a given direction. 2. magnitude. —**di•men'sion•al**, *adj.*

di•min'ish, *v.* lessen; reduce. —**dim'i•nu'tion**, *n.*

di•min'u•en'do (di min'yōō en'dō), *adj., adv. Music.* gradually reducing in loudness.

di•min'u•tive, *adj.* 1. small. 2. denoting smallness, etc. —*n.* 3. diminutive form, as of word.

dim'i•ty, *n., pl.* **-ties.** thin cotton fabric.

dim'ple, *n.* small hollow, esp. in cheek.

din, *n., v.*, **dinned, dinning.** —*n.* 1. confused noise. —*v.* 2. assail with din.

dine, *v.*, **dined, dining.** 1. eat dinner or another meal. 2. provide dinner.

din'er, *n.* 1. person who dines. 2. railroad dining car. 3. restaurant shaped like such a car.

din'ghy (ding'gē), *n., pl.* **-ghies.** small boat. Also, **din'gey, din'gy.**

din'gy (-jē), *adj.,* **-gier, -giest.** dark; dirty.

din'ner, *n.* main meal.

di'no•saur, *n.* extinct reptile.

dint, *n.* 1. force. 2. dent.

di'o•cese (dī'ə sēs'), *n.* district under a bishop. —**di•oc'e•san,** *adj., n.*

di•ox'ide (dī ok'sīd, -sid), *n.* oxide with two atoms of oxygen.

dip, *v.,* **dipped, dipping,** *n.* —*v.* 1. plunge temporarily in liquid. 2. bail or scoop. 3. slope down. —*n.* 4. act of dipping. 5. downward slope. 6. substance into which something is dipped.

diph•the'ri•a (dif thēr'ē ə), *n.* infectious disease of air passages, esp. throat.

diph'thong (dif'-), *n.* sound containing two vowels.

di•plo'ma, *n.* document of academic qualifications.

di•plo'ma•cy, *n., pl.* **-cies.** 1. conduct of international relations. 2. skill in negotiation. —**dip'lo•mat',** *n.*

dip'lo•mat'ic, *adj.* 1. of diplomacy. 2. tactful. —**dip'lo•mat'i•cal•ly,** *adv.*

dip'per, *n.* 1. one that dips. 2. ladle.

dip'so•ma'ni•a, *n.* morbid craving for alcohol. —**dip'so•ma'ni•ac,** *n.*

dire, *adj.,* **direr, direst.** dreadful.

di•rect', *v.* 1. guide. 2. command. 3. manage. 4. address. —*adj.* 5. straight. 6. straightforward. —**di•rect'ly,** *adv.* —**di•rect'ness,** *n.* —**di•rec'tor,** *n.*

di•rec•tion, *n.* 1. act of directing. 2. line along which a thing lies or moves. —**di•rec'tion•al,** *adj.*

di•rec'tive, *n.* order or instruction from authority.

di•rec'to•ry, *n., pl.* **-ries.** guide to locations or telephone numbers.

dire'ful, *adj.* dire.

dirge, *n.* funeral song.

dir'i•gi•ble, *n.* airship that can be steered.

dirk, *n.* dagger.

dirt, *n.* 1. filthy substance. 2. earth.

dirt'y, *adj.* **dirtier, dirtiest,** *v.,* **dirtied, dirtying.** —*adj.* 1. soiled. 2. indecent. —*v.* 3. soil. —**dirt'i•ness,** *n.*

dis, *v.,* **dissed, dissing.** *Slang.* 1. show disrespect for. 2. disparage.

dis-, prefix indicating: 1. reversal, as *disconnect.* 2. negation or lack, as *distrust.* 3. removal, as *disbar.*

dis•a'ble, *v.,* **-bled, -bling.** damage capability of. —**dis'a•bil'i•ty,** *n.*

dis•a•buse', *v.,* **-bused, -busing.** free from deception.

dis'ad•van'tage, *n.* 1. unfavorable circumstance. 2. injury. —**dis'ad'van•ta'geous,** *adj.*

dis'af•fect', *v.* alienate. —**dis'af•fec'tion,** *n.*

dis'a•gree', *v.* **-greed, -greeing.** differ in opinion. —**dis'a•gree'ment,** *n.*

dis'a•gree'a•ble, *adj.* unpleasant. —**dis'a•gree'a•bly,** *adv.*

dis'ap•pear', *v.* 1. vanish. 2. cease to exist. —**dis'ap•pear'ance,** *n.*

dis'ap•point', *v.* fail to fulfill hopes or wishes of. —**dis'ap•point'ment,** *n.*

dis'ap•prove', *v.,* **-proved, -proving.** condemn; censure. —**dis'ap•prov'al,** *n.*

dis•arm', *v.* 1. deprive of arms. 2. reduce one's own armed power. —**dis•ar'ma•ment,** *n.*

dis'ar•range', *v.,* **-ranged, -ranging.** disorder. —**dis'ar•range'ment,** *n.*

dis'ar•ray', *n.* lack of order.

dis•as'ter, *n.* extreme misfortune. —**dis•as'trous,** *adj.*

dis'a•vow', *v.* disown. —**dis'a•vow'al,** *n.* —**dis'a•vow'er,** *n.*

dis•band', *v.* terminate as organization. —**dis•band'ment,** *n.*

dis•bar', *v.,* **-barred, -barring.** expel from law practice. —**dis•bar'ment,** *n.*

dis'be•lieve', *v.,* **-lieved, -lieving.** reject as untrue. —**dis'be•lief',** *n.*

dis•burse', *v.,* **-bursed, -bursing.** pay out. —**dis•burse'ment,** *n.*

disc, *n.* 1. disk 2. phonograph record.

dis•card', *v.* 1. reject. —*n.* (dis'kärd). 2. something discarded. 3. discarded state.

dis•cern' (di sûrn'), *v.* 1. see. 2. distinguish. —**dis•cern'ing,** *adj.* —**dis•cern'ment,** *n.*

dis•charge', *v.,* **-charged, -charging.** 1. rid of load. 2. send forth. 3. shoot. 4. terminate employment of. 5. fulfill. —*n.* (dis'chärj). 6. act of discharging. 7. something discharged.

dis•ci'ple (di sī'pəl), *n.* follower.

dis'ci•pline, *n., v.,* **-plined, -plining.** —*n.* 1. training in rules. 2. punishment. 3. subjection to rules. 4. branch of instruction or learning. —*v.* 5. train. 6. punish. —**dis'ci•pli•nar'y,** *adj.* —**dis'ci•pli•nar'i•an,** *n.*

disc jockey, person who plays and comments on recorded music on a radio program. Also, **disk jockey.**

dis•claim', *v.* disown.

dis•close', *v.,* **-closed, -closing.** reveal. —**dis•clo'sure,** *n.*

dis'co, *n., pl.* **-cos.** 1. discotheque. 2. heavily rhythmic style of popular music for dancing.

dis•col'or, *v.* change in color. —**dis•col'or•a'tion,** *n.*

dis•com•fit', v. 1. defeat. 2. frustrate. —**dis•com'fi•ture**, n.

dis•com'fort, n. lack of comfort.

dis'com•mode', v., **-moded, -mod•ing**. cause inconvenience to.

dis'con•cert', v. perturb.

dis'con•nect', v. break connection of.

dis•con'so•late, adj. unhappy. —**dis•con'so•late•ly**, adv.

dis'con•tent', adj. Also **dis'con•tent'ed**. 1. not contented. —n. 2. lack of contentment.

dis'con•tin'ue, v., **-tinued, -tinuing**. end; stop. —**dis'con•tin'u•ance**, n.

dis'cord, n. 1. lack of harmony. 2. disagreement; strife. —**dis•cord'ance**, n. —**dis•cord'ant**, adj.

dis'co•theque' (dis'kō tek'), n. nightclub where recorded dance music is played.

dis'count', v. 1. deduct. 2. advance money after deduction of interest. 3. disregard. 4. allow for exaggeration in. —n. 5. deduction.

dis•cour'age, v., **-aged, -aging**. 1. deprive of resolution. 2. hinder. —**dis•cour'age•ment**, n.

dis'course', n., **-coursed, -coursing**. —n. 1. talk. 2. formal discussion. —v. (dis kōrs') 3. talk.

dis•cour'te•sy, n., pl. **-sies**. 1. lack of courtesy. 2. impolite act. —**dis•cour'te•ous**, adj.

dis•cov'er, v. learn or see for first time. —**dis•cov'er•y**, n. —**dis•cov'er•a•ble**, adj. —**dis•cov'er•er**, n.

dis•cred'it, v. 1. injure reputation of. 2. give no credit to. —n. 3. lack of belief. 4. disrepute.

dis•creet', adj. wise; prudent. —**dis•creet'ly**, adv.

dis•crep'an•cy, n., pl. **-cies**. difference; inconsistency. —**dis•crep'ant**, adj.

dis•crete', adj. separate.

dis•cre'tion, n. 1. freedom of choice. 2. prudence. —**dis•cre'tion•ar'y**, adj.

dis•crim'i•nate', v., **-nated, -nating**, adj. —v. (-ā nāt'). 1. distinguish accurately. 2. show partiality for or against. —adj. (-ə nit). 3. making distinctions. —**dis•crim'i•na'tion**, n.

dis•cur'sive, adj. rambling; not wholly relevant.

dis'cus (dis'kəs), n. disk, usu. of wood, for throwing in athletic competition.

dis•cuss', v. talk about. —**dis•cus'sion**, n.

dis•dain', v., n. scorn. —**dis•dain'ful**, adj.

dis•ease', n., v., **-eased, -easing**. —n. 1. ailment. —v. 2. affect with disease.

dis'em•bark', v. land. —**dis'em•bar'ka'tion**, n.

dis'em•bod'y, v., **-bodied, -bodying**. free from the body.

dis'en•chant', v. free from enchantment or illusion. —**dis'en•chant'ment**, n.

dis'en•gage', v., **-gaged, -gaging**. separate; disconnect. —**dis'en•gage'ment**, n.

dis•fa'vor, n. 1. displeasure. 2. disregard. 3. regard or treat with disfavor.

dis•fig'ure, v., **-ured, -uring**. mar.

dis•fran'chise, v., **-chised, -chising**. deprive of franchise.

dis•gorge', v., **-gorged, -gorging**. 1. vomit forth. 2. yield up.

dis•grace', n., v., **-graced, -gracing**. —n. 1. state or cause of dishonor. —v. 2. bring shame upon. —**dis•grace'ful**, adj. —**dis•grace'ful•ly**, adv.

dis•grun'tle, v., **-tled, -tling**. make discontent.

dis•guise', v., **-guised, -guising**, n. —v. 1. conceal true identity of. —n. 2. something that disguises.

dis•gust', v. 1. cause loathing in. —n. 2. loathing.

dish, n. 1. open shallow container. 2. article of food.

dis•heart'en, v. discourage.

dis•shev'el, v., **-eled, -eling**. let hang in disorder.

dis•hon'est, adj. not honest. —**dis•hon'est•ly**, adv. —**dis•hon'es•ty**, n.

dis•hon'or, n. 1. lack of honor. 2. disgrace. —v. 3. disgrace. 4. fail to honor. —**dis•hon'or•a•ble**, adj.

dish'wash'er, n. person or machine that washes dishes.

dis•il•lu'sion, v. free from illusion. —**dis•il•lu'sion•ment**, n.

dis•in•cline', v., **-clined, -clining**. make or be averse. —**dis•in•cli•na'tion**, n.

dis•in•fect', v. destroy disease germs in. —**dis•in•fect'ant**, n., adj.

dis•in•for•ma'tion, n. false information released by a government to mislead rival nations.

dis•in•gen'u•ous, adj. lacking frankness.

dis•in•her'it, v. exclude from inheritance.

dis•in'te•grate', v., **-grated, -grating**. separate into parts. —**dis•in'te•gra'tion**, n.

dis•in'ter•est, n. indifference.

dis•in'ter•est'ed, adj. impartial. —**dis•in'ter•est'ed•ly**, adv.

dis•joint'ed, adj. 1. separated at joints. 2. incoherent.

disk, n. 1. flat circular plate. 2. phonograph record. 3. thin, round plate for storing electronic data. 4. roundish, flat anatomical part, as in the spine.

disk•ette', n. floppy disk.

disk jockey, n. disc jockey.

dis•like', v., **-liked, -liking,** n. —v. 1. regard with displeasure. —n. 2. distaste.

dis•lo•cate', v., **-cated, -cating.** 1. displace. 2. put out of order. —**dis'-lo•ca'tion,** n.

dis•lodge', v., **-lodged, -lodging.** force from place. —**dis•lodg'ment,** n.

dis•loy'al, adj. not loyal; traitorous. —**dis•loy'al•ty,** n.

dis'mal, adj. 1. gloomy. 2. terrible. —**dis'mal•ly,** adv.

dis•man'tle, v., **-tled, -tling.** 1. deprive of equipment. 2. take apart.

dis•may', v. 1. dishearten. —n. 2. disheartenment.

dis•mem'ber, v. deprive of limbs. —**dis•mem'ber•ment,** n.

dis•miss', v. 1. direct or allow to go. 2. discharge. 3. reject. —**dis•mis'sal,** n.

dis•mount', v. 1. get or throw down from saddle. 2. remove from mounting.

dis'o•be'di•ent, adj. not obedient. —**dis'o•be'di•ence,** n. —**dis'o•bey',** v.

dis•or'der, n. 1. lack of order. 2. illness or disease. —v. 3. create disorder in. —**dis•or'der•ly,** adj.

dis•or'gan•ize', v., **-ized, -izing.** throw into disorder. —**dis•or'gan•i•za'tion,** n.

dis•own', v. repudiate.

dis•par'age, v., **-aged, -aging.** speak slightly of; belittle. —**dis•par'age•ment,** n.

dis'pa•rate (dis'pər it, di spar'-). distinct in kind; dissimilar. —**dis•par'i•ty,** n.

dis•pas'sion•ate, adj. impartial; calm. —**dis•pas'sion•ate•ly,** adv.

dis•patch', v. 1. transact quickly. 3. kill. —n. 4. act of sending off. 5. killing. 6. speed. 7. message or report. —**dis•patch'er,** n.

dis•pel', v., **-pelled, -pelling.** drive off; scatter.

dis•pen'sa•ry, n., pl. **-ries.** place for dispensing medicines.

dis•pen•sa'tion, n. 1. act of dispensing. 2. divine order. 3. relaxation of law.

dis•pense', v., **-pensed, -pensing.** 1. distribute. 2. administer. 3. forgo. 4. do away. —**dis•pen'sa•ble,** adj. —**dis•pens'er,** n.

dis•perse', v., **-persed, -persing.** scatter. —**dis•per'sion, dis•per'sal,** n.

dis•pir'it•ed, adj. downhearted.

dis•place', v., **-placed, -placing.** 1. put out of place. 2. replace. —**dis•place'ment,** n.

dis•play', v., n. exhibit.

dis•please', v., **-pleased, -pleasing.** offend. —**dis•pleas'ure** (-plezh'-), n.

dis•pose', v., **-posed, -posing.** 1. arrange. 2. incline. 3. decide. 4. get rid. —**dis•pos'a•ble,** adj. —**dis•pos'al,** n.

dis'po•si'tion, n. 1. personality or mood. 2. tendency. 3. disposal.

dis'pos•sess', v. deprive of possession. —**dis'pos•ses'sion,** n.

dis'pro•por'tion, n. lack of proportion. —**dis'pro•por'tion•ate,** adj.

dis•prove', v., **-proved, -proving.** prove false.

dis•pute', v., **-puted, -puting,** n. —v. 1. argue or quarrel. —n. 2. argument; quarrel. —**dis•put'a•ble,** adj. —**dis•pu'tant,** adj., n. —**dis'pu•ta'tion,** n.

dis•qual'i•fy', v., **-fied, -fying.** make ineligible.

dis•qui'et, v. 1. disturb. —n. 2. lack of peace.

dis'qui•si'tion, n. formal discourse or treatise.

dis're•gard', v. 1. ignore. —n. 2. neglect.

dis're•pair', n. impaired condition.

dis're•pute', n. ill repute. —**dis•rep'u•ta•ble,** adj.

dis're•spect', n. lack of respect. —**dis're•spect'ful,** adj.

dis•robe', v., **-robed, -robing.** undress.

dis•rupt', v. break up. —**dis•rup'tion,** n. —**dis•rup'tive,** adj.

dis•sat'is•fy', v., **-fied, -fying.** make discontent. —**dis'sat•is•fac'tion,** n.

dis•sect', v. cut apart for examination. —**dis•sec'tion,** n.

dis•sem'ble, v., **-bled, -bling.** feign. —**dis•sem'bler,** n.

dis•sem'i•nate', v., **-nated, -nating.** scatter. —**dis•sem'i•na'tion,** n.

dis•sen'sion, n. 1. disagreement. 2. discord.

dis•sent', v. 1. disagree. —n. 2. difference of opinion. —**dis•sent'er,** n.

dis'ser•ta'tion, n. formal essay or treatise.

dis•serv'ice, n. harm or injury.

dis'si•dent, adj. 1. refusing to agree or conform. —n. 2. dissident person. —**dis'si•dence,** n.

dis•sim'i•lar, adj. not similar. —**dis•sim'i•lar'i•ty,** n.

dis•sim'u•late', v., **-lated, -lating.** disguise; dissemble. —**dis•sim'u•la'tion,** n.

dis'si·pate', v., -pated, -pating. 1. scatter. 2. squander. 3. live dissolutely. —**dis'si·pa'tion**, n.

dis·so'ci·ate', v., -ated, -ating. separate.

dis'so·lute', adj. immoral; licentious. —**dis'so·lute'ly**, adv.

dis·solve', v., -solved, -solving. 1. make solution of. 2. terminate. 3. destroy. —**dis'so·lu'tion**, n.

dis'so·nance, n. inharmonious or harsh sound. —**dis'so·nant**, adj.

dis·suade', v., -suaded, -suading. persuade against.

dis'taff, n. 1. staff for holding wool, flax, etc., in spinning. —adj. 2. of women.

dis'tance, n. 1. space between. 2. remoteness. 3. aloofness.

dis'tant, adj. 1. remote. 2. reserved. —**dis'tant·ly**, adv.

dis·taste', n. dislike; aversion. —**dis·taste'ful**, adj.

dis·tem'per, n. infectious disease of dogs and cats.

dis·tend', v. expand abnormally. —**dis·ten'tion**, n.

dis·till', v. 1. obtain by evaporation and condensation. 2. purify. 3. fall in drops. —**dis·till'er**, n. —**dis·till'er·y**, n.

dis·tinct', adj. 1. clear. 2. separate. —**dis·tinct'ly**, adv.

dis·tinc'tion, n. 1. act or instance of distinguishing. 2. discrimination. 3. difference. 4. eminence. —**dis·tinc'tive**, adj.

dis·tin'guish, v. 1. identify as different. 2. perceive. 3. make eminent.

dis·tort', v. 1. twist out of shape. 2. hide truth or true meaning of. —**dis·tor'tion**, n.

dis·tract', v. 1. divert attention of. 2. trouble. —**dis·trac'tion**, n.

dis·traught', adj. absent-minded or crazed with anxiety.

dis·tress', n. 1. pain or sorrow. 2. state of emergency. —v. 3. afflict with pain or sorrow.

dis·trib'ute, v., -uted, -uting. 1. divide in shares. 2. spread. 3. sort. —**dis'tri·bu'tion**, n. —**dis·trib'u·tor**, n.

dis'trict, n. 1. political division. 2. region.

district attorney, attorney for the government within a given district, whose job is primarily prosecuting.

dis·trust', v. 1. suspect. —n. 2. suspicion. —**dis·trust'ful**, adj.

dis·turb', v. 1. interrupt rest or peace of. 2. unsettle. —**dis·turb'ance**, n.

dis·use', n. absence of use.

ditch, n. trench; channel.

dith'er (diṯẖ' er), n. 1. flustered excitement or fear. —v. 2. fail to act resolutely; vacillate.

dit'to, n. pl. -tos, adv. —n. 1. the same. —adv. 2. as stated before.

ditto mark, mark (″) indicating repetition.

dit'ty, n. pl. -ties. simple song.

di·u·ret'ic, adj. promoting urination. —**di·u·ret'ic**, n.

di·ur'nal, adj. daily.

di'va (dē'və, -vä), n. prima donna (def. 1).

di'van, n. sofa.

dive, v., dived or dove, dived, diving, n. —v. 1. plunge into water. 2. plunge deeply. —n. 3. act of diving. —**div'er**, n.

di·verge', v., -verged, -verging. 1. move or lie in different directions. 2. differ. —**di·ver'gence**, n. —**di·ver'gent**, adj.

di'vers (dī'vərz), adj. various; sundry.

di·verse', adj. of different kinds or forms. —**di·ver'si·fy'**, v. —**di·ver'si·ty**, n. —**di·ver'si·fi·ca'tion**, n.

di·vert', v. 1. turn aside. 2. amuse. —**di·ver'sion**, n.

di·vest', v. deprive; dispossess.

di·vide', v., -vided, -viding. —v. 1. separate into parts. 2. apportion. —n. 3. zone separating drainage basins. —**di·vid'er**, n.

div'i·dend, n. 1. number to be divided. 2. share in profits.

di·vine', adj., n., v., -vined, -vining. —adj. 1. of or from God or a god. 2. religious. 3. godlike. —n. 4. theologian or clergyman. —v. 5. prophesy. 6. perceive. —**div'i·na'tion**, n.

di·vin'i·ty, n., pl. -ties. divine nature. 2. god.

di·vi'sion, n. 1. act or result of dividing. 2. thing that divides. 3. section. 4. military unit under major general. —**di·vis'i·ble**, adj. —**di·vi'sion·al**, adj. —**di·vi'sive**, adj.

di·vi'sor, n. number dividing dividend.

di·vorce', n., v., -vorced, -vorcing. —n. 1. dissolution of marriage. 2. separation. —v. 3. separate by divorce. —**di·vor'cee'** (-sē'), n.fem.

di·vulge', v., -vulged, -vulging. disclose.

Dix'ie (dik'sē), n. southern states of the U.S., esp. those that joined Confederacy.

diz'zy, adj., -zier, -ziest. 1. giddy. 2. confused. —**diz'zi·ness**, n.

D.J., disc jockey. Also, **DJ**, **deejay**.

DNA, deoxyribonucleic acid, substance that carries genes along its strands.

do, v., did, done, doing, n. —v. 1. perform; execute. 2. behave. 3. fare. 4. finish. 5. effect. 6. render. 7. suffice. —n. 8. *Informal.* social gathering. 9. (dō). first note of musical scale.

doc'ile (dos'al), adj. 1. readily taught. 2. tractable. —**do·cil'i·ty,** n.

dock, n. 1. wharf. 2. place for ship. 3. fleshy part of tail. 4. prisoner's place in courtroom. —v. 5. put into dock. 6. cut off end of. 7. deduct from (pay).

dock'et, n. 1. list of court cases. 2. label.

doc'tor, n. 1. medical practitioner. 2. holder of highest academic degree. —v. 3. treat medicinally.

doc'tri·naire', adj. traditional; orthodox.

doc'trine, n. 1. principle. 2. teachings. —**doc'tri·nal,** adj.

doc'u·ment, n. paper with information or evidence.

doc'u·men'ta·ry, adj., n., pl. -ries. —adj. 1. of or derived from documents. —n. 2. film or TV program on factual subject.

dod'der, v. shake; tremble; totter.

dodge, v., dodged, dodging. —v. 1. elude. —n. 2. act of dodging. 3. trick. —**dodg'er,** n.

do'do, n., pl. -dos, -does. extinct bird.

doe, n. female deer, etc. —**doe'skin',** n.

does (duz), v. third pers. sing. pres. indic. of **do.**

does'n't (duz'-), v. *Informal.* does not.

doff, v. remove.

dog, n., v., dogged, dogging. —n. 1. domesticated carnivore. —v. 2. follow closely.

dog'ged, adj. persistent.

dog'ger·el, n. bad verse.

dog'house', n. 1. shelter for dog. 2. place of disfavor.

dog'ma, n. system of beliefs; doctrine.

dog·mat'ic, adj. 1. of dogma. 2. opinionated. —**dog·mat'i·cal·ly,** adv.

dog'ma·tism', n. aggressive assertion of opinions.

dog'wood', n. flowering tree.

doi'ly, n., pl. -lies. small napkin.

dol'drums (dōl'-), n. pl. 1. flat calms at sea. 2. listless or depressed mood.

dole, n., v., doled, doling. —n. 1. portion of charitable gift. —v. 2. give out sparingly.

dole'ful, adj. sorrowful; gloomy. —**dole'ful·ly,** adv.

doll, n. 1. toy representing baby or other human being. 2. attractive or helpful or generous person.

dol'lar, n. monetary unit equal to 100 cents.

dol'ly, n., pl. -lies. 1. small, low cart or

truck for moving heavy loads. 2. movable platform, as for movie or television camera.

dol'or·ous, adj. grievous.

dol'phin, n. whalelike animal.

dolt, n. blockhead.

do·main', n. 1. ownership of land. 2. realm.

dome, n. spherical roof or ceiling.

do·mes'tic, adj. 1. of or devoted to the home. 2. not foreign. —n. 3. household servant. —**do·mes'ti·cal·ly,** adv.

do·mes'ti·cate', v., -cated, -cating. tame. —**do·mes'ti·ca'tion,** n.

domestic partner, unmarried person who cohabits with another and seeks benefits tax. available only to married couples.

dom'i·cile' (-sīl', -sal), n. home.

dom'i·nate', v., -nated, -nating. 1. rule. 2. tower above. —**dom'i·na'tion,** **dom'i·nance,** n. —**dom'i·nant,** adj.

dom·i·neer', v. rule oppressively.

do·min'ion, n. 1. power of governing. 2. territory governed.

dom'i·no', n., pl. -noes. oblong dotted piece used in game of dominoes.

don, v., donned, donning. put on.

do'nate, v., -nated, -nating. give. —**do·na'tion,** n.

don'key, n. 1. ass. 2. fool.

do'nor, n. giver.

doo'dle, v., -dled, -dling. make absent-minded drawings. —**doo'dler,** n.

doom, n. 1. fate. 2. ruin. 3. judgment. —v. 4. destine to trouble.

dooms'day', n. day the world ends; Judgment Day.

door, n. 1. movable barrier at entrance. 2. Also, **door'way'.** entrance. —**door'bell',** n. —**door'step',** n.

dope, n. 1. liquid substance used to prepare a surface. 2. *Informal.* narcotic. 3. *Slang.* information; news. 4. *Informal.* stupid person.

dop'ey, adj., -ier, -iest. *Informal.* 1. stupid; silly. 2. sluggish or confused, as from drug use. Also, **dop'y.**

dor'mant, adj. 1. asleep. 2. inactive. —**dor'man·cy,** n.

dor'mer, n. vertical window projecting from sloping roof.

dor'mi·to·ry, n., pl. -ries. group sleeping place.

dor'mouse', n., pl. -mice. small rodent.

dor'sal, adj. of or on the back.

do'ry, n., pl. -ries. flat-bottomed rowboat.

dose, n., v., dosed, dosing. —n. 1. quantity of medicine taken at one time. —v. 2. give doses to. —**dos'age**, n.

dos'si·er (dos'ē ā'), n. set of documents, as on criminal.

dot, n., v., **dotted**, **dotting**. —n. 1. small spot. —v. 2. mark with or make dots.

do'tard (dō'tärd), n. senile person.

dote, v., **doted**, **doting**. —v. 1. be overfond. 2. be senile. —**dot'age**, n.

dou'ble, adj., n., v., **-bled**, **-bling**. —adj. 1. twice as great, etc. 2. of two parts. 3. deceitful. —n. 4. double quantity. 5. duplicate. —v. 6. make or become double. 7. bend or fold. 8. turn back. —**doub'ly**, adv.

doub'le-cross', v. Informal. cheat or betray.

doub'le-dig'it, adj. involving two-digit numbers, esp. annual inflation rate of 10% or more.

doub'le·head'er, n. two games played on the same day in rapid succession.

double standard, moral standard that differs for two different persons or groups.

double take, delayed response, as to someone or something not immediately recognized or understood.

doub'le-talk', n. meaningless or evasive talk.

doubt (dout), v. 1. be uncertain about. —n. 2. uncertainty. —**doubt'less**, adv., adj.

doubt'ful, adj. 1. having doubts. 2. causing doubts or suspicion. —**doubt'ful·ly**, adv.

douche (dōōsh), n., v., **douched**, **douching**. —n. 1. jet of liquid, sometimes with cleansing agent, applied to a body part or cavity. —v. 2. apply a douche.

dough, n. mixture of flour, liquid, etc., for baking.

dough'nut, n. ringlike cake of fried, sweet dough. —**dough'nut·like'**, adj.

dour (dŏŏr, dour), adj. sullen.

douse, v., **doused**, **dousing**. 1. plunge; dip. 2. extinguish.

dove, n. pigeon.

dove'cote', n. structure for tame pigeons. Also, **dove'cot'**.

dove'tail', n. 1. tenon-and-mortise joint. —v. 2. join by dovetail. 3. fit together harmoniously.

dow'dy, adj. **-dier**, **-diest**. not elegant.

dow'el, n. wooden pin fitting into hole.

dow'er, n. widow's share of husband's property.

down, adv. 1. to, at, or in lower place

or state. 2. on or to ground. 3. on paper. —prep. 4. in descending direction. —n. 5. descent. 6. soft feathers. —v. 7. subdue. —**down'ward**, adv., **down'wards**, adv. —**down'ward**, adv., adv. —**down'y**, adj.

down'cast', adj. dejected.

down'er, n. Informal. 1. depressing or discouraging experience or person. 2. depressant or sedative drug.

down'fall', n. 1. ruin. 2. fall. —**down'fall'en**, adj.

down'grade', v. **-graded**, **-grading**. —v. 1. reduce in rank, classification, importance, etc. —n. 2. downward slope.

down'heart'ed, adj. dejected. —**down'heart'ed·ly**, adv.

down'hill', adv., adj. in downward direction.

down'pour', n. heavy rain.

down'right', adj. 1. thorough. —adv. 2. completely.

down'stairs', adv., adj. to or on lower floor.

down'stream', adv., adj. with current of stream.

Down syndrome, genetic disorder characterized by mental retardation, a wide, flattened skull, and slanting eyes. Also, **Down's syndrome**.

down'-to-earth', adj. objective; free of whims or fancies.

down'town', n. 1. central part of town. 2. of this part. —adv. 3. to or in this part.

down'trod'den, adj. tyrannized.

dow'ry, n., pl. **-ries**. bride's estate.

dox·ol'o·gy, n., pl. **-gies**. hymn praising God.

doze, v., **dozed**, **dozing**, n. —v. 1. sleep lightly. —n. 2. light sleep.

doz'en, n., pl. **dozen**, **dozens**. group of 12.

drab, n., adj., **drabber**, **drabbest**. —n. 1. dull brownish gray. —adj. 2. colored drab. 3. dull; uninteresting.

draft, n. 1. drawing; sketch. 2. preliminary version. 3. current of air. 4. haul. 5. swallow of liquid. 6. depth in water of a ship, etc. 7. selection for military service. 8. written request for payment. —v. 9. plan. 10. write. 11. enlist by draft. —**draft'y**, adj. —**draft·ee'**, n.

drafts'man, n. person who draws plans, etc.

drag, n., v., **dragged**, **dragging**. —v. 1. draw heavily; haul. 2. dredge. 3. trail on ground. 4. pass slowly. —n. 5. something used in dragging. 6. hindrance.

drag'net', n. 1. net dragged along bottom of river, etc. **2.** system for catching criminal.

drag'on, *n.* fabled winged reptile.

drag'on·fly', *n., pl.* **-flies.** large four-winged insect.

dra·goon', *n.* **1.** heavily armed mounted soldier, formerly common in European armies. —*v.* **2.** force; coerce.

drag race, race between automobiles accelerating from a standstill.

drain, *v.* **1.** draw or flow off gradually. **2.** empty; dry. **3.** exhaust. —*n.* **4.** channel or pipe for draining. —**drain'er,** *n.* —**drain'age,** *n.*

drake, *n.* male duck.

dram, *n.* **1.** apothecaries' weight, equal to 1/8 ounce. **2.** small drink of liquor.

dra'ma, *n.* **1.** story acted on stage. **2.** series of events with vivid elements.

dra·mat'ic, *adj.* **1.** of plays or theater. **2.** highly vivid. —**dra·mat'i·cal·ly,** *adv.*

dra·mat'ics, *n.* **1.** theatrical art. **2.** exaggerated conduct or emotion.

dram'a·tist, *n.* playwright.

dram'a·tize', *v.,* **-tized, -tizing.** put in dramatic form. —**dram'a·ti·za'tion,** *n.*

drape, *v.,* **draped, draping,** *n.* —*v.* **1.** cover with fabric. **2.** arrange in folds. —*n.* **3.** draped hanging. —**dra'per·y,** *n.*

dras'tic, *adj.* extreme. —**dras'ti·cal·ly,** *adv.*

draught (draft), *n. Brit.* draft.

draw, *v.,* **drew, drawn, drawing,** *n.* —*v.* **1.** pull; lead. **2.** take out. **3.** attract. **4.** sketch. **5.** take in. **6.** deduce. **7.** stretch. **8.** make or have as draft. —*n.* **9.** act of drawing. **10.** part that is drawn. **11.** equal score. **12.** *Informal.* attraction to public.

draw'back', *n.* disadvantage.

draw'bridge', *n.* bridge that can be drawn up.

draw'er, *n.* **1.** sliding compartment. **2.** (*pl.*) trouserlike undergarment. **3.** person who draws.

draw'ing, *n.* picture, esp. in lines.

drawl, *v.* **1.** speak slowly. —*n.* **2.** drawled utterance.

dray, *n.* low, strong cart. —**dray'man,** *n.*

dread, *v.* **1.** fear. —*n.* **2.** fear. **3.** awe. —*adj.* **4.** feared. **5.** revered.

dread'ful, *adj.* **1.** very bad. **2.** inspiring dread.

dread'ful·ly, *adv. Informal.* very.

dread'locks', *n.* hairstyle with many long, ropelike locks.

dream, *n.* **1.** ideas imagined during sleep. **2.** reverie. —*v.* **3.** have dream

(about). **4.** fancy. —**dream'er,** *n.* —**dream'y,** *adj.*

drear'y, *adj.,* **drearier, dreariest.** gloomy or boring.

dredge, *n., v.* **dredged, dredging.** —*n.* **1.** machine for moving earth at the bottom of river, etc. —*v.* **2.** use, or move with dredge. **3.** sprinkle with flour.

dregs, *n.pl.* sediment.

drench, *v.* soak.

dress, *n.* **1.** woman's garment. **2.** clothing. —*v.* **3.** clothe. **4.** ornament. **5.** prepare. **6.** treat (wounds). —**dress'mak·er,** *n.* —**dress'mak·ing,** *n.*

dress'er, *n.* **1.** bureau; chest of drawers. **2.** person who dresses another. **3.** person who dresses in a certain way.

dress'ing, *n.* **1.** sauce or stuffing. **2.** application for wound.

dress'y, *adj.,* **-ier, -iest.** fancy; stylish or formal.

drib'ble, *v.,* **-bled, -bling,** *n.* —*v.* **1.** fall in drops. **2.** bounce repeatedly. —*n.* **3.** trickling stream.

dri'er, *n.* dryer.

drift, *n.* **1.** deviation from set course. **2.** tendency. **3.** something driven, esp. into heap. —*v.* **4.** carry or be carried by currents.

drift'er, *n.* person who moves frequently from one place, home, etc., to another.

drill, *n.* **1.** boring tool. **2.** methodical training. **3.** furrow for seeds. **4.** sowing machine. **5.** strong twilled cotton. —*v.* **6.** pierce with drill. **7.** train methodically. —**drill'er,** *n.*

drink, *v.,* **drank, drunk, drinking,** *n.* —*v.* **1.** swallow liquid. **2.** swallow alcoholic liquids. —*n.* **3.** liquid for quenching thirst. **4.** alcoholic beverage. —**drink'er,** *n.*

drip, *v.,* **dripped, dripping.** **1.** fall or let fall in drops. **2.** act of dripping.

drive, *v.,* **drove, driven, driving,** *n.* —*v.* **1.** send by force. **2.** control; guide. **3.** convey or travel in vehicle. **4.** impel. —*n.* **5.** military offensive. **6.** strong effort. **7.** trip in vehicle. **8.** road for driving. —**driv'er,** *n.*

drive-in', *adj.* **1.** accommodating persons in automobiles. —*n.* **2.** a drive-in theater, bank, etc.

driv'el, *v.,* **-eled, -eling,** *n.* —*v.* **1.** let saliva flow from mouth. **2.** talk foolishly. —*n.* **3.** foolish talk.

drive'way', *n.* road on private property.

driz'zle, *v.,* **-zled, -zling,** *n.* rain in fine drops.

droll (drōl), *adj.* amusingly odd. —**droll′er•y,** *n.*

drom′e•dar′y, *n., pl.* **-daries.** one-humped camel.

drone, *v.* **droned, droning,** *n.* —*v.* 1. make humming sound. 2. speak dully. —*n.* 3. monotonous tone. 4. male of honeybee.

droop, *v.* 1. sink or hang down. 2. lose spirit. —*n.* 3. act of drooping. —**droop′y,** *adj.*

drop, *n., v.* **dropped, dropping.** —*n.* 1. small, spherical mass of liquid. 2. small quantity. 3. fall. 4. steep slope. —*v.* 5. let or let fall. 6. end; cease. 7. visit. —**drop′per,** *n.*

drop′out, *n.* student who quits before graduation.

drop′sy, *n.* excessive fluid in body.

dross, *n.* refuse.

drought (drout), *n.* dry weather. Also, **drouth.**

drove, *n.* 1. group of driven cattle. 2. crowd.

drown, *v.* suffocate by immersion in liquid.

drowse, *v.,* **drowsed, drowsing.** be sleepy. —**drow′sy,** *adj.*

drub, *v.,* **drubbed, drubbing.** 1. beat. 2. defeat.

drudge, *n., v.,* **drudged, drudging.** —*n.* 1. person doing hard, uninteresting work. —*v.* 2. do such work. —**drudg′er•y,** *n.*

drug, *n., v.,* **drugged, drugging.** —*n.* 1. therapeutic chemical. 2. narcotic. —*v.* 3. mix or affect with drug. —**drug′store,** *n.*

drug′gist, *n.* person who prepares drugs; pharmacist.

dru′id (drōō′id), *n.* (*often cap.*) member of a pre-Christian religious order in northwestern Europe. —**dru′id•ism,** *n.*

drum, *n., v.,* **drummed, drumming.** —*n.* 1. percussion musical instrument. 2. eardrum. —*v.* 3. beat on or as on drum. —**drum′mer,** *n.*

drum′stick′, *n.* 1. stick for beating a drum. 2. leg of a cooked fowl.

drunk, *adj.* intoxicated. Also, **drunk′en.**

drunk′ard, *n.* habitually drunk person.

dry, *adj.,* **drier, driest,** *v.,* **dried, drying.** —*adj.* 1. not wet. 2. rainless. 3. not yielding liquid. 4. thirsty. 5. dull; boring. 6. not expressing emotion. 7. not sweet. —*v.* 8. make or become dry. —**dry′ly,** *adv.* —**dry′ness,** *n.*

dry′-clean′, *v.* clean with solvents. —**dry′-clean′er,** *n.*

dry′er, *n.* machine for removing moisture.

dry ice, solid carbon dioxide, used esp. as a refrigerant.

dry run, rehearsal or trial.

du′al, *adj.* 1. of two. 2. double.

dub, *v.,* **dubbed, dubbing.** 1. name formally. 2. furnish (film or tape) with new sound track.

du′bi•ous, *adj.* doubtful.

du′cal, *adj.* of dukes.

duch′ess, *n.* 1. duke's wife. 2. woman equal in rank to duke.

duch′y (duch′ē), *n., pl.* **duchies.** 1. territory of duke. 2. small state.

duck, *v.* 1. plunge under water. 2. stoop or bend quickly. 3. avoid. —*n.* 4. act or instance of ducking. 5. swimming bird. 6. heavy cotton fabric. —**duck′ling,** *n.*

duck′bill′, *n.* small, egg-laying mammal.

duct, *n.* tube or canal in body.

duc′tile, *adj.* 1. readily stretched; compliant. —**duc•til′i•ty,** *n.*

dud, *n. Informal.* failure.

dude (dōōd, dyōōd), *n.* 1. man excessively concerned with his clothes; dandy. 2. *Slang.* fellow; guy. 3. urban vacationer on ranch.

dudg′eon, *n.* indignation.

due, *adj.* 1. payable. 2. proper. 3. attributable. 4. expected. —*n.* 5. something due. 6. (*sometimes pl.*) regularly payable fee for membership. —*adv.* 7. in a straight line.

du′el, *n., v.,* **-eled, -eling** —*n.* 1. prearranged combat between two persons. —*v.* 2. fight in duel. —**du′el•er, du′el•ist,** *n.*

du•et′, *n.* music for two performers.

duf′fel bag′, large, cylindrical canvas bag for carrying clothes and other belongings.

dug′out′, *n.* 1. boat made by hollowing a log. 2. roofed structure where baseball players sit when not on the field. 3. rough shelter dug in the ground, as by soldiers.

duke, *n.* 1. ruler of duchy. 2. nobleman below prince.

dul′ci•mer (dul′sə mər), *n.* musical instrument with metal strings.

dull, *adj.* 1. stupid. 2. not brisk. 3. tedious. 4. not sharp. 5. dim. —*v.* 6. make or become dull. —**dul′ly,** *adv.* —**dull′ness, dul′ness,** *n.*

du′ly, *adv.* 1. properly. 2. punctually.

dumb, *adj.* 1. temporarily unable to speak. 2. *Often Offensive.* lacking the power of speech. 3. stupid.

dumb′bell′, *n.* 1. weighted bar for exercising. 2. *Informal.* stupid person.

dum•found′, *v.* strike dumb with amazement. Also, **dumb•found′.**

dum′my, n., pl. **-mies,** adj. —n. 1. model or copy. 2. Informal. **a.** Offensive. mute. **b.** stupid person. —adj. 3. counterfeit.

dump, v. 1. drop heavily. 2. empty. —n. 3. place for dumping.

dump′ling, n. 1. mass of steamed dough. 2. dough wrapper with fruit or savory filling.

dump′y, adj., **dumpier, dumpiest.** squat. —**dump′i•ness,** n.

dun, v., **dunned, dunning,** n. —v. 1. demand payment of. —n. 2. demand for payment. 3. dull brown.

dunce, n. stupid person.

dune, n. sand hill formed by wind.

dung, n. manure; excrement.

dun′ga•ree′, n. coarse cotton fabric for work clothes (**dungarees**).

dun′geon, n. cell, esp. underground.

dunk, v. 1. dip in beverage before eating. 2. submerge briefly in liquid. 3. thrust (basketball) downward through basket.

du′o•de′num (dōō′ə dē′nəm), n. uppermost part of small intestine.

dupe, n., v., **duped, duping.** —n. 1. deceived person. —v. 2. deceive.

du′plex (dōō′pleks, dyōō-), n. 1. apartment with rooms on two floors. 2. house for two families.

du′pli•cate, adj., n., v., **-cated, -cating.** —adj. (-kit) 1. exactly like. 2. double. —n. (-kit). 3. copy. —v. (-kāt′). 4. copy. 5. double. —**du′pli•ca′tion,** n. —**du′pli•ca′tor,** n.

du•plic′i•ty (-plis′-), n., pl. **-ties.** deceitfulness.

du′ra•ble, adj. enduring. —**du′ra•bil′i•ty,** n. —**du′ra•bly,** adv.

du•ra′tion, n. continuance in time.

du•ress′, n. compulsion.

dur′ing, prep. in the course of.

dusk, n. dark twilight. —**dusk′y,** adj.

dust, n. 1. fine particles of earth, etc. 2. dead body. —v. 3. free from dust. 4. sprinkle. —**dust′y,** adj.

du′ti•ful, adj. doing one's duties. Also, **du′te•ous.** —**du′ti•ful•ly,** adv.

du′ty, n., pl. **-ties.** 1. moral or legal obligation. 2. function. 3. tax, esp. on imports.

dwarf, n. 1. abnormally small person, etc. —v. 2. make or make to seem small.

dwell, v., **dwelt** or **dwelled, dwelling.** 1. reside. 2. linger, esp. in words. —**dwell′ing,** n.

dwin′dle, v., **-dled, -dling.** shrink; lessen.

dye, n., v., **dyed, dyeing.** —n. 1. coloring material. —v. 2. color by wetting. —**dye′ing,** n. —**dy′er,** n.

dyke, n. dike.

dy•nam′ic, adj. 1. of force. 2. energetic. Also, **dy•nam′i•cal.** —**dy•nam′i•cal•ly,** adv. —**dyn′a•mism,** n.

dy′na•mite, n., v., **-mited, -miting.** —n. 1. powerful explosive. —v. 2. blow up with dynamite.

dy′na•mo, n., pl. **-mos.** machine for generating electricity.

dy′nas•ty (dī′-), n., pl. **-ties.** rulers of same family. —**dy•nas′tic,** adj.

dys′en•ter′y (dis′-), n. infectious disease of bowels.

dys•func′tion (dis fungk′shən), n. impaired or ineffective functioning. —**dys•func′tion•al,** adj.

dys•lex′i•a (dis lek′sē ə), n. impairment of ability to read. —**dys•lex′ic,** adj., n.

dys•pep′sia (dis pep′shə, -sē ə), n. indigestion. —**dys•pep′tic,** adj.

E

E, e, n. fifth letter of English alphabet.

each, adj., pron. 1. every one. —adv. 2. apiece.

ea′ger, adj. ardent. —**ea′ger•ly,** adv. —**ea′ger•ness,** n.

ea′gle, n. large bird of prey.

ea′gle-eyed′, adj. having unusually sharp eyesight.

ear, n. 1. organ of hearing. 2. grain-containing part of cereal plant.

ear′drum′, n. sensitive membrane in ear.

earl, n. nobleman ranking below marquis. —**earl′dom,** n.

ear′ly, adv., **-lier, -liest,** adj. 1. in first part of. 2. before usual time.

ear′mark′, n. 1. identifying mark. —v. 2. intend or designate.

earn, v. gain by labor or merit.

ear′nest, adj. 1. serious. —n. 2. portion given to bind bargain. —**ear′nest•ly,** adv.

earn′ings, n.pl. profits.

ear′ring′, n. ornament worn on ear lobe.

ear′shot′, n. hearing range.

earth, n. 1. planet we inhabit. 2. dry land. 3. soil.

earth′en, adj. made of clay or earth. —**earth′en•ware′,** n.

earth′ly, adj., **-lier, -liest.** of or in this world.

earth'quake', *n.* vibration of earth's surface.

earth'work', *n.* **1.** military construction formed chiefly of moved earth. **2.** work of art involving modification of large land area.

earth'worm', *n.* burrowing worm.

earth'y, *adj.*, **earthier, earthiest. 1.** practical; realistic. **2.** coarse; unrefined. —**earth'i•ness,** *n.*

ease, *n., v.,* **eased, easing.** —*n.* **1.** freedom from work, pain, etc. **2.** facility. —*v.* **3.** relieve.

ea'sel, *n.* standing support, as for picture.

ease'ment, *n.* right of one property owner to use land of another for some limited purpose.

east, *n.* **1.** direction from which sun rises. **2.** (*sometimes cap.*) region in this direction. —*adj.* **3.** toward, in, or from east. —**east'er•ly,** *adj., adv.* —**east'ern,** *adj.* —**east'ward,** *adv., adj.* —**East'ern•er,** *n.*

East'er, *n.* anniversary of resurrection of Christ.

eas'y, *adj.,* **easier, easiest. 1.** not difficult. **2.** at or giving ease. **3.** affording comfort. —**eas'i•ly,** *adv.* —**eas'i•ness,** *n.*

eas'y-go'ing, *adj.* **1.** casual; relaxed. **2.** lenient.

eat, *v.,* **ate, eating, eaten. 1.** take into the mouth and swallow. **2.** wear away or dissolve.

eaves, *n.pl.* overhanging edge of roof.

eaves'drop', *v.,* **-dropped, -dropping.** listen secretly. —**eaves'drop'per,** *n.*

ebb, *n.* **1.** fall of tide. **2.** decline. —*v.* **3.** flow back. **4.** decline.

eb'on•y, *n.* **1.** hard black wood. —*adj.* **2.** very dark.

e•bul'lient, *adj.* full of enthusiasm. —**e•bul'lience,** *n.*

ec•cen'tric (ik sen'-), *adj.* **1.** odd. **2.** off center. —*n.* **3.** odd person. —**ec'cen•tric'i•ty** (-tris'-), *n.*

ec•cle'si•as'tic, *n.* **1.** member of the clergy. —*adj.* Also, **ec•cle'si•as'ti•cal,** of church or clergy.

ech'e•lon (esh'-), *n.* level of command.

ech'o, *n., pl.* **echoes,** *v.,* **echoed, echoing.** —*n.* **1.** repetition of sound, esp. by reflection. —*v.* **2.** emit or repeat as echo.

é•clair', (ā-), *n.* cream- or custard-filled pastry.

é•clat' (ā klā'), *n.* **1.** brilliance, as of success. **2.** showy or elaborate display. **3.** acclaim.

ec•lec'tic, *adj.* chosen from various sources.

e•clipse', *n., v.,* **eclipsed, eclipsing.**

—*n.* **1.** obscuring of light of sun or moon by passage of body in front of it. **2.** oblivion. —*v.* **3.** obscure; darken.

e•clip'tic, *n.* apparent annual path of sun.

e'co•cide', *n.* widespread destruction of natural environment.

e•col'o•gy, *n.* science of relationship between organisms and environment. —**e•col'o•gist,** *n.* —**ec'o•log'i•cal,** *adj.*

e'co•nom'i•cal, *adj.* thrifty. —**e'co•nom'i•cal•ly,** *adv.*

e'co•nom'ics, *n.* production, distribution, and use of wealth. —**e'co•nom'ic,** *adj.* —**e•con'o•mist,** *n.*

e•con'o•mize', *v.,* **-mized, -mizing.** save; be thrifty.

e•con'o•my, *n., pl.* **-mies. 1.** thrifty management. **2.** system of producing and distributing weath.

ec'o•sys'tem (ek'-), *n.* distinct ecological system.

é•cru' (ā'krōō), *n.* light brown; beige. Also, **éc•ru** (ā'krōō).

ec'sta•sy, *n., pl.* **-sies. 1.** overpowering emotion. **2.** rapture. —**ec•stat'ic,** *adj.*

ec•u•men'i•cal, *adj.* **1.** universal. **2.** of or pertaining to movement for universal Christian unity. —**e•cu'men•ism,** *n.*

ec•ze'ma, *n.* itching disease of skin.

ed'dy, *n., pl.* **-dies,** *v.,* **-died, -dying.** —*n.* **1.** current at variance with main current. —*v.* **2.** whirl in eddies.

e•de'ma (i dē'mə), *n.* abnormal accumulation of fluid in tissue, cavities, or joints of body.

E'den, *n.* garden where Adam and Eve first lived; paradise.

edge, *n., v.,* **edged, edging.** —*n.* **1.** border; brink. **2.** cutting side. —*v.* **3.** border. **4.** move sidewise. —**edge'wise',** *adv.* —**edg'ing,** *n.*

edg'y, *adj.,* **edgier, edgiest.** nervous or tense.

ed'i•ble, *adj.* fit to be eaten. —**ed'i•bil'i•ty,** *n.*

e'dict, *n.* official decree.

ed'i•fice (-fis), *n.* building.

ed'i•fy', *v.,* **-fied, -fying.** instruct. —**ed'i•fi•ca'tion,** *n.*

ed'it, *v.* prepare for or direct publication of. —**ed'i•tor,** *n.*

e•di'tion, *n.* one of various printings of a book.

ed'i•to'ri•al, *n.* **1.** article in periodical presenting its point of view. —*adj.* **2.** of or written by editor.

ed'u•cate', *v.,* **-cated, -cating.** develop by instruction. —**ed'u•ca'-**

tion, n.   —**ed'u·ca'tion·al,** adj.
—**ed'u·ca'tor,** n.

eel, n. snakelike fish.

e'er, adv. Poetic. ever.

ee'rie, adj., **-rier, -riest.** weird.

ef·face', v., **-faced, -facing.** wipe out.
—**ef·face'ment,** n.

ef·fect', n. 1. result. 2. power to produce results. 3. operation. 4. (pl.) personal property. —v. 5. bring about.

ef·fec'tive, adj. 1. producing intended results. 2. actually in force.

ef·fec'tive·ly, adv. 1. in an effective way. 2. for all practical purposes.

ef·fec'tu·al, adj. 1. capable; adequate. 2. valid or binding.

ef·fem'i·nate, adj. (of a man) having feminine traits.

ef·fer·vesce', v., **-vesced, -vescing.** give off bubbles of gas. —**ef·fer·ves'cence,** n. —**ef·fer·ves'cent,** adj.

ef·fete' (i fēt'), adj. worn out.

ef·fi·ca'cious, adj. effective. —**ef'fi·ca·cy,** n.

ef·fi'cient, adj. acting effectively. —**ef·fi'cien·cy,** n. —**ef·fi'cient·ly,** adv.

ef'fi·gy, n., pl. **-gies.** visual representation of person.

ef'flu·ent (ef'lōō ant), n. 1. something that flows out. —adj. 2. flowing out.

ef'fort, n. 1. exertion of power. 2. attempt.

ef·fron'ter·y, n., pl. **-teries.** impudence.

ef·fu'sion, n. free expression of feelings. —**ef·fu'sive,** adj.

e·gal'i·tar'i·an, adj. having or wishing all persons equal in rights or status. —**e·gal'i·tar'i·an·ism,** n.

egg, n. 1. reproductive body produced by animals. —v. 2. encourage.

egg'head', n. Slang. impractical intellectual.

egg'nog', n. drink containing eggs, milk, etc.

egg'plant', n. purple, egg-shaped vegetable.

e'go, n. self.

e'go·ism, n. thinking only in terms of oneself. —**e'go·ist,** n. —**e'go·is'tic, e'go·is'ti·cal,** adj.

e'go·tism, n. vanity. —**e'go·tist,** n. —**e'go·tis'tic, e'go·tis'ti·cal,** adj.

e·gre'gious (i grē'jas), adj. flagrant.

e'gress, n. exit.

e'gret, n. kind of heron.

ei'der duck (ī'dar), large, northern sea duck yielding eiderdown.

eight, n., adj. seven plus one. —**eighth,** adj., n.

eight·een', n., adj. ten plus eight. —**eight·eenth',** adj., n.

eight'y, n., adj. ten times eight. —**eight'i·eth,** adj., n.

ei'ther (ē'thər, ī'thər), adj., pron. 1. one or the other of two. —conj. 2. (introducing an alternative.) —adv. 3. (after negative clauses joined by and, or, nor.)

e·jac'u·late', v., **-lated, -lating.** 1. exclaim. 2. discharge. —**e·jac'u·la'tion,** n.

e·ject', v. force out. —**e·jec'tion,** n.

eke, v., **eked, eking.** eke out, 1. supplement. 2. make (livelihood) with difficulty.

e·lab'o·rate, adj., v., **-rated, -rating.** —adj. (-ə rit). 1. done with care and detail. —v. (-ə rāt'). 2. supply details; work out. —**e·lab'o·ra'tion,** n.

é·lan' (ā län', ā läN'), n. lively zeal; dashing spirit.

e·lapse', v., **elapsed, elapsing.** (of time) pass; slip by.

e·las'tic, adj. 1. springy. —n. 2. material containing rubber. —**e·las'tic'i·ty** (-tis'-), n.

e·late', v., **elated, elating.** put in high spirits. —**e·la'tion,** n.

el'bow, n. 1. joint between forearm and upper arm. —v. 2. jostle.

elbow grease, hard work.

el'bow·room', n. space to move or work freely.

eld'er, adj. 1. older. —n. 2. older person. 3. small tree bearing clusters of **el'der·ber'ries.**

eld'er·ly, adj. rather old.

eld'est, adj. oldest; first-born.

e·lect', v. 1. select, esp. by vote. —adj. 2. selected. —n. 3. (pl.) persons chosen. —**e·lec'tion,** n. —**e·lec'tive,** adj.

e·lec'tion·eer', v. work for candidate in an election.

e·lec'tor·al college, body of special voters (electors) chosen to elect president and vice-president of U.S.

e·lec'tor·ate, n. voters.

e·lec·tri'cian, n. one who installs or repairs electrical systems.

e·lec·tric'i·ty (-tris'-), n. agency producing certain phenomena, as light, heat, attraction, etc. 2. electric current. —**e·lec'tric, e·lec'tri·cal,** adj. —**e·lec'tri·fy,** v.

e·lec·tro·car'di·o·gram', n. graphic record of heart action.

e·lec·tro·cute', v., **-cuted, -cuting.** kill by electricity. —**e·lec·tro·cu'tion,** n.

e·lec'trode, n. conductor through which current enters or leaves electric device.

e·lec·tro·en·ceph·a·lo·gram'   (i

lek′trō en sef′ə lə gram′), n. graphic record of brain action.

e•lec•trol′y•sis, n. decomposition by electric current. —e•lec′tro•lyt′ic, adj.

e•lec′tro•mag′net, n. device with iron or steel core made magnetic by electric current in surrounding coil.

e•lec•tro•mo′tive, adj. of or producing electric current.

e•lec′tron, n. minute particle supposed to be or contain a unit of negative electricity.

electronic mail, system for sending messages between computers. Also, e-mail.

e•lec•tron′ics, n. science dealing with development of devices involving flow of electrons. —e•lec•tron′ic, adj. —e•lec•tron′i•cal•ly, adv.

el•ee•mos′y•nar′y (el′ə-), adj. charitable.

el′e•gant, adj. luxurious or refined. —el′e•gance, n.

el′e•gy, n., pl. -gies. poem of mourning.

el′e•ment, n. 1. part of whole. 2. rudiment. 3. suitable environment. 4. (pl.) atmospheric forces. 5. substance that cannot be broken down chemically. 6. (pl.) bread and wine of the Eucharist. —el′e•men′tal, adj.

el•e•men•ta•ry, adj. of or dealing with elements or rudiments.

elementary school, school giving elementary instruction in six or eight grades.

el′e•phant, n. large mammal with long trunk and tusks.

el′e•vate′, v., -vated, -vating. 1. raise higher. 2. exalt.

el′e•va′tion, n. 1. elevated place. 2. height. 3. measured drawing of vertical face.

el′e•va′tor, n. 1. platform for lifting. 2. grain storage place.

e•lev′en, n., adj. ten plus one. —e•lev′enth, adj., n.

elf, n., pl. elves. tiny mischievous sprite. —elf′in, adj.

e•lic′it (i lis′-), v. draw forth; evoke.

e•lide′ (i līd′), v., -lided, -liding. 1. omit in pronunciation. 2. pass over; ignore. —e•li′sion (i lizh′ən), n.

el′i•gi•ble, adj. fit to be chosen; qualified. —el′i•gi•bil′i•ty, n.

e•lim′i•nate′, v., -nated, -nating. get rid of. —e•lim′i•na′tion, n.

e•lite′ (i lēt′), adj. 1. chosen or regarded as finest. —n. (sing. or pl.) elite group of persons.

e•lit′ism, n. discrimination in favor of an elite.

e•lix′ir, n. 1. preparation supposed to prolong life. 2. kind of medicine.

elk, n. large deer.

e•lipse′, n. closed plane curve forming regular oblong figure. —e•lip′ti•cal, adj.

e•lip′sis, n., pl. -ses. omission of word or words.

el′o•cu′tion, n. art of speaking in public.

e•lon′gate, v., -gated, -gating. lengthen. —e•lon′ga′tion, n.

e•lope′, v., eloped, eloping. run off with lover to be married. —e•lope′-ment, n.

el′o•quent, adj. fluent and forcible. —el′o•quence, n.

else, adv. 1. instead. 2. in addition. 3. otherwise.

else′where′, adv. somewhere else.

e•lu′ci•date′ (-lōō′sə-), v., -dated, -dating. explain.

e•lude′, v., eluded, eluding. 1. avoid cleverly. 2. baffle. —e•lu′sive, adj.

e•ma′ci•ate′ (-mā′shē-), v., -ated, -ating. make lean. —e•ma′ci•a′tion, n.

e′mail, n. electronic mail. Also, E-mail.

em′a•nate′, v., -nated, -nating. come forth. —em′a•na′tion, n.

e•man′ci•pate′, v., -pated, -pating. liberate. —e•man′ci•pa′tion, n. —e•man′ci•pa′tor, n.

e•mas′cu•late′, v., -lated, -lating. castrate.

em•balm′, v. treat (dead body) to prevent decay.

em•bank′ment, n. long earthen mound.

em•bar′go, n., pl. -goes. government restriction of movement of ships or goods.

em•bark′, v. 1. put or go on board ship. 2. start. —em′bar•ka′tion, n.

em•bar′rass, v. 1. make self-conscious or ashamed. 2. complicate. —em•bar′rass•ment, n.

em′bas′sy, n., pl. -sies. 1. ambassador and staff. 2. headquarters of ambassador.

em•bed′, v., -bedded, -bedding. fix in surrounding mass.

em•bel′lish, v. decorate. —em•bel′lish•ment, n.

em′ber, n. live coal.

em•bez′zle, v., -zled, -zling. steal (money entrusted). —em•bez′zle•ment, n. —em•bez′zler, n.

em•bit′ter, v. make bitter.

em•bla′zon, v. decorate, as with heraldic devices or emblems.

em'blem, *n.* symbol. —**em'blem·at'ic,** *adj.*

em·bod'y, *v.,* **-bodied, -bodying. 1.** put in concrete form. **2.** comprise. —**em·bod'i·ment,** *n.*

em'bo·lism, *n.* closing off of blood vessel, as by gas bubble or fat globule.

em·boss', *v.* ornament with raised design.

em·brace', *v.,* **-braced, -bracing,** *n.* —*v.* **1.** clasp in arms. **2.** accept willingly. **3.** include. —*n.* **4.** act of embracing.

em·broi'der, *v.* decorate with needlework. —**em·broi'der·y,** *n.*

em·broil', *v.* involve in strife. —**em·broil'ment,** *n.*

em'bry·o', *n., pl.* **-bryos.** organism in first stages of development. —**em'bry·on'ic,** *adj.*

em·cee' (em'sē')' *n., v.,* **-ceed, -ceeing.** —*n.* **1.** master of ceremonies; person who conducts an event, as a banquet. —*v.* **2.** serve as emcee.

e·mend', *v.* correct. —**e'men·da'tion,** *n.*

em'er·ald, *n.* green gem.

e·merge', *v.,* **emerged, emerging.** come forth or into notice. —**e·mer'gence,** *n.*

e·mer'gen·cy, *n., pl.* **-cies.** urgent occasion for action.

e·mer'i·tus, *adj.* retaining title after retirement.

em'er·y, *n.* mineral used for grinding, etc.

e·met'ic, *n.* medicine that induces vomiting.

em'i·grate', *v.,* **-grated, -grating.** leave one's country to settle in another. —**em'i·grant,** *n.* —**em'i·gra'tion,** *n.*

em'i·nence, *n.* high repute. —**em'i·nent,** *adj.*

em'is·sar'y, *n., pl.* **-saries.** agent on mission.

e·mit', *v.,* **emitted, emitting. 1.** send forth. **2.** utter.

e·mol'lient (i mol'yənt), *adj.* **1.** softening; soothing. —*n.* **2.** emollient substance.

e·mol'u·ment (-ya-), *n.* salary.

e·mo'tion, *n.* state of feeling. —**e·mo'tion·al,** *adj.*

em'pa·thy, *n.* sensitive awareness of another's feelings. —**em'pa·thize',** *v.*

em'per·or, *n.* ruler of empire. —**em'press,** *n.fem.*

em'pha·sis, *n., pl.* **-ses.** greater importance; stress. —**em·phat'ic,** *adj.* —**em'pha·size',** *v.*

em·phy·se'ma (em'fə sē'mə, -zē'-), *n.* chronic lung disease.

em'pire, *n.* nations under one ruler.

em·pir'i·cal (em pir'i kəl), *adj.* drawing on experience or observation only.

em·ploy', *v.* **1.** use or hire. —*n.* **2.** employment. —**em·ploy'ee,** *n.* —**em·ploy'er,** *n.* —**em·ploy'ment,** *n.*

em·po'ri·um, *n.* large store.

em·pow'er, *v.* **1.** authorize to act for one. **2.** enable.

emp'ty, *adj.,* **-tier, -tiest,** *v.,* **-tied, -tying.** —*adj.* **1.** containing nothing. —*v.* **2.** deprive of contents. **3.** become empty. —**emp'ti·ness,** *n.*

e'mu (ē'myōo), *n.* large flightless Australian bird.

em'u·late', *v.,* **-lated, -lating.** try to equal or excel. —**em'u·la'tion,** *n.*

e·mul'si·fy', *v.,* **-fied, -fying.** make into emulsion.

e·mul'sion, *n.* **1.** milklike mixture of liquids. **2.** light-sensitive layer on film.

en·a'ble, *v.,* **-bled, -bling.** give power, means, etc., to.

en·act', *v.* **1.** make into law. **2.** act the part of. —**en·act'ment,** *n.*

e·nam'el, *n., v.,* **-eled, -eling.** —*n.* **1.** glassy coating fused to metal, etc. **2.** paint giving an enamellike surface. **3.** outer surface of teeth. —*v.* **4.** apply enamel to.

en·am'or, *v.* cause to be in love.

en·camp', *v.,* settle in camp. —**en·camp'ment,** *n.*

en·cap'su·late', *v.,* **-lated, -lating.** place as if in a capsule; summarize; condense.

en·chant', *v.* bewitch; beguile; charm. —**en·chant'ment,** *n.*

en·chi·la'da, *n.* food consisting of a tortilla rolled around a filling, usu. with a chili-flavored sauce.

en·cir'cle, *v.,* **-cled, -cling.** surround.

en'clave, *n.* country, etc., surrounded by alien territory.

en·close', *v.,* **-closed, -closing. 1.** close in on all sides. **2.** put in envelope. —**en·clo'sure,** *n.*

en·code', *v.,* **-coded, -coding.** convert into code.

en·co'mi·um (-kō'-), *n., pl.* **-miums, -mia.** praise; eulogy.

en·com'pass, *v.* **1.** encircle. **2.** contain.

en'core, *interj.* **1.** again! bravo! —*n.* **2.** additional song, etc.

en·coun'ter, *v.* **1.** meet, esp. unexpectedly. —*n.* **2.** casual meeting. **3.** combat.

en·cour'age, *v.,* **-aged, -aging.** inspire or help. —en·cour·age·ment, n.

en·croach', v. trespass. —en·croach'ment, n.

en·cum·ber, v. impede; burden. —en·cum'brance, n.

en·cyc'li·cal (-sik'-), n. letter from Pope to bishops.

en·cy·clo·pe'di·a, n. reference book giving information on many topics. Also, en·cy·clo·pae'di·a. —en·cy·clo·pe'dic, adj.

end, n. 1. extreme or concluding part. 2. close. 3. purpose. 4. result. —v. 5. bring or come to an end. 6. result. —end'less, adj.

en·dan'ger, v. expose to danger.

en·dear', v. make beloved. —en·dear'ment, n.

en·deav'or, v., n. attempt.

en·dem'ic, adj. belonging or confined to a particular people or place.

end'ing, n. close.

en'dive, n. plant for salad.

en'do·crine (en'də krin, -krīn'), adj. 1. secreting internally into the blood or lymph. 2. of glands involved in such secretion.

en·dorse', v., -dorsed, -dorsing. 1. approve or support. 2. sign on back of (a check, etc.). —en·dorse'ment, n.

en·dow', v. 1. give permanent fund to. 2. equip. —en·dow'ment, n.

en·dure', v., -dured, -during. 1. tolerate. 2. last. —en·dur'a·ble, adj. —en·dur'ance, n.

en·e'ma, n. liquid injection into rectum.

en'e·my, n., pl. -mies. adversary; opponent.

en'er·gy, n., pl. -gies. capacity for activity; vigor. —en·er·get'ic, adj.

en'er·vate', v., -vated, -vating. weaken.

en·fee'ble, v., -bled, -bling. weaken.

en·fold', v. wrap around.

en·force', v., -forced, -forcing. compel obedience to. —en·force'ment, n.

en·fran'chise, v., -chised, -chising. admit to citizenship.

en·gage', v., -gaged, -gaging. 1. occupy. 2. hire. 3. please. 4. betroth. 5. interlock with. 6. enter into conflict with. —en·gage'ment, n.

en·gen'der (-jen'-), v. cause.

en'gine, n. 1. machine for converting energy into mechanical work. 2. locomotive.

en·gi·neer', n. 1. expert in engineering. 2. engine operator. —v. 3. contrive.

en·gi·neer'ing, n. art of practical application of physics, chemistry, etc.

Eng'lish, n. language of the people of England, Australia, the U.S., etc. —Eng'lish, adj. —Eng'lish·man, n. —Eng'lish·wom'an, n.fem.

en·grave', v., -graved, -graving. cut into hard surface for printing. —en·grav'er, n. —en·grav'ing, n.

en·gross', v. occupy wholly.

en·gulf', v. swallow up.

en·hance', v., -hanced, -hancing. increase.

e·nig'ma, n. something puzzling. —en·ig·mat'ic, adj.

en·join', v. prohibit.

en·joy', v. find pleasure in or for. —en·joy'a·ble, adj. —en·joy'ment, n.

en·large', v., -larged, -larging. make or grow larger. —en·large'ment, n.

en·light'en, v. impart knowledge to. —en·light'en·ment, n.

en·list', v. enroll for service. —en·list'ment, n.

en·liv'en, v. make active.

en masse' (än mas', äN), in a mass; all together.

en'mi·ty, n. hatred.

en·nui' (än·wē'), n. boredom.

e·nor'mi·ty, n., pl. -ties. 1. extreme wickedness. 2. grievous crime; atrocity.

e·nor'mous, adj. huge; gigantic.

e·nough', adj. 1. adequate. —n. 2. adequate amount. —adv. 3. sufficiently.

en·quire', v., -quired, -quiring. inquire. —en·quir'y, n.

en·rage', v., -raged, -raging. make furious.

en·rich', v. make rich or better. —en·rich'ment, n.

en·roll', v. take into group or organization. —en·roll'ment, n.

en route (än rōōt'), on the way.

en·sem'ble (än säm'bəl), n. assembled whole.

en·sconce' (en skons'), v., -sconced, -sconcing. settle securely or snugly.

en·shrine', v., -shrined, -shrining. cherish.

en'sign (-sīn; Mil. -sən), n. 1. flag. 2. lowest commissioned naval officer.

en·slave', v., -slaved, -slaving. make slave of. —en·slave'ment, n.

en·sue', v., -sued, -suing. follow.

en·sure', v., -sured, -suring. make certain; secure.

en·tail', v. involve.

en·tan'gle, v., -gled, -gling. involve; entrap. —en·tan'gle·ment, n.

en·tente' (än tänt'), n. 1. international agreement on policy. 2. alliance of parties to an entente.

en•ter, v. 1. come or go in. 2. begin. 3. record.

en•ter•prise, n. 1. project. 2. initiative.

en•ter•pris•ing, adj. showing initiative.

en•ter•tain, v. 1. amuse. 2. treat as guest. 3. hold in mind. —**en•ter•tain•er**, n. —**en•ter•tain•ment**, n.

en•thrall, v. 1. hold by fascination; captivate. 2. enslave.

en•thu•si•asm, n. lively interest. —**en•thu•si•as•tic**, adj.

en•tice, v., -ticed, -ticing. lure. —**en•tice•ment**, n.

en•tire, adj. whole. —**en•tire•ly**, adv. —**en•tire•ty**, n.

en•ti•tle, v., -tled, -tling. permit (one) to claim something.

en•ti•ty, n., pl. -ties. real or whole thing.

en•tomb, v. bury.

en•to•mol•o•gy, n. study of insects. —**en•to•mol•o•gist**, n.

en•tou•rage (än'tŏŏ räzh'), n. group of personal attendants.

en•trails, n.pl. internal parts of body, esp. intestines.

en•trance, n., v., -tranced, -trancing. —n. (en'trans). 1. act of entering. 2. place for entering. 3. admission. —v. (en trans'). 4. charm.

en•trap, v., -trapped, -trapping. 1. catch in a trap. 2. entice into guilty situation. —**en•trap•ment**, n.

en•treat, v. implore.

en•treat•y, n., pl. -ies. earnest request.

en•tree (än'trā), n. 1. main dish of meal. 2. privilege of entering; access.

en•trench, v. fix in strong position.

en•tre•pre•neur (än'trə prə nûr'), n. independent business manager.

en•trust, v. give in trust.

en•try, n., pl. -tries. 1. entrance. 2. recorded statement, etc. 3. contestant.

e•nu•mer•ate, v., -ated, -ating. list; count. —**e•nu•mer•a•tion**, n.

e•nun•ci•ate (-sē-), v., -ated, -ating. say distinctly. —**e•nun•ci•a•tion**, n.

en•vel•op, v. wrap; surround. —**en•vel•op•ment**, n.

en•ve•lope, n. 1. covering for letter. 2. covering; wrapper.

en•vi•ron•ment, n. surrounding things, conditions, etc.

en•vi•ron•men•tal•ist, n. person working to protect environment from pollution or destruction.

en•vi•rons, n.pl. outskirts.

en•vis•age, v., -aged, -aging. form mental picture of. Also, **en•vi•sion**.

en•voy, n. 1. diplomatic agent. 2. messenger.

en•vy, n., pl. -vies, v., -vied, -vying. —n. 1. discontent at another's good fortune. 2. thing coveted. —v. 3. regard with envy. —**en•vi•a•ble**, adj. —**en•vi•ous**, adj.

en•zyme (-zīm), n. bodily substance capable of producing chemical change in other substances.

e'on, n. long period of time.

ep•au•let (ep'ə-), n. shoulder piece worn on uniform. Also, **ep'au•lette**.

e•phem•er•al, adj. short-lived.

ep•ic, adj. 1. describing heroic deeds. —n. 2. epic poem.

ep•i•cen•ter, n. point directly above true center of earthquake.

ep•i•cure, n. connoisseur of food and drink. —**ep•i•cu•re•an**, adj., n.

ep•i•dem•ic, adj. 1. affecting many persons at once. —n. 2. epidemic disease.

ep•i•der•mis, n. outer layer of skin.

ep•i•glot•tis, n. thin structure that covers larynx during swallowing.

ep•i•gram, n. terse, witty statement. —**ep•i•gram•mat•ic**, adj.

ep•i•lep•sy, n. nervous disease often marked by convulsions. —**ep•i•lep•tic**, adj., n.

ep•i•logue, n. concluding part or speech.

e•piph•a•ny, n. 1. act of showing oneself; appearance. 2. sudden perception or realization. 3. (cap.) festival, Jan. 6, commemorating the Wise Men's visit to Christ.

e•pis•co•pa•cy, n., pl. -cies. church government by bishops.

e•pis•co•pal, adj. 1. governed by bishops. 2. (cap.) designating Anglican Church or branch of it. —**E•pis•co•pa•lian**, n., adj.

ep•i•sode, n. incident. —**ep•i•sod•ic**, adj.

e•pis•tle, n. letter.

ep•i•taph, n. inscription on tomb.

ep•i•thet, n. descriptive term for person or thing.

e•pit•o•me, n. 1. summary. 2. typical specimen. —**e•pit•o•mize**, v.

e plu•ri•bus u'num, Latin. out of many, one (motto of the U.S.).

ep•och (ep'ək), n. distinctive period of time.

ep•ox•y, n., pl. -ies. tough synthetic resin, used in glues, etc.

eq•ua•ble, adj. even; temperate. —**eq•ua•bly**, adv.

e'qual, adj., n., v., equaled, equaling. —adj. 1. alike in quantity, rank, size, etc. 2. uniform. 3. adequate. —n. 4. one that is used to. —v. 5. be equal to. —**e·qual'i·ty**, n. —**e'qual·ize**, v. —**e'qual·ly**, adv.

e·quan·im·i·ty, n. calmness.

e·quate', v., **equated**, **equating**. make or consider as equal.

e·qua'tion, n. expression of equality of two quantities.

e·qua'tor, n. imaginary circle around earth midway between poles. —**e·qua·to'ri·al**, adj.

e·ques'tri·an, adj. 1. of horse riders or horsemanship. —n. 2. Also, fem. **e·ques'tri·enne'**. horse rider.

e·qui·dis'tant, adj. equally distant.

e·qui·lat'er·al, adj. having all sides equal.

e·qui·lib'ri·um, n., pl. **-riums, -ria**. balance.

e'quine, adj. of horses.

e'qui·nox', n. time when night and day are of equal length. —**e'qui·noc'tial**, adj.

e·quip', v., **equipped**, **equipping**. furnish; provide. —**e·quip'ment**, n.

eq'ui·ta·ble, adj. just; fair. —**eq'ui·ta·bly**, adv.

eq'ui·ty, n., pl. **-ties**. 1. fairness. 2. share.

e·quiv'a·lent, adj., n. equal.

e·quiv'o·cal, adj. 1. ambiguous. 2. questionable.

e·quiv'o·cate', v., **-cated, -cating**. express oneself ambiguously or indecisively. —**e·quiv·o·ca'tion**, n.

e'ra, n. period of time.

e·rad'i·cate', v., **-cated, -cating**. remove completely. —**e·rad·i·ca'tion**, n.

e·rase', v., **erased, erasing**. rub out. —**e·ras'er**, n. —**e·ra'sure**, n.

ere, prep., conj. Archaic. before.

e·rect', adj. 1. upright. —v. 2. build. —**e·rec'tion**, n. 1. something erected. 2. erect state of an organ, as the penis. —**e·rec'tile** (i rek'tl, -til, -tīl), adj.

er'mine, n. kind of weasel.

e·rode', v., **eroded, eroding**. wear away. —**e·ro'sion**, n.

e·rog'e·nous (i roj'ə nəs), adj. sensitive to sexual stimulation.

e·rot'ic, adj. 1. of sexual love. 2. arousing sexual desire. —**e·rot'i·cal·ly**, adv. —**e·rot'i·cism**, n.

e·rot'i·ca, n.pl. erotic literature and art.

err (ûr), v. 1. be mistaken. 2. sin.

er'rand, n. special trip.

er'rant, adj. roving.

er·rat'ic, adj. uncontrolled or irregular.

er·ro'ne·ous, adj. incorrect.

er'ror, n. 1. mistake. 2. sin.

er·satz' (er zäts'), n., adj. substitute.

erst'while', adj. former.

er'u·dite', adj. learned. —**er'u·di'tion**, n.

e·rupt', v. burst forth. —**e·rup'tion**, n.

er'y·sip'e·las, n. infectious skin disease.

es'ca·late', v., **-lated, -lating**. increase in intensity or size. —**es·ca·la'tion**, n.

es'ca·la'tor, n. moving stairway.

es'ca·pade', n. wild prank.

es·cape', v., **-caped, -caping**. —v. 1. get away. 2. elude. —n. 3. act or means of escaping. —**es·cap'ee**, n.

es·cape'ment, n. part of clock that controls speed.

es·cap'ism, n. attempt to forget reality through fantasy. —**es·cap'ist**, n., adj.

es·chew', v. avoid.

es'cort, n. (es'kôrt). 1. accompanying person or persons for guidance, courtesy, etc. —v. (es kôrt'). 2. accompany as escort.

es'crow, n. legal contract kept by third person until its provisions are fulfilled.

es·cutch'eon, n. coat of arms.

ESL, English as a second language.

e·soph'a·gus, n., pl. **-gi**. tube connecting mouth and stomach.

es·o·ter'ic, adj. intended for select few.

es·pe'cial, adj. special. —**es·pe'cial·ly**, adv.

Es·pe·ran'to, n. artificial language based on major European languages.

es'pi·o·nage' (-näzh', -nij), n. work or use of spies.

es'pla·nade' (es'plə näd', -näd'), n. open level space, as for public walks.

es·pouse', v., **-poused, -pousing**. 1. advocate. 2. marry. —**es·pous'al**, n.

es·pres'so, n. strong coffee made with steam.

es·py', v., **-pied, -pying**. catch sight of.

Es·quire', n. Brit. title of respect after man's name. Abbr.: Esq.

es'say, n. 1. short nonfiction work. 2. attempt. —v. (e sā'). 3. try.

es'say·ist, n. writer of essays.

es'sence, n. 1. intrinsic nature. 2. concentrated form of substance or thought.

es·sen'tial, adj. 1. necessary. —n. 2. necessary thing.

es·sen'tial·ly, adv. basically; necessarily.

es·tab'lish, v. 1. set up permanently. 2. prove.

es·tab'lish·ment, n. 1. act of establishing. 2. institution or business. 3.

(*often cap.*) group controlling government and social institutions.

es•tate′, *n.* **1.** landed property. **2.** one's possessions.

es•teem′, *v.* **1.** regard. —*n.* **2.** opinion.

es′ter, *n.* chemical compound produced by reaction between an acid and an alcohol.

es′thete, *n.* aesthete.

es′ti•ma•ble, *adj.* worthy of high esteem.

es′ti•mate′, *v.,* -mated, -mating, *n.* —*v.* (-māt′). **1.** calculate roughly. —*n.* (es′tə mit). **2.** rough calculation. **3.** opinion. —**es′ti•ma′tion**, *n.*

es•trange′, *v.,* -tranged, -tranging. alienate.

es′tro•gen (es′trə jən), *n.* any of several female sex hormones.

es′tu•ar′y, *n., pl.* -aries. part of river affected by sea tides.

et cet′er•a (set′-), and so on. *Abbr.* etc.

etch, *v.* cut design into (metal, etc.) with acid. —**etch′ing**, *n.*

e•ter′nal, *adj.* **1.** without beginning or end. —*n.* **2.** (*cap.*) God. —**e•ter′ni•ty**, *n.* —**e•ter′nal•ly**, *adv.*

e′ther, *n.* **1.** colorless liquid used as an anesthetic. **2.** upper part of space.

e•the′re•al, *adj.* **1.** delicate. **2.** heavenly.

eth′ics, *n.pl.* principles of conduct. —**eth′i•cal**, *adj.* —**eth′i•cal•ly**, *adv.*

eth′nic, *adj.* **1.** sharing a common culture. —*n.* **2.** member of minority group.

eth•nic′i•ty, *n.* ethnic traits or association.

e′thos (ē′thos, eth′os), *n.* distinguishing character or spirit of person, group, or culture.

eth′yl, *n.* fluid containing lead, added to gasoline.

e′ti•ol′o•gy (ē′tē ol′ə jē), *n., pl.* -gies. **1.** study of causes, esp. of diseases. **2.** cause or origin, esp. of a disease.

et′i•quette′, *n.* conventions of social behavior.

é•tude′ (ā′tōōd, ā′tyōōd), *n.* musical composition played to improve technique but also for its artistic merit.

et′y•mol′o•gy, *n., pl.* -gies. history of word or words.

eu•ca•lyp′tus, *n., pl.* -ti. Australian tree.

Eu′cha•rist′ (ū′kə-), *n.* Holy Communion.

eu•gen′ics, *n.* science of improving human race.

eu′lo•gy, *n., pl.* -gies. formal praise. —**eu′lo•gize′**, *v.*

eu′nuch (-nək), *n.* castrated man.

eu′phe•mism, *n.* substitution of mild expression for blunt one. —**eu′phe•mis′tic**, *adj.*

eu•pho′ny, *n., pl.* -nies. pleasant sound. —**eu•pho′ni•ous**, *adj.*

eu•pho′ri•a (yōō fôr′ē ə), *n.* strong feeling of happiness or well-being. —**eu•phor′ic**, *adj.*

Eur•a′sian, *adj.* of or originating in both Europe and Asia, or in the two considered as one continent.

eu•re′ka (yōō rē′kə, yə-), *interj.* exclamation of triumph at a discovery.

Eu•ro•pe′an, *n.* native of Europe. —**Eu•ro•pe′an**, *adj.*

eu′tha•na′sia, *n.* mercy killing.

e•vac′u•ate′, *v.,* -ated, -ating. **1.** vacate; empty. **2.** remove. **3.** help to flee. —**e•vac′u•a′tion**, *n.*

e•vade′, *v.,* evaded, evading. avoid or escape from by cleverness. —**e•va′sion**, *n.* —**e•va′sive**, *adj.*

e•val′u•ate′, *v.,* -ated, -ating. appraise. —**e•val′u•a′tion**, *n.*

e•van•gel′i•cal, *adj.* **1.** of or in keeping with Gospel. **2.** of those Protestant churches that stress personal conversion through faith.

e•van′ge•list, *n.* **1.** preacher. **2.** One of the writers of Gospel. —**e•van′ge•lism**, *n.* —**e•van′ge•lize′**, *v.*

e•vap′o•rate′, *v.,* -rated, -rating. change into or pass off as vapor. —**e•vap′o•ra′tion**, *n.*

eve, *n.* evening before.

e′ven, *adj.* **1.** smooth. **2.** uniform. **3.** equal. **4.** divisible by 2. **5.** calm. —*adv.* **6.** hardly. **7.** indeed. —*v.* **8.** make even. —**e′ven•ly**, *adv.* —**e′ven•ness**, *n.*

eve′ning, *n.* early part of night; end of day.

e•vent′, *n.* anything that happens. —**e•vent′ful**, *adj.*

e•ven′tu•al, *adj.* final. —**e•ven′tu•al•ly**, *adv.*

e•ven′tu•al′i•ty, *n., pl.* -ties. possible event.

ev′er, *adv.* at all times.

ev′er•green′, *adj.* **1.** having leaves always green. —*n.* **2.** evergreen plant.

ev′er•last′ing, *adj.* lasting forever or indefinitely.

ev′er•y, *adj.* **1.** each. **2.** all possible. —**ev′er•y•bod′y, ev′er•y•one′**, *pron.* —**ev′er•y•thing′**, *pron.* —**ev′er•y•where′**, *adv.* —**ev′er•y•day′**, *adj.*

e•vict′, *v.* remove from property by law. —**e•vic′tion**, *n.*

ev′i•dence, *n., v.,* -denced, -dencing. —*n.* **1.** grounds for belief. —*v.* **2.** prove.

ev′i•dent, *adj.* clearly so. —**ev′i•dent•ly**, *adv.*

e′vil, *adj.* **1.** wicked. **2.** unfortunate. —**e′vil•ly**, *adv.*

e•vince', v., evinced, evincing. 1. prove. 2. show.

e•vis'cer•ate' (i vis'ə rāt', v., -ated, -ating. 1. remove entrails of. 2. deprive of vital or essential parts.

e•voke', v., evoked, evoking. call forth.

e•volve', v., evolved, evolving. develop gradually. —ev'o•lu'tion, n.

ewe (yōō), n. female sheep.

ew'er, n. wide-mouthed pitcher.

ex•ac'er•bate' (ig zas'ər bāt', ek sas'-), v., -bated, -bating. make more severe, bitter, or violent.

ex•act', adj. 1. precise; accurate. —v. 2. demand; compel. —ex•act'ly, adv. —ex•act'ing, adj. severe.

ex•ag'ger•ate', v., -ated, ating. magnify beyond truth. —ex•ag'ger•a'-tion, n.

ex•alt', v. 1. elevate. 2. extol. —ex'al-ta'tion, n.

ex•am'ine, v., -ined, -ining. 1. investigate. 2. test. 3. interrogate. —ex-am'i•na'tion, n. —ex•am'in•er, n.

ex•am'ple, n. 1. typical one. 2. model. 3. illustration.

ex•as'per•ate', v., -ated, -ating. make angry. —ex•as'per•a'tion, n.

ex•ca•vate', v., -vated, -vating. 1. dig out. 2. unearth. —ex•ca•va'tion, n.

ex•ceed', v. go beyond; surpass.

ex•ceed'ing•ly, adv. very.

ex•cel', v., -celled, -celling. be superior (to).

ex'cel•len•cy, n., pl. -cies. 1. (cap.) title of honor. 2. excellence.

ex'cel•lent, adj. remarkably good. —ex'cel•lence, n.

ex•cel'si•or, n. fine wood shavings.

ex•cept', prep. 1. Also, ex•cept'ing. excluding. —v. 2. exclude. 3. object. —ex•cep'tion, n.

ex•cep'tion•a•ble, adj. causing objections.

ex•cep'tion•al, adj. unusual. —ex-cep'tion•al•ly, adv.

ex'cerpt, n. (ek'sûrpt). 1. passage from longer writing. —v. (ik sûrpt', ek'sûrpt). 2. take (passage) from book, film, etc.

ex•cess', n. (ik ses'). 1. amount over that required. —adj. (ek'ses). 2. more than necessary, usual, or desirable. —ex•ces'sive•ly, adv.

ex•change', v., -changed, -changing. n. —v. 1. change for something else. —n. 2. act of exchanging. 3. thing exchanged. 4. trading place. —ex-change'a•ble, adj.

ex•cheq'uer, n. Brit. treasury.

ex•cise', n., -cised, -cising. —n. (ek'sīz). 1. tax on certain goods. —v. (ik sīz'). 2. cut out. —ex•ci'sion, n.

ex•cite', v., -cited, -citing. 1. stir up (emotions, etc.). 2. cause. —ex•cit'-a•ble, adj. —ex•cite'ment, n.

ex•claim', v. cry out. —ex'cla•ma'-tion, n.

ex•clude', v., -cluded, -cluding. shut out. —ex•clu'sion, n.

ex•clu'sive, adj. 1. belonging or pertaining to one. 2. excluding others. 3. stylish; chic. —ex•clu'sive•ly, adv.

ex•com•mu'ni•cate', v., -cated, -cating. cut off from membership. —ex•com•mu'ni•ca'tion, n.

ex•co'ri•ate', v., -ated, ating. denounce. —ex•co'ri•a'tion, n.

ex'cre•ment, n. bodily waste matter.

ex•cres'cence, n. abnormal growth. —ex•cres'cent, adj.

ex•crete', v., -creted, -creting. eliminate from body. —ex•cre'tion, n. —ex'cre•to'ry, adj.

ex•cru'ci•at•ing (ik skrōō'shē ā'ting), adj. 1. causing intense suffering. 2. intense or extreme.

ex'cul•pate', v., -pated, -pating. free of blame. —ex'cul•pa'tion, n.

ex•cur'sion, n. short trip.

ex•cuse', v., -cused, -cusing. —v. (ik skyōōz'). 1. pardon. 2. apologize for. 3. justify. 4. seek or grant release. —n. (ik skyōōs'). 5. reason for being excused.

ex'e•crate', v., -crated, -crating. 1. abominate. 2. curse. —ex'e•cra•ble, adj.

ex'e•cute', v., -cuted, -cuting. 1. do. 2. kill legally. —ex'e•cu'tion, n. —ex'e•cu'tion•er, n.

ex•ec'u•tive, adj. 1. responsible for directing affairs. —n. 2. administrator.

ex•ec'u•tor, n. person named to carry out provisions of a will. —ex-ec'u•trix, n. fem.

ex•em'pla•ry, adj. 1. worthy of imitation. 2. warning.

ex•em'pli•fy', v., -fied, -fying. show or serve as example. —ex•em'pli•fi•ca'tion, n.

ex•empt', v., adj. free from obligation. —ex•emp'tion, n.

ex'er•cise', n., v., -cised, -cising. —n. 1. action to increase skill or strength. 2. performance. 3. (pl.) ceremony. —v. 4. put through exercises. 5. use.

ex•ert', v. put into action. —ex•er'-tion, n.

ex•hale', v., -haled, -haling. breathe out. —ex'ha•la'tion, n.

ex•haust', v. 1. use up. 2. fatigue

greatly. —n. 3. used gases from engine. —ex•haus'tion, n.

ex•hib'it, v., n. show; display. —ex•hi•bi'tion, n.

ex•hi•bi'tion•ism', n. desire or tendency to display onself. —ex•hi•bi'tion•ist, n.

ex•hil'a•rate', v., -rated, -rating. cheer; stimulate. —ex•hil•a•ra'tion, n.

ex•hort', v. advise earnestly. —ex'hor•ta'tion, n.

ex•hume' (ig zyōom'), v., -humed, -huming. dig up dead body, etc.

ex'i•gen•cy, n., pl. -cies. urgent requirement. —ex'i•gent, adj.

ex'ile, n., v., -iled, -iling. —n. 1. enforced absence from one's country or home. 2. one so absent. —v. 3. send into exile.

ex•ist', v. be; live. —ex•ist'ence, n. —ex•ist'ent, adj.

ex•is•ten'tial, adj. of human life; based on or concerning experience.

ex•is•ten'tial•ism, n. philosophy that stresses personal liberty and responsibility. —ex•is•ten'tial•ist, n.

ex'it, n. 1. way out. 2. departure. —v. 3. leave.

ex'o•dus, n. departure.

ex of•fi'ci•o (-fish'ē-ō), because of the office one holds.

ex•on'er•ate', v., -ated, -ating. free of blame. —ex•on•er•a'tion, n.

ex•or'bi•tant (ig zôr'bi tant), adj. excessive, esp. in cost. —ex•or'bi•tance, n.

ex'or•cise', v., -cised, -cising. expel (evil spirit). —ex'or•cism', n.

ex•ot'ic, adj. foreign; alien.

ex•pand', v. increase; spread out. —ex•pan'sion, n. —ex•pan'sive, adj.

ex•panse', n. wide extent.

ex•pa'ti•ate' (-pā'shē-), v., -ated, -ating. talk or write at length.

ex•pa'tri•ate', v., -ated, -ating, n., adj. —v. (-āt'). 1. exile. 2. remove (oneself) from homeland. —n. (-ət). 3. expatriated person. —adj. (-ət). 4. exiled; banished.

ex•pect', v. look forward to. —ex•pect'an•cy, n. —ex•pect'ant, adj. —ex•pec•ta'tion, n.

ex•pec'to•rate', v., -rated, -rating. spit. —ex•pec•to•ra'tion, n.

ex•pe'di•ent, adj. 1. desirable in given circumstances. 2. conducive to advantage. 3. expedient means. —ex•pe'di•en•cy, n.

ex•pe•dite', v., -dited, -diting. speed up. —ex'pe•dit'er, n.

ex'pe•di'tion, n. 1. journey to explore or fight. 2. promptness. —ex'pe•di'tion•ar'y, adj.

ex•pe•di'tious, adj. prompt. —ex•pel', v., -pelled, -pelling. force out.

ex•pend', v. 1. use up. 2. spend. —ex•pend'i•ture, n.

ex•pend'a•ble, adj. 1. available for spending. 2. that can be sacrificed if necessary.

ex•pense', n. 1. cost. 2. cause of spending.

ex•pen'sive, adj. costing much.

ex•pe'ri•ence, n., v., -enced, -encing. —n. 1. something lived through. 2. knowledge from such things. —v. 3. have experience of.

ex•per'i•ment, n. (-a mant). 1. test to discover or check something. —v. (-ment'). 2. perform experiment. —ex•per'i•men'tal, adj.

ex•pert', n. (eks'pûrt). 1. skilled person. —adj. (ik spûrt'). 2. skilled. —ex•pert'ly, adv. —ex•pert'ness, n.

ex•per'tise' (-tēz'), n. expert skill.

ex'pi•ate', v., -ated, -ating. atone for. —ex'pi•a'tion, n.

ex•pire', v., -pired, -piring. 1. end. 2. die. 3. breathe out. —ex•pi•ra'tion, n.

ex•plain', v. 1. make plain. 2. account for. —ex'pla•na'tion, n. —ex•plan'a•to'ry, adj.

ex'ple•tive, n. exclamatory oath, usu. profane.

ex'pli•cate', v., -cated, -cating. explain in detail.

ex•plic'it (-plis'-), adj. 1. clearly stated. 2. outspoken. —ex•plic'it•ly, adv.

ex•plode', v., -ploded, -ploding. 1. burst violently. 2. disprove; discredit. —ex•plo'sion, n. —ex•plo'sive, adj.

ex'ploit, n. (eks'ploit). 1. notable act. —v. (ik sploit'). 2. use, esp. selfishly. —ex'ploi•ta'tion, n.

ex•plore', v., -plored, -ploring. examine from end to end. —ex'plo•ra'tion, n. —ex•plor'er, n. —ex•plor'a•to'ry, adj.

ex•po'nent, n. 1. person who explains. 2. symbol; typical example.

ex•port', v. (ik spōrt'). 1. send to other countries. —n. (eks'pōrt). what is sent. —ex'por•ta'tion, n.

ex•pose', v., -posed, -posing. 1. lay open to harm, etc. 2. reveal. 3. allow light to reach (film). —ex•po'sure, n.

ex•po•sé' (-zā'), n. exposure of wrongdoing.

ex'po•si'tion, n. 1. public show. 2. explanation.

ex•pos'i•to•ry (-poz'i-), *adj.* serving to expound or explain.

ex•pos'tu•late' (-pos'cha-), *v.*, **-lated, -lating.** argue protestingly. —**ex•pos'tu•la'tion,** *n.*

ex•pound', *v.* state in detail.

ex•press', *v.* 1. convey in words, art, etc. 2. press out. —*adj.* 3. definite. —*n.* 4. fast or direct train, etc. 5. delivery system. —**ex•pres'sion,** *n.* —**ex•pres'sive,** *adj.*

ex•press'way', *n.* road for high-speed traffic.

ex•pro'pri•ate', *v.*, **-ated, -ating.** take for public use. —**ex•pro'pri•a'tion,** *n.*

ex•pul'sion, *n.* act of driving out.

ex•punge', *v.*, **-punged, -punging.** obliterate.

ex'pur•gate', *v.*, **-gated, -gating.** remove objectionable parts from.

ex'qui•site, *adj.* delicately beautiful.

ex'tant, *adj.* (ek'stant), *adj.* still existing.

ex•tem'po•ra'ne•ous, *adj.* impromptu. —**ex•tem'po•re** (ik stem'pə rē), *adv.*

ex•tend', *v.* 1. stretch out. 2. offer. 3. reach. 4. increase. —**ex•ten'sion,** *n.*

ex•ten'sive, *adj.* far-reaching; broad. —**ex•ten'sive•ly,** *adv.*

ex•tent', *n.* degree of extension.

ex•ten'u•ate', *v.*, **-ated, -ating.** lessen (fault).

ex•te'ri•or, *adj.* 1. outer. —*n.* 2. outside.

ex•ter'mi•nate', *v.*, **-nated, -nating.** destroy. —**ex•ter'mi•na'tion,** *n.* —**ex•ter'mi•na'tor,** *n.*

ex•ter'nal, *adj.* outer.

ex•tinct', *adj.* no longer existing. —**ex•tinc'tion,** *n.*

ex•tin'guish, *v.* put out; end.

ex'tir•pate', *v.*, **-pated, -pating.** destroy totally; tear out by roots.

ex•tol', *v.*, **-tolled, -tolling.** praise.

ex•tort', *v.* get by force, threat, etc. —**ex•tor'tion,** *n.* —**ex•tor'tion•ate,** *adj.*

ex'tra, *adj.* additional.

ex•tract', *v.* (ik strakt'). 1. draw out. —*n.* (eks'trakt). 2. something extracted. —**ex•trac'tion,** *n.*

ex•tra•cur•ric'u•lar, *adj.* outside the regular curriculum, as of a school.

ex'tra•dite', *v.*, **-dited, -diting.** de-

liver (fugitive) to another state or nation. —**ex•tra•di'tion,** *n.*

ex•tra'ne•ous, *adj.* irrelevant. —**ex•tra'ne•ous•ly,** *adv.*

ex•traor'di•nar'y, *adj.* unusual.

ex•trap'o•late, *v.*, **-lated, -lating.** infer from something that is known.

ex'tra•sen'so•ry, *adj.* beyond one's physical senses.

ex•tra•ter•res'tri•al, *adj.* from outside the earth's limits. —*n.* extraterrestrial being.

ex•trav'a•gant, *adj.* 1. spending imprudently. 2. immoderate. —**ex•trav'a•gance,** *n.*

ex•treme', *adj.* 1. farthest from ordinary. 2. very great. 3. final or outermost. —*n.* 4. utmost degree. —**ex•treme'ly,** *adv.*

ex•trem'i•ty, *n.*, *pl.* **-ties.** 1. extreme part. 2. limb of body. 3. distress.

ex'tri•cate', *v.*, **-cated, -cating.** disentangle.

ex•trin'sic, *adj.* 1. not inherent or essential. 2. being or coming from without; external.

ex'tro•vert', *n.* outgoing person.

ex•trude', *v.*, **-truded, -truding.** 1. force or press out. 2. shape by forcing through a die. —**ex•tru'sive,** *adj.*

ex•u'ber•ant, *adj.* 1. joyful; vigorous. 2. lavish. —**ex•u'ber•ance,** *n.*

ex•ude', *v.*, **-uded, -uding.** ooze out. —**ex'u•da'tion,** *n.*

ex•ult', *v.* rejoice. —**ex•ult'ant,** *adj.* —**ex•ul•ta'tion,** *n.*

eye, *n.*, *v.*, **eyed, eying** or **eyeing.** —*n.* 1. organ of sight. 2. power of seeing. 3. close watch. —*v.* 4. watch closely. —**eye'ball',** *n.*, *v.* —**eye'sight',** *n.*

eye'brow', *n.* ridge and fringe of hair over eye.

eye'glass'es, *n.pl.* pair of lenses in a frame, worn for better vision.

eye'lash', *n.* short hair at edge of eyelid.

eye'let, *n.* small hole.

eye'lid', *n.* movable skin covering the eye.

eye'sore', *n.* something unpleasant to look at.

eye'tooth', *n.* canine tooth.

eye'wit'ness, *n.* person who sees event.

F

F, f, *n.* sixth letter of English alphabet.

fa'ble, *n.* 1. short tale with moral. 2. untrue story.

fab'ric, *n.* cloth.

fab'ri•cate', *v.*, **-cated, -cating.** 1. construct. 2. devise (lie). —**fab'ri•ca'tion,** *n.*

fab·u·lous, *adj.* 1. marvelous. 2. suggesting fables.

fa·çade (fə säd′), *n.* 1. building front. 2. superficial appearance.

face, *n., v.*, **faced, facing.** —*n.* 1. front part of head. 2. surface. 3. appearance. 4. self-respect. —*v.* 5. look toward. 6. confront. —**fa′cial**, *adj.*

face′less, *adj.* lacking distinction or identity.

face′-lift′, *n.* 1. surgery to eliminate facial sagging or wrinkling. 2. renovation to improve appearance, as of a building.

fac′et (fas′it), *n.* 1. surface of cut gem. 2. aspect.

fa·ce′tious, *adj.* joking, esp. annoyingly so.

fac·ile (fas′il), *adj.* glibly easy.

fa·cil′i·tate′, *v.*, **-tated, -tating.** make easier.

fa·cil′i·ty, *n., pl.* **-ties.** 1. thing that makes task easier. 2. dexterity.

fac′ing, *n.* decorative or protective outer material.

fac·sim·i·le (fak sim′ə lē), *n.* exact copy.

fact, *n.* truth. —**fac′tu·al**, *adj.*

fac′tion, *n.* competing internal group. —**fac′tion·al**, *adj.*

fac′tious, *adj.* causing strife.

fac′tor, *n.* 1. element. 2. one of two numbers multiplied.

fac′to·ry, *n., pl.* **-ries.** place where goods are made.

fac′ul·ty, *n., pl.* **-ties.** 1. special ability. 2. power. 3. body of teachers.

fad, *n.* temporary fashion; craze.

fade, *v.*, **faded, fading.** 1. lose freshness, color, or vitality. 2. disappear gradually.

fag, *v.*, **fagged, fagging.** *n.* —*v.* 1. exhaust. —*n.* 2. Also, **fag′got.** *Offensive.* homosexual.

fag′ot, *n.* bundle of firewood.

Fahr·en·heit (far′ən hīt′), *adj.* measuring temperature so that water freezes at 32° and boils at 212°.

fail, *v.* 1. be unsuccessful or lacking (in). 2. become weaker. 3. cease functioning. —**fail′ure**, *n.*

fail′ing, *n.* 1. weak point of character. —*prep.* 2. in the absence of.

faille (fīl, fāl), *n.* ribbed fabric.

fail′-safe′, *adj.* ensured against failure of a mechanical system, etc., or against consequences of its failure.

faint, *adj.* 1. lacking force or strength. —*v.* 2. lose consciousness briefly. —**faint′ly**, *adv.*

fair, *adj.* 1. behaving or thinking justly. 2. moderately good. 3. sunny. 4. light-hued. 5. attractive. —*n.* 6. exhibition. —**fair′ly**, *adv.* —**fair′ness**, *n.*

fair′y, *n., pl.* **fairies.** 1. tiny supernatural being. 2. *Offensive.* homosexual. —**fair′y·land′**, *n.*

fairy tale, 1. story, usu. for children, about magical creatures. 2. incredible or misleading statement or account.

faith, *n.* 1. confidence. 2. religious belief. 3. loyalty. —**faith′less**, *adj.*

faith′ful, *adj.* 1. loyal. 2. having religious belief. 3. copying accurately. —**faith′ful·ly**, *adv.* —**faith′ful·ness**, *n.*

fake, *v.*, **faked, faking.** *n., adj. Informal.* —*v.* 1. pretend or counterfeit. —*n.* 2. thing faked. 3. designed to deceive. —**fak′er**, *n.*

fa·kir (fə kēr′), *n.* Muslim or Hindu monk.

fal′con (fôl′kən), *n.* bird of prey.

fall, *v.*, **fell, fallen, falling**, *n.* —*v.* 1. descend; drop. 2. happen. —*n.* 3. descent. 4. autumn.

fal′la·cy, *n., pl.* **-cies.** 1. false belief. 2. unsound argument. —**fal·la′cious**, *adj.*

fal′li·ble, *adj.* liable to error. —**fal′li·bil′i·ty**, *n.*

fal·lo′pi·an tube, either of pair of ducts in female abdomen that transport ova from ovary to uterus. Also, **Fallopian tube.**

fall′out′, *n.* radioactive particles carried by air.

fal′low, *adj.* plowed and not seeded.

false, *adj.*, **falser, falsest.** 1. not true. 2. faithless. 3. deceptive. —**false′hood**, *n.* —**fal′si·ty**, *n.* —**fal′si·fy**, *v.*

fal·set′to, *n., pl.* **-tos.** unnaturally high voice.

fal′ter, *v.* hesitate; waver.

fame, *n.* wide reputation.

fa·mil′iar, *adj.* 1. commonly known. 2. intimate. —**fa·mil′i·ar′i·ty**, *n.* —**fa·mil′iar·ize′**, *v.*

fam·i·ly, *n., pl.* **-lies.** 1. parents and their children. 2. relatives. —**fa·mil′i·al**, *adj.*

fam′ine, *n.* scarcity of food.

fam′ish, *v.* starve.

fa′mous, *adj.* renowned; celebrated.

fan, *n., v.*, **fanned, fanning.** —*n.* 1. device for causing current of air. 2. *Informal.* devotee. —*v.* 3. blow upon with fan. 4. stir up.

fa·nat′ic, *n.* person excessively devoted to cause. —**fa·nat′i·cal**, *adj.* —**fa·nat′i·cism**, *n.*

fan′ci·er, *n.* person interested in something, as dogs.

fan′cy, *n., pl.* **-cies**, *adj.*, **-cier, -ciest**, *v.*, **-cied, -cying.** —*n.* 1. imagination.

2. thing imagined. 3. whim. 4. taste.
—adj. 5. ornamental. —v. 6. imagine.
7. crave. —fan'ci•ful, adj.

fan'cy-free', adj. free from emotional ties, esp. from love.

fan'fare', n. 1. chorus of trumpets. 2. showy flourish.

fang, n. long, sharp tooth.

fan'ny, n., pl. -nies. Informal. buttocks.

fan'ta•size', v., -sized, -sizing. have fantasies.

fan•tas'tic, adj. 1. wonderful and strange. 2. fanciful. Also, fan•tas'ti•cal. —fan•tas'ti•cal•ly, adv.

fan'ta•sy, n., pl. -sies. 1. imagination. 2. imagined thing.

far, adv., adj., farther, farthest. at or to great distance.

far'a•way', adj. 1. distant; remote. 2. preoccupied; detached; dreamy.

farce, n. light comedy.

fare, n., v., fared, faring. —n. 1. price of passage. 2. food. —v. 3. eat. 4. get along. 5. go.

Far East, countries of east and southeast Asia.

fare•well', interj., n., adj. good-by.

far'-fetched', adj. not reasonable or probable.

far'-flung', adj. 1. extending over a great distance or wide area. 2. widely distributed.

farm, n. 1. tract of land for agriculture. —v. 2. cultivate land. —farm'er, n. —farm'house', n. —farm'yard', n.

far'-off', adj. distant.

far'-out', adj. Slang. extremely unconventional.

far'-reach'ing, adj. of widespread influence.

far'row, n. 1. litter of pigs. —v. 2. (of swine) bear.

far'-sight'ed, adj. 1. seeing distant objects best. 2. planning for future.

far'ther, compar. of far. adv. 1. at or to a greater distance. —adj. 2. more distant. 3. additional.

far'thest, superl. of far. adv. 1. at or to the greatest distance. —adj. 2. most distant.

fas'ci•nate', v., -nated, -nating. attract irresistibly. —fas'ci•na'tion, n.

fas'cism (fash'iz əm), n. principle of strong undemocratic government. —fas'cist, n., adj. —fa•scis'tic, adj.

fash'ion, n. 1. prevailing style. 2. manner. —v. 3. make.

fash'ion•a•ble, adj. of the latest style. —fash'ion•a•bly, adv.

fast, adj. 1. quick; swift. 2. secure. —adv. 3. tightly. 4. swiftly. —v. 5. abstain from food. —n. 6. such abstinence.

fast'back', n. rear of automobile, curved downward.

fas'ten, v. 1. fix securely. 2. seize. —fas'ten•er, fas'ten•ing, n.

fas•tid'i•ous, adj. highly critical and demanding. —fas•tid'i•ous•ly, adv.

fast'ness, n. fortified place.

fat, n., adj., fatter, fattest. —n. 1. greasy substance. —adj. 2. fleshy. —fat'ty, adj.

fa'tal, adj. causing death or ruin. —fa'tal•ly, adv.

fa'tal•ism, n. belief in unchangeable destiny. —fa'tal•is'tic, adj.

fa•tal'i•ty, n., pl. -ties. 1. death caused by a disaster. 2. fate.

fate, n., v., fated, fating. —n. 1. destiny. 2. death or ruin. —v. 3. destine.

fate'ful, adj. involving important or disastrous events.

fa'ther, n. 1. male parent. 2. (cap.) God. 3. priest.

fa'ther-in-law', n., pl. fathers-in-law. father of one's spouse.

fa'ther•land', n. 1. one's native country. 2. land of one's ancestors.

fath'om, n. 1. nautical measure equal to six feet. —v. 2. understand.

fa•tigue', n., v., -tigued, -tiguing. —n. 1. weariness. 2. (pl.) military work clothes. —v. 3. weary.

fat'ten, v. make or grow fat or prosperous.

fat'u•ous (fach'-), adj. 1. foolish or stupid. 2. unreal. —fa•tu'i•ty, n.

fau'cet, n. valve for liquids.

fault, n. 1. defect. —faul'ty, adj.

faun, n. Roman deity, part man and part goat.

fau'na (fô'nə), n., pl. -nas, -nae (-nē). animals or animal life of particular region or period.

faux pas' (fō pä'), error, esp. social.

fa'vor, n. 1. kind act. 2. high regard. —v. 3. prefer. 4. oblige. 5. resemble. Also, fa'vour. —fa'vor•a•ble, adj. —fa'vor•ite, adj.

fa'vor•it•ism, n. preference shown toward certain persons.

fawn, n. 1. young deer. —v. 2. seek favor by servility.

fax, n. 1. method of transmitting written or graphic material by telephone or radio. 2. item transmitted in this way. —v. 3. send by fax. 4. communicate with by fax.

faze, v., fazed, fazing. Informal. daunt.

fear, n. 1. feeling of coming harm. 2. awe. —v. 3. be afraid of. 4. hold in awe. —fear'ful, adj. —fear'less, adj.

fea·si·ble, *adj.* able to be done. —**fea·si·bil'i·ty,** *n.*

feast, *n.* 1. sumptuous meal. 2. religious celebration. —*v.* 3. provide with or have feast.

feat, *n.* remarkable deed.

feath'er, *n.* one of the growths forming bird's plumage. —**feath'er·y,** *adj.*

fea'ture, *n., v.* **-tured, -turing.** —*n.* 1. part of face. 2. special part, article, etc. —*v.* 3. give prominence to.

Feb'ru·ar'y, *n., pl.* **-aries.** second month of year.

fe'ces (fē'sēz), *n.pl.* excrement.

fe'cund (fē'kund), *adj.* productive. —**fe·cun'di·ty,** *n.*

fed'er·al, *adj.* 1. of states in permanent union. 2. (*sometimes cap.*) of U.S. government.

fed'er·ate', *v.,* **-ated, -ating.** unite in league. —**fed'er·a'tion,** *n.*

fe·do'ra, *n.* soft felt hat.

fee, *n.* 1. payment for services, etc. 2. ownership.

fee'ble, *adj.,* **-bler, -blest.** weak. —**fee'bly,** *adv.*

feed, *v.,* **fed, feeding,** *n.* —*v.* 1. give food to. 2. eat. —*n.* 3. food. —**feed'er,** *n.*

feed'back', *n.* 1. return of part of output of a process to its input. 2. informative response.

feel, *v.,* **felt, feeling,** *n.* —*v.* 1. perceive or examine by touch. 2. be conscious of. 3. have emotions. —**feel'ing,** *n.*

feel'er, *n.* 1. proposal or remark designed to elicit opinion or reaction. 2. organ of touch, as an antenna.

feign (fān), *v.* pretend.

feint (fānt), *n.* 1. deceptive move. —*v.* 2. make feint.

feist'y (fī'stē), *adj.,* **feistier, feistiest.** 1. full of energy; spirited. 2. ready to argue or fight; pugnacious.

fe·lic'i·tate', *v.,* **-tated, -tating.** congratulate. —**fe·lic'i·ta'tion,** *n.*

fe·lic'i·tous, *adj.* suitable.

fe·lic'i·ty, *n., pl.* **-ties.** happiness.

fe'line (fē'līn), *adj.* 1. of or like cats. —*n.* 2. animal of the cat family.

fell, *v.* cut or strike down.

fel'low, *n.* 1. man. 2. companion. 3. equal. 4. member of learned or professional group. —**fel'low·ship',** *n.*

fel'on, *n.* criminal.

fel'o·ny, *n., pl.* **-nies.** serious crime. —**fe·lo'ni·ous,** *adj.*

felt, *n.* 1. matted fabric. —*adj.* 2. of felt.

fe'male, *adj.* 1. belonging to sex that brings forth young. —*n.* 2. female person or animal.

fem'i·nine, *adj.* of women. —**fem'i·nin'i·ty,** *n.*

fem'in·ism, *n.* support of feminine causes. —**fem'in·ist,** *adj., n.*

fe'mur (fē'-), *n.* thigh bone. **fem'o·ral,** *adj.*

fence, *n., v.* **fenced, fencing.** —*n.* 1. wall-like enclosure around open area. 2. person who receives and disposes of stolen goods. —*v.* 3. fight with sword for sport. 4. sell to a fence. —**fenc'ing,** *n.*

fend, *v.* ward off.

fend'er, *n.* metal part over automobile wheel.

fen'nel, *n.* plant related to parsley, with seeds used for flavoring.

fe'ral (fēr'əl, fer'-), *adj.* 1. in a wild state; not tamed. 2. having returned to a wild state.

fer·ment', *n.* 1. substance causing fermentation. 2. agitation. —*v.* (fer ment') 3. cause or undergo fermentation.

fer·men·ta'tion, *n.* chemical change involving effervescence or decomposition.

fern, *n.* nonflowering plant with feathery leaves.

fe·ro'cious, *adj.* savagely fierce. —**fe·roc'i·ty,** *n.*

fer'ret, *n.* 1. kind of weasel. —*v.* 2. search intensively.

Fer'ris wheel, amusement ride consisting of large upright wheel with suspended seats.

fer'rous, *adj.* of or containing iron. Also, **fer'ric.**

fer'ry, *n., pl.* **-ries,** *v.,* **-ried, -rying.** —*n.* 1. Also, **fer'ry·boat'.** boat making short crossings. 2. place where ferries operate. —*v.* 3. carry or pass in ferry.

fer'tile, *adj.* 1. producing abundantly. 2. able to bear young. —**fer·til'i·ty,** *n.* —**fer'ti·lize',** *v.* —**fer'ti·liz'er,** *n.*

fer'vent, *adj.* ardent; passionate. —**fer'ven·cy, fer'vor,** *n.*

fer'vid, *adj.* vehement.

fes'tal, *adj.* of feasts.

fes'ter, *v.* 1. generate pus. 2. rankle.

fes'ti·val, *n.* 1. celebration or feast. Also, **fes·tiv'i·ty.** —**fes'tive,** *adj.*

fes·toon', *n.* 1. garland hung between two points. —*v.* 2. adorn with festoons.

fetch, *v.* go and bring.

fetch'ing, *adj.* charming; captivating. —**fetch'ing·ly,** *adv.*

fete (fāt, fet), *n., v.,* **feted, feting.** —*n.* 1. festival. 2. party. —*v.* 3. honor with a fete.

fet'id, *adj.* stinking; rank.

fe'tish, *n.* object worshiped.

fet'lock, n. 1. part of horse's leg behind hoof. 2. tuft of hair on this part.

fet'ter, n. 1. shackle for feet. 2. (pl.) anything that restrains. 3. v. put fetters on. 4. restrain from action.

fet'tle, n. condition.

fe'tus, n. unborn offspring.

feud, n. 1. lasting hostility. —v. 2. engage in feud.

feu'dal•ism, n. system by which land is held in return for service. —**feu'dal,** adj.

fe'ver, n. bodily condition marked by high temperature, rapid pulse, etc. —**fe'ver•ish,** adj.

few, adj., n. not many.

fey (fā), adj. 1. strange; whimsical. 2. supernatural; enchanted.

fez, n., pl. **fezzes.** felt cap.

fi•an•cé' (fē'än sā'), n. betrothed man. —**fi•an•cée',** n.fem.

fi•as'co (fē as'kō), n., pl. **-cos, -coes.** failure.

fi'at (fī'ət), n. decree.

fib, n., v. **fibbed, fibbing.** —n. 1. mild lie. —v. 2. tell a fib.

fi'ber, n. 1. threadlike piece, esp. one that can be woven. 2. any of the threadlike structures that form plant or animal tissue. 3. roughage. Also, **fi'bre.** —**fi'brous,** adj. —**fi'broid,** adj.

fi'ber•glass', n. material composed of fine glass fibers.

fiber optics, technology of sending light and images through glass or plastic fibers. —**fi•ber-op'tic,** adj.

fib'u•la, n., pl. **-lae, -las.** outer thinner bone from knee to ankle.

fick'le, adj. inconstant; disloyal.

fic'tion, n. 1. narrative of imaginary events. 2. something made up. —**fic•ti'tious,** adj.

fid'dle, n., v. **-dled, -dling.** —n. 1. violin. —v. 2. play folk or popular tunes on violin. 3. trifle. —**fid'dler,** n.

fi•del'i•ty, n., pl. **-ties.** faithfulness.

fidg'et, v. 1. move restlessly. —n. 2. (pl.) restlessness.

fi•du'cial (-shal), adj. based on trust, as paper money not backed by precious metal.

fi•du'ci•ar'y (-shē-), adj., n., pl. **-aries.** adj. 1. being a trustee. 2. held in trust. —n. 3. trustee.

field, n. 1. open ground. 2. area of interest.

fiend, n. 1. devil. 2. cruel person. 3. Informal. addict. —**fiend'ish,** adj.

fierce, adj., **fiercer, fiercest.** wild; violent. —**fierce'ly,** adv.

fier'y, adj., **fierier, fieriest.** 1. of or like fire. 2. ardent.

fi•es'ta, n. festival.

fife, n. high-pitched flute.

fif'teen', n., adj. ten plus five. —**fif•teenth',** adj., n.

fifth, adj. 1. next after fourth. —n. 2. fifth part.

fifth column, traitorous group within a country.

fif'ty, n., adj. ten times five. —**fif'ti•eth,** adj., n.

fig, n. fruit of semitropical tree.

fight, n., v. **fought, fighting.** battle. —**fight'er,** n.

fig'ment, n. imagined story.

fig'ur•a•tive, adj. not literal. —**fig'ur•a•tive•ly,** adv.

fig'ure, n., v., **-ured, -uring.** —n. 1. written symbol, esp. numerical. 2. amount. 3. shape. —v. 4. compute. 5. be prominent.

fig'ure•head', n. powerless leader.

fig'ur•ine', n. miniature statue.

fil'a•ment, n. fine fiber.

fil'bert, n. kind of nut.

filch, v. steal.

file, n., v. **filed, filing.** —n. 1. storage place for documents. 2. line of persons, etc. 3. metal rubbing tool. —v. 4. arrange or keep in file. 5. march in file. 6. rub with file.

fil'i•al, adj. befitting sons and daughters.

fil'i•bus'ter, n. 1. obstruction of legislation by prolonged speaking. —v. 2. use filibuster to impede legislation.

fil'i•gree', n. ornamental work of fine wires.

fill, v. 1. make full. 2. pervade. 3. supply. —n. 4. full supply. —**fill'ing,** n.

fil•let' (fi lā'), n. narrow strip, esp. of meat or fish. Also, **fi'let.**

fil'lip, n. thing that rouses or excites.

fil'ly, n., pl. **-lies.** young female horse.

film, n. 1. thin coating. 2. roll or sheet with photographically sensitive coating. 3. motion picture. —v. 4. make motion picture of.

film'strip', n. length of film containing still pictures for projecting on screen.

film'y, adj., **filmier, filmiest.** 1. partly transparent. 2. indistinct; blurred.

fil'ter, n. 1. device for straining substances. —v. 2. remove by or pass through filter.

filth, n. 1. dirt. 2. obscenity. —**filth'y,** adj.

fin, n. winglike organ on fishes.

fi'nal, adj. last. —**fi•nal'i•ty,** n. —**fi'nal•ly,** adv.

fi•na'le (fi nä'lē), n. last part.

fi'nance' (fī nans'), n., v., **-nanced, -nancing.** —n. 1. money matters. 2. (pl.) funds. —v. 3. supply with money. —**fi•nan'cial,** adj.

fin·an·cier' (-sēr', n. professional money handler.

finch, n. small bird.

find, v. **found, finding,** n. —v. 1. come upon. 2. learn. —n. 3. discovery.

fine, adj., **finer, finest,** n., v., **fined, fining.** —adj. 1. excellent. 2. delicate; thin. —n. 3. money exacted as penalty. —v. 4. subject to fine.

fin'er·y, n. showy dress.

fi·nesse' n. artful delicacy.

fin'ger, n. one of five terminal parts of hand. —**fin'ger·nail',** n.

fin'ger·print', n. 1. impression of markings of surface of finger, used for identification. —v. 2. take or record fingerprints of.

fin'ick·y, adj., **-ickier, -ickiest.** too fussy. Also, **fin'ic·al.**

fi'nis (fin'is, fī'nis), n. end.

fin'ish, v. 1. end. 2. perfect. 3. give desired surface to. —n. 4. completion. 5. surface coating or treatment.

fiord (fyôrd, fē ôrd'), n. narrow arm of sea. Also, **fjord.**

fir, n. cone-bearing evergreen tree.

fire, n., v., **fired, firing.** —n. 1. burning. 2. ardor. 3. discharge of firearms. —v. 4. set on fire. 5. discharge. 6. *Informal.* dismiss.

fire'arm', n. gun.

fire'fight'er, n. person who fights destructive fires.

fire'fly', n., pl. **-flies.** nocturnal beetle with light-producing organ.

fire'man (fīr'mən), n., pl. **-men.** 1. firefighter. 2. person maintaining fires.

fire'place', n. semiopen place for fire.

fire'plug', n. hydrant with water for fighting fires.

fire'proof', adj. safe against fire.

fire'side', n. area close to fireplace; hearth.

fire'trap', n. dilapidated building.

fire'works', n.pl. devices ignited for display of light and noise.

firm, adj. 1. hard or stiff. 2. fixed. 3. resolute. —v. 4. make or become firm. —n. 5. business organization. —**firm'ly,** adv. —**firm'ness,** n.

fir'ma·ment, n. sky.

first, adj., adv. 1. before all others. —n. 2. first thing, etc.

first aid, immediate treatment for injuries, etc.

first class, 1. best or highest class or grade. 2. most expensive class of travel accommodation. 3. class of mail sealed against inspection. —**first'-class',** adj.

first'hand', adj., adv. from the first or original source. Also, **first'-hand'.**

fis'cal (-kəl), adj. financial.

fish, n., pl. **fish, fishes,** v. —n. 1. cold-blooded aquatic vertebrate. —v. 2. try to catch fish. —**fish'er·man,** n. —**fish'er·y,** n.

fis'sion (fish'ən), n. division into parts. —**fis'sion·a·ble,** adj.

fis'sure (fish'ər), n. narrow opening.

fist, n. closed hand.

fit, adj., **fitter, fittest,** v., **fitted, fitting,** n. —adj. 1. well suited. 2. in good condition. —v. 3. be or make suitable. 4. equip. —n. 5. manner of fitting. 6. sudden attack of illness or emotion.

fit'ful, adj. irregular.

fit'ting, adj. 1. appropriate. —n. 2. attached part. 3. trial of new clothes, etc., for fit.

five, n., adj. four plus one.

fix, v. 1. make fast or steady. 2. repair. 3. prepare. —**fix'er,** n.

fix·a'tion, n. excessive attachment or bias.

fix'ings, n.pl. *Informal.* things accompanying main item.

fix'ture, n. something fixed in place.

fizz, v., n. hiss.

fiz'zle, v., **-zled, -zling,** n. —v. 1. hiss weakly. 2. *Informal.* fail. —n. 3. act of fizzling.

fjord (fyôrd, fē ôrd'), n. fiord.

flab, n. loose, excessive flesh.

flab'ber·gast', v. *Informal.* astound.

flab'by, adj., **-bier, -biest.** limp; not firm.

flac'cid (flak'sid, flas'id), adj. flabby.

flag, n., v., **flagged, flagging.** —n. 1. cloth with symbolic colors or design. 2. plant with long narrow leaves. 3. Also, **flag'stone'.** paving stone. —v. 4. signal with flags (def. 1). 5. fall off in vigor, energy, etc.

flag'el·late' (flaj'-), v. **-lated, -lating.** whip; flog. —**flag'el·la'tion,** n.

flag'on, n. large bottle.

fla'grant, adj. glaring. —**fla'gran·cy,** n.

flag'ship', n. ship of senior naval officer.

flail, n. 1. hand instrument for threshing. —v. 2. strike or strike at as with flail.

flair, n. aptitude; talent.

flak, n. 1. antiaircraft fire. 2. critical or hostile reaction.

flake, n., v., **flaked, flaking.** —n. 1. small thin piece. —v. 2. separate into flakes.

flak'y, adj., **flakier, flakiest.** 1. of or like flakes. 2. lying or coming off in flakes. 3. *Slang.* eccentric; odd. Also, **flak'ey.** —**flak'i·ness,** n.

flam•boy′ant, *adj.* showy; colorful.

flame, *n. v.*, **flamed, flaming.** blaze.

fla•men′co (flä meng′kō, flə-), *n.* Spanish gypsy dance and music style.

fla•min′go, *n. pl.* **-gos, -goes.** tall, red, aquatic bird.

flange, *n.* projecting rim.

flank, *n.* 1. side. —*v.* 2. be at side of. 3. pass around side of.

flan′nel, *n.* soft wool fabric.

flap, *v.*, **flapped, flapping**, *n.* —*v.* 1. swing loosely and noisily. 2. move up and down. —*n.* 3. flapping movement. 4. something hanging loosely. 5. *Informal.* emotionally agitated state.

flare, *v.*, **flared, flaring.** —*v.* 1. burn with unsteady or sudden flame. 2. spread outward. —*n.* 3. signal fire.

flash, *n.* 1. brief light. 2. instant. 3. news dispatch. —*v.* 4. gleam suddenly.

flash′back′, *n.* 1. earlier event inserted out of order in a story or dramatic work. 2. abnormally vivid recollection of a past event.

flash′bulb′, *n.* bulb giving burst of light for photography.

flash′cube′, *n.* device containing four flashbulbs.

flash′light′, *n.* portable battery-powered light.

flash′y, *adj.*, **flashier, flashiest.** showy. —**flash′i•ness,** *n.*

flask, *n.* kind of bottle.

flat, *adj.*, **flatter, flattest**, *n.* —*adj.* 1. level. 2. horizontal. 3. not thick. 4. uncompromising. 5. dull. 6. below musical pitch. —*n.* 7. something flat. 8. apartment. —**flat′ly,** *adv.* —**flat′-ness,** *n.* —**flat′ten,** *v.*

flat′car′, *n.* railroad car without sides or top.

flat′ter, *v.* praise insincerely. —**flat′-ter•y,** *n.*

flat′u•lent (flach′ə lənt), *adj.* 1. having an accumulation of gas in the intestines. 2. inflated and empty; pompous.

flaunt, *v.* display boldly.

fla′vor, *n.* 1. taste. —*v.* 2. give flavor to. —**fla′vor•ing,** *n.*

flaw, *n.* defect.

flax, *n.* linen plant. —**flax′en,** *adj.*

flay, *v.* strip skin from.

flea, *n.* small, bloodsucking insect.

flea market, market, often outdoors, where used articles, antiques, etc., are sold.

fleck, *n.* 1. speck. —*v.* 2. spot.

fledg′ling, *n.* young bird.

flee, *v.*, **fled, fleeing.** run away from.

fleece, *n. v.*, **fleeced, fleecing.** —*n.* 1.

wool of sheep. —*v.* 2. swindle. —**fleec′y,** *adj.*

fleet, *n.* 1. organized group of ships, aircraft, or road vehicles. —*adj.* 2. swift.

fleet′ing, *adj.* temporary; not lasting.

flesh, *n.* 1. muscle and fat of animal body. 2. body. 3. soft part of fruit or vegetable. —**flesh′y,** *adj.*

flesh′ly, *adj.* carnal.

flex, *v.* bend. —**flex′i•ble,** *adj.* —**flex′i•bil′i•ty,** *n.*

flick, *n.* 1. light stroke. —*v.* 2. strike lightly.

flick′er, *v.* 1. glow unsteadily. —*n.* 2. unsteady light.

fli′er, *n.* aviator.

flight, *n.* 1. act or power of flying. 2. trip through air. 3. steps between two floors. 4. hasty departure.

flight′y, *adj.*, **flightier, flightiest.** capricious. —**flight′i•ness,** *n.*

flim′sy, *adj.*, **-sier, -siest.** weak or thin. —**film′si•ness,** *n.*

flinch, *v.* shrink.

fling, *v.*, **flung, flinging,** *n.* —*v.* 1. throw violently. —*n.* 2. act of flinging.

flint, *n.* hard stone that strikes sparks. —**flint′y,** *adj.*

flip, *v.*, **flipped, flipping,** *n.* —*v.* 1. move, as by snapping finger. 2. turn over with sudden stroke. —*n.* 3. such movement.

flip′pant, *adj.* pert; disrespectful. —**flip′pan•cy,** *n.*

flip′per, *n.* broad flat limb.

flirt, *v.* 1. act amorously without serious intentions. —*n.* 2. person who flirts. —**flir•ta′tion,** *n.* —**flir•ta′-tious,** *adj.*

flit, *v.*, **flitted, flitting.** move swiftly.

float, *v.* 1. rest or move on or in liquid, air, etc. —*n.* 2. something that floats. 3. decorated parade wagon.

flock, *n.* 1. group of animals. —*v.* 2. gather in flock.

floe, *n.* field of floating ice.

flog, *v.*, **flogged, flogging.** beat; whip.

flood, *n.* 1. overflowing of water. —*v.* 2. overflow or cover with water, etc.

flood′light′, *n.* artificial light for large area.

floor, *n.* 1. bottom surface of room, etc. 2. level in building. 3. right to speak. —*v.* 4. furnish with floor. 5. knock down.

floor′ing, *n.* material for floors.

flop, *v.*, **flopped, flopping,** *n.* *Informal.* —*v.* 1. fall flatly. 2. fail. 3. flap. —*n.* 4. act of flopping.

flop′py, *adj.*, **-pier, -piest.** limp. —**flop′pi•ness,** *n.*

floppy disk, thin, usu. flexible plastic

disk for storing computer data and programs.

flo'ra (flôr'ə), *n., pl.* **-ras, -rae** (-ē). plants or plant life of a particular region or period.

flo'ral, *adj.* of flowers.

flor'id, *adj.* ruddy. —**flo•rid'i•ty**, *n.*

flo'rist, *n.* dealer in flowers.

floss, *n.* 1. silky fiber from certain plants. 2. fiber for cleaning between teeth. —**floss'y**, *adj.*

flo•til'la, *n.* small fleet.

flot'sam, *n.* floating wreckage.

flounce, *v.,* **flounced, flouncing,** *n.* —*v.* 1. go with an angry fling. —*n.* 2. flouncing movement. 3. ruffle for trimming.

floun'der, *v.* 1. struggle clumsily. —*n.* 2. clumsy effort. 3. flat edible fish.

flour, *n.* finely ground meal.

flour'ish (flûr'-), *v.* 1. thrive. 2. brandish. —*n.* 3. act of brandishing. 4. decoration.

flout, *v.* mock; scorn.

flow, *v.* 1. move in stream. —*n.* 2. act or rate of flowing.

flow'er, *n.* 1. blossom; bloom. —**flow'er•y**, *adj.*

flu, *n.* influenza.

fluc'tu•ate, *v.,* **-ated, -ating.** vary irregularly. —**fluc'tu•a'tion**, *n.*

flue, *n.* duct for smoke, etc.

flu'ent, *adj.* writing and speaking with ease. —**flu'en•cy**, *n.* —**flu'ent•ly**, *adv.*

fluff, *n.* downy particles. —**fluff'y**, *adj.*

flu'id, *n.* 1. substance that flows. —*adj.* 2. liquid or gaseous.

fluke, *n.* 1. lucky chance. 2. flounder (def. 3).

flume, *n.* channel; trough.

flunk, *v. Informal.* fail, esp. in a course or examination.

flun'ky, *n., pl.* **-kies.** servant or follower.

fluo•res'cence, *n.* emission of light upon exposure to radiation, etc. —**fluo•res'cent**, *adj.*

fluorescent lamp, tubular lamp using phosphors to produce radiation of light.

fluor'i•da'tion (floor'ə dā'shən), *n.* addition of fluorides to drinking water to reduce tooth decay.

fluor•ide', *n.* chemical compound containing fluorine.

fluor'o•scope' (floor'ə-), *n.* device for examining the body with x-rays.

flur'ry, *n., pl.* **-ries.** 1. gust of wind, rain, etc. 2. agitated state.

flush, *n.* 1. rosy glow. —*v.* 2. redden. 3. wash out with water. —*adj.* 4. even

with surrounding surface. 5. well supplied.

flus'ter, *v.* confuse.

flute, *n., v.,* **fluted, fluting.** —*n.* 1. musical wind instrument. 2. groove. —*v.* 3. form flutes in.

flut'ter, *v.* 1. wave in air. —*n.* 2. agitation.

flux, *n.* 1. a flowing. 2. continuous change. 3. substance that promotes fusion of metals.

fly, *v.,* **flew, flown, flying,** *n., pl.* **flies.** —*v.* 1. move or direct through air. 2. move swiftly. —*n.* 3. winged insect. —**fly'er**, *n.*

flying saucer, disk-shaped missile or plane, thought to come from outer space.

fly'leaf', *n., pl.* **-leaves.** blank page in front or back of a book.

fly'wheel', *n.* wheel for equalizing speed of machinery.

foal, *n.* young horse.

foam, *n.* 1. mass of tiny bubbles. —*v.* 2. form foam.

fob, *n.* chain or ribbon attached to a watch.

fo'cus, *n., pl.* **-cuses, -ci** (-sī), *v.,* **-cused, -cusing.** —*n.* 1. point at which refracted rays of light, etc., meet. 2. state of sharpness for image from optical device. 3. central point. —*v.* 4. bring into focus. —**fo'cal**, *adj.*

fod'der, *n.* livestock food.

foe, *n.* enemy.

fog, *n.* thick mist. —**fog'gy**, *adj.* —**fog'gi•ness**, *n.*

fo'gy, *n., pl.* **-gies.** old-fashioned person.

foi'ble, *n.* weak point.

foil, *v.* 1. frustrate. —*n.* 2. thin metallic sheet. 3. thing that sets off another by contrast. 4. thin, pointed sword for fencing.

foist, *v.* impose unjustifiably.

fold, *v.* 1. bend over upon itself. 2. wrap. 3. collapse. —*n.* 4. folded part. 5. enclosure for sheep.

fold'er, *n.* 1. folded printed sheet. 2. outer cover.

fo'li•age, *n.* leaves.

fo'li•o', *n., pl.* **-ios.** 1. sheet of paper folded once. 2. book printed on such sheets.

folk, *n.* people.

folk'lore', *n.* customs and beliefs of people.

folk'lor•ist, *n.* expert on folklore. —**folk'lor•is'tic**, *adj.*

folk song, 1. song originating among the common people. 2. song of similar character written by a known composer.

folk'sy, *adj.,* **-sier, -siest.** *Informal.*

suggesting genial simplicity. —**folk′-si·ness,** *n.*

fol′li·cle, *n.* 1. seed vessel. 2. small cavity, sac, or gland.

fol′low, *v.* 1. come or go after. 2. conform to. 3. work at. 4. move along. 5. watch or understand. 6. result.

fol′low·er, *n.* 1. person who follows. 2. disciple.

fol′low·ing, *n.* group of admirers or disciples.

fol′low-through′, *n.* 1. last part of a motion, as after a ball has been struck. 2. act of continuing a plan, program, etc., to completion.

fol′ly, *n., pl.* **-lies.** foolishness.

fo·ment′, *v.* foster.

fond, *adj.* 1. having affection. 2. foolish. —**fond′ness,** *n.*

fon′dant, *n.* sugar paste used in candies.

fon′dle, *v.,* **-dled, -dling.** caress.

fon·due′, *n.* dip of melted cheese, liquor, and seasonings.

font (font), *n.* 1. receptacle for baptismal water. 2. printing type style.

food, *n.* what is taken in for nourishment.

fool, *n.* 1. person acting stupidly. —*v.* 2. trick. 3. act frivolously. —**fool′ish,** *adj.*

fool′har′dy, *adj.,* **-dier, -diest.** rash.

fool′proof′, *adj.* proof against accident.

foot, *n., pl.* **feet,** *n.* 1. part of leg on which body stands. 2. unit of length equal to 12 inches. 3. lowest part; base. —*v.* 4. walk. —**foot′-print′,** *n.*

foot′ball′, *n.* game played with pointed leather ball.

foot′hill′, *n.* hill at foot of mountains.

foot′hold′, *n.* 1. secure place for foot to rest. 2. firm basis for progress.

foot′ing, *n.* 1. secure position. 2. basis for relationship.

foot′loose′, *adj.* free to go or travel about.

foot′man, *n.* male servant.

foot′note′, *n.* note at foot of page.

foot′-pound′, *n.* work done by force of one pound moving through distance of one foot.

foot′step′, *n.* sound of walking.

fop, *n.* haughty, overdressed man. —**fop′pish,** *adj.*

for, *prep.* 1. with the purpose of. 2. in the interest of. 3. in place of. 4. in favor of. 5. during. —*conj.* 6. seeing that. 7. because.

for′age, *n., v.,* **-aged, -aging.** —*n.* 1. food for stock. —*v.* 2. search for supplies.

for′ay, *n.* raid.

for·bear′, *v.,* **-bore, -borne, -bearing.** 1. refrain from. 2. be patient. —**for·bear′ance,** *n.*

for·bid′, *v.,* **-bade** or **-bad, -bidden** or **-bid, -bidding.** give order against.

for·bid′ding, *adj.* intimidating or discouraging.

force, *n., v.,* **forced, forcing.** —*n.* 1. strength. 2. coercion. 3. armed group. 4. influence. —*v.* 5. compel. 6. make yield. —**force′ful,** *adj.*

for′ceps, *n.* medical tool for seizing and holding.

for′ci·ble, *adj.* by means of force. —**for′ci·bly,** *adv.*

ford, *n.* 1. place for crossing water by wading. —*v.* 2. cross at ford.

fore, *adj., adv.* 1. at the front. 2. earlier. —*n.* 3. front.

fore′arm′, *n.* arm between elbow and wrist.

fore′bear′, *n.* ancestor.

fore·bode′, *v.,* **-boded, -boding.** portend.

fore′cast′, *v.,* **-cast, -casting,** *n.* 1. predict. —*n.* 2. prediction.

fore′cas·tle (fōk′səl, fōr′kas′əl), *n.* forward part of vessel's upper deck.

fore·close′, *v.,* **-closed, -closing.** deprive of the right to redeem (mortgage, etc.). —**fore·clo′sure,** *n.*

fore′fa′ther, *n.* ancestor. —**fore′-moth′er,** *n.fem.*

fore′front′, *n.* foremost place.

fore′gone′ conclusion, inevitable result.

fore′ground′, *n.* nearest area.

fore′head, *n.* part of face above eyes.

for′eign, *adj.* 1. of or from another country. 2. from outside. —**for′eign·er,** *n.*

fore′man, *n., pl.* **-men.** person in charge of work crew or jury.

fore′most′, *adj., adv.* first.

fore′noon′, *n.* daylight time before noon.

fo·ren′sic, *adj.* of or for public discussion or courtroom procedure.

fore′play′, *n.* sexual stimulation leading to intercourse.

fore′run′ner, *n.* predecessor.

fore·see′, *v.,* **-saw, -seen, -seeing.** see beforehand. —**fore′sight′,** *n.*

fore·shad′ow, *v.* indicate beforehand.

fore′skin′, *n.* skin on end of penis.

for′est, *n.* land covered with trees. —**for′est·er,** *n.* —**for′est·ry,** *n.*

fore·stall′, *v.* thwart by earlier action.

fore·tell′, *v.,* **-told, -telling.** predict.

fore′thought′, *n.* 1. prudence. 2. previous calculation.

for·ev′er, *adv.* always.

fore·warn′, *v.* warn in good time.

fore'word', *n.* introductory statement.

for'feit, *n.* 1. penalty. —*v.* 2. lose as forfeit. —*adj.* 3. forfeited. —**for'fei·ture,** *n.*

forge, *n.*, *v.* forged, forging. —*n.* 1. place for heating metal before shaping. —*v.* 2. form by heating and hammering. 3. imitate fraudulently. 4. move ahead persistently. —**forg'er,** *n.* —**for'ger·y,** *n.*

for·get', *v.* -got, -gotten, -getting. fail to remember. —**for·get'ful,** *adj.*

for·get'-me-not', *n.* small plant with blue flowers.

for·give', *v.* -gave, -given, -giving. grant pardon. —**for·giv'a·ble,** *adj.* —**for·give'ness,** *n.*

for·go', *v.* -went, -gone, -going. do without.

fork, *n.* 1. pronged instrument. 2. point of division. —*v.* 3. branch.

fork'lift', *n.* vehicle with two power-operated prongs for lifting heavy weights.

for·lorn', *adj.* abandoned.

form, *n.* 1. shape. 2. mold. 3. custom; standard practice. 4. document to be filled in. —*v.* 5. shape. —**form'a·tive,** *adj.*

for'mal, *adj.* 1. according to custom or standard practice. 2. ceremonious. 3. precisely stated. —**for'mal·ly,** *adv.* —**for'mal·ize',** *v.*

form·al'de·hyde', *n.* solution used as disinfectant.

for·mal'i·ty, *n.*, *pl.* -ties. 1. accordance with custom. 2. act done as matter of standard practice.

for'mat, *n.*, *v.* -matted, -matting. —*n.* 1. general design or arrangement. —*v.* 2. prepare (computer disk) for writing and reading.

for·ma'tion, *n.* 1. act or instance of forming. 2. material that forms. 3. pattern of ships, aircraft, etc., moving together.

form'a·tive, *adj.* 1. giving or acquiring form. 2. relating to formation and development.

for'mer, *adj.* 1. earlier. 2. first-mentioned. —**for'mer·ly,** *adv.*

for'mi·da·ble, *adj.* awesome.

for'mu·la, *n.*, *pl.* -las, -lae. 1. scientific description in figures and symbols. 2. set form of words.

for'mu·late', *v.* -lated, -lating. state systematically. —**for·mu·la'tion,** *n.*

for'ni·cate', *v.* -cated, -cating. have illicit sexual relations. —**for·ni·ca'tion,** *n.* —**for'ni·ca'tor,** *n.*

for·sake', *v.* -sook, -saken, -saking. desert; abandon.

for·swear', *v.* -swore, -sworn, -swearing. 1. renounce. 2. perjure.

for·syth'i·a, *n.* shrub bearing yellow flowers.

fort, *n.* fortified place.

forte, (fôrt), *n.* 1. one's strong point. —*adv.* (fôr'tā). 2. *Music.* loudly.

forth, *adv.* 1. onward. 2. into view. 3. abroad.

forth'com'ing, *adj.* about to appear.

forth'right', *adj.* direct in manner or speech.

forth'with', *adv.* at once.

for'ti·fi·ca'tion, *n.* defensive military construction.

for'ti·fy', *v.*, -fied, -fying. strengthen.

for·tis'si·mo', *adj.*, *adv. Music.* very loud.

for'ti·tude', *n.* patient courage.

fort'night', *n.* two weeks.

for'tress, *n.* fortified place.

for·tu'i·tous (-tyōō'-), *adj.* accidental. —**for·tu'i·tous·ly,** *adv.* —**for·tu'i·ty,** *n.*

for'tu·nate, *adj.* lucky. —**for'tu·nate·ly,** *adv.*

for'tune, *n.* 1. wealth. 2. luck.

for'ty, *n.*, *adj.* ten times four. —**for'ti·eth,** *adj.*, *n.*

fo'rum, *n.* assembly for public discussion.

for'ward, *adv.* 1. onward. Also, **for'wards.** —*adj.* 2. advanced. 3. bold. —*v.* 4. send on.

fos'sil, *n.* petrified remains of animal or plant. —**fos'sil·ize',** *v.*

fos'ter, *v.* 1. promote growth. —*adj.* 2. reared in a family but not related.

foul, *adj.* 1. filthy; dirty. 2. abominable. 3. unfair. —*n.* 4. violation of rules in game. —*v.* 5. make or become foul. 6. entangle. —**foul'ly,** *adv.*

found, *v.* establish.

foun·da'tion, *n.* 1. base for building, etc. 2. organization endowed for public benefit. 3. act of founding.

found'er, *v.* 1. fill with water and sink. 2. go lame. —*n.* 3. person who founds.

found'ling, *n.* abandoned child.

found'ry, *n.*, *pl.* -ries. place where molten metal is cast.

foun'tain, *n.* 1. spring of water. 2. source. Also, **fount.**

four, *n.*, *adj.* three plus one. —**fourth,** *n.*, *adj.*

four'teen', *n.*, *adj.* ten plus four. —**four'teenth',** *adj.*, *n.*

fowl, *n.* bird, esp. hen or rooster.

fox, *n.* carnivorous animal of dog family.

fox'glove', *n.* tall plant with bell-shaped flowers.

fox'hole', n. small pit used for cover in battle.

fox trot, dance for couples.

fox'y, adj. **foxier, foxiest. 1.** cunning. **2.** Slang. physically attractive.

foy'er, n. lobby.

fra'cas (frā'-), n. tumult.

frac'tion, n. part of whole. —**frac'tion·al,** adj.

frac'tious, adj. unruly.

frac'ture, n., v., **-tured, -turing.** break or crack.

frag'ile, adj. easily damaged. —**fra·gil'i·ty,** n.

frag'ment, n. **1.** broken part. **2.** bit. —v. **3.** break into fragments. —**frag'men·tar'y,** adj.

fra'grance, n. pleasant smell. —**fra'grant,** adj.

frail, adj. weak; fragile. —**frail'ty,** n.

frame, n., v., **framed, framing.** —n. **1.** enclosing border. **2.** skeleton. —v. **3.** devise. **4.** put in frame. —**frame'work',** n.

franc (frangk), n. French coin.

fran'chise (-chīz), n. **1.** right to vote. **2.** right to do business.

frank, adj. **1.** candid. —v. **2.** mail without charge.

frank'furt·er, n. small sausage.

frank'in·cense' (-sens'), n. aromatic resin.

fran'tic, adj. wildly excited. —**fran'ti·cal·ly,** adv.

fra·ter'nal, adj. brotherly.

fra·ter'ni·ty, n., pl. **-ties.** male society.

frat'er·nize', v., **-nized, -nizing.** associate fraternally or intimately. —**frat'er·ni·za'tion,** n.

frat'ri·cide' (fa'tri sīd', frā'-), n. **1.** act of killing one's brother. **2.** person who kills his or her brother. —**frat'ri·cid'al,** adj.

fraud, n. trickery. —**fraud'u·lent,** adj. —**fraud'u·lent·ly,** adv.

fraught, adj. full; charged.

fray, n. **1.** brawl. —v. **2.** ravel.

fraz'zle, n., v., **-zled, -zling.** n. Informal. —v. **1.** fray. **2.** fatigue. —n. **3.** state of fatigue.

freak, n. abnormal phenomenon, person, or animal.

freck'le, n. small brownish spot on skin.

free, adj., **freer, freest,** v., **freed, freeing.** —adj. **1.** having personal rights or liberty. **2.** independent. **3.** open. **4.** provided without charge. —adv. **5.** without charge. —v. **6.** make free. —**free'dom,** n.

free'boot'er, n. pirate.

free'-for-all', n. Informal. brawl; melee.

free'lance', adj., n., v., **-lanced, -lancing.** adj. **1.** hiring out one's work job by job. —n. **2.** Also, **free'lanc'er.** freelance worker. —v. **3.** work as freelance.

free'load', v. Informal. take advantage of the generosity of others; accept free food, lodging, etc. —**free'load'er,** n.

Free'ma'son, n. member of secret fraternal association for mutual assistance and promotion of brotherly love. —**Free'ma'son·ry,** n.

free'think'er, n. person with original religious opinions.

free'way', n. major highway.

freeze, v., **froze, frozen, freezing,** —v. **1.** harden into ice. **2.** fix (prices, etc.) at a specific level. **3.** make unnegotiable. —n. **4.** act or instance of freezing. —**freez'er,** n.

freight, n. **1.** conveyance of goods. **2.** goods conveyed. **3.** price paid.

freight'er, n. ship carrying mainly freight.

French, n. language or people of France. —**French,** adj. —**French'man,** n. —**French'wom'an,** n.fem.

French fries, strips of potato that have been deep-fried.

French horn, coiled brass wind instrument.

fre·net'ic, adj. frantic.

fren'zy, n., pl. **-zies.** wild excitement. —**fren'zied,** adj.

fre'quen·cy, n., pl. **-cies. 1.** state of being frequent. **2.** rate of recurrence. **3.** Physics. number of cycles in a unit of time.

fre'quent, adj. **1.** occurring often. —v. **2.** (fri kwent'). **2.** visit often.

fres'co (fres'kō), n., pl. **-coes, -cos.** painting on damp plaster.

fresh, adj. **1.** new. **2.** not salt. **3.** Informal. impudent. —**fresh'en,** v. —**fresh'ly,** adv. —**fresh'ness,** n.

fresh'et, n. sudden flood.

fresh'man, n., pl. **-men.** first-year student.

fret, n., v., **fretted, fretting.** —n. **1.** vexation. **2.** interlaced design. **3.** metal or wood ridge across strings of an instrument, as a guitar. —v. **4.** ornament with fret. **5.** worry. —**fret'ful,** adj. —**fret'work',** n.

Freud'i·an (froi'dē ən), adj. **1.** of or relating to psychoanalytic theories of Sigmund Freud. —n. **2.** person, esp. a psychoanalyst, who follows Freud's theories.

fri'a·ble, adj. crumbly.

fri'ar, n. member of Roman Catholic monastic order.

fric'as·see', n. stewed meat or fowl.

fric'tion, n. **1.** act or effect of rubbing

together. 2. conflict. —**fric'tion•al**, adj.

Fri'day, n. sixth day of week.

friend, n. 1. person attached to another by personal regard. 2. (cap.) Quaker; member of **Society of Friends**, a Christian sect. —**friend'ly**, adj. —**friend'ship**, n.

frieze (frēz), n. decorative, often carved band, as around a room.

frig'ate (frig'it), n. 1. fast sailing warship. 2. destroyerlike warship.

fright, n. 1. sudden fear. 2. shocking thing. —**fright'en**, v

fright'ful, adj. 1. causing fright. 2. Informal. ugly; tasteless.

fright'ful•ly, adv. Informal. very.

frig'id, adj. 1. very cold. 2. coldly disapproving. 3. lacking sexual appetite. —**fri•gid'i•ty, frig'id•ness**, n.

frill, n. 1. ruffle. 2. unnecessary feature. —v. 3. ruffle. —**frill'y**, adj.

fringe, n. border of lengths of thread, etc.

frip'per•y, n., pl. -**peries**. cheap finery.

frisk, v. leap playfully. —**frisk'y**, adj.

frit'ter, v. 1. squander little by little. —n. 2. fried batter cake.

friv'o•lous, adj. not serious or appropriate. —**fri•vol'i•ty**, n.

frizz, n. v. curl.

fro, adv. from; back.

frock, n. 1. dress. 2. loose robe.

frog, n. 1. small, tailless, web-footed amphibian. 2. hoarseness.

frol'ic, n., v., -**icked**, -**icking**. —n. 1. fun; gaiety. —v. 2. play merrily.

from, prep. 1. out of. 2. because of. 3. starting at.

frond, n. divided leaf.

front, n. 1. foremost part. 2. area of battle. 3. appearance; pretense. 4. false operation concealing illegal activity. —adj. 5. of or at the front. —v. 6. face. —**fron'tal**, adj.

front'age, n. front extent of property.

fron•tier', n. 1. border of a country. 2. outer edge of civilization. —**fron•tiers'man**, n.

fron'tis•piece', n. picture preceding title page.

frost, n. 1. state of freezing. 2. cover of ice particles. —v. 3. cover with frost or frosting. —**frost'y**, adj.

frost'bite', n. gangrenous condition caused by extreme cold.

frost'ing, n. 1. sweet preparation for covering cakes. 2. lusterless finish for glass, etc.

froth, n., v. foam. —**froth'y**, adj.

fro'ward, adj. perverse.

frown, v. 1. show concentration or displeasure on face. —n. 2. frowning look.

frow'zy, adj. **frowzier**, **frowziest**. slovenly.

fruc'ti•fy', v., -**fied**, -**fying**. 1. bear fruit. 2. make productive. —**fruc'ti•fi•ca'tion**, n.

fru'gal, adj. thrifty. —**fru•gal'i•ty**, n.

fruit, n. 1. edible product of a plant. 2. result.

fruit'ful, adj. productive; successful.

fruit'less, adj. vain; without success.

fru•i'tion, n. attainment.

frus'trate', v., -**trated**, -**trating**. thwart. —**frus•tra'tion**, n.

frus'tum, n. segment of conical solid with parallel top and base.

fry, v., **fried**, **frying**, n., pl. **fries**, (for 4) **fry**. —v. 1. cook in fat over direct heat. —n. 2. something fried. 3. feast of fried things. 4. young of fishes.

fuch'sia (fyōō'sha), n. plant with drooping flowers.

fudge, n. kind of candy.

fuel, n., v., **fueled**, **fueling**. —n. 1. substance that maintains fire. —v. 2. supply with or take in fuel.

fu'gi•tive, n. 1. fleeing person. —adj. 2. fleeing. 3. impermanent.

fugue (fyōōg), n. musical composition in which themes are presented by different voices in turn. —**fu'gal**, adj.

ful'crum, n., pl. -**crums**, -**cra**. support on which lever turns.

ful•fill', v. 1. carry out. 2. satisfy. —**ful•fill'ment, ful•fil'ment**, n.

full, adj. 1. filled. 2. complete. 3. abundant. —adv. 4. completely. 5. very. —**ful'ly**, adv. —**full'ness**, n.

full'-fledged', adj. fully developed.

ful'mi•nate', v., -**nated**, -**nating**. —v. 1. explode loudly. 2. issue denunciations. —n. 3. explosive chemical salt. —**ful'mi•na'tion**, n.

ful'some, adj. excessive.

fum'ble, v., -**bled**, -**bling**, n. —v. 1. grope clumsily. 2. drop. —n. 3. act of fumbling.

fume, n., v., **fumed**, **fuming**. —n. 1. vapor. —v. 2. emit or expose to fumes. 3. show anger.

fu'mi•gate', v., -**gated**, -**gating**. disinfect with fumes. —**fu'mi•ga'tion**, n.

fun, n. play; joking.

func'tion, n. 1. proper activity. 2. formal social gathering. —v. 3. act; operate. —**func'tion•al**, adj.

func'tion•ar'y, n., pl. -**aries**. official.

fund, n. 1. stock of money. —v. 2. pay for.

fun'da•men'tal, adj. 1. basic. —n. 2. basic principle. —**fun'da•men'tal•ly**, adv.

fun·da·men·tal·ist, n. believer in literal interpretation of a religious text, as the Bible. —**fun·da·men·tal·ism**, n.

fu·ner·al, n. burial rite. —**fu·ner·al**, adj.

fu·ne're·al, adj. 1. mournful. 2. of funerals.

fun·gus, n. pl. -gi (-jī). plant of group including mushrooms and molds. —**fun'gous**, adj.

funk, n. Informal. fear or depression.

fun'nel, n. v. -neled, -neling. —n. 1. cone-shaped part. 2. smokestack of vessel. —v. 3. channel or focus.

fun'ny, adj. -nier, -niest. 1. amusing. 2. Informal. strange.

fur, n. v. furred, furring. —n. 1. thick hairy skin of animal. 2. garment made of fur. —v. 3. trim with fur. —**fur'ry**, adj.

fur·be·low', n. showy trimming.

fu'ri·ous, adj. 1. full of fury. 2. violent. —**fu'ri·ous·ly**, adv.

furl, v. roll tightly.

fur'long, n. ⅛ of mile; 220 yards.

fur'lough, n. 1. leave of absence. 2. temporary layoff from work. —v. 3. give a furlough to.

fur'nace, n. structure in which to generate heat.

fur'nish, v. 1. provide. 2. fit out with furniture.

fur'nish·ing, n. 1. article of furniture, etc. 2. clothing accessory.

fur'ni·ture, n. tables, chairs, beds, etc.

fu'ror, n. general excitement.

fur'ri·er, n. dealer or worker in furs.

fur'row, n. 1. trench made by plow. 2. wrinkle. —v. 3. make furrows in.

fur'ther, adv. 1. to a greater distance or extent. 2. moreover. —adj. 3. more. —v. 4. promote. —**fur'ther·ance**, n.

fur·ther·more', adv. in addition.

fur'thest, adj. 1. most distant or remote. —adv. 2. to greatest distance.

fur'tive, adj. stealthy. —**fur'tive·ly**, adv. —**fur'tive·ness**, n.

fu'ry, n. pl. -ries. 1. violent passion, esp. anger. 2. violence.

furze, n. low evergreen shrub.

fuse, n. v. fused, fusing. —n. 1. safety device that breaks an electrical connection under excessive current. 2. Also, **fuze**. device for igniting explosive. —v. 3. blend, esp. by melting together. —**fu'si·ble**, adj. —**fu'sion**, n.

fu'se·lage' (fyoo'sə läzh'), n. framework of an airplane.

fu·sil·lade' (fyoo'sə läd'), n. simultaneous gunfire.

fuss, n. 1. needless concern or activity. —v. 2. make or put into fuss. —**fuss'y**, adj.

fus'ty, adj. -tier, -tiest. 1. moldy; musty. 2. old-fashioned; out-of-date.

fu'tile, adj. useless; unsuccessful. —**fu·til'i·ty**, n.

fu'ton (foo'ton), n. thin, quiltlike mattress used for sleeping or as seating.

fu'ture, n. 1. time to come. —adj. 2. that is to come. —**fu·tu'ri·ty**, n.

fuzz, n. fluff. —**fuzz'y**, adj. —**fuzz'i·ness**, n.

G

G, g, n. 1. seventh letter of English alphabet. 2. suitable for all ages: motion-picture classification.

gab, n. v., **gabbed, gabbing**. Informal. chatter. —**gab'by**, adj.

gab·ar·dine' (-dēn'), n. twill fabric.

gab'ble, v., -bled, -bling. —n. 1. rapid, unintelligible talk. —v. 2. talk gabble.

ga'ble, n. triangular wall from eaves to roof ridge.

gad, v., **gadded, gadding**. wander restlessly.

gad'fly', n., pl. -flies. annoyingly critical person.

gadg'et, n. Informal. any ingenious device.

gaff, n. 1. hook for landing fish. 2. spar on the upper edge of fore-and-aft sail.

gaffe (gaf), n. social blunder.

gag, v., **gagged, gagging**, n. —v. 1. stop up mouth to keep (person) silent. 2. suppress statements of. 3. retch. —n. 4. something that gags. 5. Informal. joke.

gage, n., v., **gaged, gaging**. —n. 1. token of challenge. 2. pledge. 3. gauge. —v. 4. gauge.

gag'gle, n. flock of geese or persons.

gai'e·ty, n. pl. -ties. merriment.

gai'ly, adv. merrily.

gain, v. 1. obtain. 2. earn. 3. improve. 4. move faster than another. —n. 5. profit. —**gain'ful**, adj.

gain'say', v. -said, -saying. contradict.

gait, n. manner of walking.

gai'ter, n. 1. covering for lower leg, worn over the shoe. 2. kind of shoe.

gal, n. Informal. girl.

ga'la, adj. festive.

gal'ax•y, n., pl. -axies. 1. (often cap.) Milky Way. 2. brilliant assemblage.

gale, n. strong wind.

gall (gôl), v. 1. chafe. 2. irritate. —n. 3. sore due to rubbing. 4. bile. 5. Informal. impudence. 6. abnormal growth on plants.

gall bladder, sac attached to the liver, in which bile is stored.

gal'lant, adj. chivalrous. —**gal'lant•ry,** n.

gall'le•on, n. large sailing vessel.

gal'ler•y, n. 1. corridor. 2. balcony. 3. place for art exhibits.

gal'ley, n. 1. vessel propelled by many oars. 2. kitchen of ship.

gal'li•vant', v. gad frivolously.

gal'lon, n. unit of capacity equal to 4 quarts.

gal'lop, v. 1. run at full speed. —n. 2. fast gait.

gal'lows, n. wooden frame for execution by hanging.

gall'stone', n. stone formed in bile passages.

ga•lore', adv. in abundance.

ga•losh'es, n.pl. overshoes.

gal•van'ic, adj. 1. producing or caused by electric current. 2. stimulating; exciting.

gal'va•nize', v. -nized, -nizing. 1. stimulate by or as by galvanic current. 2. coat with zinc.

gam'bit, n. 1. sacrificial move in chess. 2. clever tactic.

gam'ble, v., -bled, -bling. —v. 1. play for stakes at game of chance. 2. wager; risk. —n. 3. Informal. uncertain venture. —**gam'bler,** n.

gam'bol, v., -boled, -boling. v. frolic.

game, n. 1. pastime or contest. 2. wild animals, hunted for sport. —adj. 3. brave and willing. 4. lame.

gam'ete (gam'ēt), n. mature sexual reproductive cell that unites with another to form a new organism.

gam'in, n. street urchin. —**gam'ine** (-ēn), n.fem.

gam'ut, n. full range.

gam'y, adj., gamier, gamiest. 1. having the strong flavor of game, esp. slightly tainted game. 2. showing pluck; game. 3. risqué. —**gam'i•ness,** n.

gan'der, n. male goose.

gang, n. 1. group; band. 2. work crew. 3. band of criminals.

gan'gling, adj. awkwardly tall and thin.

gan'gli•on (-an), n., pl. -glia, -glions. nerve center.

gang'plank', n. temporary bridge to docked vessel.

gan'grene (gang'grēn), n. dying of tissue. —**gan'gre•nous,** adj.

gang'ster, n. member of criminal gang.

gang'way', n. 1. entrance to ship. 2. narrow passage. —interj. (gang'wā'). 3. make way!

gaol (jāl), n., v. Brit. jail.

gap, n. 1. opening; vacant space. 2. ravine.

gape, v., gaped, gaping. 1. open mouth as in wonder. 2. open wide.

gar, n. long, slim fish.

ga•rage', n. place where motor vehicles are kept or repaired.

garb, n. 1. clothes. —v. 2. clothe.

gar'bage, n. refuse; trash.

gar'ble, v., -bled, -bling. misquote or mix up.

gar'den, n. 1. area for growing plants. —v. 2. make or tend garden. —**gar'den•er,** n.

gar•de'ni•a, n. flowering evergreen shrub.

gar•gan'tu•an (gär gan'chōō ən), adj. extremely large; gigantic; colossal.

gar'gle, v., -gled, -gling, n. —v. 1. rinse throat. —n. 2. liquid for gargling.

gar'goyle, n. grotesquely carved figure.

gar'ish, adj. glaring; showy.

gar'land, n. 1. wreath of flowers, etc. —v. 2. deck with garland.

gar'lic, n. plant with edible, pungent bulb. —**gar'lick•y,** adj.

gar'ment, n. article of dress.

gar'ner, v. gather; acquire.

gar'net, n. deep-red gem.

gar'nish, v. 1. adorn. —n. 2. decoration.

gar'nish•ee', v., -nisheed, -nisheeing. attach (money or property of defendant).

gar'ret, n. attic.

gar'ri•son, n. 1. body of defending troops. —v. 2. provide with garrison.

gar•rote' (-ga rot'), n., v., -roted, -roting. —v. 1. strangulation. 2. strangle.

gar•ru•lous, adj. talkative. —**gar•ru'li•ty,** n.

gar'ter, n. fastening to hold up stocking.

gas, n., pl. gases, v. gassed, gassing. —n. 1. fluid substance, often burned for light or heat. 2. gasoline. —v. 3.

overcome with gas. —**gas'e•ous,** adj.

gash, n. **1.** long deep cut. —v. **2.** make gash in.

gas'ket, n. ring or strip used as packing.

gas'o•hol', n. mixture of gasoline and alcohol, used as auto fuel.

gas'o•line', n. inflammable liquid from petroleum, used esp. as motor fuel.

gasp, n. **1.** sudden short breath. —v. **2.** breathe in gasps.

gas'tric, adj. of stomachs.

gas'tro•nom'i•cal, adj. of good eating.

gate, n. movable hinged barrier.

gate'way', n. passage or entrance.

gath'er, v. **1.** bring or come together. **2.** infer. **3.** harvest. —n. **4.** pucker.

gauche (gōsh), adj. unsophisticated; socially clumsy.

gaud'y, adj., **gaudier, gaudiest.** vulgarly showy.

gauge (gāj), v., **gauged, gauging,** n. —v. **1.** estimate. **2.** measure. —n. **3.** standard of measure. **4.** distance between railroad rails.

gaunt, adj. haggard; bleak.

gaunt'let, n. **1.** large-cuffed glove. **2.** Also, **gant'let,** n. double row of persons beating offender passing between them.

gauze (gôz), n. transparent fabric. —**gauz'y,** adj.

gav'el, n. chairperson's mallet.

gawk, v. stare stupidly.

gawk'y, adj., **gawkier, gawkiest.** clumsy. —**gawk'i•ness.** n.

gay, adj. **gayer, gayest.** n. —adj. **1.** joyous. **2.** bright. **3.** Slang. homosexual. —n. **4.** Slang. homosexual. —**gay'ly,** adv.

gaze, v., **gazed, gazing,** n. —v. **1.** look steadily. —n. **2.** steady look.

ga•ze'bo (gǝ zā'bō, -zē'-), n., pl. **-bos, -boes.** structure, as a pavilion, on a site with a pleasant view.

ga•zelle', n. small, graceful antelope.

ga•zette', n. newspaper.

gaz'et•teer' (-tēr'), n. geographical dictionary.

gear, n. **1.** toothed wheel that engages with another. **2.** equipment. —v. **3.** connect by gears. **4.** adjust.

gee (jē), interj. (exclamation of surprise, disappointment, etc.)

gee'zer, n. odd or eccentric man, esp. an older one.

Gei'ger counter (gī'gǝr), instrument for measuring radioactivity.

gei'sha (gā'shǝ), n. Japanese woman trained to provide entertainment and companionship for men.

gel'a•tin, n. substance from animal skins, etc., used in jellies, glue, etc. —**ge•lat'i•nous,** adj.

geld'ing, n. castrated male horse.

gel'id (jel'id), adj. icy.

gem, n. precious stone.

gen•darme' (zhän'därm), n. French police officer.

gen'der, n. **1.** Gram. set of classes including all nouns, categorized as masculine, feminine, neuter. **2.** sex.

gene, n. biological unit that carries inherited traits.

ge'ne•al'o•gy, n., pl. **-gies.** study or account of ancestry.

gen'er•al, adj. **1.** of or including all. **2.** usual. **3.** undetailed. —n. **4.** highest-ranking army officer. —**gen'er•al•ly,** adv.

gen'er•al'i•ty, n., pl. **-ties.** general statement offered as accepted truth.

gen'er•al•ize', v., **-ized, -izing.** make generalities. —**gen'er•al•i•za'tion,** n.

general practitioner, doctor whose practice is not limited to any specific branch of medicine.

gen'er•ate', v., **-ated, -ating.** produce. —**gen'er•a'tive,** adj.

gen'er•a'tion, n. **1.** all individuals born in one period. **2.** such period (about 30 years). **3.** production.

gen'er•a'tor, n. device for producing electricity, gas, etc.

ge•ner'ic, adj. **1.** of entire categories. **2.** (of merchandise) unbranded.

gen'er•ous, adj. **1.** giving freely. **2.** abundant. —**gen'er•os'i•ty,** n.

gen'e•sis (jen'-), n. birth or origin.

ge•net'ics, n. science of heredity. —**ge•net'ic,** adj.

gen'ial (jēn'-), adj. openly friendly. —**ge'ni•al'i•ty,** n. —**gen'ial•ly,** adv.

ge'nie (jē'nē), n. spirit, often appearing in human form.

gen'i•tals, n.pl. sexual organs. —**gen'i•tal,** adj.

gen'i•tive (jen'i tiv), adj. n. **1.** grammatical case usu. indicating possession, origin, or other close association. —adj. **2.** of or relating to this case.

gen'ius (jēn'-), n. **1.** exceptional natural ability. **2.** person having such ability.

gen'o•cide' (jen'ǝ-), n. planned extermination of national or racial group.

gen're (zhän'rǝ), n. class or category of artistic work.

gen•teel', adj. well-bred; refined. —**gen•til'i•ty,** n.

gen'tian (jen'shǝn), n. plant with blue flowers.

gen'tile (-tīl), adj. (sometimes cap.) not Jewish or Mormon. —**gentile,** n.

gen•tle, *adj.*, **-tler, -tlest. 1.** mild; kindly. **2.** respectable. **3.** careful in handling things. —**gen'tle•ness**, *n.* —**gen'tly**, *adv.*

gen•tle•man, *n.*, *pl.* **-men. 1.** man of good breeding and manners. **2.** (used as polite term) any man.

gen•tri•fi•ca•tion, *n.* replacement of existing population by others with more wealth or status. —**gen'tri•fy**, *v.*

gen•try, *n.* wellborn people.

gen•u•flect (jen'yōō-), *v.* kneel partway in reverence. —**gen•u•flec'tion**, *n.*

gen•u•ine (-in), *adj.* real.

ge•nus (jē'-), *n.*, *pl.* **genera, genuses.** biological group including one or several species.

ge•o•des'ic dome, dome with framework of straight members that form grid.

ge•og•ra•phy, *n.* study of earth's surface, climate, etc. —**ge'o•graph'i•cal**, *adj.*

ge•ol•o•gy, *n.* science of earth's structure. —**ge•o•log'i•cal**, *adj.*

ge•om•e•try, *n.* branch of mathematics dealing with shapes. —**ge'o•met'ri•cal**, *adj.*

ge•o•pol'i•tics, *n.* study of politics in relation to geography. —**ge'o•po•lit'i•cal**, *adj.*

ge•ra'ni•um, *n.* small plant with showy flowers.

ger'bil (jûr'bal), *n.* small burrowing rodent, popular as a pet.

ger•i•at'rics (jer'-), *n.* branch of medicine dealing with aged persons. —**ger•i•at'ric**, *adj.*

germ, *n.* **1.** microscopic disease-producing organism. **2.** seed or origin.

German, *n.* native or language of Germany. —**German**, *adj.*

ger•mane', *adj.* pertinent.

German measles, rubella.

ger'mi•cide', *n.* agent that kills germs. —**ger•mi•cid'al**, *adj.*

ger'mi•nate', *v.*, **-nated, -nating.** begin to grow.

ger•on•tol•o•gy (jer'an tol'a jē, jēr'-), *n.* study of aging and problems and care of old people. —**ger•on•to•log'i•cal**, *adj.* —**ger•on•tol'o•gist**, *n.*

ger'ry•man'der (jer'-), *v.* divide into voting districts so as to give one group or area an unequal advantage.

ger'und (jer'-), *n.* noun form of a verb.

ges•ta'tion (jes-), *n.* period of being carried in womb.

ges•tic'u•late', *v.*, **-lated, -lating.** make gestures. —**ges•tic'u•la'tion**, *n.*

ges'ture, *n.*, *v.*, **-tured, -turing.** —*n.* **1.** expressive movement of body, head, etc. **2.** act demonstrating attitude or emotion. —*v.* **3.** make expressive movements.

get, *v.*, **got, got** or **gotten, getting. 1.** obtain. **2.** cause to be or do. **3.** be obliged to. **4.** arrive. **5.** become.

gew'gaw (gyōō'-), *n.* gaudy ornament.

gey'ser (gī'zar), *n.* hot spring that emits jets of water.

ghast'ly, *adj.*, **-lier, -liest. 1.** frightful. **2.** deathly pale.

gher'kin (gûr'-), *n.* **1.** small cucumber. **2.** small pickle.

ghet'to, *n.*, *pl.* **-tos, -toes. 1.** (formerly) Jewish part of city. **2.** city area in which mostly poor minorities live.

ghost, *n.* disembodied soul of dead person. —**ghost'ly**, *adj.*

ghost'writ'er, *n.* person who writes speech, book, etc., for another who is presumed to be the author.

ghoul (gōōl), *n.* **1.** spirit that preys on dead. **2.** person morbidly interested in misfortunes. —**ghoul'ish**, *adj.*

G.I., *Informal.* enlisted soldier.

gi'ant, *n.* **1.** being of superhuman size or strength. **2.** person of extraordinary accomplishments. —**gi'ant•ess**, *n.fem.*

gib'ber (jib'-), *v.* speak unintelligibly. —**gib'ber•ish**, *n.*

gib'bet (jib'-), *n.* gallows with projecting arm.

gib'bon (gib'-), *n.* small, long-armed ape.

gibe (jīb), *v.*, **gibed, gibing**, *n.* jeer.

gib'lets (jib'-), *n.pl.* heart, liver, and gizzard of a fowl.

gid'dy, *adj.*, **-dier, -diest. 1.** frivolous. **2.** dizzy.

gift, *n.* **1.** present. **2.** act of giving. **3.** power of giving. **4.** talent.

gift'ed, *adj.* talented.

gig (gig), *n.* **1.** light carriage drawn by one horse. **2.** light boat. **3.** *Slang.* single engagement, as of jazz musician. **4.** *Slang.* job.

gi•gan'tic, *adj.* like or befitting giants.

gig'gle, *v.*, **-gled, -gling**, *n.* —*v.* **1.** laugh lightly in silly way. —*n.* **2.** silly laugh.

gig•o•lo' (jig'-), *n.*, *pl.* **-los.** male professional escort.

gild, *v.*, **gilded** or **gilt, gilding.** coat with gold.

gill, *n.* **1.** breathing organ on fish. **2.** (jil). unit of liquid measure, 1/4 pint (4 fluid ounces).

gilt, n. gold used for gilding.

gim'crack' (jim'-), n. useless trifle.

gim'let (gim'-), n. small tool for boring holes.

gim'mick, n. device or trick.

gimp'y, adj., **gimpier, gimpiest.** Slang. limping or lame.

gin, n., v. **ginned, ginning.** —n. 1. flavored alcoholic drink. 2. machine for separating cotton from its seeds. 3. trap. —v. 4. put (cotton) through gin.

gin'ger, n. 1. plant with spicy root used in cookery. 2. spirit; animation.

gin'ger•bread', n. 1. cake flavored with ginger and molasses. 2. elaborate or gaudy architectural ornamentation.

gin'ger•ly, adj. 1. wary. —adv. 2. warily.

ging'ham, n. cotton fabric, usu. checked.

gin'seng (jin'-), n. plant with a medicinal root.

gi•raffe', n. tall, long-necked animal of Africa.

gird, v., **girt or girded, girding.** 1. encircle with or as with belt. 2. prepare.

gird'er, n. horizontal structural beam.

gir'dle, n., v., **-dled, -dling.** —n. 1. encircling band. 2. light corset. —v. 3. encircle.

girl, n. female child or young woman.

girl'friend', n. 1. frequent or favorite female companion; sweetheart. 2. female friend.

girl scout, member of organization for girls promoting character development, health, etc.

girth, n. 1. distance around. —v. 2. gird.

gis'mo (giz'mō), n. gadget. Also, **giz'-mo.**

gist (jist), n. essential meaning.

give, v., **gave, given, giving,** n. —v. 1. bestow. 2. emit. 3. present. 4. yield. —n. 5. elasticity.

give'a•way', n. Informal. 1. revealing act, remark, etc. 2. TV show in which contestants compete for prizes.

giv'en, adj. 1. stated; fixed. 2. inclined; disposed. 3. established fact or condition.

giz'zard, n. muscular stomach of birds.

gla'cier, n. mass of ice moving slowly down slope.

glad, adj., **gladder, gladdest.** 1. pleased; happy. 2. causing joy. —**glad'den,** v. —**glad'ness,** n.

glade, n. open space in forest.

glad'i•a'tor, n. Roman swordsman fighting for public entertainment.

glad'i•o'lus (glad'ē ō'lus), n., pl. **lus,**

li (lī), **luses.** plant bearing spikes of flowers. Also, **glad'i•o'la.**

glad'ly, adv. 1. with pleasure. 2. willingly.

glam'our, n. alluring charm. —**glam'or•ous,** adj. —**glam'or•ous•ly,** adv.

glance, v., **glanced, glancing,** n. —v. 1. look briefly. 2. strike obliquely. —n. 3. brief look.

gland, n. body organ that secretes some substance. —**glan'du•lar,** adj.

glan'ders, n. disease of horses.

glare, n., v., **glared, glaring.** —n. 1. strong light. 2. fierce look. 3. bright, smooth surface. —v. 4. shine with strong light. 5. stare fiercely.

glass, n. 1. hard, brittle, transparent substance. 2. (pl.) eyeglasses. 3. drinking vessel of glass. 4. anything made of glass. —adj. 5. of glass. —v. 6. cover with glass. —**glass'ware',** n.

glass ceiling, not generally acknowledged upper limit to professional advancement, esp. for women or minorities.

glass'y, adj., **glassier, glassiest.** 1. like glass, as in transparency. 2. without expression; dull.

glau•co'ma (glô kō'ma, glou-), n. condition of elevated fluid pressure within the eyeball, causing increasing loss of vision.

glaze, v., **glazed, glazing,** n. —v. 1. furnish with glass. 2. put glossy surface on. 3. make (eyes) expressionless. —n. 4. glossy coating.

gla'zier (-zhər), n. person who installs glass.

gleam, n. 1. flash of light. —v. 2. emit gleams.

glean, v. gather laboriously, as grain left by reapers. —**glean'ing,** n.

glee, n. joy; mirth. —**glee'ful,** adj.

glen, n. narrow valley.

glib, adj. suspiciously fluent. —**glib'ly,** adv. —**glib'ness,** n.

glide, v., **glided, gliding,** n. —v. 1. move smoothly and gradually. —n. 2. gliding movement.

glid'er, n. motorless heavier-than-air aircraft.

glim'mer, n. 1. faint unsteady light. —v. 2. shine faintly.

glimpse, n., v., **glimpsed, glimpsing.** —n. 1. brief view. —v. 2. catch glimpse of.

glint, n., v. gleam.

glis'ten, v. sparkle.

glitch, n. Informal. malfunction; hitch.

glit'ter, v. 1. reflect light with a brilliant sparkle. 2. make a brilliant show. —n. 3. sparkling light or luster. 4. showy brilliance. 5. small glittering ornaments.

glitz'y, *adj.,* **glitzier, glitziest.** *Informal.* tastelessly showy; flashy and pretentious.

gloam'ing, *n.* dusk.

gloat, *v.* gaze or speak with unconcealed triumph.

global warming, increase in the average temperature of the earth's atmosphere, causing changes in climate.

globe, *n.* 1. sphere; world. 2. sphere depicting the earth. 3. any sphere. —**glob'al,** *adj.*

glob'ule (glob'yool), *n.* small sphere. —**glob'u•lar,** *adj.*

gloom, *n.* 1. low spirits. 2. darkness.

gloom'y, *adj.,* **gloomier, gloomiest.** 1. dejected; low-spirited. 2. depressing. 3. dark; dismal.

glor•i•fied, *adj.* made to seem better than is really so.

glo'ri•fy, *v.,* **-fied, -fying.** 1. extol. 2. make glorious. —**glo'ri•fi•ca'tion,** *n.*

glo'ry, *n., pl.* **-ries,** *v.,* **-ried, -rying.** —*n.* 1. great praise or honor. 2. magnificence. 3. heaven. —*v.* 4. exult. —**glor'i•ous,** *adj.*

gloss, *n.* 1. external show. 2. shine. 3. explanation of text. —*v.* 4. put gloss on. 5. annotate. 6. explain away. —**glos'sy,** *adj.*

glos'sa•ry, *n., pl.* **-ries.** list of difficult words with definitions.

glot'tis, *n.* opening at upper part of larynx.

glove, *n., v.,* **gloved, gloving.** —*n.* 1. hand covering with sheath for each finger. —*v.* 2. cover with glove.

glow, *n.* 1. light emitted by heated substance. 2. brightness or warmth. —*v.* 3. shine.

glow'er (glou'-), *v.* 1. frown sullenly. —*n.* 2. frown.

glow'worm, *n.* kind of firefly.

glu'cose', *n.* sugar found in fruits.

glue, *n., v.,* **glued, gluing.** —*n.* 1. adhesive substance, esp. from gelatin. —*v.* 2. fasten with glue.

glum, *adj.* gloomily sullen.

glut, *v.,* **glutted, glutting.** *v.* —*n.* 1. feed or fill to excess. —*n.* 2. full supply. 3. surfeit.

glu'ten (gloo'-), *n.* substance left in flour after starch is removed.

glut'ton, *n.* greedy person. —**glut'ton•ous,** *adj.* —**glut'ton•y,** *n.*

glyc'er•in, *n.* thick liquid used as a sweetener, lotion, etc.

gnarl (närl), *n.* knot on a tree.

gnarled (närld), *adj.* bent and distorted.

gnash (nash), *v.* 1. grind (the teeth) together, as in rage.

gnat (nat), *n.* small fly.

gnaw (nô), *v.* wear away by biting.

gnome (nōm), *n.* dwarf in superstition.

gnu (noo), *n., pl.* **gnus, gnu.** African antelope.

go, *v.,* **went, gone, going.** 1. move; depart. 2. act. 3. become. 4. harmonize.

goad, *n.* 1. pointed stick. 2. stimulus. —*v.* 3. drive with goad. 4. tease; taunt.

goal, *n.* 1. aim. 2. terminal or target in race or game. 3. single score in various games.

goal'keep'er, *n.* in various games, player whose chief duty is to prevent opposition from scoring a goal. Also, **goal'tend'er;** *Informal.* **goal'ie.**

goat, *n.* horned mammal related to sheep.

goat•ee', *n.* pointed beard.

gob, *n.* 1. mass. 2. *Slang.* sailor.

gob'ble, *v.,* **-bled, -bling,** *n.* —*v.* 1. eat greedily. 2. make cry of male turkey. —*n.* 3. this cry.

gob'ble•de•gook', *n.* meaningless or roundabout speech or writing.

gob'bler, *n.* male turkey.

go'-be•tween', *n.* intermediary.

gob'let, *n.* stemmed glass.

gob'lin, *n.* elf.

God, *n.* 1. Supreme Being. 2. *(l.c.)* deity. —**god'dess,** *n.fem.*

god'ly, *adj.,* **-lier, -liest.** 1. of God or gods. 2. conforming to religion. —**god'li•ness,** *n.*

god'par'ent, *n.* sponsor of child at baptism. —**god'child',** *n.* —**god'fath'er,** *n.* —**god'moth'er,** *n.*

god'send', *n.* anything unexpected but welcome.

goes (gōz), third pers. sing. pres. indic. of **go.**

go'fer (gō'fər), *n. Slang.* employee who mainly runs errands.

gog'gles, *n.pl.* protective eyeglasses.

goi'ter, *n.* enlargement of thyroid gland, causing swelling on neck.

gold, *n.* 1. precious yellow metal. 2. bright yellow. —**gold, gold'en,** *adj.*

gold'en•rod', *n.* plant bearing clusters of yellow flowers.

gold'fish', *n.* small, gold-colored fish.

golf, *n.* game played on outdoor course with special clubs and small ball.

gon•do'la (gon'də lə, gon dō'lə), *n.* 1. narrow canal boat used in Venice. 2. low-sided freight car. —**gon•do•lier'** (-lēr'), *n.*

gon'er, *n. Informal.* person or thing that is dying, lost, or past recovery.

gong, *n.* brass or bronze disk sounded with soft hammer.

gon•or•rhe'a (gon'ə rē'ə), *n.* contagious venereal disease.

good, *adj.* 1. morally excellent. 2. of high or adequate quality. 3. kind. 4. skillful. —*n.* 5. benefit. 6. excellence. 7. (*pl.*) possessions. 8. (*pl.*) cloth.

good'ly, *adj.,* **-lier, -liest.** numerous; abundant.

good'-by', *interj., n., pl.* **-bys.** farewell. Also, **good'-bye'.**

good'will', *n.* friendly feelings or intentions.

Good Friday, Friday before Easter.

goof, *Informal.* —*n.* 1. fool. 2. blunder. —*v.* 3. blunder. —**goof'y,** *adj.*

goon, *n. Slang.* 1. hoodlum hired to threaten or commit violence. 2. stupid, foolish, or awkward person.

goose, *n., pl.* **geese.** web-footed water bird.

goose'ber'ry, *n., pl.* **-ries.** tart, edible acid fruit.

goose flesh, bristling of hair on the skin, as from cold or fear. Also, **goose pimples, goose bumps.**

go'pher, *n.* burrowing rodent.

gore, *n., v.,* **gored, goring.** —*n.* 1. clotted blood. 2. triangular insert of cloth. —*v.* 3. pierce with horn or tusk. 4. finish with gores (def. 2). —**gor'y,** *adj.*

gorge, *n., v.,* **gorged, gorging.** —*n.* 1. narrow rocky cleft. —*v.* 2. stuff with food.

gor'geous, *adj.* splendid.

go•ril'la, *n.* large African ape.

gos'ling, *n.* young goose.

gos'pel, *n.* 1. teachings of Christ and apostles. 2. absolute truth.

gos'sa•mer, *n.* 1. filmy cobweb. —*adj.* 2. like gossamer.

gos'sip, *n., v.,* **-siped, -siping.** —*n.* 1. idle talk, esp. about others. 2. person given to gossip. —*v.* 3. talk idly about others.

Goth'ic, *adj.* 1. of a style of European architecture from the 12th to 16th centuries. 2. (*often l.c.*) of a style of literature marked by gloomy settings and mysterious or sinister events.

gouge, *n., v.,* **gouged, gouging.** —*n.* 1. chisel with hollow blade. —*v.* 2. dig out with gouge. 3. extract by coercion. —**goug'er,** *n.*

gou'lash, *n.* seasoned meat stew.

gourd (gôrd), *n.* dried shell of kind of cucumber.

gour•mand' (gŏŏr mänd'), *n.* enthusiastic or greedy eater.

gour'met (gŏŏr'mā), *n.* lover of fine food.

gout, *n.* painful disease of joints. —**gout'y,** *adj.*

gov'ern, *v.* 1. rule. 2. influence. 3. regulate.

gov'ern•ess, *n.* woman who teaches children in their home.

gov'ern•ment, *n.* 1. system of rule. 2. political governing body. —**gov'ern•men'tal,** *adj.*

gov'er•nor, *n.* 1. person who governs. 2. device that controls speed.

gown, *n.* 1. woman's dress. 2. loose robe.

grab, *v.,* **grabbed, grabbing,** —*v.* 1. seize eagerly. —*n.* 2. act of grabbing.

grace, *n., v.,* **graced, gracing.** —*n.* 1. beauty of form, movement, etc. 2. goodwill. 3. God's love. 4. prayer said at table. —*v.* 5. lend grace to; favor. —**grace'ful,** *adj.* —**grace'less,** *adj.*

gra'cious, *adj.* kind.

gra•da'tion, *n.* change in series of stages.

grade, *n., v.,* **graded, grading.** —*n.* 1. degree in a scale. 2. scholastic division. 3. Also, **gra'di•ent.** slope. —*v.* 4. arrange in grades. 5. level.

grade school, elementary school.

grad'u•al, *adj.* changing, moving, etc., by degrees. —**grad'u•al•ly,** *adv.*

grad'u•ate, *n., adj. v.,* **-ated, -ating.** —*n.* (-it). 1. recipient of diploma. —*adj.* (-it). 2. graduated. 3. of or involved in academic study beyond the baccalaureate level. —*v.* (-āt'). 4. receive or confer diploma or degree. 5. mark in measuring degrees. —**grad'u•a'tion,** *n.*

graf•fi'ti (-fē'tē), *n.pl., sing.* **-to.** casual markings written or sketched on sidewalk, public wall, etc.

graft, *n.* 1. twig, etc., inserted in another plant to unite with it. 2. profit through dishonest use of one's position. —*v.* 3. make graft. 4. make dishonest profits. —**graft'er,** *n.*

gra'ham, *adj.* made of unsifted wholewheat flour.

Grail (grāl), *n.* in medieval legend, the cup or chalice used at the last supper of Christ with the apostles.

grain, *n.* 1. seed of cereal plant. 2. particle. 3. pattern of wood fibers. —**grain'y,** *adj.*

gram, *n.* metric unit of weight.

gram'mar, *n.* 1. features of a language as a whole. 2. knowledge or usage of the preferred forms in speaking or writing. —**gram•mat'i•cal,** *adj.* —**gram•mar'i•an,** *n.*

gran'a•ry (gran'-), *n., pl.* **-ries.** storehouse for grain.

grand, *adj.* 1. large; major. 2. impressive.

grand'child', *n.* child of one's son

or daughter. —**grand'son'**, n. —**grand'daugh'ter**, n.fem.

gran•dee' (-dē'), n. nobleman.

gran'deur, n. imposing greatness.

gran•di•ose', adj. grand or pompous.

grand jury, jury designated to determine if a law has been violated and whether the evidence warrants prosecution.

grand'par'ent, n. parent of parent. —**grand'fa'ther**, n. —**grand'moth'er**, n.fem.

grand'stand', n. 1. sloped open-air place for spectators. —v. 2. conduct oneself or perform to impress onlookers.

grange, n. farmers' organization.

gran'ite, n. granular rock.

gra•no'la, n. cereal of dried fruit, grains, nuts, etc.

grant, v. 1. bestow. 2. admit. —n. 3. thing granted.

gran'u•late', v., -lated, -lating. form into granules. —**gran•u•la'tion**, n.

gran'ule, n. small grain. —**gran'u•lar**, adj.

grape, n. smooth-skinned fruit that grows in clusters on grapevine.

grape'fruit', n. large yellow citrus fruit.

grape'vine', n. 1. vine on which grapes grow. 2. person-to-person route by which gossip or information spreads.

graph, n. diagram showing relations by lines, etc.

graph'ic, adj. 1. vivid. 2. of writing, painting, etc. —**graph'i•cal•ly**, adv.

graph'ite (-īt), n. soft, dark mineral.

grap'nel, n. hooked device for grasping.

grap'ple, v., -pled, -pling. —n. 1. hook for grasping. —v. 2. try to grasp. 3. try to cope.

grasp, v. 1. seize and hold. 2. understand. —n. 3. act of gripping. 4. mastery.

grasp'ing, adj. greedy.

grass, n. 1. ground-covering herbage. 2. cereal plant.

grass'hop'per, n. leaping insect.

grass roots, ordinary citizens, as contrasted with leadership or elite. —**grass'-roots'**, adj.

grate, v., grated, grating, n. —v. 1. irritate. 2. make harsh sound. 3. rub into small bits. —n. 4. Also, **grat'ing**. metal framework. —**grat'er**, n.

grate'ful, adj. 1. thankful. 2. welcome as news. —**grate'ful•ly**, adv.

grat'i•fy', v., -fied, -fying. please. —**grat'i•fi•ca'tion**, n.

gra'tis (grat'is), adv., adj. free of charge.

grat'i•tude', n. thankfulness.

gra•tu'i•tous (-tōō'-), adj. 1. free of charge. 2. without reasonable cause.

gra•tu'i•ty, n., pl. -ties. tip.

grave, n., adj. graver, gravest. —n. 1. place of or excavation for burial. —adj. 2. solemn. 3. important. —**grave'yard'**, n.

grav'el, n. small stones.

grav'el•ly, adj. 1. made up of or like gravel. 2. harsh-sounding; raspy.

grav'i•ta'tion, n. force of attraction between bodies. —**grav'i•tate'**, v.

grav'i•ty, n., pl. -ties. 1. force attracting bodies to the earth's center. 2. serious character.

gra'vy, n., pl. -vies. juices from cooking meat.

gray, n. 1. color between black and white. —adj. 2. of this color. 3. ambiguous. 4. vaguely depressing.

gray matter, nerve tissue of brain and spinal cord.

graze, v., grazed, grazing. 1. feed on grass. 2. brush in passing.

grease, n., v., greased, greasing. —n. 1. animal fat. 2. fatty or oily matter. —v. 3. put grease on or in. —**greas'y**, adj.

great, adj. 1. very large. 2. important. —**great'ly**, adv.

Great Dane, large, powerful dog.

grebe (grēb), n. diving bird.

greed, n. excessive desire. —**greed'y**, adj.

Greek, n. native or language of Greece. —**Greek**, adj.

green, adj. 1. of color of vegetation. 2. unripe. 3. inexperienced. —n. 4. green color. 5. grassy land.

green'belt', n. area of woods, parks, or open land surrounding a community.

green'er•y, n., pl. -eries. plants; foliage.

green'house', n. building where plants are grown.

greenhouse effect, heating of atmosphere resulting from absorption by certain gases of solar radiation.

greet, v. 1. address in meeting. 2. react to; receive. —**greet'ing**, n.

gre•gar'i•ous (gri gâr'-), adj. fond of company.

grem'lin, n. mischievous elf.

gre•nade', n. explosive hurled missile.

gren'a•dier', n. Brit. member of special infantry regiment.

grey, n., adj. gray.

grey'hound', n. slender fleet-footed dog.

grid, n. 1. covering of crossed bars. 2. system of crossed lines.

grid′dle, *n.* shallow frying pan or plate.

grid′i·ron′, *n.* 1. grill. 2. football field.

grid′lock′, *n.* 1. complete stoppage of movement due to traffic blocking all intersections. 2. stoppage of a process, as legislation.

grief, *n.* keen sorrow.

griev′ance, *n.* 1. wrong. 2. complaint against wrong.

griev′ous, *adj.* causing grief, pain, etc.

grieve, *v.*, **grieved, grieving.** feel sorrow; inflict sorrow on.

grif′fin, *n.* monster of fable with head and wings of eagle and body of lion. Also, **gryph′on.**

grill, *n.* 1. barred utensil for broiling. —*v.* 2. broil on grill. 3. question persistently.

grille (gril), *n.* ornamental metal barrier.

grim, *adj.*, **grimmer, grimmest.** 1. stern. 2. harshly threatening. —**grim′ly**, *adv.* —**grim′ness**, *n.*

gri·mace′ (*n.* grim′as, *v.* gri mās′), *n.*, *v.*, **-maced, -macing.** smirk.

grime, *n.* dirt. —**grim′y**, *adj.*

grin, *v.*, **grinned, grinning.** —*v.* 1. smile openly and broadly. —*n.* 2. broad smile.

grind, *v.*, **ground, grinding.** —*v.* 1. wear, crush, or sharpen by friction. 2. turn crank. —*n.* 3. *Informal.* dreary routine. —**grind′stone**, *n.*

grip, *n.*, *v.*, **gripped, gripping.** —*n.* 1. grasp. 2. handclasp. 3. small suitcase. 4. handle. —*v.* 5. grasp.

gripe, *v.*, **griped, griping**, *n.* —*v.* 1. grasp. 2. produce pain in bowels. 3. *Informal.* complain. —*n.* 4. *Informal.* complaint.

grippe (grip), *n.* influenza.

gris′ly, *adj.*, **-lier, -liest.** gruesome.

grist, *n.* grain to be ground. —**grist′-mill′**, *n.*

gris′tle, *n.* cartilage.

grit, *n.*, *v.*, **gritted, gritting.** —*n.* 1. fine particles. 2. courage. —*v.* 3. cause to grind together. —**grit′ty**, *adj.*

grits, *n.pl.* ground grain.

griz′zly, *adj.*, **-zlier, -zliest.** gray, as hair or fur. Also, **griz′zled.**

grizzly bear, large bear of western U.S. and Canada, with coarse, gray-tipped fur.

groan, *n.* 1. moan of pain, derision, etc. —*v.* 2. utter groans. —**groan′er**, *n.*

gro′cer, *n.* dealer in foods, etc.

gro′cer·y, *n.*, *pl.* **-ceries.** 1. store selling food. 2. (*usually pl.*) food bought at such a store.

grog′gy, *adj.*, **-gier, -giest.** dizzy. —**grog′gi·ness**, *n.*

groin, *n.* hollow where thigh joins abdomen.

grom′met, *n.* eyelet.

groom, *n.* 1. person in charge of horses or stables. 2. bridegroom. —*v.* 3. make neat.

grooms′man, *n.*, *pl.* **-men.** attendant of bridegroom.

groove, *n.*, *v.*, **grooved, grooving.** —*n.* 1. furrow. —*v.* 2. form groove in.

grope, *v.*, **groped, groping.** feel blindly.

gross, *adj.* 1. before deductions. 2. flagrant. —*n.* 3. amount before deductions. 4. twelve dozen. —**gross′ly**, *adv.* —**gross′ness**, *n.*

gro·tesque′, *adj.* 1. fantastically ugly or absurd. 2. fantastic.

grot′to, *n.*, *pl.* **-tos, -toes.** cave.

grouch, *Informal.* —*v.* 1. sulk. —*n.* 2. sulky person. 3. sullen mood. —**grouch′y**, *adj.*

ground, *n.* 1. earth's solid surface. 2. tract of land. 3. motive. 4. (*pl.*) dregs. 5. rational basis. —*adj.* 6. of or on ground. —*v.* 7. instruct in elements. 8. run aground.

ground′hog′, *n.* woodchuck.

ground′work′, *n.* basic work.

group, *n.* 1. number of persons or things placed or considered together. —*v.* 2. place in or form group.

grouse, *n.* game bird of America and Britain.

grout (grout), *n.* thin, coarse mortar, used as between tiles.

grove, *n.* small wood.

grov′el, *v.*, **-eled, -eling.** humble oneself, esp. by crouching.

grow, *v.*, **grew, grown, growing.** increase in size; develop. —**grow′er**, *n.*

growl, *n.* 1. guttural, angry sound. —*v.* 2. utter growls.

grown′up′, *n.* adult.

growth, *n.* 1. act of growing. 2. something that has grown.

grub, *n.*, *v.*, **grubbed, grubbing.** —*n.* 1. larva. 2. drudge. 3. *Informal.* food. —*v.* 4. dig.

grub′by, *adj.*, **-bier, -biest.** 1. dirty. 2. sordid. —**grub′bi·ness**, *n.*

grudge, *n.* lasting malice.

gru′el, *n.* thin cereal.

gru·el·ing, *adj.* exhausting.

grue′some, *adj.* revoltingly sinister.

gruff, *adj.* surly.

grum′ble, *v.*, **-bled, -bling.** murmur in discontent. —**grum′bler**, *n.*

grump′y, *adj.*, **grumpier, grumpiest.** surly.

grun•gy (grun'jē), *adj.*, **-gier, -giest.** *Slang.* dirty or run-down.

grunt, *n.* **1.** guttural sound. **2.** *Slang.* foot soldier. **3.** *Slang.* low-ranking worker. —*v.* **4.** utter grunts.

gryph'on, *n.* griffin.

gua'no (gwä'nō), *n.* manure, chiefly from excrement of sea birds.

guar•an•tee', *n., v.*, **-teed, -teeing.** —*n.* **1.** pledge given as security. —*v.* **2.** pledge. **3.** assure. Also, **guar'an•ty'.** —**guar•an'tor'**, *n.*

guard, *v.* **1.** watch over. —*n.* **2.** person who guards. **3.** body of guards. **4.** close watch.

guard'i•an, *n.* **1.** person who guards. **2.** person entrusted with care of another.

gua'va (gwä'və), *n.* large yellow fruit of tropical tree.

gu'ber•na•to'ri•al, *adj.* of governors.

guer•ril'la (gə ril'ə), *n.* soldier belonging to an independent group.

guess, *v.* **1.** form opinion on incomplete evidence. **2.** be right in such opinion. —*n.* **3.** act of guessing.

guess'work', *n.* **1.** act of guessing. **2.** conclusions from guesses.

guest, *n.* **1.** visitor. **2.** customer at hotel, restaurant, etc.

guf•faw', *n.* **1.** loud laughter. —*v.* **2.** laugh loudly.

guid'ance, *n.* **1.** act or instance of guiding. **2.** advice over period of time.

guide, *v.*, **guided, guiding,** *n.* **1.** show the way. —*n.* **2.** one that guides.

guided missile, radio-controlled aerial missile.

guide'line', *n.* guide or indication of future course of action.

gui'don (gī'don), *n.* small flag.

guild, *n.* commercial organization for common interest.

guile, *n.* cunning. —**guile'less,** *adj.*

guil'lo•tine' (gil'ə tēn'), *n.* machine for beheading.

guilt, *n.* fact or feeling of having committed a wrong. —**guilt'y,** *adj.*

guin'ea fowl (gin'ē), *n.* plump domesticated fowl. Also, **guinea hen.**

guinea pig, *n.* **1.** South American rodent. **2.** subject of experiment.

guise (gīz), *n.* outward appearance.

gui•tar', *n.* stringed musical instrument.

gulch, *n.* ravine.

gulf, *n.* **1.** arm of sea. **2.** abyss.

gull, *n.* **1.** web-footed sea bird. **2.** dupe. —*v.* **3.** cheat; trick.

gul'let, *n.* throat.

gul'li•ble, *adj.* easily deceived. —**gul'li•bil'i•ty,** *n.*

gul'ly, *n., pl.* **-lies.** deep channel cut by running water.

gulp, *v.* **1.** swallow in large mouthfuls. —*n.* **2.** act of gulping.

gum, *n., v.*, **gummed, gumming.** —*n.* **1.** sticky substance from plants. **2.** chewing gum. **3.** tissue around teeth. —*v.* **4.** smear with gum. —**gum'my,** *adj.*

gum'bo, *n., pl.* **-bos.** soup made with okra.

gump'tion, *n.* **1.** initiative; resourcefulness. **2.** courage; spunk.

gun, *n., v.*, **gunned, gunning.** —*n.* **1.** tubular weapon which shoots missiles with explosives. —*v.* **2.** hunt with gun. —**gun'ner,** *n.* —**gun'ner•y,** *n.*

gun'cot'ton, *n.* explosive made of cotton and acids.

gung'-ho', *adj. Informal.* thoroughly enthusiastic and loyal.

gunk (gungk), *n. Slang.* sticky or greasy matter.

gun'ny, *n., pl.* **-nies.** coarse material used for sacks.

gun'pow'der, *n.* explosive mixture.

gun'wale (gun'əl), *n.* upper edge of vessel's side.

gup'py, *n., pl.* **-pies.** tiny tropical fish.

gur'gle, *v.*, **-gled, -gling,** *n.* —*v.* **1.** flow noisily. —*n.* **2.** sound of gurgling.

gu'ru, *n.* **1.** Hindu spiritual teacher. **2.** any respected leader.

gush, *v.* **1.** flow or emit suddenly. **2.** talk effusively. —*n.* **3.** sudden flow. —**gush'y,** *adj.*

gush'er, *n.* jet of petroleum from underground.

gus'set, *n.* angular insertion, as in clothing.

gust, *n.* **1.** blast of wind. **2.** outburst. —**gust'y,** *adj.*

gus'ta•to'ry, *adj.* of taste.

gus'to, *n., pl.* **-toes.** keen enjoyment.

gut, *n., v.*, **gutted, gutting.** —*n.* **1.** intestine. **2.** (*pl.*) *Informal.* courage. —*v.* **3.** destroy interior of.

gut'ter, *n.* channel for leading off rainwater.

gut'tur•al, *adj.* **1.** of or in throat. —*n.* **2.** guttural sound. —**gut'tur•al•ly,** *adv.*

guy, *n.* **1.** rope, etc., used to guide or steady object. **2.** *Informal.* fellow.

guz'zle, *v.*, **-zled, -zling.** drink greedily.

gym•na'si•um (jim-), *n., pl.* **-siums, -sia.** place for physical exercise. *Informal,* **gym.**

gym'nast, *n.* performer of gymnastics.

gym•nas'tics, *n.pl.* physical exercises. —**gym•nas'tic,** *adj.*

gy•ne•col′o•gy (gī′nə-), *n.* branch of medicine dealing with care of women. —**gy•ne•col′o•gist,** *n.*

gyp (jip), *v.,* **gypped, gypping.** *Informal.* cheat.

gyp′sum, *n.* soft, common mineral.

Gyp′sy, *n., pl.* **-sies.** member of wandering people.

gy′rate, *v.,* **-rated, -rating.** whirl. —**gy•ra′tion,** *n.*

gy′ro•scope′ (jī′rə-), *n.* rotating wheel mounted to maintain absolute direction in space.

H

H, h, *n.* eighth letter of English alphabet.

ha′be•as cor′pus (hā′bē ə kôr′pəs), writ requiring that arrested person be brought before court to determine whether he or she is legally detained.

hab′er•dash•er•y, *n., pl.* **-eries.** shop selling men's furnishings. —**hab′er•dash′er,** *n.*

hab′it, *n.* 1. customary practice or act. 2. garb. —**ha•bit′u•al** (hə bich′ōō al), *adj.* —**ha•bit′u•al•ly,** *adv.* —**ha•bit′u•a′tion,** *n.*

hab′it•a•ble, *adj.* able to be inhabited. —**hab′it•a•bly,** *adv.*

hab′i•tant, *n.* resident.

hab′i•tat′, *n.* natural dwelling place.

hab′i•ta′tion, *n.* place of abode.

ha•bit′u•ate′, *v.,* **-ated, -ating.** accustom; make used to.

ha•bit′u•é′ (hə bich′ōō ā′), *n.* habitual visitor.

hack, *v.* 1. cut or chop roughly. 2. cough sharply. —*n.* 3. cut or notch. 4. artistic drudge. 5. vehicle for hire. —*adj.* 6. trite; routine.

hack′er, *n. Slang.* 1. computer enthusiast who is especially proficient. 2. computer user who tries to gain unauthorized access to systems.

hack′ney, *n., pl.* **-neys.** horse or carriage for hire.

hack′neyed, *adj.* trite; common.

hack′saw′, *n.* saw for cutting metal.

had′dock, *n.* food fish of northern Atlantic.

haft, *n.* handle.

hag, *n.* repulsive old woman.

hag′gard, *adj.* gaunt with fatigue.

hag′gle, *v.,* **-gled, -gling.** argue over price.

hail, *n.* 1. ice pellets (**hail′stones′**) falling from sky. 2. shout. 3. salutation. —*v.* 4. pour down hail. 5. greet. 6. call out to.

hair, *n.* 1. filament on human head, animal body, etc. 2. hairs collectively. —**hair′y,** *adj.* —**hair′i•ness,** *n.* —**hair′dres′ser,** *n.* —**hair′pin′,** *n.*

hair′breadth′, *n.* narrow margin of safety. Also, **hairs′breadth′.**

hair′cut′, *n.* 1. act of cutting hair. 2. style in which hair is cut or worn.

hair′do′, *n., pl.* **-dos.** hair arrangement.

hair′rais′ing, *adj.* frightening; terrifying.

hair′spray′, *n.* liquid spray for holding the hair in place.

hair′style′, *n.* way of cutting or arranging hair. —**hair′styl′ist,** *n.*

hal′cy•on (hal′sē ən), *adj.* peaceful; happy; carefree.

hale, *v.,* **haled, haling.** *adj.* —*v.* 1. summon forcibly. —*adj.* 2. healthy.

half, *n., pl.* **halves,** *adj., adv.* —*n.* 1. one of two equal parts. —*adj.* 2. being half. 3. incomplete. —*adv.* 4. partly.

half′-baked′, *adj.* 1. not sufficiently planned or prepared. 2. foolish.

half′-breed′, *n. Offensive.* offspring of parents of two races.

half brother, brother related through one parent only.

half′-heart′ed, *adj.* unenthusiastic. —**half′-heart′ed•ly,** *adv.* —**half′-heart′ed•ness,** *n.*

half sister, sister related through one parent only.

half′way′, *adv.* 1. to the midpoint. 2. partially or almost. —*adj.* 3. midway. 4. partial or inadequate.

halfway house, residence for persons released from hospital, prison, etc., to ease their return to society.

half′-wit′, *n.* stupid or foolish person. —**half′-wit′ted,** *adj.*

hal′i•but, *n.* large edible fish.

hal•i•to′sis, *n.* offensive breath.

hall, *n.* 1. corridor. 2. large public room.

hal•le•lu′jah (-lōō′yə), *interj.* Praise ye the Lord! Also, **hal•le•lu′iah.**

hall′mark′, *n.* 1. mark or indication of genuineness, quality, etc. 2. distinguishing characteristic.

hal′low, *v.* consecrate.

Hal′low•een′, *n.* the evening of October 31, observed by children who dress in costumes. Also, **Hal′lowe′en′.**

hal·lu·ci·na'tion, n. illusory perception.

hall'way', n. corridor.

ha'lo, n., pl. **-los, -loes.** radiance surrounding a head.

halt, v. 1. falter; limp. 2. stop. —adj. 3. lame. —n. 4. stop.

hal'ter, n. 1. strap for horse. 2. noose. 3. woman's top, tied behind the neck and across the back.

halve, v., **halved, halving.** divide in half.

ham, n. meat from rear thigh of hog.

ham'burg·er, n. sandwich of ground beef in bun.

ham'let, n. small village.

ham'mer, n. 1. tool for pounding. —v. 2. pound with hammer. —**ham'mer·er,** etc.

ham'mock, n. hanging bed of canvas, etc.

ham'per, v. 1. impede. —n. 2. large basket.

ham'ster, n. small burrowing rodent kept as a pet.

ham'string', n., v., **-strung, -stringing.** —n. 1. tendon behind the knee. —v. 2. disable by cutting hamstring. 3. make powerless or ineffective.

hand, n. 1. terminal part of arm. 2. worker. 3. side as viewed from certain point. 4. style of handwriting. 5. pledge of marriage. 6. cards held by player. —v. 7. pass by hand.

hand'bag', n. woman's purse.

hand'ball', n. ball game played against a wall.

hand'bill', n. small printed notice, usu. distributed by hand.

hand'book', n. small guide or manual.

hand'cuff', n. 1. shackle for wrist. —v. 2. put handcuff on.

hand'ful, n. 1. amount hand can hold. 2. difficult problem.

hand'gun', n. pistol.

hand'i·cap', n., v., **-capped, -capping.** —n. 1. disadvantage. —v. 2. subject to disadvantage.

hand'i·craft', n. 1. manual skill. 2. work or products requiring such skill. Also, **hand'craft'.**

hand'i·work', n. 1. work done by hand. 2. personal work or accomplishment.

hand'ker·chief (hang'kər-), n. small cloth for wiping face, etc.

han'dle, n., v., **-dled, -dling.** —n. 1. part to be grasped. —v. 2. feel or grasp. 3. manage. 4. Informal. endure. 5. deal in. —**han'dler,** n.

hand'made', adj. made individually by worker.

hand'out', n. 1. something given to a beggar. 2. item of publicity.

hand'some', adj. 1. of fine appearance. 2. generous.

hand'-to-mouth', adj. providing bare existence; precarious.

hand'writ'ing, n. writing done by hand.

hand'y, adj., **handier, handiest.** 1. convenient. 2. dexterous. 3. useful.

han'dy·man', n., pl. **-men.** worker at miscellaneous physical chores.

hang, v., **hung** or **hanged, hanging.** —v. 1. suspend. 2. suspend by neck until dead. —n. 3. manner of hanging. —**hang'ing,** n. —**hang'man,** n. —**hang'er,** n.

hang'ar, n. shed, esp. for aircraft.

hang glider, kitelike glider for soaring through the air from hilltops, etc.

hang'nail', n. small piece of partially detached skin around fingernail.

hang'o'ver, n. ill feeling from too much alcohol.

hang'up', n. Informal. obsessive problem.

hank, n. skein of yarn.

han'ker, v. yearn.

han'som, n. two-wheeled covered cab.

Ha'nuk·kah (hä'-), n. annual Jewish festival.

hap'haz'ard, adj. 1. accidental. —adv. 2. by chance.

hap'less, adj. unlucky.

hap'pen, v. occur. —**hap'pen·ing,** n.

hap'py, adj., **-pier, -piest.** 1. pleased; glad. 2. pleasurable. 3. bringing good luck. —**hap'pi·ly,** adv. —**hap'pi·ness,** n.

ha·rangue', n., v., **-rangued, -ranguing.** —n. 1. vehement speech. —v. 2. address in harangue.

ha·rass' (ha ras', har'əs), v. annoy; disturb. —**har'ass·ment,** n.

har'bin·ger (-bin jər), n. v. herald.

har'bor, n. 1. sheltered water for ships. 2. shelter. —v. 3. give shelter.

hard, adj. 1. firm; not soft. 2. difficult. 3. severe. 4. indisputable. —**hard'en,** v. —**hard'ness,** n.

hard'-bit'ten, adj. tough; stubborn.

hard'-boiled', adj. 1. boiled long enough for yolk and white to solidify. 2. not sentimental; tough.

hard'-core', adj. 1. unalterably committed. 2. graphic; explicit.

hard'hat', n. 1. worker's helmet. 2. working-class conservative.

hard'head'ed, adj. 1. practical; realistic; shrewd. 2. obstinate; willful.

hard'ly, adv. barely.

hard'ship, n. severe toil, oppression, or need.

hard'tack', n. hard biscuit.

hard'ware', n. 1. metalware. 2. the machinery of a computer.

hard'wood', n. hard, compact wood of various, chiefly deciduous, trees.

har'dy, adj. **-dier, -diest. 1.** fitted to endure hardship. **2.** daring. **—har'di·ness,** n.

hare, n. mammal resembling rabbit.

hare'brained' adj. foolish.

hare'lip', n. split upper lip.

har'em (hâr'əm), n. **1.** women's section of Muslim palace. **2.** the women there.

hark, v. listen. Also, **hark'en.**

har'lot, n. prostitute. **—har'lot·ry,** n.

harm, n. **1.** injury. **2.** evil. **—v. 3.** injure. **—harm'ful,** adj.

harm'less, adj. **1.** causing no harm. **2.** immune from legal action. **—harm'less·ly,** adv. **—harm'less·ness,** n.

har·mon'i·ca, n. musical reed instrument.

har'mo·ny, n., pl. **-nies. 1.** agreement. **2.** combination of agreeable musical sounds. **—har·mon'ic,** adj. **—har'mo·nize',** v. **—har·mo'ni·ous,** adj.

har'ness, n. **1.** horse's working gear. **—v. 2.** put harness on.

harp, n. **1.** plucked musical string instrument. **—v. 2.** dwell persistently in one's words. **—harp'ist, harp'er,** n.

har·poon', n. **1.** spear used against whales. **—v. 2.** strike with harpoon.

harp'si·chord', n. keyboard instrument with plucked strings.

har'ri·er, n. hunting dog.

har'row, n. **1.** implement for leveling or breaking up plowed land. **—v. 2.** draw a harrow over. **3.** distress.

har'ry, v., **-ried, -rying.** harass.

harsh, adj. **1.** rough. **2.** unpleasant. **3.** highly severe. **—harsh'ly,** adv. **—harsh'ness,** n.

hart, n. male deer.

har'vest, n. **1.** gathering of crops. **2.** season for this. **3.** crop. **—v. 4.** reap. **—har'vest·er,** n.

has (haz), v. third pers. sing. pres. indic. of **have.**

hash, n. **1.** chopped meat and potatoes. **2.** Slang. hashish. **—v. 3.** chop.

hash'ish, n. narcotic of Indian hemp.

hasn't, contraction of **has not.**

hasp, n. clasp for door, lid, etc.

has'sle, n., v., **-sled, -sling.** Informal. **—n. 1.** disorderly dispute. **2.** troublesome situation. **—v. 3.** bother; harass.

has'sock, n. cushion used as footstool, etc.

has'ten, v. hurry. **—haste, hast'i·ness,** n. **—hast'y,** adj. **—hast'i·ly,** adv.

hat, n. covering for head. **—hat'ter,** n.

hatch, v. **1.** bring forth young from egg. **2.** be hatched. **—n. 3.** cover for opening.

hatch'et, n. small ax.

hatch'way', n. opening in ship's deck.

hate, v., **hated, hating,** n. **—v. 1.** feel or show enmity toward. **—n. 2.** Also, **ha'tred.** strong dislike.

hate'ful, adj. **1.** full of hate. **2.** arousing hate. **—hate'ful·ly,** adv. **—hate'ful·ness,** n.

haugh'ty, adj., **-tier, -tiest.** disdainfully proud. **—haugh'ti·ly,** adv. **—haugh'ti·ness,** n.

haul, v. **1.** pull; drag. **—n. 2.** pull. **3.** distance of carrying. **4.** thing hauled. **5.** something gained.

haunch, n. hip.

haunt, v. **1.** visit often, esp. as ghost. **—n. 2.** place of frequent visits.

have, v., **had, having. 1.** possess; contain. **2.** get. **3.** be forced or obligated. **4.** be affected by. **5.** give birth to.

ha'ven, n. **1.** harbor. **2.** place of shelter.

haven't, contraction of **have not.**

hav'er·sack', n. bag for rations, etc.

hav'oc, n. devastation.

hawk, n. **1.** bird of prey. **—v. 2.** hunt with hawks. **3.** peddle.

haw'ser, n. cable for mooring or towing ship.

haw'thorn', n. small tree with thorns and small, bright fruit.

hay, n. grass cut and dried for fodder. **—hay'field',** n. **—hay'stack',** n.

hay fever, disorder of eyes and respiratory tract, caused by pollen.

hay'wire', adj. Informal. amiss.

haz'ard, n., v. risk. **—haz'ard·ous,** adj.

haze, v., **hazed, hazing.** v. **1.** play abusive tricks on. **—n. 2.** mistlike obscurity. **—ha'zy,** adj.

ha'zel, n. **1.** tree bearing edible nut (**ha'zel·nut'**). **2.** light reddish brown.

H'-bomb', n. hydrogen bomb.

he, pron. **1.** male mentioned. **—n. 2.** male.

head, n. **1.** part of body joined to trunk by neck. **2.** leader. **3.** top or foremost part. **—adj. 4.** at the head. **5.** leading or main. **—v. 6.** lead. **7.** move in certain direction.

head'ache', n. **1.** pain in upper part of head. **2.** worrying problem.

head'ing, n. caption.

head'line', n. title of newspaper article.

head'long', adj., adv. in impulsive manner.

head'quar'ters, n. center of command or operations.

head'strong', adj. willful.

head'way', n. progress.

head'y, *adj.* **headier, headiest. 1.** impetuous. **2.** intoxicating.

heal, *v.* **1.** restore to health. **2.** get well.

health, *n.* **1.** soundness of body. **2.** physical condition. **—health'ful,** *adj.* **—health'y,** *adj.*

heap, *n., v.* pile.

hear, *v.,* **heard, hearing. 1.** perceive by ear. **2.** listen. **3.** receive report. **—hear'er,** *n.* **—hear'ing,** *n.*

heark'en, *v.* listen.

hear'say', *n.* gossip; indirect report.

hearse, *n.* funeral vehicle.

heart, *n.* **1.** muscular organ keeping blood in circulation. **2.** seat of life or emotion. **3.** compassion. **4.** vital part. **—heart'less,** *adj.* **—heart'less•ly,** *adv.* **—heart'less•ness,** *n.*

heart'ache', *n.* grief.

heart attack, sudden insufficiency of oxygen supply to heart that results in heart muscle damage.

heart'burn', *n.* burning sensation in stomach and esophagus, sometimes caused by rising stomach acid.

heart'en, *v.* encourage.

heart'-rend'ing, *adj.* causing sympathetic grief.

hearth, *n.* place for fires.

heart'y, *adj.* **heartier, heartiest. 1.** cordial. **2.** genuine. **3.** vigorous. **4.** substantial. **—heart'i•ly,** *adv.*

heat, *n.* **1.** warmth. **2.** form of energy raising temperature. **3.** intensity of emotion. **4.** sexual arousal, esp. female. **—v. 5.** make or become hot. **6.** excite. **—heat'er,** *n.*

heat'ed, *adj.* **1.** supplied with heat. **2.** emotionally charged.

heath, *n.* **1.** Also, **heath'er.** low evergreen shrub. **2.** uncultivated land overgrown with shrubs.

hea'then, *n., adj.* pagan.

heave, *v.,* **heaved, heaving. —v. 1.** raise with effort. **2.** lift and throw. **3.** *Slang.* vomit. **4.** rise and fall. **—n. 5.** act or instance of heaving.

heav'en, *n.* **1.** abode of God, angels, and spirits of righteous dead. **2.** (*often pl.*) sky. **3.** bliss. **—heav'en•ly,** *adj.*

heav'y, *adj.* **heavier, heaviest. 1.** of great weight. **2.** substantial. **3.** clumsy; indelicate. **—heav'i•ly,** *adv.* **—heav'i•ness,** *n.*

heav'y-du'ty, *adj.* made for hard use.

heav'y-hand'ed, *adj.* tactless; clumsy.

heav'y-heart'ed, *adj.* preoccupied with sorrow or worry. **—heav'y-heart'ed•ness,** *n.*

heav'y-set', *adj.* large in body.

He'brew, *n.* **1.** member of people of ancient Palestine. **2.** their language, now the national language of Israel. **—He'brew,** *adj.*

heck'le, *v.,* **-led, -ling.** harass with questions, etc. **—heck'ler,** *n.*

hec'tare (hek'târ), *n.* 10,000 square meters (2.47 acres.)

hec'tic, *adj.* marked by excitement, passion, etc. **—hec'ti•cal•ly,** *adv.*

hec'tor, *v., n.* bully.

hedge, *n., v.,* **hedged, hedging. —n. 1.** Also, **hedge'row'.** fence of bushes or small trees. **—v. 2.** surround with hedge. **3.** offset (risk, bet, etc.)

hedge'hog', *n.* spiny European mammal.

he'don•ist, *n.* person living for pleasure. **—he'do•nis'tic,** *adj.* **—he'don•ism,** *n.*

heed, *v.* **1.** notice. **2.** pay serious attention to. **—heed,** *n.* **—heed'ful,** *adj.* **—heed'less,** *adj.*

heel, *n.* **1.** back of foot below ankle. **2.** part of shoe, etc., covering this. **—v. 3.** furnish with heels. **4.** lean to one side.

hef'ty, *adj.,* **-tier, -tiest. 1.** heavy. **2.** sturdy.

he•gem'o•ny (hi jem'ə nē), *n., pl.* **-nies.** domination or leadership.

heif'er (hef'ər), *n.* young cow without issue.

height, *n.* **1.** state of being high. **2.** altitude. **3.** apex. **—height'en,** *v.*

Heim'lich maneuver (hīm'lik), procedure to aid choking person by applying pressure to upper abdomen.

hei'nous (hā'nəs), *adj.* hateful.

heir (âr), *n.* inheritor. **—heir'ess,** *n.fem.*

heir'loom', *n.* possession long kept in family.

heist (hīst), *Slang.* **—n. 1.** robbery. **—v. 2.** rob.

hel'i•cop'ter, *n.* heavier-than-air craft lifted by horizontal propeller.

he'li•o•trope' (hē'lē ə trōp'), *n.* **1.** shrub with fragrant flowers. **2.** light purple color.

he'lix (hē'liks), *n., pl.* **hel'i•ces** (hel'ə sēz'), **helixes.** spiral.

hell, *n.* abode of condemned spirits. **—hell'ish,** *adj.*

hel•lo', *interj.* (exclamation of greeting.)

helm, *n.* **1.** control of rudder. **2.** steering apparatus. **—helms'man,** *n.*

hel'met, *n.* protective head covering.

help, *v.* **1.** aid. **2.** save. **3.** relieve. **4.** avoid. **—n. 5.** aid; relief. **6.** helping person or thing. **—help'er,** *n.* **—help'ful,** *adj.*

help'less, *adj.* unable to act for oneself.

hel'ter-skel'ter, *adv.* in a disorderly way.

hem, v., **hemmed, hemming,** n. —v. 1. confine. 2. fold and sew down edge of cloth. —n. 3. hemmed border.

hem'i·sphere', n. 1. half the earth or sky. 2. half sphere. —**hem'i·spher'i·cal,** adj.

hem'lock, n. 1. coniferous tree. 2. poisonous plant of parsley family.

he·mo·phil'i·a (hē'mə fil'ē ə), n. genetic disorder characterized by prolonged or excessive bleeding. —**he'mo·phil'i·ac',** n.

hem'or·rhage (hem'ə rij), n. discharge of blood.

hem'or·rhoid' (hem'ə roid'), n. (usually pl.) painful dilation of blood vessels in anus.

hemp, n. tall herb whose fiber is used for rope, etc.

hen, n. 1. female domestic fowl. 2. female bird. —**hen'ner·y,** n.

hence, adv. 1. therefore. 2. from now on. 3. from this place, etc.

hence'forth', adv. from now on.

hench'man, n., pl. **-men.** 1. associate in wrongdoing. 2. trusted attendant.

hen'na, n. red dye.

hep'a·ti'tis (hep'ə tī'tis), n. inflammation of the liver.

her, pron. 1. objective case of **she.** —adj. 2. of or belonging to female.

her'ald, n. 1. messenger or forerunner. 2. proclaimer. —v. 3. proclaim. 4. give promise of.

her'ald·ry, n. art of devising and describing coats of arms, tracing genealogies, etc. —**he·ral'dic,** adj.

herb (ûrb, hûrb), n. annual flowering plant with nonwoody stem. —**her·ba'ceous,** adj. —**herb'al,** adj.

herb'age, n. 1. nonwoody plants. 2. leaves and stems of herbs.

herb'i·cide (hûr'bə sīd', ûr'-), n. substance for killing plants, esp. weeds. —**herb·i·ci'dal,** adj.

her'cu·le·an (hûr'kyə lē'ən, hûr kyōō'lē-), adj. 1. requiring extraordinary strength or effort. 2. having extraordinary strength, courage, or size.

herd, n. 1. animals feeding or moving together. —v. 2. go in herd. 3. tend herd. —**herd'er, herds'man,** n.

here, adv. 1. in or to this place. 2. present.

here'af·ter, adv. 1. in the future. —n. 2. future life.

here'by', adv. by this.

he·red'i·tar'y, adj. 1. passing from parents to offspring. 2. of heredity. 3. by inheritance. —**he·red'i·tar'i·ly,** adv.

he·red'i·ty, n. transmission of traits from parents to offspring.

here·in', adv. in this place.

her'e·sy, n., pl. **-sies.** unorthodox opinion or doctrine. —**her'e·tic,** n. —**he·ret'i·cal,** adj.

here·to·fore', adv. before now.

here·with', adv. along with this.

her'it·age, n. 1. inheritance. 2. traditions and history.

her·maph'ro·dite' (hûr maf'rə dīt'), n. animal or plant with reproductive organs of both sexes. —**her·maph'ro·dit'ic,** adj.

her·met'ic, adj. airtight. Also, **hermet'i·cal.** —**her·met'i·cal·ly,** adv.

her'mit, n. recluse.

her'mit·age, n. hermit's abode.

her'ni·a (hûr'nē ə), n. rupture in abdominal wall, etc.

he'ro, n., pl. **-roes.** 1. man of valor, nobility, etc. 2. main male character in story. —**her'oine,** n.fem. —**he·ro'ic, he·ro'i·cal,** adj. —**her'o·ism',** n.

her'o·in, n. morphinelike drug.

her'on, n. long-legged wading bird.

her'pes (hûr'pēz), n. viral disease characterized by blisters on skin or mucous membranes.

her'ring, n. north Atlantic food fish.

hers, pron. 1. form of possessive **her.** 2. her belongings or family.

her·self', pron. emphatic or reflexive form of **her.**

hertz, n., pl. **hertz.** radio frequency of one cycle per second.

hes'i·tate', v., **-tated, -tating.** 1. hold back in doubt. 2. pause. 3. stammer. —**hes'i·tant,** adj. —**hes'i·ta'tion, hes'i·tan·cy,** n.

het'er·o·dox', adj. unorthodox. —**het'er·o·dox'y,** n.

het'er·o·ge'ne·ous, adj. 1. unlike. 2. varied.

het'er·o·sex'u·al, adj. sexually attracted to opposite sex. —**het'er·o·sex'u·al,** n.

hew, v., **hewed, hewed** or **hewn, hewing.** 1. chop or cut. 2. cut down. —**hew'er,** n.

hex, v. 1. cast spell on. 2. bring bad luck to. —n. 3. spell; charm; jinx.

hex'a·gon', n. six-sided polygon. —**hex·ag'o·nal,** adj.

hey'day', n. time of greatest vigor.

hi·a'tus (hī ā'təs), n., pl. **-tuses, -tus.** break or interruption in a series, action, etc.

hi'ber·nate', v., **-nated, -nating.** spend winter in dormant state. —**hi'ber·na'tion,** n.

hic'cup, n. 1. sudden involuntary drawing in of breath. —v. 2. have hiccups. Also, **hic'cough** (hik'up).

hick, *n.* provincial, unsophisticated person.

hick'o•ry, *n., pl.* **-ries.** tree bearing edible nut (**hickory nut**)

hide, *v.,* hid, hidden or hid, hiding, *n.* —*v.* 1. conceal or be concealed. —*n.* 2. animal's skin.

hid'e•ous, *adj.* 1. very ugly. 2. revolting.

hie, *v.,* hied, hieing or hying. *Archaic.* go hastily.

hi'er•ar•chy, *n., pl.* **-chies.** graded system of officials.

hi'er•o•glyph'ic, *adj.* Also, **hi'er•o•glyph'i•cal.** 1. of picture writing, as among ancient Egyptians. —*n.* 2. hieroglyphic symbol.

high, *adj.* 1. tall. 2. lofty. 3. expensive. 4. shrill. 5. *Informal.* exuberant with drink or drugs. 6. greater than normal. 7. elevated in pitch. —*adv.* 8. at or to high place, rank, etc.

high'brow', *n.* 1. cultured person. —*adj.* typical of a highbrow.

high fidelity, reproduction of sound without distortion. —**high' fi•del'i•ty,** *adj.*

high'-flown', *adj.* 1. pretentious. 2. bombastic.

high'-hand'ed, *adj.* overbearing.

high'lands (-lăndz), *n.* elevated part of country.

high'light', *v.* 1. emphasize. —*n.* 2. important event, scene, etc. 3. area of strong reflected light.

high'ly, *adv.* 1. in high place, etc. 2. very; extremely

high'ness, *n.* 1. high state. 2. (*cap.*) title of royalty.

high'rise', *n.* high building. —**high-rise,** *adj.*

high'road', *n.* highway.

high' school', *n.* school for grades 9 through 12.

high'-spir'it•ed, *adj.* lively; vivacious.

high'-strung', *adj.* nervous.

high'-tech', *n.* 1. technology using highly sophisticated and advanced equipment and techniques. —*adj.* 2. using or suggesting high-tech.

high'way', *n.* main road.

high'way•man, *n., pl.* **-men.** highway robber.

hi'jack', *v.* seize (plane, truck, etc.) by force. —**hi'jack'er,** *n.*

hike, *v.,* hiked, hiking, *n.* —*v.* 1. walk long distance. —*n.* 2. long walk. —**hik'er,** *n.*

hi•lar'i•ous, *adj.* 1. very funny. 2. very cheerful. —**hi•lar'i•ous•ly,** *adv.* —**hi•lar'i•ty,** *n.*

hill, *n.* high piece of land. —**hill'y,** *adj.*

hill'bil•ly, *n., pl.* **-lies.** Sometimes Of-

fensive. 1. Southern mountaineer. 2. yokel; rustic.

hill'ock, *n.* little hill.

hilt, *n.* sword handle.

him, *pron.* objective case of **he.**

him•self', *pron.* reflexive or emphatic form of **him.**

hind, *adj.* 1. rear. —*n.* 2. female deer.

hin'der, *v.* 1. retard. 2. stop. —**hin'drance,** *n.*

hind'most', *adj.* last.

hind'sight', *n.* keen awareness of how one should have avoided past mistakes.

Hin'du, *n.* adherent of Hinduism. —**Hindu,** *adj.*

Hin'du•ism, *n.* a major religion of India.

hinge, *n., v.,* hinged, hinging. —*n.* 1. joint on which door, lid, etc., turns. —*v.* 2. depend. 3. furnish with hinges.

hint, *n.* 1. indirect suggestion. —*v.* 2. give hint.

hin'ter•land', *n.* area remote from cities.

hip, *n.* 1. projecting part of each side of body below waist. —*adj. Slang.* 2. familiar with the latest or particular ideas, styles, etc.

hip'-hop', *n. Slang.* popular subculture of usu. black urban youth, esp. as characterized by rap music.

hip'pie, *n.* person of 1960s who rejected conventional cultural and moral values.

hip'po•drome', *n.* arena, esp. for horse events.

hip'po•pot'a•mus, *n., pl.* **-muses, -mi.** large African water mammal.

hire, *v.,* hired, hiring, *n.* —*v.* 1. purchase services or use of. —*n.* 2. payment for services or use.

hire'ling, *n.* person whose loyalty can be bought.

hir'sute (hûr'sōot), *adj.* hairy.

his, *pron.* 1. possessive form of **he.** 2. his belongings.

His•pan'ic, *n.* person of Spanish or Latin-American descent. —**Hispanic,** *adj.*

hiss, *v.* 1. make prolonged *s* sound. 2. express disapproval in this way. —*n.* 3. hissing sound.

his•tor'ic, *adj.* 1. Also, **his•tor'i•cal.** of history. 2. important in or surviving from the past. —**his•tor'i•cal•ly,** *adv.*

his'to•ry, *n., pl.* **-ries.** 1. knowledge, study, or record of past events. 2. pattern of events determining future. —**his•to'ri•an,** *n.*

his'tri•on'ics, *n.pl.* exaggerated, esp. melodramatic, behavior. —**his'tri•on'ic,** *adj.*

hit, v., **hit, hitting**, n. —v. 1. strike. 2. collide with. 3. meet. 4. guess. —n. 5. collision. 6. blow. 7. success. 8. *Slang.* murder. —**hit'ter,** n.

hitch, v. 1. fasten. 2. harness to cart, etc. 3. raise or move jerkily. —n. 4. fastening or knot. 5. obstruction. 6. jerk.

hitch'hike', v., **-hiked, -hiking.** beg a ride. —**hitch'hik'er,** n.

hith'er, adv. to this place. —**hith'er-ward,** adv.

hith'er-to', adv. until now.

HIV, human immunodeficiency virus, a cause of AIDS.

hive, n. shelter for bees.

hives, n.pl. eruptive skin condition.

HMO, pl. **HMOs, HMO's.** health maintenance organization, health care plan that provides comprehensive services to subscribers.

hoa'gie, n. mixed sandwich in long roll. Also, **hoa'gy.**

hoard, n. 1. accumulation for future use. —v. 2. accumulate as hoard. —**hoard'er,** n.

hoarse, adj. gruff in tone.

hoar'y, adj. 1. white with age or frost. 2. old. Also, **hoar.**

hoax, n. 1. mischievous deception. —v. 2. deceive; trick.

hob'ble, v., **-bled, -bling.** 1. limp. 2. fasten legs to prevent free movement.

hob'by, n., pl. **-bies.** favorite avocation or pastime.

hob'by-horse', n. 1. rocking toy for riding. 2. favorite subject for discussion.

hob'nob', v., **-nobbed, -nobbing.** associate on social terms.

ho'bo, n., pl. **-bos, -boes.** tramp; vagrant.

hock, n. joint in hind leg of horse, etc.

hock'ey, n. game played with bent clubs (**hockey sticks**) and ball or disk.

ho'cus-po'cus, n. 1. sleight of hand. 2. trickery.

hod, n. 1. trough for carrying mortar, bricks, etc. 2. coal scuttle.

hodge'podge', n. mixture; jumble.

hoe, n., v., **hoed, hoeing.** —n. 1. implement for breaking ground, etc. —v. 2. use hoe on.

hog, n., v., **hogged, hogging.** —n. 1. domesticated swine. 2. greedy or filthy person. —v. 3. take greedily.

hogs'head', n. large cask.

hog'tie', v., **-tied, -tying.** 1. tie with all four feet or arms together. 2. hamper; thwart.

hog'wash', n. nonsense; bunk.

hoi' pol·loi', common people; the masses.

hoist, v. 1. lift, esp. by machine. —n. 2. hoisting apparatus. 3. act or instance of lifting.

hold, v., **held, holding,** n. —v. 1. have in hand. 2. possess. 3. sustain. 4. adhere. 5. celebrate. 6. restrain or detain. 7. believe. 8. consider. —n. 9. grasp. 10. influence. 11. cargo space below ship's deck. —**hold'er,** n. —**hold'ing,** n.

hold'up', n. 1. delay. 2. robbery at gunpoint.

hole, n., v., **holed, holing.** —n. 1. opening. 2. cavity. 3. burrow. 4. in golf, one of the cups into which the ball is to be driven. —v. 5. drive into hole.

hol'i-day', n. 1. day or period without work. —adj. 2. festive.

ho'li-ness, n. holy state or character.

hol'lan-daise', n. rich egg-based sauce.

hol'low, adj. 1. empty within. 2. sunken. 3. dull. 4. unreal. —n. 5. cavity. —v. 6. make hollow.

hol'ly, n., pl. **-lies.** shrub with bright red berries.

hol'ly-hock', n. tall flowering plant.

hol'o-caust', (hol'ə kôst'), n. 1. great destruction, esp. by fire. 2. (*cap.*) Nazi killing of Jews during World War II.

hol'o-gram', n. three-dimensional image made by a laser.

ho-log'ra-phy, n. process of making holograms.

hol'ster, n. case for pistol.

ho'ly, adj., **-lier, -liest.** 1. sacred. 2. dedicated to God.

Holy Ghost, third person of Trinity. Also, **Holy Spirit.**

hom'age, n. reverence or respect.

home, n. 1. residence. 2. native place or country. —adv. 3. to or at home. —**home'land',** n. —**home'ward,** adv., adj. —**home'less,** adj. —**home'made',** adj.

home'ly, adj., **-lier, -liest.** 1. plain; not beautiful. 2. simple; without pretense.

ho'me·op'a·thy, n. method of treating disease with small doses of drugs that in a healthy person would cause symptoms like those of the disease. —**ho'me·o·path'ic,** adj.

home'sick', adj. longing for home. —**home'sick'ness,** n.

home'spun', adj. 1. spun at home. 2. unpretentious. —n. 3. cloth made at home.

home'stead', n. dwelling with its land and buildings.

home'y, adj., **homier, homiest.** cozy.

hom'i-cide', n. killing of one person by another. —**hom'i-cid'al,** adj.

hom'i-ly, n., pl. **-lies.** sermon.

hom′i•ny, *n.* 1. hulled corn. 2. coarse flour from corn.

ho′mo•ge′ne•ous, *adj.* 1. unvaried in content. 2. alike. —**ho′mo•ge•ne′i•ty**, *n.*

ho•mog′e•nize′, *v.*, **-nized, -nizing.** form by mixing and emulsifying.

hom′o•nym, *n.* word like another in sound, but not in meaning.

ho′mo•pho′bi•a, *n.* unreasoning fear or hatred of homosexuals and homosexuality.

ho′mo•sex′u•al, *adj.* 1. sexually attracted to same sex. —*n.* 2. homosexual person. —**ho′mo•sex′u•al′i•ty**, *n.*

hon′cho, *n., pl.* **-chos.** *Slang.* 1. leader; boss. 2. important or influential person.

hone, *n., v.,* **honed, honing.** —*n.* 1. fine whetstone. —*v.* 2. sharpen to fine edge.

hon′est, *adj.* 1. trustworthy. 2. sincere. 3. virtuous. —**hon′es•ty**, *n.*

hon′ey, *n.* sweet fluid produced by bees (**hon′ey•bees′**).

hon′ey•comb′, *n.* wax structure built by bees to store honey.

hon′ey•dew′ melon, sweet musk-melon.

hon′eyed (-ēd), *adj.* sweet or flattering, as speech.

hon′ey•moon′, *n.* holiday trip of newly married couple. —**hon′ey•moon′er**, *n.*

hon′ey•suck′le, *n.* shrub bearing tubular flowers.

honk, *n.* 1. sound of automobile horn. 2. nasal sound of goose, etc. —*v.* 3. make such sound.

hon′or, *n.* 1. public or official esteem. 2. something as token of this. 3. good reputation. 4. high ethical character. 5. chastity. —*v.* 6. revere. 7. confer honor. 8. show respect for. 9. accept as valid.

hon′or•a•ble, *adj.* 1. worthy of honor. 2. of high principles. —**hon′or•a•bly**, *adv.*

hon′or•ar′y, *adj.* conferred as honor.

hood, *n.* 1. covering for head and neck. 2. automobile engine cover. 3. hoodlum.

hood′lum, *n.* violent petty criminal.

hood′wink′, *v.* deceive.

hoof, *n., pl.* **hoofs, hooves.** horny covering of animal foot.

hook, *n.* 1. curved piece of metal for catching, etc. 2. fishhook. 3. sharp curve. —*v.* 4. seize, etc., with hook.

hook′er, *n. Slang.* prostitute, esp. one who solicits on the street.

hook′up′, *n.* connection of parts or

apparatus into circuit, network, machine, or system.

hoop, *n.* circular band.

hoot, *v.* 1. shout in derision. 2. (of owl) utter cry. —*n.* 3. owl's cry. 4. shout of derision.

hop, *v.,* **hopped, hopping**, *n.* —*v.* 1. leap, esp. on one foot. —*n.* 2. such a leap. 3. twining plant bearing cones used in brewing. 4. (*pl.*) the cones of this plant.

hope, *n., v.,* **hoped, hoping.** —*n.* 1. feeling that something desired is possible. 2. object of this. 3. confidence. —*v.* 4. look forward to with hope. —**hope′ful**, *adj.* —**hope′less**, *adj.*

hop′per, *n.* funnel-shaped trough for grain, etc.

horde, *n.* 1. multitude. 2. nomadic group.

hore′hound′, *n.* herb bearing bitter juice.

ho•ri′zon, *n.* apparent boundary between earth and sky.

hor′i•zon′tal, *adj.* 1. at right angles to vertical. 2. level. —*n.* 3. horizontal line, etc.

hor′mone, *n.* endocrine gland secretion that activates specific organ, mechanism, etc.

horn, *n.* 1. hard growth on heads of cattle, goats, etc. 2. hornlike part. 3. musical wind instrument. —**horn′y**, *adj.*

hor′net, *n.* large wasp.

horn′pipe′, *n.* 1. lively dance. 2. music for it.

hor′o•scope′, *n.* chart of heavens used in astrology.

hor•ren′dous, *adj.* dreadful; horrible.

hor′ri•ble, *adj.* dreadful. —**hor′ri•bly**, *adv.*

hor′rid, *adj.* abominable.

hor′ror, *n.* intense fear or repugnance. —**hor′ri•fy′**, *v.*

hors d'oeuvre (ôr dûrv′), *n., pl.* **-d'oeuvres** (-dûrv′). tidbit served before meal.

horse, *n.* 1. large domesticated quadruped. 2. cavalry. 3. frame with legs for bearing work, etc. —**horse′-back′**, *n., adv.* —**horse′man**, *n.* —**horse′wo•man**, *n.fem.* —**horse′hair′**, *n.*

horse′play′, *n.* rough or boisterous play.

horse′pow′er, *n.* unit of power, equal to 550 foot-pounds per second.

horse′rad′ish, *n.* cultivated plant with pungent root.

horse′shoe′, *n.* 1. U-shaped iron plate nailed to horse's hoof. 2. arrangement in this form. 3. (*pl.*) game in which horseshoes are tossed.

hor·ti·cul·ture, n. cultivation of gardens. **—hor·ti·cul·tur·ist,** n.

ho·san·na, interj. praise the Lord!

hose, n. 1. stockings. 2. flexible tube for water, etc.

ho·sier·y (-zha rē), n. stockings.

hos·pice (hos′pis), n. 1. shelter for pilgrims, strangers, etc. 2. facility for supportive care of dying persons.

hos·pi·ta·ble, adj. showing hospitality. **—hos·pi·ta·bly,** adv.

hos·pi·tal, n. institution for treatment of sick and injured. **—hos·pi·tal·ize′,** v.

hos·pi·tal·i·ty, n., pl. **-ties.** warm reception of guests, etc.

host, n. 1. entertainer of guests. 2. great number. 3. (cap.) bread consecrated in Eucharist. **—host′ess,** n.fem.

hos′tage, n. person given or held as security.

hos′tel, n. inexpensive transient lodging.

hos′tile (-tal), adj. 1. opposed; unfriendly. 2. of enemies. **—hos·til′i·ty,** n.

hot, adj., **hotter, hottest.** 1. of high temperature. 2. feeling great heat. 3. sharp-tasting. 4. ardent.

hot′bed′, n. 1. covered and heated bed of earth for growing plants. 2. place where something thrives and spreads.

hot′-blood′ed, adj. excitable.

hot dog, 1. frankfurter. 2. Slang. person who acts flamboyantly; show-off.

ho·tel′, n. house offering food, lodging, etc.

hot′head′, n. impetuous or rash person.

hot′house′, n. greenhouse.

hot line, system for instantaneous communications of major importance.

hot rod, Slang. car (usu. old) with speeded-up engine.

hound, n. 1. hunting dog. **—v. 2.** hunt or track.

hour, n. period of 60 minutes. **—hour′ly,** adj., adv.

hour′glass′, n. timepiece operating by visible fall of sand.

house, n., v., **housed, housing. —n.** (hous). 1. building, esp. for residence, rest, etc. 2. family. 3. legislative or deliberative body. 4. commercial firm. **—v.** (houz). 5. provide with a house.

house′bro′ken, adj. trained to excrete outdoors or to behave appropriately indoors.

house′fly′, n., pl. **-flies.** common insect.

house′hold′, n. 1. people of house. **—adj.** 2. domestic.

house′keep′er, n. person who manages a house. **—house′keep′ing,** n.

house′warm′ing, n. party to celebrate moving into a new home.

house′wife′, n., pl. **-wives.** woman in charge of household. **—house′wife′ly,** adj.

house′work′, n. work done in housekeeping.

hous′ing, n. 1. dwellings collectively. 2. container.

hov′el, n. small mean dwelling.

hov′er, v. 1. stay fluttering or suspended in air. 2. linger about.

Hov·er·craft′, n. Trademark. vehicle that can skim over water on cushion of air.

how, adv. 1. in what way. 2. to, at, or in what extent, price, or condition. 3. why.

how·ev′er, conj. 1. nevertheless. **—adv.** 2. to whatever extent.

how′itz·er, n. short-barreled cannon for firing shells at an elevated angle.

howl, v. 1. utter loud long cry. 2. wail. **—n.** 3. cry of wolf, etc. 4. wail.

hub, n. central part of wheel.

hub′bub, n. confused noise.

hu′bris (hyōō′bris, hōō′-), n. excessive pride or self-confidence.

huck′le·ber′ry, n., pl. **-ries.** dark blue or black edible berry of heath shrub.

huck′ster, n. peddler.

hud′dle, v., **-dled, -dling,** n. **—v.** 1. crowd together. **—n.** 2. confused heap or crowd.

hue, n. 1. color. 2. outcry.

huff, n. fit of anger.

hug, v., **hugged, hugging,** n. **—v.** 1. clasp in arms. 2. stay close to. **—n.** 3. tight clasp.

huge, adj., **huger, hugest.** very large in size or extent. **—huge′ly,** adv. **—huge′ness,** n.

hu′la (hōō′la), n. Hawaiian dance with intricate arm movements.

hulk, n. hull remaining from old ship.

hulk′ing, adj. bulky; clumsy. Also, **hulk′y.**

hull, n. 1. outer covering of seed or fruit. 2. body of ship. **—v.** 3. remove hull of.

hul′la·ba·loo′, n., pl. **-loos.** Informal. uproar.

hum, v., **hummed, humming,** n. **—v.** 1. make low droning sound. 2. sing with closed lips. 3. be busy or active. **—n.** 4. indistinct murmur.

hu′man, adj. 1. of or like people or their species. **—n.** 2. Also, **human being.** a person.

i'dol, *n.* object worshiped or adored. —**i'dol·ize',** *v.*

i·dol'a·try, *n., pl.* **-tries.** worship of idols. —**i·dol'a·ter,** *n.* —**i·dol'a·trous,** *adj.*

i'dyll, *n.* composition describing simple pastoral scene. Also, **i'dyl.** —**i·dyl'lic,** *adj.*

if, *conj.* 1. in case that. 2. whether. 3. though.

ig'loo, *n., pl.* **-loos.** snow hut.

ig'ne·ous, *adj.* 1. produced by great heat. 2. of fire.

ig·nite', *v.,* **-nited, -niting.** set on or catch fire. —**ig·ni'tion,** *n.*

ig·no'ble, *adj.* 1. dishonorable. 2. humble. —**ig·no'bly,** *adv.*

ig·no·min'i·ous, *adj.* 1. humiliating. 2. contemptible. —**ig'no·min'y,** *n.*

ig'no·ra'mus (-rā'-), *n.* ignorant person.

ig'no·rant, *adj.* 1. lacking knowledge. 2. unaware. —**ig'no·rance,** *n.*

ig·nore', *v.,* **-nored, -noring.** disregard.

i·gua'na (i gwä'nə), *n.* large tropical lizard.

ilk, *n.* family or kind.

ill, *adj.* 1. not well; sick. 2. evil. 3. unfavorable. —*n.* 4. evil; harm. 5. ailment. —*adv.* 6. badly. 7. with difficulty.

ill'-ad·vised', *adj.* showing bad judgment.

ill'-bred', *adj.* rude.

il·le'gal, *adj.* unlawful. —**il·le'gal·ly,** *adv.*

il·leg'i·ble, *adj.* hard to read. —**il·leg'i·bil'i·ty,** *n.*

il·le·git'i·mate, *adj.* 1. unlawful. 2. born out of wedlock. —**il·le·git'i·ma·cy,** *n.*

il·lib'er·al, *adj.* 1. not generous. 2. narrow in attitudes or beliefs.

il·lic'it, *adj.* unlawful; not allowed.

il·lit'er·ate, *adj.* 1. unable to read and write. —*n.* 2. illiterate person. —**il·lit'er·a·cy,** *n.*

ill'ness, *n.* bad health.

il·log'i·cal, *adj.* not logical. —**il·log'i·cal·ly,** *adv.*

ill'-treat', *v.* abuse. —**ill'-treat'ment,** *n.*

il·lu'mi·nate', *v.,* **-nated, -nating.** supply with light. Also, **il·lu'mine.** —**il·lu'mi·na'tion,** *n.*

il·lu'sion, *n.* false impression or appearance. —**il·lu'sive,** **il·lu'so·ry,** *adj.*

il·lus'trate', *v.,* **-trated, -trating.** 1. explain with examples, etc. 2. furnish with pictures. —**il·lus·tra'tion,** *n.*

—**il·lus'tra·tive,** *adj.* —**il·lus'tra·tor,** *n.*

il·lus'tri·ous, *adj.* 1. famous. 2. glorious.

im-, *prefix.* variant of **in-**.

im'age, *n.* 1. likeness. 2. idea. 3. conception of one's character. —*v.* 4. mirror.

im'age·ry, *n., pl.* **-ries.** 1. mental images collectively. 2. use of figures of speech.

im·ag·ine, *v.,* **-ined, -ining.** 1. form mental images. 2. think; guess. —**im·ag'i·na'tion,** *n.* —**im·ag'i·na'tive,** *adj.* —**im·ag'i·nary,** *adj.* —**im·ag'i·na·ble,** *adj.*

i·mam' (i mäm'), *n.* Muslim religious leader.

im·bal'ance, *n.* lack of balance.

im·be·cile (-sil), *n.* 1. *Obsolete.* a retarded person having a mental age of up to eight years. 2. a foolish or stupid person. —**im·be·cil'i·ty,** *n.*

im·bibe', *v.,* **-bibed, -bibing.** drink. —**im·bib'er,** *n.*

im·bro'glio (-brōl'yō), *n., pl.* **-glios.** complicated affair.

im·bue', *v.,* **-bued, -buing.** 1. inspire. 2. saturate.

im'i·tate', *v.,* **-tated, -tating.** 1. copy. 2. counterfeit. —**im'i·ta'tive,** *adj.* —**im'i·ta'tor,** *n.* —**im'i·ta'tion,** *n.*

im·mac'u·late, *adj.* 1. spotlessly clean. 2. pure.

im'ma·nent, *adj.* being within. —**im'ma·nence,** *n.*

im·ma·te'ri·al, *adj.* 1. unimportant. 2. spiritual.

im·ma·ture', *adj.* not mature. —**im'ma·tu'ri·ty,** *n.*

im·meas'ur·a·ble, *adj.* limitless. —**im·meas'ur·a·bly,** *adv.*

im·me'di·ate, *adj.* 1. without delay. 2. nearest. 3. present. —**im·me'di·a·cy,** *n.* —**im·me'di·ate·ly,** *adv.*

im·me·mo'ri·al, *adj.* beyond memory or record.

im·mense', *adj.* 1. vast. 2. boundless. —**im·men'si·ty,** *n.* —**im·mense'ly,** *adv.*

im·merse', *v.,* **-mersed, -mersing.** 1. plunge into liquid. 2. absorb, as in study. —**im·mer'sion,** *n.*

im'mi·grant, *n.* person who immigrates.

im'mi·grate', *v.,* **-grated, -grating.** come to new country. —**im'mi·gra'tion,** *n.*

im'mi·nent, *adj.* about to happen. —**im'mi·nence,** *n.*

im·mo'bile, *adj.* not moving. —**im'mo·bil'i·ty,** *n.* —**im·mo'bi·lize',** *v.*

im·mod'er·ate, *adj.* excessive. —**im· mod'er·ate·ly,** *adv.*

im·mod'est, *adj.* not modest. —**im· mod'es·ty,** *n.*

im'mo·late, *v.,* -lated, -lating. 1. sacrifice. 2. destroy by fire. —**im'mo· la'tion,** *n.*

im·mor'al, *adj.* not moral. —**im·mo· ral'i·ty,** *n.* —**im·mor'al·ly,** *adv.*

im·mor'tal, *adj.* 1. not subject to death or oblivion. —*n.* 2. immortal being. —**im·mor·tal'i·ty,** *n.* —**im· mor'tal·ize',** *v.*

im·mov'a·ble, *adj.* 1. fixed. 2. unchanging.

im·mune', *adj.* 1. protected from disease. 2. exempt. —**im·mu'ni·ty,** *n.* —**im'mu·nize',** *v.*

immune system, network of cells and tissues that protects the body from pathogens and foreign substances.

im·mu·nol'o·gy, *n.* branch of science dealing with the immune system, immunity from disease, etc. —**im·mu· nol'o·gist,** *n.*

im·mure', *v.,* -mured, -muring. confine within walls.

im·mu'ta·ble, *adj.* unchangeable. —**im·mu'ta·bil'i·ty,** *n.*

imp, *n.* 1. little demon. 2. mischievous child. —**imp'ish,** *adj.*

im·pact', *n.* 1. collision. 2. influence; effect. —*v.* 3. collide with. 4. have effect.

im·pair', *v.* damage; weaken. —**im· pair'ment,** *n.*

im·pale', *v.,* -paled, -paling. fix upon sharp stake, etc.

im·pal'pa·ble, *adj.* that cannot be felt or understood.

im·pan'el, *v.,* -eled, -eling. list for jury duty.

im·part', *v.* 1. tell. 2. give.

im·par'tial, *adj.* unbiased. —**im'par· ti·al'i·ty,** *n.* —**im·par'tial·ly,** *adv.*

im·pass'a·ble, *adj.* not able to be passed through or along.

im'passe (-pas), *n.* deadlock.

im·pas'sioned, *adj.* full of passion.

im·pas'sive, *adj.* 1. emotionless. 2. calm. —**im·pas'sive·ly,** *adv.*

im·pa'tience, *n.* lack of patience. —**im·pa'tient,** *adj.* —**im·pa'tient· ly,** *adv.*

im·peach', *v.* charge with misconduct in office. —**im·peach'ment,** *n.*

im·pec'ca·ble, *adj.* faultless. —**im· pec'ca·bly,** *adv.*

im·pe·cu'ni·ous, *adj.* without money.

im·pede', *v.,* -peded, -peding. hinder. —**im·ped'i·ment,** *n.*

im·ped·i·men'ta, *n.pl.* baggage, etc., carried with one.

im·pel', *v.,* -pelled, -pelling. urge forward.

im·pend', *v.* be imminent.

im·pen'e·tra·ble, *adj.* that cannot be penetrated. —**im·pen'e·tra·bil' i·ty,** *n.* —**im·pen'e·tra·bly,** *adv.*

im·per'a·tive, *adj.* 1. necessary. 2. *Gram.* denoting command.

im'per·cep'ti·ble, *adj.* 1. very slight. 2. not perceptible. —**im'per·cep'ti· bly,** *adv.*

im·per'fect, *adj.* 1. having defect. 2. not complete. 3. *Gram.* denoting action in progress. —**im·per·fec'tion,** *n.* —**im·per'fect·ly,** *adv.*

im·pe'ri·al (-pēr'-), *adj.* of an empire or emperor.

im·pe'ri·al·ism', *n.* policy of extending rule over other peoples. —**im· pe'ri·al·ist,** *n., adj.* —**im·pe'ri·al· is'tic,** *adj.*

im·per'il, *v.,* -iled, -iling. endanger.

im·pe'ri·ous, *adj.* domineering. —**im·pe'ri·ous·ly,** *adv.*

im·per'ish·a·ble, *adj.* immortal; not subject to decay. —**im·per'ish·a· bly,** *adv.*

im·per'me·a·ble, *adj.* not permitting penetration. —**im·per'me·a·bil'i· ty,** *n.*

im·per'son·al, *adj.* without personal reference or bias. —**im·per'son·al· ly,** *adv.*

im·per'son·ate', *v.,* -ated, -ating. act the part of. —**im·per'son·a'tion,** *n.* —**im·per'son·a'tor,** *n.*

im·per'ti·nence, *n.* 1. rude presumption. 2. irrelevance. —**im·per'ti· nent,** *adj.* —**im·per'ti·nent·ly,** *adv.*

im·per·turb'a·ble, *adj.* calm.

im·per'vi·ous, *adj.* 1. not allowing penetration. 2. incapable of being affected. —**im·per'vi·ous·ly,** *adv.*

im·pe·ti'go (im'pi tī'gō), *n.* contagious skin infection characterized by pustules.

im·pet'u·ous, *adj.* rash or hasty. —**im·pet'u·os'i·ty,** *n.* —**im·pet'· u·ous·ly,** *adv.*

im'pe·tus, *n.* 1. stimulus. 2. force of motion.

im·pi'e·ty, *n., pl.* -ties. 1. lack of piety. 2. act showing this. —**im·pi' ous,** *adj.*

im·pinge', *v.,* -pinged, -pinging. 1. strike; collide 2. encroach.

im'pi·ous (im'pē ə, im pī'-), *adj.* 1. not pious; irreligious. 2. disrespectful.

imp'ish, *adj.* implike; mischievous.

im·pla'ca·ble, *adj.* not to be placated.

im•plant′, v. instill. —n. (im′plant).
2. device or material used to repair or replace part of the body.

im•plau′si•ble, adj. not plausible.
—**im•plau′si•bil′i•ty,** n.

im•ple′ment, n. 1. instrument or tool.
—v. 2. put into effect.

im•pli′cate, v.. -cated, -cating. involve as guilty.

im•pli•ca′tion, n. 1. act of implying.
2. thing implied. 3. act of implicating.

im•plic′it (-plis′it), adj. 1. unquestioning; complete. 2. implied. —**im•plic′it•ly,** adv.

im•plode′, v.. -ploded, -ploding.
burst inward. —**im•plo′sion,** n.

im•plore′, v.. -plored, -ploring. urge or beg.

im•ply′, v.. -plied, -plying. 1. indicate.
2. suggest.

im•po•lite′, adj. rude.

im•pol′i•tic, adj. not wise or prudent.

im•pon′der•a•ble, adj. that cannot be weighed, measured, or evaluated.

im•port′, v. 1. bring in from another country. 2. matter; signify. —n. (im′pört). 3. anything imported. 4. significance. —**im′por•ta′tion,** n. —**im•port′er,** n.

im•por′tant, adj. 1. of some consequence. 2. prominent. —**im•por′tance,** n.

im•por•tune′ (-tyo͞on′), v.. -tuned, -tuning. beg persistently. —**im•por′tu•nate,** adj.

im•pose′, v.. -posed, -posing. 1. set as obligation. 2. intrude (oneself). 3. deceive. —**im′po•si′tion,** n.

im•pos′ing, adj. impressive.

im•pos′si•ble, adj. that cannot be done or exist. —**im•pos′si•bil′i•ty,** n. —**im•pos′si•bly,** adv.

im′post, n. tax or duty.

im•pos′tor, n. person who deceives under false name. Also, **im•pos′ter.** —**im•pos′ture,** n.

im•po•tence, n. 1. lack of power. 2. lack of sexual powers. —**im′po•tent,** adj.

im•pound′, v. seize by law.

im•pov′er•ish, v. make poor.

im•prac′ti•ca•ble, adj. incapable of being put into practice or use.

im•prac′ti•cal, adj. not usable or useful.

im′pre•ca′tion, n. curse.

im•pre•cise′, adj. not precise.

im•preg′na•ble, adj. resistant to or proof against attack.

im•preg′nate, v.. -nated, -nating. 1. make pregnant. 2. saturate. —**im′preg•na′tion,** n.

im′pre•sa′ri•o, n. person who orga-

nizes or manages entertainment events, as opera.

im•press′, v. 1. affect with respect, etc. 2. fix in mind. 3. stamp. 4. force into public service. —n. (im′pres). 5. act of impressing. —**im•pres′sive,** adj.

im•pres′sion, n. 1. effect on mind or feelings. 2. notion. 3. printed or stamped mark.

im•pres′sion•a•ble, adj. easily influenced, esp. emotionally. —**im•pres′sion•a•bly,** adv.

im•pres′sion•ism, n. (often cap.) style of 19th-century painting characterized by short brush strokes to represent the effect of light on objects. —**im•pres′sion•ist,** n., adj. —**im•pres′sion•is′tic,** adj.

im•pri•ma′tur (im′pri mä′tər, -mā′-), n. 1. permission to print or publish. 2. sanction; approval.

im′print, n. 1. mark made by pressure. 2. sign of event, etc., making impression.

im•pris′on, v. put in prison. —**im•pris′on•ment,** n.

im•prob′a•ble, adj. unlikely. —**im•prob′a•bil′i•ty,** n.

im•promp′tu, adj.. adv. without preparation.

im•prop′er, adj. not right, suitable, or proper. —**im′pro•pri′e•ty,** n. —**im•prop′er•ly,** adv.

im•prove′, v.. -proved, -proving. make or become better. —**im•prove′ment,** n.

im•pro•vise′, v.. -vised, -vising. prepare for or perform at short notice. —**im′pro•vi•sa′tion,** n.

im•pru′dent, adj. not prudent; unwise.

im′pu•dent, adj. shamelessly bold. —**im′pu•dence,** n. —**im′pu•dent•ly,** adv.

im•pugn′ (-pyo͞on′), v. cast doubt on.

im′pulse, n. 1. inciting influence. 2. sudden inclination. —**im•pul′sive,** adj.

im•pu′ni•ty, n. exemption from punishment.

im•pure′, adj. 1. not pure. 2. immoral. —**im•pu′ri•ty,** n.

im•pute′, v.. -puted, -puting. attribute.

in, prep. 1. within. 2. into. 3. while; during. 4. into some place. —adv. 5. inside; within.

in-, common prefix meaning "not" or "lacking." See list on following pages.

in′ad•vert′ent, adj. 1. heedless. 2. unintentional. —**in′ad•vert′ence,** n.

in·al·ien·a·ble, *adj.* not to be taken away or transferred.

in·ane, *adj.* silly.

in·ar·tic·u·late, *adj.* not clear in expression.

in'as·much' as, 1. seeing that. 2. to the extent that.

in·au·gu·rate, *v.*, **-rated, -rating.** 1. induct into office. 2. begin. **—in·au'gu·ral,** *adj.* **—in·au·gu·ra'tion,** *n.*

in'board, *adj., adv.* 1. inside a hull or aircraft. 2. nearer the center, as of an airplane.

in'born', *adj.* present at birth; innate.

in'breed', *v.* produce by repeated breeding of closely related individuals. **—in'breed'ing,** *n.* **—in'bred',** *adj.*

in·can·des·cence (-des'əns), *n.* glow of intense heat. **—in·can·des'cent,** *adj.*

in·can·ta'tion, *n.* 1. magic ritual. 2. spell.

in·ca·pac'i·tate, *v.*, **-tated, -tating.** make unfit. **—in·ca·pac'i·ty,** *n.*

in·car'cer·ate, *v.*, **-ated, -ating.** imprison. **—in·car·cer·a'tion,** *n.*

in·car'nate (-nit), *adj.* embodied in flesh. **—in·car·na'tion,** *n.*

in·cen'di·ar·y (-sen'-), *adj., n., pl.* **-aries.** —*adj.* 1. of or for setting fires. 2. arousing strife. —*n.* 3. person who maliciously sets fires.

in·cense', *v.*, **-censed, -censing.** *n.* —*v.* (in sens') 1. enrage. —*n.* (in' sens). 2. substance burned to give a sweet odor.

in·cen'tive, *n.* stimulus; motivation.

in·cep'tion, *n.* beginning.

in·ces'sant, *adj.* uninterrupted. **—in·ces'sant·ly,** *adv.*

in'cest, *n.* sexual relations between close relatives. **—in·ces'tu·ous,** *adj.*

inch, *n.* unit of length, 1/12 foot.

in·cho'ate (-kō'it), *adj.* just begun; incomplete.

in'ci·dence, *n.* range of occurrence or effect.

in'ci·dent, *n.* 1. happening. 2. side event. —*adj.* 3. likely. 4. naturally belonging. **—in'ci·den'tal,** *adj.*, *n.* **—in'ci·den'tal·ly,** *adv.*

in·cin'er·ate, *v.*, **-ated, -ating.** burn to ashes. **—in·cin'er·a'tor,** *n.*

in·cip'i·ent (-sip'-), *adj.* beginning. **—in·cip'i·ence,** *n.*

in·cise' (-sīz'), *v.*, **-cised, -cising.** cut into; engrave. **—in·ci'sion,** *n.*

in·ci'sive, *adj.* 1. sharp. 2. uncomfortably sharp, as criticism.

in·ci'sor, *n.* cutting tooth.

in·cite', *v.*, **-cited, -citing.** urge to action.

in·cline', *v.*, **-clined, -clining,** *n.* —*v.* 1. tend. 2. slant. 3. dispose. —*n.* (in klīn). 4. slanted surface. **—in·cli·na'tion,** *n.*

in·close', *v.*, **-closed, -closing.** enclose.

in·clude', *v.*, **-cluded, -cluding.** 1. contain. 2. have among others. **—in·clu'sion,** *n.* **—in·clu'sive,** *adj.*

in·cog'ni·to (in kog'ni tō'), *adj., adv.* using assumed name.

in'come, *n.* money received.

in·com·mu'ni·ca'do (in'kə myōō'ni kä'dō), *adj., adv.* without means of communicating with others.

in·com'pa·ra·ble, *adj.* unequaled. **—in·com'pa·ra·bly,** *adv.*

in·con·sid'er·ate, *adj.* thoughtless.

in·con'ti·nent, *adj.* 1. unable to control bodily discharges. 2. lacking sexual self-restraint. **—in·con'ti·nence,** *n.*

in·cor'po·rate, *v.*, **-rated, -rating.** 1. form a corporation. 2. include as part. **—in·cor·po·ra'tion,** *n.*

in·cor·ri·gi·ble, *adj.* not to be reformed.

in·crease', *v.*, **-creased, -creasing,** *n.* —*v.* 1. make or become more or greater. —*n.* (in'krēs). 2. instance of increasing. 3. growth or addition. **—in·creas'ing·ly,** *adv.*

in·cred'i·ble, *adj.* unbelievable; amazing. **—in·cred'i·bly,** *adv.*

in·cred'u·lous, *adj.* not believing.

---

in'a·bil'i·ty
in'ac·ces'si·ble
in·ac'cu·ra·cy
in·ac'cu·rate
in·ac'tive
in·ad'e·qua·cy
in·ad'e·quate
in·ad·mis'si·ble
in·ad·vis'a·ble
in·an'i·mate
in·ap·pro'pri·ate

in·apt'i·tude'
in·ar·tis'tic
in·at·ten'tion
in·at·ten'tive
in·au'di·ble
in·aus·pi'cious
in·cal'cu·la·ble
in·ca'pa·ble
in·ca·pac'i·ty
in·cau'tious
in·ci·vil'i·ty

in·cre·ment, n. addition; increase. —**in·cre·men'tal**, adj.

in·crim'i·nate, v., -nated, -nating. charge with or involve in crime. —**in·crim·i·na'tion**, n.

in·crust', v. cover with crust or outer layer. —**in·crus·ta'tion**, n.

in'cu·bate', v., -bated, -bating. keep warm, as eggs for hatching. —**in·cu·ba'tion**, n.

in'cu·ba'tor, n. 1. heated case for incubating. 2. apparatus in which premature infants are cared for.

in·cul'cate, v., -cated, -cating. teach; instill.

in·cum'bent, adj. 1. obligatory. —n. 2. office holder. —**in·cum'ben·cy**, n.

in·cur', v., -curred, -curring. bring upon oneself.

in·cur'sion, n. raid.

in·debt'ed, adj. obligated by debt. —**in·debt'ed·ness**, n.

in·de·ci'sion, n. inability to decide.

in·deed', adv. 1. in fact. —interj. 2. (used to express surprise, contempt, etc.)

in·de·fat'i·ga·ble, adj. tireless.

in·del'i·ble, adj. that cannot be erased.

in·dem'ni·fy', v., -fied, -fying. compensate for or insure against loss, etc. —**in·dem'ni·ty**, n.

in·dent', v. 1. notch. 2. set back from margin. —**in·den·ta'tion**, **in·den'tion**, n.

in·den'ture (in den'chər) n., v., -tured, -turing. —n. 1. contract, esp. one by which apprentice is bound to service. —v. 2. bind by indenture.

in·de·pend'ent, adj. 1. free. 2. not influenced by or dependent on others. —**in·de·pend'ence**, n.

in·de·struct'i·ble, adj. that cannot be destroyed.

in'dex, n., pl. -dexes, -dices, v. —n. 1. list of names, topics, etc., with page references. 2. indicator. —v. 3. provide with index.

In'di·an, n. 1. native of India. 2. Also, **Amer'ican In'dian**. member of the aboriginal peoples of N. and S. America. —**Indian**, adj.

in'di·cate', v., -cated, -cating. 1. be a sign of. 2. point to. —**in·di·ca'tion**, n. —**in·dic'a·tive**, adj. —**in'di·ca'tor**, n.

in·dict' (-dīt'), v. charge with crime. —**in·dict'ment**, n.

in·dif'fer·ent, adj. 1. without interest or concern. 2. moderate. —**in·dif'fer·ence**, n.

in·dig'e·nous (-dij'ə nəs), adj. native.

in'di·gent, adj. needy; destitute. —**in'di·gence**, n.

in·di·ges'tion, n. difficulty in digesting food.

in·dig·na'tion, n. righteous anger. —**in·dig'nant**, adj.

in·dig'ni·ty, n., pl. -ties. 1. loss of dignity. 2. cause of this.

in'di·go', n., pl. -gos, -goes. blue dye.

in·dis·crim'i·nate, adj. done at random; haphazard

in'dis·pose', v., -posed, -posing. 1. make ill. 2. make unwilling.

in'dite', v., -dited, -diting. write.

in·di·vid'u·al, adj. 1. single; particular. 2. of or for one only. —n. 3. single person, animal, or thing. —**in·di·vid·u·al'i·ty**, n. —**in·di·vid'u·al·ly**, adv.

in·di·vid'u·al·ist, n. person dependent only on self.

in·doc'tri·nate', v., -nated, -nating. train to accept doctrine. —**in·doc'tri·na'tion**, n.

in'do·lent, adj. lazy. —**in'do·lence**, n.

in·dom'i·ta·ble, adj. that cannot be conquered or dominated.

in'door', adj. done, used, etc., inside a building. —**in'doors'**, adv.

in·du'bi·ta·ble, adj. undoubted. —**in·du'bi·ta·bly**, adv.

in·duce', v., -duced, -ducing. 1. persuade; influence. 2. cause; bring on. —**in·duce'ment**, n.

in·duct', v. bring into office, military service, etc.

in·duc·tion, n. 1. reasoning from particular facts. 2. act of inducting. —**in·duc′tive**, adj.

in·dulge′, v., -dulged, -dulging. 1. accommodate whims, appetites, etc., of. 2. accommodate one's own whims, appetites, etc. —**in·dul′gence**, n. —**in·dul′gent**, adj.

in·dus′tri·al·ist, n. owner of industrial plant.

in·dus′tri·al·ize′, v., -ized, -izing. convert to modern industrial methods.

in·dus′tri·ous, adj. hard-working. —**in·dus′tri·ous·ly**, adv.

in′dus·try, n., pl. -tries. 1. trade or manufacture, esp. with machinery. 2. diligent work. —**in·dus′tri·al**, adj.

in·e·bri·ate, v., -ated, -ating, n. —v. (in ē′brī āt′). 1. make drunk. —n. (-it). 2. drunken person.

in·ef′fa·ble, adj. that cannot be described.

in·ef·fec′tu·al, adj. futile; unsatisfactory.

in·ept′, adj. careless; unskilled.

in·eq′ui·ty, n., pl. -ties. injustice.

in·ert′, adj. 1. without inherent power to move, resist, or act. 2. slow-moving. —**in·er′tia**, n.

in·ev′i·ta·ble, adj. not to be avoided. —**in·ev′i·ta·bil′i·ty**, n. —**in·ev′i·ta·bly**, adv.

in·ex′o·ra·ble, adj. unyielding. —**in·ex′o·ra·bly**, adv.

in·ex′pli·ca·ble, adj. not to be explained.

in·ex′tri·ca·ble, adj. that cannot be freed or disentangled. —**in·ex′tri·ca·bly**, adv.

in·fal′li·ble, adj. never failing or making mistakes. —**in·fal′li·bly**, adv.

in·fa′mous, adj. of evil repute. —**in′fa·mous·ly**, adv.

in′fa·my, n., pl. -mies. evil repute. —**in′fa·mous**, adj.

in′fant, n. small baby. —**in′fan·cy**, n. —**in′fan·tile′**, adj.

in′fan·try, n., pl. -tries. soldiers who fight on foot. —**in′fan·try·man**, n.

in·fat′u·ate′, v., -ated, -ating. inspire with foolish passion.

in·fect′, v. affect, esp. with disease germs. —**in·fec′tion**, n.

in·fec′tious, adj. spreading readily.

in·fer′, v., -ferred, -ferring. conclude or deduce. —**in·fer′ence**, n.

in·fe′ri·or, adj. 1. less good, important, etc. —n. 2. person inferior to another. —**in·fe′ri·or′i·ty**, n.

in·fer′nal, adj. 1. of hell. 2. *Informal.* outrageous

in·fest′, v. overrun; trouble. —**in′fes·ta′tion**, n.

in′fi·del, n. unbeliever.

in′field′, n. 1. area of baseball field inside base lines. 2. players in infield. —**in′field′er**, n.

in′fight′ing, n. conflict within group.

in·fil′trate, v., -trated, -trating. pass in, as by filtering. —**in′fil·tra′tion**, n.

in′fi·nite, adj. 1. vast; endless. —n. 2. that which is infinite. —**in·fin′i·ty**, n.

in·fin′i·tes′i·mal, adj. immeasurably small.

in·fin′i·tive, n. simple form of verb.

in·firm′, adj. feeble; weak. —**in·fir′mi·ty**, n.

in·fir′ma·ry, n., pl. -ries. hospital.

in·flame′, v., -flamed, -flaming. 1. set afire. 2. redden. 3. excite. 4. cause bodily reaction marked by redness, pain, etc. —**in·flam′ma·ble**, adj. —**in·flam′ma·to′ry**, adj. —**in′flam·ma′tion**, n.

in·flate′, v., -flated, -flating. 1. swell or expand with air or gas. 2. increase unduly.

in·fla′tion, n. 1. rise in prices when currency or credit expands faster than available goods or services. 2. act of inflating. —**in·fla′tion·ar′y**, adj.

in·flect′, v. 1. bend. 2. modulate. 3. display forms of a word. —**in·flec′tion**, n. —**in·flec′tion·al**, adj.

in·flict′, v. impose harmfully. —**in·flic′tion**, n.

in′flu·ence, n., v., -enced, -encing. —n. 1. power to affect another. 2. something that does this. —v. 3.

move, affect, or sway. —**in·flu·en′·tial,** *adj.*

in′flu·en′za, *n.* acute contagious disease caused by virus.

in′flux, *n.* instance of flowing in.

in′fo·mer′cial, *n.* program-length television commercial designed to appear to be standard programming rather than an advertisement.

in·form′, *v.* supply with information. —**in·form′ant,** *n.* —**in·form′er,** *n.* —**in·form′a·tive,** *adj.*

in′for·ma′tion, *n.* factual knowledge. —**in·for·ma′tion·al,** *adj.*

information superhighway, large-scale communications network linking computers, television sets, etc.

in′fo·tain′ment, *n.* broadcasting or publishing that strives to treat factual matter in an entertaining way, as by dramatizing or fictionalizing real events.

in·frac′tion, *n.* violation.

in′fra·red′, *n.* part of invisible spectrum.

in′fra·struc′ture, *n.* 1. basic framework of system or organization. 2. basic facilities, as transportation and communications systems.

in·fringe′, *v.,* **-fringed, -fringing.** violate; encroach. —**in·fringe′ment,** *n.*

in·fu′ri·ate′, *v.,* **-ated, -ating.** enrage.

in·fuse′, *v.,* **-fused, -fusing.** 1. instill. 2. steep. —**in·fu′sion,** *n.*

in·gen′ious (-jēn′-), *adj.* inventive; clever. —**in·ge·nu′i·ty,** *n.*

in·gen′u·ous (-jen′-), *adj.* artlessly sincere.

in·gest′ (-jest′), *v.* take into the body, as food or liquid. —**in·ges′tion,** *n.*

in′got (ing′gət), *n.* cast mass of metal.

in·grained′, *adj.* fixed firmly.

in·grate′, *n.* ungrateful person.

in·gra′ti·ate′ (-grā′shē āt′), *v.,* **-ated, -ating.** get (oneself) into someone's good graces.

in·gre′di·ent, *n.* element or part of mixture.

in′gress, *n.* entrance.

in·hab′it, *v.* live in. —**in·hab′it·ant,** *n.*

in·hale′, *v.,* **-haled, -haling.** breathe in. —**in·ha·la′tion,** *n.*

in·here′, *v.,* **-hered, -hering.** be inseparable part or element. —**in·her′ent,** *adj.*

in·her′it, *v.* become heir to. —**in·her′it·ance,** *n.*

in·hib′it, *v.* restrain or hinder. —**in′·hi·bi′tion,** *n.*

in·hu′man, *adj.* 1. brutal. 2. not human. —**in·hu·man′i·ty,** *n.*

in·im′i·cal, *adj.* 1. adverse. 2. hostile.

in·im′i·ta·ble, *adj.* not to be imitated.

in·iq′ui·ty, *n., pl.* **-ties.** 1. wicked injustice. 2. sin. —**in·iq′ui·tous,** *adj.*

in·i′tial, *adj., n., v.,* **-tialed, -tialing.** —*adj.* 1. of or at beginning. —*n.* 2. first letter of word. —*v.* 3. sign with initials of one's name.

in·i′ti·ate′, *v.,* **-ated, -ating.** 1. begin. 2. admit with ceremony. —**in·i′ti·a′tion,** *n.*

in·i′ti·a·tive, *n.* 1. beginning action. 2. readiness to begin action.

in·ject′, *v.* force, as into tissue. —**in·jec′tion,** *n.* —**in·jec′tor,** *n.*

in·junc′tion, *n.* order or admonition.

in·jure, *v.,* **-jured, -juring.** 1. hurt. 2. do wrong to. —**in·ju′ri·ous,** *adj.* —**in′ju·ry,** *n.*

ink, *n.* 1. writing fluid. —*v.* 2. mark with ink. —**ink′y,** *adj.*

ink′ling, *n.* hint.

in′land, *adj.* 1. of or in the interior of a region. 2. not foreign. —*adv.* 3. of or toward inland area. —*n.* 4. inland area.

in′-law′, *n.* relative by marriage.

in·lay′, *v.,* **-laid, -laying.** —*v.* (in lā′.) 1. ornament with design set in surface. —*n.* (in′lā′.) 2. inlaid work.

in′let, *n.* narrow bay.

in′mate′, *n.* person confined in prison, hospital, etc.

in′most′, *adj.* farthest within. Also, **in′ner·most′.**

inn, *n.* 1. hotel. 2. tavern.

in·nards, *n.pl.* 1. internal parts of the

---

in·dis·tinct′
in′dis·tin·guish·a·ble
in·di·vis·i·ble
in·ed′i·ble
in·ef·fec′tive
in′ef·fi′cien·cy
in′ef·fi′cient
in·el′i·gi·ble
in′e·qual′i·ty
in·eq′ui·ta·ble
in′es·cap′a·ble

in·es′ti·ma·ble
in·ex′act′
in′ex·cus′a·ble
in′ex·haust′i·ble
in′ex·pen′sive
in′ex·pe′ri·enced
in′ex·pres′si·ble
in·fea′si·ble
in·fe·lic′i·tous
in·fer′tile
in′fi·del′i·ty

body. 2. internal parts, structure, etc., of something. **—in•scru'ta•bil'i•ty,** n.

in•nate', adj. natural; born into one.

in'ner, adj. 1. being farther within. 2. spiritual.

inner city, central part of city, often deteriorating.

in'ning, n. Baseball. one round of play for both teams.

in'no•cence, n. 1. freedom from guilt. 2. lack of worldly knowledge. **—in'no•cent,** adj., n.

in•noc'u•ous, adj. harmless.

in'no•vate', v., -vated, -vating. bring in something new. **—in'no•va'tion,** n. **—in'no•va'tor,** n. **—in'no•va'tive,** adj.

in•nu•en'do, n., pl. -dos, -does. hint of wrong.

in•nu'mer•a•ble, adj. 1. very numerous. 2. that cannot be counted.

in•oc'u•late', v., -lated, -lating. immunize with disease in mild form. **—in•oc'u•la'tion,** n.

in•or'di•nate, adj. excessive. **—in•or'di•nate•ly,** adv.

in'pa•tient, n. patient who stays in hospital while receiving care or treatment.

in'put', n., v., -putted or -put, -putting. **—n. 1.** power, etc., supplied to machine. 2. information given computer. **—v. 3.** enter (data) into computer.

in'quest, n. legal inquiry, esp. by coroner.

in•quire', v., -quired, -quiring. 1. ask. 2. make investigation. **—in•quir'y,** n.

in•qui•si'tion, n. investigation. **—in•quis'i•tor,** n.

in•quis'i•tive, adj. having great curiosity.

in'road', n. encroachment.

in•sane', adj. mentally deranged. **—in•san'i•ty,** n.

in•sa'ti•a•ble, adj. impossible to satisfy.

in•scribe', v., -scribed, -scribing. 1. write or engrave. 2. dedicate. **—in•scrip'tion,** n.

in•scru'ta•ble, adj. that cannot be

understood. **—in•scru'ta•bil'i•ty,** n.

in'sect, n. small six-legged animal with body in three parts.

in•sec'ti•cide', n. chemical for killing insects.

in•sem'i•nate', v., -nated, -nating. 1. sow seed in. 2. impregnate. **—in•sem'i•na'tion,** n.

in•sen'sate, adj. without feeling.

in•sen'si•ble, adj. 1. incapable of feeling or perceiving. 2. not aware; unconscious. 3. not perceptible by the senses.

in•sert', v. 1. put or set in. **—n.** (in'sûrt). 2. something inserted. **—in•ser'tion,** n.

in'shore', adj. 1. on or close to the shore. **—adv.** 2. toward the shore.

in'side', prep., adv. 1. within. **—n.** (in'sīd'). 2. inner part. **—adj.** (in'sīd'). 3. inner.

in•sid'er, n. 1. member of certain organization, society, etc. 2. person who has influence, esp. because privy to confidential information.

in•sid'i•ous, adj. artfully treacherous.

in'sight', n. discernment.

in•sig'ni•a, n.pl. badges of rank, honor, etc.

in•sin'u•ate', v., -ated, -ating. 1. hint slyly. 2. put into mind. 3. make one's way artfully. **—in•sin'u•a'tion,** n.

in•sip'id, adj. without distinctive qualities; vapid.

in•sist', v. be firm or persistent. **—in•sist'ence,** n. **—in•sist'ent,** adj.

in'so•far', adv. to such extent.

in'so•lent, adj. boldly rude. **—in'so•lence,** n.

in•sol'vent, adj. without funds to pay one's debts. **—in•sol'ven•cy,** n.

in•som'ni•a, n. sleeplessness.

in'so•much', adv. 1. to such a degree (that). 2. inasmuch (as).

in•sou'ci•ant (in sōō'sē ənt). adj. free from concern or anxiety. **—in•sou'ci•ance,** n.

in•spect', v. view critically or officially. **—in•spec'tion,** n.

---

in•flex'i•ble	in•ju•di'cious
in•for'mal	in•jus'tice
in'for•mal'i•ty	in•of•fen'sive
in•fre'quen•cy	in•op'er•a•tive
in•fre'quent	in•op•por'tune'
in•glo'ri•ous	in•or•gan'ic
in•grat'i•tude'	in•se•cure'
in•har•mon'ic	in•sen'si•tive
in•har•mo'ni•ous	in•sep'a•ra•ble
in•hos'pi•ta•ble	in•sig•nif'i•cance
in•hu•mane'	in•sig•nif'i•cant

in·spec'tor, *n.* **1.** person with duty to inspect. **2.** minor police official.

in·spire', *v.* **-spired, -spiring. 1.** arouse (emotion, etc.). **2.** prompt to extraordinary actions. **3.** inhale. **—in'spi·ra'tion,** *n.* **in·spi·ra'tion·al,** *adj.*

in·stall', *v.* **1.** put in position for use. **2.** establish. **—in·stal·la'tion,** *n.*

in·stall'ment, *n.* division, as of payment or story. Also, **in·stal'ment.**

in·stance, *n.,* **-stanced, -stancing.** **—n. 1.** case; example. **—v. 2.** cite.

in·stant, *n.* **1.** moment. **2.** point of time now present. **—adj. 3.** immediate. **—in'stant·ly,** *adv.*

in·stan·ta'ne·ous, *adj.* occurring, etc., in an instant. **—in'stan·ta'ne·ous·ly,** *adv.*

in·stead', *adv.* in another's place.

in'step', *n.* upper arch of foot.

in'sti·gate', *v.,* **-gated, -gating.** incite to action. **—in'sti·ga'tion,** *n.* **—in'sti·ga'tor,** *n.*

in·still', *v.* introduce slowly. Also, **in·stil'.** **—in·still'ment,** *n.*

in'stinct, *n.* natural impulse or talent. **—in·stinc'tive,** *adj.*

in'sti·tute', *v.,* **-tuted, -tuting,** *n.* **—v. 1.** establish. **2.** put into effect. **—n. 3.** society or organization. **4.** established law, custom, etc.

in'sti·tu'tion, *n.* **1.** organization with public purpose. **2.** established tradition, etc. **3.** act of instituting. **—in'sti·tu'tion·al,** *adj.*

in·struct', *v.* **1.** order. **2.** teach. **—in·struc'tion,** *n.* **—in·struc'tive,** *adj.* **—in·struc'tor,** *n.*

in'stru·ment, *n.* **1.** tool. **2.** device for producing music. **3.** means; agent. **4.** legal document. **—in'stru·men'tal,** *adj.* **—in'stru·men·tal'i·ty,** *n.*

in'su·lar, *adj.* **1.** of islands. **2.** narrow in viewpoint. **—in'su·lar'i·ty,** *n.*

in'su·late', *v.,* **-lated, -lating.** cover with nonconducting material. **—in'su·la'tion,** *n.* **—in'su·la'tor,** *n.*

in'su·lin, *n.* synthetic hormone used to treat diabetes.

in·sult', *v.* **1.** treat with open con-

tempt. **—n.** (in'sult). **2.** such treatment.

in·su'per·a·ble, *adj.* that cannot be overcome.

in·sure', *v.,* **-sured, -suring. 1.** make certain. **2.** guarantee payment in case of harm to or loss of. **—in·sur'ance,** *n.* **—in·sur'er,** *n.*

in·sur'gent, *n.* **1.** rebel. **—adj. 2.** rebellious.

in'sur·rec'tion, *n.* armed revolt.

in·tact', *adj.* undamaged; whole.

in'take', *n.* **1.** point at which something is taken in. **2.** what is taken in.

in'te·ger (-jar), *n.* **1.** whole number. **2.** entity.

in'te·gral, *adj.* **1.** necessary to completeness. **2.** entire.

in'te·grate', *v.,* **-grated, -grating. 1.** bring into whole. **2.** complete. **3.** abolish segregation by race. **—in'te·gra'tion,** *n.*

in·teg'ri·ty, *n.* **1.** soundness of character; honesty. **2.** perfect condition.

in·teg'u·ment, *n.* skin, rind, etc.

in'tel·lect', *n.* **1.** understanding. **2.** mental capacity.

in'tel·lec'tu·al, *adj.* **1.** of intellect. **2.** devising or employing concepts in dealing with problems. **—n. 3.** person who pursues intellectual interests. **—in'tel·lec'tu·al·ly,** *adv.*

in·tel'li·gence, *n.* **1.** ability to learn and understand. **2.** news. **3.** gathering of secret information. **—in·tel'li·gent,** *adj.*

in·tel'li·gi·ble, *adj.* understandable. **—in·tel'li·gi·bil'i·ty,** *n.* **—in·tel'li·gi·bly,** *adv.*

in·tend', *v.* plan; design.

in·tense', *adj.* **1.** extremely powerful. **2.** emotional. **—in·ten'si·fy,** *v.* **—in·ten'si·ty,** *n.*

in·ten'sive, *adj.* thoroughgoing.

in·tent', *n.* **1.** purpose. **—adj. 2.** firmly concentrated. **3.** firmly purposeful. **—in·tent'ly,** *adv.*

in·ten'tion, *n.* **1.** purpose. **2.** meaning. **—in·ten'tion·al,** *adj.*

in·ter' (-tûr'), *v.,* **-terred, -terring.** bury.

in'sin·cere'
in'sin·cer'i·ty
in'sol'u·ble
in'sta·bil'i·ty
in'sub·or'di·nate
in'sub·or'di·na'tion
in'suf·fer·a·ble
in'suf·fi'cient
in'sup·press'i·ble
in'sur·mount'a·ble
in'sus·cep'ti·ble

in·tan'gi·ble
in·tem'per·ance
in·tem'per·ate
in·tol'er·a·ble
in·tol'er·ance
in·tol'er·ant
in·var'i·a·ble
in·vis'i·ble
in·vis'i·bly
in·vol'un·tar'y
in·vul'ner·a·ble

in•ter•act′, v. act upon one another. —**in•ter•ac′tion**, n. —**in•ter•ac′tive**, adj.

in•ter•cede′, v., **-ceded, -ceding.** act or plead in behalf. —**in•ter•ces′sion,** n.

in•ter•cept′, v. stop or check passage. —**in•ter•cep′tion,** n. —**in•ter•cep′tor,** n.

in•ter•change′, v., **-changed, -changing,** n. —v. (in′tər chānj′). 1. exchange. 2. alternate. —n. (in′tər chānj′). 3. act or place of interchanging.

in•ter•con′ti•nen′tal, adj. 1. between or among continents. 2. capable of traveling between continents.

in′ter•course′, n. 1. dealings. 2. sexual relations.

in′ter•de•pend′ent, adj. mutually dependent. —**in′ter•de•pend′ence,** n.

in•ter•dict′, n. 1. decree that prohibits. —v. (in′tər dikt′). 2. prohibit. —**in′ter•dic′tion,** n.

in′ter•est, n. 1. feeling of attention, curiosity, etc. 2. business or ownership. 3. benefit. 4. payment for use of money. —v. 5. excite or hold interest of.

in′ter•face′, n. 1. surface forming common boundary between two spaces. 2. common boundary between people, concepts, etc. 3. computer hardware or software that communicates information between entities, as between computer and user. —v. 4. interact or coordinate smoothly.

in′ter•fere′, v., **-fered, -fering.** 1. hamper. 2. intervene. 3. meddle. —**in′ter•fer′ence,** n.

in′ter•im, n. meantime. —adj. 2. temporary.

in•te′ri•or, adj. 1. inside. 2. inland. —n. 3. interior part.

in•ter•ject′, v. add or include abruptly.

in′ter•jec′tion, n. 1. act of interjecting. 2. something interjected. 3. interjected word that forms a complete utterance, as indeed!

in′ter•lace′, v., **-laced, -lacing.** unite by or as if by weaving together; intertwine.

in′ter•lard′, v. mix in.

in′ter•lock′, v., lock, join, or fit together closely.

in′ter•loc′u•tor, n. participant in conversation.

in′ter•loc′u•to′ry, adj. 1. of or in conversation. 2. Law. not final.

in′ter•lop′er, n. intruder.

in′ter•lude′, n. 1. intervening episode, time, etc. 2. performance in intermission.

in•ter•mar′ry, v., **-ried, -rying.** 1. (of groups) become connected by marriage. 2. marry outside one's religion, ethnic group, etc. —**in′ter•mar′riage,** n.

in′ter•me′di•ar′y, adj., n., pl. **-aries.** —adj. 1. intermediate. —n. 2. person negotiating between others.

in′ter•me′di•ate, adj. being or acting between two others.

in•ter′ment, n. burial.

in′ter•mez′zo (in′tər met′sō, -med′zō), n., pl. **-mezzos, -mezzi.** short musical composition, as between divisions of a longer work.

in′ter•mi′na•ble, adj. seeming to be without end; endless. —**in•ter′mi•na•bly,** adv.

in′ter•mis′sion, n. interval between acts in drama, etc.

in′ter•mit′tent, adj. alternately ceasing and starting again.

in•tern′, v. 1. hold within certain limits; confine. —n. (in′tûrn). 2. Also, **in′terne.** resident assistant physician on hospital staff. —**in•tern′ment,** n.

in•ter′nal, adj. 1. interior; inner. 2. not foreign; domestic. —**in•ter′nal•ly,** adv.

internal medicine, branch of medicine dealing with diagnosis and nonsurgical treatment of diseases.

in′ter•na′tion•al, adj. 1. among nations. 2. of many nations.

in′ter•na′tion•al•ism, n. principle of international cooperation. —**in′ter•na′tion•al•ist,** n.

in′ter•na′tion•al•ize′, v., **-ized, -izing.** 1. make international. 2. bring under international control.

in′ter•ne′cine (-nē′sīn), adj. 1. of conflict within a group. 2. mutually destructive.

Internet, n. Trademark. large computer network linking smaller networks worldwide.

in′tern•ist, n. doctor specializing in internal medicine.

in′ter•play′, n. reciprocal action.

in′ter•po•late′, v., **-lated, -lating.** insert to alter or clarify meaning. —**in′ter•po•la′tion,** n.

in′ter•pose′, v., **-posed, -posing.** 1. place between things. 2. intervene.

in•ter′pret, v. 1. explain. 2. construe. 3. translate. —**in•ter′pre•ta′tion,** n. —**in•ter′pret•er,** n.

in′ter•ra′cial, adj. of, for, or between persons of different races.

in•ter′ro•gate′, v., **-gated, -gating.**

question. —in·ter·ro·ga'tion, n. —in·ter·rog·a·tive, adj. —in·ter'ro·ga·tor, n.

in·ter·rupt', v. break in; stop. —in·ter·rup'tion, n.

in·ter·sect', v. divide by crossing; cross.

in·ter·sec'tion, n. 1. place where two or more roads meet. 2. act or fact of intersecting.

in·ter·sperse' (-spûrs'), v., -spersed, -spersing. 1. scatter at random. 2. vary with something scattered.

in·ter·state', adj. involving number of states.

in·ter·stice (-tûr'stis), n. chink or opening.

in·ter·twine', v., -twined, -twining. unite by twining together.

in·ter·val, n. 1. intervening time or space. 2. difference in musical pitch between two tones.

in·ter·vene', v., -vened, -vening. 1. come or be between. 2. mediate. —in·ter·ven'tion, n. —in·ter·ven'tion·ist, n.

in·ter·view', n. 1. conversation to obtain information. 2. meeting. —v. 3. have interview with. —in'ter·view·er, n.

in·tes·tate', adj. 1. without having made a will. 2. not disposed of by will.

in·tes'tine, n. lower part of alimentary canal. —in·tes'ti·nal, adj.

in'ti·mate, adj., n., v., -mated, -mating. —adj. 1. close; friendly. 2. private. 3. thorough. —n. 4. intimate friend. —v. (-māt') 5. imply. —in'ti·ma·cy, n. —in'ti·ma'tion, n. —in'ti·mate·ly, adv.

in·tim'i·date', v., -dated, -dating. make timid; frighten. —in·tim'i·da'tion, n.

in'to, prep. to inside of.

in·tone', v., -toned, -toning. 1. use particular spoken tone. 2. chant. —in·to·na'tion, n.

in·tox'i·cate', v., -cated, -cating. affect with or as with alcoholic liquor. —in·tox'i·ca'tion, n.

in·trac'ta·ble, adj. stubborn; unmanageable.

in·tra·mu'ral, adj. within one school.

in·tran'si·gent (-sa jant), adj. uncompromising. —in·tran'si·gence, n.

in·tran'si·tive, adj. (of verb) not having a direct object.

in·tra·ve'nous, adj. within or into vein.

in·trep'id, adj. fearless. —in·tre·pid'i·ty, n.

in'tri·cate, adj. complicated. —in'tri·ca·cy, n.

in·trigue' (in trēg'), v., -trigued, -triguing, n. —v. 1. interest by puzzling. 2. plot. —n. 3. crafty design or plot.

in·trin'sic, adj. inherent; basic. —in·trin'si·cal·ly, adv.

in·tro·duce', v., -duced, -ducing. 1. bring to notice, use, etc. 2. be preliminary to. 3. make (person) known to another. —in·tro·duc'tion, n. —in'tro·duc'to·ry, adj.

in·tro·spec'tion, n. examination of one's own thoughts and motives. —in·tro·spec'tive, adj.

in'tro·vert', n. person concerned chiefly with inner thoughts or feelings. —in'tro·ver'sion, n.

in·trude', v., -truded, -truding. come or bring in without welcome. —in·trud'er, n. —in·tru'sion, n. —in·tru'sive, adj.

in·tu·i'tion, n. instinctive perception. —in·tu'i·tive, adj.

in·un·date', v., -dated, -dating. flood. —in·un·da'tion, n.

in·ure' (in yŏŏr'), v., -ured, -uring. accustom; harden.

in·vade', v., -vaded, -vading. enter as an enemy. —in·vad'er, n. —in·va'sion, n.

in'va·lid, n. 1. sick person. —adj. 2. sick. 3. for invalids. 4. (in val'id) not valid. —in·val'i·date', v.

in·val'u·a·ble, adj. beyond valuing; priceless.

in·vec'tive, n. 1. censure. 2. harsh taunts or accusations.

in·veigh' (-vā'), v. attack violently in words.

in·vei'gle (-vē'gal -vā'-), v. -gled, -gling. lure into action.

in·vent', v. devise (something new). —in·ven'tion, n. —in·ven'tive, adj. —in·ven'tor, n.

in'ven·to·ry, n., pl. -tories. list or stock of goods.

in·verse', adj. 1. reversed. 2. opposite. 3. inverted.

in·vert', v. 1. turn upside down. 2. reverse. 3. make contrary. —in·ver'sion, n.

in·ver'te·brate (-brit), n. 1. without backbone. 2. invertebrate animal.

in·vest', v. 1. spend money, esp. so as to get larger amount in return. 2. give or devote (time, etc.). 3. furnish with power or authority. —in·vest'ment, n. —in·ves'tor, n.

in•ves'ti•gate', v., **-gated, -gating.** examine in detail. —**in•ves'ti•ga'tion,** n. —**in•ves'ti•ga'tor,** n.

in•vet'er•ate, adj. confirmed in habit.

in•vid'i•ous, adj. **1.** likely to arouse envy. **2.** offensively unjust.

in•vig'or•ate', v., **-ated, -ating.** give vigor to.

in•vin'ci•ble, adj. unconquerable. —**in•vin'ci•bil'i•ty,** n.

in•vi'o•la•ble, adj. that must not or cannot be violated. —**in•vi'o•la•bil'i•ty,** n.

in•vi'o•late, adj. **1.** not hurt or desecrated. **2.** uninhabited.

in•vite', v., **-vited, -viting. 1.** ask politely. **2.** act so as to make likely. **3.** attract. —**in'vi•ta'tion,** n.

in vi'tro (in vē'trō), developed or maintained in a controlled nonliving environment, as a laboratory vessel.

in•vo•ca'tion, n. prayer for aid, guidance, etc.

in'voice, n., v., **-voiced, -voicing.** —n. **1.** list with prices of goods sent to buyer. —v. **2.** list on invoice.

in•voke', v., **-voked, -voking. 1.** beg for. **2.** call on in prayer. **3.** cite as authoritative.

in•volve', v., **-volved, -volving. 1.** include as necessary. **2.** complicate. **3.** implicate. **4.** engross. —**in•volve'ment,** n.

in'ward, adv. **1.** Also, **in'wards.** toward the interior. —adj. **2.** toward the interior. **3.** inner. —n. **4.** inward part.

i'o•dine', n. nonmetallic element used in medicine.

i'on, n. electrically charged particle.

i'on•ize' (ī'a nīz'), v., **-nized, -nizing. 1.** separate or change into ions. **2.** produce ions in. **3.** become ionized. —**i'on•i•za'tion,** n.

i•on'o•sphere (ī on'a sfēr'), n. outermost region of earth's atmosphere, consisting of ionized layers.

i•o'ta (ī ō'ta), n. very small quantity.

IOU, written acknowledgment of debt.

IQ, intelligence quotient.

ip'e•cac', n. drug from root of South American shrub.

i•ras'ci•ble (i ras'a bal), adj. easily angered.

ire, n. anger. —**i'rate,** adj.

ir'i•des'cence (-des'ans), n. play of rainbowlike colors. —**ir'i•des'cent,** adj.

i'ris, n. **1.** colored part of the eye. **2.** perennial plant with showy flowers.

I'rish, n. language or people of Ireland. —**I'rish,** adj.

irk, v. vex; annoy. —**irk'some,** adj.

i'ron, n. **1.** metallic element. **2.** implement for pressing cloth. **3.** (pl.) shackles. —adj. **4.** of or like iron. —v. **5.** press with iron (def. 2).

iron curtain, (formerly) barrier between Communist and non-Communist areas.

i'ro•ny, n., pl. **-nies. 1.** figure of speech in which meaning is opposite to what is said. **2.** outcome contrary to expectations. —**i•ron'i•cal,** i•ron'ic, adj. —**i•ron'i•cal•ly,** adv.

ir•ra'di•ate', v., **-ated, -ating. 1.** illuminate. **2.** expose to radiation. **3.** enlighten. —**ir•ra'di•a'tion,** n.

ir•ra'tion•al, adj. without reason or judgment.

ir•rec'on•cil'a•ble, adj. **1.** that cannot be brought into agreement. **2.** bitterly opposed.

ir're•deem'a•ble, adj. that cannot be redeemed.

ir•re•duc'i•ble, adj. that cannot be reduced.

ir•ref'u•ta•ble, adj. not refutable.

ir•reg'u•lar, adj. **1.** not symmetrical. **2.** not fixed. **3.** not conforming to rule or normality. —**ir•reg'u•lar'i•ty,** n.

ir•rel'e•vant, adj. not relevant. —**ir•rel'e•vance,** n.

ir•re•li'gious, adj. **1.** not religious. **2.** hostile to religion.

ir•rep'a•ra•ble, adj. that cannot be rectified. —**ir•rep'a•ra•bly,** adv.

ir're•press'i•ble, adj. that cannot be repressed. —**ir're•press'i•bly,** adv.

ir're•proach'a•ble, adj. blameless.

ir're•sist'i•ble, adj. not to be withstood.

ir•res'o•lute', adj. undecided.

ir're•spec'tive, adj. without regard to.

ir•re•spon'si•ble, adj. not concerned with responsibilities.

ir're•triev'a•ble, adj. that cannot be recovered.

ir•rev'er•ent, adj. lacking respect.

ir•rev'o•ca•ble, adj. not to be revoked or annulled.

ir'ri•gate', v., **-gated, -gating.** supply with water. —**ir'ri•ga'tion,** n.

ir'ri•ta•ble, adj. easily angered. —**ir'ri•ta•bil'i•ty,** n.

ir'ri•tate', v., **-tated, -tating. 1.** anger or vex. **2.** make sensitive. **3.** excite to action. —**ir'ri•ta'tion,** n. —**ir'ri•tant,** n.

ir•rup'tion, n. **1.** bursting in. **2.** invasion.

is, v. third pers. sing. pres. indic. of **be.**

i'sin•glass', n. **1.** transparent substance from some fish. **2.** mica.

Is•lam', *n.* religious faith founded by Muhammad (A.D. 570–632).

is•land, *n.* body of land surrounded by water.

isle, *n.* small island.

is•let (ī'lit), *n.* very small island.

ism, *n.* doctrine.

i'so•bar (ī'sə bär'), *n.* line on map connecting points at which barometric pressure is the same.

i'so•late, *v.* **-lated, -lating.** set apart. —**i'so•la'tion**, *n.*

i'so•la'tion•ist, *n.* person opposed to participation in world affairs. —**i'so•la'tion•ism,** *n.*

i'so•met'rics, *n.pl.* exercises in which one body part is tensed against another. —**i'so•met'ric**, *adj.*

i•sos'ce•les (ī sos'ə lēz'), *adj.* (of triangle) having two sides equal.

i'so•tope', *n.* one of two or more forms of an element that vary in atomic weight.

is'sue, *v.* **-sued, -suing,** —*v.* 1. send out. 2. publish. 3. distribute. 4. emit. 5. emerge. —*n.* 6. act of issuing. 7. thing issued. 8. point in question. 9. offspring. 10. result. —**is'su•ance,** *n.*

isth'mus (is'məs), *n.* strip of land surrounded by water and connecting two larger bodies.

it, *pron.* third pers. sing. neuter pronoun.

I•tal'ian, *n.* native or language of Italy. —**Italian,** *adj.*

i•tal'ic, *n.* printing type that slopes to right. Also, **i•tal'ics.** —**i•tal'i•cize'**, *v.* —**i•tal'ic,** *adj.*

itch, *v.* 1. feel irritation of skin. —*n.* 2. itching sensation. 3. restless desire.

i'tem, *n.* separate article.

i'tem•ize', *v.* **-ized, -izing.** state by items; list. —**i'tem•i•za'tion,** *n.*

it'er•ate, *v.* **-ated, -ating.** say or do repeatedly. —**it'er•a'tion,** *n.* —**it'er•a'tive,** *adj.*

i•tin'er•ant, *adj.* 1. traveling. —*n.* 2. person who goes from place to place.

i•tin'er•ar'y, *n. pl.* **-aries.** 1. route. 2. plan of travel.

its, *adj.* possessive form of **it.**

it's, contraction of **it is.**

it•self', *pron.* reflexive form of **it.**

i'vo•ry, *n. pl.* **-ries.** 1. hard white substance in tusks of elephant, etc. 2. yellowish white.

i'vy, *n. pl.* **ivies.** climbing evergreen vine. —**i'vied,** *adj.*

J

J, j, *n.* tenth letter of English alphabet.

jab, *v.* **jabbed, jabbing,** *n.* poke; thrust.

jab'ber, *v.* 1. talk rapidly or indistinctly. —*n.* 2. such talk.

jack, *n.* 1. lifting device. 2. person. 3. knave in playing cards. 4. male. 5. flag; ensign. —*v.* 6. raise with jack.

jack'al, *n.* wild dog of Asia and Africa.

jack'ass', *n.* 1. male donkey. 2. fool.

jack'et, *n.* 1. short coat. 2. any covering.

jack-in-the-box', *n., pl.* **-boxes.** toy consisting of box from which figure springs up when the lid is opened.

jack'knife', *n.* folding pocket knife.

jack'pot', *n.* cumulative prize in contest, lottery, etc.

jack rabbit, large rabbit of western America.

Ja•cuz'zi (jə kōō'zē), *n., pl.* **-zis.** *Trademark.* brand name for type of whirlpool bath.

jade, *n., v.,* **jaded, jading.** —*n.* 1. valuable green stone. 2. old horse. —*v.* 3. weary.

jag, *n.* 1. projection; ragged edge. 2. *Slang.* drunken spree. —**jag'ged,** *adj.*

jag'uar (-wär), *n.* large South American wildcat.

jail, *n.* 1. prison. —*v.* 2. put in prison. —**jail'er,** *n.*

ja•lop'y, *n., pl.* **-pies.** old, decrepit automobile.

jam, *v.,* **jammed, jamming,** *n.* —*v.* 1. push or squeeze. 2. make or become unworkable. —*n.* 3. people or objects jammed together. 4. *Informal.* difficult situation. 5. preserve of entire fruit.

jamb, *n.* side post of door or window.

jam•bo•ree', *n.* 1. merry gathering.

jan'gle, *v.,* **-gled, -gling,** *n.* —*v.* 1. sound harshly. —*n.* 2. harsh sound.

jan'i•tor, *n.* caretaker of building. —**jan'i•tress,** *n. fem.*

Jan•u•ar'y, *n.* first month of year.

Jap•a•nese', *n., pl.* **-nese.** native or language of Japan. —**Japanese,** *adj.*

jar, *n., v.,* **jarred, jarring.** —*n.* 1. broad-mouthed bottle. 2. unpleasant sound. 3. sudden shock or shake. —*v.* 4. shock or shake. 5. conflict.

jar'gon, *n.* language meaningful only to particular trade, etc.

jas'mine, *n.* fragrant shrub.

jas'per, *n.* precious quartz.

jaun·dice (jôn'-), *n.* illness causing yellowed skin, etc.

jaun·diced, *adj.* 1. skeptical. 2. envious.

jaunt, *n.* short trip.

jaun·ty, *adj.* **-tier, -tiest.** sprightly. —**jaun·ti·ly**, *adv.* —**jaun·ti·ness**, *n.*

jave·lin, *n.* spear.

jaw, *n.* either of two bones forming mouth.

jaw·bone', *n., v.* **-boned, -boning.** —*n.* 1. bone of the jaw. —*v.* 2. influence by persuasion, esp. by public appeal.

jay, *n.* noisy colorful bird.

jay·walk', *v.* cross street improperly. —**jay·walk'er**, *n.*

jazz, *n.* 1. popular music of black American origin. 2. *Slang.* insincere or pretentious talk.

jazz·y, *adj.* **jazzier, jazziest.** 1. of or like jazz music. 2. fancy or flashy.

jeal·ous, *adj.* 1. resentful of another's success, etc. 2. vigilant, esp. against rivalry. —**jeal·ous·y**, *n.*

jeans, *n.pl.* cotton trousers.

Jeep, *n. Trademark.* small rugged type of automobile.

jeer, *v.* 1. deride. —*n.* 2. deriding shout.

Je·ho'vah, *n.* God.

je·june' (ji joon'), *adj.* 1. lacking interest or significance; insipid. 2. lacking maturity; childish.

jell (jel), *v.* 1. become like jelly in consistency. 2. become clear or definite.

jel'ly, *n., pl.* **-lies**, *v.* **-lied, -lying.** —*n.* 1. soft, semisolid food, as fruit juice boiled down with sugar. —*v.* 2. make into, or provide with, jelly.

jel'ly·fish', *n., pl.* **-fish, -fishes.** marine animal with soft, jellylike body.

jen'ny, *n., pl.* **-nies.** 1. spinning machine. 2. female donkey, wren, etc.

jeop'ard·ize' (jep'-), *v.* **-ized, -izing.** risk; endanger. —**jeop'ard·y**, *n.*

jerk, *n.* 1. quick, sharp thrust, pull, etc. 2. *Slang.* stupid, naïve person. —*v.* 3. give jerk to. —**jerk'y**, *adj.*

jer·ry-built', *adj.* flimsily made.

jer'sey, *n.* type of sweater or shirt.

jest, *n., v.* joke; banter. —**jest'er**, *n.*

Je'sus, *n.* founder of Christian religion. Also called **Jesus Christ.**

jet, *n., v.*, **jetted, jetting**, *adj.* —*n.* 1. stream under pressure. 2. Also, **jet plane.** plane operated by jet propulsion. —*v.* 3. spout. —*adj.* 4. deep black.

jet lag, fatigue after jet flight to different time zone.

jet propulsion, propulsion of plane, etc., by reactive thrust of jet. —**jet' pro·pelled'**, *adj.*

jet'sam, *n.* goods thrown overboard to lighten distressed ship.

jet'ti·son, *v.* cast (jetsam) out.

jet'ty, *n., pl.* **-ties.** wharf; pier.

Jew, *n.* 1. follower of Judaism. 2. descendant of Biblical Hebrews. —**Jew'ish**, *adj.*

jew'el, *n.* precious stone; gem. —**jew'el·er**, *n.* —**jew'el·ry**, *n.*

jib, *n.* triangular sail on forward mast.

jibe, *v.* **jibed, jibing.** 1. gibe. 2. *Informal.* be consistent.

jif'fy, *n., pl.* **-fies.** short time.

jig, *n., v.* **jigged, jigging.** —*n.* 1. lively folk dance. —*v.* 2. dance a jig.

jig'gle, *v.* **-gled, -gling.** —*v.* 1. move back and forth, etc. —*n.* 2. act of jiggling.

jig'saw', *n.* saw with narrow vertical blade for cutting curves, patterns, etc.

jigsaw puzzle, set of irregularly cut flat pieces that form a picture when fitted together.

jilt, *v.* reject (a previously encouraged suitor).

jim'my, *n., pl.* **-mies**, *v.* **-mied, -mying.** —*n.* 1. short crowbar. —*v.* 2. force open with or as if with a jimmy.

jin'gle, *v.* **-gled, -gling**, *n.* —*v.* 1. make repeated clinking sound. —*n.* 2. clink; tinkle. 3. very simple verse.

jin·rik'i·sha (jin rik'shô), *n.* rickshaw. Also, **jin·rik'sha.**

jinx, *n.* 1. cause of bad luck. —*v.* 2. cause bad luck.

jit'ter·bug', *n.* acrobatic jazz dance.

jit'ters, *n.pl. Informal.* nervousness. —**jit'ter·y**, *adj.*

jive (jīv), *n., v.* **jived, jiving.** —*n.* 1. swing music or early jazz. 2. deceptive or meaningless talk. —*v.* 3. *Slang.* fool or kid.

job, *n., v.* **jobbed, jobbing.** —*n.* 1. piece of work. 2. employment. —*v.* 3. sell wholesale. —**job'less**, *adj.*

job'ber, *n.* 1. wholesaler. 2. dealer in odd lots of merchandise.

jock, *n. Informal.* 1. athlete. 2. enthusiast.

jock'ey, *n.* 1. rider of race horses. —*v.* 2. maneuver.

jo·cose', *adj.* jesting; merry. Also, **jo·cund.** —**jo·cos'i·ty**, *n.*

joc'u·lar, *adj.* joking.

jodh'purs (jod'parz), *n.pl.* riding breeches.

jog, *n., v.* **jogged, jogging**, *n.* —*v.* 1. nudge; shake. 2. run at slow, steady pace. —*n.* 3. nudge. 4. steady pace. 5. projection.

join, *v.* 1. put together. 2. become member of.

join'er, *n.* 1. assembler of woodwork. 2. *Informal.* person who likes to join clubs, etc. —**join'er•y,** *n.*

joint, *n.* 1. place or part in which things join. 2. movable section. 3. cheap, sordid place. 4. *Slang.* marijuana cigarette. —*adj.* 5. shared or sharing. —*v.* 6. join or divide at joint. —**joint'ly,** *adv.*

joist, *n.* floor beam.

joke, *n., v.,* **joked, joking.** —*n.* 1. amusing remark, story, etc. —*v.* 2. make or tell joke. 3. speak only to amuse. —**jok'er,** *n.* —**jok'ing•ly,** *adv.*

jol'ly, *adj.,* **-lier, -liest,** *v.,* **-lied, -lying,** *adv.* —*adj.* 1. gay; merry. —*v.* 2. try to keep (someone) in good humor. —*adv.* 3. *Brit. Informal.* very. —**jol'li•ness, jol'li•ty,** *n.*

jolt, *v., n.* jar; shake.

jon'quil, *n.* fragrant yellow or white narcissus.

josh, *v. Informal.* tease.

jos'tle, *v.,* **-tled, -tling.** —*v.* 1. push rudely. —*n.* 2. rude push.

jot, *n., v.,* **jotted, jotting.** —*n.* 1. bit. —*v.* 2. write.

jour'nal, *n.* 1. daily record. 2. periodical. 3. part of shaft in contact with bearing.

jour'nal•ism, *n.* newspaper writing. —**jour'nal•ist,** *n.* —**jour'nal•is'tic,** *adj.*

jour'ney, *n.* 1. act or course of traveling. —*v.* 2. travel.

jour'ney•man, *n., pl.* **-men.** hired skilled worker.

joust (joust), *n.* fight between mounted knights.

jo'vi•al, *adj.* vigorously cheerful. —**jo'vi•al'i•ty,** *n.*

jowl, *n.* jaw or cheek.

joy, *n.* gladness; delight. —**joy'ful, joy'ous,** *adj.*

ju'bi•lant, *adj.* rejoicing. —**ju'bi•la'tion,** *n.*

ju'bi•lee', *n.* celebration, esp. of anniversary.

Ju'da•ism', *n.* religion of the Jewish people.

judge, *n., v.,* **judged, judging.** —*n.* 1. person who decides cases in court of law. 2. person making authoritative decisions. 3. discriminating person; connoisseur. —*v.* 4. decide on. —**judg'er,** *n.*

judg'ment, *n.* 1. decision, as in court of law. 2. good sense.

ju•di'cial, *adj.* 1. of justice, courts of law, or judges. 2. thoughtful; wise. —**ju•di'cial•ly,** *adv.*

ju•di'ci•ar•y, *n., pl.* **-aries,** *adj.* —*n.* 1.

legal branch of government. —*adj.* 2. of judges, etc.

ju•di'cious, *adj.* wise; prudent.

ju'do, *n.* martial art based on jujitsu.

jug, *n.* 1. container for liquids. 2. *Slang.* prison.

jug'ger•naut' (jug'ər nôt', -not'), *n.* any large, overpowering, irresistible force.

jug'gle, *v.,* **-gled, -gling.** perform tricks tossing things. —**jug'gler,** *n.*

jug'u•lar, *adj.* 1. of the neck. —*n.* 2. large vein in neck.

juice, *n.* liquid part of plant, fruit, etc. —**juic'y,** *adj.*

ju•jit'su, *n.* Japanese method of wrestling and self-defense.

juke box, coin-operated phonograph.

Ju•ly', *n.* seventh month of year.

jum'ble, *n., v.,* **-bled, -bling.** —*n.* 1. confused mixture. —*v.* 2. make jumble of.

jum'bo, *adj.* very large.

jump, *v.* 1. spring up; leap. 2. raise. —*n.* 3. spring; leap. 4. rise. 5. *Informal.* advantage.

jump'er, *n.* 1. one that jumps. 2. sleeveless dress worn over blouse.

jump'suit', *n.* 1. one-piece suit worn by parachutist. 2. garment fashioned after it.

jump'y, *adj.* **jumpier, jumpiest.** nervous. —**jump'i•ly,** *adv.* —**jump'i•ness,** *n.*

junc'tion, *n.* 1. union. 2. place of joining.

junc'ture, *n.* 1. point of time. 2. crisis. 3. joint.

June, *n.* sixth month of year.

jun'gle, *n.* wildly overgrown tropical land.

jun'ior, *adj.* 1. younger. 2. lower. —*n.* 3. third-year high school or college student.

junior high school, school usu. encompassing grades 7 through 9.

ju'ni•per, *n.* coniferous evergreen shrub or tree.

junk, *n.* 1. useless material; rubbish. 2. type of Chinese ship. 3. narcotics, esp. heroin. —*v.* 4. discard.

jun'ket, *n.* 1. custard. 2. pleasure excursion. 3. trip by government official at public expense. —*v.* 4. entertain.

junk'ie, *n. Informal.* 1. drug, esp. heroin, addict. 2. person who craves or is enthusiastic for something.

jun'ta (hŏŏn'tä), *n.* military group that seizes power and rules.

Ju'pi•ter, *n.* 1. chief Roman god. 2. largest of sun's planets.

ju·ris·dic·tion, *n.* authority, range of control, etc., of judge or the like. **—ju'ris·dic'tion·al,** *adj.*

ju'ris·pru'dence, *n.* science of law.

ju'rist, *n.* expert in law.

ju'ror, *n.* member of jury. Also, **ju'ryman,** *fem.* **ju'ry·wom'an.**

ju'ry, *n., pl.* **-ries.** group of persons selected to make decisions, esp. in law court.

just, *adj.* 1. fair; right. 2. legal. 3. true. —*adv.* 4. exactly. 5. barely. 6. only. **—just'ly,** *adv*

jus'tice, *n.* 1. fairness; rightness. 2. administration of law. 3. high judge.

justice of the peace, local public officer who performs marriages, tries minor cases, etc.

jus'ti·fy', *v.* **-fied, -fying.** 1. show to be true, right, etc. 2. defend. **—jus'ti·fi·ca'tion,** *n.* **—jus'ti·fi'a·ble,** *adj.*

jut, *v.,* jutted, jutting, *n.* —*v.* 1. project. —*n.* 2. projection.

jute, *n.* East Indian plant whose fibers are used for fabrics, etc.

ju've·nile, *adj.* 1. young. —*n.* 2. young person. 3. youthful theatrical role. 4. book for children.

jux'ta·pose', *v.* **-posed, -posing.** place close for comparison.

K

K, k, *n.* eleventh letter of English alphabet.

kai'ser (kī'-), *n.* German emperor.

kale, *n.* type of cabbage.

ka·lei'do·scope' (-lī'-), *n.* optical device in which colored bits change patterns continually. **—ka·lei'do·scop'ic,** *adj.*

kan'ga·roo', *n., pl.* **-roos, -roo.** Australian marsupial with long hind legs used for leaping.

ka'pok, *n.* silky down from seeds of certain tropical trees, used in pillows, etc.

ka·put' (-pŏŏt'), *adj. Informal.* 1. extinct. 2. out of order.

ka'ra·o'ke (kar'ē ō'kē), *n.* act of singing along to a music video, esp. one from which original vocals have been eliminated.

kar'at, *n.* 1/24 part: unit for measuring purity of gold.

ka·ra'te (kə rä'tē), *n.* Japanese technique of unarmed combat.

kar'ma, *n.* fate as the result of one's actions in successive incarnations.

ka'ty·did, *n.* large green grasshopper.

kay'ak (kī'ak), *n.* Eskimo canoe, esp. of skin.

ka·zoo', *n.* tubular musical toy that vibrates and buzzes when one hums into it.

keel, *n.* 1. central framing member of ship's bottom. —*v.* 2. fall sideways.

keen, *adj.* 1. sharp. 2. excellent. 3. intense. 4. eager. —*v.* 5. wail; lament. **—keen'ly,** *adv.* **—keen'ness,** *n.*

keep, *v.,* kept, keeping, *n.* —*v.* 1. continue. 2. detain. 3. support. 4. maintain. 5. withhold. 6. observe. 7. last. —*n.* 8. board and lodging. **—keep'er,** *n.*

keep'ing, *n.* 1. conformity. 2. care.

keep'sake', *n.* souvenir.

keg, *n.* small barrel.

kelp, *n.* large brown seaweed.

ken, *n.* knowledge.

ken'nel, *n.* 1. doghouse. 2. establishment where dogs are boarded and cared for.

ker'chief, *n.* cloth head covering.

ker'nel, *n.* center part of nut.

ker'o·sene', *n.* type of oil.

ketch'up, *n.* catchup.

ket'tle, *n.* pot for boiling liquids, etc.

ket'tle·drum', *n.* large drum with round copper bottom.

key, *n.* 1. part for operating lock. 2. explanation. 3. operating lever. 4. musical tonality. 5. reef. —*adj.* 6. chief. —*v.* 7. intensify; excite.

key'board', *n.* 1. row of keys on piano, computer, etc. —*v.* 2. insert (data) into computer.

key'note', *n.* 1. basic note of a musical piece; tonic. 2. theme of meeting, etc.

key'stone', *n.* stone forming summit of arch.

khak'i (kak'ē), *adj.* *n.* yellowish brown.

khan (kän), *n.* Asian ruler.

kib·butz' (-bŏŏts'), *n., pl.* **-but'zim.** Israeli collective community.

kib'itz·er, *n. Informal.* person offering unwanted advice. **—kib'itz,** *v.*

kick, *v.* 1. strike with foot. 2. recoil. 3. *Informal.* complain. —*n.* 4. act or result of kicking. 5. *Informal.* thrill.

kick'back', *n.* portion of an income given, often secretly, to someone who made the income possible.

kick'off', *n.* 1. kick that begins play in football or soccer. 2. beginning of anything.

kid, *n., v.,* kidded, kidding. —*n.* 1. young goat. 2. leather from its skin. 3. *Informal.* child. —*v.* 4. *Informal.* fool; tease.

kid'nap, v., **-napped** or **-naped**, **-napping** or **-naping**. abduct, esp. for ransom. —**kid'nap·er**, n.

kid'ney, n. 1. gland that secretes urine. 2. kind.

kill, v. 1. end life of; murder. 2. destroy; cancel. —n. 3. animal slain. —**kill'er**, n.

kiln (kil, kiln), n. large furnace for making bricks, etc.

kil'o·cy'cle, n. kilohertz.

kil'o·gram', n. 1000 grams. Also, **kilo**.

kil'o·hertz', n., pl. **-hertz**. radio frequency of 1000 cycles per second. Also, formerly, **kil'o·cy'cle**.

kil'o·li'ter (-lē'-), n. 1000 liters.

ki·lom'e·ter, n. 1000 meters.

kil'o·watt', n. 1000 watts.

kilt, n. man's skirt, worn in Scotland.

ki·mo'no (-na), n., pl. **-nos**. loose dressing gown.

kin, n. relatives. Also, **kins'folk'**. —**kins'man**, n. —**kins'wom'an**, n.fem. —**kin'ship**, n.

kind, adj. 1. compassionate; friendly. —n. 2. type; group. —**kind'ness**, n.

kin'der·gar'ten, n. school for very young children.

kin'dle, v., **-dled, -dling**. 1. set afire. 2. rouse.

kin'dling, n. material for starting fire.

kind'ly, adj., **-lier, -liest**, adv. —adj. 1. kind; gentle. —adv. 2. in kind manner. 3. cordially; favorably. —**kind'li·ness**, n.

kin'dred, adj. 1. related; similar. —n. 2. relatives.

kin'e·scope', n. 1. television tube. 2. filmed recording of television show.

ki·net'ic, adj. of or caused by motion.

king, n. supreme male ruler. —**king'ly**, adj.

king'dom, n. government ruled by king or queen.

king'fish·er, n. colorful, fish-eating bird.

king'-size', adj. extra large.

kink, n., v. twist; curl. —**kink'y**, adj.

ki·osk (kē'osk), n. small open structure where newspapers, refreshments, etc., are sold.

kip'per, n. salted, dried fish.

kis'met (kiz'met), n. fate.

kiss, v. 1. touch with lips in affection, etc. —n. 2. act of kissing. 3. type of candy.

kit, n. set of tools, supplies, etc.

kitch'en, n. room for cooking. —**kitch'en·ware'**, n.

kitch'en·ette', n. small, compact kitchen.

kite, n. 1. light, paper-covered frame flown in wind on long string. 2. type of falcon.

kith and kin, friends and relations.

kitsch (kich), n. something tawdry designed to appeal to undiscriminating persons.

kit'ten, n. young cat. Also, **kit'ty**.

kit'ten·ish, adj. playfully coy or cute.

klep'to·ma'ni·a, n. irresistible desire to steal. —**klep'to·ma'ni·ac'**, n.

knack, n. special skill.

knap'sack', n. supply bag carried on back.

knave, n. dishonest rascal. —**knav'ish**, adj.

knead (nēd), v. mix (dough).

knee, n. middle joint of leg.

knee'cap', n. flat bone at front of knee.

knee'-jerk', adj. Informal. reacting in an automatic, habitual way.

kneel, v., **knelt** or **kneeled, kneeling**. be on one's knees.

knell, n. slow, deep sound of bell.

knick'ers, n.pl. type of breeches.

knick'knack', n. trinket.

knife, n., pl. **knives**. cutting blade in handle.

knight, n. 1. chivalrous medieval soldier of noble birth. 2. holder of honorary rank. 3. piece in chess. —v. 4. name a man a knight. —**knight'hood**, n. —**knight'ly**, adj., adv.

knit, v., **knitted** or **knit, knitting**. form netlike fabric. —**knit'ting**, n.

knob, n. rounded handle. —**knob'by**, adj.

knock, v. 1. strike hard; pound. 2. Informal. criticize. —n. 3. hard blow, etc. 4. Informal. criticism. —**knock'er**, n.

knoll (nōl), n. small hill.

knot, n., v., **knotted, knotting**. —n. 1. intertwining of cords to bind. 2. cluster. 3. lump. 4. hard mass where branch joins tree trunk. 5. one nautical mile per hour. —v. 6. tie or tangle. —**knot'ty**, adj.

knout, n. whip.

know, v., **knew, known, knowing**. —v. 1. understand, remember, or experience. —n. 2. Informal. state of knowledge, esp. of secrets. —**know'a·ble**, adj.

know'-how', n. Informal. skill.

knowl'edge, n. facts, etc., known.

knowl'edge·a·ble, adj. well-informed.

knuck'le, n. 1. joint of a finger. —v. 2. **knuckle down**, apply oneself earnestly. 3. **knuckle under**, submit; yield.

kohl·ra'bi (kōl'rä'bē), n., pl. **-bies**. variety of cabbage.

ko'la (kō'lə), *n.* tropical African tree grown for its nuts, used to flavor soft drinks.

kook (kook), *n. Slang.* eccentric. —**kook'y,** *adj.*

Ko·ran', *n.* sacred scripture of Islam.

Ko·re'an (kə rē'ən), *n.* native or language of Korea.

ko'sher, *adj.* (among Jews) permissible to eat.

kow'tow', *v.* act obsequiously.

kryp'ton, *n.* inert gas, an element found in very small amounts in the atmosphere.

ku'dos (-dōs, -dōz), *n.* praise; glory.

kud'zu (kood'zoo), *n.* fast-growing vine planted for fodder and to retain soil.

kum'quat, *n.* small citrus fruit of Chinese shrub.

kung' fu', Chinese technique of unarmed combat.

L

L, l, *n.* twelfth letter of English alphabet.

la'bel, *n., v.,* **-beled, -beling.** —*n.* 1. tag bearing information. —*v.* 2. put label on.

la'bi·um, *n., pl.* **-bia.** folds of skin bordering the vulva. —**la'bi·al,** *adj.*

la'bor, *n.* 1. bodily toil; work. 2. childbirth. 3. workers as a group. —*v.* 4. work. Also, *Brit.* **la'bour.** —**la'bor·er,** *n.*

la'bored, *adj.* done with difficulty.

lab'o·ra·to·ry, *n., pl.* **-ries.** place for scientific work.

la·bo'ri·ous, *adj.* involving much labor.

lab'y·rinth (lab'ə-), *n.* 1. maze. 2. internal ear.

lac, *n.* resinous secretion of Asian insect.

lace, *n., v.,* **laced, lacing.** —*n.* 1. fancy network of threads. 2. cord. —*v.* 3. fasten with lace. —**lac'y,** *adj.*

lac'er·ate' (las'ə-), *v.,* **-ated, -ating.** tear; mangle. —**lac'er·a'tion,** *n.*

lach'ry·mal (lak'rə məl), *adj.* of or producing tears.

lach'ry·mose', *adj.* tearful.

lack, *n.* 1. deficiency. —*v.* 2. be wanting.

lack'a·dai'si·cal, *adj.* listless.

lack'ey, *n.* servile follower.

lack'lus'ter, *adj.* uninteresting.

la·con'ic (la kon'ik), *adj.* using few words. —**la·con'i·cal·ly,** *adv.*

lac'quer, *n.* 1. kind of varnish. —*v.* 2. coat with lacquer.

la·crosse' (lə krôs'), *n.* game of ball played with long rackets.

lac'tic, *adj.* of or from milk.

la·cu'na (lə kyoo'nə), *n., pl.* **-nae** (-nē). **-nas.** 1. cavity. 2. gap.

lad, *n.* boy.

lad'der, *n.* structure of two sidepieces with steps between.

lad'en, *adj.* loaded heavily.

lad'ing, *n.* cargo; freight.

la'dle, *n., v.,* **-dled, -dling.** —*n.* 1. large deep-bowled spoon. —*v.* 2. dip with ladle.

la'dy, *n., pl.* **-dies.** 1. woman of refinement. 2. mistress of household. 3. title of noblewoman. —**la'dy·like',** *adj.*

la'dy·bug', *n.* small spotted beetle. Also, **la'dy·bird'.**

la'dy·fin'ger, *n.* small oblong cake.

lag, *v.,* **lagged, lagging,** *n.* —*v.* 1. move slowly or belatedly. —*n.* 2. instance of lagging.

la'ger (lä'gər), *n.* kind of beer.

lag'gard, *adj.* 1. lagging. —*n.* 2. person who lags.

la·goon', *n.* shallow pond connected with river, lake, or sea.

laid'-back', *adj. Informal.* relaxed; easygoing.

lair, *n.* den of beast.

lais'sez-faire' (les'ā fer'), *adj.* without interfering in trade, others' affairs, etc.

la'i·ty, *n.* laypersons.

lake, *n.* large body of water enclosed by land.

la'ma, *n.* Tibetan or Mongolian Buddhist priest.

La·maze' method (lə mäz'), method by which expectant mother is prepared for birth by classes, exercises, etc.

lamb, *n.* young sheep.

lam·baste' (lam bāst', -bast'), *v.,* **-basted, -basting.** *Informal.* 1. beat severely. 2. reprimand harshly.

lam'bent, *adj.* flickering or glowing lightly. —**lam'ben·cy,** *n.*

lame, *adj.,* **lamer, lamest,** *v.,* **lamed, laming.** —*adj.* 1. crippled. 2. inadequate. —*v.* 3. make lame.

la·mé' (la mā', lä-), *n.* ornamental fabric with metallic threads.

la·ment', *v.* 1. mourn; regret. —*n.* 2. Also, **lam'en·ta'tion.** expression of lament. —**lam'en·ta·ble,** *adj.*

lam'i·na, *n., pl.* **-nae** (-nē), **-nas.** thin layer.

lam′i•nate′, v., **-nated, -nating,** adj. —v. **1.** split into thin layers. **2.** cover or form with layers. —adj. **3.** Also, **lam′i•nat′ed.** made of layers. —**lam′i•na′tion,** n.

lamp, n. light source. —**lamp′shade′,** n. —**lamp′post′,** n.

lamp′black′, n. pigment from soot.

lam•poon′, n. vicious satire. —v. **2.** satirize.

lam′prey, n. eellike fish.

lance, n., v., **lanced, lancing.** —n. **1.** long spear. —v. **2.** open with lancet.

lan′cet, n. sharp-pointed surgical tool.

land, n. **1.** part of the earth's surface above water. **2.** region. —v. **3.** bring or come to land. **4.** fall to earth or floor.

lan′dau (-dô), n. carriage with folding top.

land′fall′, n. **1.** approach to or sighting of land. **2.** land sighted or reached.

land′fill′, n. **1.** area of land built up from material, as refuse, deposited on it. **2.** material deposited on landfill.

land′ing, n. **1.** act of one that lands. **2.** place for landing persons and goods. **3.** platform between stairs.

land′locked′, adj. **1.** shut in completely or almost completely by land. **2.** having no access to sea. **3.** living in waters shut off from sea.

land′lord′, n. person who owns and leases property. —**land′la′dy,** n.fem.

land′lub′ber, n. person unused to sea.

land′mark′, n. **1.** prominent object serving as a guide. **2.** anything prominent of its kind.

land′scape′, n., v., **-scaped, -scaping.** —n. **1.** broad view of rural area. —v. **2.** arrange trees, shrubs, etc., for effects.

land′slide′, n. fall of earth or rock.

lane, n. narrow road.

lan′guage, n. **1.** speech. **2.** any means of communication.

lan′guid, adj. without vigor.

lan′guish, v. **1.** be or become weak. **2.** pine. —**lan′guor,** n. —**lan′guor•ous,** adj.

lank, adj. lean; gaunt. Also, **lank′y.**

lan′o•lin, n. fat from wool.

lan′tern, n. case for enclosing light.

lan′yard (lan′yard), n. short rope.

lap, v., **lapped, lapping,** n. —v. **1.** lay or lie partly over. **2.** wash against. **3.** take up with tongue. —n. **4.** overlapping part. **5.** one circuit of racecourse. **6.** part of body of sitting person from waist to knees.

la•pel′, n. folded-back part on front of a garment.

lap′i•dar′y, n., pl. **-daries,** adj. —n. **1.** worker in gems. —adj. **2.** meticulous in detail.

lap′in, n. rabbit.

lap′is laz′u•li (lap′is laz′ŏŏ lē, -lī′, laz′yŏŏ-), n. **1.** deep blue semiprecious gem. **2.** sky-blue color; azure.

lapse, n., v., **lapsed, lapsing.** —n. **1.** slight error; negligence. **2.** slow passing. —v. **3.** pass slowly. **4.** make error. **5.** slip downward. **6.** become void.

lap′top′, n. portable microcomputer that fits on the lap.

lar′ce•ny, n., pl. **-nies.** theft.

larch, n. tree of pine family.

lard, n. **1.** rendered fat of hogs. —v. **2.** apply lard to.

lard′er, n. pantry.

large, adj., **larger, largest. 1.** great in size or number. **2. at large,** a. at liberty. **b.** in general.

large′ly, adv. **1.** in large way. **2.** generally.

lar•gess′, n. generous gifts. Also, **lar•gesse′.**

lar′go, adv. Music. slowly.

lar′i•at, n. long, noosed rope.

lark, n. **1.** small songbird. **2.** frolic.

lark′spur, n. plant with flowers on tall stalks.

lar′va, n., pl. **-vae** (-vē). young of insect between egg and pupal stages. —**lar′val,** adj.

lar′yn•gi′tis (-jī′-), n. inflammation of larynx.

lar′ynx, n., pl. **-ynges, -ynxes.** cavity at upper end of windpipe. —**la•ryn′ge•al,** adj.

la•sa′gna (lə zän′yə, lä-), n. baked dish of wide strips of pasta layered with cheese, tomato sauce, and usu. meat. Also, **la•sa′gne.**

las•civ′i•ous (lə siv′-), adj. lewd.

la′ser, n. device for amplifying radiation of frequencies of visible light.

lash, n. **1.** flexible part of whip. **2.** blow with whip. **3.** eyelash. —v. **4.** strike with or as with lash. **5.** bind.

lass, n. girl.

las′si•tude′, n. **1.** listlessness. **2.** indifference.

las′so, n., pl. **-sos, soes,** v., **-soed, -soing.** —n. **1.** lariat. —v. **2.** catch with lasso.

last, adj. **1.** latest. **2.** final. —adv. **3.** most recently. **4.** finally. —n. **5.** that which is last. **6.** foot-shaped form on which shoes are made or repaired. —v. **7.** continue. —**last′ly,** adv.

latch, n. **1.** device for fastening door or gate. —v. **2.** fasten with latch.

late, adj., adv., **later, latest. 1.** after proper time. **2.** being or lasting well along in time. **3.** recent. **4.** deceased.

late'ly, *adv.* recently.

la'tent, *adj.* hidden; dormant. —**la'ten·cy,** *n.*

lat'er·al, *adj.* on or from the side.

la'tex, *n.* milky plant juice yielding rubber.

lath (lath), *n.* **1.** narrow wood strip. **2.** material for holding plaster. —*v.* **3.** cover with laths.

lathe (lāṯẖ), *n.* machine for turning wood, etc., against a shaping tool.

lath'er, *n.* **1.** froth made with soap and water. **2.** froth from sweating. —*v.* **3.** form or cover with lather.

Lat'in, *n.* **1.** language of ancient Rome. **2.** member of any people speaking Latin-based language. —**Latin,** *adj.*

Latin America, countries in South and Central America where Spanish or Portuguese is spoken. —**Lat'in-A·mer'i·can,** *adj.*

La·ti'no (la tē'nō, la-), *n.* Hispanic.

lat'i·tude' (-trēn'), *n.* **1.** distance from equator. **2.** freedom.

la·trine' (-trēn'), *n.* toilet, esp. in army.

lat'ter, *adj.* **1.** being second of two. **2.** later.

lat'tice, *n.* structure of crossed strips. —**lat'tice·work',** *n.*

laud, *v.* praise. —**laud'a·ble,** *adj.* —**laud'a·to'ry,** *adj.*

lau'da·num (lô'də nəm), *n.* tincture of opium.

laugh, *v.* **1.** express mirth audibly. —*n.* **2.** act or sound of laughing. —**laugh'ter,** *n.*

laugh'a·ble, *adj.* ridiculous.

laugh'ing·stock', *n.* object of ridicule.

launch, *v.* **1.** set afloat. **2.** start. **3.** throw. —*n.* **4.** large open motorboat.

launch pad, platform for launching rockets. Also, **launch'ing pad.**

laun'der, *v.* wash and iron. —**laun'der·er,** *n.* —**laun'dress,** *n.fem.*

laun'dry, *n., pl.* **-dries. 1.** clothes, etc., to be washed. **2.** place where clothes, etc., are laundered.

lau're·ate (lôr'ē it, lor'-), *n.* person who has been honored in a particular field.

lau'rel, *n.* **1.** small glossy evergreen tree. **2.** (*pl.*) honors.

la'va, *n.* molten rock from volcano.

lav'a·to'ry, *n., pl.* **-ries. 1.** bathroom. **2.** washbowl.

lave, *v.,* **laved, laving.** bathe.

lav'en·der, *n.* **1.** pale purple. **2.** fragrant shrub yielding **oil of lavender.**

lav'ish, *adj.* **1.** extravagant. —*v.* **2.** expend or give abundantly. —**lav'ish·ly,** *adv.*

law, *n.* **1.** rules under which people live. **2.** rule. **3.** legal action. —**law'a·bid'ing,** *adj.* —**law'less,** *adj.* —**law'mak'er,** *n.*

law'ful, *adj.* permitted by law. —**law'ful·ly,** *adv.*

lawn, *n.* **1.** grass-covered land kept mowed. **2.** thin cotton or linen fabric.

law'suit', *n.* prosecution of claim in court.

law'yer, *n.* person trained in law.

lax, *adj.* **1.** careless. **2.** slack. —**lax'i·ty,** *n.*

lax'a·tive, *adj.* **1.** mildly purgative. —*n.* **2.** laxative agent.

lay, *v.,* **laid, laying,** *n., adj.* —*v.* **1.** put down. **2.** produce eggs. **3.** ascribe. **4.** devise. **5.** pt. of **lie.** —*n.* **6.** position. **7.** song. —*adj.* **8.** not clerical or professional. —**lay'man, lay'per·son,** *n.* —**lay'wom·an,** *n.fem.*

lay'a·way plan, method of purchasing in which store reserves item until customer has completed a series of payments.

lay'er, *n.* one thickness.

lay·ette', *n.* outfit for newborn child.

lay'out', *n.* arrangement.

la'zy, *adj.,* **-zier, -ziest. 1.** unwilling to work. **2.** slow-moving. —**la'zi·ly,** *adv.* —**la'zi·ness,** *n.*

leach, *v.* **1.** soak through or in. **2.** dissolve from a material by soaking in.

lead (lēd *for 1–4;* led *for 5–7*), *v.,* **led, leading,** *n.* —*v.* **1.** guide by going before or with. **2.** influence. **3.** afford passage. —*n.* **4.** foremost place or part. **5.** heavy malleable metal. **6.** plummet. **7.** graphite used in pencils. —**lead'en,** *adj.* —**lead'er,** *n.* —**lead'er·ship',** *n.*

leaf, *n., pl.* **leaves,** *v.* —*n.* **1.** flat green part on stem of plant. **2.** thin sheet. —*v.* **3.** thumb through. —**leaf'y,** *adj.*

leaf'let, *n.* **1.** pamphlet. **2.** small leaf.

league, *n., v.,* **leagued, leaguing.** —*n.* **1.** alliance; pact. **2.** unit of distance, about three miles. —*v.* **3.** unite in league.

leak, *n.* **1.** unintended hole. —*v.* **2.** pass or let pass through leak. **3.** allow to be known unofficially. —**leak'age,** *n.* —**leak'y,** *adj.*

lean, *v.,* **leaned** *or* **leant, leaning,** *adj.* —*v.* **1.** bend. **2.** depend. **3.** inclination. **4.** lean flesh. —*adj.* **5.** not fat. —**lean'ness,** *n.*

leap, *v.,* **leaped** *or* **leapt, leaping,** *n.* —*v.* **1.** spring through air; jump. —*n.* **2.** jump.

leap year, year of 366 days.

learn, *v.* acquire knowledge or skill. —**learn'er,** *n.* —**learn'ing,** *n.*

learn'ed, adj. knowing much; scholarly.

lease, n., v., **leased, leasing.** —n. 1. contract conveying property for certain time. —v. 2. get by means of lease.

leash, n. line for holding dog.

least, adj. 1. smallest. —n. 2. least amount, etc. —adv. 3. to least extent, etc.

leath'er, n. prepared skin of animals. —**leath'er•y,** adj.

leave, v., **left, leaving,** n. —v. 1. depart from. 2. let remain or be. 3. have remaining. 4. bequeath. —n. 5. permission. 6. farewell. 7. furlough.

leav'en (lev'-), n. 1. Also, **leav'en•ing.** fermenting agency to raise dough. —v. 2. produce fermentation.

lech'er•ous (lech'ar as), adj. lustful. —**lech'er•y,** n. —**lech'er,** n.

lec'tern, n. stand for speaker's papers.

lec'ture, n., v. —**tured, -turing.** —n. 1. instructive speech. —v. 2. give lecture. —**lec'tur•er,** n.

ledge, n. narrow shelf.

ledg'er, n. account book.

lee, n. 1. shelter. 2. side away from the wind. 3. (pl.) dregs. —**lee,** adj. —**lee'-ward,** adj., adv., n.

leech, n. bloodsucking worm.

leek, n. plant resembling onion.

leer, n. 1. sly or insinuating glance. —v. 2. look with leer.

lee'way' (-ā'), n. 1. Naut. drift due to wind. 2. extra time, space, etc.

left, adj. 1. on side toward west when facing north. 2. still present; remaining. —n. 3. left side. 4. political side favoring liberal or radical reform. —**left'-hand',** adj. —**left'-hand•ed,** adj. —**left'ist,** n., adj.

leg, n. 1. one of limbs supporting a body. 2. any leglike part.

leg'a•cy, n., pl. **-cies.** anything bequeathed.

le'gal, adj. of or according to law. —**le•gal'i•ty,** n. —**le'gal•ize',** v.

leg•a•tee', n. person bequeathed legacy.

le•ga'tion, n. 1. diplomatic minister and staff. 2. official residence of minister.

le•ga'to (la gā'to), adj., adv. Music. smooth and connected; without breaks.

leg'end, n. 1. story handed down by tradition. 2. inscription. —**leg'end•ar'y,** adj.

leg'er•de•main' (lej'ar də mān'), n. sleight of hand.

leg'ging, n. covering for leg.

leg'i•ble, adj. easily read. —**leg'i•bil'i•ty,** n. —**leg'i•bly,** adv.

le'gion, n. 1. military unit. 2. multitude. —**le'gion•naire',** n.

leg'is•late', v., **-lated -lating.** 1. make laws. 2. effect by law. —**leg'is•la'tion,** n. —**leg'is•la'tive,** adj. —**leg'is•la'tor,** n.

leg'is•la•ture, n. law-making body.

le•git'i•mate, adj. 1. lawful. 2. after right or established principles. 3. born to a married couple. —**le•git'i•ma•cy,** n.

le•git'i•mize', v., **-mized, -mizing.** show to be or treat as legitimate.

leg•ume' (leg'yōōm), n. plant of group including peas and beans. —**le•gu'mi•nous,** adj.

lei (lā), n. wreath of flowers for neck.

lei'sure (lē'zhar), n. 1. freedom from work. —adj. 2. unoccupied; at rest. —**lei'sure•ly,** adj. unhurried.

lem'ming, n. small rodent, noted for periodic mass migrations.

lem'on, n. 1. yellowish fruit of citrus tree. 2. Informal. person or thing, esp. a newly bought product, that is defective or unsatisfactory.

lem•on•ade', n. beverage of lemon juice and sweetened water.

le'mur (lē'mar), n. small monkeylike animal.

lend, v., **lent, lending.** 1. give temporary use of. 2. give; provide. —**lend'er,** n.

length, n. size or extent from end to end. —**length'en,** v. —**length'wise',** adv., adj. —**length'y,** adj.

le'ni•ent, adj. merciful; not severe. —**le'ni•ence,** le'ni•en•cy, n.

lens, n., pl. **lenses.** glass for changing convergence of light rays.

Lent, n. season of fasting preceding Easter. —**Lent'en,** adj.

len'til, n. pealike plant.

le'o•nine' (lē'a nīn'), adj. of or like the lion.

leop'ard, n. large fierce spotted animal.

le'o•tard' (lē'a tärd'), n. tight one-piece garment worn by acrobats, dancers, etc.

lep'er (lep'ar), n. person afflicted with leprosy.

lep're•chaun', n. Irish sprite.

lep'ro•sy, n. disease marked by skin ulcerations.

les'bi•an (lez'-), n. 1. female homosexual. —adj. 2. pertaining to female homosexuals.

le'sion (lezhan), n. 1. injury. 2. morbid change in bodily organ.

less, adj. 1. to smaller extent. Also, **les'ser.** 2. smaller. 3. lower in importance. —n. 4. Also, **lesser.**

smaller amount, etc. —*prep.* 5. minus. —**less'en,** *v.*

les•see', *n.* one granted a lease.

les'ser, *adj.* 1. compar. of **little.** 2. minor.

les'son, *n.* 1. something to be studied. 2. reproof. 3. useful experience.

les'sor, *n.* one granting a lease.

lest, *conj.* for fear than.

let, *v.,* **let, letting,** *n.* —*v.* 1. permit. 2. rent out. 3. contract for work. —*n.* 4. hindrance.

let'down', *n.* 1. disappointment. 2. decrease in volume, force, energy, etc.

le'thal, *adj.* deadly.

leth'ar•gy, *n., pl.* **-gies.** drowsy dullness. —**le•thar'gic,** *adj.*

let'ter, *n.* 1. written communication. 2. written component of word. 3. actual wording. 4. (*pl.*) literature. —*v.* 5. write with letters.

let'tered, *adj.* literate; learned.

let'ter•head', *n.* 1. printed information at top of letter paper. 2. paper with a letterhead.

let'tuce, *n.* plant with large leaves used in salad.

let'up', *n.* cessation; pause; relief.

leu•ke'mi•a, *n.* cancerous disease of blood cells.

lev'ee, *n.* 1. embankment to prevent floods. 2. (Also, le vē'). reception.

lev'el, *adj., n., v.,* **-eled, -eling.** —*adj.* 1. even. 2. horizontal. 3. well-balanced. —*n.* 4. height; elevation. 5. level position. 6. device for determining horizontal plane. —*v.* 7. make or become level. 8. aim. —**lev'el•er,** *n.*

lev'er, *n.* bar moving on fixed support to exert force.

lev'er•age, *n.* power or action of lever.

le•vi'a•than (-vī'-), *n.* 1. in the Bible, a sea monster. 2. something of immense size or power.

lev'i•tate', *v.,* **-tated, -tating.** rise or cause to rise into the air, esp. in apparent defiance of gravity. —**lev'i•ta'tion,** *n.*

lev'i•ty, *n.* lack of seriousness.

lev'y, *v.,* **levied, levying,** *n., pl.* **levies.** —*v.* 1. raise or collect by authority. 2. make (war). —*n.* 3. act of levying. 4. something levied.

lewd, *adj.* obscene. —**lewd'ly,** *adv.* —**lewd'ness,** *n.*

lex'i•cog'ra•phy, *n.* writing of dictionaries. —**lex'i•cog'ra•pher,** *n.*

lex'i•con, *n.* dictionary.

li'a•bil'i•ty, *n., pl.* **-ties.** 1. debt. 2. disadvantage. 3. state of being liable.

li'a•ble, *adj.* 1. likely. 2. subject to obligation or penalty.

li'ai•son' (lē'ə zon'), *n.* 1. contact to

ensure cooperation. 2. intimacy; affair.

li'ar, *n.* person who tells lies.

li'bel, *n., v.,* **-beled, -beling.** —*n.* 1. defamation in writing or print. —*v.* 2. publish libel against. —**li'bel•ous,** *adj.*

lib'er•al, *adj.* 1. favoring extensive individual liberty. 2. tolerant. 3. generous. —*n.* 4. liberal person. —**lib'er•al•ism,** *n.* —**lib'er•al'i•ty,** *n.* —**lib'er•al•ize',** *v.*

liberal arts, college courses comprising the arts, humanities, and natural and social sciences.

lib'er•ate', *v.,* **-ated, -ating.** set free. —**lib'er•a'tion,** *n.* —**lib'er•a'tor,** *n.*

lib'er•tar'i•an, *n.* person who advocates liberty in thought or conduct.

lib'er•tine' (-tēn'), *n.* dissolute person.

lib'er•ty, *n., pl.* **-ties.** 1. freedom; independence. 2. right to use place. 3. impertinent freedom.

li•bi'do (-bē-), *n., pl.* **-dos.** 1. sexual desire. 2. instinctual energies and drives derived from the id. —**li•bid'i•nous,** *adj.*

li'brar•y, *n., pl.* **-ries.** 1. place for collection of books, etc. 2. collection of books, etc. —**li•brar'i•an,** *n.*

li•bret'to (li-), *n., pl.* **-tos, -ti.** words of musical drama.

li'cense, *n., v.,* **-censed, -censing.** —*n.* 1. formal permission. 2. undue freedom. —*v.* 3. grant license to. Also, **li'cence.**

li•cen'tious, *adj.* lewd; lawless.

li'chen (lī'kən), *n.* crustlike plant on rocks, trees, etc.

lic'it (lis'it), *adj.* lawful.

lick, *v.* 1. pass tongue over. 2. *Informal.* beat or defeat. —*n.* 3. act of licking. 4. place where animals lick salt.

lic'o•rice, *n.* plant root used in candy, etc.

lid, *n.* 1. movable cover. 2. eyelid.

lie, *n., v.,* **lied, lying.** —*n.* 1. deliberately false statement. —*v.* 2. tell lie.

lie, *v.,* **lay, lain, lying,** *n.* —*v.* 1. assume or have reclining position. 2. be or remain. —*n.* 3. manner of lying.

lie detector, polygraph.

lief, *adv.* gladly.

liege (lēj), *n.* 1. lord. 2. vassal.

lien (lēn), *n.* right in another's property as payment on claim.

lieu (lōō), *n.* stead.

lieu•ten'ant, *n.* 1. commissioned officer in army or navy. 2. aide. —**lieu•ten'an•cy,** *n.*

life, *n., pl.* **lives.** 1. distinguishing quality of animals and plants. 2. period of being alive. 3. living things. 4.

mode of existence. **5.** animation. —**life′long′**, *adj.* —**life′time′**, *n.* —**life′less**, *adj.*

life′boat′, *n.* boat carried on ship to save passengers in the event of sinking.

life′guard′, *n.* person employed to protect swimmers, as at a beach.

life preserver, buoyant device to keep a person afloat.

lif′er, *n.* person serving a term of imprisonment for life.

life′sav′er, *n.* person or thing that saves from death or a difficult situation. —**life′sav′ing**, *adj.*

life′-size′, *adj.* of the actual size of a person, etc.

life′style′, person's general pattern of living. Also, **life′-style′**.

life′-sup•port′, *adj.* of equipment or techniques that sustain or substitute for essential body functions.

lift, *v.* **1.** move or hold upward. **2.** raise or rise. —*n.* **3.** act of lifting. **4.** help. **5.** ride. **6.** exaltation. **7.** *Brit.* elevator.

lift′-off′, *n.* departure from ground by rocket, etc., under own power.

lig′a•ment, *n.* band of tissue.

light, *n., adj., v.* **1.** *lighted* or *lit, lighting.* —*n.* **1.** that which makes things visible or gives illumination. **2.** daylight. **3.** aspect. **4.** enlightenment. —*adj.* **5.** not dark. **6.** not heavy. **7.** not serious. —*v.* **8.** ignite. **9.** illuminate. **10.** alight; land. **11.** happen (upon). —**light′ly,** *adv.* —**light′ness,** *n.*

light′en, *v.* **1.** become or make less dark. **2.** lessen in weight. **3.** mitigate. **4.** cheer.

light′er, *n.* **1.** something that lights. **2.** barge.

light′-heart′ed, *adj.* cheerful; without worry.

light′-head′ed, *adj.* as if about to faint.

light′house′, *n.* tower displaying light to guide mariners.

light′ning, *n.* flash of light in sky caused by electrical discharge.

lightning rod, metal rod to divert lightning from a structure into the ground.

light′-year′, *n.* distance that light travels in one year.

lig′nite (lig′nīt), *n.* kind of coal.

like, *v., liked, liking, adj., prep., conj., n.* —*v.* **1.** find agreeable. **2.** wish. —*adj.* **3.** resembling; similar to. —*prep.* **4.** in like manner with. —*conj.* **5.** *Informal.* as; as if. —*n.* **6.** like person or thing; match. **7.** preference. —**lik′a•ble, like′a•ble,** *adj.*

like′ly, *adj., -lier, -liest, adv.* —*adj.* **1.** probable. **2.** suitable; promising.

—*adv.* **3.** probably. —**like′li•hood′,** *n.*

lik′en, *v.* compare.

like′ness, *n.* **1.** image; picture. **2.** fact of being like.

like′wise′, *adv.* **1.** also. **2.** in like manner.

li′lac (lī′lak), *n.* fragrant flowering shrub.

lilt, *n.* rhythmic cadence.

lil′y, *n., pl. lilies.* bulbous plant with erect stems and showy flowers.

li′ma bean, flat, edible bean.

limb, *n.* **1.** jointed part of an animal body. **2.** branch.

lim′ber, *adj.* **1.** flexible; supple. —*v.* **2.** make or become limber.

lim′bo, *n., pl. -bos.* **1.** region on border of hell or heaven. **2.** state of oblivion. **3.** midway state or place. **4.** dance involving bending backward to pass under horizontal bar.

Lim′burg•er, *n.* soft strong cheese.

lime, *n., v., limed, liming.* —*n.* **1.** oxide of calcium, used in mortar, etc. **2.** small, greenish, acid fruit of tropical tree. —*v.* **3.** treat with lime.

lime′light′, *n.* **1.** public notice; fame. **2.** strong light formerly used on stage.

lim′er•ick (lim′-), *n.* humorous fiveline verse.

lime′stone′, *n.* rock consisting chiefly of powdered calcium.

lim′it, *n.* **1.** farthest extent; boundary. —*v.* **2.** fix or keep within limits. —**lim′it•less**, *adj.*

lim′it•ed, *adj.* **1.** restricted **2.** (of trains, etc.) making few stops. **3.** limited train, etc.

lim•ou•sine (lim′ə zēn′), *n.* luxurious automobile for several passengers.

limp, *v.* **1.** walk unevenly. —*n.* **2.** lame movement. —*adj.* **3.** not stiff or firm.

lim′pet, *n.* small cone-shelled marine animal.

lim′pid, *adj.* clear.

linch′pin′, *n.* **1.** pin inserted through end of axle to keep wheel on. **2.** something that holds various parts of structure together.

lin′den, *n.* tree with heart-shaped leaves.

line, *n., v., lined, lining.* —*n.* **1.** long thin mark. **2.** row; series. **3.** course of action, etc. **4.** boundary. **5.** string, cord, etc. **6.** occupation. —*v.* **7.** form line. **8.** mark with line. **9.** cover inner side of.

lin′e•age (lin′ē ij), *n.* ancestry.

lin′e•al, *adj.* **1.** of direct descent. Also, **lin′e•ar.** in or of a line.

lin′e•a•ment, *n.* feature, as of face.

lin′en, *n.* **1.** fabric made from flax. **2.** articles of linen or cotton.

lin'er, *n.* 1. ship or airplane on regular route. 2. lining.

line'-up', *n.* order.

lin'ger, *v.* 1. stay on. 2. persist. 3. delay.

lin•ge•rie (län'zhə rā'), *n.* women's undergarments.

lin'go, *n., pl.* **-goes.** *Informal.* language.

lin'gual, *adj.* 1. of the tongue. 2. of languages.

lin•gui'ni (-gwē'nē), *n. pl.* pasta in slender flat form.

lin'guist, *n.* person skilled in languages.

lin•guis'tics, *n.* science of language. —**lin•guis'tic,** *adj.*

lin'i•ment, *n.* liquid applied to bruises, etc.

lin'ing, *n.* inner covering.

link, *n.* 1. section of chain. 2. bond. —*v.* 3. unite. —**link'age,** *n.*

links, *n.pl.* golf course.

lin'net, *n.* small songbird.

li•no'le•um, *n.* floor covering made of cork, oil, etc.

Lin'o•type', *n. Trademark.* keyboard machine for casting solid type.

lin'seed', *n.* seed of flax.

lin'sey-wool'sey, *n.* fabric of linen and wool.

lint, *n.* bits of thread.

lin'tel, *n.* beam above door or window.

li'on, *n.* 1. large tawny animal of Africa and Asia. 2. person of note. —**li'on•ess,** *n.fem.*

li'on•ize', *v.,* **-ized, -izing.** treat as a celebrity.

lip, *n.* 1. fleshy margin of the mouth. 2. projecting edge. 3. *Slang.* impudent talk.

lip•o•suc'tion (lip'ə suk'shən, lī'pə-), *n.* surgical withdrawal of excess fat from under skin.

lip reading, method of understanding spoken words by interpreting speaker's lip movements.

lip service, insincere profession of friendship, admiration, support, etc.

lip'stick', *n.* coloring for lips.

liq'ue•fy', *v.,* **-fied, -fying.** become liquid. —**liq'ue•fac'tion,** *n.*

li•queur' (li kûr'), *n.* strong sweet alcoholic drink.

liq'uid, *n.* 1. fluid of molecules remaining together. —*adj.* 2. of or being a liquid. 3. in or convertible to cash.

liq'ui•date', *v.,* **-dated, -dating.** 1. settle, as debts. 2. convert into cash. 3. eliminate. —**liq'ui•da'tion,** *n.*

liq'uor, *n.* 1. alcoholic beverage. 2. liquid.

lisle (līl), *n.* strong linen or cotton thread.

lisp, *n.* 1. pronunciation of *s* and *z* like *th.* —*v.* 2. speak with lisp.

list, *n.* 1. series of words, names, etc. 2. inclination to side. —*v.* 3. make or enter on list. 4. incline.

lis'ten, *v.* attend with ear. —**lis'ten•er,** *n.*

list'less, *adj.* spiritless.

lit'a•ny, *n., pl.* **-nies.** 1. form of prayer. 2. prolonged, tedious account.

li'ter (lē'-), *n.* metric unit of capacity, = 1.0567 U.S. quarts. Also, *Brit.,* **li'tre.**

lit'er•al, *adj.* 1. in accordance with strict meaning of words. 2. exactly as written or stated. —**lit'er•al•ly,** *adv.*

lit'er•al-mind'ed, *adj.* interpreting without imagination.

lit'er•ar'y, *adj.* of books and writings.

lit'er•ate, *adj.* 1. able to read and write. 2. educated. —*n.* 3. literate person. —**lit'er•a•cy,** *n.*

lit'er•a•ture, *n.* writings, esp. those of notable expression and thought.

lithe (līth), *adj.* limber. Also, **lithe'some.**

lith'i•um (lith'ē əm), *n.* soft silverwhite metallic element.

lith'o•graph', *n.* print made from prepared stone or plate. —**li•thog'ra•pher,** *n.* —**li•thog'ra•phy,** *n.*

lit'i•gant, *n.* person engaged in lawsuit.

lit'i•gate', *v.,* **-gated, -gating.** carry on lawsuit. —**lit'i•ga'tion,** *n.*

lit'mus, *n.* blue coloring matter turning red in acid solution.

litmus test, use of single issue or factor as basis for judgment.

lit'ter, *n.* 1. disordered array. 2. young from one birth. 3. stretcher. 4. bedding for animals. 5. scattered rubbish, etc. —*v.* 6. strew in disorder.

lit'ter•bug', *n.* person who litters public places with trash.

lit'tle, *adj.,* **-tler, -tlest.** 1. small. 2. mean. —*adv.* 3. not much. —*n.* 4. small amount.

lit'ur•gy (lit'ər jē), *n., pl.* **-gies.** form of worship. —**li•tur'gi•cal,** *adj.*

liv'a•ble, *adj.* habitable or endurable.

live (liv for *1–5*; līv for *6–8*), *v.,* **lived, living,** —*v.* 1. be alive. 2. endure in reputation. 3. rely for food, etc. 4. dwell. 5. pass (life). —*adj.* 6. alive. 7. energetic. 8. effective.

live'li•hood', *n.* means of supporting oneself.

live'ly, *adj.,* **-lier, -liest,** *adv.* —*adj.* 1. active; spirited. —*adv.* 2. vigorously. —**live'li•ness,** *n.*

liv′er, n. abdominal organ that secretes bile.

liv′er•wurst′, n. liver sausage.

liv′er•y, n., pl. **-eries.** 1. uniform of male servants. 2. keeping of horses for hire.

live′stock′, n. domestic farm animals.

liv′id, adj. 1. dull blue. 2. furious.

liv′ing, adj. 1. live. 2. sufficient for living. —n. 3. condition of life. 4. livelihood.

living will, document stipulating that no extraordinary measures be taken to prolong signer's life during terminal illness.

liz′ard, n. four-legged reptile.

lla′ma (lä′ma), n. South American animal.

lo, interj. behold!

load, n. 1. cargo; anything carried. 2. charge of firearm. —v. 3. put load on. 4. oppress. 5. charge (firearm). —**load′er,** n.

loaf, n., pl. **loaves,** v. —n. 1. shaped mass of bread, etc. —v. 2. idle. —**loaf′er,** n.

loam, n. loose fertile soil.

loan, n. 1. act of lending. 2. something lent. —v. 3. lend.

loath, adj. reluctant.

loathe, v. **loathed, loathing.** feel disgust at; despise. —**loath′some,** adj.

lob, v. **lobbed, lobbing.** —v. 1. strike or hurl in a high curve. —n. 2. tennis ball so struck.

lob′by, n., pl. **-bies,** v. **-bied, -bying.** —n. 1. vestibule or entrance hall. 2. group that tries to influence legislators. —v. 3. try to influence legislators. —**lob′by•ist,** n.

lobe, n. roundish projection. —**lo′bar,** **lo′bate,** adj.

lob′ster, n. edible marine shellfish.

lo′cal, adj. 1. of or in particular area. —n. 2. local branch of trade union. 3. train that makes all stops. —**lo′cal•ly,** adv.

lo•cale′ (-kal′), n. setting; place.

lo•cal′i•ty, n., pl. **-ties.** place; area.

lo′cal•ize′, v., **-ized, -izing.** confine to particular place. —**lo′cal•i•za′tion,** n.

lo′cate, v., **-cated, -cating.** find or establish place of.

lo•ca′tion, n. 1. act or instance of locating. 2. place where something is.

lock, n. 1. fastener preventing unauthorized access. 2. place in canal, etc., for moving vessels from one water level to another. 3. part of firearm. 4. tress of hair. —v. 5. secure with lock. 6. shut in or out. 7. join firmly.

lock′er, n. closet with lock.

lock′et, n. small case worn on necklace.

lock′jaw′, n. disease in which jaws become tightly locked; tetanus.

lock′out′, n. business closure to force acceptance of employer's terms of work.

lock′smith′, n. person who makes or repairs locks.

lo′co, adj. Slang. crazy.

lo′co•mo′tion, n. act of moving about.

lo′co•mo′tive, n. engine that pulls railroad cars.

lo′cust, n. 1. kind of grasshopper. 2. flowering American tree.

lo•cu′tion (lō kyōō′shan), n. phrase; expression.

lode, n. veinlike mineral deposit.

lode′star′, n. star that shows the way.

lode′stone′, n. magnetic stone. Also, **load′stone′.**

lodge, n., v. **lodged, lodging.** —n. 1. hut or house. 2. members or meeting place of fraternal organization. —v. 3. live or house temporarily. 4. fix or put; become fixed. —**lodg′er,** n.

lodg′ing, n. 1. temporary housing. 2. (pl.) rooms.

lodg′ment, n. 1. lodging. 2. something lodged. Also, **lodge′ment.**

loft, n. attic or gallery.

loft′y, adj., **loftier, loftiest.** 1. tall. 2. exalted or elevated. —**loft′i•ly,** adv.

log, n., v. **logged, logging.** —n. 1. trunk of felled tree. 2. Also, **log′-book′,** record of events. —v. 3. fell and cut up trees. 4. record in log. 5. **log in** or **on,** gain access to secured computer system. —**log′ger,** n.

lo′gan•ber′ry, n., pl. **-ries.** dark red acid fruit.

log′a•rithm, n. Math. symbol of number of times a number must be multiplied by itself to equal a given number.

loge (lōzh), n. box in theater.

log′ger•head′, n. 1. stupid person. 2. **at loggerheads,** disputing.

log′ic, n. science of reasoning. —**log′i•cal,** adj. —**log′i•cal•ly,** adv. —**lo•gi′cian,** n.

lo•gis′tics, n. science of military supply. —**lo•gis′tic, lo•gis′ti•cal,** adj.

lo′go, n. representation or symbol of company name, trademark, etc. Also, **lo′go•type′.**

lo′gy (lō′gē), adj., **-gier, -giest.** heavy; dull.

loin, n. part of body between ribs and hipbone.

loi′ter, v. linger. —**loi′ter•er,** n.

loll, v. 1. recline indolently. 2. hang loosely.

lol'li·pop', *n.* hard candy on stick.

lone, *adj.* alone.

lone'ly, *adj.* -li·er, -li·est. 1. alone. 2. wishing for company. 3. isolated. —**lone'li·ness**, *n.*

lone'some, *adj.* 1. depressed by solitude. 2. lone.

long, *adj.* 1. of great or specified length. —*adv.* 2. for long space of time. —*v.* 3. yearn. —**long'ing**, *n.*

lon·gev'i·ty (lon jev'-), *n.* long life.

long'hand', *n.* ordinary handwriting.

lon'gi·tude', *n.* distance east and west on earth's surface.

lon'gi·tu'di·nal, *adj.* 1. of longitude. 2. lengthwise.

long'shore'man, *n.* person who loads and unloads vessels. —**long'shore'wom·an**, *n.fem.*

long shot, 1. racehorse, team, etc., with little chance for winning. 2. undertaking with little chance for success.

long'-wind'ed, *adj.* speaking or spoken at excessive length.

look, *v.* 1. direct the eyes. 2. seem. 3. face. 4. seek. —*n.* 5. act of looking. 6. appearance.

looking glass, mirror.

look'out', *n.* 1. watch. 2. person for keeping watch. 3. place for keeping watch.

loom, *n.* 1. device for weaving fabric. —*v.* 2. weave on loom. 3. appear as large and indistinct.

loon, *n.* diving bird.

loon'y, *adj.* **loon·i·er**, **loon·i·est.** *Informal.* 1. lunatic; insane. 2. extremely foolish.

loop, *n.* 1. circular form from length of material or line. —*v.* 2. form a loop.

loop'hole', *n.* 1. small opening in wall, etc. 2. means of evasion.

loose, *adj.*, **looser**, **loosest**, *v.*, **loosed**, **loosing**. —*adj.* 1. free; unconfined. 2. not firm or tight. 3. not exact. 4. dissolute. —*v.* 5. free. 6. shoot (missiles). —**loos'en**, *v.* —**loose'ly**, *adv.* —**loose'ness**, *n.*

loot, *n.* 1. spoils. —*v.* 2. plunder. —**loot'er**, *n.*

lop, *v.*, **lopped**, **lopping**. cut off.

lope, *v.*, **loped**, **loping**, *n.* —*v.* 1. move or run with easy, long stride. —*n.* 2. long, easy stride.

lop'sid'ed, *adj.* uneven.

lo·qua'cious, *adj.* talkative. —**lo·quac'i·ty** (-kwas'ə tē), *n.*

lord, *n.* 1. master. 2. British nobleman. 3. (*cap.*) God. 4. (*cap.*) Jesus Christ. —*v.* 5. domineer. —**lord'ly**, *adj.* —**lord'ship**, *n.*

lore, *n.* learning.

lor·gnette' (lôr nyet'), *n.* eyeglasses on long handle.

lor'ry, *n.*, *pl.* -ries. *Brit.* truck.

lose, *v.*, **lost**, **losing**. 1. fail to keep. 2. misplace. 3. be deprived of. 4. fail to win. —**los'er**, *n.*

loss, *n.* 1. disadvantage from losing. 2. something lost. 3. waste.

lot, *n.* 1. object drawn to decide question by chance. 2. allotted share. 3. piece of land. 4. large amount or number.

lo'tion, *n.* medicinal liquid for skin.

lot'ter·y, *n.*, *pl.* -ter·ies. sale of tickets on prizes to be awarded by lots.

lot'to, *n.* 1. game of chance similar to bingo. 2. lottery in which players choose numbers that are matched against those of the official drawing.

lo'tus, *n.* water lily of Egypt and Asia.

loud, *adj.* 1. strongly audible. 2. obtrusive. —**loud'ly**, *adv.* —**loud'ness**, *n.*

loud'-mouth', *n.* a braggart, gossip, etc. —**loud'-mouthed'**, *adj.*

loud'speak'er, *n.* device for reproducing sound at higher volume.

lounge, *v.*, **lounged**, **lounging**, *n.* —*v.* 1. pass time idly. 2. loll. —*n.* 3. kind of sofa. 4. public parlor.

louse, *n.*, *pl.* **lice**. bloodsucking insect.

lous'y, *adj.*, **lousier**, **lousiest.** 1. *Informal.* bad; poor. 2. troubled with lice. —**lous'i·ness**, *n.*

lout, *n.* boor.

lou'ver (lōō'vər), *n.* arrangement of slits for ventilation.

lov'a·ble, *adj.* attracting love. Also, **love'a·ble**. —**lov'a·bly**, *adv.*

love, *n.*, *v.*, **loved**, **loving**. —*n.* 1. strong affection. 2. sweetheart. —*v.* 3. have love for. —**lov'er**, *n.* —**love'less**, *adj.* —**lov'ing·ly**, *adv.*

love'ly, *adj.* -li·er, -li·est. charming.

love'sick', *adj.* sick from intensity of love.

low, *adj.* 1. not high or tall. 2. prostrate. 3. weak. 4. humble or inferior. 5. not loud. —*adv.* 6. in or to low position. 7. in quiet tone. —*n.* 8. something that is low. 9. moo. —*v.* 10. moo.

low'brow', *n.* 1. uncultured person. —*adj.* 2. typical of a lowbrow.

low'down', *n.* 1. real and unadorned facts. —*adj.* (low'down'). 2. contemptible; mean.

low'er, (lō'ər *for 1, 2*; lou'ər *for 3–5*), *v.* 1. reduce or diminish. 2. make or become lower. 3. be threatening. 4. frown. —*n.* 5. lowering appearance.

low'-key', *adj.* restrained; understated.

low'ly, *adj.*. -li·er, -li·est. humble; meek.

lox, n. salmon cured in brine.

loy·al, adj. faithful. **—loy'al·ty,** n.

loz'enge (loz'inj), n. 1. flavored candy, often medicated. 2. diamond shape.

LSD, lysergic acid diethylamide, a powerful psychedelic drug.

lub'ber, n. clumsy person.

lu'bri·cant, n. lubricating substance.

lu'bri·cate, v., **-cated, -cating.** oil or grease, esp. to diminish friction. **—lu·bri·ca'tion,** n. **—lu'bri·ca·tor,** n. **—lu'bri·cant,** adj., n.

lu·bri·cious (-brish'əs), adj. 1. lewd. 2. slippery. Also, **lu·bri·cous** (-kəs).

lu'cid (lōo'sid), adj. 1. bright. 2. clear in thought or expression. 3. rational. **—lu·cid'i·ty, lu'cid·ness,** n. **—lu'cid·ly,** adv.

luck, n. 1. chance. 2. good fortune. **—luck'less,** adj.

luck'y, adj. **luckier, luckiest.** having or due to good luck. **—luck'i·ly,** adv.

lu'cra·tive, adj. profitable.

lu'cre (lōo'kər), n. gain or money.

lu'di·crous, adj. ridiculous. **—lu'di·crous·ly,** adv.

luff, v. 1. sail into wind. **—**n. 2. act of luffing.

lug, v., **lugged, lugging,** n. **—**v. 1. pull or carry with effort. 2. haul. **—**n. 3. projecting handle.

luge (lōozh), n., v., **luged, luging. —**n. 1. small racing sled for one or two persons. **—**v. 2. race on a luge.

lug'gage, n. baggage.

lu·gu·bri·ous (lōo gōo'-), adj. excessively mournful or gloomy.

luke'warm', adj. slightly warm.

lull, v. 1. soothe, esp. to sleep. **—**n. 2. brief stillness.

lull'a·by, n., pl. **-bies.** song to lull baby.

lum·ba'go, n. muscular pain in back.

lum'ber, n. 1. timber made into boards, etc. **—**v. 2. cut and prepare timber. 3. encumber. 4. move heavily. **—lum'ber·man,** n.

lum'ber·jack', n. person who fells trees.

lu'mi·nar·y, n., pl. **-naries.** 1. celestial body. 2. person who inspires many.

lu'min·es'cent, adj. luminous at relatively low temperatures. **—lu·min·es'cence,** n.

lu'mi·nous, adj. giving or reflecting light. **—lu·mi·nos'i·ty,** n.

lump, n. 1. irregular mass. 2. swelling. 3. aggregation. **—**adj. 4. including many. **—**v. 5. put together. 6. endure. **—lump'y,** adj.

lu'na·cy, n., pl. **-cies.** insanity.

lu'nar, adj. 1. of or according to moon. 2. Also, **lu'nate.** crescent-shaped.

lu'na·tic, n. 1. insane person. **—**adj. 2. for the insane. 3. crazy.

lunch, n. 1. Also, **lunch'eon.** light meal, esp. at noon. **—**v. 2. eat lunch.

lunch'eon·ette', n. restaurant for quick, simple lunches.

lung, n. respiratory organ.

lunge, n., v., **lunged, lunging. —**n. 1. sudden forward movement. **—**v. 2. make lunge.

lu'pus (lōo'pəs), n. any of several diseases characterized by skin eruptions.

lurch, n. 1. sudden lean to one side. 2. helpless plight. **—**v. 3. make lurch.

lure, n., v., **lured, luring. —**n. 1. bait. **—**v. 2. decoy; entice.

lu'rid, adj. 1. glaringly lighted. 2. intended to be exciting; sensational.

lurk, v. 1. loiter furtively. 2. exist unperceived.

lus'cious (lush'əs), adj. delicious.

lush, adj. 1. tender and juicy. 2. abundant.

lust, n. 1. strong desire. **—**v. 2. have strong desire. **—lust'ful,** adj.

lus'ter, n. gloss; radiance. Also, **lus'tre. —lus'trous,** adj.

lust'y, adj., **lustier, lustiest.** vigorous. **—lust'i·ly,** adv.

lute, n. stringed musical instrument.

Lu'ther·an, adj. Protestant sect named for Martin Luther.

lux·u'ri·ant (lug zhŏor'ē ənt), adj. profuse; abundant. **—lux·u'ri·ance,** n.

lux·u'ri·ate' (-ē āt'), v., **-ated, -ating.** revel; delight.

lux'u·ry (luk'shə rē), n., pl. **-ries.** something enjoyable but not necessary. **—lux·u'ri·ous,** adj.

ly·ce'um, n. hall for lectures, etc.

lye, n. alkali solution.

ly'ing-in', n. 1. of or for childbirth. **—**n. 2. childbirth.

lymph, n. yellowish matter from body tissues. **—lym·phat'ic,** adj.

lynch, v. put to death without legal authority.

lynx, n., pl. **lynxes, lynx.** kind of wildcat.

lyre, n. ancient harplike instrument.

lyr'ic, adj. Also, **lyr'i·cal.** 1. (of poetry) musical. 2. of or writing such poetry. 3. ardently expressive. **—**n. 4. lyric poem. 5. (pl.) words for song. **—lyr'i·cal·ly,** adv. **—lyr'i·cism,** n.

M

M, m, *n.* thirteenth letter of English alphabet.

ma'am, *n. Informal.* mother.

ma'am, *n. Informal.* madam.

ma•ca'bre, *adj.* gruesome.

mac•ad'am, *n.* road-making material containing broken stones. **—mac•ad'am•ize',** *v.*

mac•a•ro'ni, *n.* 1. tube-shaped food made of wheat. 2. 18th-century fop.

mac'a•roon', *n.* small cookie, usually containing almonds.

ma•caw', *n.* tropical American parrot.

mace, *n.* 1. spiked war club. 2. staff of office. 3. spice from part of nutmeg seed. 4. (*cap.*) *Trademark.* chemical for subduing rioters, etc.

ma•che'te (mə shet'ē), *n.* heavy knife.

Mach'i•a•vel'li•an (mak'-), *adj.* wily.

mach'i•na'tion (mak'-), *n.* cunning plan.

ma•chine', *n.* 1. apparatus or mechanical device. 2. group controlling political organization.

machine gun, firearm capable of firing continuous stream of bullets.

ma•chin'er•y, *n., pl.* **-eries.** machines or mechanisms.

ma•chin'ist, *n.* operator of powered tool, ship's engines, etc.

ma•chis'mo (-chēz'-), *n.* exaggerated masculinity as basis for code of behavior.

ma'cho (mä'-), *adj.* exaggeratedly virile.

mack'er•el, *n.* common food fish.

mack'i•naw', *n.* short, heavy, woolen coat.

mack'in•tosh', *n.* raincoat of rubberized cloth.

mac'ra•mé', *n.* decorative work of knotted cords.

mac•ro•bi•ot'ic, *adj.* of or giving long life.

mac'ro•cosm, *n.* universe.

mad, *adj.* **madder, maddest.** 1. insane. 2. *Informal.* angry. 3. violent. **—mad'man',** *n.* **—mad'den,** *v.* **—mad'ly,** *adv.* **—mad'ness,** *n.*

mad'am, *n.* 1. female term of address. 2. woman in charge of brothel.

mad'ame, *n., pl.* **mesdames** (mä dam'). French term of address for a married woman.

mad'e•moi•selle' (mad'mwa zel'), *n., pl.* **mademoiselles, mesdemoiselles.** French term of address for unmarried woman.

Ma•don'na, *n.* Virgin Mary.

mad'ras, *n.* light cotton fabric.

mad'ri•gal, *n.* song for several voices unaccompanied.

mael'strom (māl'-), *n.* 1. whirlpool. 2. confusion.

maes'tro (mīs'-), *n., pl.* **-tros.** master, esp. of music.

Ma'fi•a, *n.* criminal society.

mag•a•zine', *n.* 1. periodical publication. 2. storehouse for ammunition, etc. 3. cartridge receptacle in repeating weapon.

ma•gen'ta (-jen'-), *n.* reddish purple.

Ma'gi (mā'jī), *n.pl. Bible.* the three wise men.

mag'ic, *n.* 1. seemingly supernatural production of effects. **—adj.** Also, **mag'i•cal.** 2. of magic. 3. enchanting. **—ma•gi'cian,** *n.*

mag•is•te'ri•al, *adj.* masterlike; authoritative.

mag'is•trate', *n.* civil public official.

mag'ma, *n.* molten material beneath the earth's surface, from which igneous rocks and lava are formed.

mag•nan'i•mous, *adj.* generous; high-minded. **—mag•na•nim'i•ty,** *n.*

mag'nate, *n.* business leader.

mag•ne'sia, *n.* magnesium oxide, used as laxative.

mag•ne'si•um (-zē-), *n.* light, silvery, metallic element.

mag'net, *n.* metal body that attracts iron or steel. **—mag•net'ic,** *adj.*

mag'net•ism, *n.* 1. characteristic property of magnets. 2. science of magnets. 3. great personal charm. **—mag'net•ize',** *v.*

mag•ne'to, *n., pl.* **-tos.** small electric generator.

mag•nif'i•cence, *n.* 1. splendor; grandeur. 2. nobility. 3. supreme excellence. **—mag•nif'i•cent,** *adj.*

mag'ni•fy', *v.,* **-fied, -fying.** 1. increase apparent size. 2. enlarge. **—mag'ni•fi•ca'tion,** *n.* **—mag'ni•fi'er,** *n.*

mag•nil'o•quent, *adj.* grandiose or pompous in expression. **—mag•nil'o•quence,** *n.*

mag'ni•tude', *n.* 1. size or extent. 2. brightness, as of star.

mag•no'li•a, *n.* tree with large, usually fragrant, flowers.

mag'pie', *n.* black-and-white bird that steals.

ma•ha•ra'jah, *n.* (formerly) ruling

prince in India. —**ma•ha•ra'nee,** n.fem.

ma•hat'ma (mə hät'mə, -hat'-), n. person, esp. in India, held in highest esteem for wisdom and saintliness.

mah'-jongg', n. Chinese game.

ma•hog'a•ny, n., pl. **-nies.** tropical American tree.

Ma•hom'et, n. Muhammad.

maid, n. 1. unmarried woman. 2. female servant.

maid'en, n. 1. young unmarried woman. —adj. 2. of maidens. 3. unmarried. 4. initial. —**maid'en•ly,** adj. —**maid'en•li•ness,** n.

mail, n. 1. material delivered by postal system. 2. postal system. 3. armor, usually flexible. —adj. 4. of mail. —v. 5. send by mail. —**mail'box',** n. —**mail'man',** n.

maim, v. cripple; impair.

main, adj. 1. chief; principal. —n. 2. chief pipe or duct. 3. strength. 4. ocean. —**main'ly,** adv.

main'frame', n. large computer, often the hub of a system serving many users.

main'land', n. continental land rather than island.

main'spring', n. chief spring of mechanism.

main'stay', n. chief support.

main'stream', n. customary trend of behavior, opinion, etc.

main•tain', v. 1. support. 2. assert. 3. keep in order. —**main'te•nance,** n.

mai'tre d'hô'tel' (me'tr dō tel'), headwaiter. Also, **mai'tre d''** (mā'tər dē').

maize (māz), n. corn.

maj'es•ty, n., pl. **-ties.** 1. regal grandeur. 2. sovereign. —**ma•jes'tic,** adj. —**ma•jes'ti•cal•ly,** adv.

ma•jol'i•ca, n. kind of pottery.

ma'jor, n. 1. army officer above captain. 2. person of legal age. —adj. 3. larger or more important.

ma'jor•do'mo, n. steward.

ma'jor•ette', n. female leader of marchers.

major general, army officer above brigadier general.

ma•jor'i•ty, n., pl. **-ties.** 1. greater number. 2. full legal age.

make, v., **made, making,** n. —v. 1. bring into existence; form. 2. cause; force. 3. earn. 4. accomplish. —n. 5. style. 6. manufacture. —**mak'er,** n.

make'-be•lieve', n. 1. pretending to oneself that fanciful thing is true. —adj. 2. fictitious.

make'shift', n., adj. substitute.

make'up', n. 1. cosmetics. 2. organization; composition.

mal•ad•just'ment, n. 1. faulty adjustment. 2. inability to adapt to social conditions. —**mal•ad•just'ed,** adj.

mal'ad•min'is•ter, v. mismanage.

mal'a•droit', adj. awkward.

mal'a•dy, n., pl. **-dies.** illness.

ma•laise' (-lāz'), n. 1. bodily weakness or discomfort. 2. vague uneasiness.

ma•lar'i•a, n. mosquito-borne disease. —**ma•lar'i•al,** adj.

mal'con•tent', n. dissatisfied person.

mal de mer', seasickness.

male, adj. 1. of sex that begets young. —n. 2. male person, etc.

male•dic'tion, n. curse.

male•fac'tor, n. person who does wrong.

ma•lev'o•lent, adj. wishing evil. —**ma•lev'o•lence,** n.

mal•fea'sance (-fē'-), n. misconduct in office.

mal•formed', adj. badly formed. —**mal•for•ma'tion,** n.

mal'ice, n. evil intent. —**ma•li'cious,** adj.

ma•lign' (-līn'), v. 1. speak ill of. —adj. 2. evil.

ma•lig'nan•cy, n., pl. **-cies.** 1. malignant state. 2. cancerous growth.

ma•lig'nant, adj. 1. causing harm or suffering. 2. deadly.

ma•lin'ger, v. feign sickness. —**ma•lin'ger•er,** n.

mall, n. 1. shaded walk. 2. covered shopping center.

mal'lard, n. wild duck.

mal'le•a•ble, adj. 1. that may be hammered or rolled into shapes. 2. readily influenced. —**mal'le•a•bil'i•ty, mal'le•a•ble•ness,** n.

mal'let, n. wooden-headed hammer.

mal•nu•tri'tion, n. improper nutrition.

mal•o'dor•ous, adj. smelling bad.

mal•prac'tice, n. improper professional behavior.

malt, n. germinated grain used in liquor-making.

mal•treat', v. abuse.

ma'ma, n. Informal. mother.

mam'bo (mäm'bō), n. Latin-American dance style.

mam'mal, n. vertebrate animal whose young are suckled.

mam'ma•ry, adj. of breasts.

mam'mon, n. 1. material wealth; riches. 2. greed for riches.

mam'moth, n. 1. large extinct kind of elephant. —adj. 2. huge.

mam'my, n., pl. **-mies.** Informal. mother.

man, n., pl. **men,** v., **manned, man•ning.** —n. 1. male human being. 2.

person. 3. human race. —v. 4. supply with crew. 5. serve.

man'a·cle, n., v., **-cled, -cling.** handcuff.

man'age, v., **-aged, -aging.** 1. take care of. 2. direct. —**man'age·a·ble,** adj. —**man'ag·er,** n. —**man·a·ge'ri·al,** adj.

man'age·ment, n. 1. direction; control. 2. persons in charge.

ma·ña'na (mä nyä'nä), n. Spanish. tomorrow.

man'a·tee' (man'a tē'), n. plant-eating aquatic mammal. Also, **sea cow.**

man·da·rin, n. 1. public official in Chinese Empire. 2. (cap.) spoken form of Chinese language.

man'date, n. 1. authority over territory granted to nation by other nations. 2. territory under such authority. 3. command, as to take office. —**man'date,** v.

man·da·to·ry, adj. officially required.

man·di·ble, n. bone comprising the lower jaw.

man·do·lin', n. plucked stringed musical instrument.

man'drake, n. narcotic herb.

man'drel, n. rod or axle in machinery.

man'drill, n. kind of baboon.

mane, n. long hair at neck of some animals.

ma·neu'ver (-nōō'-), n. 1. planned movement, esp. in war. —v. 2. change position by maneuver. 3. put in certain situation by intrigue. —**ma·neu'ver·a·ble,** adj.

man'ful, adj. resolute. —**man'ful·ly,** adv.

man'ga·nese', n. hard metallic element.

mange (mānj), n. skin disease of animals. —**man'gy,** adj.

man'ger, n. trough for feeding stock.

man'gle, v., **-gled, -gling,** n. —v. 1. disfigure, esp. by crushing. 2. put through mangle. —n. 3. device with rollers for removing water in washing clothes.

man'go, n., pl. **-goes.** fruit of tropical tree.

man'grove, n. kind of tropical tree.

man'han·dle, v., **-dled, -dling.** handle roughly.

man·hat'tan, n. cocktail of whiskey and vermouth.

man'hole', n. access hole to sewer, drain, etc.

man'hood, n. 1. manly qualities. 2. state of being a man.

ma·ni'a, n. 1. great excitement. 2. violent insanity.

ma·ni'ac', n. lunatic. —**ma·ni'a·cal** (-nī'-), adj.

man'ic, adj. irrationally excited or lively.

man'i·cure', n. skilled care of fingernails and hands. —**man'i·cure',** v. —**man'i·cur'ist,** n.

man'i·fest', adj. 1. evident. —v. 2. show plainly. —n. 3. list of cargo and passengers. —**man·i·fes·ta'tion,** n.

man·i·fes'to, n., pl. **-toes.** public declaration of philosophy or intentions.

man'i·fold', adj. 1. of many kinds or parts. —v. 2. copy.

man'i·kin, n. model of human body.

Ma·nil'a paper, strong, light brown or buff paper.

ma·nip'u·late', v., **-lated, -lating.** handle with skill or cunning. —**ma·nip·u·la'tion,** n. —**ma·nip'u·la'tor,** n.

man·kind', n. 1. human race. 2. men.

man'ly, adj., **-lier, -liest.** virile.

man'na, n. divine food.

man'ne·quin (-kin), n. model for displaying clothes.

man'ner, n. 1. way of doing, acting, etc. 2. (pl.) way of acting in society. 3. sort.

man'ner·ism, n. peculiarity of manner.

man'ner·ly, adj. polite.

man'nish, adj. like a man.

man'-of-war', n., pl. **men-of-war.** warship.

man'or, n. large estate. —**ma·no'ri·al,** adj.

man'pow'er, n. available labor force.

man'sard, n. roof with two slopes of different pitch on all sides.

manse, n. house and land of parson.

man'serv'ant, n. male servant, as valet.

man'sion, n. stately house.

man'slaugh'ter, n. unlawful killing of person without malice.

man'tel, n. ornamental structure around fireplace.

man·til'la, n. lace head scarf of Spanish women.

man'tis, n. kind of carnivorous insect.

man'tle, n., v., **-tled, -tling.** —n. 1. loose cloak. —v. 2. envelop. 3. blush.

man'tra, n. Hindu or Buddhist verbal formula for recitation.

man'u·al, adj. 1. of or done with hands. —n. 2. small informational book. 3. typewriter powered solely by typist's hands. —**man'u·al·ly,** adv.

man·u·fac'ture, n., v., **-tured, -turing.** —n. 1. making of things, esp. in great quantity. 2. thing made. —v. 3. make. —**man·u·fac'tur·er,** n.

ma·nure', n., v., **-ured, -uring.** —n. 1. fertilizer, esp. dung. —v. 2. apply manure to.

man•u•script′, n. handwritten or typed document.

man′y, adj. 1. comprising a large number; numerous. —n. 2. large number.

Mao′ism (mou′iz əm), n. theories and policies of Chinese Communist leader Mao Zedong. —**Mao′ist**, n., adj.

map, n., v., **mapped, mapping.** —n. 1. flat representation of earth, etc. —v. 2. show by map. 3. plan.

ma′ple, n. northern tree.

mar, v., **marred, marring.** damage.

ma•ra′ca, n. gourd-shaped rattle filled with seeds or pebbles, used as rhythm instrument.

mar′a•schi′no (-skē′-), n. cordial made from fermented juice of wild cherry.

maraschino cherry, cherry preserved in real or imitation maraschino.

mar′a•thon′, n. long contest, esp. a foot race of 26 miles, 385 yards.

ma•raud′, v. plunder. —**ma•raud′er**, n.

mar′ble, n. 1. crystalline limestone used in sculpture and building. 2. small glass ball used in children's game. —adj. 3. of marble.

march, v. 1. walk with measured tread. 2. advance. —n. 3. act of marching. 4. distance covered in marching. 5. music for marching.

March, n. third month of year.

Mar′di Gras (mär′dē grä′, grä′), the day before Lent, often celebrated as a carnival.

mare, n. female horse.

mar′ga•rine (-jə-), n. oleomargarine.

mar′gin, n. 1. edge. 2. amount more than necessary. 3. difference between cost and selling price. —**mar′gin•al**, adj.

mar′i•gold′, n. common, yellow-flowered plant.

ma′ri•jua′na (mä′rə wä′nə), n. plant whose leaves contain a narcotic.

ma•rim′ba, n. xylophone with chambers for resonance.

ma•ri′na (-rē′-), n. docking area for small boats.

mar′i•nate′, v. **-nated, -nating.** season by steeping. Also, **mar′i•nade′**.

ma•rine′, adj. 1. of the sea. —n. 2. member of U.S. Marine Corps. 3. fleet of ships.

Marine Corps, military branch of U.S. Navy.

mar′i•ner, n. sailor.

mar′i•o•nette′, n. puppet on strings.

mar′i•tal, adj. of marriage. —**mar′i•tal•ly**, adv.

mar′i•time′, adj. of sea or shipping.

mar•jo•ram, n. herb used as seasoning.

mark, n. 1. any visible sign. 2. object aimed at. 3. rating; grade. —v. 4. be feature of. 5. put mark on, as grade or price. 6. pay attention to. —**mark′er**, n.

marked, adj. 1. conspicuous. 2. ostentatious. 3. singled out for revenge. —**mark′ed•ly**, adv.

mar′ket, n. 1. place for selling and buying. —v. 2. sell or buy. —**mar′ket•a•ble**, adj.

mar′ket•place′, n. 1. open area where market is held. 2. the world of business, trade, and economics.

marks′man, n., pl. **-men.** good shooter. —**marks′man•ship′**, n. —**marks′wom•an**, n.fem.

mark′up′, n. price increase by retailer.

mar′lin, n. large game fish.

mar′ma•lade′, n. fruit preserve.

mar′mo•set′, n. small, tropical American monkey.

mar′mot (-mət), n. bushy-tailed rodent.

ma•roon′, n., adj. 1. dark brownish-red. —v. 2. abandon ashore.

mar•quee′ (-kē′), n. projecting shelter over outer door.

mar′quis (-kwis), n. rank of nobility below duke. Also, Brit. **mar′quess.** —**mar•quise′** (-kēz′), n.fem.

mar′qui•sette′ (-ki zet′), n. delicate open fabric.

mar′riage, n. 1. legal union of man and woman. 2. wedding. —**mar′riage•a•ble**, adj.

mar′row, n. soft interior tissue of bone.

mar′ry, v., **-ried, -rying.** take, give, or unite in marriage; wed.

Mars, n. 1. Roman god of war. 2. one of the planets.

marsh, n. low, wet land. —**marsh′y**, adj.

mar′shal, n., v., **-shaled, -shaling.** —n. 1. federal officer. —v. 2. rally; organize.

marsh′mal′low, n. gelatinous confection.

mar•su′pi•al, n. animal carrying its young in pouch, as the kangaroo. —**mar•su′pi•al**, adj.

mart, n. market.

mar′ten, n. small, American, fur-bearing animal.

mar′tial, adj. warlike; military. —**mar′tial•ly**, adv.

mar′tin, n. bird of swallow family.

mar′ti•net′, n. stern disciplinarian.

mar•ti′ni (-tē′nē), n. cocktail of gin and vermouth.

mar′tyr, n. 1. person who willingly

dies or suffers for a belief. —v. 2. make martyr of. —**mar'tyr·dom**, n.

mar'vel, n. v., -veled, -veling. —n. 1. wonderful thing. —v. 2. wonder (at). —**mar'vel·ous**, adj.

Marx'ism, n. doctrine of eventually classless society; communism. —**Marx'ist**, n., adj.

mar'zi·pan', n. confection of almond paste and sugar.

mas·car'a, n. cosmetic for eyelashes.

mas'cot, n. source of good luck.

mas'cu·line, adj. of or like men. —**mas'cu·lin'i·ty**, n.

mash, n. 1. soft pulpy mass. —v. 2. crush.

mash'ie, n. golf club.

mask, n. 1. disguise for face. —v. 2. disguise.

mas'och·ism (mas'ə kiz'əm), n. willful suffering. —**mas'och·ist**, n. —**mas'och·is'tic**, adj.

ma'son, n. builder with stone, brick, etc. —**ma'son·ry**, n.

mas'quer·ade', n., v., -aded, -ading. —n. 1. disguise. 2. party at which guests wear disguise. —v. 3. wear disguise. —**mas'quer·ad'er**, n.

mass, n. 1. body of coherent matter. 2. quantity or size. 3. weight. 4. (cap.) celebration of the Eucharist. 5. **the masses**, ordinary or common people as a whole. —v. 6. form into a mass. —adj. 7. of or affecting the masses. 8. done on a large scale.

mas'sa·cre, n., v., -cred, -cring. —n. 1. killing of many. —v. 2. slaughter.

mas·sage', n., v., -saged, -saging. —n. 1. treat body by rubbing or kneading. —v. 2. such treatment. —**mas·seur'** (mə sûr'), n. —**mas·seuse'** (mə sōōs'), n.fem.

mas'sive, adj. large; heavy. —**mas'sive·ly**, adv.

mast, n. upright pole.

mas·tec'to·my, n., pl. -mies. surgical removal of a breast.

mas'ter, n. 1. person in control. 2. employer or owner. 3. skilled person. —adj. 4. chief. —v. 5. conquer.

mas'ter·ful, adj. asserting power or authority. —**mas'ter·ful·ly**, adv.

mas'ter·ly, adj. highly skilled.

mas'ter·mind', n. 1. supreme planner. —v. 2. plan as mastermind.

mas'ter·piece', n. work of highest skill.

master's degree, academic degree awarded to student who has completed at least one year of graduate study.

master sergeant, noncommissioned officer of highest rank.

mas'ter·y, n., pl. -teries. control; skill.

mas'ti·cate', v., -cated, -cating. chew. —**mas'ti·ca'tion**, n.

mas'tiff, n. powerful dog.

mas'to·don', n. large extinct elephantlike mammal.

mas'toid, n. protuberance of bone behind ear.

mas'tur·bate', v., -bated, -bating. practice sexual self-gratification. —**mas'tur·ba'tion**, n.

mat, n., v., matted, matting, adj. —n. 1. covering for floor or other surface. 2. border for picture. 3. padding. 4. thick mass. 5. matte. —v. 6. cover with mat. 7. form into mat. —adj. 8. matte.

mat'a·dor', n. bullfighter.

match, n. 1. short stick chemically tipped to strike fire. 2. person or thing resembling or equaling another. 3. game. 4. marriage. —v. 5. equal. 6. fit together. 7. arrange marriage for.

match'less, adj. unequaled. —**match'less·ly**, adv.

match'mak'er, n. arranger of marriages.

mate, n., v., mated, mating. —n. 1. one of pair. 2. officer of merchant ship. 3. assistant. 4. female member of couple. —v. 5. join; pair.

ma'ter, n. Brit. Informal. mother.

ma·te'ri·al, n. 1. substance of which thing is made. 2. fabric. —adj. 3. physical. 4. pertinent. —**ma·te'ri·al·ly**, adv.

ma·te'ri·al·ism', n. 1. devotion to material objects or wealth. 2. belief that all reality is material. —**ma·te'ri·al·ist**, n. —**ma·te'ri·al·is'tic**, adj.

ma·te'ri·al·ize', v., -ized, -izing. give or assume material form.

ma·te'ri·el', n. supplies, esp. military.

ma·ter'ni·ty, n. motherhood. —**ma·ter'nal**, adj.

math'e·mat'ics, n. science of numbers. —**math'e·mat'i·cal**, adj. —**math'e·ma·ti'cian**, n.

mat'i·née' (-nā'), n. afternoon performance.

mat'ins, n. morning prayer.

ma'tri·arch', n. female ruler. —**ma'tri·ar'chy**, n.

ma·tric'u·late', v., -lated, -lating. enroll. —**ma·tric'u·la'tion**, n.

mat'ri·mo'ny, n., pl. -nies. marriage. —**mat'ri·mo'ni·al**, adj.

ma'trix (mā'triks, ma'-), n., pl. -trices (-tri sēz'), -trixes. 1. place or point where something originates. 2. mold; model.

ma'tron, n. 1. married woman, esp. one who is mature and dignified. 2.

female institutional officer. **—ma´tron•ly,** adj.

matte (mat), adj. **1.** having a dull surface, without luster. **—n. 2.** dull surface or finish. Also, **mat.**

mat´ter, n. **1.** material. **2.** affair or trouble. **3.** pus. **4.** importance. **—v. 5.** be of importance.

mat´ter-of-fact´, adj. objective; realistic.

mat´ting, n. mat of rushes.

mat´tock, n. digging implement with one broad and one pointed end.

mat´tress, n. thick filled case for sleeping on.

ma•ture´ (-tyŏŏr´), adj. **-turer, -turest,** v., **-tured, -turing. —adj. 1.** grown or developed. **2.** adult in manner or thought. **3.** payable. **—v. 4.** become or make mature. **—ma•tu´ri•ty,** n. **—ma•ture´ly,** adv. **—mat´u•ra´tion,** n.

maud´lin, adj. weakly sentimental.

maul, v. handle roughly.

mau•so•le´um, n., pl. **-leums, -lea.** tomb in form of building.

mauve (mōv), n. pale purple.

mav´er•ick, n. **1.** unbranded calf. **2.** nonconformist.

maw, n. mouth.

mawk´ish, adj. sickly sentimental. **—mawk´ish•ly,** adv. **—mawk´ish•ness,** n.

max´im, n. general truth.

max´i•mum, n. **1.** greatest degree or quantity. **—adj. 2.** greatest possible.

may, v., pt. **might.** (auxiliary verb of possibility or permission).

May, n. fifth month of year.

may´be, adv. perhaps.

May´day´, n. international radio distress call.

may´hem, n. random violence.

may•on•naise´, n. salad dressing made chiefly of egg yolks, oil, and vinegar. Also, Informal, **may´o.**

may´or, n. chief officer of city. **—may´or•al•ty,** n.

maze, n. confusing arrangement of paths.

ma•zur´ka, n. lively Polish dance.

me, pers. pronoun. objective case of I.

mead, n. liquor of fermented honey.

mead´ow, n. level grassland.

mead´ow•lark´, n. common American songbird.

mea´ger, adj. poor; scanty. Also, **mea´gre.**

meal, n. **1.** food served or eaten. **2.** coarse grain. **—meal´y,** adj.

meal´y-mouthed´, adj. avoiding candid speech.

mean, v., **meant, meaning,** adj., n. **—v. 1.** intend (to do or signify). **2.** sig-

nify. **—adj. 3.** poor; shabby. **4.** hostile; malicious. **5.** middle. **—n. 6.** (pl.) method of achieving purpose. **7.** (pl.) money or property. **8.** intermediate quantity. **—mean´ness,** n.

me•an´der, v. wander aimlessly.

mean´ing, n. **1.** significance. **—adj. 2.** significant. **—mean´ing•ful,** adj. **—mean´ing•less,** adj. **—mean´ing•ly,** adv.

mean´time´, n. **1.** time between. **—adv.** Also, **mean´while´. 2.** in time between.

mea´sles, n. infectious disease marked by small red spots.

mea´sly, adj., **-slier, -sliest.** Informal. miserably small.

meas´ure, v., **-ured, -uring.** n. **—v. 1.** ascertain size or extent. **—n. 2.** process of measuring. **3.** dimensions. **4.** instrument or system of measuring. **5.** action. **—meas´ur•a•ble,** adj. **—meas´ure•ment,** n.

meas´ured, adj. in distinct sequence.

meat, n. **1.** flesh of animals used as food. **2.** edible part of fruit, nut, etc. **3.** essential part; gist.

meat´y, adj., **meatier, meatiest. 1.** with much meat. **2.** rewarding attention.

Mec´ca (mek´ə), n. **1.** city in Saudi Arabia, spiritual center of Islam. **2.** (often l.c.) place that attracts many.

me•chan´ic, n. skilled worker with machinery.

me•chan´i•cal, adj. of or operated by machinery. **—me•chan´i•cal•ly,** adv.

me•chan´ics, n. science of motion and of action of forces on bodies.

mech´an•ism´, n. **1.** structure of machine. **2.** piece of machinery. **—mech´a•nist,** n.

mech´a•nis´tic, adj. of or like machinery.

mech´a•nize´, v., **-nized, -nizing.** adapt to machinery. **—mech´a•ni•za´tion,** n.

med´al, n. badgelike metal object given for merit.

med´al•ist, n. winner of a medal.

me•dal´lion, n. large medal or medallike ornament.

med´dle, v., **-dled, -dling.** interfere; tamper. **—med´dler,** n. **—med´dle•some,** adj.

me´di•a, n. pl. the means of mass communication, as radio, television, and newspapers.

me´di•an, adj., n. middle.

me´di•ate´, v., **-ated, -ating.** settle (dispute) between parties. **—me•di•a´tion,** n. **—me´di•a´tor,** n.

med'ic, *n. Informal.* doctor or medical aide.

Med'i•caid, *n.* state- and federal-supported medical care for low-income persons.

med'i•cal, *adj.* 1. of medicine. 2. curative. **—med'i•cal•ly,** *adv.*

me•dic'a•ment, *n.* healing substance.

Med'i•care', *n.* government-supported medical insurance for those 65 years old or more.

med'i•cate', *v.,* **-cated, -cating.** treat with medicine. **—med'i•ca'tion,** *n.*

me•dic'i•nal (-dis'-), *adj.* curative; remedial. **—me•dic'i•nal•ly,** *adv.*

med'i•cine, *n.* 1. substance used in treating disease. 2. art of preserving or restoring physical health.

medicine man, among American Indians, person believed to have magical powers.

me•di•e'val, *adj.* of the Middle Ages. Also, **me'di•ae'val.**

me•di•e'val•ism, *n.* 1. a characteristic of the Middle Ages. 2. devotion to medieval ideals, etc.

me•di•e'val•ist, *n.* 1. expert in medieval history, etc. 2. one devoted to medieval ideals.

me'di•o'cre, *adj.* undistinguished. **—me'di•oc'ri•ty,** *n.*

med'i•tate', *v.,* **-tated, -tating.** think intensely; consider. **—med'i•ta'tion,** *n.* **—med'i•ta'tive,** *adj.*

me'di•um, *n., pl.* **-diums** *for 1–5,* **-dia** *for 1–3, 5, adj.* **—***n.* 1. something intermediate or moderate. 2. means of doing. 3. environment. 4. person believed able to communicate with dead. 5. means of mass communication. **—***adj.* 6. intermediate.

med'ley, *n.* mixture, as of tunes.

meek, *adj.* submissive.

meer'schaum (mir'sham), *n.* claylike mineral, used for tobacco pipes.

meet, *v.,* **met, meeting,** *n., adj.* **—***v.* 1. come into contact with. 2. make acquaintance of. 3. satisfy. **—***n.* 4. equal. 5. meeting, esp. for sport. **—***adj.* 6. proper.

meet'ing, *n.* 1. a coming together. 2. persons gathered.

meg'a-, *prefix.* 1. one million. 2. large.

meg'a•hertz', *n., pl.* **-hertz.** *Elect.* one million cycles per second.

meg'a•lo•ma'ni•a, *n.* delusion of greatness, riches, etc.

meg'a•lop'o•lis, *n.* very large urbanized area. Also, **me•gap'o•lis.**

meg'a•phone', *n.* cone-shaped device for magnifying sound.

meg'a•ton', *n.* one million tons, esp. of TNT as equivalent in explosive force.

mel'an•cho'li•a, *n.* mental disease marked by great depression.

mel'an•chol'y, *n., pl.* **-cholies.** 1. low spirits; depression. **—***adj.* 2. sad.

mé•lange' (mā länj'), *n.* mixture.

me•lee (mā'lā), *n.* confused, general fight.

mel'io•rate' (mēl'ya rāt'), *v.,* **-rated, -rating.** improve. **—mel'io•ra'tion,** *n.* **—mel'io•ra'tive,** *adj.*

mel•lif'lu•ous, *adj.* soft and sweet in speech.

mel'low, *adj.* 1. soft and rich. 2. genial. **—***v.* 3. make or become mellow.

me•lo'de•on, *n.* reed organ.

me•lo'di•ous, *adj.* tuneful.

mel'o•dra'ma, *n.* play emphasizing theatrical effects and strong emotions. **—mel'o•dra•mat'ic,** *adj.*

mel'o•dy, *n., pl.* **-dies.** arrangement of musical sounds. **—me•lod'ic,** *adj.*

mel'on, *n.* edible fruit of certain annual vines.

melt, *v.,* **melted, melted** or **molten, melting.** 1. make or become liquid, esp. by heat. 2. soften.

melt'down', *n.* melting of nuclear reactor core, causing escape of radiation.

melting pot, place where blending of peoples, races, or cultures takes place.

mel'ton, *n.* smooth woolen fabric.

mem'ber, *n.* 1. part of structure or body. 2. one belonging to organization. **—mem'ber•ship',** *n.*

mem'brane, *n.* thin film of tissue in animals and plants.

me•men'to, *n., pl.* **-tos, -toes.** reminder.

mem'oir (-wär), *n.* 1. (*pl.*) personal recollection. 2. biography.

mem'o•ra•bil'i•a, *n.pl.* souvenirs.

mem'o•ra•ble, *adj.* worth remembering. **—mem'o•ra•bly,** *adv.*

mem'o•ran'dum, *n., pl.* **-dums, -da.** written statement or reminder. Also, **mem'o.**

me•mo'ri•al, *n.* 1. something honoring memory of a person or event. **—***adj.* 2. serving as memorial.

mem'o•rize', *v.,* **-rized, -rizing.** commit to memory.

mem'o•ry, *n., pl.* **-ries.** 1. faculty of remembering. 2. something that is remembered. 3. length of time of recollection. 4. reputation after death. 5. capacity of computer to store information.

men'ace, *v.,* **-aced, -acing,** *n.* **—***v.* 1. threaten evil to. **—***n.* 2. something that threatens.

mé•nage' (mā näzh'), *n.* household.

me·nag'er·ie, *n.* collection of animals.

mend, *v.* repair; improve. **—mend'er,** *n.*

men·da'cious, *adj.* untruthful. **—men·dac'i·ty,** *n.*

men'di·cant, *n.* beggar.

me'ni·al, *adj.* 1. humble; servile. **—***n.* 2. servant.

men·in·gi'tis (-jī'-), *n.* inflammation of membranes surrounding brain and spinal cord.

men'o·pause', *n.* cessation of menses, usually between ages of 45 and 50.

me·no'rah (mə nôr'ə), *n.* symbolic candelabrum used by Jews during Hanukkah.

men'ses (-sēz), *n.pl.* monthly discharge of blood from uterus. **—men'stru·al,** *adj.* **—men'stru·ate',** *v.* **—men·stru·a'tion,** *n.*

men'sur·a·ble (-shar-), *adj.* measurable. **—men'su·ra'tion,** *n.*

men'swear', *n.* clothing for men.

men'tal, *adj.* of or in mind. **—men'tal·ly,** *adv.*

men·tal'i·ty, *n., pl.* **-ties.** 1. mental ability. 2. characteristic mental attitude.

men'thol, *n.* colorless alcohol from peppermint oil. **—men'thol·at'ed,** *adj.*

men'tion, *v.* 1. speak or write of. **—***n.* 2. reference. **—men'tion·a·ble,** *adj.*

men'tor, *n.* adviser; teacher.

men'u, *n.* list of dishes that can be served.

me·ow', *n.* 1. sound cat makes. **—***v.* 2. make such sound.

mer'can·tile' (-tēl, -tīl), *adj.* of or engaged in trade.

mer'ce·nar'y (-sə-), *adj., n., pl.* **-naries.** **—***adj.* 1. acting only for profit. **—***n.* 2. hired soldier.

mer'cer·ize', *v.,* **-ized, -izing.** treat (cottons) for greater strength.

mer'chan·dise', *n., v.,* **-dised, -dising.** **—***n.* 1. goods; wares. **—***v.* 2. buy and sell.

mer'chant, *n.* person who buys and sells goods for profit.

merchant marine, commercial vessels of nation.

mer·cu'ri·al, *adj.* 1. of mercury. 2. sprightly. 3. changeable in emotion.

mer'cu·ry, *n.* 1. heavy metallic element. 2. (*cap.*) one of the planets. 3. (*cap.*) Roman god of commerce and messenger to other gods.

mer'cy, *n., pl.* **-cies.** 1. pity; compassion. 2. act of compassion. **—mer'ci·ful,** *adj.* **—mer'ci·less,** *adj.*

mere, *adj.* only; simple. **—mere'ly,** *adv.*

mer'e·tri'cious, *adj.* falsely attractive.

merge, *v.,* **merged, merging.** combine. **—merg'er,** *n.*

me·rid'i·an, *n.* circle on earth's surface passing through the poles.

me·ringue' (-rang'), *n.* egg whites and sugar beaten together.

me·ri'no, *n., pl.* **-nos.** kind of sheep.

mer'it, *n.* 1. excellence or good quality. **—***v.* 2. deserve. **—mer'i·to'ri·ous,** *adj.*

mer'maid', *n.* imaginary sea creature, half woman and half fish. **—mer'man',** *n.masc.*

mer'ry, *adj.,* **-rier, -riest.** gay; joyous. **—mer'ri·ly,** *adv.* **—mer'ri·ment,** *n.*

mer'ry-go-round', *n.* revolving amusement ride.

mer'ry·mak'ing, *n.* festivities; hilarity. **—mer'ry·mak'er,** *n.*

me'sa (mā'-), *n.* high, steep-walled plateau.

mesh, *n.* 1. open space of net. 2. net itself. 3. engagement of gears. **—***v.* 4. catch in mesh. 5. engage. 6. match or interlock.

mes'mer·ize', *v.,* **-ized, -izing.** hypnotize. **—mes'mer·ism,** *n.*

mes·quite' (-kēt'), *n.* common tree of southwest U.S.

mess, *n.* 1. dirty or disorderly condition. 2. group taking meals together regularly. 3. meals so taken. **—***v.* 4. disorder; make dirty. 5. eat in company. **—mess'y,** *adj.*

mes'sage, *n.* communication.

mes'sen·ger, *n.* bearer of message.

Mes·si'ah, *n.* 1. expected deliverer. 2. (in Christian theology) Jesus Christ.

mes·ti'zo (mes tē'zō), *n., pl.* **-zos, -zoes.** person part-Spanish, part-Indian. Also, **mes·ti'za,** *fem.*

me·tab'o·lism', *n.* biological processes of converting food into living matter and matter into energy. **—met'a·bol'ic,** *adj.*

met'al, *n.* 1. elementary substance such as gold or copper. 2. mettle. **—me·tal'lic,** *adj.* **—met'al·ware',** *n.*

met'al·lur'gy, *n.* science of working with metals. **—met'al·lur'gist,** *n.*

met'a·mor'phose, *v.,* **-phosed, -phosing.** transform.

met'a·mor'pho·sis, *n., pl.* **-ses.** change.

met'a·phor, *n.* figure of speech using analogy. **—met'a·phor'i·cal,** *adj.*

met'a·phys'ics, *n.* branch of philosophy concerned with ultimate nature of reality. **—met'a·phys'i·cal,** *adj.* **—met'a·phy·si'cian,** *n.*

me·tas'ta·size', *v.,* **-sized, -sizing.**

spread from one to another part of the body. —me•tas′ta•sis′, n. —met′a•stat′ic, adj.

mete, v., meted, meting. allot.

me′te•or, n. celestial body passing through earth's atmosphere. —me•te•or′ic, adj.

me′te•or•ite′, n. meteor reaching earth.

me′te•or•ol′o•gy, n. science of atmospheric phenomena, esp. weather. —me′te•or•olog′i•cal, adj. —me′te•orol′o•gist, n.

me′ter, n. 1. unit of length in metric system, equal to 39.37 inches. 2. rhythmic arrangement of words. 3. device for measuring flow. —v. 4. measure. Also, Brit., me′tre. —met′ric, met•ri•cal, adj.

meth′a•done′, n. synthetic narcotic used in treating heroin addiction.

meth′ane, n. colorless, odorless, flammable gas.

meth′a•nol′, n. colorless liquid used as solvent, fuel, or antifreeze. Also, meth′yl alcohol.

meth′od, n. system of doing. —me•thod′i•cal, me•thod′ic, adj. —me•thod′i•cal•ly, adv.

me•tic′u•lous, adj. minutely careful.

mé′tier′ (mā′tyā), n. field of activity in which one has special ability. Also, me′tier.

met′ric, adj. of decimal system of weights and measures, based on meter and gram. —met′ri•cize′, v. —met′ri•ca′tion, n.

met′ro•nome′, n. device for marking tempo.

me•trop′o•lis, n. great city.

met′ro•pol′i•tan, adj. 1. of or in city. 2. of cities and urban areas.

met′tle, n. 1. spirit. 2. disposition.

mew (myoō), n. 1. cry of a cat. —v. 2. emit a mew.

mews, n. street with dwellings converted from stables.

Mex′i•can, n. native of Mexico. —Mexican, adj.

mez′za•nine′, n. low story between two main floors; balcony.

mez′zo•so•pran′o (met′sō-, med′zo-), n. voice, musical part, or singer intermediate in range between soprano and contralto.

mi•as′ma (mī-), n., pl. -mata, -mas. vapors from decaying organic matter.

mi′ca, n. shiny mineral occurring in thin layers.

mi′cro-, prefix. 1. extremely small. 2. one millionth.

mi′crobe, n. microorganism, esp. one causing disease.

mi′cro•chip′, n. chip (def. 3).

mi′cro•com•put′er, n. compact computer with less capability than minicomputer.

mi′cro•cosm, n. world in miniature.

mi′cro•fiche′ (-fēsh′), n. small sheet of microfilm.

mi′cro•film′, n. 1. very small photograph of book page, etc. —v. 2. make microfilm of.

mi•crom′e•ter, n. device for measuring minute distances.

mi′cro•or′gan•ism′, n. microscopic organism.

mi′cro•phone′, n. instrument for changing sound waves into changes in electric current.

mi′cro•scope′, n. instrument for inspecting minute objects.

mi′cro•scop′ic, adj. 1. of microscopes. 2. extremely small.

mi′cro•wave′, n. 1. short radio wave used in radar, cooking, etc. 2. oven that uses microwaves to generate heat in the food. —v. 3. cook in microwave oven.

mid, adj. 1. middle. —prep. 2. amid.

mid′day′, n. noon.

mid′dle, adj. 1. equally distant from given limits. 2. medium. —n. 3. middle part.

Middle Ages, period of European history, about A.D. 476 to 1500.

middle class, class of people intermediate between the poor and the wealthy, usu. educated working people.

Middle East, area including Israel and Arab countries of NE Africa and SW Asia.

mid′dle•man′, n. merchant who buys direct from producer.

middle school, school encompassing grades 5 or 6 through 8.

mid′dling, adj. 1. medium. —n. 2. (pl.) coarse parts of grain.

mid′dy, n., pl. -dies. blouse with square back collar.

midge, n. minute fly.

midg′et, n. very small person or thing.

mid′land, n. interior of country.

mid′night′, n. 12 o'clock at night.

mid′point′, n. point at or near the middle.

mid′riff, n. part of body between the chest and abdomen.

mid′ship•man, n., pl. -men. rank of student at U.S. Naval or Coast Guard academy.

midst, n. middle.

mid′sum•mer, n. 1. middle of the summer. 2. summer solstice, around June 21.

mid′way′, adj., adv. 1. in or to middle.

—*n.* 2. area of rides, games, shows, etc., at carnival.

mid'wife', *n., pl.* **-wives.** woman who assists at childbirth.

mien (mēn), *n.* air; bearing.

miff, *n.* 1. petty quarrel. —*v.* 2. offend.

might, *v.* 1. pt. of **may.** —*n.* 2. strength; power.

might'y, *adj.* **mightier, mightiest,** *adv.* —*adj.* 1. powerful; huge. —*adv.* 2. *Informal.* very. —**might'i•ness,** *n.*

mi'graine, *n.* painful headache.

mi'grate, *v.,* **-grated, -grating.** go from one region to another. —**mi•gra'tion,** *n.* —**mi'gra•to'ry,** *adj.* —**mi'grant,** *adj., n.*

mi•ka'do, *n., pl.* **-dos.** a title of emperor of Japan.

mike, *n. Informal.* microphone.

mil, *n.* one thousandth of inch.

mi•la'dy, *n., pl.* **-dies.** English noblewoman (often used as term of address).

milch, *adj.* giving milk.

mild, *adj.* gentle; temperate. —**mild'ly,** *adv.* —**mild'ness,** *n.*

mil'dew', *n.* 1. discoloration caused by fungus. —*v.* 2. affect with mildew.

mile, *n.* unit of distance, equal on land to 5280 ft.

mile'age, *n.* 1. miles traveled. 2. travel allowance.

mile'stone', *n.* 1. marker showing road distance. 2. important event.

mi•lieu' (mēl yœ'), *n., pl.* **-lieus, -lieux.** environment.

mil'i•tant, *adj.* warlike; aggressive.

mil'i•ta•rism, *n.* military spirit. 2. domination by military. —**mil'i•ta•rist,** *n.* —**mil'i•ta•ris'tic,** *adj.*

mil'i•ta•rize', *v.,* **-ized, -izing.** equip with military weapons.

mil'i•tar'y, *adj., n., pl.* **-taries.** *adj.* 1. of armed forces, esp. on land. —*n.* 2. armed forces or soldiers collectively.

mil'i•tate', *v.,* **-tated, -tating.** act (for or against).

mi•li'tia (-lish'ə), *n.* organization for emergency military service. —**mi•li'tia•man,** *n.*

milk, *n.* 1. white liquid secreted by female mammals to feed their young. —*v.* 2. draw milk from. —**milk'y,** *adj.* —**milk'maid',** *n.* —**milk'man',** *n.*

milk'weed', *n.* plant with milky juice.

Milk'y Way', *Astron.* galaxy containing sun and earth.

mill, *n.* 1. place where manufacturing is done. 2. device for grinding. 3. one tenth of a cent. —*v.* 4. grind or treat with mill. 5. groove edges of (coin). 6. move about in confusion. —**mill'er,** *n.*

mil•len'ni•um, *n., pl.* **-niums, -nia.** 1. future period of joy. 2. future reign of Christ on earth.

mil'let, *n.* cereal grass.

mil'li•gram', *n.* one thousandth of gram.

mil'li•li'ter, *n.* one thousandth of liter.

mil'li•me'ter, *n.* one thousandth of meter.

mil'li•ner, *n.* person who makes or sells women's hats.

mil'li•ner'y, *n.* 1. women's hats. 2. business or trade of a milliner.

mil'lion, *n., adj.* 1000 times 1000. —**mil'lionth,** *adj., n.*

mil'lion•aire', *n.* person having million dollars or more.

mill'stone', *n.* 1. stone for grinding grain. 2. heavy mental or emotional burden.

milt, *n.* male secretion of fish.

mime, *n.* pantomimist; clown.

mim'e•o•graph', *n.* 1. stencil device for duplicating. —*v.* 2. copy with mimeograph.

mim'ic, *v.,* **-icked, -icking,** *n.* —*v.* 1. imitate speech or actions of. —*n.* 2. person who mimics. —**mim'ic•ry,** *n.*

mi•mo'sa, *n.* semitropical tree or shrub.

min•a•ret', *n.* tower for calling Muslims to prayer.

mince, *v.,* **minced, mincing.** 1. chop fine. 2. speak, move, or behave with affected elegance. —**minc'ing•ly,** *adv.*

mince'meat', *n.* cooked mixture of finely chopped meat, raisins, spices, etc., used in pies.

mind, *n.* 1. thinking or feeling part of human or animal. 2. intellect. 3. inclination. —*v.* 4. heed; obey.

mind'ful, *adj.* careful.

mind'less, *adj.* 1. heedless. 2. without intelligence.

mine, *pron., n., v.,* **mined, mining.** —*pron.* 1. possessive form of I. —*n.* 2. excavation in earth for getting out metals, coal, etc. 3. stationary explosive device used in war. —*v.* 4. dig or work in mines. 5. lay explosive mines. —**min'er,** *n.*

min'er•al, *n.* 1. inorganic substance. 2. substance obtained by mining. —*adj.* 3. of minerals.

min'er•al•o•gy, *n.* science of minerals. —**min'er•al•og'i•cal,** *adj.* —**min'er•al'o•gist,** *n.*

mineral water, water containing dissolved mineral salts or gases.

min'e•stro'ne (min'i strō'nē), *n.* thick vegetable soup.

min'gle, v., **-gled, -gling.** associate; mix.

min'i, n. something small of its kind.

min'i·a·ture, n. **1.** greatly reduced form. **2.** tiny painting. —adj. **3.** on small scale.

min'i·a·tur·ize', v., **-ized, -izing.** make in or reduce to very small size. —**min'i·a·tur·i·za'tion,** n.

min'i·com·put'er, n. computer with capabilities intermediate between those of microcomputer and mainframe.

min'im, n. smallest unit of liquid measure.

min'i·mize', v., **-mized, -mizing.** make minimum.

min'i·mum, n. **1.** least possible quantity, degree, etc. —adj. **2.** Also, **min'i·mal.** least; lowest.

min'ion, n. servile follower.

min'is·ter, n. **1.** person authorized to conduct worship. **2.** government representative abroad. **3.** head of governmental department. —v. **4.** give care. —**min'is·te'ri·al,** adj. —**min'is·tra'tion,** n.

min'is·try, n., pl. **-tries. 1.** religious calling. **2.** clergy. **3.** duty or office of a department of government. **4.** body of executive officials. **5.** act of ministering.

mink, n. semiaquatic fur-bearing animal.

min'now, n. tiny fish.

mi'nor, adj. **1.** lesser in size, importance, etc. **2.** under legal age. —n. **3.** person under legal age.

mi·nor'i·ty, n., pl. **-ties. 1.** smaller number or part. **2.** relatively small population group. **3.** state or time of being under legal age.

min'strel, n. **1.** musician or singer, esp. in Middle Ages. **2.** comedian in blackface.

mint, n. **1.** aromatic herb. **2.** place where money is coined. —v. **3.** make coins.

min·u·end', n. number from which another is to be subtracted.

min·u·et', n. stately dance.

mi'nus, prep. **1.** less. —adj. **2.** less than.

mi·nus'cule' (min'əs-), adj. tiny.

min·ute, n. **1.** sixty seconds. **2.** (pl.) record of proceedings. —adj. (mī nyōōt'). **3.** extremely small. **4.** attentive to detail. —**mi·nute'ly,** adv.

mi·nu'ti·ae' (-shē ē'), n.pl. trifling matters.

minx, n. saucy girl.

mir'a·cle, n. supernatural act or effect. —**mi·rac'u·lous,** adj.

mi·rage', n. atmospheric illusion in

which images of far-distant objects are seen.

mire, n., v., **mired, miring.** —n. **1.** swamp. **2.** deep mud. —v. **3.** stick fast in mire. **4.** soil with mire. —**mir'y,** adj.

mir'ror, n. **1.** reflecting surface. —v. **2.** reflect.

mirth, n. gaiety, —**mirth'ful,** adj. —**mirth'less,** adj.

mis'ad·ven'ture, n. mishap.

mis'an·thrope', n. hater of humanity. —**mis'an·throp'ic,** adj.

mis'ap·ply', v., **-plied, -plying.** use wrongly. —**mis'ap·pli·ca'tion,** n.

mis'ap·pre·hend', v. misunderstand. —**mis'ap·pre·hen'sion,** n.

mis'ap·pro'pri·ate', v., **-ated, -ating.** use wrongly as one's own. —**mis·ap·pro'pri·a'tion,** n.

mis'be·got'ten, adj. ill-conceived.

mis'be·have', v., **-haved, -having.** behave badly. —**mis'be·hav'ior,** n.

mis·cal'cu·late', v., **-lated, -lating.** judge badly. —**mis·cal·cu·la'tion,** n.

mis·car'riage, n. **1.** premature birth resulting in death of fetus. **2.** failure.

mis·car'ry, v., **-ried, -rying. 1.** go wrong. **2.** have miscarriage.

mis'ce·ge·na'tion (mis'i jə-), n. sexual union between members of different races.

mis'cel·la'ne·ous, adj. unclassified; various. —**mis'cel·la·ny,** n.

mis·chance', n. bad luck.

mis'chief, n. **1.** trouble, caused willfully. **2.** tendency to tease. —**mis'chie·vous,** adj.

mis'con·ceive', v., **-ceived, -ceiving.** misunderstand. —**mis'con·cep'tion,** n.

mis·con'duct, n. improper or illegal conduct.

mis'con·strue', v., **-strued, -struing.** misinterpret.

mis'cre·ant, n. villain.

mis·deed', n. immoral deed.

mis'de·mean'or, n. minor offense.

mi'ser, n. hoarder of wealth. —**mi'ser·ly,** adj.

mis'er·a·ble, adj. **1.** wretched. **2.** deplorable. **3.** contemptible. —**mis'er·a·bly,** adv.

mis'er·y, n., pl. **-eries.** wretched condition.

mis·fire', v., **-fired, -firing.** fail to fire.

mis·fit', n. **1.** poor fit. **2.** (mis'fit'). maladjusted person.

mis·for'tune, n. bad luck.

mis·giv'ing, n. apprehension; doubt.

mis·guide', v., **-guided, -guiding.** guide wrongly.

mis'hap, n. unlucky accident.

mish'mash (mish'mäsh'), n. jumble; hodgepodge.

mis·in·form', v. give false information to. —**mis·in·for·ma'tion**, n.

mis·in·ter'pret, v. interpret wrongly. —**mis·in·ter·pre·ta'tion**, n.

mis·judge', v., **-judged**, **-judging**. judge wrongly. —**mis·judg'ment**, n.

mis·lay', v., **-laid**, **-laying**. 1. put in place later forgotten. 2. misplace

mis·lead', v., **-led**, **-leading**. 1. lead in wrong direction. 2. lead into error, as in conduct.

mis·man'age, v., **-aged**, **-aging**. manage badly. —**mis·man'age·ment**, n.

mis·no'mer, n. misapplied name.

mi·sog'y·ny (-soj'ə-), n. hatred of women. —**mi·sog'y·nist**, n.

mis·place', v., **-placed**, **-placing**. 1. forget location of. 2. place unwisely.

mis·print', n. error in printing.

mis·pro·nounce', v., **-nounced**, **-nouncing**. pronounce wrongly. —**mis·pro·nun·ci·a'tion**, n.

mis·quote', v., **-quoted**, **-quoting**. quote incorrectly. —**mis·quo·ta'tion**, n.

mis·read' (-rēd'), v., **-read** (red'), **-reading**. 1. read wrongly. 2. misinterpret

mis·rep·re·sent', v. give wrong idea of. —**mis·rep·re·sen·ta'tion**, n.

mis·rule', n. bad or unwise rule. —**mis·rule'**, v.

miss, v. 1. fail to hit, catch, meet, do, etc. 2. note or feel absence of. —n. 3. (cap.) title of respect for unmarried woman. 4. girl. 5. failure to hit, catch, etc.

mis'sal, n. book of prayers, etc., for celebrating Mass.

mis·shap'en, adj. deformed.

mis'sile, n. object thrown or shot, as lance or bullet.

mis'sion, n. 1. group sent abroad for specific work. 2. duty. 3. air operation against enemy. 4. missionary post.

mis'sion·ar·y, n., pl. **-aries**, adj. —n. 1. person sent to propagate religious faith. —adj. 2. of religious missions.

mis'sive, n. written message.

mis·spell', v. spell wrongly.

mis·state', v., **-stated**, **-stating**. state wrongly. —**mis·state'ment**, n.

mis·step', n. error.

mist, n. light, thin fog. —**mist'y**, adj.

mis·take', n., v., **-took**, **-taken**, **-taking**. n. 1. error in judgment, action, or belief. —v. 2. take or regard wrongly. 3. misunderstand. 4. be in error.

Mis'ter, n. title of respect for man. Abbr.: **Mr.**

mis'tle·toe', n. parasitic plant.

mis·treat', v. treat badly. —**mis·treat'ment**, n.

mis'tress, n. 1. female head of household. 2. female owner. 3. woman illicitly acting as wife.

mis·tri'al, n. trial ended without verdict because of legal error or inability of jury to agree on verdict.

mis·trust', n. lack of trust. —**mis·trust'**, v.

mis·un·der·stand', v., **-stood**, **-standing**. understand wrongly. —**mis·un·der·stand'ing**, n.

mis·use', n., v., **-used**, **-using**. —n. (-yōōs'). 1. improper use. —v. (-yōōz'). 2. use badly or wrongly. 3. abuse.

mite, n. 1. tiny parasitic insect. 2. small thing or bit.

mi'ter, v. 1. join two pieces on diagonal. —n. 2. such joint. 3. tall cap worn by bishops. Also, Brit., **mi'tre**.

mit'i·gate, v., **-gated**, **-gating**. make less severe.

mitt, n. thick glove.

mit'ten, n. fingerless glove.

mix, v., mixed or **mixt**, **mixing**, n. —v. 1. put together; combine. 2. associate. 3. confuse. —n. 4. mixture. 5. mess. —**mix'ture**, n.

mix'-up', n. state of confusion.

mne·mon'ic (nē-), adj. aiding memory.

moan, n. 1. low groan. —v. 2. utter moans.

moat, n. deep, water-filled ditch around fortification.

mob, n., v., **mobbed**, **mobbing**. —n. 1. crowd, esp. disorderly one. —v. 2. attack as a mob.

mo'bile, adj. 1. capable of moving or being moved. —n. (-bēl). 2. abstract sculpture with parts that move, as with breezes. —**mo·bil'i·ty**, n.

mo'bi·lize', v., **-lized**, **-lizing**. make ready for war. —**mo'bi·li·za'tion**, n.

moc'ca·sin, n. 1. soft shoe. 2. poisonous snake.

mo'cha (-ka), n. 1. kind of coffee. 2. flavoring made from coffee and chocolate.

mock, v. 1. mimic or ridicule. —n. 2. derision. —adj. 3. imitation.

mock'er·y, n., pl. **-ies**. 1. derision. 2. dishonest imitation; travesty.

mock'ing·bird', n. songbird with imitative voice.

mock'-up', n. scale model.

mod, adj. Informal. fashionably up-to-date.

mode, n. prevailing style. —**mod'ish,** adj.

mod'el, n., adj. v., **-eled, -eling.** —n. 1. standard for imitation. 2. person who poses, as for artist or photographer. —adj. 3. serving as model. —v. 4. pattern after model. 5. wear as model. 6. form.

mo'dem (mō'dəm, -dem), n. device enabling transmission of data from or to a computer via telephone or other communication lines.

mod'er·ate, adj., n., v., **-ated, -ating.** —adj. (-it). 1. not extreme. —n. (-it). 2. person having moderate views. —v. (-ə rāt'). 3. make or become less violent, intense, etc. 4. preside over. —**mod·er·a'tion,** n. —**mod'er·ate·ly,** adv.

mod'er·a'tor, n. director of group discussion.

mod'ern, adj. of recent time. —**mo·der'ni·ty,** n. —**mod'ern·ize',** v. —**mod'ern·i·za'tion,** n.

mod'ern·is'tic, adj. following modern trends. —**mod'ern·ism,** n.

mod'est, adj. 1. humble in estimating oneself. 2. simple; moderate. 3. decent; moral. —**mod'es·ty,** n. —**mod'est·ly,** adv.

mod'i·cum, n. small amount.

mod'i·fy, v., **-fied, -fying.** alter or moderate. —**mod'i·fi·ca'tion,** n. —**mod'i·fi'er,** n.

mo·diste' (-dēst'), n.fem. maker of women's attire.

mod'u·late', v., **-lated, -lating.** 1. soften. 2. Radio. alter (electric current) in accordance with sound waves. 3. alter the pitch or key of. —**mod'u·la'tion,** n.

mod'ule, n. 1. unit of measure. 2. building unit. 3. self-contained element of spacecraft. —**mod'u·lar,** adj.

mo'gul (mō'gəl), n. 1. powerful or influential person. 2. bump on ski slope.

mo'hair', n. fabric from fleece of the Angora goat.

Mo·ham'med·an·ism, n. Islam. —**Mo·ham'med·an,** n., adj.

moi'e·ty, n., pl. **-ties.** half; any part.

moil, n., v. labor.

moist, adj. damp. —**mois'ten,** v.

mois'ture, n. dampness; small beads of water.

mo'lar, n. broad back tooth.

mo·las'ses, n. thick, dark syrup produced in refining sugar.

mold, n. 1. form for shaping molten or plastic material. 2. thing so formed. 3. fungus growth on animal or vegetable matter. 4. loose rich earth. —v. 5. shape or form. 6.

become or make covered with mold (def. 3). —**mold'y,** adj.

mold'er, v. 1. decay. —n. 2. person who molds.

mold'ing, n. decorative strip with special cross section.

mole, n. 1. small, congenital spot on skin. 2. small, furred, underground mammal. 3. spy who works against government or agency he or she is employed by. —**mole'skin',** n.

mol'e·cule', n. smallest physical unit of a chemical element or compound. —**mo·lec'u·lar,** adj. —**mol'lusc.**

mole'hill', n. 1. small mound of earth raised by moles. 2. something small and insignificant.

mo·lest', v. 1. annoy by interfering with. 2. make indecent sexual advances to. —**mo'les·ta'tion,** n.

moll, n. Slang. female companion of gangster.

mol'li·fy, v., **-fied, -fying.** appease in temper.

mol'lusk, n. hard-shelled invertebrate animal. Also, **mol'lusc.**

mol'ly·cod'dle, v., **-dled, -dling.** pamper.

molt, v. shed skin or feathers.

mol'ten, adj. melted.

mo·lyb'de·num (ma lib'də nəm), n. silver-white metallic element used in alloys.

mo'ment, n. 1. short space of time. 2. importance.

mo'men·tar'y, adj. very brief in time. —**mo'men·tar'i·ly,** adv.

mo·men'tous, adj. important.

mo·men'tum, n., pl. **-ta, -tums.** force of moving body.

mon'ad, n. one-celled organism.

mon'arch, n. hereditary sovereign.

mon'ar·chy, n., pl. **-chies.** 1. government by monarch. 2. country governed by monarch. —**mon'ar·chism,** n.

mon'as·ter'y, n., pl. **-teries.** residence of monks. —**mo·nas'tic,** adj. —**mo·nas'ti·cism,** n.

Mon'day, n. second day of week.

mon'e·tar'y, adj. of money.

mon'ey, n., pl. **moneys, monies.** 1. pieces of metal or certificates issued as medium of exchange. 2. wealth.

mon'eyed (-ēd), adj. wealthy.

mon'gol·ism, n. Offensive. (earlier term for) Down syndrome.

Mon'gol·oid', adj. designating division of human race including most peoples of eastern Asia.

mon'goose, n., pl. **-gooses.** carnivorous animal of Asia.

mon'grel, n. 1. animal or plant result-

ing from crossing of different breeds.
—*adj.* 2. of mixed breeds.

mon'i·tor, *n.* 1. pupil who assists teacher. —*v.* 2. check continuously.

mon'i·to'ry, *adj.* warning.

monk, *n.* man who is a member of a religious order.

mon'key, *n.* 1. mammal strongly resembling a human being. —*v.* 2. trifle idly.

monkey wrench, 1. wrench with adjustable jaws. 2. something that interferes with process or operation.

mon'o·chrome', *adj.* of one color. Also, **mon'o·chro·mat'ic.**

mon'o·cle, *n.* eyeglass for one eye.

mo·nog'a·my, *n.* marriage of one woman with one man. —**mo·nog'a·mous,** *adj.* —**mo·nog'a·mist,** *n.*

mon'o·gram', *n.* design made of one's initials. —**mon'o·grammed,** *adj.*

mon'o·graph', *n.* treatise on one subject.

mon'o·lith', *n.* structure of single block of stone. —**mon'o·lith'ic,** *adj.*

mon'o·logue', *n.* talk by single speaker. Also, **mon'o·log.** —**mon'o·log·ist,** *n.*

mon'o·ma'ni·a, *n.* obsessive zeal for or interest in single thing. —**mon'o·ma'ni·ac,** *n.*

mon'o·nu·cle·o'sis (-nōō'klē ō'sis, -nyōō'-), *n.* infectious disease characterized by fever, swelling of lymph nodes, etc.

mon'o·plane', *n.* airplane with one wing on each side.

mo·nop'o·ly, *n., pl.* **-lies.** 1. exclusive control. 2. commodity, etc., so controlled. 3. company having such control. —**mo·nop'o·lis'tic,** *adj.* —**mo·nop'o·lize',** *v.*

mon'o·rail', *n.* 1. single rail serving as track for wheeled vehicles. 2. car or train moving on such a rail.

mon'o·syl'la·ble, *n.* word of one syllable. —**mon'o·syl·lab'ic,** *adj.*

mon'o·the·ism, *n.* doctrine or belief that there is only one God. —**mon'o·the'ist,** *n., adj.* —**mon'o·the·is'tic,** *adj.*

mon'o·tone', *n.* single tone of unvarying pitch.

mo·not'o·ny, *n.* wearisome uniformity. —**mo·not'o·nous,** *adj.*

mon·sieur' (mə syœ'), *n., pl.* **messieurs'** (mā-). French term of address for man.

mon·si'gnor (mon sē'nyər), *n., pl.* **-gnors, -gno'ri** (mon sē nyô'rē). title of certain dignitaries of Roman Catholic Church.

mon·soon', *n.* seasonal wind of Indian Ocean.

mon'ster, *n.* 1. animal or plant of abnormal form. 2. wicked creature. 3. anything huge.

mon·stros'i·ty, *n., pl.* **-ties.** something grotesquely abnormal.

mon'strous, *adj.* 1. huge. 2. frightful.

mon·tage' (-täzh'), *n.* blending of elements from several pictures into one.

month, *n.* any of twelve parts of calendar year.

month'ly, *adj., n., pl.* **-lies,** *adv.* —*adj.* 1. occurring, appearing, etc., once a month. 2. lasting for a month. —*n.* 3. periodical published once a month. —*adv.* 4. once a month. 5. by the month.

mon'u·ment, *n.* memorial structure.

mon'u·men'tal, *adj.* 1. imposing. 2. serving as monument.

moo, *n.* 1. sound cow makes. —*v.* 2. utter such sound.

mooch, *Slang.* 1. try to get without paying. —*n.* 2. Also, **mooch'er.** person who mooches.

mood, *n.* frame of mind.

mood'y, *adj.,* **moodier, moodiest.** of uncertain mood. —**mood'i·ly,** *adv.*

moon, *n.* 1. body which revolves around earth monthly. 2. month. —*v.* 3. gaze dreamily.

moon'light, *n.* 1. light from moon. —*v.* 2. work at second job after principal one.

moon'shine', *n.* illegally made liquor. —**moon'shin'er,** *n.*

moon'stone', *n.* pearly gem.

moor, *v.* 1. secure (ship), as at a dock. —*n.* 2. *Brit.* open peaty wasteland.

moor'ing, *n.* 1. (*pl.*) cables, etc., by which ship is moored. 2. place where ship is moored.

moose, *n., pl.* **moose.** large animal of deer family.

moot, *adj.* debatable.

mop, *n., v.,* **mopped, mopping.** —*n.* 1. piece of cloth, etc., fastened to stick, for washing or dusting. —*v.* 2. clean with mop. 3. *Mil.* **mop up,** destroy final resisting elements.

mope, *v.,* **moped, moping.** be in low spirits.

mo'ped, *n.* motorized bicycle.

mop'pet, *n.* child.

mo·raine' (-rān'), *n.* mass of stone, etc., left by glacier.

mor'al, *adj.* 1. of or concerned with right conduct. 2. virtuous. —*n.* 3. (*pl.*) principles of conduct. 4. moral lesson. —**mor'al·ist,** *n.* —**mor'al·is'tic,** *adj.*

mo·rale', *n.* spirits; mood.

mo·ral'i·ty, *n.* **1.** conformity to rules of right conduct. **2.** moral quality.

mor'al·ize', *v.,* **-ized, -izing.** think or pronounce on moral questions.

mor'al·ly, *adv.* **1.** according to morals. **2.** in one's honest belief.

mo·rass', *n.* swamp.

mor·a·to'ri·um, *n., pl.* **-ria, -riums. 1.** legal permission to delay payment of debts. **2.** any temporary cessation.

mor'bid, *adj.* **1.** unwholesome. **2.** of disease. **—mor·bid'i·ty,** *n.* **—mor'bid·ly,** *adv.*

mor'dant, *adj.* **1.** sarcastic; biting. **2.** burning; corrosive.

more, *adj.* **1.** in greater amount or degree. **2.** additional. *—n.* **3.** additional or greater quantity or degree. *—adv.* **4.** in addition.

more·o'ver, *adv.* besides.

mo'res (môr'āz), *n.pl.* social and moral customs of group.

mor·ga·nat'ic, *n.* designating marriage between royal person and commoner.

morgue, *n.* place where corpses are taken for identification.

mor'i·bund', *adj.* dying.

Mor'mon·ism, *n.* religion founded in U.S. in 1830. **—Mor'mon,** *n., adj.*

morn, *n.* morning.

morn'ing, *n.* **1.** first part of day. *—adj.* **2.** done, or occurring, in the morning.

morn'ing-glo'ry, *n., pl.* **-ries.** vine with funnel-shaped flowers.

morning sickness, nausea occurring early in the day during the first months of pregnancy.

mo·roc'co, *n.* fine leather.

mo'ron, *n.* stupid person. **—mo·ron'ic,** *adj.*

mo·rose', *adj.* gloomily ill-humored. **—mo·rose'ly,** *adv.* **—mo·rose'ness,** *n.*

Mor'phe·us, *n.* classical god of dreams.

mor'phine (-fēn), *n.* narcotic found in opium.

mor·phol'o·gy (môr fol'ə jē), *n.* **1.** branch of biology dealing with form and structure of organisms. **2.** form and structure of an organism.

mor'row, *n. Poetic.* the next day.

Morse, *n.* telegraphic code of long and short signals.

mor'sel, *n.* small amount.

mor'tal, *adj.* **1.** liable to death. **2.** causing death. **3.** to death. *—n.* **4.** human being. **—mor'tal·ly,** *adv.*

mor·tal'i·ty, *n., pl.* **-ties. 1.** mortal nature. **2.** relative death rate.

mor'tar, *n.* **1.** bowl in which drugs, etc., are pulverized. **2.** short cannon. **3.** material used to bind masonry.

mort'gage (môr'-), *n., v.,* **-gaged, -gaging.** *—n.* **1.** conditional transfer of property as security for debt. *—v.* **2.** put mortgage on. **—mort'ga·gee',** *v.* **—mort'ga·gor,** *n.*

mor·ti'cian, *n.* undertaker.

mor'ti·fy', *v.,* **-fied, -fying. 1.** humiliate. **2.** subject (body) to austerity. **—mor'ti·fi·ca'tion,** *n.*

mor'tise, *n., v.,* **-tised, -tising.** *—n.* **1.** slot in wood for tenon. *—v.* **2.** fasten by mortise.

mor'tu·ar'y (-chōo-), *n., pl.* **-aries.** place where bodies are prepared for burial.

mo·sa'ic, *n.* design made of small pieces of colored stone, glass, etc.

mo'sey, *v. Informal.* stroll.

Mos'lem, *n., adj.* Muslim.

mosque (mosk), *n.* Muslim place of prayer.

mos·qui'to, *n., pl.* **-toes, -tos.** common biting insect.

moss, *n.* small, leafy-stemmed plant growing on rocks, etc. *—v.* **2.** cover with moss. **—moss'y,** *adj.*

most, *adj.* **1.** in greatest amount. **2.** majority of. *—n.* **3.** greatest quantity. *—adv.* **4.** to greatest extent.

most'ly, *adv.* **1.** in most cases. **2.** in greater part.

mote, *n.* small particle.

mo·tel', *n.* roadside hotel for automobile travelers.

moth, *n.* insect, some of whose larvae eat cloth.

moth'ball', *n.* ball of camphor, etc., for repelling moths.

moth'er, *n.* **1.** female parent. **2.** head of group of nuns. **3.** stringy substance forming on fermenting liquids. *—adj.* **4.** of, like, or being mother. **5.** native. *—v.* **6.** act as or like mother to. **—moth'er·hood',** *n.* **—moth'er·ly,** *adj.*

moth'er-in-law', *n., pl.* **mothers-in-law.** mother of one's spouse.

moth'er·land', *n.* **1.** one's native land. **2.** land of one's ancestors.

moth'er-of-pearl', *n.* inner layer of certain shells.

mo·tif' (-tēf'), *n.* recurring subject or theme.

mo'tile (mōt'l, mō'til), *adj. Biology.* capable of moving spontaneously. **—mo·til'i·ty,** *n.*

mo'tion, *n.* **1.** process of changing position. **2.** action or power of movement. **3.** formal proposal made in meeting. *—v.* **4.** indicate by gesture. **—mo'tion·less,** *adj.*

motion picture, series of photographs projected so rapidly that objects seem to be moving.

mo·ti·vate, v., -vated, -vating. give motive to. —**mo'ti·va'tion**, n.

mo·tive, n. 1. purpose; goal. —adj. 2. of or causing motion.

mot'ley, adj. widely, often grotesquely, varied.

mo'tor, n. 1. small, powerful engine. —adj. 2. of or causing motion. 3. of or operated by motor. —v. 4. travel by automobile.

mo'tor·boat', n. boat run by motor.

mo'tor·cade', n. procession of automobiles.

mo'tor·car', n. automobile.

mo'tor·cy'cle, n. heavy motor-driven bicycle.

mo'tor·ist, n. automobile driver.

mo'tor·ize', v., -ized, -izing. furnish with motors or motor-driven vehicles.

mot'tle, v., -tled, -tling. mark with spots or blotches.

mot'to, n., pl. -toes, -tos. phrase expressing one's guiding principle.

mould, n. mold.

mould'er, v. molder.

moult, v., n. molt.

mound, n. heap of earth; hill.

mount, v. 1. go up; get on; rise. 2. prepare for use or display. 3. fix in setting. —n. 4. act or manner of mounting. 5. horse for riding. 6. Also, **mounting**, support, setting, etc. 7. hill.

moun'tain, n. lofty natural elevation on earth's surface. —**moun'tain·ous**, adj.

mountain bike, bicycle designed for off-road use, usu. having smaller frame and wider tires.

moun·tain·eer', n. 1. mountain climber. 2. dweller in mountains. —**moun'tain·eer'ing**, n.

mountain lion, cougar.

moun'te·bank', n. charlatan.

mourn, v. grieve; feel or express sorrow (for). —**mourn'er**, n. —**mourn'ful**, adj. —**mourn'ing**, n.

mouse, n., pl. **mice**, v., **moused**, **mousing**. —n. 1. small gray rodent. 2. palm-sized device used to select items on computer screen. —v. (mouz). 3. hunt for mice.

mousse (mōōs), n. 1. frothy dessert. 2. foamy preparation used to style hair.

mous·tache', n. mustache.

mous'y, adj., **mousier**, **mousiest**. drably quiet in manner or appearance. —**mous'i·ness**, n.

mouth, n., adj., v. —n. 1. opening through which animal takes in food. 2. any opening. —v. 3. utter pompously or dishonestly. —**mouth'ful**, n.

mouth organ, harmonica.

mouth'piece', n. 1. piece at or forming mouth. 2. person, newspaper, etc., speaking for others.

mouth'-wa'tering, adj. appetizing, as in appearance or aroma.

move, v., **moved**, **moving**, n. —v. 1. change place or position. 2. change one's abode. 3. advance. 4. make formal proposal in meeting. 5. affect emotionally. —n. 6. act of moving. 7. purposeful action. —**mov·a·ble**, adj., n. —**mov'er**, n.

move'ment, n. 1. act or process of moving. 2. trend in thought. 3. works of mechanism. 4. principal division of piece of music.

moving picture, motion picture. Also, **mov'ie**.

mow, v., **mowed**, **mowed** or **mown**, **mowing**, n. (mō). 1. cut (grass, etc.). 2. kill indiscriminately. —n. (mou). 3. place in barn where hay, etc., are stored. —**mow'er**, n.

moz·za·rel'la (mot's rel'lä, mōt'-), n. mild, white semisoft cheese.

Mr. (mis'tər), pl. **Messrs.** (mes'ərz) mister; title of address for man.

MRI, magnetic resonance imaging: process of producing images of the body using strong magnetic field and low-energy radio waves.

Mrs. (mis'iz, miz'iz), pl. **Mmes.** (mā däm', -dam') title of address for married woman.

Ms. (miz), title of address for woman not to be distinguished as married or unmarried.

much, adj. 1. in great quantity or degree. —n. 2. great quantity. 3. notable thing. —adv. 4. greatly. 5. generally.

mu'ci·lage, n. gummy adhesive. —**mu·ci·lag'i·nous**, adj.

muck, n. 1. filth. 2. moist barn refuse. —**muck'y**, adj.

muck'rake', v., -raked, -raking. expose scandal. —**muck'rak'er**, n.

mu'cous (-kəs), adj. 1. secreting mucus. 2. of like mucus.

mucous membrane, membrane lining internal surface of organ.

mu'cus, n. sticky secretion of mucous membrane.

mud, n. 1. wet soft earth. 2. scandalous or malicious statements or information. —**mud'dy**, adj., v.

mud'dle, v., -dled, -dling. —v. 1. mix up; confuse. —n. 2. confusion.

mu·ez'zin (myōō ez'in, moo-), n. crier who summons Muslims to prayer.

muff, n. 1. tubular covering of fur, etc., for hands. —v. 2. bungle. 3. drop (ball) after catching.

muf′fin, *n.* small round bread.

muf′fle, *v.,* **-fled, -fling,** *n.* —*v.* 1. wrap in scarf, cloak, etc. 2. deaden (sound). —*n.* 3. something that muffles.

muf′fler, *n.* 1. heavy neck scarf. 2. device for deadening sound, as on engine.

muf′ti, *n.* civilian dress.

mug, *n., v.,* **mugged, mugging.** —*n.* 1. drinking cup. 2. *Slang.* face. —*v.* 3. assault, usually with intent to rob. 4. *Slang.* grimace. —**mug′ger,** *n.*

mug′gy, *adj.,* **-gier, -giest.** hot and humid.

mug shot, photograph of the face of a criminal suspect.

Mu•ham′mad, *n.* founder of Islam, A.D. 570–632.

mu•lat′to, *n., pl.* **-toes.** 1. person with one white and one black parent. 2. person with mixed black and white ancestry.

mul′ber•ry, *n., pl.* **-ries.** tree, the leaves of some of whose species are used as food by silkworms.

mulch, *n.* 1. loose covering of leaves, straw, etc., on plants. —*v.* 2. surround with mulch.

mulct (mulkt), *v.* 1. deprive of by trickery. 2. fine.

mule, *n.* 1. offspring of donkey and mare. 2. woman's house slipper.

mul′ish, *adj.* obstinate.

mull, *v.* 1. study or ruminate (over). 2. heat and spice.

mul′lah, *n.* Muslim religious teacher.

mul•lein (-in), *n.* tall, woolly-leaved weed.

mul′let, *n.* common food fish.

mul′li•gan, *n.* stew of meat and vegetables.

mul•ti•far′i•ous, *adj.* many and varied.

mul•ti•na′tion•al, *n.* 1. corporation with operations in many countries. —*adj.* 2. pertaining to several nations or multinationals.

mul′ti•ple, *adj.* 1. consisting of or involving many. —*n.* 2. number evenly divisible by stated other number.

mul•ti•pli•cand′, *n.* number to be multiplied by another.

mul•ti•plic′i•ty, *n., pl.* **-ties.** great number or variety.

mul′ti•ply, *v.,* **-plied, -plying.** 1. increase the number of. 2. add (number) to itself a stated number of times. —**mul′ti•pli′er,** *n.* —**mul′ti•pli•ca′tion,** *n.*

mul′ti•tude, *n.* great number.

mul•ti•tu′di•nous, *adj.* 1. numerous. 2. having many parts.

mum, *adj.* silent.

mum′ble, *v.,* **-bled, -bling,** *n.* —*v.* 1. speak quietly and unintelligibly. —*n.* 2. mumbling sound.

mum′bo jum′bo, 1. strange ritual. 2. senseless language.

mum′mer, *n.* 1. person in festive disguise. 2. actor.

mum′mer•y, *n., pl.* **-meries.** mere show.

mum′my, *n., pl.* **-mies.** dead body treated to prevent decay.

mumps, *n.pl.* infectious disease marked by swelling of salivary glands.

munch, *v.* chew.

mun•dane′, *adj.* commonplace.

mu•nic′i•pal, *adj.* of a city.

mu•nic′i•pal′i•ty, *n., pl.* **-ties.** self-governing city.

mu•nif′i•cent, *adj.* extremely generous. —**mu•nif′i•cence,** *n.* —**mu•nif′i•cent•ly,** *adv.*

mu•ni′tions, *n.* weapons and ammunition used in war.

mu′ral, *n.* 1. picture painted on wall. —*v.* 2. of walls.

mur′der, *n.* 1. unlawful willful killing. —*v.* 2. commit murder. —**mur′der•er,** *n.* —**mur′der•ess,** *n.fem.* —**mur′der•ous,** *adj.*

murk, *n.* darkness.

murk′y, *adj.,* **murkier, murkiest.** dark and gloomy. —**murk′i•ness,** *n.*

mur′mur, *n.* 1. low, continuous, indistinct sound. 2. complaint. —*v.* 3. speak softly or indistinctly. 4. complain.

mur′rain (mûr′in), *n.* disease of cattle.

mus′ca•dine, *n.* American grape.

mus′cat, *n.* sweet grape.

mus•ca•tel′, *n.* wine made from muscat grapes.

mus′cle, *n., v.,* **-cled, -cling.** —*n.* 1. bundle of fibers in animal body that contract to produce motion. 2. brawn. —*v.* 3. *Informal.* force one's way. —**mus′cu•lar,** *adj.*

muscular dys′tro•phy (dis′tra fē), hereditary disease characterized by gradual wasting of muscles.

muse, *v.,* **mused, musing.** 1. reflect quietly. 2. say or think meditatively.

Muse, *n.* one of nine goddesses of the arts.

mu•se′um, *n.* place for permanent public exhibits.

mush, *n.* 1. meal boiled in water until thick, used as food. 2. anything soft. 3. *Informal.* maudlin sentiment. —*v.* 4. travel on foot, esp. over snow with dog team. —**mush′y,** *adj.*

mush′room, *n.* 1. fleshy fungus, usually umbrella-shaped, sometimes edible. —*adj.* 2. growing rapidly. —*v.* 3. grow quickly.

mu'sic, *n.* 1. art of arranging sounds for effect by rhythm, melody, etc. 2. score of musical composition. —**mu·si'cian,** *n.*

mus'i·cal, *adj.* 1. of music. 2. pleasant-sounding. 3. sensitive to or skilled in music. —*n.* 4. Also, **mus'ical com'e·dy,** a play with music. —**mus·i·cal·ly,** *adv.*

mu·si·col'o·gy, *n.* scholarly or scientific study of music. —**mu'si·col'o·gist,** *n.*

music video, videotape featuring dramatized rendition of popular song.

musk, *n.* animal secretion, used in perfume. —**musk'y,** *adj.*

mus'ket, *n.* early rifle.

mus·ket·eer', *n.* soldier armed with musket.

musk·mel'on, *n.* sweet edible melon.

musk'rat', *n.* large aquatic American rodent.

Mus'lim (muz'-), *n.* 1. follower of Islam. —*adj.* 2. of or pertaining to Islam.

mus'lin, *n.* plain-weave cotton fabric.

muss, *Informal.* —*n.* 1. disorder; mess. —*v.* 2. rumple. —**muss'y,** *adj.*

mus'sel, *n.* bivalve mollusk, sometimes edible.

must, *aux. v.* 1. be obliged to. 2. may be assumed to. —*adj.* 3. necessary. —*n.* 4. anything necessary. 5. new wine not yet fermented.

mus'tache, *n.* hair growing on upper lip. Also, **mus·ta'chio** (-shō).

mus'tang, *n.* small wild horse of western U.S.

mus'tard, *n.* pungent yellow powder made from seeds of mustard plant.

mus'ter, *v.* 1. assemble, as troops; gather. —*n.* 2. assembly.

mus'ty, *adj.* **-tier, -tiest.** stale-smelling. —**mus'ti·ness,** *n.*

mu'ta·ble, *adj.* subject to change. —**mu·ta·bil'i·ty,** *n.*

mu'tant (myōō'nt), *n.* 1. organism resulting from mutation. —*adj.* 2. undergoing or resulting from mutation.

mu'tate (myōō'tāt), *v.* **-tated, -tating.** change or cause to change.

mu·ta'tion, *n.* 1. sudden change in genetic characteristic. 2. individual or species characterized by such change. 3. change.

mute, *adj.,* **muter, mutest,** *n., v.,* **muted, muting.** —*adj.* 1. silent. 2. in-

capable of speech. —*n.* 3. person unable to utter words. 4. device for muffling musical instrument. —*v.* 5. deaden sound of.

mu'ti·late, *v.,* **-lated, -lating.** injure by depriving of or damaging part. —**mu'ti·la'tion,** *n.*

mu'ti·ny, *n., pl.* **-nies,** *v.,* **-nied, -nying.** revolt against lawful authority. —**mu'ti·neer',** *n.* —**mu'ti·nous,** *adj.*

mutt, *n. Slang.* mongrel dog.

mut'ter, *v.* 1. speak low and indistinctly; grumble. —*n.* 2. act or sound of muttering.

mut'ton, *n.* flesh of sheep, used as food.

mu'tu·al (-chōō-), *adj.* 1. done, etc., by two or more in relation to each other; reciprocal. 2. common. —**mu'tu·al·ly,** *adv.*

muz'zle, *n., v.,* **-zled, -zling.** —*n.* 1. mouth of firearm. 2. mouth part of animal's head. 3. cage for this. —*v.* 4. put muzzle on. 5. silence; gag.

my, *pron.* possessive form of I used before noun.

my'na, *n.* Asiatic bird sometimes taught to talk.

my·o'pi·a, *n.* near-sightedness. —**my·op'ic,** *adj.*

myr'i·ad, *n., adj.* 1. very great number. 2. ten thousand.

myr'i·a·pod', *n.* many-legged worm.

myrrh (mûr), *n.* aromatic substance from certain plants.

myr'tle, *n.* 1. evergreen shrub. 2. periwinkle (def. 2).

my·self', *pron., pl.* **ourselves.** 1. intensive form of I or me. 2. reflexive form of me.

mys'ter·y, *n., pl.* **-teries.** 1. anything secret, unknown, or unexplained. 2. obscurity. 3. secret rite. —**mys·te'ri·ous,** *adj.* —**mys·te'ri·ous·ly,** *adv.*

mys'tic, *adj.* Also, **mys'ti·cal.** 1. mysterious or occult. 2. spiritual. —*n.* 3. believer in mysticism.

mys'ti·cism, *n.* doctrine of direct spiritual intuition of God, truth, etc.

mys'ti·fy, *v.,* **-fied, -fying.** bewilder purposely. —**mys'ti·fi·ca'tion,** *n.*

mys·tique' (mi stēk'), *n.* aura of mystery or power.

myth, *n.* 1. legendary story, person, etc. 2. false popular belief. —**myth'i·cal, myth'ic,** *adj.* —**myth'i·cal·ly,** *adv.*

my·thol'o·gy, *n., pl.* **-gies.** body of myths. —**myth·o·log'i·cal,** *adj.*

N

N, n, *n.* fourteenth letter of English alphabet.

nab, *v.,* **nabbed, nabbing.** *Informal.* seize; arrest.

na'bob, *n.* wealthy, influential, or powerful person.

na·celle' (-sel'), *n.* enclosed shelter for aircraft engine.

na'cre (nā'kər), *n.* mother-of-pearl. **—na'cre·ous,** *adj.*

na'dir (nā'dər), *n.* **1.** lowest point. **2.** point of celestial sphere directly below given point.

nag, *v.,* **nagged, nagging,** *n.* **—v. 1.** scold constantly. **—n. 2.** person who nags. **3.** old horse.

nai'ad (nā'ad), *n.* water nymph.

nail, *n.* **1.** slender piece of metal for holding pieces of wood together. **2.** horny plate at end of finger or toe. **—v. 3.** fasten with nails. **4.** *Informal.* secure or seize.

na·ive' (nä ēv'), *adj.* **1.** simple; unsophisticated. Also, **na·ïve'.**

na·ive·té' (-tā'), *n.* artless simplicity. Also, **na·ïve·té'.**

na'ked, *adj.* **1.** without clothing or covering. **2.** (of eye) unassisted in seeing. **3.** plain. **—na'ked·ness,** *n.*

name, *n., v.,* **named, naming. —n. 1.** word or words by which a person, place, or thing is designated. **2.** reputation. **3.** behalf or authority. **—v. 4.** give name to. **5.** specify. **6.** appoint. **—nam'a·ble, na'me·a·ble,** *adj.* **—nam'er,** *n.* **—name'less,** *adj.*

name'ly, *adv.* that is to say.

name'sake, *n.* one having same name as another.

nan'ny, *n., pl.* **-nies.** child's nursemaid.

nanny goat, female goat.

nap, *n., v.,* **napped, napping. —n. 1.** short sleep. **2.** short, fuzzy fibers on the surface of cloth. **—v. 3.** raise fuzz on. **4.** have short sleep.

na'palm (nā'pām), *n.* **1.** highly incendiary jellylike substance used in bombs, etc. **—v. 2.** bomb or attack with napalm.

nape, *n.* back of neck.

naph'tha (naf'-), *n.* petroleum derivative, used as solvent, fuel, etc.

naph'tha·lene (naf'-), *n.* white crystalline substance used in mothballs, etc.

nap'kin, *n.* piece of cloth or paper used at table to wipe lips or fingers.

narc (närk), *n. Slang.* government narcotics agent.

nar·cis'sism, *n.* excessive admiration of oneself. **—nar'cis·sis'tic,** *adj.*

nar·cis'sus, *n.* spring-blooming plant, as daffodil or jonquil.

nar·cot'ic, *adj.* **1.** sleep-inducing. **—n. 2.** substance that dulls pain, induces sleep, etc. **3.** addictive drug, esp. an illegal one.

nar'rate, *v.,* **-rated, -rating.** tell. **—nar·ra'tion,** *n.* **—nar'ra·tor,** *n.*

nar'ra·tive, *n.* **1.** story of events. **—adj. 2.** that narrates. **3.** of narration.

nar'row, *adj.* **1.** not broad or wide. **2.** literal or strict in interpreting rules, etc. **3.** minute. **—v. 4.** make or become narrow. **—n. 5.** narrow place, thing, etc. **—nar'row-mind'ed,** *adj.*

nar'whal (-wəl), *n.* Arctic whale.

NASA (nas'ə), *n.* National Aeronautics and Space Administration.

na'sal, *adj.* **1.** of noses. **2.** spoken through nose. **—n. 3.** nasal sound. **—na'sal·ly,** *adv.*

nas'cent (nas'ənt, nā'sənt), *adj.* beginning to exist or develop. **—nas'cence,** *n.*

na·stur'tium, *n.* garden plant with yellow, orange, and red flowers.

nas'ty, *adj.,* **-tier, -tiest. 1.** disgustingly unclean. **2.** objectionable. **—nas'ti·ly,** *adv.* **—nas'ti·ness,** *n.*

na'tal, *adj.* of one's birth.

na'tion, *n.* **1.** people living in one territory under same government. **2.** people related by tradition or ancestry. **—na'tion·al,** *adj.,* *n.* **—na'tion·al·ly,** *adv.*

na'tion·al·ism, *n.* devotion to one's nation. **—na'tion·al·ist,** *n., adj.* **—na'tion·al·is'tic,** *adj.*

na'tion·al'i·ty, *n., pl.* **-ties. 1.** condition of being member of a nation. **2.** nation.

na'tion·al·ize, *v.,* **-ized, -izing.** bring under national control or ownership. **—na'tion·al·i·za'tion,** *n.*

na'tion·wide', *adj., adv.* across entire nation.

na'tive, *adj.* **1.** belonging to by birth, nationality, or nature. **2.** of natives. **3.** being the place of origin of a person or thing. **—n. 4.** person, animal, or plant native to region.

na·tiv'i·ty, *n., pl.* **-ties.** birth.

NATO (nā'tō), *n.* North Atlantic Treaty Organization.

nat'ty, *adj.,* **-tier, -tiest.** smart; trim.

nat'u·ral, *adj.* **1.** of, existing in, or formed by nature. **2.** to be expected in circumstances. **3.** without affectation.

4. *Music.* neither sharp nor flat. —**nat'u·ral·ly,** *adv.* —**nat'u·ral·ness,** *n.*

nat'u·ral·ism, *n.* artistic or literary style that represents objects or events as they occur in nature or real life. —**nat'u·ral·is'tic,** *adj.*

nat'u·ral·ist, *n.* 1. student of nature. 2. adherent of naturalism.

nat'u·ral·ize', *v.,* **-ized, -izing.** 1. confer citizenship upon. 2. introduce to region. —**nat'u·ral·i·za'tion,** *n.*

na'ture, *n.* 1. material world. 2. universe. 3. character of person or thing.

naught, *n.* zero.

naugh'ty, *adj.,* **-tier, -tiest.** 1. disobedient; bad. 2. improper. —**naugh'ti·ly,** *adv.* —**naugh'ti·ness,** *n.*

nau'sea (nô'sha), *n.* 1. feeling of impending vomiting. 2. disgust. —**nau'se·ate',** *v.* —**nau'seous,** *adj.*

nau'ti·cal, *adj.* of ships, sailors, or navigation.

nau'ti·lus, *n.* mollusk having pearly shell.

na'val, *adj.* of ships or navy.

nave, *n.* main lengthwise part of church.

na'vel, *n.* pit in center surface of belly.

nav'i·gate', *v.,* **-gated, -gating.** 1. traverse (water or air). 2. direct on a course. —**nav'i·ga'tion,** *n.* —**nav'i·ga'tor,** *n.* —**nav'i·ga·ble,** *adj.*

na'vy, *n., pl.* **-vies.** all of a nation's warships, with their crews.

nay, *adv.,* *n.* no.

Na'zi (nä'tsē), *n.* member of the National Socialist party in Germany, headed by Adolf Hitler. —**Na'zism,** *n.*

neap tide, tide having lowest high point.

near, *adv.* 1. close by. —*adj.* 2. close. 3. intimate. —*v.* 4. approach. —**near'ness,** *n.*

near'by', *adj., adv.* close by.

near'ly, *adv.* almost; in close agreement.

near'sight'ed, *adj.* seeing distinctly only at short distance. —**near'-sight'ed·ness,** *n.*

neat, *adj.* 1. orderly. 2. skillful. 3. undiluted. —**neat'ly,** *adv.* —**neat'ness,** *n.*

neb, *n.* bill or beak.

neb'u·la, *n., pl.* **-lae** (-lē'), **-las.** luminous mass of gas or far-distant stars. —**neb'u·lar,** *adj.*

neb'u·lous, *adj.* 1. hazy; vague. 2. cloudlike.

nec'es·sar'y, *adj., n., pl.* **-saries.** —*adj.* 1. that cannot be dispensed with. 2. required by facts or reason;

unavoidable. —*n.* 3. something necessary. —**nec'es·sar'i·ly,** *adv.*

ne·ces'si·tate', *v.,* **-tated, -tating.** make necessary.

ne·ces'si·ty, *n., pl.* **-ties.** 1. something necessary. 2. fact of being necessary. 3. poverty.

neck, *n.* 1. part connecting head and trunk. —*v.* 2. *Slang.* play amorously.

neck'er·chief, *n.* cloth worn around neck.

neck'lace, *n.* ornament of gems, etc., worn around neck.

neck'tie', *n.* cloth strip worn under collar and tied in front.

ne·crol'o·gy, *n., pl.* **-gies.** list of persons who have died.

nec'ro·man'cy, *n.* magic. —**nec'ro·manc'er,** *n.*

ne·cro'sis, *n.* death of tissue or of organ.

nec'tar, *n.* 1. sweet secretion of flower. 2. drink of gods.

nec'tar·ine', *n.* downless peach.

nee (nā), *adj.* (of woman) born; having as maiden name. Also, **née.**

need, *n.* 1. requirement. 2. condition marked by necessity, as poverty. —*v.* 3. depend absolutely or strongly. 4. be obliged. —**need'ful,** *adj.* —**need'less,** *adj.*

nee'dle, *n., v.,* **-dled, -dling.** —*n.* 1. slender pointed implement for sewing, knitting, etc. 2. anything similar, as indicator or gauge. 3. hypodermic syringe. —*v.* 4. prod; tease.

nee'dle·point', *n.* embroidery on canvas.

nee'dle·work', *n.* art or product of working with a needle, esp. in embroidery.

needs, *adv.* necessarily.

need'y, *adj.,* **needier, neediest.** very poor. —**need'i·ness,** *n.*

ne'er'-do-well', *n.* person who habitually fails.

ne·far'i·ous, *adj.* wicked.

ne·gate', *v.,* **-gated, -gating.** deny; nullify. —**ne·ga'tion,** *n.*

neg'a·tive, *adj.* 1. expressing denial or refusal. 2. undistinguished. 3. *Math.* minus. 4. *Photog.* having light and shade reversed. —*n.* 5. negative statement, etc. 6. *Photog.* negative image. —**neg'a·tive·ly,** *adv.*

ne·glect', *v.* 1. disregard; fail to do. —*n.* 2. disregard; negligence. —**ne·glect'ful,** *adj.*

neg'li·gee' (-zhā'), *n.* woman's house robe.

neg'li·gent, *adj.* neglectful. —**neg'li·gence,** *n.*

neg'li·gi·ble, *adj.* unimportant.

ne·go'ti·a·ble (-shē-), *adj.* transferable, as securities. —**ne·go·ti·a·bil·i·ty,** *n.*

ne·go·ti·ate (-shē āt′), *v.*, **-ated, -ating.** 1. deal with; bargain. 2. dispose of. —**ne·go·ti·a′tion,** *n.* —**ne·go′ti·a′tor,** *n.*

Ne′gro, *n., pl.* **-groes.** member of racial group having brown to black skin; a black. —**Ne′gro,** *adj.* —**Ne′groid,** *adj.*

neigh, *n.* 1. cry of horse; whinny. —*v.* 2. make cry of horse.

neigh′bor, *n.* 1. person or thing near another. —*v.* 2. be near. —**neigh′bor·ly,** *adj.*

neigh′bor·hood, *n.* 1. surrounding area. 2. district having separate identity.

nei′ther (nē′ᵺ ər, nī′ᵺ ər), *conj., adj.* not either.

nem′e·sis, *n., pl.* **-ses.** cause of one's downfall.

Ne′o·lith′ic, *adj.* of the later Stone Age.

ne·ol′o·gism (-jiz′əm), *n.* new word or phrase.

ne′on, *n.* gas used in electrical signs.

ne′o·phyte′, *n.* beginner.

neph′ew, *n.* son of one's brother or sister.

ne·phri′tis, *n.* inflammation of the kidneys. —**ne·phrit′ic** (-frit′ik), *adj.*

nep′o·tism, *n.* official favoritism toward one's relatives.

nerd, *n. Slang.* 1. dull, ineffectual, or unattractive person. 2. person devoted to nonsocial pursuit.

nerve, *n., v.,* **nerved, nerving.** —*n.* 1. bundle of fiber that conveys impulses between brain and other parts of body. 2. courage. 3. *Informal.* presumption. 4. (*pl.*) anxiety; unease. —*v.* 5. give courage to.

nerve gas, poison gas that interferes with nerve functions, respiration, etc.

nerv′ous, *adj.* 1. of nerves. 2. having or caused by disordered nerves. 3. anxious; uneasy. —**nerv′ous·ly,** *adv.* —**nerv′ous·ness,** *n.*

nerv′y, *adj.,* **nervier, nerviest.** *Informal.* presumptuous.

nest, *n.* 1. place used by bird or other creature for rearing its young. 2. group of things fitting tightly together. —*v.* 3. settle in nest. 4. fit one within another.

nest egg, money saved for emergencies, retirement, etc.

nes′tle, *v.,* **-tled, -tling.** lie close and snug.

net, *adj., n., v.,* **netted, netting.** —*adj.* 1. exclusive of loss, expense, etc. —*n.* 2. net profit. 3. Also, **net′ting.** lace-

like fabric of uniform mesh. 4. bag of such fabric. —*v.* 5. gain as clear profit. 6. cover with net. 7. ensnare.

neth′er, *adj.* lower. —**neth′er·most,** *adj.*

net′tle, *n., v.,* **-tled, -tling.** —*n.* 1. plant with stinging hairs. —*v.* 2. irritate; sting.

net′work′, *n.* 1. netlike combination. 2. group of associated radio or television stations, etc. 3. any system of interconnected elements. —*v.* 4. share information informally with others who have common interests.

neu′ral (nyŏŏr′əl), *adj.* of nerves or nervous system.

neu·ral′gia, *n.* sharp pain along nerve.

neu·ri′tis, *n.* inflammation of nerve. —**neu·rit′ic,** *adj.*

neu·rol′o·gy, *n.* study of nerves. —**neu·rol′o·gist,** *n.* —**neu′ro·log′i·cal,** *adj.*

neu′ron (nŏŏr′on, nyŏŏr′-), *n.* cell that is basic to nervous system.

neu·ro′sis, *n., pl.* **-ses.** psychoneurosis. —**neu·rot′ic,** *adj., n.*

neu′ter, *adj.* 1. neither male nor female. —*v.* 2. spay or castrate. —**neu′ter,** *n.*

neu′tral, *adj.* 1. taking no side in controversy. 2. not emphatic or positive. —*n.* 3. neutral person or state. —**neu·tral′i·ty,** *n.* —**neu′tral·ize′,** *v.* —**neu′tral·ly,** *adv.* —**neu′tral·i·za′tion,** *n.*

neu′tron, *n.* particle in nucleus of atom.

nev′er, *adv.* not ever.

nev′er·the·less′, *adv.* in spite of what has been said.

new, *adj.* 1. of recent origin or existence. 2. unfamiliar. —*adv.* 3. recently; freshly. —**new′ly,** *adv.* —**new′ness,** *n.*

new′el, *n.* post at the head or foot of stair.

New England, group of states in northeast U.S.

new′fan′gled, *adj.* of a new kind or fashion.

new′ly·wed′, *n.* newly married person.

news, *n.* report of recent event, situation, etc.

news′cast′, *n.* radio or television broadcast of news. —**news′cast′er,** *n.*

news′let′ter, *n.* small informative periodical for specialized group.

news′man′, *n.* journalist. Also, **news′wom′an,** *n.fem.*

news′pa′per, *n.* periodical containing

news, etc. —**news'pa'per•man'**, n. —**news'pa'per•wom'an**, n.fem.

news'print', n. paper on which newspapers are printed.

news'reel', n. motion picture of news events.

news'stand', n. sales booth for periodicals, etc.

news'wor'thy, adj. interesting enough to warrant press coverage. —**news'wor'thi•ness**, n.

newt, n. salamander.

new wave, movement that breaks with traditional values, etc.

new year, 1. (cap.) first day of year. **2.** year approaching.

next, adj. **1.** nearest after. —adv. **2.** in nearest place after. **3.** at first subsequent time.

next'-door', adj. in the next house, apartment, etc.

nex'us, n., pl. **nexus**. link or series.

ni'a•cin, n. nicotinic acid.

nib, n. **1.** beak of bird. **2.** pen point.

nib'ble, v., **-bled, -bling.** —v. **1.** bite off in small bits. —n. **2.** small morsel.

nib'lick, n. golf club.

nice, adj. **nicer, nicest. 1.** agreeable. **2.** precise. **3.** fastidious. —**nice'ly**, adv.

ni'ce•ty, n., pl. **-ties. 1.** subtle point. **2.** refinement.

niche (nich), n. **1.** recess in wall. **2.** proper role or vocation.

nick, n. **1.** notch or hollow place in surface. **2.** precise or opportune moment. —v. **3.** make nick in.

nick'el, n. **1.** hard silver-white metal. **2.** five-cent coin.

nick'el•o'de•on, n. **1.** early, cheap motion-picture house. **2.** coin-operated automatic piano, etc.

nick'name', n., v., **-named, -naming.** —n. **1.** name used informally. —v. **2.** give nickname to.

nic'o•tine' (-tēn'), n. alkaloid found in tobacco.

nic'o•tin'ic acid, vitamin from nicotine, used against pellagra.

niece, n. daughter of one's brother or sister.

nif'ty, adj., **-tier, -tiest.** Informal. smart; fine.

nig'gard•ly, adj. **1.** stingy. **2.** meanly small.

nigh, adv., adj. near.

night, n. period between sunset and sunrise.

night'cap', n. **1.** alcoholic drink taken at the end of an evening. **2.** cap worn while sleeping.

night'club', n. establishment open at night, offering food, drink, and entertainment.

night'fall', n. coming of night.

night'gown', n. gown for sleeping. Also, **night'dress'**.

night'hawk', n. nocturnal American bird.

night'in•gale', n. small European bird noted for male's song.

night'ly, adj., adv. every night.

night'mare', n. **1.** bad dream. **2.** harrowing event.

night owl, n. person who often stays up late at night.

night'shade', n. plant sometimes used in medicine.

night'shirt', n. loose shirtlike garment worn in bed.

ni'hil•ism (nī'ə liz'əm), n. total disbelief in principles. —**ni'hil•ist**, n. —**ni'hil•is'tic**, adj.

nil, n. nothing.

nim'ble, adj., **-bler, -blest.** agile; quick. —**nim'bly**, adv. —**nim'ble•ness**, n.

nim'bus, n., pl. **-bi** (-bī), **-buses. 1.** halo. **2.** rain cloud.

nim'rod, n. hunter.

nin'com•poop', n. fool.

nine, n., adj. eight plus one. —**ninth**, n., adj.

nine'pins', n.pl. bowling game played with nine wooden pins.

nine'teen', n., adj. ten plus nine. —**nine'teenth'**, n., adj.

nine'ty, n., adj. ten times nine. —**nine'ti•eth**, adj., n.

nin'ny, n., pl. **-nies.** fool.

nip, v., **nipped, nipping.** n. —v. **1.** pinch or bite. **2.** check growth of. **3.** affect sharply. **4.** sip. —n. **5.** pinch. **6.** biting quality. **7.** sip. —**nip'py**, adj.

nip and tuck, closely contested.

nip'ple, n. **1.** milk-discharging protuberance on breast. **2.** nipple-shaped object.

nir•va'na (nir vä'nə), n. **1.** (in Buddhism) freedom from all passion. **2.** state of bliss; salvation.

nit, n. egg of louse.

ni'ter, n. white salt used in gunpowder, etc. Also, **ni'tre**.

nit'-pick', v. Informal. argue or find fault pettily.

ni'trate, n. **1.** salt of nitric acid. **2.** fertilizer containing nitrates.

ni'tro•gen, n. colorless, odorless, tasteless gas, used in explosives, fertilizers, etc.

ni'tro•glyc'er•in, n. colorless, highly explosive oil.

ni'trous, adj. **1.** of niter. **2.** Also, **ni'tric.** containing nitrogen.

nit'ty-grit'ty, n. Slang. essentials of situation.

nit'wit', n. simpleton.

nix, adv. Informal. no.

no, adv., n., pl. **noes,** adj. —adv. **1.** word used to express dissent, denial, or refusal. —n. **2.** negative vote. —adj. **3.** not any.

no·bil'i·ty, n., pl. **-ties. 1.** noble class. **2.** noble quality.

no'ble, adj., **-bler, -blest,** n. —adj. **1.** of high rank by birth. **2.** admirable or magnificent. —n. **3.** person of noble rank. —**no'ble·man,** n. —**no'ble·wom'an,** n.fem. —**no'bly,** adv.

no'bod·y, n., pl. **-bodies. 1.** no one. **2.** one of no importance.

noc·tur'nal, adj. **1.** of night. **2.** occurring or active by night.

noc'turne, n. dreamy or pensive musical composition.

nod, v., **nodded, nodding,** n. —v. **1.** incline head briefly. **2.** become sleepy. **3.** sway gently. **4.** be absent-minded. —n. **5.** brief inclination of head, as in assent.

node, n. **1.** protuberance. **2.** difficulty. **3.** joint in plant stem.

nod'ule, n. small knob or lump. —**nod'u·lar,** adj.

no'-fault', adj. (of auto accident insurance, divorces, etc.) effective without establishing fault.

nog'gin, n. **1.** small mug. **2.** Informal. head.

noise, n., v., **noised, nois·ing.** —n. **1.** sound, esp. loud or harsh. —v. **2.** spread rumors. —**noise'less,** adj. —**nois'y,** adj. —**nois'i·ly,** adv. —**nois'i·ness,** n.

noi'some, adj. offensive or noxious.

no'mad, n. wanderer. —**no·mad'ic,** adj.

nom de plume (nom' də ploom'), name assumed by writer.

no'men·cla'ture (-klā'chər), n. set or system of names.

nom'i·nal, adj. **1.** in name only; so-called. **2.** trifling. —**nom'i·nal·ly,** adv.

nom'i·nate', v., **-nated, -nating. 1.** propose as candidate. **2.** appoint. —**nom'i·na'tion,** n. —**nom'i·na'tor,** n.

nom'i·na·tive, adj. **1.** denoting noun or pronoun used as the subject of a sentence. —n. **2.** nominative case.

nom'i·nee', n. one nominated.

non·a·ge·nar'i·an, n. person 90 to 99 years old.

nonce, n. present occasion.

non'cha·lant' (non'shə länt'), adj. **1.** coolly unconcerned. —**non'cha·lance',** n. —**non'cha·lant'ly,** adv.

non'com·mis'sioned, adj. Mil. not commissioned.

non'com·mit'tal, adj. not committing oneself. —**non'com·mit'tal·ly,** adv.

non' com·pos men'tis, Law. not of sound mind.

non·con·duc'tor, n. substance that does not readily conduct heat, electricity, etc.

non·con·form'ist, n. person who refuses to conform.

non·de·script', adj. of no particular kind.

none, pron. sing. and pl. **1.** not one; not any. —adv. **2.** in no way.

non·en'ti·ty, n., pl. **-ties. 1.** unimportant person or thing. **2.** nonexistent thing.

none'the·less', adv. nevertheless.

no'-no', n. Informal. forbidden thing.

non·pa·reil' (non'pə rel'), adj. **1.** having no equal. —n. **2.** person or thing without equal.

non·par'ti·san, adj. **1.** not taking sides. **2.** belonging to no party.

non·plus', v. puzzle completely.

non·prof'it, adj. not established for the purpose of making a profit.

non·sec·tar'i·an, adj. of no one sect. —**nonsectarian.**

non'sense, n. **1.** senseless or absurd words or action. **2.** anything useless. —**non·sen'si·cal,** adj.

non se'qui·tur, statement unrelated to preceding one.

non'stop', adj., adv. without intermediate stops. Also, **non-stop.**

non·sup·port', n. failure to provide financial support.

non·vi'o·lence, n. policy of refraining from using violence, as in political protest.

noo'dle, n. thin strip of dough, cooked in soup, etc.

nook, n. **1.** corner of room. **2.** secluded spot.

noon, n. 12 o'clock in daytime. —**noon'time',** n. —**noon'tide',** n.

no one, not anyone.

noose, n., v., **noosed, noosing.** —n. **1.** loop with running knot that pulls tight. —v. **2.** catch by noose.

nor, conj. or not: used with **neither.**

Nor'dic, n. person marked by tall stature, blond hair, and blue eyes. —**Nor'dic,** adj.

norm, n. standard.

nor'mal, adj. **1.** of standard type; usual. **2.** at right angles. —n. **3.** standard; average. **4.** perpendicular line. —**nor'mal·cy, nor·mal'i·ty,** n. —**nor'mal·ize',** v. —**nor'mal·i·za'tion,** n. —**nor'mal·ly,** adv.

normal school, school for training teachers.

north, n. **1.** cardinal point of compass,

on one's right facing the setting sun.
2. territory in or to north. —*adj.* 3. toward, in, or from north. —*adv.* 4. toward north. —**north'er•ly**, *adj.*, *adv.* —**north'ern**, *adj.* —**north'ern•er**, *n.* —**north'ward**, *adv.*

north•east', *n.* point or direction midway between north and east. —**north'east'**, *adj.*, *adv.* —**north'east'ern**, *adj.*

north•west', *n.* point or direction midway between north and west. —**north'west'**, *adj.*, *adv.* —**north'west'ern**, *adj.*

nose, *n.*, *v.*, **nosed, nosing.** —*n.* 1. part of head containing nostrils. 2. sense of smell. 3. projecting part. —*v.* 4. smell. 5. pry or head cautiously.

nose'dive', *n.* 1. downward plunge. —*v.* 2. go into a nosedive.

nose'gay', *n.* small bouquet.

nos•tal'gia, *n.* yearning for past. —**nos•tal'gic**, *adj.*

nos'tril, *n.* external opening of nose for breathing and smelling.

nos'trum, *n.* medicine allegedly having special powers.

nos'y, *adj.*, **nosier, nosiest.** *Informal.* unduly inquisitive. Also, **nos'ey.**

not, *adv.* word expressing negation, denial, or refusal.

no'ta•ble, *adj.* 1. worthy of note; important. —*n.* 2. prominent person. —**no'ta•bly**, *adv.*

no'ta•rize', *v.*, **-rized, -rizing.** authenticate by notary.

no'ta•ry, *n.*, *pl.* **-ries.** official authorized to verify documents. Also, **notary public.**

no•ta'tion, *n.* 1. note. 2. special symbol. —**no•ta'tion•al**, *adj.*

notch, *n.* 1. angular cut. —*v.* 2. make notch in.

note, *n.*, *v.*, **noted, noting.** —*n.* 1. brief record, comment, etc. 2. short letter. 3. importance. 4. notice. 5. paper promising payment. 6. musical sound or written symbols. —*v.* 7. write down. 8. notice. —**note'book'**, *n.*

not'ed, *adj.* famous.

note'wor'thy, *adj.* notable.

noth'ing, *n.* 1. not anything. 2. trivial action, thing, etc. —*adv.* 3. not at all.

no'tice, *n.*, *v.*, **-ticed, -ticing.** —*n.* 1. information; warning. 2. note, etc., that informs or warns. 3. attention; heed. —*v.* 4. pay attention to; perceive. 5. mention. —**no'tice•a•ble**, *adj.* —**no'tice•a•bly**, *adv.*

no'ti•fy', *v.*, **-fied, -fying.** give notice to. —**no'ti•fi•ca'tion**, *n.*

no'tion, *n.* 1. idea; conception. 2.

opinion. 3. whim. 4. (*pl.*) small items, as pins or threads.

no•to'ri•ous, *adj.* widely known, esp. unfavorably. —**no•to•ri'e•ty**, *n.*

not'with•stand'ing, *prep.* 1. in spite of. —*adv.* 2. nevertheless. —*conj.* 3. although.

nou'gat (nōō'gət), *n.* pastelike candy with nuts.

nought, *n.* naught.

noun, *n.* word denoting person, place, or thing.

nour'ish, *v.* sustain with food. —**nour'ish•ment**, *n.*

nov'el, *n.* 1. long fictitious narrative. —*adj.* 2. unfamiliar. —**nov'el•ist**, *n.*

nov'el•ty, *n.*, *pl.* **-ties.** 1. unfamiliarity. 2. unfamiliar or amusing thing.

No•vem'ber, *n.* eleventh month of year.

nov'ice, *n.* 1. beginner. 2. person just received into a religious order.

no•vi'ti•ate (-vish'ē it), *n.* probationary period in religious order.

No'vo•caine', *n. Trademark.* local anesthetic.

now, *adv.* 1. at present time. 2. immediately. —*conj.* 3. since. —*n.* 4. the present.

now'a•days', *adv.* in these times.

no'where', *adv.* not anywhere.

nox'ious, *adj.* harmful.

noz'zle, *n.* projecting spout.

nth (enth), *adj.* utmost.

nu'ance (nyoo'äns), *n.* shade of expression, etc.

nub, *n.* gist.

nu'bile (nyoo'bil, -bīl), *adj.* (of a young woman) 1. marriageable. 2. sexually developed and attractive.

nuclear energy, energy released by reactions within atomic nuclei, as in nuclear fission or fusion.

nuclear physics, branch of physics dealing with atoms.

nu'cle•us, *n.*, *pl.* **-clei, -cleuses.** 1. central part about which other parts are grouped. 2. central body of living cell. 3. central core of atom. —**nu'cle•ar**, *adj.*

nude, *adj.* 1. naked. —*n.* 2. naked human figure, esp. in art.

nudge, *v.*, **nudged, nudging**, *n.* —*v.* 1. push slightly. —*n.* 2. slight push.

nud'ism, *n.* practice of going naked for health. —**nud'ist**, *n.*

nu'ga•to'ry, *adj.* 1. trifling. 2. futile.

nug'get, *n.* lump.

nui'sance, *n.* annoying thing or person.

nuke, *n.*, *v.*, **nuked, nuking.** *Slang.*

—n. 1. nuclear weapon or power plant. —v. 2. attack with nuclear weapons.

null, adj. of no effect.

null'i•fy', v., **-fied, -fying. 1.** make null. 2. make legally void. —**nul'li•fi•ca'tion,** n.

numb, adj. 1. deprived of feeling or movement. —v. 2. make numb. —**numb'ness,** n.

num'ber, n. 1. sum of group of units. 2. numeral. 3. one of series or group. 4. large quantity. —v. 5. mark with number. 6. count. 7. amount to in numbers.

num'ber•less, adj. too numerous to count.

nu'mer•al, n. 1. word or sign expressing number. —adj. 2. of numbers.

nu'mer•ate', v., **-ated, -ating.** number; count. —**nu'mer•a'tion,** n.

nu'mer•a'tor, n. part of fraction written above the line, showing number to be divided.

nu•mer'i•cal, adj. of, denoting, or expressed by number. —**nu•mer'i•cal•ly,** adv.

nu'mer•ous, adj. very many.

nu'mis•mat'ics, n. science of coins and medals.

num'skull', n. Informal. dunce. Also, **numb'skull'.**

nun, n. woman living with religious group under strict vows.

nun'ci•o' (nun'shē ō'), n., pl. **-cios.** diplomatic representative of a Pope.

nun'ner•y, n., pl. **-neries.** convent.

nup'tial, adj. 1. of marriage. —n. 2. (pl.) marriage ceremony.

nurse, n., v., **nursed, nursing.** —n. 1. person who cares for sick or children. —v. 2. tend in sickness. 3. look after carefully. 4. suckle.

nurs'er•y, n., pl. **-eries. 1.** room set apart for young children. 2. place where young trees or plants are grown.

nursery school, school for children below kindergarten age.

nur'ture, v., **-tured, -turing,** n. —v. 1. feed and care for during growth. —n. 2. upbringing. 3. nourishment.

nut, n. 1. dry fruit consisting of edible kernel in shell. 2. the kernel. 3. perforated, threaded metal block used to screw on end of bolt, etc. —**nut'crack'er,** n. —**nut'shell',** n.

nut'meg, n. aromatic seed of East Indian tree.

nu'tri•a (nyoo'trē ə), n. fur resembling beaver.

nu'tri•ent, adj. 1. nourishing. —n. 2. nutrient substance.

nu'tri•ment, n. nourishment.

nu•tri'tion, n. 1. process of nourishing or being nourished. 2. study of dietary requirements. 3. process by which organism converts food into living tissue. —**nu•tri'tious,** nu'tri•tive, adj. —**nu•tri'tion•al,** adj. —**nu•tri'tion•ist,** n.

nuts, adj. Informal. crazy.

nut'ty, adj., **-tier, -tiest. 1.** tasting of or like nuts. 2. Informal. insane; senseless. —**nut'ti•ness,** n.

nuz'zle, v., **-zled, -zling. 1.** thrust nose (against). 2. cuddle.

ny'lon, n. 1. tough, elastic synthetic substance used for yarn, bristles, etc. 2. (pl.) stockings of nylon.

nymph, n. 1. beautiful goddess living in woodlands, waters, etc. 2. beautiful young woman.

nym'pho•ma'ni•a, n. uncontrollable sexual desire in women. —**nym'pho•ma'ni•ac',** n.

O

O, o, n. 1. fifteenth letter of English alphabet. —interj. 2. expression of surprise, gladness, pain, etc. 3. word used before name in archaic form of address.

o', prep. abbreviated form of **of.**

oaf, n. clumsy, rude person. —**oaf'ish,** adj.

oak, n. tree having hard wood. —**oak'en,** adj.

oa'kum, n. loose fiber used in calking seams.

oar, n. 1. flat-bladed shaft for rowing boat. —v. 2. row. —**oars'man,** n.

oar'lock', n. support on gunwale for oar.

o•a'sis, n., pl. **-ses.** fertile place in desert.

oat, n. cereal grass having edible seed.

oath, n. 1. solemn affirmation; vow. 2. curse.

oat'meal', n. 1. meal made from oats. 2. cooked breakfast food made from this.

ob'bli•ga'to (ob'li•gä'tō), n., pl. **-tos, -ti** (-tē). musical line performed by single instrument accompanying a solo part.

ob'du•rate, adj. stubborn; not sorry or penitent. —**ob'du•ra•cy,** n.

o•bei'sance (-bā'-), *n.* **1.** bow or curtsy. **2.** homage.

ob'e•lisk, *n.* tapering, four-sided monumental shaft.

o•bese' (ō bēs'), *adj.* very fat. —**o•bes'i•ty,** *n.*

o•bey', *v.* **1.** do as ordered by. **2.** respond to, as controls. —**o•be'di•ence,** *n.* —**o•be'di•ent,** *adj.* —**o•be'di•ent•ly,** *adv.*

ob•fus'cate (-fus'kāt), *v.,* **-cated, -cating.** confuse; make unclear. —**ob•fus•ca'tion,** *n.*

o•bit'u•ar•y, *n., pl.* **-aries.** notice of death.

ob'ject, *n.* **1.** something solid. **2.** thing or person to which attention is directed. **3.** end; motive. **4.** noun or pronoun that represents goal of action. —*v.* (əb jekt'). **5.** make protest. —**ob•jec'tion,** *n.* —**ob•jec'tor,** *n.*

ob•jec'tion•a•ble, *adj.* causing disapproval; offensive.

ob•jec'tive, *n.* **1.** something aimed at. **2.** objective case. —*adj.* **3.** real or factual. **4.** unbiased. **5.** being object of perception or thought. **6.** denoting word used as object of sentence. —**ob•jec'tive•ly,** *adv.* —**ob•jec•tiv'i•ty,** *n.*

ob'jur•gate, *v.,* **-gated, -gating.** scold. —**ob'jur•ga'tion,** *n.* —**ob•jur•ga•to•ry,** *adj.*

ob•late', *adj.* (of spheroid) flattened at poles.

ob•la'tion, *n.* offering; sacrifice.

ob'li•gate, *v.,* **-gated, -gating.** bind morally or legally. —**ob'li•ga'tion,** *n.* —**ob•lig'a•to•ry,** *adj.*

o•blige', *v.,* **obliged, obliging. 1.** require; bind. **2.** place under debt of gratitude.

o•blig'ing, *adj.* willing to help.

ob•lique' (ə blēk'), *adj.* **1.** slanting. **2.** indirect. —**ob•lique'ly,** *adv.* —**ob•liq'ui•ty,** *n.*

ob•lit'er•ate, *v.,* **-ated, -ating.** remove all traces of. —**ob•lit'er•a'tion,** *n.*

ob•liv'i•on, *n.* **1.** state of being forgotten. **2.** forgetfulness. —**ob•liv'i•ous,** *adj.*

ob'long, *adj.* **1.** longer than broad. —*n.* **2.** oblong rectangle.

ob'lo•quy, *n.* **1.** public disgrace. **2.** abuse.

ob•nox'ious, *adj.* offensive. —**ob•nox'ious•ly,** *adv.*

o'boe, *n.* wind instrument. —**o'bo•ist,** *n.*

ob•scene', *adj.* offensive to decency. —**ob•scene'ly,** *adv.* —**ob•scen'i•ty,** *n.*

ob•scu'rant•ism, *n.* willful obscuring

of something presented to public. —**ob•scu'rant•ist,** *n., adj.*

ob•scure', *adj. v.,* **-scured, -scuring.** —*adj.* **1.** not clear. **2.** not prominent. **3.** dark. —*v.* **4.** make obscure. —**ob•scu•ra'tion,** *n.* —**ob•scu'ri•ty,** *n.* —**ob•scure'ly,** *adv.*

ob•se'qui•ous, *adj.* servilely deferential.

ob'se•quy, *n., pl.* **-quies.** funeral rite.

ob•serv'ance, *n.* **1.** act of observing or conforming. **2.** due celebration. —**ob•serv'ant,** *adj.*

ob•serv'a•to•ry, *n., pl.* **-ries.** place equipped for observing stars, etc.

ob•serve', *v.,* **-served, -serving. 1.** see; notice; watch. **2.** remark. **3.** pay respect to or perform duly. —**ob'ser•va'tion,** *n.* —**ob•serv'er,** *n.*

ob•sess', *v.* be constantly in thoughts of. —**ob•ses'sion,** *n.* —**ob•ses'sive,** *adj.*

ob•sid'i•an (əb sid'ē ən), *n.* dark volcanic glass.

ob'so•les'cent (-les'ənt), *adj.* becoming obsolete. —**ob'so•les'cence,** *n.*

ob'so•lete', *adj.* no longer in use.

ob'sta•cle, *n.* something in the way.

ob•stet'rics, *n.* branch of medicine concerned with childbirth. —**ob•stet'ri•cian,** *n.* —**ob•stet'ric,** *adj.*

ob'sti•nate, *adj.* **1.** firm; stubborn. **2.** not yielding to treatment. —**ob'sti•na•cy,** *n.* —**ob'sti•nate•ly,** *adv.*

ob•strep'er•ous, *adj.* unruly.

ob•struct', *v.* block; hinder. —**ob•struc'tion,** *n.* —**ob•struc'tive,** *adj.* —**ob•struc'tion•ism,** *n.* perverse desire to be obstructive. —**ob•struc'tion•ist,** *n., adj.*

ob•tain', *v.* **1.** get or acquire. **2.** prevail. —**ob•tain'a•ble,** *adj.*

ob•trude', *v.,* **-truded, -truding.** thrust forward; intrude. —**ob•tru'sion,** *n.* —**ob•tru'sive,** *adj.*

ob•tuse', *adj.* **1.** blunt; not rounded. **2.** not perceptive. **3.** (of angle) between 90° and 180°.

ob'verse, *n.* **1.** front. **2.** side of coin having principal design. **3.** counterpart. —*adj.* (ob vûrs'). **4.** facing. **5.** corresponding.

ob'vi•ate, *v.,* **-ated, -ating.** take preventive measures against; avoid.

ob'vi•ous, *adj.* **1.** readily perceptible. **2.** not subtle. —**ob'vi•ous•ly,** *adv.* —**ob'vi•ous•ness,** *n.*

oc•a•ri'na (ok'ə rē'nə), *n.* egg-shaped wind instrument.

oc•ca'sion, *n.* **1.** particular time. **2.** important time. **3.** opportunity. **4.** reason. —*v.* **5.** give cause for. —**oc•ca'sion•al,** *adj.* —**oc•ca'sion•al•ly,** *adv.*

Oc·ci·dent (ok′sə-), n. West, esp. Europe and Americas. —**Oc′ci·den′tal**, adj., n.

oc·clude, v., -cluded, -cluding. close; shut. —**oc·clu′sion**, n.

oc·cult′, adj. 1. outside ordinary knowledge. —n. 2. occult matters.

oc·cu·pa·tion, n. 1. trade; calling. 2. possession. 3. military seizure. —**oc′cu·pa′tion·al**, adj.

oc·cu·py, v., -pied, -pying. 1. inhabit or be in. 2. require as space. 3. take possession of. 4. hold attention of. —**oc′cu·pan·cy**, n. —**oc′cu·pant**, n.

oc·cur′, v., -curred, -curring. 1. take place. 2. appear. 3. come to mind. —**oc·cur′rence**, n.

o·cean, n. 1. large body of salt water covering much of earth. 2. any of its five main parts. —**o·ce·an′ic**, adj.

o·cean·og·ra·phy, n. study of oceans. —**o·ce·a·nog′ra·pher**, n. —**o′ce·a·nog′ra·pher**, n.

o·ce·lot (ō′sə-), n. small American wildcat.

o·cher (ō′kər), n. yellow-to-red earth used as pigment. Also, **o′chre.**

o′clock′, adv. of or by the clock.

oc·ta·gon′, n. plane figure with eight sides and eight angles.

oc·tane, n. colorless liquid hydrocarbon found in petroleum.

oc·tave, n. Music. 1. eighth tone from given tone. 2. interval between two tones.

oc·ta·vo (-tā′-), n., pl. -vos. book whose pages are printed 16 to a sheet.

oc·tet′, n. group of eight, esp. musicians. Also, **oc·tette′.**

Oc·to·ber, n. tenth month of year.

oc·to·ge·nar′i·an, n. person 80 to 89 years old.

oc·to·pus, n., pl. -puses, -pi. large, soft-bodied, eight-armed sea mollusk.

oc′u·lar, adj. of eyes.

oc′u·list, n. doctor skilled in eye-treatment.

OD (ō′dē′), n., pl. **ODs** or **OD's**, v., **OD'd** or **ODed**, **OD'ing**. Slang. —n. 1. overdose of a drug, esp. a fatal one. —v. 2. take a drug overdose.

odd, adj. 1. eccentric; bizarre. 2. additional; not part of set. 3. not evenly divisible by two.

odd′ball′, n. Informal. peculiar person or thing.

odd′i·ty, n., pl. -ties. 1. queerness. 2. odd person or thing.

odds, n. 1. chances; probability for or against. 2. state of disagreement. 3. odd things.

odds′-on′, adj. most likely.

ode, n. poem of praise.

o′di·ous, adj. hateful.

o′di·um, n. 1. discredit; reproach. 2. hatred.

o·dom′e·ter (ō-), n. instrument that measures distance traveled.

o′dor, n. quality that affects sense of smell; scent. —**o′dor·ous**, adj.

o′dor·if′er·ous, adj. having odor, esp. unpleasant.

od′ys·sey (od′ə sē), n. long, adventurous journey.

o′er, prep., adv. Poetic. over.

of, prep. particle indicating: 1. being from. 2. belonging to.

off, adv. 1. up or away. 2. deviating. 3. out of operation or effect. —prep. 4. up or away from. —adj. 5. no longer in operation or effect. 6. in error. 7. one's way.

of′fal, n. refuse; garbage; carrion.

off′beat′, adj. Informal. unconventional.

off′-col′or, adj. 1. not having the usual color. 2. of questionable taste; risqué.

of·fend′, v. displease greatly.

of·fend′er, n. 1. person who offends. 2. person who commits crime.

of·fense′, n. 1. wrong; sin. 2. displeasure. 3. attack. Also, **of·fence′.** —**of·fen′sive**, adj., n.

of·fer, v. 1. present. 2. propose; suggest. —n. 3. proposal; bid. —**of′fer·ing**, n.

of′fer·to′ry, n., pl. -ries. 1. Rom. Cath. Ch. offering to God of bread and wine during Mass. 2. collection of religious service.

off′hand′, adj. 1. Also, **off′hand′ed.** done without previous thought; informal. 2. curt; brusque. —**off′hand′**, **off′hand′ed·ly**, adv.

of′fice, n. 1. place of business. 2. position of authority or trust. 3. duty; task. 4. religious service.

of′fi·cer, n. person of rank or authority.

of·fi′cial, n. 1. person who holds office. —adj. 2. authorized. 3. pertaining to public office. —**of·fi′cial·ly**, adv.

of·fi′ci·ate, v., -ated, -ating. perform official duties. —**of·fi′ci·a′tor**, n.

of·fi′cious, adj. too forward in offering unwanted help.

off′ing, n. 1. distant area. 2. foreseeable future.

off′-key′, adj. 1. not in tune. 2. somewhat incongruous or abnormal.

off′set′, v., -set, -setting. compensate for.

off′shoot′, n. branch.

off'shore', adj., adv. in water and away from shore.

off'spring', n. children or descendants.

oft, adv. Poetic. often.

of'ten, adv. 1. frequently. 2. in many cases.

o'gle, v., ogled, ogling, n. —v. 1. eye with impertinent familiarity. —n. 2. ogling glance.

o'gre (ō'gər), n. 1. hideous giant who eats human flesh. 2. cruel or barbarous person. —**o'gre•ish**, adj. —**o'gress**, n.fem.

oh, interj. (exclamation of surprise, etc.)

ohm (ōm), n. unit of electrical resistance.

oil, n. 1. greasy combustible liquid used for lubricating, heating, etc. —v. 2. supply with oil. —adj. 3. of oil. —**oil'er**, n. —**oil'y**, adj.

oil'cloth', n. fabric made waterproof with oil.

oint'ment, n. salve.

OK, adj., adv., v., **OK'd**, **OK'ing**, n., pl. **OK's.** —adj., adv. 1. all right; correct. —v. (ō'kā') 2. approve. —n. (ō'kā') 3. agreement or approval. Also, **O.K.**, **o'kay'.**

o'kra, n. tall garden plant with edible pods.

old, adj. 1. far advanced in years or time. 2. of age. 3. Also, **old'en.** former; ancient. 4. experienced. —n. 5. former time.

old'-fash'ioned, adj. having style, ideas, etc., of an earlier time.

old hand, person with long experience.

old hat, old-fashioned; dated.

old'ster, n. Informal. elderly person.

old'-tim'er, n. Informal. elderly person.

Old World, Europe, Asia, and Africa. —**old'-world'**, adj.

o'le•ag'i•nous (ō'lē aj'ə nəs), adj. 1. oily. 2. unctuous; fawning.

o'le•an'der, n. poisonous evergreen flowering shrub.

o'le•o•mar'ga•rine (-jə rin, -rēn'), n. edible fat made of vegetable oils and skim milk. Also, **o'le•o'**, **o'le•o•mar'ga•rin.**

ol•fac'to•ry, adj. pertaining to sense of smell.

ol'i•garch' (-gärk'), n. ruler in an oligarchy.

ol'i•gar'chy, n., pl. -**chies.** government by small group. —**ol'i•gar'chic**, adj.

ol'ive, n. 1. evergreen tree valued for its small, oily fruit. 2. fruit of this tree. 3. yellowish green.

om'buds•man', n., pl. -**men.** official

who investigates private individuals' complaints against government. Also, fem. **om'buds•wom'an.**

om'e•let, n. eggs beaten with milk and fried or baked. Also, **om'e•lette.**

o'men, n. sign indicative of future.

om'i•nous, adj. threatening evil. —**om'i•nous•ly**, adv.

o•mit', v., omitted, omitting. 1. leave out. 2. fail to do, etc. —**o•mis'sion**, n.

om'ni•bus', n., pl. -**buses.** 1. bus. 2. anthology.

om•nip'o•tent, adj. almighty. —**om•nip'o•tence**, n.

om'ni•pres'ent, adj. present everywhere at once.

om•nis'cient (om nish'ənt), adj. knowing all things. —**om•nis'cience**, n.

om•niv'o•rous, adj. eating all kinds of foods.

on, prep. particle expressing: 1. position in contact with supporting surface. 2. support; reliance. 3. situation or direction. 4. basis. —adv. 5. onto a thing, place, or person. 6. forward. 7. into operation. —adj. 8. near.

once, adv. 1. formerly. 2. single time. 3. at any time. —conj. 4. if ever; whenever.

once'-o'ver, n. Informal. quick survey.

on•col'o•gy, n. branch of medical science dealing with tumors and cancer. —**on•col'o•gist**, n.

on'com'ing, adj. approaching.

one, adj. 1. single. 2. some. 3. common to all. —n. 4. first and lowest whole number. 5. single person or thing. —pron. 6. person or thing.

one'ness, n. unity.

on'er•ous (on'-), adj. burdensome.

one•self', pron. person's self. Also, **one's self.**

one'-sid'ed, adj. 1. with all advantage on one side. 2. biased.

one'-time', adj. being such before; former.

one'-track', adj. Informal. obsessed with one subject.

one'-way', adj. moving or allowing movement in one direction only.

on'go'ing, adj. in progress; continuing.

on'ion, n. common plant having edible bulb.

on'-line', adj. operating under the direct control of, or connected to, a main computer.

on'look'er, n. spectator; witness.

on'ly, adv. 1. alone; solely. 2. merely. —adj. 3. sole. —conj. 4. but.

on'rush', n. rapid advance.

on'set', n. 1. beginning. 2. attack.

on'slaught', n. attack.

on'to, prep. upon; on.

on•tog'e•ny (on toj'ə nē), n. development of an individual organism.

on•tol'o•gy, n. branch of metaphysics studying existence or being.

o'nus (ō'nəs), n. burden.

on'ward, adv. 1. toward or at point ahead. —adj. 2. moving forward.

on'yx, n. quartz occurring in varicolored bands.

ooze, v., **oozed, oozing**, n. —v. 1. leak out slowly; exude. —n. 2. something that oozes. 3. soft mud.

o•pac'i•ty (ō pas'-), n., pl. **-ties.** state of being opaque.

o'pal, n. precious stone, often iridescent.

o'pal•es'cent, adj. with opallike play of color. —o'pal•es'cence, n.

o•paque' (ō pāk'), adj. 1. not transmitting light. 2. not shining. 3. not clear.

OPEC (ō'pek), n. Organization of Petroleum Exporting Countries.

o'pen, adj. 1. not shut. 2. not enclosed or covered. 3. available; accessible. 4. candid. —v. 5. make or become open. 6. begin. 7. come apart. —n. 8. any open space.

o'pen-and-shut', adj. easily solved or decided; obvious.

o'pen-hand'ed, adj. generous.

o'pen•ing, n. 1. unobstructed or unoccupied place. 2. gap or hole. 3. beginning. 4. opportunity.

o'pen-mind'ed, adj. without prejudice. —o'pen-mind'ed•ness, n.

open shop, business in which union membership is not a condition of employment.

op'er•a, n. sung drama. —op'er•at'ic, adj.

op'er•a•ble, adj. 1. able to be operated. 2. curable by surgery.

op'er•ate', v., **-ated, -ating.** 1. work or run. 2. exert force or influence. 3. use surgery. —op'er•a'tion, n. —op'er•a'tor, n.

op'er•a'tion•al, adj. 1. concerning operations. 2. in working order. 3. in operation.

op'er•a•tive, n. 1. worker. 2. detective. 3. spy. —adj. 4. effective.

op'er•et'ta, n. light opera.

oph•thal'mi•a (of thal'mē ə), n. inflammation of eye.

oph•thal•mol'o•gy, n. branch of medicine dealing with eye. —oph'thal•mol'o•gist, n.

o'pi•ate (ō'pē it), n. medicine containing opium.

o•pin'ion, n. unproven belief or judgment.

o•pin'ion•at'ed, adj. conceitedly stubborn in opinions.

o'pi•um, n. narcotic juice of poppy.

o•pos'sum, n. pouched mammal of southern U.S.

op•po'nent, n. 1. person on opposite side in contest. 2. person opposed to something.

op'por•tune', adj. appropriate; timely.

op'por•tun'ism, n. unprincipled use of opportunities. —op'por•tun'ist, n. —op'por•tun•is'tic, adj.

op'por•tu'ni•ty, n., pl. **-ties.** temporary possible advantage.

op•pose', v., **-posed, -posing.** 1. resist or compete with. 2. hinder. 3. set as an obstacle. 4. cause to disfavor something. —op'po•si'tion, n.

op'po•site, adj. 1. in corresponding position on other side. 2. completely different. —n. 3. one that is opposite. —op'po•si'tion, n.

op•press', v. 1. weigh down. 2. treat harshly as matter of policy. —op•pres'sion, n. —op•pres'sive, adj. —op•pres'sor, n.

op•pro'bri•um, n. disgrace and reproach. —op•pro'bri•ous, adj.

op'tic, adj. of eyes.

op'ti•cal, adj. 1. acting by means of sight and light. 2. made to assist sight. 3. visual. 4. of optics. —op'ti•cal•ly, adv.

op•ti'cian, n. maker of eyeglasses.

op'tics, n. branch of science dealing with light and vision.

op'ti•mal, adj. optimum.

op'ti•mism, n. 1. disposition to hope for best. 2. belief that good will prevail over evil. —op'ti•mist, n. —op'ti•mis'tic, adj.

op'ti•mum, adj., n. best.

op'tion, n. 1. power of choosing or deciding. 2. choice made. —op'tion•al, adj.

op•tom'e•try, n. art of testing eyes for eyeglasses. —op•tom'e•trist, n.

op'u•lent, adj. wealthy. —op'u•lence, n.

o'pus (ō'pəs), n., pl. **opera.** work, esp. musical, usually numbered.

or, conj. (particle used to connect alternatives.)

or'a•cle, n. 1. answer by the gods to question. 2. medium giving the answer. —o•rac'u•lar, adj.

o'ral, adj. 1. spoken. 2. of mouths. —o'ral•ly, adv.

or'ange, n. 1. round, reddish-yellow citrus fruit. 2. reddish yellow.

or'ange•ade', n. drink with base of orange juice.

o·rang'-u·tan', *n.* large, long-armed ape. Also, **o·rang'-ou·tang'**, **o·rang'**.

o·ra'tion, *n.* formal speech.

or'a·tor, *n.* eloquent public speaker.

or'a·to'ri·o, *n., pl.* **-ri·os.** religious work for voices and orchestra in dramatic form.

or'a·to·ry, *n., pl.* **-ries. 1.** eloquent speaking. **2.** small room for prayer. **—or'a·tor'i·cal**, *adj.*

orb, *n.* **1.** sphere. **2.** any of heavenly bodies.

or'bit, *n.* **1.** path of planet, etc., around another body. **2.** cavity in skull for eyeball. **—or'bit·al**, *adj.*

or'chard, *n.* plot of fruit trees.

or'ches·tra, *n.* **1.** *Music.* large company of instrumental performers. **2.** space in theater for musicians. **3.** main floor of theater. **—or·ches'tral**, *adj.*

or'ches·trate, *v.*, **-trated, -trating.** arrange music for orchestra. **—or'ches·tra'tion**, *n.*

or'chid (ôr'kid), *n.* **1.** tropical plant with oddly shaped blooms. **2.** light purple.

or·dain', *v.* **1.** invest as a member of the clergy. **2.** appoint or direct.

or·deal', *n.* severe test.

or'der, *n.* **1.** authoritative command. **2.** harmonious arrangement. **3.** group bound by common religious rules. **4.** list of goods or services desired. **5.** give an order. **6.** arrange.

or'der·ly, *adj., adv., n., pl.* **-lies.** *—adj.* **1.** methodical. **2.** well-behaved. *—adv.* **3.** according to rule. *—n.* **4.** hospital attendant. **—or'der·li·ness**, *n.*

or'di·nal, *adj.* showing position in series, as *first, second,* etc. *—n.* **2.** ordinal number.

or'di·nance, *n.* law.

or'di·nar·y, *adj., n., pl.* **-naries.** *—adj.* **1.** usual; normal. *—n.* **2.** ordinary condition, etc. **—or'di·nar·i·ly**, *adv.*

or'di·na'tion, *n.* act or ceremony of ordaining. Also, **or·dain'ment.**

ord'nance, *n.* military weapons of all kinds.

ore, *n.* metal-bearing rock.

o·reg'a·no, *n.* plant with leaves used as seasoning.

or'gan, *n.* **1.** large musical keyboard instrument sounded by air forced through pipes, etc. **2.** part of animal or plant with specific function. **3.** means of communication. **—or'gan·ist**, *n.*

or'gan·dy, *n., pl.* **-dies.** thin stiff cotton fabric.

or·gan'ic, *adj.* **1.** of carbon compounds. **2.** of living organisms. **3.** of animals or produce raised or grown without synthetic fertilizers, pesticides, etc. **—or·gan'i·cal·ly**, *adv.*

or'gan·ism, *n.* anything living or formerly alive.

or'gan·ize', *v.*, **-ized, -izing.** form into coordinated whole; systematize. **—or'gan·i·za'tion**, *n.* **—or'gan·iz'er**, *n.* **—or'gan·i·za'tion·al**, *adj.*

or'gasm, *n.* sexual climax.

or'gy, *n., pl.* **-gies.** wild revelry. **—or'gi·as'tic**, *adj.*

o'ri·ent, *n.* (ôr'ē ant). **1.** (*cap.*) countries of Asia. *—v.* (ôr'ē ent'). **2.** set facing certain way. **3.** inform about one's situation. **—O·ri·en'tal**, *adj.* **—o'ri·en·ta'tion**, *n.*

o'ri·en·teer'ing, *n.* sport of finding way across unfamiliar country.

or'i·fice (ôr'ə fis), *n.* opening.

o·ri·ga'mi (ôr'i gä'mē), *n.* Japanese art of folding paper into decorative or representational forms.

or'i·gin, *n.* **1.** source. **2.** beginning. **3.** circumstances of birth or ancestry.

o·rig'i·nal, *adj.* **1.** first. **2.** novel. **3.** being new work. **4.** capable of creating something original. *—n.* **5.** primary form. **6.** thing copied or imitated. **7.** beginning. **—o·rig'i·nal'i·ty**, *n.*

o·rig'i·nal·ly, *adv.* **1.** at first. **2.** in original manner.

o·rig'i·nate', *v.*, **-nated, -nating. 1.** come to be. **2.** give origin to. **—o·rig'i·na'tor**, *n.* **—o·rig'i·na'tion**, *n.*

o'ri·ole', *n.* bright-colored bird of Europe and America.

or'i·son (ôr'i zan), *n.* prayer.

Or'lon, *n. Trademark.* synthetic fabric resembling nylon.

or'na·ment, *n.* (ôr'na mant). **1.** something added to beautify. *—v.* (ôr'na ment'). **2.** adorn; decorate. **—or'na·men'tal**, *adj.* **—or'na·men·ta'tion**, *n.*

or'nate', *adj.* elaborately ornamented. **—or·nate'ly**, *adv.*

or'ner·y, *adj. Informal.* ill-tempered.

or·ni·thol'o·gy, *n.* study of birds. **—or'ni·thol'o·gist**, *n.* **—or'ni·tho·log'i·cal**, *adj.*

o'ro·tund', *adj.* **1.** rich and clear in voice. **2.** pompous; bombastic.

or'phan, *n.* **1.** child whose parents are both dead. *—adj.* **2.** of or for orphans. *—v.* **3.** bereave of parents.

or'phan·age, *n.* home for orphans.

or'ris, *n.* kind of iris.

or·tho·don'tics, *n.* branch of dentistry dealing with prevention and correction of irregular teeth. Also, **or'-**

tho·don'ti·a. —**or'tho·don'tic,** adj. —**or'tho·don'tist,** n.

or'tho·dox', adj. 1. sound and correct in doctrine. 2. conventional. 3. (cap.) of Christian churches common in eastern Europe and adjacent areas. —**or'tho·dox'y,** n.

or·thog'ra·phy, n., pl. **-phies.** spelling. —**or'tho·graph'ic,** or **tho·graph'i·cal,** adj.

or·tho·pe'dics, n. branch of medicine dealing with the skeletal system. —**or'tho·pe'dist,** or **or'tho·pe'dic,** adj.

os'cil·late' (os'ə-), v., **-lated, -lating.** swing to and fro. —**os'cil·la'tion,** n. —**os'cil·la'tor,** n.

os'cu·late' (os'kyə-), v., **-lated, -lating.** kiss. —**os'cu·la'tion,** n. —**os'cu·la·to'ry,** adj.

o'sier (ō'zhər), n. tough flexible twig.

os'mi·um, n. hard, heavy metallic element used in alloys.

os·mo'sis, n. diffusion of liquid through membrane.

os'prey, n. large hawk.

os'se·ous, adj. of, like, or containing bone.

os'si·fy', v., **-fied, -fying.** make or become bone. —**os'si·fi·ca'tion,** n.

os·ten'si·ble, adj. merely apparent or pretended. —**os·ten'si·bly,** adv.

os·ten·ta'tion, n. pretentious display. —**os·ten·ta'tious,** adj.

os'te·o·path'y, n. treatment of disease by manipulating affected part. —**os'te·o·path',** n. —**os'te·o·path'ic,** adj.

os'te·o·po·ro'sis (os'tē ō pə rō'sis), n. disorder in which bones become increasingly porous, brittle, and subject to fracture.

os'tra·cize' (os'trə sīz'), v., **-cized, -cizing.** exclude from society; banish. —**os'tra·cism,** n.

os'trich, n. large, swift-footed, flightless bird.

oth'er, adj. 1. additional. 2. different. 3. being remaining one. 4. former. —pron. 5. other person or thing.

oth'er·wise', adv. 1. in other ways or circumstances. —adj. 2. of other sort.

o'ti·ose' (ō'shē ōs'), adj. 1. idle. 2. futile.

ot'ter, n. aquatic mammal.

ot'to·man, n. low, cushioned seat.

ought, aux. v. 1. be bound by obligation or reasoning. 2. cipher (0).

ounce, n. unit of weight equal to 1/16 lb. avoirdupois or 1/12 lb. troy.

our, pron. possessive form of **we,** used before noun.

ours, pron. possessive form of **we,** used predicatively.

our·selves', pron. 1. reflexive substitute for **us.** 2. intensive or substitute for **we** or **us.**

oust, v. eject; force out.

oust'er, n. ejection.

out, adv. 1. away from some place. 2. so as to emerge or project. 3. until conclusion. 4. to depletion. 5. so as to be extinguished, etc. —adj. 6. away from some place. 7. extinguished, etc. —prep. 8. out from. 9. away along. —n. 10. means of evasion.

out'age (ou'tij), n. 1. interruption or failure in supply of power.

out'-and-out', adj. utter; thorough.

out'board', adj., adv. on exterior of ship or boat.

out'bound', adj. headed for the open sea.

out'break', n. 1. sudden occurrence. 2. riot.

out'burst', n. bursting forth.

out'cast', n. exiled or rejected person.

out'class', v. outdo in excellence.

out'come', n. consequence.

out'crop', n. emerging stratum at earth's surface.

out'cry', n., pl. **-cries.** expression of distress or protest.

out·dat'ed, adj. obsolete.

out·dis'tance, v., **-tanced, -tancing.** leave behind, as in racing.

out·do', v., **-did, -done, -doing.** surpass.

out'door', adj. done or occurring in open air. —**out'doors',** adv., n.

out'er, adj. 1. farther out. 2. on outside.

outer space, 1. space beyond the earth's atmosphere. 2. space beyond the solar system.

out'field', n. part of baseball field beyond diamond. —**out'field'er,** n.

out'fit', n., v., **-fitted, -fitting.** —n. 1. set of articles for any purpose. 2. organized group of persons. —v. 3. equip. —**out'fit'ter,** n.

out'flank', v. go beyond flank of.

out'go', n., pl. **-goes.** expenditure.

out'go·ing, adj. 1. departing. 2. retiring from a position or office. 3. friendly; sociable.

out'grow', v., **-grew, -grown, -growing.** grow too large or mature for.

out'growth', n. 1. natural result. 2. offshoot.

out'house', n. separate building serving as toilet.

out'ing, n. pleasure trip.

out·land'ish, adj. strange.

out'last', v. endure after.

out'law', n. 1. habitual criminal. 2. person excluded from protection of law. —v. 3. prohibit by law. 4. deny protection of law to. —**out·law'ry**, *n.*

out·lay', *n.* expenditure.

out·let', *n.* 1. opening or passage out. 2. market for goods.

out·line', *n., v., -lined, -lining.* —n. 1. line by which object is bounded. 2. drawing showing only outer contour. 3. general description. —v. 4. draw or represent in outline.

out·live', *v., -lived, -living.* live longer than.

out·look', *n.* 1. view from place. 2. mental view. 3. prospect.

out·ly'ing, *adj.* remote.

out·mod'ed, *adj.* obsolete.

out·num'ber, *v.* be more numerous than.

out'-of-date', *adj.* obsolete.

out'-of-doors', *adv.* 1. outdoor. —n. 2. outdoors.

out·pa'tient, *n.* patient visiting hospital to receive treatment.

out·post', *n.* 1. sentinel station away from main army. 2. place away from main area.

out·put', *n.* 1. production. 2. quantity produced.

out·rage', *n., v., -raged, -raging.* —n. 1. gross violation of law or decency. —v. 2. subject to outrage. —**out·ra'geous**, *adj.*

ou·tré' (ōō trā'), *adj.* unconventional; bizarre.

out·right', *adj.* 1. utter; thorough. —adv. (out'rīt'). 2. without concealment; completely.

out·set', *n.* beginning.

out·side', *n.* 1. outer side, aspect, etc. 2. space beyond enclosure. —adj. 3. being, done, etc., on the outside. —adv. 4. on or to the outside. —prep. (out'sīd'). 5. at the outside of.

out·sid'er, *n.* person not belonging.

out·skirts', *n.pl.* bordering parts.

out·smart', *v. Informal.* outwit.

out·spo'ken, *adj.* candid.

out·spread', *adj.* extended.

out·stand'ing, *adj.* 1. prominent. 2. not yet paid.

out·strip', *v., -stripped, -stripping.* 1. excel. 2. outdistance.

out'take', *n.* segment of film or recording edited from published version.

out'ward, *adj.* 1. external. —adv. 2. Also, **out'wards**. toward the outside. —**out'ward·ly**, *adv.*

out·weigh', *v.* exceed in importance.

out·wit', *v., -witted, -witting.* defeat by superior cleverness.

out·worn', *adj.* 1. no longer vital or appropriate. 2. useless because of wear.

o'val, *adj.* egg-shaped; elliptical. Also, **o'vate**.

o'va·ry, *n., pl. -ries.* female reproductive gland. —**o·var'i·an**, *adj.*

o·va'tion, *n.* enthusiastic applause.

ov'en, *n.* chamber for baking or drying.

o'ver, *prep.* 1. above in place, authority, etc. 2. on. 3. across; through. 4. in excess of. 5. concerning. 6. during. —adv. 7. so as to affect whole surface. 8. above. 9. again. —adj. 10. finished. 11. remaining. 12. upper. 13. surplus.

o'ver·age' (ō'vər ij), *n.* 1. surplus. —adj. (ō'vər āj'). 2. beyond desirable age.

o'ver·all', *adj.* 1. including everything. —n. 2. (pl.) loose, stout trousers.

o'ver·awe', *v., -awed, -awing.* dominate with impressiveness or force.

o'ver·bear'ing, *adj.* arrogant; domineering.

o'ver·blown', *adj.* 1. overdone; excessive. 2. pretentious.

o'ver·board', *adv.* over side of ship into water.

o'ver·cast', *adj.* 1. cloudy. 2. gloomy.

o'ver·coat', *n.* coat worn over ordinary clothing.

o'ver·come', *v., -came, -come, -coming.* defeat; overpower.

o'ver·do', *v., -did, -done, -doing.* 1. do to excess. 2. exaggerate.

o'ver·dose', *n., v., -dosed, -dosing.* —n. 1. excessive dose. —v. 2. take an excessive dose.

o'ver·draw', *v., -drew, -drawn, -drawing.* draw upon (account, etc.) in excess of one's balance. —**o'ver·draft'**, *n.*

o'ver·drive', *n.* arrangement of gears providing propeller speed greater than engine crankshaft speed.

o'ver·due', *adj.* due some time before.

o'ver·flow', *v., -flowed, -flown, -flowing.* —v. 1. flow or run over; flood. —n. (ō'vər flō'). 2. instance of overflowing. 3. something that runs over.

o'ver·grow', *v., -grew, -grown, -growing.* cover with growth.

o'ver·hand', *adv.* with hand above shoulder.

o'ver·hang', *v., -hung, -hanging, n.* —v. 1. project over. 2. threaten. —n. (ō'vər hang'). 3. projection.

o'ver·haul', *v.* 1. investigate thoroughly, as for repair. 2. overtake. —n. 3. complete examination.

o'ver·head', *adv.* 1. aloft. —n. (ō'vər hed'). 2. general business expense.

o·ver·hear', v., **-heard, -hearing.** hear without speaker's intent.

o·ver·joyed', adj. very happy.

o·ver·kill', n. 1. *Mil.* ability to kill more, esp. by nuclear weapons, than is needed for victory. 2. any greatly excessive amount.

o·ver·land', adv. adj. across open country.

o·ver·lap', v., **-lapped, -lapping.** n. —v. 1. extend over and beyond. —n. (ō'vər lap'). 2. overlapping part.

o·ver·lay', v., **-laid, -laying.** n. —v. 1. spread over. —n. 2. something used in overlaying.

o·ver·look', v. 1. fail to notice. 2. afford view over.

o·ver·ly, adv. *Informal.* excessively.

o·ver·night', adv. 1. during the night. 2. on previous night. —adj. 3. done, made, etc., during the night. 4. staying for one night.

o·ver·pass', n. bridge crossing other traffic.

o·ver·pow·er, v. 1. overwhelm in feeling. 2. subdue.

o·ver·rate', v., **-rated, -rating.** esteem too highly.

o·ver·reach', v. 1. extend beyond. 2. defeat (oneself), as by excessive eagerness.

o·ver·re·act', v. react too emotionally. —**o·ver·re·ac'tion**, n.

o·ver·ride', v., **-rode, -ridden, -riding.** prevail over; supersede.

o·ver·rule', v., **-ruled, -ruling.** rule against.

o·ver·run', v., **-ran, -run, -running.** 1. swarm over. 2. overgrow.

o·ver·seas', adv. over or across the sea.

o·ver·see', v., **-saw, -seen, -seeing.** supervise. —**o·ver·se'er**, n.

o·ver·shad·ow, v. be more important than.

o·ver·shoe', n. shoe worn over another shoe to keep out wet or cold.

o·ver·sight', n. 1. error of neglect. 2. supervision.

o·ver·sleep', v., **-slept, -sleeping.** sleep beyond desired time.

o·ver·state', v., **-stated, -stating.** exaggerate in describing. —**o·ver·state'ment**, n.

o·ver·step', v., **-stepped, -stepping.** exceed.

o·ver·stuffed', adj. (of furniture) having the frame padded and covered.

o·vert', adj. 1. not concealed. 2. giving perceptible cause or provocation.

o·ver·take', v., **-took, -taking.** catch up with.

o·ver-the-coun·ter, adj. 1. not listed on or traded through an organized securities exchange. 2. sold legally without a prescription.

o·ver·throw', v., **-threw, -thrown, -throwing.** n. —v. 1. defeat; put end to. —n. (ō'vər thrō'). 2. act of overthrowing.

o·ver·time', n. time worked in addition to regular hours. —**o·ver·time'**, adv., adj.

o·ver·tone', n. 1. additional meaning. 2. musical tone added to basic tone.

o·ver·ture', n. 1. offer. 2. musical prelude to opera, etc.

o·ver·turn', v. 1. tip off base. 2. defeat.

o·ver·view', n. overall perception or description.

o·ver·ween·ing, adj. conceited.

o·ver·weight', n. 1. excess of weight. —adj. (ō'vər wāt'). 2. weighing more than is normal.

o·ver·whelm', v. 1. weigh upon overpoweringly; crush. 2. stun, as with attention.

o·ver·work', v., **-worked** or **-wrought, -working.** n. —v. 1. work too hard. —n. (ō'vər wûrk'). 2. work beyond one's strength.

o·ver·wrought', adj. highly excited.

o'void, adj. egg-shaped.

ov·u·late', v., **-lated, -lating.** produce and discharge eggs (ova) from ovary. —**ov·u·la'tion**, n.

o'vum, n., pl. **ova.** female reproductive cell.

owe, v., **owed, owing.** be obligated to pay or give to another.

owl, n. nocturnal bird of prey. —**owl'ish**, adj.

owl'et, n. small owl.

own, adj. 1. of or belonging to. —v. 2. possess. 3. acknowledge. —**own'er**, n. —**own'er·ship**, n.

ox, n., pl. **oxen.** adult castrated male bovine.

ox'blood', n. deep, dull red color.

ox'ford, n. low shoe laced over instep.

ox'ide, n. compound of oxygen and another element.

ox'i·dize', v., **-dized, -dizing.** 1. add oxygen to. 2. rust. —**ox'i·di·za'tion**, **ox·i·da'tion**, n.

ox·y·a·cet'y·lene' (ok'sē ə set'ə lēn'), adj. denoting a mixture of oxygen and acetylene used for cutting and welding steel.

ox'y·gen, n. colorless, odorless gas necessary to life and fire.

oys'ter, n. edible, irregularly shaped mollusk.

o'zone, n. form of oxygen present in upper atmosphere.

P

P, p, *n.* sixteenth letter of English alphabet.

pace, *n., v.,* **paced, pacing.** —*n.* 1. rate of movement or progress. 2. variable linear measure, about 30 inches. 3. step or gait. —*v.* 4. set pace for. 5. step slowly and regularly. —**pac'er,** *n.*

pace'mak'er, *n.* 1. one that sets pace. 2. electrical device for controlling heartbeat.

pach'y·derm' (pak'ə-), *n.* thick-skinned mammal, as the elephant.

pa·cif'ic, *adj.* peaceful.

pac'i·fism, *n.* principle of abstention from violence. —**pac'i·fist,** *n.* —**pac·i·fis'tic,** *adj.*

pac'i·fy, *v.,* **-fied, -fying.** 1. calm. 2. appease. —**pac·i·fi'er,** *n.* —**pac·i·fi·ca'tion,** *n.*

pack, *n.* 1. bundle. 2. group or complete set. —*v.* 3. make into compact mass. 4. fill with objects. 5. cram. —**pack'er,** *n.*

pack'age, *n., v.,* **-aged, -aging.** —*n.* 1. bundle; parcel. 2. container. —*v.* 3. put into package.

pack'et, *n.* 1. small package. 2. passenger boat, esp. with fixed route.

pact, *n.* agreement.

pad, *n., v.,* **padded, padding.** —*n.* 1. soft, cushionlike mass. 2. bound package of writing paper. 3. dull sound of walking. —*v.* 4. furnish with padding. 5. expand with false or useless matter. 6. walk with dull sound.

pad'ding, *n.* material with which to pad.

pad'dle, *n., v.,* **-dled, -dling.** —*n.* 1. short oar for two hands. —*v.* 2. propel with paddle. 3. play in water.

pad'dock, *n.* enclosed field for horses.

pad'dy, *n., pl.* **-dies.** rice field.

pad'lock, *n.* 1. portable lock with U-shaped shackle. —*v.* 2. lock with padlock. 3. forbid access to.

pae'an (pē'ən), *n.* song of praise.

pa'gan, *n.* 1. worshiper of idols. —*adj.* 2. idolatrous; heathen. —**pa'gan·ism,** *n.*

page, *n., v.,* **paged, paging.** —*n.* 1. written or painted surface. 2. boy servant. —*v.* 3. number pages of. 4. seek by calling by name.

pag'eant, *n.* elaborate spectacle. —**pag'eant·ry,** *n.*

pag'i·nate, *v.,* **-nated, -nating.** number the pages of (a book, etc.). —**pag·i·na'tion,** *n.*

pa·go'da, *n.* Far Eastern temple tower, esp. Buddhist.

pail, *n.* cylindrical container for liquids; bucket.

pain, *n.* 1. bodily or mental suffering. 2. (*pl.*) effort. 3. penalty. —*v.* 4. hurt. —**pain'ful,** *adj.* —**pain'ful·ly,** *adv.* —**pain'less,** *adj.*

pain'kil·ler, *n.* something, esp. an analgesic, that relieves pain.

pains'tak'ing, *adj.* very careful.

paint, *n.* 1. liquid coloring matter used as coating. —*v.* 2. represent in paint. 3. apply paint to. —**paint'er,** *n.* —**paint'ing,** *n.*

pair, *n., pl.* **pairs, pair,** *v.* —*n.* 1. combination of two, esp. matching. —*v.* 2. form or arrange in pairs.

pais'ley, *n.* fabric woven in colorful, detailed pattern.

pa·jam'as, *n.pl.* two-piece nightclothes.

pal, *n. Informal.* comrade.

pal'ace, *n.* official residence of sovereign.

pal'an·quin' (-kēn'), *n.* enclosed chair or bed carried on men's shoulders.

pal'at·a·ble, *v.* agreeable to taste.

pal'ate, *n.* 1. roof of mouth. 2. sense of taste. —**pal'a·tal,** *adj.*

pa·la'tial, *adj.* splendidly built or furnished. —**pa·la'tial·ly,** *adv.*

pa·la'ver, *n.* 1. conference. 2. flattery. 3. idle talk.

pale, *adj.,* **paler, palest,** *v.,* **paled, paling.** —*adj.* 1. without intensity of color; near-white. 2. dim. —*v.* 3. become or make pale. —*n.* 4. stake; picket. 5. bounds. 6. enclosed area.

Pa'le·o·lith'ic, *adj.* denoting early Stone Age.

pa'le·on·tol'o·gy, *n.* science of early life forms, as represented by fossils.

pal'ette (pal'it), *n.* board on which painter lays and mixes colors.

pal'frey (pôl'-), *n., pl.* **-freys.** riding horse.

pal'i·mo·ny, *n.* alimony awarded to member of unmarried couple.

pal'ing, *n.* pale fence.

pal'i·sade', *n.* 1. fence of pales. 2. line of tall cliffs.

pall (pôl), *n.* 1. cloth spread over coffin. 2. something seen or felt as gloomy. —*v.* 3. become wearisome or distasteful.

pall'bear·er, *n.* person who attends the coffin at funeral.

pal'let, *n.* 1. straw mattress. 2. implement for shaping, used by potters. 3. projecting lip on panel.

pal'li·ate', *v.,* **-ated, -ating.** mitigate; excuse. —**pal'li·a'tive,** *n., adj.*

pal′lid, adj. pale.

pal′lor, n. paleness.

palm n. 1. inner surface of hand. 2. tall, unbranched tropical tree. 3. conceal in palm of hand.

pal·met′to, n., pl. -tos, -toes. species of palm.

palm′is·try, n. art of telling fortunes from patterns of lines on palms of hands.

palm′y, adj., **palmier**, **palmiest**. thriving.

pal′o·mi′no (-mē′-), n., pl. -nos. light-tan horse.

pal′pa·ble, adj. obvious; tangible. —**pal′pa·bly**, adv.

pal′pi·tate′, v., -tated, -tating. pulsate with unnatural rapidity. —**pal′·pi·ta′tion**, n.

pal′sy (pôl′zē), n., pl. -sies, v., -sied, -sying. —n. 1. paralysis. 2. muscular condition with tremors. —v. 3. afflict with palsy.

pal′try, adj., -trier, -triest. trifling.

pam′pas, n. vast South American plains.

pam′per, v. indulge; coddle.

pam′phlet, n. 1. thin booklet, cheaply printed. 2. argumentative treatise.

pam′phlet·eer′, n. writer of pamphlets.

pan, n., v., **panned**, **panning**. —n. 1. broad shallow metal dish for cooking. —v. 2. wash (gravel, etc.) in seeking gold. 3. Informal. criticize harshly. 4. swivel camera horizontally to record panorama.

Pan, n. Greek god of shepherds.

pan′a·ce′a (-sē′a), n. cure-all.

pa·nache′ (pa nash′, -näsh′), n. grand or flamboyant manner; flair.

pan′cake′, n. flat fried batter cake.

pan′cre·as, n. gland near stomach secreting a digestive fluid. —**pan′cre·at′ic**, adj.

pan′da, n. bearlike Asiatic animal.

pan·dem′ic, adj. epidemic over large area.

pan′de·mo′ni·um, n. uproar.

pan′der, n. 1. person who caters to base passions of others. —v. 2. act as pander. —**pan′der·er**, n.

pane, n. glass section of window.

pan′e·gyr′ic (-jir′ik), n. eulogy.

pan′el, n., v., -eled, -eling. —n. 1. bordered section of wall, door, etc. 2. list of persons called for jury duty. 3. public discussion group. —v. 4. arrange in or ornament with panels. —**pan′el·ing**, n. —**pan′el·ist**, n.

pang, n. sudden feeling of distress.

pan′han′dle, v., -dled, -dling. Informal. beg. —**pan′han′dler**, n.

pan′ic, n. demoralizing terror.

—**pan′ick·y**, adj. —**pan′ic-strick′·en**, adj.

pan′i·cle, n. loose flower cluster.

pan′o·ply, n., pl. -plies. 1. impressive display. 2. suit of armor.

pan′o·ram′a, n. 1. view over wide area. 2. continuously changing scene. —**pan′o·ram′ic**, adj.

pan′sy, n., pl. -sies. 1. species of violet. 2. Brit. (Offensive.) homosexual.

pant, v. 1. breathe hard and quickly. 2. long eagerly.

pan′ta·loons′, n.pl. Archaic. trousers.

pan′the·ism, n. religious belief or philosophical doctrine that identifies God with the universe. —**pan′the·is′tic**, adj.

pan′the·on, n. 1. building with tombs or memorials of a nation's illustrious dead. 2. heroes of a nation, etc., as a group.

pan′ther, n. cougar, puma, or leopard.

pan′ties, n.pl. women's underpants. Also, **pan′ty**.

pan′to·graph′, n. instrument for copying traced figures on any scale.

pan′to·mime′, n., v., -mimed, -miming. —n. 1. expression by mute gestures. 2. play in this form. —v. 3. express in pantomime. —**pan′to·mim′ist**, n.

pan′try, n., pl. -tries. room for kitchen supplies.

pants, n.pl. Informal. trousers.

panty hose, one-piece stockings plus panties for women.

pan′zer, adj. 1. (esp. in German army) armored. —n. 2. tank or other armored vehicle.

pap, n. soft food.

pa′pa, n. father.

pa′pa·cy, n., pl. -cies. office or dignity of the pope.

pa′pal, adj. of the pope.

pa·paw (pô′pô), n. small North American tree.

pa·pa′ya, n. melonlike tropical American fruit.

pa′per, n. 1. thin fibrous sheet for writing, etc. 2. document. 3. treatise. 4. newspaper. —v. 5. decorate with wallpaper. —adj. 6. of paper. —**pa′per·y**, adj. —**pa′per·weight′**, n.

pa′per·back′, n. book cheaply bound in paper.

pa′pier-mâ·ché′ (pā′pər mə shā′), n. molded paper pulp.

pa·pil′la, n., pl. -lae (pil′ē). small protuberance, as those concerned with touch, taste, and smell. —**pap′il·lar′y**, adj.

pa′pist, n., adj. Disparaging. Roman Catholic. —**pa′pism**, n.

pa•poose′, *n.* North American Indian baby. Also, **pap•poose′**.

pap•ri′ka (pa prē′-), *n.* mild spice from dried ground fruit of a pepper plant.

Pap test, test for cancer of the cervix.

pa•py′rus (-pī′-), *n., pl.* -**ri.** tall aquatic plant made into paper by ancient Egyptians.

par, *n.* 1. equality in value or standing. 2. average amount, etc. 3. in golf, standard number of strokes for one hole or complete course.

par′a•ble, *n.* allegory conveying moral.

pa•rab′o•la, *n.* a U-shaped curve, surface, object, etc. —**par•a•bol′ic,** *adj.*

par′a•chute′, *n., v.,* -**chuted,** -**chuting.** —*n.* 1. umbrellalike apparatus used to fall safely through air. —*v.* 2. drop or fall by parachute. —**par′a•chut′ist,** *n.*

pa•rade′, *n., v.,* -**raded,** -**rading.** —*n.* 1. public procession or assembly for display. —*v.* 2. march in display. 3. display ostentatiously. —**pa•rad′er,** *n.*

par′a•digm (-dīm′, -dim), *n.* example or pattern.

par′a•dise′, *n.* 1. heaven. 2. garden of Eden. 3. best place or condition.

par′a•dox′, *n.* true statement that appears self-contradictory. —**par•a•dox′i•cal,** *adj.*

par′af•fin, *n.* waxy substance from petroleum, used in candles, etc.

par′a•gon′, *n.* model of excellence.

par′a•graph′, *n.* 1. distinct portion of written or printed matter, begun on new line. —*v.* 2. divide into paragraphs.

par′a•keet′, *n.* small parrot.

par′a•le′gal, *n.* attorney's assistant, trained to perform certain legal tasks but not licensed to practice law.

par′al•lax′, *n.* apparent displacement of object viewed due to changed position of viewer.

par′al•lel′, *adj., n., v.,* -**leled,** -**leling.** —*adj.* 1. having same direction. 2. having same characteristics. —*n.* 3. anything parallel. —*v.* 4. be parallel to.

par′al•lel′o•gram, *n.* a four-sided figure whose opposite sides are parallel.

pa•ral′y•sis, *n., pl.* -**ses.** loss of voluntary muscular control. —**par•a•lyt′ic,** *n., adj.* —**par′a•lyze′,** *v.*

par′a•med′ic, *n.* person performing paramedical services.

par′a•med′i•cal, *adj.* practicing medicine in secondary capacity.

pa•ram′e•ter, *n.* determining factor.

par′a•mil′i•ta•ry, *adj.* of organizations operating in place of or in addition to a regular military force.

par′a•mount′, *adj.* greatest; utmost.

par′a•mour′, *n.* lover of married person.

par′a•noi′a, *n.* mental disorder marked by systematized delusions ascribing hostile intentions to other persons. —**par′a•noi′ac,** *adj., n.*

par′a•pet, *n.* wall at edge of roof or terrace.

par′a•pher•na′lia, *n.pl.* 1. equipment. 2. belongings.

par′a•phrase′, *v.,* -**phrased,** -**phrasing,** *n.* —*v.* 1. restate in other words. —*n.* 2. such restatement.

par′a•ple′gi•a (-plē′-), *n.* paralysis of lower part of body. —**par′a•pleg′ic** (-plēj′-), *n., adj.*

par′a•pro•fes′sion•al, *adj.* engaged in profession in partial or secondary capacity. —**paraprofessional,** *n.*

par′a•site′, *n.* animal or plant that lives on another organism. —**par•a•sit′ic,** *adj.*

par′a•sol′, *n.* sun umbrella.

par′a•troops′, *n.* force of soldiers (**paratroopers**) who reach battle by parachuting from planes.

par′boil′, *v.* precook.

par′cel, *n., v.,* -**celed,** -**celing.** —*n.* 1. goods wrapped together; bundle. 2. part. —*v.* 3. divide.

parch, *v.* dry by heat.

par•chee′si, *n.* game resembling backgammon.

parch′ment, *n.* skin of sheep, etc., prepared for writing on.

par′don, *n.* 1. polite indulgence. 2. forgiveness. —*v.* 3. excuse; forgive. —**par′don•a•ble,** *adj.*

pare, *v.,* **pared, paring.** cut off outer part of.

par•e•gor′ic, *n.* soothing medicine.

par′ent, *n.* father or mother. —**pa•ren′tal,** *adj.* —**par′ent•hood′,** *n.*

par′ent•age, *n.* descent.

pa•ren′the•sis, *n., pl.* -**ses.** 1. upright curves ( ) used to mark off interpolation. 2. material so interpolated. —**par•en•thet′ic,** **par•en•thet′i•cal,** *adj.* —**par•en•thet′i•cal•ly,** *adv.*

pa•re′sis, *n.* incomplete paralysis.

par•fait′ (pär fā′), *n.* frothy frozen dessert.

pa•ri′ah (-rī′-), *n.* outcast.

par′i•mu•tu•el, *n.* form of betting on races.

par′ish, *n.* ecclesiastical district. —**pa•rish′ion•er,** *n.*

par′i•ty, *n.* 1. equality. 2. similarity. 3. guaranteed level of farm prices.

park, n. 1. tract of land set apart for public. —v. 2. place vehicle.

par′ka, n. hooded garment.

Par′kin·son′s disease, neurological disease characterized by tremors, esp. of fingers and hands, shuffling, and muscular rigidity.

park′way′, n. broad thoroughfare with dividing strip or side strips planted with trees, etc.

par′lance, n. way of speaking.

par′lay, v. reinvest original amount and its earnings.

par′ley, n. 1. conference between combatants. —v. 2. hold parley.

par′lia·ment, n. 1. legislative body, esp. (cap.) of United Kingdom.

par′lia·men′ta·ry, adj. 1. of, by, or having a parliament. 2. in accordance with rules of debate.

par′lor, n. room for receiving callers.

Par′me·san′, n. hard, dry Italian cheese.

pa·ro′chi·al, adj. 1. of a parish. 2. narrow; provincial. —**pa·ro′chi·al·ism**, n.

par′o·dy, n., pl. -dies, v., -died, -dying. —n. 1. humorous imitation. —v. 2. imitate in ridicule.

pa·role′, n., v., -roled, -roling. —n. 1. conditional release from prison. —v. 2. put on parole. —**pa·rol·ee′** (-rō′lē′), n.

par′ox·ysm, n. sudden violent outburst. —**par′ox·ys′mal**, adj.

par·quet′ (-kā′), n. floor of inlaid design.

par′ri·cide′ (-sīd′), n. crime of killing one's father.

par′rot, n. 1. hook-billed, bright-colored bird capable of being taught to talk. —v. 2. repeat senselessly.

par′ry, v., -ried, -rying, n., pl. -ries. —v. 1. ward off; evade. —n. 2. act of parrying.

parse, v., parsed, parsing. describe (word or sentence) grammatically.

par′si·mo′ny, n. excessive frugality. —**par′si·mo′ni·ous**, adj.

pars′ley, n. garden herb used in seasoning.

pars′nip, n. plant with white edible root.

par′son, n. member of the clergy.

par′son·age, n. house provided for parson.

part, n. 1. portion of a whole. 2. share. 3. (pl.) personal qualities. —v. 4. separate.

par·take′, v., -took, -taken, -taking. have share.

par′tial, adj. 1. being part; incomplete. 2. biased. 3. especially fond. —**par′tial·i·ty**, n. —**par′tial·ly**, adv.

par·tic′i·pate′, v., -pated, -pating. take part; share (in). —**par·tic′i·pant**, n., adj. —**par·tic′i·pa′tor**, n. —**par·tic′i·pa′tion**, n.

par′ti·ci·ple, n. adjective derived from verb. —**par′ti·cip′i·al**, adj.

par′ti·cle, n. 1. tiny piece. 2. functional word.

par·tic′u·lar, adj. 1. pertaining to some one person, thing, etc. 2. noteworthy. 3. attentive to details. —n. 4. detail. —**par·tic′u·lar·ly**, adv.

part′ing, n. departure or separation.

par′ti·san, n. 1. adherent. 2. guerrilla.

par·ti′tion, n. 1. division into portions. 2. interior wall. —v. 3. divide into parts.

part′ly, adv. not wholly.

part′ner, n. 1. sharer; associate. 2. joint owner. —**part′ner·ship′**, n.

par′tridge, n. game bird.

part′-time′, adj. 1. involving or working less than the usual or full time. —adv. 2. on a part-time basis.

par·tu·ri′tion, n. childbirth.

par′ty, n., pl. -ties. 1. group of people with common purpose. 2. social gathering. 3. person concerned.

pas′chal (pas′kəl), adj. of Passover or Easter.

pa·sha′, n. (formerly) Turkish official.

pass, v., passed, passed or past, passing, n. —v. 1. go past, by, or through. 2. omit. 3. approve. 4. convey. 5. proceed. 6. go by; elapse. 7. die. 8. be accepted. 9. go unchallenged. —n. 10. narrow route through barrier. 11. permission or license. 12. free ticket. 13. state of affairs. —**pass′er**, n.

pas′sa·ble, adj. adequate. —**pas′sa·bly**, adv.

pas′sage, n. 1. section of writing, etc. 2. freedom to pass. 3. movement; transportation. 4. corridor. 5. lapse. 6. act of passing. —**pas′sage·way**, n.

pass′book′, n. booklet recording depositor's bank balance, etc.

pas·sé′ (pa sā′), adj. out-of-date.

pas′sen·ger, n. traveler on vehicle or craft.

pass′er·by′, n., pl. passersby. person who passes by.

pass′ing, adj. brief; transitory.

pas′sion, n. 1. very strong emotion. 2. sexual love. 3. (cap.) sufferings of Christ. —**pas′sion·ate**, adj. —**pas′sion·ate·ly**, adv. —**pas′sion·less**, adj.

pas′sive, adj. 1. not in action. 2. acted upon. 3. submitting without resistance. 4. designating voice of verbs indicating subject acted upon. —**pas′-**

sive•ly, adv. **—pas'sive•ness, pas•siv'i•ty,** n.

pass'key, n. master key.

Pass'o•ver, n. annual Jewish festival.

pass'port, n. official document giving permission to travel abroad.

pass'word, n. secret word used to gain access.

past, adj. 1. gone by, as in time. 2. of an earlier time. 3. designating a tense or verb formation showing time gone by. —n. 4. time or events gone by. 5. past tense. —adv. 6. so as to pass by. —prep. 7. after. 8. beyond.

pas'ta (päs'-), n. Italian flour-and-egg mixture, as spaghetti or macaroni.

paste, n., v., **pasted, pasting.** —n. 1. soft sticky mixture. 2. shiny glass used for gems. —v. 3. fasten with paste. **—past'y,** adj.

paste'board', n. firm board made of layers of paper.

pas•tel', n. soft color.

pas'tern, n. part of a horse's foot between the fetlock and the hoof.

pas'teur•ize', v., **-ized, -izing.** heat (milk, etc.) to destroy certain bacteria. **—pas'teur•i•za'tion,** n.

pas•tiche' (-tēsh'), n. artistic work made up of borrowed pieces.

pas•tille' (-tēl') n. flavored or medicated lozenge.

pas'time', n. diversion.

pas'tor, n. minister.

pas'to•ral, adj. 1. having rural charm. 2. of shepherds. 3. of pastors.

pas'to•rale' (-räl'), n. dreamy musical composition.

pas•tra'mi (-trä'-), n. seasoned smoked or pickled beef.

pas'try, n., pl. **-tries.** food made of rich paste, as pies.

pas'tur•age, n. grazing ground.

pas'ture, n., v., **-tured, -turing.** —n. 1. grassy ground for grazing cattle. —v. 2. graze on pasture.

pat, v., **patted, patting,** n., adj., adv. —v. 1. strike gently with flat object, hand, etc. —n. 2. light stroke. 3. small mass. —adj. 4. apt; to the point. —adv. 5. perfectly. 6. unwaveringly.

patch, n. 1. piece of material used to mend or protect. 2. any small piece. —v. 3. mend, esp. with patches. **—patch'work',** n.

patch'y, adj., **patchier, patchiest.** irregular in surface or quality. **—patch'i•ness,** n.

pate, n. crown of head.

pâ•té' (pä tāl', pa-), n. paste of puréed or chopped meat, liver, etc.

pa•tel'la, n., pl. **-tellae** (-tel'ē). kneecap.

pat'ent, n. 1. exclusive right to make,

use, and sell invention. —adj. 2. protected by patent. 3. (also pā'tant). evident; plain. —v. 4. secure patent on.

patent leather, hard, glossy, smooth leather.

pa•ter'nal, adj. 1. fatherly. 2. related through father. **—pa•ter'nal•ly,** adv.

pa•ter'nal•ism, n. benevolent control. **—pa•ter•nal•is'tic,** adj.

pa•ter'ni•ty, n. fatherhood.

pa•ter•nos'ter, n. Lord's Prayer.

path, n. 1. Also, **path'way.** narrow way. 2. route. 3. course of action.

pa•thet'ic, adj. arousing pity. **—pa•thet'i•cal•ly,** adv.

path'o•gen (path'ə jən, -jen'), n. disease-producing agent. **—path'o•gen'ic,** adj.

path'o•log'i•cal, adj. sick; morbid. **—path'o•log'i•cal•ly,** adv.

pa•thol'o•gy, n. study of disease. **—pa•thol'o•gist,** n.

pa'thos (pā'-), n. quality or power of arousing pity.

pa'tient, n. 1. person under care of a doctor. —adj. 2. enduring pain, annoyance, or delay calmly. **—pa'tience,** n. **—pa'tient•ly,** adv.

pat'i•na (pə tē'na), n. film on old bronze, etc.

pa'ti•o', n., pl. **-tios.** inner open court.

pat'ois (pat'wä, pä'twä), n. regional form of a language.

pa'tri•arch', n. 1. venerable old man. 2. male head of tribe or family. **—pa'tri•ar'chal,** adj.

pa'tri•ar'chy, n., pl. **-chies.** family group ruled by a father.

pa•tri'cian, n. 1. aristocrat. —adj. 2. aristocratic.

pat'ri•mo'ny, n., pl. **-nies.** inherited estate.

pa'tri•ot, n. person who loves, supports, and defends his or her country. **—pa'tri•ot'ic,** adj. **—pa'tri•ot'ism,** n. **—pa'tri•ot'i•cal•ly,** adv.

pa•trol', v., **-trolled, -trolling,** n. —v. 1. pass through in guarding. —n. 2. person or group assigned to patrol.

pa•trol'man, n., pl. **-men.** police officer who patrols specific area.

pa'tron, n. 1. supporter. 2. regular customer.

pa'tron•age, n. 1. support by patron. 2. political control of appointments to office.

pa'tron•ize', v., **-ized, -izing.** 1. buy from, esp. regularly. 2. treat condescendingly.

pat'ter, v. 1. move or strike with slight tapping sounds. 2. speak glibly. —n.

3. pattering sound. 4. rapid, glib speech.

pat'tern, *n.* 1. surface design. 2. characteristic mode of development, etc. 3. model for copying. —*v.* 4. make after pattern.

pat'ty, *n., pl.* **-ties.** 1. thin, round piece of ground or minced food, as of meat. 2. little pie or wafer.

pau'ci•ty (pô'sə tē), *n.* scarceness.

paunch, *n.* belly, esp. when large. —**paunch'y,** *adj.*

pau'per, *n.* poor person.

pause, *n., v.,* **paused, pausing.** —*n.* 1. temporary stop. —*v.* 2. make pause.

pave, *v.,* **paved, paving.** 1. cover with solid road surface. 2. prepare. —**pave'ment,** *n.*

pa•vil'ion, *n.* 1. light open shelter. 2. tent.

paw, *n.* 1. foot of animal with nails or claws. —*v.* 2. strike or scrape with paw.

pawl, *n.* pivoted bar engaging with teeth of ratchet wheel.

pawn, *v.* 1. deposit as security for loan. —*n.* 2. state of being pawned. 3. piece used in chess. —**pawn'shop',** *n.*

pawn'bro'ker, *n.* person who lends money on pledged articles.

pay, *v.,* **paid, paying,** *n.* —*v.* 1. give money required to. 2. give as compensation. 3. yield profit. 4. let out (rope). —*n.* 5. wages. 6. paid employ. —**pay'a•ble,** *adj.* —**pay•ee',** *n.* —**pay'er,** *n.* —**pay'ment,** *n.*

pay'load', *n.* 1. revenue-producing freight, etc. 2. contents to be carried.

pay'off', *n.* 1. *Informal.* final consequence. 2. awaited payment.

PC, *n., pl.* **PCs** or **PC's.** personal computer. 2. politically correct.

pea, *n.* round edible seed of common legume.

peace, *n.* freedom from war, trouble, or disturbance. —**peace'mak'er,** *n.* —**peace'time',** *n.*

peace'ful, *adj.* 1. at peace. 2. desiring peace. Also, **peace'a•ble.** —**peace'ful•ly,** *adv.* —**peace'ful•ness,** *n.*

peach, *n.* sweet juicy pinkish fruit.

pea'cock', *n.* male of peafowl, having iridescent tail feathers of green, blue, and gold.

pea'fowl', *n.* bird of pheasant family.

pea'hen', *n.* female peafowl.

pea jacket, short heavy coat worn by mariners.

peak, *n.* 1. pointed top. 2. highest point.

peaked, *adj.* 1. having peak. 2. (pē'kid). sickly, haggard.

peal, *n.* 1. loud prolonged sound, as of

bells or thunder. 2. set of bells. —*v.* 3. sound in a peal.

pea'nut', *n.* pod or edible seed of leguminous plant that ripens underground.

pear, *n.* elongated edible fruit.

pearl, *n.* hard, smooth, near-white gem formed within shell of an oyster. —**pearl'y,** *adj.*

peas'ant, *n.* farmer or farm worker.

peat, *n.* organic soil dried for fuel. —**peat'y,** *adj.*

peb'ble, *n.* small, rounded stone. —**peb'bly,** *adj.*

pe•can' (pi kän', -kan'), *n.* smooth-shelled nut.

pec•ca•dil'lo, *n., pl.* **-loes, -los.** trifling sin.

pec'ca•ry, *n., pl.* **-ries.** wild American pig.

peck, *v.* 1. strike with beak. —*n.* 2. pecking stroke. 3. dry measure of eight quarts.

pec'tin, *n.* substance in ripe fruit that forms jelly when evaporated.

pec'to•ral, *adj.* 1. of the chest. —*n.* 2. pectoral muscle or organ.

pec'u•late', *v.,* **-lated, -lating.** embezzle. —**pec'u•la'tion,** *n.*

pe•cul'iar, *adj.* 1. strange; odd. 2. uncommon. 3. exclusive. —**pe•cu'li•ar'i•ty,** *n.* —**pe•cul'iar•ly,** *adv.*

pe•cu'ni•ar'y, *adj.* of money.

ped'a•gogue', *n.* teacher. —**ped'a•go'gy,** *n.* —**ped'a•gog'ic, ped'a•gog'i•cal,** *adj.* —**ped'a•gog'i•cal•ly,** *adv.*

ped'al, *n., adj.,* **-aled, -aling,** *adj.* —*n.* 1. lever worked by foot. —*v.* 2. work pedals of. —*adj.* 3. (pē'dal). of feet.

ped'ant, *n.* person excessively concerned with details. —**pe•dan'tic,** *adj.* —**ped'ant•ry,** *n.*

ped'dle, *v.,* **-dled, -dling.** carry about for sale. —**ped'dler,** *n.*

ped'er•as'ty, *n.* sexual relations between a man and a boy. —**ped'er•ast',** *n.*

ped'es•tal, *n.* base for column, statue, etc.

pe•des'tri•an, *n.* 1. walker. —*adj.* 2. walking. 3. prosaic.

pe•di•at'rics, *n.* study of care and diseases of children. —**pe•di•a•tri'cian,** *n.* —**pe•di•at'ric,** *adj.*

ped'i•cure' (ped'i kyŏor'), *n.* professional care of the feet, as trimming of toenails.

ped'i•gree', *n.* 1. certificate of ancestry. 2. ancestry. —**ped'i•greed',** *adj.*

ped'i•ment, *n.* gablelike architectural feature.

pe•dom'e•ter, *n.* instrument that measures distance walked.

peek, v., n. peep (defs. 1–3; 5).

peel, v. 1. remove or lose skin, bark, etc. —n. 2. skin of fruit, etc.

peen, n. sharp end of hammer head.

peep, v. 1. look through small opening. 2. look furtively. 3. show slightly. 4. utter shrill little cry. —n. 5. quick look. 6. weak sound. —**peep'er,** n.

peer, n. 1. equal. 2. noble. —v. 3. look closely.

peer'age, n. 1. rank of peer. 2. list of peers.

peer'less, adj. without equal. —**peer'less·ness,** n.

peeve, v., peeved, peeving. annoy; vex.

pee'vish, adj. discontented; cross.

pee·wee, n. Informal. person or thing that is unusually small.

peg, n., v., pegged, pegging. —n. 1. pin of wood, metal, etc. —v. 2. fasten with pegs.

pe·jo·ra·tive (pi jôr'ə tiv, -jor'-), adj. disparaging; negative.

Pe'king·ese' (pē'kə nēz'), n., pl. -ese. long-haired Chinese dog with flat muzzle. Also, **Pe'kin·ese'.**

pe'koe, n. black tea.

pel'i·can, n. large-billed bird.

pel·la'gra (pə lā'-), n. chronic disease from inadequate diet.

pel'let, n. little ball.

pell'-mell', adv. in disorderly haste.

pel·lu'cid (pə loo'sid), adj. 1. translucent. 2. clear.

pelt, v. 1. throw. 2. assail. —n. 3. blow with something thrown. 4. skin of beast.

pel'vis, n. 1. basinlike cavity in lower part of body trunk. 2. bones forming this cavity. —**pel'vic,** adj.

pen, n., v., penned or (for 4) pent, penning. —n. 1. instrument for writing with ink. 2. small enclosure. —v. 3. write with pen. 4. confine in pen.

pe'nal (pē'nəl), adj. of, given as, or subject to punishment. —**pe'nal·ize',** v.

pen'al·ty, n., pl. -ties. 1. punishment. 2. disadvantage.

pen'ance, n. punishment as penitence for sin.

pence, n. Brit. pl. of penny.

pen'chant, n. liking.

pen'cil, n. enclosed stick of graphite, etc., for marking.

pend, v. remain undecided.

pend'ant, n. 1. hanging ornament. 2. match; counterpart.

pend'ent, adj. hanging.

pend'ing, prep. 1. until. —adj. 2. undecided.

pen'du·lous, adj. hanging.

pen'du·lum, n. weight hung to swing freely.

pen'e·trate', v., -trated, -trating. 1. pierce; permeate. 2. enter. 3. understand; have insight. —**pen'e·tra·ble,** adj. —**pen'e·tra'tion,** n.

pen'guin, n. flightless aquatic bird.

pen·i·cil'lin (pen'ə sil'in), n. antibacterial substance produced in certain molds.

pen·in'su·la, n. piece of land nearly surrounded by water. —**pen·in'su·lar,** adj.

pe'nis, n. male organ of copulation and urination.

pen'i·tent, adj. 1. sorry for sin or fault. —n. 2. penitent person. —**pen'i·tence,** n.

pen·i·ten'tia·ry, n., pl. -ries. prison.

pen'knife', n. small pocket knife.

pen'man, n., pl. -men. person skilled in writing. —**pen'man·ship',** n.

pen name, writer's pseudonym.

pen'nant, n. flag, usually tapered. Also, **pen'non.**

pen'ny, n., pl. -nies, Brit. pence. small coin, equal to one cent in the U.S. and Canada, and to 1/100 pound in United Kingdom. —**pen'ni·less,** adj.

pen'ny·weight', n. (in troy weight) 24 grains, or 1/20 of an ounce.

pe·nol'o·gy, n. science of punishment of crime and management of prisoners. —**pe·nol'o·gist,** n.

pen pal, person with whom one keeps up exchange of letters.

pen'sion, n. 1. fixed periodic payment for past service, etc. 2. (pän sē ôn'). (in France) boarding house or school. —v. 3. give pension to.

pen'sion·er, n. person receiving pension.

pen'sive, adj. gravely thoughtful. —**pen'sive·ly,** adv. —**pen'sive·ness,** n.

pent, adj. confined.

pen'ta·gon', n. plane figure having five sides and five angles.

pen·tam'e·ter, n. verse or line of five feet.

Pen'ta·teuch' (-tōok', -tyōok'), n. Bible. first five books of the Old Testament.

Pen'te·cost', n. 1. Christian festival; Whitsunday. 2. Jewish festival.

pent'house', n. rooftop apartment or dwelling.

pent'-up', adj. restrained; confined.

pe'nult, n. next to last syllable of word.

pe·nul'ti·mate (pi nul'tə mit), adj. being or occurring next to last.

pe·num'bra, n., pl. -brae, -bras. partial shadow outside complete shadow of celestial body in eclipse. —**pe·num′bral,** *adj.*

pe·nu·ri·ous (pa nyŏŏr′-), *adj.* 1. meanly stingy. 2. in great poverty.

pen′u·ry, *n.* poverty.

pe′on, *n.* 1. unskilled worker. 2. worker in bondage to pay off debts.

pe′on·age, *n.* labor in bondage.

pe′o·ny, *n., pl.* -nies. perennial plant with large showy flowers.

peo′ple, *n., v.* -pled, -pling. —*n.* 1. body of persons constituting nation or ethnic group. 2. persons in general. 3. person's relatives. —*v.* 4. populate.

pep, *n., v.* pepped, pepping. *Informal.* —*n.* 1. vigor. —*v.* 2. give vigor to. —**pep′py,** *adj.*

pep′per, *n.* 1. pungent condiment from dried berries of certain plants. 2. hollow, edible, green-to-red fruit of certain plants. —*v.* 3. season with pepper. 4. pelt with shot or missiles. —**pep′per·y,** *adj.*

pep′per·mint′, *n.* aromatic oil of herb, used as flavoring.

pep′sin, *n.* juice secreted in stomach that digests proteins.

pep′tic, *adj.* digestive.

per, *prep.* through; for; by means of.

per′ad·ven′ture, *adv.* *Archaic.* maybe.

per·am′bu·late′, *v.,* -lated, -lating. walk about or through. —**per·am′bu·la′tion,** *n.*

per·am′bu·la·tor, *n.* baby carriage.

per·cale′, *n.* smooth, closely woven cotton fabric.

per cap′i·ta, by or for each person.

per·ceive′, *v.,* -ceived, -ceiving. 1. gain knowledge of by seeing, hearing, etc. 2. understand. —**per·ceiv′a·ble, per·cep′ti·ble,** *adj.*

per·cent′, *n.* number of parts in each hundred. Also, **per cent.**

per·cent′age, *n.* 1. proportion or rate per hundred. 2. *Informal.* profit; advantage.

per·cept′, *n.* result of perceiving.

per·cep′tion, *n.* 1. act or faculty of perceiving. 2. intuition; insight. 3. result or product of perceiving.

per·cep′tive, *adj.* 1. keen. 2. showing perception.

perch, *n.* 1. place for roosting. 2. linear measure of 5½ yards. 3. square rod (30¼ sq. yards). 4. common food fish. —*v.* 5. set or rest on perch.

per·chance′, *adv. Poetic.* maybe; by chance.

per′co·late′, *v.,* -lated, -lating. filter through. —**per′co·la′tion,** *n.*

per′co·la·tor, *n.* kind of coffee pot.

per·cus′sion, *n.* 1. violent impact.

2. sounded by striking. —**per·cus′sion·ist,** *n.*

per di′em (par dē′əm), *adv.* 1. by the day. —*n.* 2. daily pay or allowance for expenses. 3. person paid by the day. —*adj.* 4. paid by the day.

per·di′tion, *n.* ruin; hell.

per′e·gri·nate′, *v.,* -nated, -nating. travel on foot. —**per′e·gri·na′tion,** *n.*

per·emp′to·ry, *adj.* permitting no denial or refusal. —**per·emp′to·ri·ly,** *adv.* —**per·emp′to·ri·ness,** *n.*

per·en′ni·al, *adj.* 1. lasting indefinitely. 2. living more than two years. —*n.* 3. perennial plant. —**per·en′ni·al·ly,** *adv.*

per′fect, *adj.* 1. complete; faultless; correct. 2. *Gram.* denoting action already completed. —*n.* 3. *Gram.* perfect tense. —*v.* (par fekt′). 4. finish; improve; make faultless. —**per·fec′tion,** *n.* —**per′fect·ly,** *adv.*

per·fec′tion·ism, *n.* insistence on perfection. —**per·fec′tion·ist,** *n.*

per′fi·dy, *n., pl.* -dies. treachery; faithlessness. —**per·fid′i·ous,** *adj.*

per′fo·rate′, *v.,* -rated, -rating. make holes through. —**per′fo·ra′tion,** *n.*

per·force′, *adv.* of necessity.

per·form′, *v.* 1. carry out; do. 2. act, as on stage. —**per·for′mance,** *n.* —**per·form′er,** *n.*

per·fume′, *n., v.,* -fumed, -fuming. —*n.* 1. sweet-smelling liquid. 2. sweet smell. —*v.* (par fyoom′). 3. impart fragrance to.

per·func′to·ry, *adj.* done without care or attention. —**per·func′to·ri·ly,** *adv.* —**per·func′to·ri·ness,** *n.*

per·haps′, *adv.* maybe.

per′i·car′di·um, *n.* membranous sac enclosing the heart.

per′i·gee′ (-jē′), *n.* point nearest earth in orbit of a heavenly body.

per′i·he′li·on, *n.* point nearest sun in orbit of a planet or comet.

per′il, *n.* 1. danger. 2. endanger. —**per′il·ous,** *adj.*

per·im′e·ter, *n.* 1. outer boundary of plane figure. 2. length of boundary. —**per′i·met′ric, per′i·met′ri·cal,** *adj.*

per′i·od, *n.* 1. portion of time. 2. mark (.) ending declarative sentence, etc.

per′i·od′ic, *adj.* recurring regularly or intermittently. —**pe′ri·od′i·cal·ly,** *adv.*

pe′ri·od′i·cal, *n.* 1. publication issued at regular intervals. —*adj.* 2. periodic.

per′i·o·don′tal (per′ē ə don′tl), *adj.* of or concerning bone, tissue, and gums surrounding and supporting teeth.

per'i•pa•tet'ic, adj. walking or traveling about; itinerant.

pe•riph'er•al, adj. **1.** located on periphery. **2.** only partly relevant.

pe•riph'er•y, n., pl. **-eries. 1.** external boundary. **2.** external surface.

per'i•scope', n. optical instrument consisting of a tube in which mirrors or prisms reflect to give a view from below or behind an obstacle.

per'ish, v. **1.** die, esp. violently. **2.** decay. **—per'ish•a•ble,** adj., n.

per'i•to•ni'tis (-nī'-), n. inflammation of the abdominal wall.

per'i•win'kle, n. **1.** edible marine snail. **2.** trailing evergreen plant.

per'jure, v., **-jured, -juring.** make (oneself) guilty of perjury. **—per'jur•er,** n.

per'ju•ry, n., pl. **-ries.** false statement made willfully under oath.

perk, v. **1.** move or raise jauntily. **2.** become lively. **3.** perquisite. **—perk'y,** adj.

per'ma•nent, adj. **1.** lasting indefinitely. **—**n. **2.** Also, **perm.** wave or curl set in hair by chemicals or heat. **—per'ma•nence, per'ma•nen•cy,** n. **—per'ma•nent•ly,** adv.

per'me•ate', v., **-ated, -ating.** penetrate; pervade. **—per'me•a'tion,** n. **—per'me•a•ble,** adj.

per•mis'sion, n. authorization granting request. **—per•mis'si•ble,** adj. **—per•mis'si•bly,** adv.

per•mis'sive, adj. **1.** giving permission. **2.** loose or lax in discipline.

per•mit', v., **-mitted, -mitting.** —v. (par mit'). **1.** allow; agree to. **2.** afford opportunity. **—**n. (pûr'mit). **3.** written order giving permission.

per•mu•ta'tion, n. alteration; change in order.

per•ni'cious, adj. **1.** highly hurtful. **2.** deadly.

per'o•ra'tion, n. concluding part of speech.

per•ox'ide, n. **1.** oxide containing large amount of oxygen. **2.** antiseptic liquid (**hydrogen peroxide**).

per•pen•dic'u•lar, adj. **1.** upright; vertical. **2.** meeting given line at right angles. **—**n. **3.** perpendicular line or position.

per'pe•trate', v., **-trated, -trating.** commit (crime, etc.). **—per'pe•tra'tion,** n. **—per'pe•tra'tor,** n.

per•pet'u•al, adj. **1.** lasting forever. **2.** unceasing. **—per•pet'u•ate',** v. **—per•pe•tu'i•ty,** n. endless duration.

per•plex', v. **1.** confuse mentally. **—per•plex'i•ty,** n.

per'qui•site, n. incidental profit in addition to fixed pay.

per se (pûr sā', sē', par), by, of, for, or in itself; intrinsically.

per'se•cute', v., **-cuted, -cuting.** oppress persistently, esp. for one's beliefs. **—per'se•cu'tion,** n. **—per'se•cu'tor,** n.

per'se•vere', v., **-vered, -vering.** continue steadfastly. **—per'se•ver'ance,** n.

per'si•flage' (pûr'sə fläzh', pâr'-), n. light, bantering talk.

per•sim'mon, n. soft, astringent fruit.

per•sist', v. **1.** continue firmly in spite of opposition. **2.** endure. **—per•sist'ence,** n. **—per•sist'ent,** adj. **—per•sist'ent•ly,** adv.

per'son, n. **1.** human being. **2.** individual personality. **3.** body.

per'son•a•ble, adj. attractive in appearance and manner.

per'son•age, n. distinguished person.

per'son•al, adj. **1.** of, by, or relating to a certain person. **2.** Gram. denoting class of pronouns that refer to speaker, person addressed, or thing spoken of. **3.** Law. of property that is movable. **—per'son•al•ly,** adv.

personal computer, microcomputer designed for individual use, as for word processing.

per'son•al'i•ty, n., pl. **-ties. 1.** distinctive personal character. **2.** famous person.

per'son•al•ize', v., **-ized, -izing. 1.** make personal. **2.** treat as if human.

per•son'i•fy', v., **-fied, -fying. 1.** attribute personal character to. **2.** embody; typify. **3.** impersonate. **—per•son'i•fi•ca'tion,** n.

per'son•nel', n. employees.

per•spec'tive, n. **1.** art of depicting on surface so as to show space relationships. **2.** mental view.

per'spi•ca'cious, adj. mentally keen. **—per'spi•cac'i•ty,** n.

per•spic'u•ous, adj. clear to understanding. **—per'spi•cu'i•ty,** n.

per•spire', v., **-spired, -spiring.** sweat. **—per'spi•ra'tion,** n.

per•suade', v., **-suaded, -suading. 1.** prevail on to act as suggested. **2.** convince. **—per•sua'sive,** adj.

per•sua'sion, n. **1.** act or power of persuading. **2.** conviction or belief. **3.** religious system.

pert, adj. bold; saucy. **—pert'ly,** adv. **—pert'ness,** n.

per•tain', v. have reference; belong.

per'ti•na'cious, adj. holding tenaciously to purpose, opinion, etc.

per'ti•nent, adj. relevant. **—per'ti•**

nence, per'ti•nen•cy, n. —per'ti•nent•ly, adv.

per•turb', v. disturb greatly. —per'tur•ba'tion, n.

pe•ruse' (-rōōz'), v., -rused, -rusing. read, esp. with care. —pe•ru'sal, n.

per•vade', v., -vaded, -vading. extend or be present throughout. —per•va'sive, adj.

per•verse', adj. 1. stubbornly contrary. 2. counter to what is considered normal. —per•ver'si•ty, n. —per•verse'ly, adv.

per•vert', v. 1. turn from right or moral course or use. —n. (pûr'vûrt), n. 2. perverted person. —per•ver'sion, n.

pes'ky, adj., -kier, -kiest. annoying; troublesome.

pe'so (pā'sō), n. monetary unit and coin of Mexico, Cuba, etc.

pes'si•mism, n. 1. disposition to expect worst. 2. belief that all things tend to evil. —pes'si•mist, n. —pes'si•mis'tic, adj. —pes'si•mis'ti•cal•ly, adv.

pest, n. troublesome person, animal, or thing.

pes'ter, v. annoy; harass.

pes'ti•cide, n. poison used to kill harmful insects, weeds, etc.

pes'ti•lence, n. deadly epidemic disease. —pes'ti•lent, adj.

pes'tle, n. instrument for pounding or crushing.

pet, n., adj., v., petted, petting. —n. 1. tame animal that is cared for affectionately. 2. favorite. 3. fit of peevishness. —adj. 4. treated as pet. —v. 5. indulge or fondle.

pet'al, n. leaf of blossom.

pe'ter, v. Informal. diminish gradually.

pet'it (pet'ē), adj. Law. petty.

pe•tite' (-tēt'), adj. (of woman) tiny.

pe•ti'tion, n. 1. request, esp. formal one. —v. 2. present petition. —pe•ti'tion•er, n.

pet'rel, n. small oceanic bird.

pet'ri•fy, v., -fied, -fying. 1. turn into stone. 2. paralyze with fear.

pet•ro•dol'lars, n.pl. money surpluses of petroleum-exporting countries.

pet'rol, n. Brit. gasoline.

pe•tro'le•um, n. oily liquid occurring naturally: source of gasoline, kerosene, paraffin, etc.

pe•trol'o•gy, n. study of rocks.

pet'ti•coat, n. underskirt.

pet'tish, adj. petulant.

pet'ty, adj., -tier, -tiest. 1. small or trivial. 2. small-minded. —pet'ti•ness, n.

pet'u•lant (pech'-), adj. showing impatient irritation. —pet'u•lance, n.

pe•tu'ni•a, n. plant with funnel-shaped flowers.

pew, n. enclosed bench or seats in church.

pe•wee, n. any of certain small birds.

pew'ter, n. alloy containing much tin.

PG, parental guidance recommended: motion-picture classification.

pha'e•ton (fā'ə tən), n. open carriage or automobile.

pha'lanx, n., pl. -lanxes, -langes (fə lan'jēz). 1. compact body, as of troops, etc. 2. any of bones of fingers or toes.

phal'lus, n., pl. phalli. 1. penis. 2. image of penis as symbol of fertility. —phal'lic, adj.

phan'tasm, n. apparition.

phan•tas•ma•go'ri•a, n. shifting series of illusions.

phan'tom, n. 1. dreamlike or ghostlike image; apparition. —adj. 2. unreal.

Phar'aoh (fâr'ō), n. title of ancient Egyptian kings.

Phar'i•see', n. 1. member of ancient Jewish sect. 2. (l.c.) self-righteous person.

phar•ma•ceu'ti•cal (-sōō'-), adj. pertaining to pharmacy. Also, phar'ma•ceu'tic.

phar•ma•col'o•gy, n. study of drugs. —phar•ma•col'o•gist, n.

phar•ma•co•poe'ia (-pē'ə), n. authoritative book on medicines.

phar'ma•cy, n., pl. -cies. 1. art or practice of preparing medicines. 2. place for dispensing medicines. —phar'ma•cist, n.

phar'ynx, n., pl. pharynges (fə rin'jēz), pharynxes. tube connecting mouth and nasal passages with esophagus. —pha•ryn'ge•al, adj.

phase, n. 1. stage of change. 2. aspect of changing time.

phase'out', n. gradual dismissal or termination.

pheas'ant, n. large, long-tailed, bright-colored bird.

phe•no•bar'bi•tal', n. white powder used as sedative.

phe'nol, n. carbolic acid. —phe•no'lic, adj.

phe•nom'e•non', n., pl. -ena. 1. something observable. 2. extraordinary thing or person. —phe•nom'e•nal, adj. —phe•nom'e•nal•ly, adv.

phi'al, n. vial.

phi•lan'der, v. (of man) make love lightly. —phi•lan'der•er, n.

phi•lan'thro•py, n., pl. -pies. 1. love of humanity. 2. benevolent act, work, or institution. —phil'an•throp'ic,

phil'an·throp'i·cal, *adj.* —**phi·lan'thro·pist,** *n.*

phi·lat'e·ly, *n.* collection and study of postage stamps, etc. —**phil'a·tel'ic,** *adj.* —**phi·lat'e·list,** *n.*

phil·har·mon'ic, *adj.* 1. music-loving. —*n.* 2. large orchestra.

phil'is·tine' (fil'ə stēn'), *n.* person indifferent to art or culture.

phi·lol'o·gy, *n.* linguistics. —**phi·lol'o·gist,** *n.*

phi·los'o·pher, *n.* 1. person versed in philosophy. 2. person guided by reason. 3. person who remains calm under difficulties.

phi·los'o·phy, *n.,* *pl.* -phies. 1. study of truths underlying being and knowledge. 2. system of philosophical belief. 3. principles of particular field of knowledge or action. 4. calmness. —**phil'o·soph'ic, phil'o·soph'i·cal,** *adj.* —**phi·los'o·phize',** *v.*

phil'ter, *n.* magic potion.

phle·bi'tis (flə bī'tis), *n.* inflammation of a vein.

phle·bot'o·my, *n.,* *pl.* -mies. *Med.* practice of opening a vein to let blood. —**phle·bot'o·mize',** *v.*

phlegm (flem), *n.* 1. thick mucus secreted in the respiratory passages. 2. apathy.

phleg·mat'ic, *adj.* unemotional or unenthusiastic. —**phleg·mat'i·cal·ly,** *adv.*

phlox, *n.* garden plant with showy flowers.

pho'bi·a, *n.* morbid fear.

phoe'be (fē'bē), *n.* small American bird.

Phoe'bus (fē'-), *n.* Apollo as the sun god.

phoe'nix (fē'niks), *n.* mythical bird burning, then rising reborn from its ashes.

phone, *n.,* *v.,* phoned, phoning. *Informal.* telephone.

pho·net'ics, *n.* science of speech sounds. —**pho·net'ic,** *adj.* —**pho·net'i·cal·ly,** *adv.*

phon'ics, *n.* method of teaching reading and spelling based on phonetics.

pho'no·graph', *n.* sound-producing machine using records. —**pho'no·graph'ic,** *adj.*

pho'ny, *adj.,* -nier, -niest, *n.,* *pl.* -nies. *Informal.* —*adj.* 1. false; fraudulent. —*n.* 2. something phony. —**pho'ni·ness,** *n.*

phos'gene (-jēn), *n.* poisonous gas.

phos'phate, *n.* 1. salt of phosphoric acid. 2. fertilizer containing phosphorus.

phos'phor (fos'fər), *n.* substance showing luminescence when struck by ultraviolet light, etc.

phos'pho·resce', *v.,* -resced, -rescing. be luminous without perceptible heat. —**phos'pho·res'cence,** *n.* —**phos'pho·res'cent,** *adj.*

phos'pho·rus, *n.* solid nonmetallic element present in all forms of life. —**phos·phor'ic, phos'pho·rous,** *adj.*

pho'to, *n.,* *pl.* -tos. *Informal.* photograph.

pho'to·cop'y, *n.,* *pl.* -copies. photographic copy. —**pho'to·cop'y,** *v.*

pho'to·e·lec'tric, *adj.* of or using electrical effects produced by light.

pho'to·en·grav'ing, *n.* process of obtaining a relief-printing surface by photographic reproduction. —**pho'to·en·grav'er,** *n.*

pho'to·gen'ic (-jen'-), *adj.* looking attractive in photographs.

pho'to·graph', *n.* 1. picture produced by photography. —*v.* 2. take photograph. —**pho·tog'ra·pher,** *n.*

pho·tog'ra·phy, *n.* process of obtaining images on sensitized surface by action of light. —**pho'to·graph'ic,** *adj.*

pho'to·sen'si·tive, *adj.* sensitive to light.

Pho'to·stat', *n.* 1. *Trademark.* camera for photographing documents, etc. 2. *(l.c.)* the photograph. —*v.* 3. *(l.c.)* make photostatic copy. —**pho'to·stat'ic,** *adj.*

pho'to·syn'the·sis, *n.* conversion by plants of carbon dioxide and water into carbohydrates, aided by light and chlorophyll.

phrase, *n.,* *v.,* phrased, phrasing. —*n.* 1. sequence of words used as unit. 2. minor division of musical composition. —*v.* 3. express in particular way.

phra'se·ol'o·gy, *n.* 1. manner of verbal expression. 2. expressions.

phre·net'ic, *adj.* frenetic.

phre·nol'o·gy, *n.* theory that mental powers are shown by shape of skull. —**phre·nol'o·gist,** *n.*

phy'lum, *n.,* *pl.* -la. primary classification of plants or animals.

phys'ic, *n.* medicine, esp. one that purges.

phys'i·cal, *adj.* 1. of the body. 2. of matter. 3. of physics. —*n.* 4. examination of the body, as by a physician. —**phys'i·cal·ly,** *adv.*

physical therapy, treatment of physical disability or pain by techniques such as exercise or massage.

phy·si'cian, *n.* medical doctor.

phys'ics, *n.* science of matter, motion, energy, and force. —**phys'i·cist,** *n.*

phys•i•og•no•my, n., pl. **-mies.** face.

phys•i•og•ra•phy, n. study of earth's surface.

phys•i•ol•o•gy, n. science dealing with functions of living organisms. —**phys•i•o•log′i•cal**, adj. —**phys′i•ol′o•gist**, n. —**phys′i•o•log′i•cal•ly**, adv.

phys•i•o•ther′a•py, n. treatment of disease by massage, exercise, etc.

phy•sique′ (-zēk′), n. physical structure.

pi (pī), n. the Greek letter π, used as symbol for ratio of circumference to diameter.

pi•a•nis′si•mo, adj. Music. very softly.

pi•an′o, n., pl. **-anos.** —adj. —n. 1. Also, **pi•an′o•for′te.** musical keyboard instrument in which hammers strike upon metal strings. —adv. (pē ä′nō). 2. Music. softly. —**pi•an′ist**, n.

pi•az′za, n. 1. open public square, esp. in Italy. 2. veranda.

pi′ca (pī′-), n. 1. size of printing type. 2. unit of measure in printing (about 1/6 inch).

pic•a•resque′, adj. of a form of fiction that humorously describes adventures of roguish hero.

pic′a•yune′, adj. petty; insignificant.

pic•ca•lil′li, n. spiced vegetable relish.

pic′co•lo, n., pl. **-los.** small shrill flute.

pick, v. 1. choose. 2. gather; pluck. 3. dig or break into, esp. with pointed instrument. 4. nibble listlessly. —n. 5. choice. 6. right to choose. 7. Also, **pick′ax′, pick′axe′.** sharp-pointed tool for breaking rock, etc. —**pick′er**, n.

pick′er•el, n. small pike.

pick′et, n. 1. pointed post or stake. 2. demonstrator from labor union in front of workplace. 3. body of troops posted to warn of enemy attack. —v. 4. enclose with pickets. 5. put pickets in front of.

pick′le, n., v., **-led**, **-ling.** —n. 1. cucumber, etc., preserved in spiced vinegar. 2. predicament. —v. 3. preserve in vinegar or brine.

pick′pock′et, n. person who steals from others' pockets.

pick′up′, n. 1. ability to accelerate rapidly. 2. small open-body truck.

pick′y, adj. **pickier, pickiest.** extremely fussy or finicky.

pic′nic, n., v., **-nicked**, **-nicking.** —n. 1. outing and meal in the open. —v. 2. have picnic. —**pic′nick•er**, n.

pic′ture, n., v., **-tured**, **-turing.** —n. 1. painting, photograph, etc., on flat surface. 2. motion picture. —v. 3. represent in picture. 4. imagine. —**pic•to′ri•al**, adj.

pic′tur•esque′, adj. visually charming or quaint.

pid′dling, adj. trivial; negligible.

pidg′in (pij′in), n. language developed to allow speakers of two different languages to communicate, primarily a simplified form of one of the languages.

pidgin English, English trade jargon used in Orient, West Africa, etc.

pie, n. baked dish of fruit, meat, etc., in pastry crust.

pie′bald′, adj. having patches of different colors.

piece, n., v., **pieced**, **piecing.** —n. 1. limited or single portion. 2. one part of a whole. 3. artistic work. 4. rifle or cannon. —v. 5. make or enlarge by joining pieces.

piece′meal′, adv. 1. gradually. 2. into fragments.

piece′work′, n. work done and paid for by the piece.

pied, adj. many-colored.

pie′plant′, n. rhubarb.

pier, n. 1. structure at which vessels are moored. 2. masonry support.

pierce, v., **pierced**, **piercing.** 1. make hole or way into or through. 2. make (hole) in.

pi′e•ty, n. quality of being pious.

pig, n. 1. swine, esp. young. 2. oblong bar of metal. —**pig′gish**, adj.

pi′geon, n. short-legged bird with compact body.

pi′geon•hole′, n., v., **-holed**, **-holing.** —n. 1. small compartment, as in desk, etc. —v. 2. classify. 3. put aside and ignore.

pi′geon-toed′, adj. having toes or feet turned inward.

pig′gy•back′, adv. 1. on the back or shoulders. —adj. 2. astride the back or shoulders. 3. attached to or allied with something else. 4. relating to the carrying of truck trailers on trains.

pig′head′ed, adj. perversely stubborn.

pig iron, crude iron from blast furnace.

pig′ment, n. coloring matter. —**pig′men•tar′y**, adj.

pig•men•ta′tion, n. coloration.

pig′my, n., pl. **-mies.** pygmy.

pig′pen′, n. 1. pen for keeping pigs. 2. filthy or untidy place. Also, **pig′sty′.**

pig′tail′, n. hanging braid at back of head.

pike, n. 1. large slender fresh-water fish. 2. metal-headed shaft. 3. highway.

pik'er, *n. Slang.* person who does things cheaply or meanly.

pi'laf (pē'läf, pi läf'), *n.* Middle Eastern rice dish. Also, **pi'laff.**

pi·las'ter, *n.* shallow decorative imitation of column.

pile, *n., v.,* **piled, piling.** —*n.* 1. heap. 2. device for producing energy by nuclear reaction. 3. Also, **pil'ing.** upright driven into ground as foundation member or to retain earth. 4. hair; down; wool; fur. 5. nap (def. 2). 6. *pl.* hemorrhoids. —*v.* 7. lay in pile. 8. accumulate.

pil'fer, *v.* steal, esp. from storage. —**pil'fer·age,** *n.*

pil'grim, *n.* 1. traveler, esp. to sacred place. 2. (*cap.*) early Puritan settler of Massachusetts. —**pil'grim·age,** *n.*

pill, *n.* small mass of medicine to be swallowed.

pil'lage, *v.,* **-laged, -laging,** *n.* plunder.

pil'lar, *n.* upright shaft of masonry.

pill'box', *n.* 1. small fort. 2. box for pills.

pil'lo·ry, *n., pl.* **-ries,** *v.,* **-ried, -rying.** —*n.* 1. wooden framework used to confine and expose offenders. —*v.* 2. put in pillory. 3. expose to public contempt.

pil'low, *n.* bag of feathers, etc., used as support for head. —**pil'low·case',** *n.*

pi'lot, *n.* 1. operator of aircraft or ship. 2. expert in navigation. —*v.* 3. steer; guide. —*adj.* 4. experimental.

pi·men'to, *n., pl.* **-tos.** dried fruit of tropical tree; allspice.

pi·mien'to (-myen'-), *n., pl.* **-tos.** variety of garden pepper.

pimp, *n., v.* —*n.* 1. manager of prostitutes. —*v.* 2. act as pimp.

pim'per·nel', *n.* variety of primrose.

pim'ple, *n.* small swelling on skin. —**pim'ply,** *adj.*

pin, *n., v.,* **pinned, pinning.** —*n.* 1. slender pointed piece of metal, wood, etc., for fastening. —*v.* 2. fasten with pin. 3. hold fast; bind.

pin'a·fore', *n.* 1. child's apron. 2. sleeveless dress.

pince'-nez' (pans' nā'), *n., pl.* **pince-nez.** pair of eyeglasses supported by spring pinching the nose.

pin'cers, *n.* gripping tool with two pivoted limbs.

pinch, *v.* 1. squeeze, as between finger and thumb. 2. cramp or affect sharply. 3. economize. —*n.* 4. act of pinching; nip. 5. tiny amount. 6. distress; emergency. —**pinch'er,** *n.*

pinch'-hit', *v.* **-hit, -hitting.** substitute.

pine, *v.,* **pined, pining.** —*v.* 1. long painfully. 2. fail in health from grief, etc. —*n.* 3. cone-bearing evergreen tree with needle-shaped leaves. —**pin'y,** *adj.*

pine'ap'ple, *n.* edible fruit of tropical plant.

pin'feath'er, *n.* undeveloped feather.

Ping'-Pong', *n. Trademark.* variety of tennis played on table.

pin'ion (-yən), *n.* 1. feather or wing. 2. small cogwheel. —*v.* 3. bind (the arms).

pink, *n.* 1. pale red. 2. fragrant garden flower. 3. highest degree. —**pink,** *adj.*

pink'eye', *n.* contagious inflammation of membrane covering eye.

pin'na·cle, *n.* 1. lofty peak or position. 2. pointed summit.

pi'noch'le (pē'nuk əl, -nok-), *n.* game using 48 cards.

pin'point', *v.* identify precisely.

pin'stripe', *n.* very thin stripe in fabric.

pint, *n.* liquid and dry measure equal to one-half quart.

pin'tle, *n.* pin or bolt.

pin'to, *adj., n., pl.* **-tos.** —*adj.* 1. piebald. —*n.* 2. piebald horse.

pinto bean, bean with pinkish mottled seeds.

pin'up', *n.* large photograph of sexually attractive person.

pin'wheel', *n.* windmill-like toy that spins on stick.

pi·o·neer', *n.* 1. early arrival in new territory. 2. first one in any effort. —*v.* 3. act as pioneer.

pi'ous, *adj.* 1. reverential; devout. 2. sacred. —**pi'ous·ly,** *adv.* —**pi'ous·ness,** *n.*

pip, *n.* 1. small fruit seed. 2. spot on playing card, domino, etc. 3. disease of fowls.

pipe, *n., v.,* **piped, piping.** —*n.* 1. tube for conveying fluid. 2. tube with bowl at one end for smoking tobacco. 3. tube used in or as musical instrument. —*v.* 4. play on pipe. 5. convey by pipe. —**pip'er,** *n.* —**pipe'line',** *n.*

pip'ing, *n.* 1. pipes. 2. sound of pipes. 3. kind of trimming.

pip'pin, *n.* kind of apple.

pip'squeak', *n. Informal.* small or unimportant person.

pi'quant (pē'kənt), *adj.* agreeably sharp. —**pi'quan·cy,** *n.*

pique (pēk), *v.,* **piqued, piquing,** *n.* —*v.* 1. arouse resentment in. 2. excite (curiosity, etc.). —*n.* 3. irritated feeling.

pi·qué' (pi kā'), *n.* corded cotton fabric.

pi'ra·cy, *n., pl.* **-cies.** 1. robbery at sea. 2. illegal use of patented or copyrighted material. —**pi'rate,** *n., v.*

pi·ra·nha (pi ran´ya, -ran´-, -ra´na), *n., pl.* **-nhas, -nha.** small, fiercely predatory fish of South American rivers.

pir·ou·ette (pir´ōō et´), *v.,* **-etted, -etting,** *n.* 1. whirl about on the toes. —*n.* 2. such whirling.

pis·ca·to·ri·al (pis´ka-), *adj.* of fishing.

pis·ta·chi·o (pis tä´shē ō´), *n., pl.* **-chios.** nut with edible greenish kernel.

pis´til, *n.* seed-bearing organ of flower.

pis´tol, *n.* short hand-held gun.

pis´ton, *n.* part moving back and forth under pressure in engine cylinder.

pit, *n., v.,* **pitted, pitting.** —*n.* 1. hole in ground or other surface. 2. hollow in body. 3. part of main floor of theater. 4. stone of fruit. —*v.* 5. mark with pits. 6. set in enmity or opposition. 7. remove pit from.

pi´ta (pē´tä, -ta), *n.* round, flat Middle Eastern bread with pocket.

pitch, *v.* 1. throw. 2. set at certain point. 3. fall forward. 4. drop and rise, as ship. —*n.* 5. relative point or degree. 6. musical tone. 7. slope. 8. sticky dark substance from coal tar. 9. sap that exudes from bark of pines.

pitch´blende´, *n.* mineral: principal ore of uranium and radium.

pitched, *adj.* fought with all available troops.

pitch´er, *n.* 1. container with spout for liquids. 2. person who pitches.

pitch´fork´, *n.* sharp-tined fork for handling hay.

pit´e·ous, *adj.* pathetic.

pit´fall´, *n.* trap; hazard.

pith, *n.* 1. spongy tissue. 2. essence. 3. strength. —**pith´y,** *adj.* —**pith´i·ness,** *n.*

pit´i·a·ble, *adj.* 1. deserving pity. 2. contemptible. —**pit´i·a·bly,** *adv.*

pit´i·ful, *adj.* 1. deserving pity. 2. exciting contempt. 3. full of pity. —**pit´i·ful·ly,** *adv.* —**pit´i·ful·ness,** *n.*

pit´tance, *n.* meager income.

pi·tu´i·tar´y (pi tyōō´ə ter´ē), *adj.* denoting gland at base of brain.

pit´y, *n., pl.* **pities,** *v.,* **pitied, pitying.** —*n.* 1. sympathetic sorrow. 2. cause for regret. —*v.* 3. feel pity for. —**pit´i·less,** *adj.* —**pit´i·less·ly,** *adv.*

piv´ot, *n.* 1. short shaft on which something turns. —*v.* 2. turn on or provide with pivot. —**piv´ot·al,** *adj.*

pix´el, *n.* smallest element of image in video display system.

pix´y, *n., pl.* **pixies.** fairy. Also, **pix´ie.**

pi·zazz´, *n. Informal.* 1. energy; vigor. 2. dash; flair. Also, **piz·zazz´.**

piz´za (pēt´sa), *n.* dish of cheese, tomato sauce, etc., on baked crust.

piz·zer·i´a (pēt´sə rē´ə), *n.* restaurant serving mainly pizza.

piz´zi·ca´to (pit´si kä´tō), *adj. Music.* played by plucking strings with fingers.

plac´a·ble, *adj.* forgiving.

plac´ard, *n.* public notice posted or displayed.

pla´cate, *v.,* **-cated, -cating.** appease. —**pla·ca´tion,** *n.*

place, *n., v.,* **placed, placing.** —*n.* 1. particular portion of space. 2. function. 3. social standing. 4. stead. —*v.* 5. put in place. 6. identify from memory. —**place´ment,** *n.*

pla·ce´bo (pla sē´bō), *n., pl.* **-bos, -boes.** pill, etc., containing no medication, given to reassure patient.

pla·cen´ta (-sen´-), *n.* organ in uterus which attaches to and nourishes fetus.

plac´er, *n.* surface gravel containing gold particles.

plac´id, *adj.* serene. —**pla·cid´i·ty,** *n.* —**plac´id·ly,** *adv.*

pla´gia·rize´ (plā´jə rīz´), *v.,* **-rized, -rizing.** copy and claim as one's own work of another. —**pla´gia·rism,** *n.* —**pla´gia·rist,** *n.*

plague, *n., v.,* **plagued, plaguing.** —*n.* 1. often fatal epidemic disease. 2. affliction or vexation. —*v.* 3. trouble; annoy.

plaid (plad), *n.* 1. fabric woven in many-colored cross bars. —*adj.* 2. having such pattern.

plain, *adj.* 1. distinct. 2. evident. 3. candid. 4. ordinary; unpretentious. 5. without pattern. 6. flat. —*adv.* 7. clearly. 8. candidly. —*n.* 9. level area. —**plain´ly,** *adv.* —**plain´ness,** *n.*

plain´clothes´man, *n., pl.* **-men.** police officer who wears civilian clothes on duty.

plaint, *n.* complaint.

plain´tiff, *n.* one who brings suit in court.

plain´tive, *adj.* melancholy. —**plain´tive·ly,** *adv.* —**plain´tive·ness,** *n.*

plait, *n., v.* 1. braid. 2. pleat.

plan, *n., v.,* **planned, planning.** —*n.* 1. scheme of action or arrangement. 2. drawing of projected structure. —*v.* 3. make plan. —**plan´ner,** *n.*

plane, *n., adj., v.,* **planed, planing.** —*n.* 1. flat surface. 2. level. 3. airplane. 4. sharp-bladed tool for smoothing. —*adj.* 5. flat. —*v.* 6. glide. 7. smooth with plane.

plan'et, *n.* solid heavenly body revolving about sun. **—plan'e·tar'y,** *adj.*

plan·e·tar'i·um, *n., pl.* **-iums, -ia.** 1. optical device that projects a representation of heavens on a dome. 2. museum with such device.

plank, *n.* 1. long flat piece of timber. 2. point in political platform.

plank'ton, *n.* microscopic organisms floating in water, mostly algae and protozoa.

plant, *n.* 1. any member of vegetable group of living things. 2. equipment for business or process. —*v.* 3. set in ground for growth. 4. furnish with plants. **—plant'er,** *n.* **—plant'like',** *adj.*

plan'tain (-tin), *n.* 1. tropical banana-like plant. 2. common flat-leaved weed.

plan'tar (plan'tər), *adj.* of the soles of the feet.

plan·ta'tion, *n.* large farm, esp. with one crop.

plaque (plak), *n.* 1. monumental tablet. 2. sticky, whitish film formed on tooth surfaces.

plas'ma, *n.* clear liquid part of blood or lymph.

plas'ter, *n.* 1. pasty composition of lime, sand, and water for covering walls, etc. 2. medicinal preparation spread on cloth and applied to body. —*v.* 3. cover or treat with plaster.

plaster of Paris, form of gypsum in powdery form, used in making plasters and casts.

plas'tic, *adj.* 1. of or produced by molding. 2. moldable. 3. three-dimensional. —*n.* 4. organic material that is hardened after shaping. **—plas·tic'i·ty,** *n.*

plastic surgery, branch of surgery dealing with repair, replacement, or reshaping of malformed, injured, or lost parts of body.

plate, *n.* 1. shallow round dish for food. 2. gold or silver ware. 3. sheet of metal used in printing. 4. shaped holder for false teeth. —*v.* 5. coat with metal. **—plat'er,** *n.*

pla·teau', *n., pl.* **-teaus, -teaux.** raised plain.

plat'form, *n.* 1. raised flooring or structure. 2. set of announced political principles.

plat'i·num, *n.* precious, malleable metallic element.

plat'i·tude', *n.* trite remark. **—plat'i·tud'i·nous,** *adj.*

pla·ton'ic, *adj.* without sexual involvement.

pla·toon', *n.* small military or police unit.

plat'ter, *n.* large shallow dish for serving meat, etc.

plat'y·pus (-ə pəs), *n., pl.* **-puses, -pi.** duckbill.

plau'dit (plô'dit), *n.* (*usu. pl.*) applause.

plau'si·ble, *adj.* apparently true, reasonable, or trustworthy. **—plau'si·bil'i·ty,** *n.* **—plau'si·bly,** *adv.*

play, *n.* 1. dramatic composition. 2. action for recreation. 3. fun. 4. change. 5. freedom of movement. —*v.* 6. act in a play. 7. engage in game. 8. perform on musical instrument. 9. amuse oneself. 10. move about lightly. **—play'er,** *n.* **—play'ful,** *adj.* **—play'ful·ly,** *adv.* **—play'ful·ness,** *n.* **—play'go'er,** *n.* **—play'mate',** *n.*

play'back', *n.* 1. reproduction of a sound or video recording. 2. apparatus used in producing playbacks.

play'boy', *n.* man who pursues life of pleasure without responsibilities or attachments.

play'ground', *n.* area used esp. by children, for outdoor recreation.

play'house', *n.* 1. theater. 2. small house for children to play in.

play'-off', *n.* extra game played to break a tie.

play'thing', *n.* toy.

play'wright', *n.* writer of plays.

pla'za, *n.* public square, esp. in Spanish-speaking countries.

plea, *n.* 1. defense; justification. 2. entreaty.

plead, *v.,* **pleaded** or **pled, pleading.** 1. make earnest entreaty. 2. allege formally in court. 3. argue (case at law). 4. allege in justification. **—plead'er,** *n.*

pleas'ant, *adj.* agreeable; pleasing. **—pleas'ant·ly,** *adv.*

pleas'ant·ry, *n., pl.* **-ries.** good-humored remark.

please, *v.,* **pleased, pleasing.** be or act to pleasure of; seem good. **—pleas'ing·ly,** *adv.*

pleas'ure, *n.* 1. enjoyment. 2. person's will or desire.

pleat, *n.* 1. double fold of cloth. —*v.* 2. fold in pleats.

ple·be'ian (plə bē'ən), *adj.* of common people.

pleb'i·scite' (-sīt'), *n.* direct vote by citizens on public question.

plec'trum, *n., pl.* **-tra, -trums.** object for picking strings of musical instrument.

pledge, *n., v.,* **pledged, pledging. —***n.* 1. solemn promise. 2. property delivered as security on a loan. **3.** toast. —*v.* **4.** bind by pledge. **5.** promise. **6.** deliver as pledge.

ple'na•ry, *adj.* full; complete.

plen'i•po•ten'ti•ar'y (-shē er'ē), *n., pl.* **-aries,** *adj.* —*n.* **1.** diplomat with full authority. —*adj.* **2.** having full authority.

plen'i•tude, *n.* abundance.

plen'ty, *n.* **1.** abundant supply. —*adv. Informal.* **2.** very. —**plen'te•ous, plen'ti•ful,** *adj.*

pleth'o•ra, *n.* superabundance.

pleu'ri•sy, *n.* inflammation of chest membranes.

Plex'i•glas', *n. Trademark.* light, durable transparent plastic.

pli'a•ble, *adj.* easily bent or influenced. —**pli'a•bil'i•ty,** *n.* —**pli'a•bly,** *adv.*

pli'ant, *adj.* pliable. —**pli'an•cy,** *n.*

pli'ers, *n.pl.* small pincers.

plight, *n.* **1.** distressing condition. —*v.* **2.** promise.

plod, *v.*, **plodded, plodding. 1.** walk heavily. **2.** work laboriously. —**plod'der,** *n.*

plop, *v.*, **plopped, plopping.** —*v.* **1.** drop with sound like that of object hitting water. **2.** drop with direct impact. —*n.* **3.** plopping sound or fall.

plot, *n., v.*, **plotted, plotting.** —*n.* **1.** secret scheme. **2.** main story of fictional work. **3.** small area of ground. —*v.* **4.** plan secretly. **5.** mark (chart course) on. **6.** divide into plots. —**plot'ter,** *n.*

plov'er (pluv'ər), *n.* shore bird.

plow, *n.* **1.** implement for cutting and turning soil. **2.** similar implement for removing snow. —*v.* **3.** cut or turn with plow. **4.** force way, as through water. Also, **plough.** —**plow'man,** *n.*

plow'share', *n.* blade of plow.

ploy, *n.* maneuver to gain advantage; stratagem; ruse.

pluck, *v.* **1.** pull out from fixed position. **2.** sound (strings of musical instrument). —*n.* **3.** pull or tug. **4.** courage.

pluck'y, *adj.*, **pluckier, pluckiest.** courageous.

plug, *n., v.*, **plugged, plugging.** —*n.* **1.** object for stopping hole. **2.** device on electrical cord that establishes contact in socket. **3.** *Slang.* advertisement; favorable mention. —*v.* **4.** stop with or insert plug. **5.** *Slang.* advertise or mention favorably. **6.** work steadily. —**plug'ger,** *n.*

plum, *n.* **1.** oval juicy fruit. **2.** deep purple. **3.** *Informal.* favor widely desired. —**plum'like',** *adj.*

plumb, *n.* **1.** plummet. —*adj.* **2.** per-

pendicular. —*adv.* **3.** vertically. **4.** exactly. **5.** *Informal.* completely. —*v.* **6.** make vertical. **7.** measure depth of.

plumb'ing, *n.* system of water pipes, etc. —**plumb'er,** *n.*

plume, *n., v.*, **plumed, pluming.** —*n.* **1.** feather, esp. large one. **2.** ornamental tuft. —*v.* **3.** preen. **4.** furnish with plumes. —**plum'age,** *n.*

plum'met, *n.* **1.** weight on line for sounding or establishing verticals. —*v.* **2.** plunge.

plump, *adj.* **1.** somewhat fat or thick. —*v.* **2.** make or become plump. **3.** fall or drop heavily. —*adv.* **4.** heavy fall. **5.** directly. **6.** heavily.

plun'der, *v.* **1.** rob by open violence. —*n.* **2.** act of plundering. **3.** loot.

plunge, *v.*, **plunged, plunging.** —*v.* **1.** dip suddenly. **2.** rush. **3.** pitch forward. —*n.* **4.** dive.

plung'er, *n.* **1.** pistonlike part moving within the cylinder of certain machines. **2.** device with handle and suction cup, used to unclog drains.

plu'ral, *adj.* **1.** of, being, or containing more than one. —*n.* **2.** plural form. —**plur'al•ize',** *v.*

plu'ral•ism, *n.* condition in which minority groups participate in dominant society, yet maintain their cultural differences.

plu•ral'i•ty, *n., pl.* **-ties. 1.** excess of votes given leading candidate over next candidate. **2.** majority.

plus, *prep.* **1.** increased by. —*adj.* **2.** involving addition. **3.** positive. —*n.* **4.** something additional.

plush, *n.* long-piled fabric.

plu'to•crat', *n.* **1.** wealthy person. **2.** member of wealthy governing class. —**plu•to•cra'cy,** *n.*

plu•to'ni•um, *n.* radioactive element.

ply, *v.*, **plied, plying,** *n., pl.* **plies.** —*v.* **1.** work with hand. **2.** carry on, as trade. **3.** supply or offer something repeatedly. **4.** travel regularly. —*n.* **5.** fold; thickness.

ply'wood', *n.* board of thin sheets of wood glued together.

p.m., after noon. Also, **P.M.**

PMS, premenstrual syndrome, physical and emotional changes that may be experienced in the several days before menstruation.

pneu•mat'ic (nyōō-), *adj.* **1.** of air or other gases. **2.** operated by or filled with air. —**pneu•mat'i•cal•ly,** *adv.*

pneu•mo'ni•a, *n.* inflammation of lungs.

poach, *v.* **1.** take game or fish illegally. **2.** cook (eggs, fruit, etc.) in hot water. —**poach'er,** *n.*

pock, n. mark on skin from smallpox, etc.

pock'et, n. **1.** small bag sewed into garment. **2.** pouch; cavity. —adj. **3.** small. —v. **4.** put into one's pocket. **5.** take as profit. **6.** suppress.

pock'et·book', n. purse.

pod, n., v., **podded, podding.** —n. **1.** seed covering. —v. **2.** produce pod.

po·di'a·try, n. diagnosis and treatment of foot disorders. —**po·di'a·trist,** n.

po'di·um, n., pl. **-diums, -dia.** small raised platform.

po'em, n. composition in verse.

po'et, n. —**po'et·ess,** n.fem.

po'et·ry, n. rhythmical composition of words. —**po·et'ic, po·et'i·cal,** adj.

po·grom' (pə grum'), n. organized massacre, esp. of Jews.

poign'ant (poin'yant), adj. keenly distressing. —**poign'an·cy,** n.

poin·set'ti·a (poin set'ē ə), n. tropical plant with scarlet flowers.

point, n. **1.** sharp end. **2.** projecting part. **3.** dot. **4.** definite position or time. **5.** compass direction. **6.** basic reason, assertion, etc. **7.** detail. **8.** unit of printing measure. —v. **9.** indicate. **10.** direct. —**point'less,** adj.

point'-blank', adj. **1.** direct; plain. —adv. **2.** directly.

point'er, n. **1.** one that points. **2.** long stick for pointing. **3.** breed of hunting dog.

poise, n., v., **poised, poising.** —n. **1.** balance. **2.** composure. —v. **3.** balance. **4.** be in position for action.

poi'son, n. **1.** substance that kills or harms seriously. —v. **2.** harm with poison. —**poi'son·er,** n. —**poi'son·ous,** adj.

poison ivy, 1. vine or shrub having shiny leaves with three leaflets. **2.** rash caused by touching poison ivy.

poke, v., **poked, poking,** n. thrust.

pok'er, n. **1.** rod for poking fires. **2.** card game.

pok'er-faced', adj. showing no emotion or intention.

pok'y, adj., **pokier, pokiest.** Informal. slow; dull. Also, **poke'y.** —**pok'i·ness,** n.

po'lar, adj. **1.** arctic or antarctic. **2.** in opposition or contrast. **3.** of magnetic poles. —**po·lar'i·ty,** n.

polar bear, large white bear of arctic regions.

pole, n., v., **poled, poling.** —n. **1.** long slender piece, esp. of wood. **2.** unit of length equal to 16 1/2 ft.; rod. **3.** square rod, 30 1/4 sq. yards. **4.** each end of axis. **5.** each end of magnet,

etc., showing strongest opposite force. **6.** (cap.) native or citizen of Poland. —v. **7.** propel with a pole.

pole'cat', n. small bad-smelling mammal, esp. the skunk.

po·lem'ics (lem'iks), n. art or practice of argument. —**po·lem'ic,** n., adj.

pole vault, athletic event in which vault over horizontal bar is performed with aid of long pole.

po·lice', n., v., **-liced, -licing.** —n. **1.** organized civil force for enforcing law. —v. **2.** keep in order. —**po·lice'man,** n. —**po·lice'wom·an,** n.fem.

pol'i·cy, n., pl. **-cies. 1.** definite course of action. **2.** insurance contract.

pol·i·o·my·e·li'tis (pōl'ē ō mī'ə lī'tis), n. infantile paralysis. Also, **po'li·o'.**

pol'ish (pol'-), v. **1.** make or become smooth and glossy. —n. **2.** polishing substance. **3.** gloss. **4.** refinement.

Pol'ish (pōl'-), n. **1.** language or people of Poland. —adj. **Polish,** adj.

po·lite', adj. showing good manners; refined. —**po·lite'ly,** adv. —**po·lite'ness,** n.

pol'i·tic, adj. **1.** prudent; expedient. **2.** political.

politically correct, marked by a typically progressive orthodoxy on issues of race, sex, etc. —**political correctness.**

pol·i·tick'ing, n. political self-aggrandizement.

pol'i·tics, n. **1.** science or conduct of government. **2.** political affairs, methods, or principles. —**po·lit'i·cal,** adj. —**pol'i·ti'cian,** n. —**po·lit'i·cal·ly,** adv.

pol'ka, n. lively dance.

polka dot, pattern of dots on fabric.

poll, n. **1.** voting or votes at election. **2.** list of individuals, as for voting. **3.** (pl.) place of voting. **4.** analysis of public opinion. —v. **5.** receive votes. **6.** vote. **7.** ask opinions of.

pol'len, n. powdery fertilizing element of flowers. —**pol'li·nate,** v. —**pol'li·na'tion,** n.

poll'ster, n. person who takes public-opinion polls.

pol·lute', v., **-luted, -luting.** contaminate or make foul. —**pol·lu'tion,** n. —**pol·lut'ant,** n.

po'lo, n., pl. **-los.** game played on horseback.

pol·o·naise' ('-nāz'), n. slow dance.

pol'ter·geist' (pōl'tər gīst'), n. boisterous, often destructive ghost.

pol·troon', n. coward.

pol·y·an·dry, *n.* practice of having more than one husband at a time.

pol·y·es·ter, *n.* artificial material for plastics and synthetics.

pol·y·eth·yl·ene, *n.* plastic polymer used esp. for containers, electrical insulation, and packaging.

po·lyg·a·my, *n.* practice of having many spouses, esp. wives, at one time. —**po·lyg·a·mist,** *n.* —**po·lyg·a·mous,** *adj.*

pol·y·glot, *adj.* able to speak, write, or read several languages.

pol·y·gon, *n.* figure having three or more straight sides. —**po·lyg·o·nal,** *adj.*

pol·y·graph, *n.* instrument recording variations in certain body activities, sometimes used to detect lying in response to questions.

pol·y·he·dron, *n., pl.* **-drons, -dra.** solid figure having four or more sides.

pol·y·mer, *n.* compound formed by the combination of various molecules, with water, alcohol, or the like eliminated.

pol·yp, *n.* 1. projecting growth from mucous surface. 2. simple, sedentary aquatic animal form.

pol·y·phon·ic, *adj.* having many musical parts.

pol·y·syl·lab·ic, *adj.* consisting of many syllables.

pol·y·un·sat·u·rat·ed, *adj.* of a class of animal or vegetable fats associated with low cholesterol content.

po·made, *n.* scented hair ointment.

pome·gran·ate (pom'gran'it), *n.* red, many-seeded fruit of Asiatic tree.

pom·mel (pum'al), *n., v.* **-meled, -meling.** —*n.* 1. knob. —*v.* 2. strike; beat.

pomp, *n.* stately display.

pom·pa·dour (-dôr'), *n.* arrangement of hair brushed up high from forehead.

pom·pom, *n.* ornamental tuft.

pomp·ous, *adj.* affectedly dignified or serious. —**pom·pos'i·ty, pomp·ous·ness,** *n.* —**pomp'ous·ly,** *adv.*

pon·cho, *n., pl.* **-chos.** blanketlike cloak.

pond, *n.* small lake.

pon·der, *v.* meditate.

pon·der·ous, *adj.* heavy; not graceful.

pone, *n.* unleavened corn bread.

pon·gee (-jē'), *n.* silk fabric.

pon·iard (pon'yard), *n.* dagger.

pon·tiff, *n.* 1. pope. 2. chief priest; bishop. —**pon·tif'i·cal,** *adj.*

pon·tif'i·cate, *v.,* **-cated, -cating.** speak with affected air of authority.

pon·toon', *n.* floating support.

po·ny, *n., pl.* **-nies.** small horse.

po·ny·tail, *n.* hair gathered and fastened at the back of the head, so as to hang freely there.

poo·dle, *n.* kind of dog with thick, curly hair.

pool, *n.* 1. body of still water. 2. group of persons or things available for use. 3. game resembling billiards. —*v.* 4. put into common fund.

poop, *n.* upper deck on afterpart of a ship.

poor, *adj.* 1. having little wealth. 2. wanting. 3. inferior. 4. unfortunate. —*n.* 5. poor persons. —**poor'ly,** *adv.* —**poor'ness,** *n.*

pop, *v.,* **popped, popping,** *n., adv.* —*v.* 1. make or burst with a short, quick sound. 2. shoot. —*n.* 3. short, quick sound. 4. effervescent soft drink. —*adv.* 5. suddenly.

pop'corn, *n.* kind of corn whose kernels burst in dry heat.

pope, *n. (often cap.)* head of Roman Catholic Church.

pop'lar, *n.* any of certain fast-growing trees.

pop'lin, *n.* corded fabric.

pop'o·ver, *n.* very light muffin.

pop'py, *n., pl.* **-pies.** showy-flowered herbs, one species of which yields opium.

pop'u·lace, *n.* people of a place.

pop'u·lar, *adj.* 1. generally liked and approved. 2. of the people. 3. prevalent. —**pop'u·lar'i·ty,** *n.* —**pop'u·lar·ize',** *v.* —**pop'u·lar·ly,** *adv.*

pop'u·late, *v.,* **-lated, -lating.** inhabit.

pop'u·la'tion, *n.* 1. total number of persons inhabiting given area. 2. body of inhabitants.

pop'u·lism, *n.* political philosophy or movement promoting the interests of the common people. —**pop'u·list,** *n., adj.*

pop'u·lous, *adj.* with many inhabitants.

por'ce·lain, *n.* glassy ceramic ware; china.

porch, *n.* exterior shelter on building.

por'cine (pôr'sīn), *adj.* of or like swine.

por'cu·pine, *n.* rodent with stout quills.

pore, *v.,* **pored, poring,** *n.* —*v.* 1. ponder or read intently. —*n.* 2. minute opening in skin.

por'gy, *n., pl.* **-gies.** fleshy salt-water food fish.

pork, *n.* flesh of hogs as food.

pork barrel, government funds available for popular local improvements.

por·nog'ra·phy, *n.* obscene literature

or art. —**por'no•graph'ic,** *adj.*
—**por•nog'ra•pher,** *n.*

po'rous, *adj.* permeable by water, air,
etc. —**po'rous•ness, po•ros'i•ty,** *n.*

por'poise, *n.* gregarious aquatic mammal.

por'ridge, *n.* boiled cereal.

por'rin•ger, *n.* round dish for soup,
etc.

port, *n.* 1. place where ships load and
unload. 2. harbor. 3. left side of vessel, facing forward. 4. sweet red wine.
—**port,** *adj.*

port'a•ble, *adj.* readily carried.
—**port•a•bil'i•ty,** *n.*

por'tage, *n.* 1. overland route between
navigable streams. act of carrying.

por'tal, *n.* door or gate, esp. a large
one.

por•tend', *v.* indicate beforehand.

por'tent, *n.* 1. omen. 2. ominous significance. —**por•ten'tous,** *adj.*

por'ter, *n.* 1. railroad attendant in
parlor or sleeping car. 2. baggage carrier. 3. person who cleans or maintains building, store, etc.

por'ter•house', *n.* choice cut of beef-
steak.

port•fo'li•o', *n., pl.* **-lios.** 1. portable
case for papers, etc. 2. cabinet post.

port'hole', *n.* opening in ship's side.

por'ti•co', *n., pl.* **-coes, -cos.** roof
supported by columns.

por•tiere' (pōr tyâr', -târ'), *n.* curtain
hung in doorway. Also, **por•tière'.**

por'tion, *n.* 1. part of a whole. 2.
share. —*v.* 3. divide into shares.

port'ly, *adj.,* **-lier, -liest.** 1. fat. 2.
stately. —**port'li•ness,** *n.*

por'trait, *n.* picture, sculpture, etc.,
showing specific person. —**por'trai•-
ture,** *n.*

por•tray', *v.* represent faithfully, as in
picture. —**por•tray'al,** *n.*

Por'tu•guese', *n., pl.* **-guese.** native
or language of Portugal. —**Portu•-
guese,** *adj.*

por'tu•lac'a (pōr'chə lak'ə), *n.* low-
growing garden plant.

pose, *v.,* **posed, posing,** *n.* —*v.* 1. assume or feign physical position, atti-
tude, or character. 2. take or give specific position. 3. ask (question). —*n.*
4. position or character assumed.

po'ser, *n.* 1. person who poses, as for
artist. 2. difficult question.

po•seur' (pō zûr'), *n.* affected person.

posh, *adj.* elegant; luxurious.

pos'it (poz'it), *v.* lay down or assume
as a fact or principle; postulate.

po•si'tion, *n.* 1. place or attitude. 2.
belief or argument on question. 3. social or organizational standing. 4.
job. —*v.* 5. place.

pos'i•tive, *adj.* 1. explicit; not deny-
ing or questioning. 2. emphatic. 3.
confident. 4. showing features and
shades of original. 5. *Gram.* denoting
first degree of comparison. 6. denoting more than zero. 7. deficient in
electrons. 8. revealing presence of
thing tested for. —*n.* 9. something
positive. —**pos'i•tive•ly,** *adv.*
—**pos'i•tive•ness,** *n.*

pos'se (pos'ē), *n.* body of persons assisting sheriff.

pos•sess', *v.* 1. have under ownership
or domination. 2. have as quality. 3.
obsess or craze. 4. (of man) succeed in
having sexual relations with. —**pos•-
ses'sor,** *n.* —**pos•ses'sion,** *n.*

pos•ses'sive, *adj.* 1. denoting possession. 2. obsessed with dominating another.

pos'si•ble, *adj.* that may be, happen,
etc. —**pos'si•bil'i•ty,** *n.* —**pos'si•-
bly,** *adv.*

pos'sum, *n.* opossum.

post, *n.* 1. upright support. 2. position
of duty or trust. 3. station for soldiers
or traders. 4. *Chiefly Brit.* mail. —*v.*
5. put up. 6. station at post. 7. *Chiefly
Brit.* mail. 8. enter in ledger. 9. hasten. 10. inform. —*adv.* 11. with speed.

post'age, *n.* charge for mailing.

post'al, *adj.* concerning mail.

post•bel'lum, *adj.* after war, esp. U.S.
Civil War.

post'card', *n.* small card usu. having
picture on one side and space for
stamp, address, and message on the
other.

post'er, *n.* large public notice.

pos•te'ri•or, *adj.* 1. situated behind.
2. later. —*n.* 3. buttocks.

pos•ter'i•ty, *n.* descendants.

post'grad'u•ate, *adj.* 1. of or consisting of postgraduates. —*n.* 2. student
taking advanced work after graduation.

post'haste', *adv.* speedily.

post•hu'mous (pos'chə məs), *adj.* 1.
published after author's death. 2.
born after father's death. —**post'hu•-
mous•ly,** *adv.*

post'man, *n.* mail carrier.

post'mark', *n.* official mark on mail
showing place and time of mailing.
—**post'mark',** *v.*

post'mas'ter, *n.* official in charge of
post office.

post me•rid'i•em', afternoon.

post•mor'tem, *adj.* 1. following
death. —*n.* 2. examination of dead
body.

post office, government office responsible for postal service.

post•paid', adv., adj. with postage paid in advance.

post•par'tum, adj. following childbirth.

post•pone', v., **-poned, -poning.** delay till later. —**post•pone'ment,** n.

post'script', n. note added to letter after signature.

pos'tu•late', v., **-lated, -lating,** n. —v. (pos'chǝ lāt') 1. require. 2. assume without proof. —n. (-lit.) 3. something postulated.

pos'ture, n., v., **-tured, -turing.** —n. 1. position of the body. —v. 2. place in particular position. 3. behave affectedly; pose.

post'war', adj. after a war.

po'sy, n., pl. **-sies.** flower or bouquet.

pot, n., v., **potted, potting.** —n. 1. round deep container for cooking, etc. 2. total stakes at cards. 3. Slang. marijuana. —v. 4. put into pot.

po'ta•ble, adj. drinkable.

pot'ash', n. potassium carbonate, esp. from wood ashes.

po•tas'si•um, n. light metallic element.

po•ta'tion, n. drink.

po•ta'to, n., pl. **-toes.** edible tuber of common garden plant.

pot'bel'ly, n., pl. **-lies.** belly that sticks out. —**pot'bel'lied**, adj.

po'tent, adj. 1. powerful. 2. (of a male) capable of sexual intercourse. —**po'tence, po'ten•cy**, n. —**po'-tent•ly**, adv.

po'ten•tate', n. powerful person, as a sovereign.

po•ten'tial, adj. 1. possible. 2. latent. —n. 3. possibility, esp. for development. —**po•ten'ti•al'i•ty**, n. —**po•ten'tial•ly**, adv.

poth'er, n., v. fuss.

po'tion, n. drink.

pot'luck', n. 1. meal to which participants bring food to be shared. 2. whatever happens to be available.

pot'pour•ri' (pō'pǝ rē'), n. miscellany.

pot'shot', n. 1. casual or aimless shot. 2. random or incidental criticism.

pot'ter, n. 1. person who makes earthen pots. —v. 2. putter (def 1).

pot'ter•y, n., pl. **-teries.** ware made of clay and baked.

pouch, n. 1. bag or sack. 2. baglike sac.

poul'tice (pōl'tis), n. soft moist mass applied as medicament.

poul'try, n. domestic fowls.

pounce, v., **pounced, pouncing**, n. —v. 1. swoop down or spring sud-

denly. 2. seize eagerly. —n. 3. sudden swoop.

pound, n., pl. **pounds, pound**, v. —n. 1. unit of weight: in U.S., **pound avoirdupois** (16 ounces) and **pound troy** (12 ounces). 2. British monetary unit. 3. enclosure for stray animals. —v. 4. strike repeatedly and heavily. 5. crush by pounding.

pound cake, rich, sweet cake.

pour, v. 1. cause to flow; flow. —n. 2. abundant flow.

pout, v. 1. look sullen. —n. 2. sullen look or mood.

pov'er•ty, n. 1. poorness. 2. lack.

pow'der, n. 1. solid substance crushed to fine loose particles. —v. 2. reduce to powder. 3. apply powder to. —**pow'der•y**, adj.

pow'er, n. 1. ability to act; strength. 2. faculty. 3. authority; control. 4. person, nation, etc., having great influence. 5. mechanical energy. 6. product of repeated multiplications of number by itself. 7. magnifying capacity of an optical instrument. —**pow'er•ful**, adj. —**pow'er•ful•ly**, adv. —**pow'er•less**, adj. —**pow'er•less•ly**, adv.

pow'wow', n. Informal. conference.

pox, n. disease marked by skin eruptions.

prac'ti•ca•ble, adj. able to be put into practice; feasible.

prac'ti•cal, adj. 1. of or from practice. 2. useful. 3. level-headed. 4. concerned with everyday affairs. 5. virtual. —**prac'ti•cal'i•ty**, n. —**prac'ti•cal•ly**, adv.

prac'tice, n., v., **-ticed, -ticing.** —n. 1. habit; custom. 2. actual performance. 3. repeated performance in learning. 4. professional activity. —v. 5. Also, Brit. **prac'tise.** 5. do habitually or as profession. 6. be proficient in acquiring skill. —**prac'ticed**, adj.

prac•ti'tion•er, n. person engaged in a profession.

prag•mat'ic, adj. concerned with practical values and results. —**prag'ma•tist**, n. —**prag•mat'i•cal•ly**, adv.

prai'rie, n. broad flat treeless grassland.

prairie dog, burrowing squirrel of western North America.

praise, n., v., **praised, praising.** —n. 1. words of admiration or strong approval. 2. grateful homage. —v. 3. give praise to. 4. worship. —**praise'-wor'thy**, adj. —**prais'er**, n.

pra'line', n. confection of caramelized nuts and sugar.

pram, n. Brit. Informal. baby carriage.

prance, v., **pranced, prancing**, n. —v. 1. step about gaily or proudly. —n. 2. act of prancing. —**pranc'er**, n.

prank, n. playful trick. —**prank'ster**, n.

prate, v., **prated, prating**. talk foolishly.

prat'tle, v. —**tled, -tling**, n. —v. 1. chatter foolishly or childishly. —n. 2. chatter. —**prat'tler**, n.

prawn, n. large shrimplike shellfish.

pray, v. make prayer.

prayer, n. 1. devout petition to or spiritual communication with God. 2. petition. —**prayer'ful**, adj.

pre-, prefix. before or earlier.

preach, v. 1. advocate. 2. deliver (sermon). —**preach'er**, n.

pre·am'ble, n. introductory declaration.

pre·car'i·ous, adj. uncertain; dangerous. —**pre·car'i·ous·ly**, adv.

pre·cau'tion, n. prudent advance measure. —**pre·cau'tion·ar·y**, adj.

pre·cede', v., **-ceded, -ceding**. go before. —**prec'e·dence**, n.

prec'e·dent, n. past case used as example or guide.

pre'cept, n. rule of conduct.

pre·cep'tor, n. teacher.

pre'cinct, n. bounded or defined area.

pre'cious, adj. 1. valuable. 2. beloved. 3. affectedly refined. —**pre'cious·ly**, adv.

prec'i·pice (pres'ə pəs), n. sharp cliff.

pre·cip'i·tate', v., **-tated, -tating**, adj., n. —v. 1. hasten occurrence of. 2. separate (solid from solution). 3. condense (as vapor into rain). 4. fling down. —adj. (-tit). 5. rash or impetuous; hasty. —n. (-tit). 6. substance precipitated. 7. condensed moisture. —**pre·cip'i·ta'tion**, n.

pre·cip'i·tous, adj. 1. like a precipice. 2. precipitate.

pré·cis' (prā sē'), n. summary.

pre·cise', adj. 1. definite; exact. 2. distinct. 3. strict. —**pre·ci'sion**, **pre·cise'ness**, n. —**pre·cise'ly**, adv.

pre·clude', v., **-cluded, -cluding**. prevent. —**pre·clu'sion**, n. —**pre·clu'sive**, adj.

pre·co'cious, adj. forward in development. —**pre·coc'i·ty**, n.

pre'·Co·lum'bi·an, adj. of the period before the arrival of Columbus in the Americas.

pre·cur'sor, n. 1. predecessor. 2. harbinger.

pre·da'cious, adj. predatory. Also, **pre·da'ceous**.

pred'a·tor, n. animal that preys.

pred'a·to·ry (pred'ə tōr'ē), adj. 1.

plundering. 2. feeding on other animals.

pred·e·ces'sor, n. one who precedes another.

pre·des'ti·na'tion, n. 1. determination beforehand. 2. destiny. —**pre·des'tine**, v.

pre·dic'a·ment, n. trying or dangerous situation.

pred'i·cate', v., **-cated, -cating**, adj., n. —v. (-kāt'). 1. declare. 2. find basis for. —adj. (-kit). 3. Gram. belonging to predicate. —n. (-kit). 4. Gram. part of sentence that expresses what is said of subject. —**pred'i·ca'tion**, n.

pre·dict', v. tell beforehand. —**pre·dic'tion**, n. —**pre·dict'a·ble**, adj. —**pre·dic'tor**, n.

pre·di·lec'tion (pred'-), n. preference.

pre·dom'i·nate', v., **-nated, -nating**. 1. be more powerful or common. 2. control. —**pre·dom'i·nance**, n. —**pre·dom'i·nant**, adj. —**pre·dom'i·nant·ly**, adv.

pre·em'i·nent, adj. superior; outstanding. —**pre·em'i·nence**, n. —**pre·em'i·nent·ly**, adv.

pre·empt', v. 1. acquire or reserve before others. 2. occupy to establish prior right to buy. Also, **pre-empt'**. —**pre·emp'tion**, n.

preen, v. 1. trim or clean (feathers or fur). 2. dress (oneself) carefully.

pre·fab'ri·cate', v., **-cated, -cating**. construct in parts before final assembly elsewhere. —**pre·fab'ri·ca'tion**, n. —**pre'fab**, n. Informal.

pref'ace, n., v., **-aced, -acing**. —n. 1. preliminary statement. —v. 2. provide with or serve as preface. —**pref'a·to'ry**, adj.

pre'fect, n. magistrate.

pre·fer', v., **-ferred, -ferring**. 1. like better. 2. present (criminal charge, etc.).

pref'er·a·ble, adj. more desirable. —**pref'er·a·bly**, adv.

pref'er·ence, n. 1. liking of one above others. 2. person or thing preferred. 3. granting of advantage to one especially. —**pref'er·en'tial**, adj.

pre·fer'ment, n. promotion.

pre'fix, n. 1. syllable or syllables put before word to qualify its meaning. —v. (prē fiks'). 2. put before.

preg'nant, n. 1. being with child. 2. filled; fraught. 3. momentous. —**preg'nan·cy**, n.

pre·hen'sile (-sil), adj. adapted for grasping.

pre·his·tor'ic, adj. of time before recorded history.

prej'u·dice, *n.*, *v.*, **-diced, -dicing.** —*n.* **1.** opinion formed without specific evidence. **2.** disadvantage. —*v.* **3.** affect with prejudice. —**prej'u·di'·cial**, *adj.*

prel'ate, *n.* high church official.

pre·lim'i·nar'y, *adj.*, *n.*, *pl.* **-naries.** —*adj.* **1.** introductory. —*n.* **2.** preliminary stage or action.

prel'ude, *n.* **1.** *Music.* **a.** preliminary to more important work. **b.** brief composition, esp. for piano. **2.** preliminary to major action or event.

pre·mar'i·tal, *adj.* before marriage.

pre·ma'ture', *adj.* **1.** born, occurring, or maturing too soon. **2.** overhasty. —**pre·ma·ture'ly**, *adv.* —**pre·ma·ture'ness, pre·ma·tu'ri·ty**, *n.*

pre·med'i·tate, *v.*, **-tated, -tating.** plan in advance. —**pre·med'i·ta'·tion**, *n.*

pre·mier' (pri mēr'), *n.* **1.** prime minister. —*adj.* **2.** chief.

pre·miere' (pri mēr'), *n.* first public performance.

prem'ise, *n.* **1.** (*pl.*) building with its grounds. **2.** statement from which conclusion is drawn.

pre'mi·um, *n.* **1.** contest prize. **2.** bonus. **3.** periodic insurance payment.

pre·mo·ni'tion, *n.* foreboding. —**pre·mon'i·to'ry**, *adj.*

pre·na'tal, *adj.* before birth or before giving birth.

pre·oc'cu·py', *v.*, **-pied, -pying.** engross completely. —**pre·oc'cu·pa'·tion**, *n.*

pre·or·dain', *v.* decree in advance.

prep, *v.*, **prepped, prepping. 1.** get ready; prepare. **2.** attend preparatory school.

preparatory school, private secondary school preparing students for college. Also, **prep school.**

pre·pare', *v.*, **-pared, -paring. 1.** make or get ready. **2.** manufacture. —**prep'a·ra'tion**, *n.* —**pre·par'a·to'ry**, *adj.* —**pre·par'ed·ness**, *n.*

pre·pon'der·ant, *adj.* superior in force or numbers. —**pre·pon'der·ance**, *n.*

prep'o·si'tion, *n.* word placed before noun or adjective to indicate relationship of space, time, means, etc. —**prep'o·si'tion·al**, *adj.*

pre·pos·sess'ing, *adj.* impressing favorably.

pre·pos'ter·ous, *adj.* absurd.

prep'py, *n.*, *pl.* **-pies**, *adj.*, **-pier, -piest.** —*n.* **1.** student or graduate of a preparatory school. **2.** person who dresses or acts like a preppy. —*adj.* **3.** of or characteristic of a preppy.

pre·req'ui·site, *adj.* **1.** required in advance. —*n.* **2.** something prerequisite.

pre·rog'a·tive, *n.* special right or privilege.

pres'age (pres'ij), *v.*, **-aged, -aging. 1.** portend. **2.** predict.

pres'by·te'ri·an, *adj.* **1.** (of religious group) governed by presbytery. **2.** (*cap.*) designating Protestant church so governed. —*n.* **3.** (*cap.*) member of Presbyterian Church.

pres'by·ter'y, *n.*, *pl.* **-teries.** body of church elders and (in Presbyterian churches) ministers.

pre'school', *adj.* **1.** of or for children between infancy and kindergarten age. —*n.* **2.** school or nursery for preschool children.

pre'science (prē'shē ans), *n.* foresight. —**pre'scient**, *adj.*

pre·scribe', *v.*, **-scribed, -scribing. 1.** order for use, as medicine. **2.** order. —**pre·scrip'tion**, *n.* —**pre·scrip'tive**, *adj.*

pres'ence, *n.* **1.** fact of being present. **2.** vicinity. **3.** perceived personal quality, esp. when impressive.

presence of mind, ability to think clearly and act appropriately, as during a crisis.

pres'ent, *adj.* **1.** being or occurring now. **2.** being at particular place. **3.** *Gram.* denoting action or state now in progress. —*n.* **4.** present time. **5.** *Gram.* present tense. **6.** thing bestowed as gift. —*v.* (pri zent'). **7.** give, bring, or offer. **8.** exhibit. —**pres'en·ta'tion**, *n.*

pre·sent'a·ble, *adj.* suitable in looks, dress, etc. —**pre·sent'a·bly**, *adv.*

pre·sen'ti·ment, *n.* feeling of something impending, esp. evil.

pres'ent·ly, *adv.* **1.** at present. **2.** soon.

pre·sent'ment, *n.* presentation.

pre·serve', *v.*, **-served, -serving.** —*v.* **1.** keep alive. **2.** keep safe. **3.** maintain. **4.** prepare (food) for long keeping. —*n.* **5.** (*pl.*) preserved fruit. **6.** place where game is protected. —**pres'er·va'tion**, *n.* —**pre·serv'a·tive**, *n.*, *adj.* —**pre·serv'er**, *n.*

pre·side', *v.*, **-sided, -siding.** act as chairman.

pres'i·dent, *n.* **1.** highest executive of republic. **2.** chief officer. —**pres'i·den·cy**, *n.*

press, *v.* **1.** act upon with weight or force. **2.** oppress; harass. **3.** insist upon. **4.** urge to hurry or comply. —*n.* **5.** newspapers, etc., collectively. **6.** device for pressing or printing. **7.** crowd. **8.** urgency. —**press'er**, *n.*

press'ing, adj. urgent.

pres'sure, n. 1. exertion of force by one body upon another. 2. harassment. 3. urgency.

pressure cooker, pot with airtight lid, for cooking quickly by steam under pressure.

pressure group, group that tries to influence legislation in a particular way.

pres·ti·dig·i·ta'tion (-dij'ə-), n. sleight of hand. **—pres'ti·dig·i·ta'tor,** n.

pres·tige' (-tēzh'), n. distinguished reputation.

pres'to, adv. Music. quickly.

pre·sume' (-zōōm'), v., **-sumed, -suming.** 1. take for granted. 2. act with unjustified boldness. **—pre·sum'a·ble,** adj. **—pre·sum'a·bly,** adv. **—pre·sump'tion** (-zump'-), n. **—pre·sump'tu·ous,** adj.

pre·sup·pose', v., **-posed, -posing.** assume. **—pre·sup·po·si'tion,** n.

pre·teen', n. 1. child between 10 and 13 years old. 2. of or for preteens.

pre·tend', v. 1. make false appearance or claim. 2. make believe. 3. claim, as sovereignty. **—pre·tend'er,** n. **—pre·tense',** n.

pre·ten'sion, n. 1. ostentation. 2. act of pretending. **—pre·ten'tious,** adj. **—pre·ten'tious·ly,** adv. **—pre·ten'tious·ness,** n.

pret'er·it, Gram. **—adj.** 1. denoting action in past. **—n.** 2. preterit tense.

pre·ter·nat'u·ral, adj. supernatural.

pre'text, n. ostensible reason; excuse.

pret'ty, adj., **-tier, -tiest,** adv. **—adj.** 1. pleasingly attractive. **—adv.** 2. moderately. 3. very. **—pret'ti·fy,** v. **—pret'ti·ly,** adv. **—pret'ti·ness,** n.

pret'zel, n. crisp elongated or knotted biscuit.

pre·vail', v. 1. be widespread. 2. exercise persuasion. 3. gain victory.

prev'a·lent, adj. widespread; general. **—prev'a·lence,** n.

pre·var'i·cate, v., **-cated, -cating.** speak evasively; lie. **—pre·var'i·ca'tion,** n. **—pre·var'i·ca'tor,** n.

pre·vent', v. 1. hinder; stop. **—pre·vent'a·ble, pre·vent'i·ble,** adj. **—pre·ven'tion,** n. **—pre·ven'tive, pre·vent'a·tive,** adj., n.

pre'view, n., v. view or show in advance.

pre'vi·ous, adj. occurring earlier. **—pre'vi·ous·ly,** adv.

prey, n. 1. animal hunted as food by another animal. 2. victim. **—v.** 3. seize prey. 4. victimize another. 5. be obsessive.

price, n., v., **priced, pricing. —n.** 1. amount for which thing is sold. 2. value. **—v.** 3. set price on. 4. Informal. ask the price of.

price'less, adj. too valuable to set price on.

pric'ey, adj., **pricier, priciest.** Informal. high-priced. **—pric'i·ness,** n.

prick, n. 1. puncture by pointed object. **—v.** 2. pierce. 3. point.

prick'le, n. 1. sharp point. **—prick'ly,** adj.

pride, n., v., **prided, priding. —n.** 1. high opinion of worth of oneself or that associated with oneself. 2. self-respect. 3. that which one is proud of. 4. group of lions. **—v.** 5. feel pride. **—pride'ful,** adj.

priest, n. person authorized to perform religious rites; member of clergy. **—priest'ess,** n.fem. **—priest'hood,** n.

prig, n. self-righteous person. **—prig'gish,** adj.

prim, adj. stiffly proper. **—prim'ly,** adv. **—prim'ness,** n.

pri'ma don'na (prē'mə don'ə), 1. principal female opera singer. 2. temperamental person.

pri'ma fa'ci·e (prī'mə fā'shē ē', fā'shē), Law. sufficient to establish a fact unless rebutted.

pri'mal, adj. 1. first; original. 2. most important.

pri'ma·ry, adj., n., pl. **-ries. —adj.** 1. first in importance or in order. 2. earliest. **—n.** 3. preliminary election for choosing party candidates.

pri'mate (-māt), n. 1. high church official. 2. mammal of order including humans, apes, and monkeys.

prime, adj., n., v., **primed, priming. —adj.** 1. first in importance or quality. 2. original. **—n.** 3. best stage or part. **—v.** 4. prepare for special purpose or function.

prime minister, chief minister in some governments.

prim'er, n. elementary book, esp. for reading.

prime time, hours, usu. between 7 and 11 P.M., considered to have largest television audience.

pri·me'val, adj. of earliest time.

prim'i·tive, adj. 1. earliest. 2. simple; unrefined. **—prim'i·tive·ly,** adv. **—prim'i·tive·ness,** n.

pri·mor'di·al (prī môr'dē əl), adj. existing at or from the very beginning.

primp, v. dress fussily.

prim'rose, n. early-flowering garden perennial.

prince, n. high-ranking male member of royalty. **—prin'cess,** n.fem.

prince'ly, *adj.* lavish.

prin'ci·pal, *adj.* 1. chief. —*n.* 2. chief; leader. 3. head of school. 4. person authorizing another to act for him. 5. capital sum, distinguished from interest. —**prin'ci·pal·ly,** *adv.*

prin'ci·pal'i·ty, *n.,* *pl.* **-ties.** state ruled by prince.

prin'ci·ple, *n.* 1. rule of conduct or action. 2. fundamental truth or doctrine. 3. fundamental cause or factor.

print, *v.* 1. reproduce from inked types, plates, etc. 2. write in letters like those of print. 3. produce (photograph) from negative. 4. (of book) present availability for sale. 6. print lettering. 7. anything printed. —**print'er,** *n.* —**print'a·ble,** *adj.*

print'out, *n.* printed output of computer.

pri'or, *adj.* 1. earlier. —*adv.* 2. previously. —*n.* 3. officer in religious house. —**pri'or·ess,** *n.fem.* —**pri'o·ry,** *n.*

pri·or'i·ty, *n.,* *pl.* **-ties.** 1. state of being earlier. 2. precedence.

prism (priz'əm), *n.* transparent body for dividing light into its spectrum. —**pris·mat'ic,** *adj.*

pris'on, *n.* building for confinement of criminals. —**pris'on·er,** *n.*

pris'sy, *adj.,* **-sier, -siest.** excessively or affectedly proper. —**pris'si·ness,** *n.*

pris'tine (-tēn), *adj.* original; pure.

pri'vate, *adj.* 1. belonging to particular person or group. 2. free of outside knowledge or intrusion. —*n.* 3. soldier of lowest rank. —**pri'va·cy,** *n.* —**pri'vate·ly,** *adv.*

pri·va·teer', *n.* privately owned vessel commissioned to fight. —**pri·va·teer'ing,** *n.*

pri·va'tion, *n.* lack; need.

priv'i·lege, *n.,* *v.,* **-leged, -leging.** —*n.* 1. special advantage. —*v.* 2. grant privilege to.

priv'y, *adj.,* *n.,* *pl.* **privies.** —*adj.* 1. participating in shared secret. 2. private. —*n.* 3. outdoor toilet.

prize, *n.,* *v.,* **prized, prizing.** —*n.* 1. reward for victory, superiority, etc. 2. thing worth striving for. —*v.* 3. esteem highly.

pro, *n.,* *pl.* **pros,** *adv.* —*n.* 1. argument in favor of something. 2. *Informal.* professional. —*adv.* 3. in favor of a plan, etc.

prob'a·ble, *adj.* 1. likely to occur, etc. 2. affording ground for belief. —**prob'a·bil'i·ty,** *n.* —**prob'a·bly,** *adv.*

pro'bate, *n.,* *adj.,* *v.,* **-bated, -bating.** —*n.* 1. authentication of will. —*adj.* 2. of probate. —*v.* 3. establish validity.

pro·ba'tion, *n.* 1. act of testing. 2. period of such testing. 3. conditional release, as from prison. 4. period in which to redeem past failures or mistakes. —**pro·ba'tion·ar'y,** *adj.*

probe, *v.,* **probed, probing,** *n.* —*v.* 1. examine thoroughly. —*n.* 2. surgical instrument for exploring wounds, etc. —**prob'er,** *n.*

pro'bi·ty, *n.* honesty.

prob'lem, *n.* matter involving uncertainty or difficulty. —**prob'lem·at'ic, prob'lem·at'i·cal,** *adj.*

pro·bos'cis (-bos'is), *n.,* *pl.* **-cises.** flexible snout, as elephant's trunk.

pro·ce'dure (-sē'jər), *n.* course of action. —**pro·ce'dur·al,** *adj.*

pro·ceed', *v.* 1. go forward. 2. carry on action. 3. issue forth. —*n.* (prō'sēd). 4. (*pl.*) sum derived from sale, etc.

pro·ceed'ing, *n.* 1. action or conduct. 2. (*pl.*) a. records of society. b. legal action.

proc'ess, *n.* 1. series of actions toward given end. 2. continuous action. 3. legal summons. 4. projecting growth. —*v.* 5. treat by particular process.

pro·ces'sion, *n.* ceremonial movement; parade.

pro·ces'sion·al, *n.* 1. hymn sung during procession. 2. hymnal.

pro-choice', *adj.* supporting the right to legalized abortion.

pro·claim', *v.* announce publicly. —**proc'la·ma'tion,** *n.*

pro·cliv'i·ty, *n.,* *pl.* **-ties.** natural tendency.

pro·cras'ti·nate', *v.,* **-nated, -nating.** delay from temperamental causes. —**pro·cras'ti·na'tion,** *n.* —**pro·cras'ti·na'tor,** *n.*

pro·cre'ate', *v.,* **-ated, -ating.** produce or have offspring. —**pro'cre·a'tion,** *n.*

proc'tor, *n.* 1. person who watches over students at examinations. —*v.* 2. supervise or monitor.

pro·cure', *v.* **-cured, -curing.** 1. get; obtain. 2. cause. 3. hire prostitutes. —**pro·cure'ment,** *n.*

pro·cur'er, *n.* 1. one that procures. 2. Also, **pro·cur'ess,** *fem.* person who arranges for prostitution.

prod, *v.,* **prodded, prodding,** *n.* —*v.* 1. poke. 2. incite; goad. —*n.* 3. poke. 4. goading instrument.

prod'i·gal, *adj.* 1. wastefully extravagant. 2. lavish. —*n.* 3. spendthrift.

prod'i·gal'i·ty, *n.* 1. extravagance; lavishness.

pro·di·gious -(dij'əs), *adj.* huge; wonderful.

prod·i·gy, *n., pl.* **-gies. 1.** very gifted person. **2.** wonderful thing.

pro·duce', *v.,* **-duced, -ducing,** *n.* —*v.* **1.** bring into existence; create. **2.** bear, as young, fruit. **3.** exhibit. —*n.* (prō'dōōs). **4.** product. **5.** agricultural products. —**pro·duc'er**, *n.* —**pro·duc'tion**, *n.* —**pro·duc'tive**, *adj.* —**pro·duc·tiv'i·ty**, *n.*

prod'uct, *n.* **1.** thing produced; result. **2.** result obtained by multiplying.

pro·fane', *adj., v.,* **-faned, -faning.** —*adj.* **1.** irreverent toward sacred things. **2.** secular. —*v.* **3.** defile. **4.** treat (sacred thing) with contempt. —**prof·a·na'tion**, *n.*

pro·fan'i·ty, *n., pl.* **-ties. 1.** profane quality. **2.** blasphemous or vulgar language.

pro·fess', *v.* **1.** declare. **2.** affirm faith in. **3.** claim.

pro·fes'sion, *n.* **1.** learned vocation. **2.** declaration; assertion.

pro·fes·sion·al, *adj.* **1.** following occupation for gain. **2.** of or engaged in profession. —*n.* **3.** professional person. —**pro·fes'sion·al·ly**, *adv.*

pro·fes'sor, *n.* college teacher of highest rank. —**pro·fes·so'ri·al**, *adj.*

prof'fer, *v., n.* offer.

pro·fi'cient, *adj.* expert. —**pro·fi'cien·cy**, *n.* —**pro·fi'cient·ly**, *adv.*

pro'file, *n.* **1.** side view. **2.** informal biographical sketch.

prof'it, *n.* **1.** pecuniary gain from business transaction. **2.** net gain after costs. **3.** benefit. —*v.* **4.** gain advantage. **5.** make profit. —**prof'it·a·ble**, *adj.* —**prof'it·a·bly**, *adv.* —**prof'it·less**, *adj.*

prof'it·eer', *n.* **1.** person who makes unfair profit. —*v.* **2.** act as profiteer.

prof'li·gate -(git), *adj.* **1.** immoral. **2.** extravagant. —**prof'li·ga·cy**, *n.*

pro for'ma, done as a matter of form or for the sake of form.

pro·found', *adj.* **1.** thinking deeply. **2.** intense. **3.** deep. —**pro·found'ly**, *adv.* —**pro·fun'di·ty**, *n.*

pro·fuse', *adj.* extravagant; abundant. —**pro·fuse'ly**, *adv.* —**pro·fu'sion**, **pro·fuse'ness**, *n.*

pro·gen'i·tor, *n.* ancestor.

prog'e·ny, *n.pl.* children; offspring.

pro·ges'ter·one', *n.* female hormone that prepares uterus for fertilized ovum.

prog·no'sis, *n., pl.* **-noses** -(nō'sēz). medical forecast.

prog·nos'ti·cate', *v.,* **-cated,**
-**cating.** predict. —**prog·nos'ti·ca'tion**, *n.*

pro'gram, *n., v.,* **-grammed, -gramming.** —*n.* **1.** plan of things to do. **2.** schedule of entertainments. **3.** television or radio show. **4.** plan for computerized problem solving. —*v.* **5.** make program for or including. —**pro'gram·mer**, *n.*

prog'ress, *n.* **1.** advancement. **2.** permanent improvement. **3.** growth. —*v.* (prə gres'). **4.** make progress. —**pro·gres'sion**, *n.* —**pro·gres'sive**, *adj., n.* —**pro·gres'sive·ly**, *adv.*

pro·hib'it, *v.* forbid; prevent.

pro·hi·bi'tion, *n.* **1.** act of prohibiting. **2.** (*cap.*) period, 1920–33, when manufacture and sale of alcoholic drinks was forbidden in U.S. —**pro·hi·bi'tion·ist**, *n.*

pro·hib'i·tive, *adj.* **1.** serving to prohibit. **2.** too expensive.

proj'ect, *n.* **1.** something planned. —*v.* (prə jekt'). **2.** plan; contemplate. **3.** impel forward. **4.** display upon surface, as motion picture or map. **5.** extend out; protrude. —**pro·jec'tion**, *n.* —**pro·jec'tor**, *n.*

pro·jec'tile, *n.* object fired with explosive force.

pro·le·tar'i·at, *n.* working or impoverished class. —**pro·le·tar'i·an**, *adj., n.*

pro·life', *adj.* opposed to legalized abortion.

pro·lif'er·ate', *v.,* **-ated, -ating.** spread rapidly. —**pro·lif'er·a'tion**, *n.*

pro·lif'ic, *adj.* productive.

pro·lix', *adj.* tediously long and wordy. —**pro·lix'i·ty**, *n.*

pro'logue, *n.* introductory part of novel, play, etc.

pro·long', *v.* lengthen.

prom, *n.* formal dance at high school or college.

prom·e·nade' -(nād', -näd'), *n., v.,* **-naded, -nading.** —*n.* **1.** leisurely walk. **2.** space for such walk. —*v.* **3.** take promenade.

prom'i·nent, *adj.* **1.** conspicuous. **2.** projecting. **3.** well-known. —**prom'i·nence**, *n.* —**prom'i·nent·ly**, *adv.*

pro·mis'cu·ous, *adj.* **1.** having numerous casual sexual partners. **2.** indiscriminate. —**pro·mis·cu'i·ty**, *n.* —**pro·mis'cu·ous·ly**, *adv.*

prom'ise, *n., v.,* **-ised, -ising.** —*n.* **1.** assurance that one will act as specified. **2.** indication of future excellence. —*v.* **3.** assure by promise. **4.** afford ground for expectation. —**prom'is·ing**, *adj.*

prom·is·so·ry, *adj.* containing promise, esp. of payment.

prom·on·to·ry, *n., pl.* -ries. high peak projecting into sea or overlooking low land.

pro·mote', *v.*, -moted, -moting. 1. further progress of. 2. advance. 3. organize. —**pro·mot'er**, *n.* —**pro·mo'tion**, *n.*

prompt, *adj.* 1. ready to act. 2. done at once. —*v.* 3. incite to action. 4. suggest (action, etc.). —**prompt'er**, *n.* —**prompt'ly**, *adv.* —**prompt'ness**, **promp'ti·tude'**, *n.*

prom·ul·gate', *v.*, -gated, -gating. proclaim formally. —**prom·ul·ga'tion**, *n.* —**prom'ul·ga'tor**, *n.*

prone, *adj.* 1. likely; inclined. 2. lying flat, esp. face downward.

prong, *n.* point.

pro'noun', *n.* word used as substitute for noun. —**pro·nom'i·nal**, *adj.*

pro·nounce', *v.*, -nounced, -nouncing. 1. utter, esp. precisely. 2. declare to be. 3. announce. —**pro·nounce'ment**, *n.*

pro·nounced', *adj.* 1. strongly marked. 2. decided.

pron'to, *adv.* promptly; quickly.

pro·nun·ci·a'tion, *n.* production of sounds of speech.

proof, *n.* 1. evidence establishing fact. 2. standard strength, as of liquors. 3. trial printing. —*adj.* 4. resisting perfectly.

proof'read', *v.*, -read, -reading. read (printers' proofs, etc.) to mark errors. —**proof'read'er**, *n.*

prop, *n., v.*, propped, propping. —*n.* 1. rigid support. 2. propeller. —*v.* 3. support with prop.

prop·a·gan'da, *n.* doctrines disseminated by organization. —**prop'a·gan'dist**, *n.* —**prop'a·gan'dize**, *v.*

prop'a·gate', *v.*, -gated, -gating. 1. reproduce; cause to reproduce. 2. transmit (doctrine, etc.). —**prop'a·ga'tion**, *n.*

pro'pane, *n.* colorless flammable gas, used esp. as fuel.

pro·pel', *v.*, -pelled, -pelling. drive forward. —**pro·pel'lant**, **pro·pel'lent**, *n.*

pro·pel'ler, *n.* screwlike propelling device.

pro·pen'si·ty, *n., pl.* -ties. inclination.

prop'er, *adj.* 1. suitable; fitting. 2. correct. 3. designating particular person, place, or thing. —**prop'er·ly**, *adv.*

prop'er·ty, *n., pl.* -ties. 1. that which one owns. 2. attribute.

proph'e·sy (-sī), *v.*, -sied, -sying.

foretell; predict. —**proph'e·cy** (-sē), *n.*

proph'et, *n.* 1. person who speaks for God. 2. inspired leader. 3. person who predicts. —**pro·phet'ic**, *adj.* —**pro·phet'i·cal·ly**, *adv.*

pro·phy·lax'is (prō'fə lak'sis), *n.* protection from or prevention of disease. —**pro·phy·lac'tic**, *adj., n.*

pro·pin'qui·ty, *n.* nearness.

pro·pi'ti·ate' (prə pish'ē āt'), *v.*, -ated, -ating. appease.

pro·pi'tious, *adj.* favorable. —**pro·pi'tious·ly**, *adv.*

pro·po'nent, *n.* advocate; supporter.

pro·por'tion, *n.* 1. comparative or proper relation of dimensions or quantities. 2. symmetry. 3. (*pl.*) dimensions. —*v.* 4. adjust in proper relation. —**pro·por'tion·al**, *adj.*

pro·por'tion·ate, *adj.* being in due proportion. —**pro·por'tion·ate·ly**, *adv.*

pro·pos'al, *n.* 1. proposition. 2. offer of marriage.

pro·pose', *v.*, -posed, -posing. 1. suggest. 2. intend. 3. offer marriage.

prop·o·si'tion, *n.* 1. proposed plan. 2. statement that affirms or denies. 3. proposal of illicit sex. —*v.* 4. make proposition to.

pro·pound', *v.* offer for consideration.

pro·pri'e·tor, *n.* owner or manager. —**pro·pri'e·tar'y**, *adj.*

pro·pri'e·ty, *n., pl.* -ties. 1. appropriateness. 2. (*pl.*) morality; correctness.

pro·pul'sion, *n.* propelling force.

pro·rate', *v.*, -rated, -rating. divide proportionally.

pro·sa'ic, *adj.* commonplace. —**pro·sa'i·cal·ly**, *adv.*

pro·scribe', *v.*, -scribed, -scribing. prohibit. —**pro·scrip'tion**, *n.*

prose, *n.* ordinary language; not verse.

pros'e·cute', *v.*, -cuted, -cuting. 1. begin legal proceedings against. 2. go on with (task, etc.). —**pros'e·cu'tion**, *n.* —**pros'e·cu'tor**, *n.*

pros'e·lyte (pros'ə līt'), *n., v.*, -lyted, -lyting. convert. —**pros'e·lyt·ize'**, *v.*

pros'o·dy (pros'ə dē), *n., pl.* -dies. study of poetic meters and versification.

pros'pect, *n.* 1. likelihood of success. 2. outlook; view. 3. potential customer. —*v.* 4. search. —**pros·pec'tive**, *adj.* —**pros'pec·tor**, *n.*

pro·spec'tus, *n.* description of new investment or purchase.

pros'per, *v.* be successful. —**pros·per'i·ty**, *n.* —**pros'per·ous**, *adj.* —**pros'per·ous·ly**, *adv.*

pros'tate, *n.* gland in males at base of bladder.

pros•the•sis (pros thē'sis), *n.*, *pl.* **-ses** (-sēz). device that substitutes for or supplements missing or defective body part. **—pros•thet'ic,** *adj.*

pros'ti•tute, *n.*, *v.*, **-tuted, -tuting.** **—n.** 1. person who engages in sexual intercourse for money. **—v.** 2. put to base use. **—pros'ti•tu'tion,** *n.*

pros'trate, *v.*, **-trated, -trating,** *adj.* **—v.** 1. lay (oneself) down, esp. in humility. 2. exhaust. *—adj.* 3. lying flat. 4. helpless. 5. exhausted. **—pros•tra'tion,** *n.*

pros'y, *adj.* **prosier, prosiest.** dull.

pro•tag'o•nist, *n.* main character.

pro•tect', *v.* defend, as from attack or annoyance. **—pro•tec'tion,** *n.* **—pro•tec'tive,** *adj.* **—pro•tec'tive•ly,** *adv.* **—pro•tec'tor,** *n.*

pro•tec'tor•ate, *n.* relation by which strong state partly controls weaker state. 2. such weaker state.

pro'té•gé' (prō'tə zhā'), *n.* one under friendly patronage of another. **—pro'té•gée',** *n.fem.*

pro'tein, *n.* nitrogenous compound required for life processes.

pro'test, *n.* 1. objection. *—v.* (prə test'). 2. express objection. 3. declare. **—prot'es•ta'tion,** *n.*

Prot'es•tant, *n.* Christian who belongs to a church that began by breaking away from the Roman Catholic Church in the 16th century. **—Prot'es•tant•ism',** *n.*

pro'to•col', *n.* diplomatic etiquette.

pro'ton, *n.* part of atom bearing positive charge.

pro'to•plasm', *n.* basis of living matter.

pro'to•type', *n.* model or typical version. **—pro'to•typ'i•cal,** *adj.*

pro•to•zo'an (-zō'ən), *n.*, *pl.* **-zoans, -zoa.** any of various one-celled organisms that usu. obtain nourishment by ingesting food rather than by photosynthesis.

pro•tract', *v.* lengthen. **—pro•trac'tion,** *n.*

pro•trac'tor, *n.* instrument for measuring angles.

pro•trude', *v.*, **-truded, -truding.** project; extend. **—pro•tru'sion,** *n.* **—pro•tru'sive,** *adj.*

pro•tu'ber•ant, *adj.* bulging out. **—pro•tu'ber•ance,** *n.*

proud, *adj.* 1. having pride. 2. arrogant. 3. magnificent. **—proud'ly,** *adv.*

prove, *v.*, **proved, proving.** 1. establish as fact. 2. test. 3. be or become ultimately. **—prov'a•ble,** *adj.*

prov'e•nance, *n.* place or source of origin.

prov'en•der, *n.* fodder.

prov'erb, *n.* wise, long-current saying. **—pro•ver'bi•al,** *adj.*

pro•vide', *v.*, **-vided, -viding.** 1. supply. 2. yield. 3. prepare beforehand. **—pro•vid'er,** *n.*

pro•vid'ed, *conj.* if.

prov'i•dence, *n.* 1. God's care. 2. economy.

prov'i•dent, *adj.* showing foresight; prudent.

prov'i•den'tial, *adj.* coming as godsend.

prov'ince, *n.* 1. administrative unit of country. 2. sphere.

pro•vin'cial, *adj.* 1. of province. 2. narrow-minded; unsophisticated.

pro•vi'sion, *n.* 1. something stated as necessary or binding. 2. act of providing. 3. what is provided. 4. arrangement beforehand. 5. (*pl.*) food supply. *—v.* 6. supply with provisions. **—pro•vi'sion•al,** *adj.* temporary.

pro•vi'so, *n.*, *pl.* **-sos, -soes.** something required in agreement.

pro•vo'ca•teur' (prə vok'ə tûr', -tŏŏr'), *n.* person who provokes trouble, esp. as an agent for the police or a foreign power.

pro•voke', *v.*, **-voked, -voking.** 1. exasperate. 2. arouse. **—prov'o•ca'tion,** *n.* **—pro•voc'a•tive,** *adj.* **—pro•voc'a•tive•ly,** *adv.*

pro'vost marshal (prō'vō), *Mil.* head of police.

prow, *n.* fore part of ship or aircraft.

prow'ess, *n.* 1. exceptional ability. 2. bravery.

prowl, *v.* roam or search stealthily. **—prowl'er,** *n.*

prox•im'i•ty, *n.* nearness.

prox'y, *n.*, *pl.* **proxies.** agent.

prude, *n.* person overly concerned with proprieties. **—prud'ish,** *adj.*

pru'dence, *n.* practical wisdom; caution. **—pru'dent, pru•den'tial,** *adj.*

prune, *v.*, **pruned, pruning,** *n.* *—v.* 1. cut off (branches, etc.). *—n.* 2. kind of plum, often dried.

pru'ri•ent (prŏŏr'ē ənt), *adj.* having lewd thoughts. **—pru'ri•ence,** *n.*

pry, *v.*, **pried, prying,** *n.* *—v.* 1. look or inquire too curiously. 2. move with lever. *—n.* 3. act of prying. 4. prying person. 5. lever.

psalm, *n.* sacred song.

pseu'do (sōō'dō), *adj.* false; imitation.

pseu'do•nym, *n.* false name used by writer.

pso•ri'a•sis (sə rī'ə sis), *n.* chronic,

inflammatory skin disease characterized by scaly patches.

psy·che (sī′kē), n. human soul or mind.

psy·che·del·ic (sī′kə del′ik), adj. noting a mental state of extreme feelings, distorted sense perceptions, hallucinations, etc.

psy·chi·a·try, n. science of mental diseases. —**psy·chi·at′ric**, adj. —**psy·chi′a·trist**, n.

psy·chic, adj. 1. of the psyche. 2. pertaining to an apparently nonphysical force or agency. —n. 3. person sensitive to psychic influences.

psy·cho·a·nal′y·sis, n. 1. study of conscious and unconscious psychological processes. 2. treatment of psychoneuroses according to such study. —**psy·cho·an′a·lyze**, v. —**psy·cho·an′a·lyst**, n.

psy·chol′o·gy, n. science of mental states and behavior. —**psy·cho·log′i·cal**, adj. —**psy·cho·log′i·cal·ly**, adv. —**psy·chol′o·gist**, n.

psy·cho·neu·ro′sis, n., pl. -**ses**. emotional disorder. —**psy·cho·neu·rot′ic**, adj. n.

psy·cho·path′a·thy (-kop′-), n., pl. -**thies**. mental disease. —**psy·cho·path′ic**, adj. —**psy·cho·path′**, n.

psy·cho′sis, n., pl. -**ses**. severe mental disease. —**psy·chot′ic**, adj.

psy·cho·so·mat′ic, adj. (of physical disorder) caused by one's emotional state.

psy·cho·ther′a·py, n., pl. -**pies**. treatment of mental disorders. —**psy·cho·ther′a·pist**, n.

ptar′mi·gan (tär′-), n. species of mountain grouse.

pter′o·dac′tyl (ter′ə dak′til), n. extinct flying reptile.

pto·maine (tō′-), n. substance produced during decay of plant and animal matter.

pub, n. Brit. Informal. tavern.

pu′ber·ty (pyōō′-), n. sexual maturity.

pu′bic, adj. of or near the genitals.

pub′lic, adj. 1. of or for people generally. 2. open to view or knowledge of all. —n. 3. people. —**pub′lic·ly**, adv.

pub·li·ca′tion, n. 1. publishing of book, etc. 2. item published.

pub·lic′i·ty, n. 1. public attention. 2. material promoting this.

pub′li·cize′, v., -**cized**, -**cizing**. bring to public notice. —**pub′li·cist**, n.

pub′lish, v. 1. issue (book, paper, etc.) for general distribution. 2. announce publicly. —**pub′lish·er**, n.

puck, n. black rubber disk hit into goal in hockey.

puck′er, v., n. wrinkle.

puck′ish, adj. mischievous.

pud′ding (pŏŏd′-), n. soft dish, usually dessert.

pud′dle (pud′-), n., v., -**dled**, -**dling**. —n. 1. small pool of water, esp. dirty water. —v. 2. fill with puddles.

pudg′y, adj. pudgier, pudgiest. short and fat. —**pudg′i·ness**, n.

pueb′lo (pweb′lō), n., pl. -**los**. village of certain Southwestern Indians.

pu′er·ile (pyōō′ər il), adj. childish. —**pu·er·il′i·ty**, n.

puff, n. 1. short quick blast, as of wind. 2. inflated part. 3. anything soft and light. —v. 4. blow with puffs. 5. breathe hard and fast. 6. inflate. —**puff′y**, adj.

puf′fin, n. sea bird.

pug, n. kind of dog.

pu′gil·ism, n. boxing. —**pu′gil·ist**, n.

pug·na′cious, adj. fond of fighting. —**pug·nac′i·ty**, n.

pug nose, short, broad, somewhat turned-up nose.

puke, v., **puked**, **puking**, n. Slang. vomit.

pul·chri·tude′, n. beauty.

pull, v. 1. draw; haul. 2. tear. 3. move with force. —n. 4. act of pulling. 5. force. 6. handle. 7. Informal. influence in politics, etc.

pul′let, n. young hen.

pul′ley, n. wheel for guiding rope.

Pull′man, n. railroad sleeping car.

pull′o·ver′, adj. 1. designed to be put on by being drawn over the head. —n. 2. pullover garment.

pul′mo·nar′y, adj. of lungs.

pulp, n. 1. soft fleshy part, as of fruit or tooth. 2. any soft mass. —v. 3. make or become pulp. —**pulp′y**, adj.

pul′pit, n. platform in church from which service is conducted or sermon is preached.

pul′sar (-sär), n. source of pulsating radio energy among stars.

pul′sate, v., -**sated**, -**sating**. throb. —**pul·sa′tion**, n.

pulse, n., v., **pulsed**, **pulsing**. —n. 1. steady beat of arteries caused by heart's contractions. —v. 2. pulsate.

pul′ver·ize′, v., -**ized**, -**izing**. reduce to powder. —**pul′ver·i·za′tion**, n.

pu′ma, n. cougar.

pum′ice, n. porous volcanic glass used as abrasive.

pum′mel, v., -**meled**, -**meling**. strike; beat.

pump, n. 1. apparatus for raising or driving fluids. 2. light low shoe. —v. 3. raise or drive with pump. 4. Informal. try to get information from.

pum·per·nick'el, *n.* hard, sour rye bread.

pump'kin, *n.* large orange fruit of garden vine.

pun, *n.*, *v.* **punned, punning.** —*n.* 1. play with words alike in sound but different in meaning. —*v.* 2. make pun. —**pun'ster**, *n.*

punch, *n.* 1. thrusting blow. 2. tool for piercing material. 3. sweetened beverage. —*v.* 4. hit with thrusting blow. 5. drive (cattle). 6. cut or indent with punch. —**punch'er**, *n.*

punch'y, *adj.* **punchier, punchiest.** 1. befuddled; dazed, as if having been punched. 2. vigorously effective; forceful.

punc·til'i·ous, *adj.* exact or careful in conduct.

punc'tu·al, *adj.* on time. —**punc·tu·al'i·ty**, *n.* —**punc'tu·al·ly**, *adv.*

punc'tu·ate', *v.*, **-ated, -ating.** 1. mark with punctuation. 2. accent periodically.

punc'tu·a'tion, *n.* use of commas, semicolons, etc.

punc'ture, *n.*, *v.*, **-tured, -turing.** —*n.* 1. perforation. —*v.* 2. perforate with pointed object.

pun'dit, *n.* learned person; sage.

pun'gent, *adj.* 1. sharp in taste. 2. biting. —**pun'gen·cy**, *n.* —**pun'gent·ly**, *adv.*

pun'ish, *v.* subject to pain, confinement, loss, etc., for offense. —**pun'ish·a·ble**, *adj.* —**pun'ish·ment**, *n.*

pu'ni·tive, *adj.* punishing.

punk, *n.* 1. substance that will smolder, used esp. to light fires. 2. *Slang.* something or someone worthless or unimportant. 3. *Slang.* young ruffian; hoodlum. 4. Also, **punk rock.** rock music marked by loudness and aggressive, often abusive, lyrics. 5. style of clothing, etc., suggesting defiance of social norms. —*adj.* 6. *Informal.* poor in quality. 7. of punk rock or punk style.

punt, *n.* 1. kick in football. 2. shallow flat-bottomed boat. —*v.* 3. kick (dropped ball) before it touches ground. 4. propel (boat) with pole.

pu'ny, *adj.*, **-nier, -niest.** small and weak.

pup, *n.* young dog.

pu'pa (pyōō'pə), *n.*, *pl.* **-pae, -pas.** insect in stage between larva and winged adult. —**pu'pal**, *adj.*

pu'pil, *n.* 1. person being taught. 2. opening in iris of eye.

pup'pet, *n.* 1. doll or figure manipulated by hand or strings. 2. person, government, etc., whose actions are controlled by another.

pup'py, *n.*, *pl.* **-pies.** young dog.

pur'chase, *v.*, **-chased, -chasing.** *n.* —*v.* 1. buy. —*n.* 2. acquisition by payment. 3. what is purchased. 4. leverage. —**pur'chas·er**, *n.*

pure, *adj.* **purer, purest.** 1. free from anything different or hurtful. 2. abstract. 3. absolute. 4. chaste. —**pure'ly**, *adv.* —**pure'ness**, *n.*

pure'bred, *adj.* 1. having ancestors over many generations from a recognized breed. —*n.* 2. purebred animal.

pu·rée' (pyŏŏ rā'), *n.*, *v.*, **-réed, -réeing.** —*n.* 1. cooked food that has been sieved or blended. —*v.* 2. make purée of.

pur'ga·to'ry, *n.*, *pl.* **-ries.** 1. *Rom. Cath. Theol.* condition or place of purification, after death, from venial sins. 2. any condition or place of temporary punishment.

purge, *v.*, **purged, purging,** *n.* —*v.* 1. cleanse; purify. 2. rid. 3. clear by causing evacuation. —*n.* 4. act or means of purging. —**pur·ga'tion**, *n.* —**pur'ga·tive**, *adj.*, *n.*

pu'ri·fy, *v.*, **-fied, -fying.** make or become pure. —**pu·ri·fi·ca'tion**, *n.*

Pu'rim (pŏŏr'im), *n.* Jewish commemorative festival.

Pu'ri·tan, *n.* 1. member of strict Protestant group originating in 16th-century England. 2. (*l.c.*) person of strict morality or religious views. —**pu·ri·tan'i·cal**, *adj.*

pu'ri·ty, *n.* condition of being pure.

purl, *v.* knit with inverted stitch.

pur'loin', *v.* steal.

pur'ple, *n.* 1. color blended of red and blue. —*adj.* 2. of or like purple.

pur·port', *v.* 1. claim. 2. imply. —*n.* (pŭr'pōrt). 3. meaning.

pur'pose, *n.*, *v.*, **-posed, -posing.** —*n.* 1. object; aim; intention. —*v.* 2. intend. —**pur'pose·ful**, *adj.* —**pur'pose·less**, *adj.*

purr, *v.* 1. utter low continuous sound, as by cat. —*n.* 2. this sound.

purse, *n.*, *v.*, **pursed, pursing.** —*n.* 1. small case for carrying money. 2. sum of money offered as prize. —*v.* 3. pucker.

purs'er, *n.* financial officer.

pur·su'ant, *adv.* according.

pur·sue', *v.*, **-sued, -suing.** 1. follow to catch. 2. carry on (studies, etc.). —**pur·su'ance**, *n.* —**pur·su'er**, *n.*

pur·suit', *n.* 1. act of pursuing. 2. quest. 3. occupation.

pu'ru·lent (pyŏŏr'ə lant), *adj.* full of pus. —**pu'ru·lence**, *n.*

pur·vey', *v.* provide; supply. —**pur·vey'ance**, *n.* —**pur·vey'or**, *n.*

pur'view (pŭr'vyōō), *n.* 1. range of

operation, authority, or concern. **2.** range of vision, insight, or understanding.

pus, *n.* liquid matter found in sores, etc.

push, *v.* **1.** exert force on to send away. **2.** urge. —*n.* **3.** act of pushing. **4.** strong effort. —**push'er,** *n.*

push'o'ver, *n. Informal.* one easily victimized or overcome.

pus'sil·lan'i·mous, *adj.* cowardly.

puss'y, *n., pl.* **pussies.** cat. Also, **puss.**

puss'y·foot', *v.* **1.** go stealthily. **2.** act timidly or irresolutely.

pussy willow, small American shrub.

pus'tule (-chōol), *n.* pimple containing pus.

put, *v.,* **put, putting.** —*v.* **1.** move or place. **2.** set, as to task. **3.** express. **4.** apply. **5.** impose. **6.** throw. —*n.* **7.** throw.

pu'ta·tive, *adj.* reputed.

pu'tre·fy', *v.,* **-fied, -fying.** rot. —**pu'tre·fac'tion,** *n.*

pu'trid, *adj.* rotten.

putsch (pōoch), *n.* sudden political revolt or uprising.

putt, *v.* **1.** strike (golf ball) gently and carefully. —*n.* **2.** such stroke.

put'ter, *v.* **1.** busy oneself ineffectively. —*n.* **2.** club for putting.

put'ty, *n., v.,* **-tied, -tying.** —*n.* **1.** cement of whiting and linseed oil. —*v.* **2.** secure with putty.

puz'zle, *n., v.,* **-zled, -zling.** —*n.* **1.** device or question offering difficulties. —*v.* **2.** perplex. —**puz'zle·ment,** *n.*

pyg'my, *n., pl.* **-mies.** dwarf.

py'lon, *n.* tall thin structure.

py'or·rhe'a, *n.* disease of gums.

pyr'a·mid, *n.* **1.** solid with triangular sides meeting in point. —*v.* **2.** increase gradually. —**py·ram'i·dal,** *adj.*

pyre, *n.* heap of wood, esp. for burning corpse.

py'rite, *n.* common yellow mineral of low value.

py'ro·ma'ni·a, *n.* mania for setting fires. —**py'ro·ma'ni·ac',** *n.*

py'ro·tech'nics, *n.* fireworks. —**py'ro·tech'nic,** *adj.*

py'thon, *n.* large snake that kills by constriction.

Q

Q, q, *n.* seventeenth letter of English alphabet.

Q.E.D., which was to be shown or demonstrated.

quack, *n.* pretender to medical skill. —**quack'er·y,** *n.*

quad'ran'gle, *n.* **1.** plane figure with four angles and four sides. **2.** Also, *Informal,* **quad.** enclosed four-sided area. —**quad·ran'gu·lar,** *adj.*

quad'rant, *n.* **1.** arc of 90°. **2.** instrument for measuring altitudes.

quad'ra·phon'ic, *adj.* of sound reproduced through four recording tracks.

quad'ri·lat'er·al, *adj.* **1.** four-sided. —*n.* **2.** four-sided plane figure.

qua·drille' (kwə dril'), *n.* square dance for four couples.

quad'ri·ple'gi·a (kwod'rə plē'jē ə, -jə), *n.* paralysis of the entire body below the neck. —**quad'ri·ple'gic,** *n., adj.*

quad'ru·ped', *n.* four-footed animal.

quad·ru'ple, *adj., n., v.,* **-pled, -pling.** —*adj.* **1.** of four parts. **2.** four times as great. **3.** number, etc., four times as great as another. —*v.* **4.** increase fourfold.

quad·ru'plet, *n.* one of four children born at one birth.

quad·ru'pli·cate, *n.* group of four copies.

quaff (kwaf), *v.* drink heartily.

quag'mire', *n.* boggy ground.

qua'hog (kwô'hog, kō'-), *n.* edible American clam.

quail, *n., pl.* **quails, quail,** *v.* —*n.* **1.** game bird resembling domestic fowls. —*v.* **2.** lose courage; show fear.

quaint, *adj.* pleasingly odd. —**quaint'ly,** *adv.* —**quaint'ness,** *n.*

quake, *v.,* **quaked, quaking,** *n.* —*v.* **1.** tremble. —*n.* **2.** earthquake.

Quak'er, *n.* member of Society of Friends.

qual'i·fy', *v.,* **-fied, -fying. 1.** make proper or fit. **2.** modify. **3.** mitigate. **4.** show oneself fit. —**qual'i·fi·ca'tion,** *n.*

qual'i·ty, *n., pl.* **-ties. 1.** characteristic. **2.** relative merit. **3.** excellence. —**qual'i·ta'tive,** *adj.*

quality time, time devoted exclusively to nurturing cherished person or activity.

qualm (kwäm), *n.* **1.** misgiving; scruple. **2.** feeling of illness.

quan'da·ry, *n., pl.* **-ries.** dilemma.

quan'ti·ty, *n., pl.* **-ties. 1.** amount; measure. **2.** *Math.* something having magnitude. —**quan'ti·ta'tive,** *adj.*

quan'tum, *n., pl.* **-ta,** *adj.* —*n.* **1.** quantity or amount. **2.** *Physics.* very small, indivisible quantity of energy. —*adj.* 3. sudden and significant.

quar'an·tine', *n.*, *v.*, **-tined**, **-tining.** —*n.* 1. strict isolation to prevent spread of disease. —*v.* 2. put in quarantine.

quar'rel, *n.*, *v.*, **-reled**, **-reling.** —*n.* 1. angry dispute. —*v.* 2. disagree angrily. —**quar'rel·some**, *adj.*

quar'ry, *n.*, *pl.* **-ries**, *v.*, **-ried**, **-rying.** —*n.* 1. pit from which stone is taken. 2. object of pursuit. —*v.* 3. get stone from quarry.

quart, *n.* measure of capacity: in liquid measure, 1/4 gallon; in dry measure, 1/8 peck.

quar'ter, *n.* 1. one of four equal parts. 2. coin worth 25 cents. 3. (*pl.*) place of residence. 4. mercy. —*v.* 5. divide into quarters. 6. lodge. —*adj.* 7. being a quarter.

quar'ter·back', *n.* position in football.

quarter horse, strong, agile horse capable of great speed over short distances.

quar'ter·ly, *adj.*, *n.*, *pl.* **-lies**, *adv.* —*adj.* 1. occurring, etc., each quarter year. —*n.* 2. quarterly publication. —*adv.* 3. once each quarter year.

quar'ter·mas'ter, *n.* 1. military officer in charge of supplies, etc. 2. naval officer in charge of signals, etc.

quar·tet', *n.* group of four. Also, **quar·tette'.**

quar'to, *n.*, *pl.* **-tos.** book page printed from sheets folded twice.

quartz, *n.* common crystalline mineral.

qua'sar (kwā'zär), *n.* astronomical source of powerful radio energy.

quash, *v.* subdue; suppress.

qua'si (kwā'zī), *adj.* resembling; to be regarded as if.

quat'rain, *n.* four-line stanza.

qua'ver, *v.* 1. quiver. 2. speak tremulously. —*n.* 3. quavering tone.

quay (kē), *n.* landing beside water.

quea'sy (kwē'zē), *adj.*, **-sier**, **-siest.** 1. nauseated. 2. uneasy.

queen, *n.* 1. wife of king. 2. female sovereign. 3. fertile female of bees, ants, etc. —*v.* 4. reign as queen.

queer, *adj.* 1. strange; odd. —*n.* 2. Offensive. homosexual. —*v.* 3. Slang. ruin; impair. —**queer'ly**, *adv.* —**queer'ness**, *n.*

queil, *v.* suppress.

quench, *v.* slake or extinguish.

quer'u·lous, *adj.* peevish.

que'ry (kwēr'ē), *n.*, *pl.* **-ries**, *v.*, **-ried**, **-rying.** question.

quest, *n. v.* search.

ques'tion, *n.* 1. sentence put in a form

to elicit information. 2. problem for discussion or dispute. —*v.* 3. ask a question. 4. doubt. —**ques'tion·a·ble**, *adj.* —**ques'tion·er**, *n.*

ques'tion·naire', *n.* list of questions.

queue (kyōō), *n.*, *v.*, **queued**, **queuing.** —*n.* 1. line of persons. 2. braid of hair hanging down the back. —*v.* 3. form in a line.

quib'ble, *v.*, **-bled**, **-bling**, —*v.* 1. speak ambiguously in evasion. 2. make petty objections. —*n.* 3. act of quibbling. —**quib'bler**, *n.*

quiche (kēsh), *n.* pielike dish of cheese, onion, etc.

quick, *adj.* 1. prompt; done promptly. 2. swift. 3. alert. —*n.* 4. living persons. 5. sensitive flesh. —*adv.* 6. quickly. —**quick'ly**, *adv.* —**quick'ness**, *n.*

quick'en, *v.* 1. hasten. 2. rouse. 3. become alive.

quick'lime', *n.* untreated lime.

quick'sand', *n.* soft sand yielding easily to weight.

quick'sil'ver, *n.* mercury.

quid, *n.* 1. portion for chewing. 2. *Brit. Informal.* one pound sterling.

quid pro quo, *pl.* **quid pro quos, quids pro quo.** something given or taken for something else.

qui·es'cent (kwī·es'ənt), *adj.* resting; inactive. —**qui·es'cence**, *n.*

qui'et, *adj.* 1. being at rest. 2. peaceful. 3. silent. 4. restrained. —*v.* 5. make or become quiet. 6. tranquillity. —**qui'et·ly**, *adv.* —**qui'et·ness**, *n.*

qui'e·tude', *n.*

qui·e'tus (kwī·ē'təs), *n.* 1. final settlement. 2. release from life.

quill, *n.* large feather.

quilt, *n.* padded and lined bed covering.

quince, *n.* yellowish acid fruit.

qui'nine, *n.* bitter substance used esp. in treating malaria.

quin·tes'sence, *n.* essential substance. —**quin'tes·sen'tial**, *adj.*

quin·tet', *n.* group of five. Also, **quin·tette'.**

quin·tu'plet, *n.* one of five children born at one birth.

quip, *n.*, *v.*, **quipped**, **quipping.** —*n.* 1. witty or sarcastic remark. —*v.* 2. make quip.

quire, *n.* set of 24 uniform sheets of paper.

quirk, *n.* peculiarity.

quis'ling, *n.* traitor.

quit, *v.*, **quitted**, **quitting.** 1. stop. 2. leave. 3. relinquish. —**quit'ter**, *n.*

quit'claim', *n.* 1. transfer of one's interest. 2. give up claim to.

quite, *adv.* 1. completely. 2. really.

quits, *adj.* with no further payment or revenge due.

quit'tance, *n.* **1.** requital. **2.** discharge from debt.

quiv'er, *v.* **1.** tremble. —*n.* **2.** trembling. **3.** case for arrows.

quix·ot'ic, *adj.* extravagantly idealistic; impractical.

quiz, *v.,* quizzed, quizzing, *n. pl.* quizzes. —*v.* **1.** question. —*n.* **2.** informal questioning.

quiz'zi·cal, *adj.* **1.** comical. **2.** puzzled. —**quiz'zi·cal·ly,** *adv.*

quoit, *n.* flat ring thrown to encircle peg in game of quoits.

quon'dam, *adj.* former.

Quon'set hut, *n. Trademark.* semicylindrical metal shelter with end walls.

quo'rum, *n.* number of members needed to transact business legally.

quo'ta, *n.* proportional share due.

quote, *v.,* quoted, quoting, *n.* —*v.* **1.** repeat verbatim. **2.** cite. **3.** state (price of). —*n.* **4.** *Informal.* quotation. —**quo·ta'tion,** *n.* —**quot'a·ble,** *adj.*

quoth, *v. Archaic.* said.

quo·tid'i·an (kwō tid'ē ən), *adj.* **1.** daily. **2.** ordinary; everyday.

quo'tient, *n. Math.* number of times one quantity is contained in another.

R

R, r, *n.* **1.** eighteenth letter of English alphabet. **2.** those less than 17 years old must be accompanied by adult: motion-picture classification.

rab'bi, *n.* Jewish religious leader. —**rab·bin'ic, rab·bin'i·cal,** *adj.*

rab'bit, *n.* small, long-eared mammal.

rab'ble, *n.* mob.

rab'id, *adj.* **1.** irrationally intense. **2.** having rabies. —**rab'id·ly,** *adv.*

ra'bies (rā'bēz), *n.* fatal disease transmitted by bite of infected animal.

rac·coon', *n.* small nocturnal carnivorous mammal.

race, *n., v.,* raced, racing. —*n.* **1.** contest of speed. **2.** onward course or flow. **3.** group of persons of common origin. **4.** any class or kind. —*v.* **5.** engage in race. **6.** move swiftly. —**rac'er,** *n.* —**ra'cial,** *adj.*

ra·ceme' (rā sēm'), *n.* cluster of flowers along stem.

rac'ism, *n.* hatred of or prejudice against another race.

rack, *n.* **1.** framework to hold various articles. **2.** toothed bar engaging with teeth of pinion. **3.** instrument of torture. **4.** destruction. —*v.* **5.** torture. **6.** strain.

rack'et, *n.* **1.** noise. **2.** illegal or dishonest business. **3.** Also, **rac'quet.** framed network used as bat in tennis, etc.

rack·e·teer', *n.* criminal engaged in racket.

rac'on·teur' (rak'on tûr'), *n.* skilled storyteller.

ra·coon', *n.* raccoon.

rac'quet·ball, *n.* game similar to handball, played with rackets on four-walled court.

rac'y, *adj.,* racier, raciest. **1.** lively. **2.** risqué. —**rac'i·ness,** *n.*

ra'dar, *n.* electronic device capable of locating unseen objects by radio wave.

ra'di·al, *adj.* of rays or radii.

ra'di·ant, *adj.* **1.** emitting rays of light. **2.** bright; exultant. **3.** emitted in rays, as heat. —**ra'di·ance,** *n.* —**ra'di·ant·ly,** *adv.*

ra'di·ate', *v.* **-ated, -ating. 1.** spread like rays from center. **2.** emit or issue in rays. —**ra'di·a'tion,** *n.*

ra'di·a'tor, *n.* heating device.

rad'i·cal, *adj.* **1.** fundamental. **2.** favoring drastic reforms. —*n.* **3.** person with radical ideas. **4.** atom or group of atoms behaving as unit in chemical reaction. —**rad'i·cal·ism,** *n.* —**rad'i·cal·ly,** *adv.*

ra'di·o', *n., pl.* **-dios. 1.** way of transmitting sound by electromagnetic waves, without wires. **2.** apparatus for sending or receiving such waves.

ra'di·o·ac'tive, *adj.* emitting radiation from the atomic nucleus, as radium, for example, does. —**ra'di·o·ac·tiv'i·ty,** *n.*

ra'di·ol'o·gy, *n.* use of radiation, as x-rays, for medical diagnosis and treatment. —**ra'di·ol'o·gist,** *n.*

rad'ish, *n.* crisp root of garden plant, eaten raw.

ra'di·um, *n.* radioactive metallic element.

ra'di·us, *n., pl.* **-dii, -diuses. 1.** straight line from center of a circle to circumference. **2.** one of the bones of the forearm.

ra'don (rā'don), *n.* inert gaseous element produced by decay of radium.

raf'fi·a, *n.* fiber made from leafstalks of a Madagascan palm.

raff'ish, *adj.* **1.** jaunty; rakish. **2.** gaudily vulgar or cheap; tawdry.

raf'fle, *n., v.,* **-fled, -fling.** —*n.* **1.** lottery in which chances are sold. —v. 2. dispose of by raffle.

raft, n. floating platform of logs, etc.

raft'er, n. framing member of roof.

rag, n. worthless bit of cloth, esp. one torn. —**rag'ged,** adj.

rag·a·muf'fin, n. ragged child.

rage, n., v., **raged, raging.** —n. 1. violent anger. 2. object of popular enthusiasm. —v. 3. be violently angry. 4. prevail violently.

rag'lan, n. loose garment with sleeves continuing to collar.

ra·gout' (ra gōō'), n. stew.

rag'weed', n. plant whose pollen causes hay fever.

raid, n. 1. sudden attack. —v. 2. attack suddenly. —**raid'er,** n.

rail, n. 1. horizontal bar, used as barrier, support, etc. 2. one of pair of railroad tracks. 3. railroad as means of transport. 4. wading bird. —v. 5. complain bitterly.

rail'ing, n. barrier of rails and posts.

rail'ler·y, n. banter.

rail'road', n. 1. road with fixed rails on which trains run. —v. 2. transport by means of a railroad. 3. coerce into hasty action or decision.

rail'way', n. Chiefly Brit. railroad.

rai'ment, n. clothing.

rain, n. 1. water falling from sky in drops. 2. rainfall. —v. 3. fall or send down as rain. —**rain'y,** adj.

rain'bow', n. arc of colors sometimes seen in sky opposite sun during rain. —**rain'bow·like,** adj.

rain'coat', n. waterproof coat.

rain'fall', n. amount of rain.

raise, v., **raised, raising.** —v. 1. lift up. 2. set upright. 3. cause to appear. 4. grow. 5. collect. 6. rear. 7. cause (dough) to expand. 8. end (siege). —9. increase, esp. in pay.

rai'sin, n. dried sweet grape.

ra'jah (-ja), n. (formerly) Indian king or prince.

rake, n., v., **raked, raking.** —n. 1. long-handled implement with teeth for gathering or smoothing ground. 2. dissolute person. 3. slope. —v. 4. gather, smooth, etc., with rake. 5. fire guns the length of (target).

rak'ish, adj. 1. jaunty. 2. dissolute.

ral'ly, v., **-lied, -lying,** n., pl. **-lies.** —v. 1. bring into order again. 2. call or come together. 3. revive. 4. come to aid. —n. 5. renewed order. 6. renewal of strength. 7. mass meeting.

ram, n., v., **rammed, ramming.** —n. 1. male sheep. 2. device for battering, forcing, etc. —v. 3. strike forcibly.

RAM, random-access memory: computer memory available for creating,

loading, and running programs and manipulating and temporarily storing data.

ram'ble, v., **-bled, -bling,** n. —v. 1. stroll idly. 2. talk vaguely. —n. 3. leisurely stroll. —**ram'bler,** n.

ram·bunc'tious, adj. difficult to control or handle; wildly boisterous.

ram'i·fy', v., **-fied, -fying.** divide into branches. —**ram'i·fi·ca'tion,** n.

ramp, n. sloping surface between two levels.

ram'page, n., v., **-paged, -paging.** —n. 1. (ram'pāj). violent behavior. —v. 2. (ram pāj'). move furiously about.

ramp'ant, adj. 1. vigorous; unrestrained. 2. standing on hind legs.

ram'part, n. mound of earth raised as bulwark.

ram'rod', n. rod for cleaning or loading gun.

ram·shack'le, adj. rickety.

ranch, n. large farm, esp. for raising stock. —**ranch'er,** n.

ran'cid (-sid), adj. stale. —**ran·cid'i·ty,** n.

ran'cor (rang'kar), n. lasting resentment. —**ran'cor·ous,** adj.

ran'dom, adj. without aim or consistency.

ran'dy, adj., **randier, randiest.** sexually aroused; lustful.

range, n., v., **ranged, ranging.** —n. 1. limits; extent. 2. place for target shooting. 3. distance between gun and target. 4. row. 5. mountain chain. 6. grazing area. 7. cooking stove. —v. 8. arrange. 9. pass over (area). 10. vary.

rang'er, n. 1. warden of forest tract. 2. civil officer who patrols large area.

rang'y (rān'jē), adj., **rangier, rangiest.** slender and long-limbed.

rank, n. 1. class, group, or standing. 2. high position. 3. row. 4. (pl.) enlisted personnel. —v. 5. arrange. 6. put or be in particular rank. 7. be senior in rank. —adj. 8. growing excessively. 9. offensively strong in smell. 10. utter. 11. grossly vulgar. —**rank'ly,** adv. —**rank'ness,** n.

ran'kle, v., **-kled, -kling.** irritate.

ran'sack, v. search thoroughly.

ran'som, n. 1. sum demanded for prisoner. —v. 2. pay ransom for.

rant, v. 1. speak wildly. —n. 2. violent speech. —**rant'er,** n.

rap, v., **rapped, rapping,** n. —v. 1. strike quickly and sharply. —n. 2. sharp blow. 3. popular music marked by rhythmical intoning of rhymed verses over repetitive beat. —**rap'per,** n.

ra·pa'cious, adj. plundering; greedy.

rape, n., v., **raped, raping.** —n. 1. forcing of sexual intercourse on someone. 2. abduction or seizure. —v. 3. commit rape on. 4. abduct or seize. —**rap'ist,** n.

rap'id, adj. swift. —n. 2. (pl.) swift-moving part of river. —**ra·pid'i·ty,** **rap·id·ness,** n. —**rap'id·ly,** adv.

ra·pi'er (rā'pē ər), n. slender sword.

rap·ine (rap'in), n. plunder.

rap·port' (ra pôr'), n. sympathetic relationship.

rapt, adj. engrossed.

rap'ture, n. ecstatic joy. —**rap'tur·ous,** adj.

rare, adj., **rarer, rarest.** 1. unusual. 2. thin, as air. 3. (of meat) not thoroughly cooked. —**rar'i·ty,** n. —**rare'ly,** adv. —**rare'ness,** n.

rare'bit (râr'bit), n. dish of melted cheese.

rar'e·fy, v., **-fied, -fying.** make or become thin, as air.

rar'ing, adj. very eager or anxious.

ras'cal, n. dishonest person. —**ras·cal'i·ty,** n.

rash, adj. 1. thoughtlessly hasty. —n. 2. skin eruption. —**rash'ly,** adv. —**rash'ness,** n.

rash'er, n. thin slice of bacon or ham.

rasp, v. 1. scrape, as with file. 2. irritate. 3. speak gratingly. —n. 4. coarse file. 5. rasping sound. —**rasp'y,** adj.

rasp'ber·ry (raz'-), n., pl. **-ries.** small juicy red or black fruit.

rat, n. rodent larger than mouse.

ratch'et, n. wheel or bar having teeth that catch pawl to control motion.

rate, n., v., **rated, rating.** —n. 1. charge in proportion to something that varies. 2. degree of speed, etc. —v. 3. estimate or fix rate. 4. consider; judge.

rath'er, adv. 1. somewhat. 2. in preference. 3. on the contrary.

rat'i·fy, v., **-fied, -fying.** confirm formally.

ra'tio (shō-, shē ō'), n., pl. **-tios.** relative number or extent; proportion.

ra·ti·oc·i·na'tion (rash'ē os'-), n. reasoning.

ra'tion, n. 1. fixed allowance. —v. 2. apportion. 3. put on ration.

ra'tion·al, adj. 1. sensible. 2. sane. —**ra'tion·al·ly,** adv. —**ra'tion·al'i·ty,** n.

ra'tion·ale' (rash'ə nal'), n. reasonable basis for action.

ra'tion·al·ism, n. advocacy of precise reasoning as source of truth. —**ra'tion·al·ist,** n. —**ra'tion·al·is'tic,** adj.

ra'tion·al·ize', v., **-ized, -izing.** 1.

find reason for one's behavior or attitude. 2. make rational. —**ra'tion·al·i·za'tion,** n.

rat·tan', n. hollow stem of climbing palm.

rat'tle, v., **-tled, -tling,** n. —v. 1. make series of short sharp sounds. 2. chatter. 3. *Informal.* disconcert. —n. 4. sound of rattling. 5. child's toy that rattles.

rat'tle·snake', n. venomous American snake.

rau'cous (rô'kəs), adj. 1. hoarse; harsh. 2. rowdy; disorderly. —**rau'cous·ly,** adv.

raun'chy, adj. **-chier, -chiest.** 1. vulgar; smutty. 2. lecherous. 3. dirty; slovenly.

rav'age, v., **-aged, -aging.** ruin. —**rav'ag·er,** n.

rave, v., **raved, raving.** talk wildly.

rav'el, v. 1. disengage threads. 2. tangle. 3. make clear. —n. 4. tangle. 5. disengaged thread.

ra'ven, n. large shiny black bird.

rav'en·ous, adj. very hungry; greedy.

ra·vine', n. deep, narrow valley.

ra·vi·o'li, n. small pockets of pasta filled esp. with cheese or meat.

rav'ish, v. 1. fill with joy. 2. rape. —**rav'ish·er,** n. —**rav'ish·ment,** n.

raw, adj. 1. in the natural state. 2. uncooked. 3. open. 4. untrained. —n. 5. raw condition or substance. —**raw'ness,** n.

raw'hide', n. untanned hide, as of cattle.

ray, n. 1. narrow beam of light. 2. trace. 3. line outward from center. 4. flat-bodied broad-sea fish.

ray'on, n. silklike synthetic fabric.

raze, v., **razed, razing.** demolish.

ra'zor, n. sharp-edged instrument for shaving.

razz, v. make fun of; mock.

re, n. 1. (rā) *Music.* second tone of scale. —prep. 2. (rē) with reference to.

re-, prefix indicating: 1. repetition, as *reprint, rearm.* 2. withdrawal.

reach, v. 1. come to. 2. be able to touch. 3. extend. —n. 4. act of reaching. 5. extent.

re·act', v. 1. act upon each other. 2. respond.

re·ac'tion, n. 1. extreme political conservatism. 2. responsive action. 3. chemical change. —**re·ac'tion·ar'y,** n., adj.

re·ac'tor, n. 1. one that reacts. 2. apparatus for producing useful nuclear energy.

read, v., **read, reading.** 1. observe and understand (printed matter, etc.). 2.

register. 3. utter aloud (something written or printed). 4. obtain and store, as in computer memory. **—read′a•ble**, adj. **—read′er**, n. **—read′er•ship**, n.

read′ing, n. 1. amount read at one time. 2. interpretation of written or musical work.

read′y, adj., **readier, readiest**, v., **readied, readying**, n. —adj. 1. fully prepared. 2. willing. 3. apt. —v. 4. make ready. —n. 5. state of being ready. **—read′i•ly**, adv. **—read′i•ness**, n.

read′y-made′, adj. ready for use when bought.

re′al, adj. 1. actual. 2. genuine. 3. denoting immovable property. **—re•al′i•ty**, **re′al•ness**, n. **—re′al•ly**, adv.

real estate, land with buildings, etc., on it. Also, **re′al•ty**.

re′al•ist, n. person accepting things as they are. **—re′al•is′tic**, adj.

re′al•ize′, v., **-ized, -izing**. 1. understand clearly. 2. make real. 3. get as profit. **—re′al•i•za′tion**, n.

realm (relm), n. 1. kingdom. 2. special field.

Re′al•tor, n. Trademark. real estate broker.

ream, n. 1. twenty quires of paper. —v. 2. enlarge (hole) with a **ream′er**. **—ream′er**, n.

reap, v. harvest. **—reap′er**, n.

rear, n. 1. back part. —adj. 2. of or at rear. —v. 3. care for to maturity. 4. raise; erect. 5. rise on hind legs.

rear admiral, naval officer above captain.

re•arm′, v. arm again. **—re•arm′a•ment**, n.

rea′son, n. 1. cause for belief, act, etc. 2. sound judgment. 3. sanity. —v. 4. think or argue logically. 5. infer. **—rea′son•ing**, n. **—rea′son•er**, n.

rea′son•a•ble, adj. showing sound judgment. **—rea′son•a•bly**, adv.

re′as•sure′, v., **-sured, -suring**. restore confidence of. **—re′as•sur′ance**, n.

re′bate, n., **-bated, -bating**, n. —v. 1. return (part of amount paid). —n. 2. amount rebated.

re•bel′, v., **-belled, -belling**. —v. (ri bel′). 1. rise in arms against one's government. 2. resist any authority. —n. (reb′əl). 3. one who rebels. **—re•bel′lion**, n. **—re•bel′lious**, adj.

re•bound′, v. 1. bound back after impact. —n. (rē′bound′). 2. act of rebounding.

re•buff′, n. 1. blunt check or refusal. —v. 2. check; repel.

re•buke′, v., **-buked, -buking**, n. reprimand.

re′bus, n. puzzle in which pictures and symbols combine to represent a word.

re•but′, v., **-butted, -butting**. refute. **—re•but′tal**, n.

re•cal′ci•trant (ri kal′sə trənt), adj. resisting control. **—re•cal′ci•trance**, n.

re•call′, v. 1. remember. 2. call back. 3. withdraw. —n. 4. act of recalling.

re•cant′, v. retract.

re′cap, n., v., **-capped, -capping**. —n. 1. recapitulation. 2. tire reconditioned by adding strip of new rubber. —v. 3. recapitulate. 4. recondition a tire.

re′ca•pit′u•late (-pich′ə-), v., **-lated, -lating**. review; sum up. **—re′ca•pit′u•la′tion**, n.

re•cede′, v., **-ceded, -ceding**. move or appear to move back.

re•ceipt′, n. 1. written acknowledgment of receiving. 2. (pl.) amount received. 3. act of receiving.

re•ceiv′a•ble, adj. still to be paid.

re•ceive′, v., **-ceived, -ceiving**. 1. take (something offered or delivered). 2. experience. 3. welcome (guests). 4. accept.

re•ceiv′er, n. 1. one that receives. 2. device, as radio, that receives electrical signals and converts them to sound, etc. 3. person put in charge of property in litigation. **—re•ceiv′er•ship′**, n.

re′cent, adj. happening, etc., lately. **—re′cen•cy**, n. **—re′cent•ly**, adv.

re•cep′ta•cle, n. container.

re•cep′tion, n. 1. act of receiving. 2. fact or manner of being received. 3. social function.

re•cep′tion•ist, n. person who receives callers in an office.

re•cep′tive, adj. quick to understand and consider ideas.

re•cess′, n. 1. temporary cessation of work. 2. alcove. 3. (pl.) inner part. —v. 4. take or make recess.

re•ces′sion, n. 1. withdrawal. 2. economic decline.

re•ces′sion•al, n. music played at end of church service.

re•cher′ché (rə shâr′shā, rə shâr shā′), adj. 1. very rare or choice. 2. affectedly refined.

re•cid′i•vism (ri sid′ə viz′əm), n. repeated or habitual relapse, as into crime.

rec′i•pe′, n. formula, esp. in cookery.

re•cip′i•ent, n. 1. receiver. —adj. 2. receiving.

re•cip′ro•cal, adj. 1. mutual. —n. 2.

thing in reciprocal position. —**re•cip′ro•cal•ly,** *adv.*

re•cip′ro•cate′, *v.,* -**cated,** -**cating.**
1. give, feel, etc., in return. 2. move alternately backward and forward. —**re•cip′ro•ca′tion,** *n.*

rec′i•proc′i•ty, *n.* interchange.

re•cit′al, *n.* musical entertainment.

re•cite′, *v.,* -**cited,** -**citing.** 1. repeat from memory. 2. narrate. —**rec′i•ta′tion,** *n.*

reck′less, *adj.* careless. —**reck′less•ly,** *adv.* —**reck′less•ness,** *n.*

reck′on, *v.* 1. calculate. 2. esteem. 3. *Informal.* suppose. 4. deal (with). —**reck′on•er,** *n.*

reck′on•ing, *n.* 1. settling of accounts. 2. navigational calculation.

re•claim′, *v.* make usable, as land. —**rec′la•ma′tion,** *n.*

re•cline′, *v.,* -**clined,** -**clining.** lean back.

rec′luse, *n.* person living in seclusion.

re•cog′ni•zance, *n.* bond pledging one to do a particular act.

rec′og•nize′, *v.,* -**nized,** -**nizing.** 1. identify or perceive from previous knowledge. 2. acknowledge formally. 3. greet. —**rec′og•ni′tion,** *n.* —**rec′og•niz′a•ble,** *adj.*

re•coil′, *v.* 1. shrink back. 2. spring back. —*n.* 3. act of recoiling.

rec′ol•lect′, *v.* remember. —**rec′ol•lec′tion,** *n.*

rec′om•mend′, *v.* 1. commend as worthy. 2. advise. —**rec′om•men•da′tion,** *n.*

rec′om•pense′, *v.,* -**pensed,** -**pensing,** *n.* —*v.* 1. repay or reward for services, injury, etc. —*n.* 2. such compensation.

rec′on•cile′, *v.,* -**ciled,** -**ciling.** 1. bring into agreement. 2. restore to friendliness. —**rec′on•cil′i•a′tion,** *n.* —**rec′on•cil′a•ble,** *adj.*

rec′on•dite′ (rek′ən dīt′), *adj.* 1. very profound, difficult, or abstruse. 2. known by few; esoteric.

re′con•noi′ter, *v.* search area, esp. for military information. —**re•con′nais•sance** (ri kon′ə səns), *n.*

re•cord′, *v.* 1. set down in writing. 2. register for mechanical reproduction. —*n.* (rek′ərd). 3. what is recorded. 4. object from which sound is mechanically reproduced. 5. best rate, etc., yet attained. —*adj.* (rek′ərd). 6. making or being a record. —**re•cord′er,** *n.* —**re•cord′ing,** *n.*

re•count′, *v.* 1. narrate. 2. count again. —*n.* (rē′kount′). 3. a second count.

re•coup′ (ri kⁿp′), *v.* recover; make up.

re•course′, *n.* resort for help.

re•cov′er, *v.* 1. get back. 2. reclaim. 3. regain health. —**re•cov′er•a•ble,** *adj.* —**re•cov′er•y,** *n.*

rec′re•a′tion, *n.* refreshing enjoyment. —**rec′re•a′tion•al,** *adj.*

re•crim′i•nate′, *v.,* -**nated,** -**nating.** accuse in return. —**re•crim′i•na′tion,** *n.*

re′cru•des′cence, *n.* breaking out again after inactivity. —**re′cru•des′cent,** *adj.*

re•cruit′, *n.* 1. new member of military or other group. —*v.* 2. enlist.

rect′an•gle, *n.* parallelogram with four right angles. —**rect•an′gu•lar,** *adj.*

rec′ti•fy′, *v.,* -**fied,** -**fying.** correct. —**rec′ti•fi•a•ble,** *adj.* —**rec′ti•fi′er,** *n.*

rec′ti•lin′e•ar, *adj.* 1. forming straight line. 2. formed by straight lines.

rec′ti•tude′, *n.* rightness of behavior.

rec′tor, *n.* 1. member of clergy in charge of parish, etc. 2. head of university, etc.

rec′to•ry, *n., pl.* -**ries.** parsonage.

rec′tum, *n.* lowest part of intestine. —**rec′tal,** *adj.*

re•cum′bent, *adj.* lying down. —**re•cum′ben•cy,** *n.*

re•cu′per•ate′ (-kⁿ′-), *v.,* -**ated,** -**ating.** regain health. —**re•cu′per•a′tion,** *n.*

re•cur′, *v.,* -**curred,** -**curring.** 1. occur again. 2. return in thought, etc. —**re•cur′rence,** *n.* —**re•cur′rent•ly,** *adv.*

re•cy′cle, *v.,* -**cled,** -**cling.** treat (refuse) to extract reusable material.

red, *n., adj.* **redder, reddest.** —*n.* 1. color of blood. 2. leftist radical in politics. —*adj.* 3. of or like red. 4. radically to left in politics. —**red′den,** *v.*

red′-blood′ed, *adj.* vigorous; virile.

re•deem′, *v.* 1. pay off. 2. recover. 3. fulfill. 4. deliver from sin by sacrifice. —**re•deem′er,** *n.* —**re•demp′tion,** *n.* —**re•demp′tive,** *adj.*

red′-hand′ed, *adj., adv.* in the act of wrongdoing.

red′head′, *n.* person with red hair. —**red′head′ed,** *adj.*

red herring, something intended to distract attention from the real problem or issue.

red′-hot′, *adj.* 1. red with heat. 2. violent; furious. 3. very fresh or new.

red′-let′ter, *adj.* memorable.

red′lin′ing, *n.* refusal by banks to grant mortgages in specified urban areas.

red'o·lent, *adj.* 1. odorous. 2. suggestive. —**red'o·lence,** *n.*

re·doubt', *n.* small isolated fort.

re·doubt'a·ble, *adj.* 1. evoking fear; formidable. 2. commanding respect.

re·dound', *v.* occur as result.

re·dress', *v.* 1. set right (a wrong). —*n.* (rē'dres). 2. act of redressing.

red tape, excessive attention to prescribed procedure.

re·duce', *v.,* **-duced, -ducing.** 1. make less in size, rank, etc. 2. put into simpler form or state. 3. remove body weight. —**re·duc'i·ble,** *adj.* —**re·duc'tion,** *n.* —**re·duc'er,** *n.*

re·dun'dant, *adj.* 1. excess. 2. wordy. —**re·dun'dance, re·dun'dan·cy,** *n.* —**re·dun'dant·ly,** *adv.*

red'wood', *n.* huge evergreen tree of California.

reed, *n.* 1. tall marsh grass. 2. musical pipe made of hollow stalk. 3. small piece of cane or metal at mouth of wind instrument. —**reed'y,** *adj.*

reef, *n.* 1. narrow ridge near the surface of water. 2. *Naut.* part of sail rolled or folded to reduce area. —*v.* 3. shorten (sail) by rolling or folding.

reef'er, *n.* 1. short heavy coat. 2. *Slang.* marijuana cigarette.

reek, *v.* 1. smell strongly and unpleasantly. —*n.* 2. such smell.

reel, *n.* 1. turning object for wound cord, film, etc. 2. lively dance. —*v.* 3. wind on reel. 4. tell easily and at length. 5. sway or stagger. 6. whirl.

reeve, *v.,* **reeved** or **rove, reeved** or **roven, reeving.** pass (rope) through hole.

re·fec'to·ry, *n., pl.* **-ries.** dining hall.

re·fer', *v.,* **-ferred, -ferring.** 1. direct attention. 2. direct or go for information. 3. apply. —**re·fer'ral,** *n.*

ref'er·ee', *n.* 1. judge. —*v.* 2. act as referee.

ref'er·ence, *n.* 1. act or fact of referring. 2. something referred to. 3. person from whom one seeks recommendation. 4. testimonial.

ref'er·en'dum, *n., pl.* **-dums, -da.** submission to popular vote of law passed by legislature.

re·fill', *v.* 1. fill again. —*n.* (rē'fil'). 2. second filling.

re·fine', *v.,* **-fined, -fining.** 1. free from impurities or error. 2. teach good manners, taste, etc. —**re·fin'er,** *n.* —**re·fine'ment,** *n.*

re·fin'er·y, *n., pl.* **-eries.** establishment for refining, esp. petroleum.

re·flect', *v.* 1. cast back. 2. show; mirror. 3. bring (credit or discredit) on one. 4. think. —**re·flec'tion,** *n.* —**re·flec'tive,** *adj.* —**re·flec'tor,** *n.*

re·flex', *adj.* 1. denoting involuntary action. 2. bent. —*n.* 3. involuntary movement.

re·flex'ive, *adj.* 1. (of verb) having same subject and object. 2. (of pronoun) showing identity with subject.

re·for'est, *v.* replant with forest trees.

re·form', *n.* 1. correction of what is wrong. —*v.* 2. change for better. —**re·form'er,** *n.* —**ref'or·ma'tion,** *n.*

re·form'a·to'ry, *n., pl.* **-ries.** prison for young offenders.

re·frac'tion, *n.* change of direction of light or heat rays in passing to another medium. —**re·fract',** *v.* —**re·frac'tive,** *adj.* —**re·frac'tor,** *n.*

re·frac'to·ry, *adj.* stubborn.

re·frain', *v.* 1. keep oneself (from). —*n.* 2. recurring passage in song, etc.

re·fresh', *v.* 1. reinvigorate, as by rest, etc. 2. stimulate. —**re·fresh'ment,** *n.* —**re·fresh'er,** *adj., n.*

re·frig'er·ate', *v.,* **-ated, -ating.** make or keep cold. —**re·frig'er·ant,** *adj., n.* —**re·frig'er·a'tion,** *n.*

re·frig'er·a'tor, *n.* cabinet for keeping food cold.

ref'uge, *n.* shelter from danger.

ref'u·gee', *n.* person who flees for safety.

re·ful'gent (ri ful'jant), *adj.* shining brightly; radiant. —**re·ful'gence,** *n.*

re·fund', *v.* 1. give back (money). —*n.* (rē'fund). 2. repayment.

re·fur'bish, *v.* renovate.

re·fuse', *v.,* **-fused, -fusing.** —*v.* 1. decline to accept. 2. deny (request). —*n.* 3. (ref'yōos). rubbish. —**re·fus'al,** *n.*

re·fute', *v.,* **-futed, -futing.** prove false or wrong. —**re·fu'ta·ble,** *adj.* —**ref'u·ta'tion,** *n.*

re·gain', *v.* get again.

re'gal, *adj.* royal.

re·gale', *v.,* **-galed, -galing.** 1. entertain grandly. 2. feast.

re·ga'li·a, *n.pl.* emblems of royalty, office, etc.

re·gard', *v.* 1. look upon with particular feeling. 2. respect. 3. look at. 4. concern. —*n.* 5. reference. 6. attention. 7. respect and liking.

re·gard'ing, *prep.* concerning.

re·gard'less, *adv.* 1. without regard; in spite of. —*adj.* 2. heedless.

re·gat'ta, *n.* 1. boat race. 2. organized series of boat races.

re·gen'er·ate', *v.,* **-ated, -ating,** *adj.* —*v.* 1. make over for the better. 2. form anew. —*adj.* (-at). 3. regenerated. —**re·gen'er·a'tion,** *n.* —**re·gen'er·a·tive,** *adj.*

re'gent, *n.* 1. person ruling in place of

sovereign. 2. university governor.
—re•gen•cy, n.

reg•gae (reg'ā), n. Jamaican music
blending blues, calypso, and rock.

re•gime' (rā zhēm'), n. system of rule.

reg•i•men', n. 1. course of diet, etc.,
for health. 2. rule.

reg•i•ment (-mant), n. 1. infantry
unit. —v. (rej'ə ment'). 2. subject to
strict, uniform discipline. —reg•i•
men'tal, adj. —reg•i•men•ta'tion,
n.

re'gion, n. area; district. —re'gion•
al, adj. —re'gion•al•ly, adv.

reg•is•ter, n. 1. written list; record. 2.
range of voice or instrument. 3. device for controlling passage of warm
air. —v. 4. enter in register. 5. show.
6. enter oneself on list of voters.
—reg•is•tra'tion, n.

reg•is•trar', n. official recorder.

reg•is•try, n., pl. -tries. 1. registra-
tion. 2. place where register is kept. 3.
register.

re•gress', v. return to previous, inferior state. —re•gres'sion, n. —re•
gres'sive, adj.

re•gret', v., -gretted, -gretting. n.
—v. 1. feel sorry about. —n. 2. feeling
of loss or sorrow. —re•gret'ta•ble,
adj. —re•gret'ful, adj.

reg•u•lar, adj. 1. usual. 2. symmetrical. 3. recurring at fixed times. 4. orderly. 5. denoting permanent army.
—n. 6. regular soldier. —reg•u•lar'-
i•ty, n. —reg•u•lar•ly, adv.

reg•u•late', v., -lated, -lating. 1. control by rule, method, etc. 2. adjust.
—reg•u•la'tion, n. —reg•u•la•tor,
n.

re•gur•gi•tate', v., -tated, -tating.
cast or surge back; pour from stomach. —re•gur•gi•ta'tion, n.

re•ha•bil•i•tate', v., -tated, -tating.
restore to good condition. —re•ha•
bil•i•ta'tion, n.

re•hash', v. 1. rework or reuse in new
form without significant change. —n.
(rē'hash'). 2. act of rehashing. 3.
something rehashed.

re•hearse', v., -hearsed, -hearsing. 1.
act or direct in practice for performance. 2. recount in detail. —re•
hears'al, n.

reign, n. 1. royal rule. —v. 2. have sovereign power or title.

re•im•burse', v., -bursed, -bursing.
repay, as for expenses. —re•im•
burse'ment, n.

rein, n. narrow strap fastened to bridle
or bit for controlling animal.

re•in•car•na'tion, n. continuation of
soul after death in new body.

rein'deer', n. large arctic deer.

re•in•force', v., -forced, -forcing.
strengthen with support, troops, etc.
—re•in•force'ment, n.

re•in•state', v., -stated, -stating. put
back into former position or state.
—re•in•state'ment, n.

re•it•er•ate', v., -ated, -ating. repeat.
—re•it•er•a'tion, n.

re•ject', v. 1. refuse or discard. —n. 2.
(rē'jekt). 2. something rejected. —re•
jec'tion, n.

re•joice', v., -joiced, -joicing. be or
make glad.

re•join', v. answer.

re•join'der, n. response.

re•ju've•nate', v., -nated, -nating.
make young and vigorous again.
—re•ju've•na'tion, n.

re•lapse', v., -lapsed, -lapsing. 1. fall
back into former state or practice.
—n. 2. act or instance of relapsing.

re•late', v., -lated, -lating. 1. tell. 2.
establish or have relation.

re•la'tion, n. 1. connection. 2. relative. 3. narrative. —re•la'tion•ship',
n.

rel'a•tive, n. 1. person connected with
another by blood or marriage. —adj.
2. comparative. 3. designating word
that introduces subordinate clause.
—rel'a•tive•ly, adv.

rel•a•tiv'i•ty, n. principle that time,
mass, etc. are relative, not absolute
concepts.

re•lax', v. 1. make or become less
tense, firm, etc. 2. slacken. —re•lax•
a'tion, n.

re•lay, n. 1. fresh supply of persons,
etc., to relieve others. —v. 2. carry
forward by relays.

re•lease', v., -leased, -leasing. —v.
1. let go; discharge. —n. 2. act or instance of releasing.

rel'e•gate', v., -gated, -gating. 1.
consign. 2. turn over. —rel'e•ga'-
tion, n.

re•lent', v. become more mild or forgiving. —re•lent'less, adj.

rel'e•vant, adj. having to do with
matter in question. —rel'e•vance, n.

re•li'a•ble, adj. trustworthy. —re•
li•a•bil'i•ty, n. —re•li'a•bly, adv.

re•li'ance, n. trust. confidence.
—re•li'ant, adj.

rel'ic, n. 1. object surviving from past.
2. personal memorial of sacred person.

re•lief', n. 1. alleviation of pain, distress, etc. 2. help. 3. pleasant change.
4. projection.

re•lieve', v., -lieved, -lieving. 1. ease;
alleviate. 2. break sameness of. 3. release or discharge from duty.

re•li'gion, n. 1. recognition and worship of controlling superhuman power. **2.** particular system of religious belief. —**re·li'gious,** *adj.* —**re·li'gious·ly,** *adv.* —**re·li'gious·ness,** *n.*

re·lin'quish, *v.* give up; surrender.

rel'i·quary (rel'i kwer´ē), *n., pl.* -**quaries.** receptacle for religious relics.

rel'ish, *n.* **1.** enjoyment. **2.** chopped pickles, etc. —*v.* **3.** take enjoyment in.

re·luc'tant, *adj.* unwilling. —**re·luc'tance,** *n.* —**re·luc'tant·ly,** *adv.*

re·ly', *v.,* -**lied, -lying.** put trust in.

re·main', *v.* **1.** continue to be. **2.** stay; be left. —*n.pl.* **3.** that which remains. **4.** corpse.

re·main'der, *n.* that which remains.

re·mand', *v.* send back, as to jail or lower court of law.

re·mark', *v.* **1.** say casually. **2.** perceive; observe. —*n.* **3.** casual comment. **4.** notice.

re·mark'a·ble, *adj.* extraordinary. —**re·mark'a·bly,** *adv.*

rem'e·dy, *n., pl.* -**dies,** *v.,* -**died, -dying,** *n., pl.* -**dies.** —*v.* **1.** cure or alleviate. **2.** correct. —*n.* **3.** something that remedies. —**re·me'di·al,** *adj.*

re·mem'ber, *v.* **1.** recall to or retain in memory. **2.** mention as sending greetings. —**re·mem'brance,** *n.*

re·mind', *v.* cause to remember. —**re·mind'er,** *n.*

rem'i·nisce' (rem'ə nis´), *v.,* -**nisced, -niscing.** recall past experiences. —**rem'i·nis'cence,** *n.* —**rem'i·nis'cent,** *adj.*

re·miss', *adj.* negligent.

re·mit', *v.,* -**mitted, -mitting. 1.** send money. **2.** pardon. **3.** abate. —**re·mis'sion,** *n.*

re·mit'tance, *n.* money, etc., sent.

re·mit'tent, *adj.* (of illness) less severe at times.

rem'nant, *n.* **1.** small remaining part. **2.** trace.

re·mod'el, *v.,* -**eled, -eling.** renovate.

re·mon'strate, *v.,* -**strated, -strating.** protest; plead in protest. —**re·mon'stra·tion,** *n.* —**re·mon'strance,** *n.*

re·morse', *n.* regret for wrongdoing. —**re·morse'ful,** *adj.* —**re·morse'less,** *adj.*

re·mote', *adj.* **1.** far distant. **2.** faint. —*n.* **3.** remote control (def. 2). —**re·mote'ly,** *adv.* —**re·mote'ness,** *n.*

remote control, 1. control of an apparatus from a distance, as by radio signals. **2.** Also, **remote.** device used for such control.

re·move', *v.,* -**moved, -moving,** —*v.* **1.** take away or off. **2.** move to another place. —*n.* **3.** distance of sep-

aration. —**re·mov'al,** *n.* —**re·mov'a·ble,** *adj.*

re·mu'ner·ate, *v.,* -**ated, -ating.** pay for work, etc. —**re·mu'ner·a'tion,** *n.* —**re·mu'ner·a'tive,** *adj.*

ren'ais·sance' (ren'ə säns´), *n.* **1.** revival. **2.** (*cap.*) cultural period marked by interest in culture of antiquity.

re'nal (rēn'l), *adj.* of or near the kidneys.

re·nas'cent (ri nā'sənt), *adj.* being reborn; springing again into being or vigor.

rend, *v.* **1.** tear apart. **2.** disturb with noise. **3.** distress.

ren'der, *v.* **1.** cause to be. **2.** do, show, or furnish. **3.** deliver officially. **4.** perform. **5.** give back. **6.** melt (fat). —**ren·di'tion,** *n.*

ren'dez·vous' (rän'də vōō´, -dā-), *n., pl.* -**vous.** appointment or place to meet.

ren'e·gade', *n.* deserter.

re·nege' (ri nig´, -neg´), *v.,* -**neged, -neging.** *Informal.* break promise.

re·new', *v.* **1.** begin or do again. **2.** make like new; replenish. —**re·new'al,** *n.*

ren'net, *n.* **1.** membrane lining stomach of calf or other animal. **2.** preparation of this used in making cheese.

re·nounce', *v.,* -**nounced, -nouncing.** give up voluntarily. —**re·nounce'ment,** *n.*

ren'o·vate', *v.,* -**vated, -vating.** repair; refurbish. —**ren'o·va'tion,** *n.*

re·nown', *n.* fame.

rent, *n.* **1.** Also, **rent'al.** payment for use of property. **2.** tear; violent break. —*v.* **3.** grant or have use of in return for rent.

rent'al, *n.* **1.** amount given or received as rent. **2.** act of renting. **3.** property rented.

re·nun'ci·a'tion, *n.* act of renouncing.

re·pair', *v.* **1.** restore to good condition. **2.** go. —*n.* **3.** work of repairing. **4.** good condition. —**rep'a·ra·ble,** *adj.*

rep'a·ra'tion, *n.* amends for injury.

rep'ar·tee', *n.* exchange of wit; banter.

re·past', *n.* meal.

re·pa'tri·ate', *v.,* -**ated, -ating.** send back to one's native country. —**re·pa'tri·a'tion,** *n.*

re·pay', *v.,* -**paid, -paying.** pay back. —**re·pay'ment,** *n.*

re·peal', *v.* **1.** revoke officially. —*n.* **2.** revocation.

re·peat', *v.* **1.** say, tell, or do again. —*n.* **2.** act of repeating. **3.** musical passage to be repeated. —re•peat′-edly, adv.

re•peat′er, n. 1. one that repeats. 2. gun firing several shots in rapid succession.

re•pel′, v., -pelled, -pelling. 1. drive back; thrust away. 2. excite disgust or suspicion. —re•pel′lent, adj., n.

re•pent′, v. feel contrition. —re•pent′ance, n. —re•pent′ant, adj. —re•pent′ant•ly, adv.

re•per•cus′sion, n. 1. indirect result. 2. echo.

rep•er•toire′ (rep′ər twär′), n. group of works that performer or company can perform. Also, rep′er•to•ry.

rep•e•ti′tion, n. repeated action, utterance, etc. —rep•e•ti′tious, adj. —rep•et′i•tive, adj.

re•place′, v., -placed, -placing. 1. take place of. 2. provide substitute for. —re•place′ment, n. —re•place′a•ble, adj.

re•plen′ish, v. make full again. —re•plen′ish•ment, n.

re•plete′, adj. abundantly filled. —re•ple′tion, n.

rep′li•ca, n. copy.

re•ply′, v., -plied, -plying, n., pl. -plies. answer.

re•port′, n. 1. statement of events or findings. 2. rumor. 3. loud noise. —v. 4. tell of (events or findings). 5. present oneself. 6. inform against. 7. write about for newspaper. —re•port′er, n.

re•pose′, n., v., -posed, -posing. —n. 1. rest or sleep. 2. tranquillity. —v. 3. rest or sleep. 4. put, as trust. —re•pose′ful, adj.

re•pos′i•to•ry, n., pl. -tories. place where things are stored.

re•pos•sess′, v. take back.

rep′re•hen′si•ble, adj. blameworthy. —rep′re•hen′si•bly, adv.

rep′re•sent′, v. 1. express; signify. 2. act or speak for. 3. portray. —rep′-re•sen•ta′tion, n. —rep′re•sen•ta′tion•al, adj.

rep′re•sent′a•tive, n. 1. one that represents another or others. 2. member of legislative body. —adj. 3. representing. 4. typical.

re•press′, v. 1. inhibit. 2. suppress. —re•pres′sive, adj. —re•pres′sion, n.

re•prieve′, v., -prieved, -prieving, n. respite.

rep′ri•mand′, n. 1. severe reproof. —v. 2. reprove severely.

re•pris′al, n. infliction of injuries in retaliation.

re•proach′, v. 1. blame; upbraid. —n.

2. blame; discredit. —re•proach′ful, adj.

rep′ro•bate′, n., adj., v., -bated, -bating. —n. 1. hopelessly bad person. —adj. 2. depraved. —v. 3. condemn. —rep′ro•ba′tion, n.

re•pro•duce′, v., -duced, -ducing. 1. copy or duplicate. 2. produce by propagation. —re•pro•duc′tion, n. —re•pro•duc′tive, adj.

re•proof′, n. censure.

re•prove′, v., -proved, -proving. blame.

rep′tile, n. creeping animal, as lizard or snake.

re•pub′lic, n. state governed by representatives elected by citizens.

re•pub′li•can, adj. 1. or favoring republic. 2. (cap.) of Republican party, one of two major political parties of U.S. —n. 3. (cap.) member of Republican party.

re•pu′di•ate′, v., -ated, -ating. reject as worthless, not binding, or false. —re•pu′di•a′tion, n.

re•pug′nant, adj. distasteful. —re•pug′nance, n.

re•pulse′, v., -pulsed, -pulsing, n. —v. 1. drive back with force. —n. 2. act of repulsing. 3. rejection. —re•pul′sion, n.

re•pul′sive, adj. disgusting.

rep′u•ta•ble, adj. of good reputation. —rep′u•ta•bly, adv.

rep′u•ta′tion, n. 1. public estimation of character. 2. good name.

re•pute′, n., v., -puted, -puting. —n. 1. reputation. —v. 2. give reputation to. —re•put′ed•ly, adv.

re•quest′, v. 1. ask for. —n. 2. act of requesting. 3. what is requested.

Req′ui•em (rek′wē əm), n. Rom. Cath. Ch. mass for dead.

re•quire′, v., -quired, -quiring. 1. need. 2. demand. —re•quire′ment, n.

req′ui•site, adj. 1. necessary. —n. 2. necessary thing.

req′ui•si′tion, n. 1. formal order or demand. —v. 2. take for official use.

re•quite′, v., -quited, -quiting. make return to or for. —re•quit′al (-kwī′-tal), n.

re′run′, n. 1. showing of motion picture or television program after its initial run. 2. the program shown.

re•scind′ (-sind′), v. annul; revoke.

res•cue, v., -cued, -cuing, n. —v. 1. free from danger, capture, etc. —n. 2. act of rescuing. —res′cu•er, n.

re•search′, n. diligent investigation. —re•search′er, n.

re•sem′ble, v., -bled, -bling. be similar to. —re•sem′blance, n.

re·sent, v. feel indignant or injured at. —**re·sent'ful**, adj. —**re·sent'ment**, n.

res·er·va'tion, n. 1. act of withholding or setting apart. 2. particular doubt or misgiving. 3. advance assurance of accommodations. 4. tract of land for use of an Indian tribe.

re·serve', v., -served, -serving, n., adj. —v. 1. keep back; set apart. —n. 2. something reserved. 3. part of military force held in readiness to support active forces. 4. reticence; aloofness. —adj. 5. kept in reserve.

re·serv'ist, n. member of military reserves.

res·er·voir' (rez'ər vôr'), n. 1. place where water is stored for use. 2. supply.

re·side', v., -sided, -siding. 1. dwell. 2. be vested, as powers.

res'i·dence, n. 1. dwelling place. 2. act or fact of residing. —**res'i·dent**, n. —**res'i·den'tial**, adj.

res'i·due', n. remainder. —**re·sid'u·al**, adj.

re·sign', v. 1. give up (job, office, etc.). 2. submit, as to fate or force. —**res'ig·na'tion**, n.

re·sil'i·ent (ri zil'yənt), adj. 1. springing back. 2. recovering readily from adversity. —**re·sil'i·ence**, n.

res'in, n. exudation from some plants, used in medicines, etc. —**res'in·ous**, adj.

re·sist', v. withstand; offer opposition to. —**re·sist'ant**, adj. —**re·sist'ance**, n. —**re·sist'er**, n.

res'o·lute', adj. determined on action or result. —**res'o·lute'ly**, adv. —**res'o·lute'ness**, n.

res'o·lu'tion, n. 1. formal expression of group opinion. 2. determination. 3. solution of problem.

re·solve', v., -solved, -solving, n. —v. 1. decide firmly. 2. state formally. 3. clear away. 4. solve. —n. 5. resolution.

res'o·nant, adj. 1. resounding. 2. rich in sound. —**res'o·nance**, n. —**res'o·nant·ly**, adv.

re·sort', v. 1. apply or turn (to) for use, help, etc. 2. go often. —n. 3. place much frequented, esp. for recreation. 4. recourse.

re·sound' (-zound'), v. echo.

re·sound'ing, adj. impressively thorough or complete.

re·source' (rē'sôrs, ri sôrs'), n. 1. source of aid or supply. 2. (pl.) wealth.

re·source'ful, adj. clever. —**re·source'ful·ly**, adv. —**re·source'ful·ness**, n.

re·spect', n. 1. detail; point. 2. reference. 3. esteem. —v. 4. hold in esteem. —**re·spect'er**, n.

re·spect'a·ble, adj. 1. worthy of respect. 2. decent. —**re·spect'a·bil'i·ty**, n. —**re·spect'a·bly**, adv.

re·spect'ful, adj. showing respect. —**re·spect'ful·ly**, adv. —**re·spect'ful·ness**, n.

re·spect'ing, prep. concerning.

re·spec'tive, adj. in order previously named. —**re·spec'tive·ly**, adv.

res'pi·ra'tor, n. apparatus to produce artificial breathing.

re·spire', v., -spired, -spiring. breathe. —**res'pi·ra'tion**, n. —**res'pi·ra·to·ry**, adj.

res'pite, n. 1. temporary relief or delay. —v. 2. relieve or cease temporarily.

re·splend'ent, adj. gleaming. —**re·splend'ence**, n.

re·spond', v. answer.

re·spond'ent, adj. 1. answering. —n. 2. Law. defendant.

re·sponse', n. reply. —**re·spon'sive**, adj. —**re·spon'sive·ly**, adv.

re·spon'si·bil'i·ty, n. pl. -ties. 1. state of being responsible. 2. obligation. 3. initiative.

re·spon'si·ble, adj. 1. causing or allowing things to happen. 2. capable of rational thought. 3. reliable. —**re·spon'si·bly**, adv.

rest, n. 1. refreshing quiet. 2. cessation from motion, work, etc. 3. support. 4. Music. interval of silence. 5. remainder; others. —v. 6. be quiet or at ease. 7. cease from motion. 8. lie or lay. 9. be based. 10. rely. 11. continue to be. —**rest'ful**, adj. —**rest'ful·ly**, adv. —**rest'ful·ness**, n. —**rest'less**, adj. —**rest'less·ly**, adv. —**rest'less·ness**, n.

res'tau·rant, n. public eating place.

res'tau·ra·teur', n. restaurant owner.

res·ti·tu'tion, n. 1. reparation. 2. return of rights, etc.

res'tive, adj. restless. —**res'tive·ly**, adv.

re·store', v., -stored, -storing. 1. bring back, as to use or good condition. 2. give back. —**re·sto·ra'tion**, n. —**re·stor'a·tive**, adj., n.

re·strain', v. 1. hold back. 2. confine.

re·straint', n. 1. restraining influence. 2. confinement. 3. constraint.

re·strict', v. confine; limit. —**re·stric'tion**, n. —**re·stric'tive**, adj.

rest room, room in public building with washbowls and toilets.

re·sult', n. 1. outcome; consequence.

—v. 2. occur as result. 3. end. —re•sult'ant, adj., n.

re•sume', v., -sumed, -suming. 1. go on with again. 2. take again. —re•sump'tion, n.

ré•su•mé' (rez' ŏŏ mā'), n. summary, esp. of education and work.

re•sur•rect', v. bring to life again. —res•ur•rec'tion, n.

re•sus•ci•tate' (-sus'ə-), v. revive. —re•sus•ci•ta'tion, n.

re•tail', n. 1. sale of goods to consumer. —v. 2. sell at retail. —re•tail'er, n.

re•tain', v. 1. keep or hold. 2. engage. —re•tain'a•ble, adj.

re•tain'er, n. 1. fee paid to secure services. 2. old servant.

re•tal'i•ate', v., -ated, -ating. return like for like, esp. evil. —re•tal'i•a'tion, n. —re•tal'i•a•to'ry, adj.

re•tard', v. delay; hinder. —re•tar•da'tion, n.

re•tard'ed, adj. 1. slow or weak in mental development. —n.pl. 2. retarded persons.

retch, v. try to vomit.

re•ten'tion, n. 1. retaining. 2. power of retaining. 3. memory. —re•ten'tive, adj.

ret'i•cent, adj. saying little. —ret'i•cence, n. —ret'i•cent•ly, adv.

ret'i•na, n. coating on back part of eyeball that receives images. —ret'i•nal, adj.

ret'i•nue' (-nyŏŏ'), n. train of attendants.

re•tire', v., -tired, -tiring. 1. withdraw. 2. go to bed. 3. end working life. —re•tire'ment, n.

re•tir'ing, adj. shy.

re•tool', v. replace tools and machinery of.

re•tort', v. 1. reply smartly. —n. 2. sharp or witty reply. 3. long-necked vessel used in distilling.

re•touch', v. improve (picture) by marking.

re•trace', v., -traced, -tracing. go back over.

re•tract', v. withdraw. —re•trac'tion, n. —re•tract'a•ble, adj.

re•tread', n. 1. tire that has new tread added. 2. Informal. person returned to former position or occupation. 3. reviving or reworking of old or familiar idea, story, etc.

re•treat', n. 1. forced withdrawal. 2. private place. —v. 3. make a retreat. 4. withdraw.

re•trench', v. reduce expenses. —re•trench'ment, n.

ret•ri•bu'tion, n. requital according to merits, esp. for evil. —re•trib'u•tive, adj.

re•trieve', v., -trieved, -trieving. 1. regain or restore. 2. make amends for. 3. recover (killed game). —n. 4. recovery. —re•triev'er, n.

ret'ro•ac'tive, adj. applying also to past. —ret'ro•ac'tive•ly, adv.

ret'ro•fit', v., -fitted, -fitting. refit with newly developed equipment.

ret'ro•grade', adj., v., -graded, -grading. —adj. 1. moving backward. —v. 2. move backward. 3. degenerate.

ret'ro•gress', v. return to earlier or more primitive condition. —ret'ro•gres'sion, n. —ret'ro•gres'sive, adj.

ret'ro•spect', n. occasion of looking back. —ret'ro•spec'tive, adj. —ret'ro•spec'tion, n.

re•turn', v. 1. go or come back to former place or condition. 2. put or bring back. 3. reply. —n. 4. act or fact of returning. 5. recurrence. 6. requital. 7. reply. 8. (often pl.) profit. 9. report. —re•turn'a•ble, adj.

re•u•nite', v., -nited, -niting. unite after separation. —re•un'ion, n.

rev, n., v., revved, revving. Informal. —n. 1. revolution (in machinery). —v. 2. increase speed of (motor).

re•vamp', v. renovate.

re•veal', v. disclose.

re•veil•le (rev'ə lē), n. Mil. signal for awakening.

rev'el, v., -eled, -eling. 1. enjoy greatly. 2. make merry. —n. 3. merrymaking. —rev'el•er, n. —rev'el•ry, n.

rev•e•la'tion, n. disclosure.

re•venge', v., -venged, -venging. —n. 1. harm in return for harm; retaliation. 2. vindictiveness. 3. take revenge. —re•venge'ful, adj. —re•veng'er, n.

rev'e•nue', n. income, esp. of government or business.

re•ver'ber•ate', v., -ated, -ating. 1. echo back. 2. reflect. —re•ver'ber•a'tion, n.

re•vere', v., -vered, -vering. hold in deep respect.

rev'er•ence, n., v., -enced, -encing. —n. 1. deep respect and awe. —v. 2. regard with reverence. —rev'er•ent, rev'er•en'tial, adj. —rev'er•ent•ly, adv.

rev'er•end, adj. title used with name of member of the clergy.

rev'er•ie, n. fanciful musing. Also, rev'er•y.

re•verse', adj., n., v., -versed, -versing. —adj. 1. opposite in position, action, etc. **2.** of or for backward motion. —*n.* **3.** reverse part, footage, etc. **4.** misfortune. —*v.* **5.** turn in the opposite position, direction, or condition. —**re·vers'i·ble,** *adj.*

re·vert', *v.* go back to earlier state, topic, etc. —**re·ver'sion.**

re·view', *n.* **1.** critical article. **2.** repeated viewing. **3.** inspection. —*v.* **4.** view again. **5.** inspect. **6.** survey. **7.** write a review of. —**re·view'er,** *n.*

re·vile', *v.,* **-viled, -viling.** speak abusively to. —**re·vile'ment,** *n.* —**re·vil'er,** *n.*

re·vise', *v.,* **-vised, -vising.** change or amend content of. —**re·vi'sion,** *n.* —**re·vis'er,** *n.*

re·vi'sion·ism, *n.* departure from accepted doctrine. —**re·vi'sion·ist,** *n., adj.*

re·vi'tal·ize', *v.,* **-ized, -izing.** bring new vitality to.

re·viv'al, *n.* **1.** restoration to life, use, etc. **2.** religious awakening. —**re·viv'al·ist,** *n.*

re·vive', *v.,* **-vived, -viving.** bring back to consciousness, use, notice, etc. —**re·viv'er,** *n.*

re·viv'i·fy, *v.,* **-fied, -fying.** bring back to life.

re·voke', *v.,* **-voked, -voking.** annul or repeal. —**rev'o·ca·ble,** *adj.* —**rev'o·ca'tion,** *n.*

re·volt', *v.* **1.** rebel. **2.** feel disgust. **3.** fill with disgust. —*n.* **4.** rebellion. **5.** loathing. —**re·volt'ing,** *adj.*

rev·o·lu'tion, *n.* **1.** overthrow of established government. **2.** fundamental change. **3.** rotation. —**rev·o·lu'tion·ar'y,** *adj., n.* —**rev·o·lu'tion·ist,** *n.*

rev·o·lu'tion·ize', *v.,* **-ized, -izing.** cause fundamental change in.

re·volve', *v.,* **-volved, -volving. 1.** turn round, as on axis. **2.** consider. —**re·volv'er,** *n.* pistol with revolving cylinder holding cartridges.

re·vue', *n.* light topical theatrical show.

re·vul'sion, *n.* violent change of feeling, esp. to disgust.

re·ward', *n.* **1.** recompense for merit, service, etc. —*v.* **2.** give reward.

rhap'so·dy, *n., pl.* **-dies. 1.** exaggerated expression of enthusiasm. **2.** irregular musical composition.

rhe'o·stat', *n.* device for regulating electric current.

rhe'sus, *n.* kind of monkey found in India.

rhet'o·ric, *n.* **1.** skillful use of language. **2.** exaggerated speech. —**rhe·tor'i·cal,** *adj.*

rhetorical question, question asked for effect, not to elicit reply.

rheu·ma'tism', *n.* disease affecting joints or muscles. —**rheu·mat'ic,** *adj., n.*

Rh factor (är′āch′), antigen in blood that may cause severe reaction in individual lacking the substance, as in a transfusion.

rhine'stone', *n.* artificial diamondlike gem.

rhi·noc'er·os, *n.* large thick-skinned mammal with horned snout.

rhi'zome (rī′zōm), *n.* rootlike stem.

rho·do·den'dron, *n.* flowering evergreen shrub.

rhom'boid, *n.* oblique-angled parallelogram with only the opposite sides equal.

rhom'bus, *n., pl.* **-buses, -bi.** oblique-angled parallelogram with all sides equal.

rhu'barb, *n.* garden plant with edible leaf stalks.

rhyme, *n., v.,* **rhymed, rhyming.** —*n.* **1.** agreement in end sounds of lines or words. **2.** verse with such correspondence. —*v.* **3.** make or form rhyme.

rhythm, *n.* movement with uniformly recurring beat. —**rhyth'mic, rhyth'mi·cal,** *adj.* —**rhyth'mi·cal·ly,** *adv.*

rib, *n., v.,* **ribbed, ribbing.** —*n.* **1.** one of the slender curved bones enclosing chest. **2.** riblike part. —*v.* **3.** furnish with ribs. **4.** *Informal.* tease.

rib'ald, *adj.* bawdy in speech. —**rib'ald·ry,** *n.*

rib'bon, *n.* strip of silk, rayon, etc.

ri·bo·fla'vin (rī′bō flā′vin), *n.* important vitamin in milk, fresh meat, eggs, etc.

rice, *n.* edible starchy grain of grass grown in warm climates.

rich, *adj.* **1.** having great possessions. **2.** abounding; fertile. **3.** costly. **4.** containing butter, eggs, cream, etc. **5.** strong; vivid. **6.** mellow. —*n.* **7.** rich people. —**rich'ly,** *adv.* —**rich'ness,** *n.*

rich'es, *n.pl.* wealth.

rick, *n.* stack of hay, etc.

rick'ets, *n.* childhood disease often marked by bone deformities.

rick·et·y, *adj.,* **-etier, -etiest.** shaky.

rick'shaw, *n.* two-wheeled passenger vehicle pulled by person.

ric·o·chet' (rik′ə shā′), *v.,* **-cheted, -cheting,** *n.* —*v.* **1.** rebound from a flat surface. —*n.* **2.** such a movement.

rid, *v.,* **rid** or **ridded, ridding.** clear or free of. —**rid'dance,** *n.*

rid'dle, *n., v.,* **-dled, -dling.** —*n.* **1.** puzzling question or matter. **2.** coarse sieve. —*v.* **3.** speak perplexingly. **4.**

pierce with many holes. 5. put through sieve.

ride, v., rode, ridden, riding, n. —v. 1. be carried in traveling. 2. sit on and manage (horse, etc.). 3. rest on something. —n. 4. journey on a horse, etc. 5. vehicle or device in which people ride for amusement.

rid'er, n. 1. person that rides. 2. clause attached to legislative bill before passage.

ridge, n., v., ridged, ridging. —n. 1. long narrow elevation. —v. 2. form with ridge.

rid'i·cule', n., v., -culed, -culing. —n. 1. derision. —v. 2. deride.

ri·dic'u·lous, adj. absurd. —ri·dic'-u·lous·ly, adv.

rife, adj. 1. widespread. 2. abounding.

riff, n. 1. repeated phrase in jazz or rock music, usu. accompanying a soloist. 2. variation or improvisation, as on an idea. —v. 3. perform a riff.

riff'raff', n. rabble.

ri'fle, n., v., -fled, -fling. —n. 1. shoulder firearm with spirally grooved barrel. —v. 2. cut spiral grooves in (gun barrel). 3. search through to rob. 4. steal. —ri'fle·man, n.

rift, n. split.

rig, v., rigged, rigging, n. —v. 1. fit with tackle and other parts. 2. put together as makeshift. 3. manipulate fraudulently or artificially. —n. 4. arrangement of masts, booms, tackle, etc. 5. equipment; outfit. —rig'ger, n.

rig'ging, n. ropes and chains that support and work masts, sails, etc.

right, adj. 1. just or good. 2. correct. 3. in good condition. 4. on side that is toward the east when one faces north. 5. straight. —n. 6. that which is right. 7. right side. 8. that justly due one. 9. conservative side in politics. —adv. 10. directly; completely. 11. set correctly. 12. in right position. 13. correct. —right'ly, adv. —right'ness, n. —right'ist, adj.

right angle, 90-degree angle.

right'eous, adj. virtuous. —right'-eous·ly, adv. —right'eous·ness, n.

right'ful, adj. belonging to or having just claim. —right'ful·ly, adv.

right of way, 1. right of one vehicle to proceed ahead of another. 2. path or route that may lawfully be used. 3. strip of land acquired for use, as by railroad.

rig'id, adj. 1. stiff; inflexible. 2. rigorous. —ri·gid'i·ty, n. —rig'id·ly, adv.

rig'ma·role', n. confused talk.

rig'or, n. 1. strictness. 2. hardship.

—rig'or·ous, adj. —rig'or·ous·ly, adv.

ri'gor mor'tis, stiffening of body after death.

rile, v., riled, riling. Informal. vex.

rill, n. small brook.

rim, n., v., rimmed, rimming. —n. 1. outer edge. —v. 2. furnish with rim.

rime, n., v., rimed, riming. —n. 1. rhyme. 2. rough white frost. —v. 3. cover with rime.

rind, n. firm covering, as of fruit or cheese.

ring, n., v., rang, rung (for 11, ringed), ringing. —n. 1. round band for a finger. 2. any circular band. 3. enclosed area. 4. group cooperating for selfish purpose. 5. ringing sound. 6. telephone call. —v. 7. sound clearly and resonantly. 8. seem; appear. 9. be filled with sound. 10. signal by bell. 11. form ring around.

ring'er, n. 1. person or thing that closely resembles another. 2. athlete entered in competition in violation of eligibility rules.

ring'lead'er, n. leader in mischief.

ring'let, n. curl of hair.

ring'worm', n. contagious skin disease.

rink, n. floor or sheet of ice for skating on.

rinse, v., rinsed, rinsing, n. —v. 1. wash lightly. —n. 2. rinsing act. 3. preparation for rinsing.

ri'ot, n. 1. disturbance by mob. 2. wild disorder. —v. 3. take part in riot. —ri'ot·ous, adj.

rip, v., ripped, ripping, n. tear. —rip'-per, n.

ripe, adj., riper, ripest. fully developed; mature. —rip'en, v. —ripe'ly, adv. —ripe'ness, n.

rip'off', n. Slang. theft or exploitation.

ri·poste' (ri pōst'), n. quick, sharp reply or reaction.

rip'ple, v., -pled, -pling, n. —v. 1. form small waves. —n. 2. pattern of small waves.

rise, v., rose, risen, rising, n. —v. 1. get up. 2. revolt. 3. appear. 4. originate. 5. move upward. 6. increase. 7. (of dough) expand. —n. 8. upward movement. 9. origin. 10. upward slope. —ris'er, n.

ris'i·ble (riz'ə bəl), adj. causing laughter.

risk, n. 1. dangerous chance. —v. 2. expose to risk. 3. take risk of. —risk'y, adj.

ris·qué' (-kā'), adj. almost immodest.

rite, n. ceremonial act.

rit'u•al, *n.* system of religious or other rites. **—rit'u•al•ism',** *n.*

ri'val, *n., adj., v.,* **-valed, -valing.** —*n.* 1. competitor. 2. equal. —*adj.* 3. being a rival. —*v.* 4. compete with. 5. match. **—ri'val•ry,** *n.*

rive, *v.,* **rived, rived** *or* **riven, riving.** split.

riv'er, *n.* large natural stream of water.

riv'et, *n., v.,* **-eted, -eting.** —*n.* 1. metal bolt hammered after insertion. —*v.* 2. fasten with rivets.

riv'u•let, *n.* small stream.

roach, *n.* cockroach.

road, *n.* 1. open way for travel. 2. Also, **road'stead'.** anchorage near shore.

road'block', *n.* 1. obstruction placed across road to halt traffic. 2. obstacle to progress.

road'run'ner, *n.* large terrestrial cuckoo of western U.S.

road show, show, as a play, performed by touring actors.

roam, *v.* wander; rove.

roan, *adj.* 1. (of horses) sorrel, chestnut, or bay with gray or white spots. —*n.* 2. roan horse.

roar, *v.* 1. make loud, deep sound. —*n.* 2. loud, deep sound. 3. loud laughter.

roast, *v.* 1. cook by dry heat. —*n.* 2. roasted meat.

rob, *v.,* **robbed, robbing.** deprive of unlawfully. **—rob'ber,** *n.* **—rob'ber•y,** *n.*

robe, *n., v.,* **robed, robing.** —*n.* 1. long loose garment. 2. wrap or covering. —*v.* 3. clothe, esp. ceremonially.

rob'in, *n.* red-breasted bird.

ro'bot, *n.* 1. humanlike machine that performs mechanical tasks. 2. person who acts in mechanical manner.

ro•bot'ics, *n.* technology of computer-controlled robots.

ro•bust', *adj.* strong and healthy.

rock, *n.* 1. mass of stone. 2. Also, **rock'n'roll.** popular music with steady, insistent rhythm. —*v.* 3. move back and forth. **—rock'y,** *adj.*

rock bottom, the very lowest point.

rock'er, *n.* curved support of cradle or **rock'ing chair.**

rock'et, *n.* tube propelled by discharge of gases from it.

ro•co'co, *n.* elaborate decorative style of many curves. **—ro•co'co,** *adj.*

rod, *n.* 1. slender shaft. 2. linear measure of 5½ yards.

ro'dent, *n.* small gnawing or nibbling mammal.

ro'de•o', *n., pl.* **-deos.** exhibition of cowboy skills.

roe, *n., pl.* **roes, roe.** 1. small old-world deer. 2. fish eggs or spawn.

roent•gen (rent'gan, -jan), *n.* unit for measuring radiation dosage.

rog'er, *interj.* (message) received.

rogue, *n.* rascal. **—ro'guish,** *adj.* **—ro'guer•y,** *n.*

roil, *v.* 1. make muddy. 2. vex. **—roil'y,** *adj.*

roist'er, *v.* 1. swagger. 2. carouse. **—roist'er•er,** *n.*

role, *n.* part of function, as of character in play. Also, **rôle.**

roll, *v.* 1. move by turning. 2. rock. 3. have deep, loud sound. 4. flatten with roller. 5. form into roll or ball. —*n.* 6. list; register. 7. anything cylindrical. 8. small cake. 9. deep long sound. **—roll'er,** *n.*

roller coaster, 1. small railroad, esp. in amusement park, that moves along winding route with steep inclines. 2. experience with sharp ups and downs.

roller skate, skate with four wheels. **—roller-skate,** *v.*

rol'lick•ing, *adj.* jolly.

ROM, read-only memory: non-modifiable part of computer memory containing programmed instructions to system.

ro•maine', *n.* kind of lettuce.

Ro'man, *n.* 1. native or citizen of Rome or Roman Empire. 2. (*l.c.*) upright style of printing type. **—Ro'man,** *adj.*

Roman Catholic Church, Christian Church of which pope (Bishop of Rome) is head. **—Roman Catholic.**

ro•mance', *n., v.,* **-manced, -mancing.** —*n.* 1. colorful, imaginative tale. 2. colorful, fanciful quality. 3. love affair. —*v.* 4. act romantically. 5. tell fanciful, false story.

Roman numerals, system of numbers using letters as symbols: I = 1, V = 5, X = 10, L = 50, C = 100, D = 500, M = 1,000.

ro•man'tic, *adj.* 1. of romance. 2. impractical or unrealistic. 3. imbued with idealism. 4. preoccupied with love. 5. passionate; fervent. 6. of a style of literature and art stressing imagination and emotion. —*n.* 7. romantic person. **—ro•man'ti•cal•ly,** *adv.*

ro•man'ti•cism, *n.* romantic spirit or artistic style or movement. **—ro•man'ti•cist,** *n.*

romp, *v., n.* frolic.

romp'ers, *n.pl.* child's loose outer garment.

rood (rood), *n.* 1. crucifix. 2. one-quarter of an acre.

roof, *n., pl.* **roofs.** 1. upper covering of

building. —v. 2. provide with roof. —**roof'er,** n.

rook (rŏŏk), n. 1. European crow. 2. chess piece; castle. —v. 3. cheat.

rook'ie, n. *Slang.* recruit or beginner.

room, n. 1. separate space within building. 2. space. —v. 3. lodge. —**room'er,** n. —**room'mate,** n. —**roomy,** adj.

roost, n. 1. perch where fowls rest at night. —v. 2. sit on roost.

roost'er, n. male chicken.

root, n. 1. part of plant growing underground. 2. embedded part. 3. origin. 4. quantity that, when multiplied by itself so many times, produces given quantity. —v. 5. establish roots. 6. implant. 7. **root out,** exterminate. 8. dig with snout. 9. *Informal.* cheer encouragingly. —**root'er,** n.

root beer, soft drink flavored with extracts of roots, barks, and herbs.

root canal, root portion of the pulp cavity of a tooth.

rope, n., v., **roped, roping.** —n. 1. strong twisted cord. —v. 2. fasten or catch with rope.

ro'sa•ry, n., pl. **-ries.** *Rom. Cath. Ch.* 1. series of prayers. 2. string of beads counted in saying rosary.

rose, n. thorny plant having showy, fragrant flowers.

ro•se' (rō zā'), n. pink wine.

rose•ate, adj. 1. rose-colored. 2. promising; bright.

rose'mar'y, n. aromatic evergreen shrub, with leaves used for seasoning.

ro•sette', n. rose-shaped ornament.

Rosh' Ha•sha'na (rōsh' hä shä'na), Jewish New Year.

ros'in, n. solid left after distilling off turpentine from pine resin.

ros'ter, n. list of persons, groups, events, etc.

ros'trum, n., pl. **-trums, -tra.** speakers' platform.

ros'y, adj., **rosier, rosiest.** 1. pinkish-red. 2. cheerful; optimistic; bright. —**ros'i•ly,** adv. —**ros'i•ness,** n.

rot, v., **rotted, rotting.** —v. 1. decay. —n. 2. decay. 3. disease marked by decay of tissue.

ro'tate, v., **-tated, -tating.** turn on or as on axis. —**ro'ta•ry,** adj. —**ro•ta'tion,** n. —**ro•ta'tor,** n.

rote, n. 1. routine way. 2. **by rote,** from memory in mechanical way.

ro•tis'ser•ie, n. rotating machine for roasting.

ro'tor, n. rotating part.

rot'ten, adj. 1. decaying. 2. corrupt. —**rot'ten•ly,** adv. —**rot'ten•ness,** n.

ro•tund', adj. round. —**ro•tun'di•ty,** n.

ro•tun'da, n. round room.

rou•é' (rōō ā'), n. dissolute man; rake.

rouge (rōōzh), n. 1. red cosmetic for cheeks and lips. 2. red polishing agent for metal. —v. 3. color with rouge.

rough, adj. 1. not smooth. 2. violent in action or motion. 3. harsh. 4. crude. —n. 5. rough thing or part. —v. 6. make rough. —**rough'ly,** adv. —**rough'ness,** n.

rough'age, n. coarse or fibrous material in food.

rou•lette' (rōō-), n. gambling game based on spinning disk.

round, adj. 1. circular, curved, or spherical. 2. complete. 3. expressed as approximate number. 4. sonorous. —n. 5. something round. 6. complete course, series, etc. 7. part of beef thigh between rump and leg. 8. song in which voices enter at intervals. 9. stage of competition, as in tournament. —adv. 10. in or as in a circle. 11. in circumference. —prep. 12. around. —v. 13. make or become round. 14. complete. 15. bring together. —**round'ness,** n.

round'a•bout', adj. indirect.

round'ly, adv. unsparingly.

round'up', n. 1. bringing together. 2. summary.

rouse, v., **roused, rousing.** stir up; arouse.

roust'a•bout', n. heavy laborer.

rout, n. 1. defeat ending in disorderly flight. —v. 2. force to flee in disorder.

route (rōōt), n., v., **routed, routing.** —n. 1. course of travel. —v. 2. send by or plan route.

rou•tine', n. 1. regular order of action. —adj. 2. like or by routine. 3. ordinary.

rove, v., **roved, roving.** wander aimlessly. —**rov'er,** n.

row (rō), v. 1. propel by oars. 2. (rou.) dispute noisily. —n. 3. trip in rowboat. 4. persons or things in line. 5. (rou). noisy dispute. —**row'boat',** n.

row'dy, adj., **-dier, -diest,** n., pl. **-dies.** —adj. 1. rough and disorderly. —n. 2. rowdy person.

roy'al, adj. of kings or queens. —**roy'al•ly,** adv.

roy'al•ist, n. person favoring royal government. —**royalist,** adj. —**roy'al•ism,** n.

roy'al•ty, n., pl. **-ties.** 1. royal persons. 2. royal power. 3. share of proceeds, paid to an author, inventor, etc.

rub, v., **rubbed, rubbing**, n. —v. 1. apply pressure or friction to in cleaning, smoothing, etc. 2. press against with friction. —n. 3. act of rubbing. 4. difficulty.

rub'ber, n. 1. elastic material from a tropical tree. 2. pl. overshoes. —**rub'-ber·ize'**, v. —**rub'ber·y**, adj.

rubber stamp, 1. stamp with rubber printing surface, for imprinting names, standard messages, etc. 2. automatic approval. —**rub'ber-stamp'**, v.

rub'bish, n. 1. waste. 2. nonsense.

rub'ble, n. broken stone.

rub'down', n. massage.

ru·bel'la (rōō bel'ə), n. usu. mild viral infection that may cause damage to fetus if contracted during pregnancy. Also, **German measles.**

ru'bi·cund' (rōō'bə kund'), adj. red.

ru'ble (rōō'bəl), n. monetary unit of Russia and of some former Soviet states.

ru'bric (rōō'brik), n. 1. title or heading. 2. class or category.

ru'by, n., pl. **-bies.** deep-red gem.

ruck'sack', n. type of knapsack.

ruck'us, n. noisy commotion; uproar.

rud'der, n. turning flat piece for steering vessel or aircraft.

rud'dy, adj., **-dier, -diest.** having healthy red color.

rude, adj., **ruder, rudest.** 1. discourteous. 2. unrefined; crude. —**rude'ly**, adv. —**rude'ness**, n.

ru'di·ment (rōō'-), n. basic thing to learn. —**ru'di·men'ta·ry**, adj.

rue, v., **rued, ruing**, n. regret. —**rue'-ful**, adj.

ruff, n. deep full collar.

ruf'fi·an, n. rough or lawless person.

ruf'fle, v., **-fled, -fling**, n. —v. 1. make uneven. 2. disturb. 3. gather in folds. 4. beat (drum) softly and steadily. —n. 5. break in evenness. 6. band of cloth, ribs, etc., gathered on one edge. 7. soft steady beat.

rug, n. floor covering.

Rug'by, n. English form of football.

rug'ged, adj. 1. roughly irregular. 2. severe. —**rug'ged·ly**, adv. —**rug'-ged·ness**, n.

ru'in, n. 1. downfall; destruction. 2. (pl.) remains of fallen building, etc. —v. 3. bring or come to ruin or ruins. —**ru'in·a'tion**, n. —**ru'in·ous**, adj.

rule, n., v., **ruled, ruling.** —n. 1. principle; regulation. 2. control. 3. ruler (def. 2). —v. 4. control. 5. decide in the manner of a judge. 6. mark with ruler. —**rul'ing**, n., adj.

rul'er, n. 1. person who rules. 2.

straight-edged strip for measuring, drawing lines, etc.

rum, n. alcoholic liquor made esp. from molasses.

rum'ba, n. Cuban dance.

rum'ble, v., **-bled, -bling**, n. —v. 1. make long, deep, heavy sound. —n. 2. such sound.

ru'mi·nant, n. 1. cud-chewing mammal, as cows. —adj. 2. cud-chewing.

ru'mi·nate', v., **-nated, -nating.** 1. chew cud. 2. meditate. —**ru'mi·na'-tion**, n.

rum'mage, v., **-maged, -maging.** search.

rummage sale, sale of miscellaneous items, esp. to raise money for charity.

rum'my, n., pl. **-mies.** 1. card game. 2. Slang. drunkard.

ru'mor, n. 1. unconfirmed but widely repeated story. —v. 2. tell as rumor.

rump, n. hind part of body.

rum'ple, v., **-pled, -pling**, n. wrinkle or ruffle.

rum'pus, n. Informal. noise; disturbance.

run, v., **ran, run, running.** —v. 1. advance quickly. 2. be candidate. 3. flow; melt. 4. extend. 5. operate. 6. be exposed to. 7. manage. —n. 8. act or period of running. 9. raveled line in knitting. 10. freedom of action. 11. scoring unit in baseball.

run'a·round', n. Informal. evasive treatment.

run'a·way', n. 1. fugitive; deserter. 2. something that has broken away from control. —adj. 3. escaped; fugitive. 4. uncontrolled.

run'-down', adj. 1. fatigued; weary. 2. fallen into disrepair. 3. (of spring-operated machine) not running because of not being wound.

rune, n. any of the characters of the alphabet used by ancient Germanic-speaking peoples. —**ru'nic**, adj.

rung, n. 1. ladder step. 2. bar between chair legs.

run'-in', n. quarrel; confrontation.

run'ner, n. 1. one that runs. 2. messenger. 3. blade of skate. 4. strip of fabric, carpet, etc.

run'ner-up', n. competitor finishing in second place.

runt, n. undersized person or thing.

run'way', n. strip where airplanes take off and land.

rup'ture, n., v., **-tured, -turing.** —n. 1. break. 2. hernia. —v. 3. break. 4. cause breach of.

ru'ral, adj. of or in the country.

ruse, n. trick.

rush, v. 1. move with speed or violence. —n. 2. act of rushing. 3. hostile attack. 4. grasslike herb growing in marshes. —*adj.* 5. requiring or marked by haste.

rush hour, time of day when many people are in transit, esp. to and from work.

rus'set, *n.* reddish brown.

Rus'sian, *n.* native or language of Russia. —**Russian,** *adj.*

rust, *n.* 1. red-orange coating that forms on iron and steel exposed to air and moisture. 2. plant disease. —*v.* 3. make or become rusty. —**rust'y,** *adj.*

rus'tic, *adj.* 1. rural. 2. simple. —*n.* 3. country person.

rus'ti•cate, *v.,* **-cated, -cating.** go to or live in the country.

rus'tle, *v.,* **-tled, -tling,** *n.* —*v.* 1. make small soft sounds. 2. steal (cattle, etc.). —*n.* 3. rustling sound. —**rus'tler,** *n.*

rut, *n., v.,* **rutted, rutting.** —*n.* 1. furrow or groove worn in the ground. 2. period of sexual excitement in male deer, goats, etc. —*v.* 3. make ruts in. 4. be in rut. —**rut'ty,** *adj.*

ru'ta•ba'ga (rōō'tə bā'gə), *n.* yellow turnip.

ruth'less, *adj.* pitiless. —**ruth'less•ness,** *n.*

RV, recreational vehicle.

rye, *n.* cereal grass used for flour, feed, and whiskey.

S

S, s, *n.* nineteenth letter of English alphabet.

Sab'bath, *n.* day of religious observance and rest, observed on Saturday by Jews and on Sunday by most Christians.

sab•bat'i•cal, *n.* 1. paid leave of absence for study. —*adj.* 2. (*cap.*) of the Sabbath.

sa'ber, *n.* one-edged sword. Also, **sa'bre.**

sa'ble, *n.* small mammal with dark-brown fur.

sab'o•tage', *n., v.,* **-taged, -taging.** —*n.* 1. willful injury to equipment, etc. —*v.* 2. attack by sabotage. —**sab'o•teur',** *n.*

sac, *n.* baglike part.

sac'cha•rin (sak'ə rin), *n.* sweet substance used as sugar substitute.

sac'cha•rine, *adj.* overly sweet.

sac•er•do'tal (sas'ər-), *adj.* priestly.

sa•chet' (-shā'), *n.* small bag of perfumed powder.

sack, *n.* 1. large stout bag. 2. bag. 3. *Slang.* dismissal. 4. plundering. —*v.* 5. put into a sack. 6. *Slang.* dismiss. 7. plunder; loot. —**sack'ing,** *n.*

sack'cloth', *n.* coarse cloth worn for penance or mourning.

sac'ra•ment, *n.* 1. solemn rite in Christian church. 2. (*cap.*) Eucharist. —**sac'ra•men'tal,** *adj.*

sa'cred, *adj.* 1. holy. 2. secured against violation. —**sa'cred•ly,** *adv.* —**sa'cred•ness,** *n.*

sac'ri•fice', *n., v.,* **-ficed, -ficing.** —*n.* 1. offer of life, treasure, etc.; to deity. 2. surrender of something for purpose. —*v.* 3. give as sacrifice. —**sac'ri•fi'cial,** *adj.*

sac'ri•lege (-lij), *n.* profanation of

anything sacred. —**sac'ri•le'gious,** *adj.*

sac'ris•tan (sak'ri stan), *n.* sexton.

sac'ris•ty, *n., pl.* **-ties.** room in church, etc., where sacred objects are kept.

sac'ro•il'i•ac', *n.* joint in lower back.

sac'ro•sanct', *adj.* sacred.

sad, *adj.* **sadder, saddest.** sorrowful. —**sad'den,** *v.* —**sad'ly,** *adv.* —**sad'ness,** *n.*

sad'dle, *n., v.,* **-died, -dling.** —*n.* 1. seat for rider on horse, etc. 2. anything resembling saddle. —*v.* 3. put saddle on. 4. burden.

sad'ism, *n.* sexual or other enjoyment in causing pain. —**sad'ist,** *n.* —**sa•dis'tic,** *adj.*

sa'do•mas'o•chism' (sā'dō mas'ə kiz'əm), *n.* sexual or other enjoyment in causing or experiencing pain. —**sa'do•mas'o•chist',** *n.* —**sa'do•mas'o•chis'tic,** *adj.*

sa•fa'ri (sə fär'ē), *n.* (in E. Africa) journey; hunting expedition.

safe, *adj.,* **safer, safest,** *n.* —*adj.* 1. secure or free from danger. 2. dependable. —*n.* 3. stout box for valuables. —**safe'ly,** *adv.* —**safe'keep'ing,** *n.*

safe'guard', *n.* 1. something that ensures safety. —*v.* 2. protect.

safe sex, sexual activity in which precautions are taken to avoid sexually transmitted diseases.

saf'fron, *n.* bright yellow seasoning.

sag, *v.,* **sagged, sagging,** *n.* —*v.* 1. bend, esp. in middle, from weight or pressure. 2. hang loosely. —*n.* 3. sagging place.

sa'ga, *n.* heroic tale.

sa·ga'cious, *adj.* shrewd and practical. —**sa·gac'i·ty,** *n.*

sage, *n., adj.,* **sager, sagest.** —*n.* 1. wise person. 2. herb with gray-green leaves used in seasoning. —*adj.* 3. wise; prudent. —**sage'ly,** *adv.* —**sage'ness,** *n.*

sage'brush', *n.* sagelike, bushy plant of dry plains of western U.S.

sa'go, *n.* starchy substance from some palms.

sa'hib (sä'ib), *n.* (in colonial India) term of respect for European.

said, *adj.* named before.

sail, *n.* 1. sheet spread to catch wind to propel vessel or windmill. 2. trip on sailing vessel. —*v.* 3. move by action of wind. 4. travel over water. —**sail'or,** *n.*

sail'fish', *n.* large fish with upright fin.

saint, *n.* holy person. —**saint'hood,** *n.* —**saint'ly,** *adj.* —**saint'li·ness,** *n.*

sake, *n.* 1. interest; account. 2. purpose. 3. (sä'kē) Japanese rice wine.

sa·laam (sa läm'), *n.* 1. Islamic salutation. 2. low bow with hand on forehead.

sal'a·ble, *adj.* subject to or fit for sale. Also, **sale'a·ble.**

sa·la'cious (-lā'shəs), *adj.* lewd.

sal'ad, *n.* dish esp. of raw vegetables or fruit.

sal'a·man·der, *n.* small amphibian.

sa·la'mi, *n.* kind of sausage.

sal'a·ry, *n., pl.* **-ries.** fixed payment for regular work. —**sal'a·ried,** *adj.*

sale, *n.* 1. act of selling. 2. opportunity to sell. 3. occasion of selling at reduced prices. —**sales'man,** *n.* —**sales'la'dy, sales'wom'an,** *n.fem.* —**sales'per'son,** *n.* —**sales'people,** *n.pl.* —**sales'room',** *n.*

sa'li·ent (sā'-), *adj.* 1. conspicuous. 2. projecting. —*n.* 3. projecting part. —**sa'li·ence,** *n.* —**sa'li·ent·ly,** *adv.*

sa'line (sā'līn), *adj.* salty. —**sa·lin'i·ty,** *n.*

sa·li'va, *n.* fluid secreted into mouth by glands. —**sal'i·var'y,** *adj.* —**sal'i·vate',** *v.*

sal'low, *adj.* having sickly complexion.

sal'ly, *n., pl.* **-lies,** *v.,* **-lied, -lying.** —*n.* 1. sudden attack by besieged troops. 2. outburst or rush. 3. witty remark. —*v.* 4. make sally.

salm'on, *n.* pink-fleshed food fish of northern waters.

sal'mo·nel'la (sal'mə nel'ə), *n., pl.* **-lae (-ē), -las.** bacillus that causes various diseases, including food poisoning.

sa·lon', *n.* 1. drawing room. 2. art gallery.

sa·loon', *n.* 1. place where intoxicating liquors are sold and drunk. 2. public room.

sal'sa (säl'sə, -sä), *n.* 1. Latin-American music with elements of jazz, rock, and soul. 2. sauce, esp. hot sauce containing chilies.

salt, *n.* 1. sodium chloride, used as mineral, in sea water, etc. 2. chemical compound derived from acid and base. 3. wit. 4. *Informal.* sailor. —*v.* 5. season or preserve with salt. —**salt'y,** *adj.*

SALT, *n.* Strategic Arms Limitation Talks.

salt'pe'ter, *n.* potassium nitrate.

sa·lu'bri·ous, *adj.* healthful. —**sa·lu'bri·ous·ly,** *adv.* —**sa·lu'bri·ty,** *n.*

sal'u·tar'y, *adj.* healthful; beneficial.

sal'u·ta'tion, *n.* 1. greeting. 2. formal opening of letter.

sa·lute', *v.,* **-luted, -luting,** *n.* —*v.* 1. express respect or goodwill, esp. in greeting. —*n.* 2. act of saluting.

sal'vage, *n., v.,* **-vaged, -vaging.** —*n.* 1. act of saving ship or cargo at sea. 2. property saved. —*v.* 3. save from shipwreck or destruction.

sal·va'tion, *n.* 1. deliverance. 2. deliverance from sin.

salve (sav), *n., v.,* **salved, salving.** —*n.* 1. ointment for sores. —*v.* 2. apply salve to.

sal'ver, *n.* tray.

sal'vi·a, *n.* plant of mint family.

sal'vo, *n., pl.* **-vos, -voes.** discharge of guns, bombs, etc., in rapid series.

Sa·mar'i·tan, *n.* compassionate and helpful person.

sam'ba (sam'bə, säm'-), *n., v.,* **-baed, -baing.** —*n.* 1. Brazilian dance of African origin. —*v.* 2. dance the samba.

same, *adj.* 1. identical or corresponding. 2. unchanged. 3. just mentioned. —*n.* 4. same person or thing. —**same'ness,** *n.*

sam'o·var', *n.* metal urn.

sam'pan, *n.* small Far Eastern boat.

sam'ple, *n., adj., v.,* **-pled, -pling.** —*n.* 1. small amount to show nature or quality. —*adj.* 2. as sample. —*v.* 3. test by sample.

sam'pler, *n.* needlework done to show skill.

sam'u·rai', *n., pl.* **-rai.** member of hereditary warrior class in feudal Japan.

san'a·to'ri·um, *n., pl.* **-riums, -ria.** sanitarium.

sanc'ti·fy', *v.,* **-fied, -fying.** 1. make holy. 2. give sanction to. —**sanc'ti·fi·ca'tion,** *n.*

sanc'ti•mo'ny, *n.* hypocritical devoutness. **—sanc'ti•mo'ni•ous,** *adj.*

sanc'tion, *n.* 1. permission or support. 2. legal action by group of states against another state. —*v.* 3. authorize; approve.

sanc'ti•ty, *n., pl.* **-ties.** 1. holiness. 2. sacred character.

sanc'tu•ar'y, *n., pl.* **-aries.** 1. holy place. 2. area around altar. 3. place of immunity from arrest or harm.

sanc'tum, *n., pl.* **-tums, -ta.** private place.

sand, *n.* 1. fine grains of rock. 2. (*pl.*) sandy region. —*v.* 3. smooth with sandpaper. **—sand'er,** *n.* **—sand'y,** *adj.*

san'dal, *n.* shoe consisting of sole and straps.

san'dal•wood', *n.* fragrant wood.

sand'blast', *v.* clean with blast of air or steam laden with sand.

sand'man', *n.* figure in folklore who puts sand in children's eyes to make them sleepy.

sand'pa'per, *n.* paper coated with sand. —*v.* 2. smooth with sandpaper.

sand'pip'er, *n.* small shore bird.

sand'stone', *n.* rock formed chiefly of sand.

sand'wich, *n.* 1. two slices of bread with meat, etc., between. —*v.* 2. insert.

sane, *adj.,* **saner, sanest.** free from mental disorder; rational. **—sane'ly,** *adv.*

san'gui•nar'y, *adj.* 1. bloody. 2. bloodthirsty.

san'guine (-gwin), *adj.* 1. hopeful. 2. red.

san'i•tar'i•um, *n., pl.* **-iums, -ia.** place for treatment of invalids and convalescents.

san'i•tar'y, *adj.* of health. **—san'i•tar'i•ly,** *adv.*

san'i•ta'tion, *n.* application of sanitary measures.

san'i•ty, *n.* 1. soundness of mind. 2. good judgment.

San'skrit, *n.* extinct language of India.

sap, *n., v.,* **sapped, sapping.** —*n.* 1. trench dug to approach enemy's position. 2. juice of woody plant. 3. *Slang.* fool. —*v.* 4. weaken; undermine. **—sap'per,** *n.*

sa'pi•ent, *adj.* wise. **—sa'pi•ence,** *n.*

sap'ling, *n.* young tree.

sap'phire, *n.* deep-blue gem.

sap'suck'er, *n.* kind of woodpecker.

sar'casm, *n.* 1. harsh derision. 2. ironical gibe. **—sar•cas'tic,** *adj.* **—sar•cas'ti•cal•ly,** *adv.*

sar•co'ma, *n., pl.* **-mas, -mata.** type of malignant tumor.

sar•coph'a•gus, *n., pl.* **-gi.** stone coffin.

sar•dine', *n.* small fish, often preserved in oil.

sar•don'ic, *adj.* sarcastic. **—sar•don'i•cal•ly,** *adv.*

sa'ri (sär'ē), *n.* length of cloth used as dress in India.

sa•rong', *n.* skirtlike garment.

sar'sa•pa•ril'la (sas'pə ril'ə), *n.* 1. tropical American plant. 2. soft drink flavored with roots of this plant.

sar•to'ri•al, *adj.* of tailors or tailoring.

sash, *n.* 1. band of cloth usually worn as belt. 2. framework for panes of window, etc.

Sas'quatch (sas'kwoch, -kwach), *n.* large, hairy humanoid creature said to inhabit wilderness areas of U.S. and Canada. Also, **Bigfoot.**

sas'sa•fras', *n.* American tree with aromatic root bark.

Sa'tan, *n.* chief evil spirit; devil. **—sa•tan'ic,** *adj.*

satch'el, *n.* handbag.

sate, *v.,* **sated, sating.** satisfy or surfeit.

sa•teen', *n.* glossy cotton fabric.

sat'el•lite', *n.* 1. body that revolves around planet. 2. subservient follower.

satellite dish, dish-shaped reflector, used esp. for receiving satellite and microwave signals.

sa'ti•ate' (-shē-), *v.,* **-ated, -ating.** surfeit. **—sa•ti•a'tion, sa•ti'e•ty,** *n.*

sat'in, *n.* glossy silk or rayon fabric. **—sat'in•y,** *adj.*

sat'ire, *n.* use of irony or ridicule in exposing vice, folly, etc. **—sa•tir'i•cal, sa•tir'ic,** *adj.* **—sa•tir'i•cal•ly,** *adv.*

sat'i•rize', *v.,* **-rized, -rizing.** subject to satire. **—sat'i•rist,** *n.*

sat'is•fy', *v.,* **-fied, -fying.** 1. fulfill desire, need, etc. 2. convince. 3. pay. **—sat'is•fac'tion,** *n.* **—sat'is•fac'to•ry,** *adj.* **—sat'is•fac'to•ri•ly,** *adv.*

sat'u•rate', *v.,* **-rated, -rating.** soak completely. **—sat'u•ra'tion,** *n.*

Sat'ur•day, *n.* seventh day of week.

Sat'urn, *n.* major planet.

sat'ur•nine' (-nīn'), *adj.* gloomy.

sa'tyr (sā'tər), *n.* 1. woodland deity, part man and part goat. 2. lecherous person.

sauce, *n.* 1. liquid or soft relish. 2. stewed fruit.

sauce'pan', *n.* cooking pan with handle.

sau·cer, n. small shallow dish.

sau·cy, adj. **-ci·er, -ciest.** impertinent. **—sau'ci·ly,** adv. **—sau'ci·ness,** n.

sauer'kraut', n. chopped fermented cabbage.

sau·na (sô'-), n. bath heated by steam.

saun·ter, v., n. stroll.

sau'sage, n. minced seasoned meat, often in casing.

sau·té' (sô tā'), v., **-téed, -téeing.** cook in a little fat.

sau·terne' (sō tûrn'), n. sweet white wine.

sav'age, adj. **1.** wild; uncivilized. **2.** ferocious. **—**n. **3.** uncivilized person. **—sav'age·ly,** adv. **—sav'age·ry,** n.

sa·van'na, n. grassy plain with scattered trees. Also, **sa·van'nah.**

sa·vant' (sa vänt'), n. learned person.

save, v., **saved, saving,** prep., conj. **—**v. **1.** rescue or keep safe. **2.** reserve. **—**prep., conj. **3.** except.

sav'ing, adj. **1.** rescuing; redeeming. **2.** economical. **—**n. **3.** economy. **4.** (pl.) money put by. **—**prep. **5.** except. **6.** respecting.

sav'ior, n. **1.** one who rescues. **2.** (cap.) Christ. Also, **sav'iour.**

sa·voir-faire' (sav'wär fâr'), n. competence in social matters.

sa'vor, v., n. taste or smell.

sa'vor·y, adj., n., pl. **-ories. —**adj. **1.** pleasing in taste or smell. **—**n. **2.** aromatic plant.

sav'vy, n., adj., **-vier, -viest. —**n. **1.** practical understanding. **—**adj. **2.** shrewd and well-informed.

saw, n. **1.** toothed metal blade. **—**v. **2.** cut with saw. **—saw'mill,** n. **—saw'-yer,** n.

sax'o·phone', n. musical wind instrument.

say, v., **said, saying,** n. **—**v. **1.** speak; declare; utter. **2.** declare as truth. **—**n. **3.** Informal. right to speak or choose.

say'ing, n. proverb.

say'-so', n., pl. **-sos.** Informal. personal assurance; word.

scab, n. **1.** crust forming over sore. **2.** worker who takes striker's place. **—**v. **3.** form scab. **—scab'by,** adj.

scab'bard, n. sheath for sword blade, etc.

sca'bies, n. infectious skin disease.

scab'rous (skab'ras), adj. **1.** having a rough surface. **2.** indecent; obscene.

scaf'fold, n. **1.** Also, **scaf'fold·ing.** temporary framework used in construction. **2.** platform on which criminal is executed.

scal'a·wag', n. rascal.

scald, v. **1.** burn with hot liquid or

steam. **2.** heat just below boiling. **—**n. **3.** burn caused by scalding.

scale, n., v., **scaled, scaling. —**n. **1.** one of flat hard plates covering fish, etc. **2.** flake. **3.** device for weighing. **4.** series of measurement units. **5.** relative measure. **6.** succession of musical tones. **—**v. **7.** remove or shed scales. **8.** weigh. **9.** climb with effort. **10.** reduce proportionately. **—scal'y,** adj. **—scal'i·ness,** n.

scal'lion, n. small green onion.

scal'lop (skol'ap, skal'-), n. **1.** bivalve mollusk. **2.** one of series of curves on a border. **—**v. **3.** finish with scallops.

scalp, n. **1.** skin and hair of top of head. **—**v. **2.** cut scalp from. **3.** buy and resell at unofficial price. **—scalp'er,** n.

scal'pel, n. small surgical knife.

scam, n., v., **scammed, scamming. —**n. **1.** fraudulent scheme; swindle. **—**v. **2.** cheat; defraud.

scamp, n. rascal.

scam'per, v. **1.** go quickly. **—**n. **2.** quick run.

scam'pi (skam'pē, skäm-), n., pl. **-pi. 1.** large shrimp. **2.** dish of scampi.

scan, v., **scanned, scanning. 1.** examine closely. **2.** glance at. **3.** analyze verse meter.

scan'dal, n. **1.** disgraceful act; disgrace. **2.** malicious gossip. **—scan'dal·ous,** adj. **—scan'dal·mon'ger,** n.

scan'dal·ize', v., **-ized, -izing.** offend; shock.

scan'ner, n. **1.** person or thing that scans. **2.** device that monitors selected radio frequencies and reproduces any signal detected. **3.** device that optically scans bar codes, etc., and identifies data.

scant, adj. barely adequate. Also, **scant'y. —scant'i·ly,** adv. **—scant'i·ness,** n.

scape'goat', n. one made to bear blame for others.

scape'grace', n. scamp; rascal.

scap'u·la, n., pl. **-lae, -las.** shoulder blade. **—scap'u·lar,** n.

scar, n., v., **scarred, scarring. 1.** mark left by wound, etc. **—**v. **2.** mark with scar.

scar'ab, n. beetle.

scarce, adj. **scarcer, scarcest. 1.** insufficient. **2.** rare. **—scar'ci·ty,** n.

scarce'ly, adv. **1.** barely. **2.** definitely not.

scare, v., **scared, scaring,** n. **—**v. **1.** frighten. **—**n. **2.** sudden fright.

scare'crow', n. object set up to frighten birds away from planted seed.

scarf, n., pl. **scarfs, scarves.** band of cloth esp. for neck.

scar·i·fy′, v., **-fied, -fying. 1.** scratch (skin, etc.). **2.** loosen (soil).

scar′let, n. bright red.

scarlet fever, contagious disease marked by fever and rash.

scar′y, adj. **-ier, -iest.** causing fear.

scat, v., **scatted, scatting.** run off.

scathe, v., **scathed, scathing.** criticize harshly.

scat·o·log′i·cal, adj. concerned with excrement or obscenity.

scat′ter, v. throw loosely about.

scav′en·ger, v., **-enged, -enging. 1.** search for food. **2.** cleanse. —**scav′en·ger,** n.

sce·nar′i·o, n., pl. **-ios.** plot outline, esp. of motion picture.

scene, n. **1.** location of action. **2.** view. **3.** subdivision of play. **4.** display of emotion. —**sce′nic,** adj.

scen′er·y, n. **1.** features of landscape. **2.** stage set.

scent, n. **1.** distinctive odor. **2.** trail marked by this. **3.** sense of smell. —v. **4.** smell. **5.** perfume.

scep′ter (sep′-), n. rod carried as emblem of royal power. Also, **scep′tre.**

scep′tic, n. skeptic.

sched′ule (skej′-), n., v., **-uled, -uling.** —n. **1.** timetable or list. —v. **2.** enter on schedule.

scheme, n., v., **schemed, scheming.** —n. **1.** plan; design. **2.** intrigue. —v. **3.** plan or plot. —**schem′er,** n. —**sche·mat′ic,** adj.

scher′zo (skert′sō), n., pl. **-zos, -zi** (-sē). playful musical movement.

schism (siz′əm), n. **1.** division within church, etc.; disunion. —**schis·mat′ic,** adj., n.

schist (shist), n. layered crystalline rock.

schiz′oid (skit′soid), adj. having personality disorder, marked by depression, withdrawal, etc.

schiz′o·phre′ni·a (skit′sə frē′nē ə), n. kind of mental disorder.

schlock (shlok), n. Informal. inferior merchandise. —**schlock′y,** adj.

schmaltz (shmälts), n. Informal. sentimental art, esp. music. —**schmaltz′y,** adj.

schol′ar, n. **1.** learned person. **2.** pupil. —**schol′ar·ly,** adj.

schol′ar·ship′, n. **1.** learning. **2.** aid granted to promising student.

scho·las′tic, adj. of schools or scholars. —**scho·las′ti·cal·ly,** adv.

school, n. **1.** place for instruction. **2.** regular meetings of teacher and pupils. **3.** believers in doctrine or theory. **4.** group of fish, whales, etc. —v.

5. educate; train. —**school′book′,** n. —**school′house′,** n. —**school′mate′,** n. —**school′room′,** n. —**school′teach′er,** n.

schoon′er, n. kind of sailing vessel.

schwa (shwä), n. vowel sound in certain unstressed syllables, as a in sofa; usually represented by ə.

sci·at′i·ca (sī-), n. neuralgia in hip and thigh. —**sci·at′ic,** adj.

sci′ence, n. systematic knowledge, esp. of physical world. —**sci′en·tif′ic,** adj. —**sci′en·tif′i·cal·ly,** adv. —**sci′en·tist,** n.

science fiction, fiction dealing with space travel, robots, etc.

scim′i·tar (sim′-), n. curved sword.

scin·til′la (sin-), n. particle, esp. of evidence.

scin′til·late′, v., **-lated, -lating.** sparkle. —**scin·til·la′tion,** n.

sci′on (sī′ən), n. **1.** descendant. **2.** shoot cut for grafting.

scis′sors, n. cutting instrument with two pivoted blades.

scle·ro′sis (sklī-), n. hardening, as of tissue. —**scle·rot′ic,** adj.

scoff, v. **1.** jeer. —n. **2.** derision. —**scoff′er,** n.

scoff′law′, n. person who flouts the law, as by ignoring traffic tickets.

scold, v. **1.** find fault; reprove. —n. **2.** scolding person.

sconce, n. wall bracket for candles, etc.

scone, n. small flat cake.

scoop, n. **1.** small deep shovel. **2.** bucket of steam shovel, etc. **3.** act of scooping. **4.** quantity taken up. **5.** Informal. earliest news report. —v. **6.** take up with scoop. **7.** Informal. best (competing news media) with scoop (def. 5).

scoot, v. go swiftly.

scoot′er, n. low two-wheeled vehicle.

scope, n. extent.

scorch, v. **1.** burn slightly. —n. **2.** superficial burn.

score, n., pl. **scores,** (for 3) **score,** v., **scored, scoring.** —n. **1.** points made in game. **2.** notch. **3.** group of twenty. **4.** account; reason. **5.** written piece of music. —v. **6.** earn points in game. **7.** notch or cut. **8.** criticize. —**scor′er,** n.

scorn, n. **1.** contempt. **2.** mockery. —v. **3.** regard or refuse with scorn. —**scorn′ful,** adj. —**scorn′ful·ly,** adv.

scor′pi·on, n. small venomous spiderlike animal.

Scot, n. native or inhabitant of Scotland. —**Scot′tish,** adj., n.pl.

Scotch, adj. **1.** (loosely) Scottish.

2. (pl.) (loosely) Scottish people. **3.** whiskey made in Scotland.

scotch, v. **1.** make harmless. **2.** put an end to.

scot'-free', adj. avoiding harm, punishment, obligation, or apprehension.

scoun'drel, n. rascal.

scour, v. **1.** clean by rubbing. **2.** range in searching.

scourge (skûrj), n., v., **scourged, scourging.** —n. **1.** whip. **2.** cause of affliction. —v. **3.** whip.

scout, n. **1.** person sent ahead to examine conditions. —v. **2.** examine as scout. **3.** reject with scorn.

scow, n. flat-bottomed, flat-ended boat.

scowl, v. **1.** fierce frown. —v. **2.** frown fiercely.

scrab'ble, v., **-bled, -bling. 1.** scratch with hands, etc. **2.** scrawl.

scrag, n. scrawny creature. —**scrag'-gy,** adj.

scrag'gly, adj., **-glier, -gliest.** shaggy.

scram, v., **scrammed, scramming.** Informal. go away quickly.

scram'ble, v., **-bled, -bling,** n. —v. **1.** move with difficulty, using feet and hands. **2.** mix together. —n. **3.** scrambling progression. **4.** struggle for possession.

scrap, n., adj., v., **scrapped, scrapping.** —n. **1.** small piece. **2.** discarded material. **3.** Informal. fight. —adj. **4.** discarded. **5.** in scraps or as scraps. —v. **6.** break up; discard. —**scrap'py,** adj.

scrap'book', n. blank book for clippings, etc.

scrape, v., **scraped, scraping,** n. —v. **1.** rub harshly. **2.** remove by scraping. **3.** collect laboriously. —n. **4.** act or sound of scraping. **5.** scraped place. **6.** predicament. —**scrap'er,** n.

scrap'ple, n. sausagelike food of pork, corn meal, and seasonings.

scratch, v. **1.** mark, tear, or rub with something sharp. **2.** strike out. —n. **3.** mark from scratching. **4.** standard. —**scratch'y,** adj.

scrawl, v. **1.** write carelessly or awkwardly. —n. **2.** such handwriting.

scraw'ny, adj., **-nier, -niest.** thin. —**scraw'ni·ness,** n.

scream, n. **1.** loud sharp cry. —v. **2.** utter screams.

screech, n. **1.** harsh shrill cry. —v. **2.** utter screeches.

screen, n. **1.** covered frame. **2.** anything that shelters or conceals. **3.** wire mesh. **4.** surface for displaying motion pictures. —v. **5.** shelter with screen. **6.** sift through screen.

screen'play', n. outline or full script of motion picture.

screw, n. **1.** machine part or fastener driving or driven by twisting. **2.** propeller. **3.** coercion. —v. **4.** hold with screw. **5.** turn as screw.

screw'ball', Slang. —n. **1.** eccentric or wildly whimsical person. —adj. **2.** eccentric or whimsical.

screw'driv'er, n. tool for turning screws.

scrib'ble, v., **-bled, -bling.** —v. **1.** write hastily or meaninglessly. —n. **2.** piece of such writing.

scribe, n. professional copyist.

scrim'mage, n., v., **-maged, -maging.** —n. **1.** rough struggle. **2.** play in football. —v. **3.** engage in scrimmage.

scrimp, v. economize.

scrip, n. certificate, paper money, etc.

script, n. **1.** handwriting. **2.** manuscript.

Scrip'ture, n. **1.** Bible. **2.** (l.c.) sacred or religious writing or book. —**scrip'tur·al,** adj.

scrod, n. young codfish or haddock.

scrof'u·la, n. tuberculous disease, esp. of lymphatic glands.

scroll, n. roll of inscribed paper.

scro'tum, n., pl. **-ta, -tums.** pouch of skin containing testicles. —**scro'tal,** adj.

scrounge, v., **scrounged, scrounging.** Informal. **1.** beg or mooch. **2.** search. —**scroung'er,** n.

scrub, v., **scrubbed, scrubbing,** n., adj. —v. **1.** clean by rubbing. —n. **2.** low trees or shrubs. **3.** anything small or poor. —adj. **4.** small or poor. —**scrub'by,** adj.

scruff, n. nape.

scru'ple, n. restraint from conscience.

scru'pu·lous, adj. **1.** having scruples. **2.** careful. —**scru'pu·lous·ly,** adv.

scru'ti·nize', v., **-nized, -nizing.** examine closely. —**scru'ti·ny,** n.

scu'ba, n. self-contained breathing device for swimmers.

scud, v., **scudded, scudding.** move quickly.

scuff, v. **1.** shuffle. **2.** mar by hard use.

scuf'fle, n., v., **-fled, -fling.** —n. **1.** rough, confused fight. —v. **2.** engage in scuffle.

scull, n. **1.** oar used over stern. **2.** light racing boat. —v. **3.** propel with scull.

scull'er·y, n., pl. **-leries.** workroom off kitchen.

sculp'ture, n. **1.** three-dimensional art of wood, marble, etc. **2.** piece of such work. —**sculp'tor,** n. —**sculp'tress,** n.fem.

scum, n. **1.** film on top of liquid. **2.** worthless persons. —**scum'my,** adj.

scup'per, n. opening in ship's side to drain off water.

scur'ril•ous, adj. coarsely abusive or derisive. —**scur'ril•ous•ly,** adv. —**scur•ril'i•ty, scur'ril•ous•ness,** n.

scur'ry, v., **-ried, -rying,** n., pl. **-ries.** hurry.

scur'vy, n., adj. **-vier, -viest.** —n. 1. disease from inadequate diet. —adj. 2. contemptible.

scut'tle, n., v., **-tled, -tling.** —n. 1. covered opening, esp. on flat roof. 2. coal bucket. —v. 3. sink intentionally. 4. scurry.

scut'tle•butt', n. Informal. rumor; gossip.

scythe (sīth), n. curved, handled blade for mowing by hand.

sea, n. 1. ocean. 2. body of salt water smaller than ocean. 3. turbulence of water. —**sea'board',** n. —**sea'shore',** n. —**sea'coast',** n. —**sea'port',** n. —**sea'go•ing,** adj.

sea cow, manatee.

sea'far•ing, n. traveling by or working at sea.

sea horse, small fish with beaked head.

seal, n., pl. **seals,** (also for 3) **seal,** —n. 1. imprinted device affixed to document. 2. means of closing. 3. marine animal with large flippers. —v. 4. affix seal to. 5. close by seal. —**seal'ant,** n.

sea level, position of the sea's surface at mean level between high and low tides.

sea lion, large seal.

seam, n. 1. line formed in sewing two pieces together. —v. 2. join with seam.

sea'man, n., pl. **-men.** sailor. —**sea'man•ship',** n.

seam'stress, n. woman who sews.

seam'y, adj., **seamier, seamiest.** 1. sordid. 2. having seams. —**seam'i•ness,** n.

sé'ance (sā'äns), n. meeting to attempt communication with spirits.

sea'plane', n. airplane equipped with floats.

sea'port', n. port for seagoing vessels.

sear, v. 1. burn or char. 2. dry up.

search, v. 1. examine, as in looking for something. 2. investigate. —n. 3. examination or investigation. —**search'er,** n.

search'light', n. device for throwing strong beam of light.

sea'sick•ness, n. nausea from motion of ship. —**sea'sick',** adj.

sea'son, n. 1. any of four distinct periods of year. 2. best or usual time. —v.

3. flavor with salt, spices, etc. —**sea'son•al,** adj.

sea'son•a•ble, adj. appropriate to time of year.

sea'son•ing, n. flavoring, as salt, spices, or herbs.

seat, n. 1. place for sitting. 2. right to sit, as in Congress. 3. site; location. 4. established center. —v. 5. place on seat. 6. find seats for. 7. install.

seat'ing, n. 1. arrangement of seats. 2. material for seats.

sea'weed', n. plant growing in sea.

sea'wor•thy, adj., **-thier, -thiest.** fit for sea travel.

se•ba'ceous (-shəs), adj. of, resembling, or secreting a fatty substance.

seb'or•rhe'a (seb'ə rē'ə), n. abnormally heavy discharge from sebaceous glands.

se•cede', v., **-ceded, -ceding.** withdraw from nation, alliance, etc. —**se•ces'sion,** n.

se•clude', v., **-cluded, -cluding.** locate in solitude. —**se•clu'sion,** n.

sec'ond, adj. 1. next after first. 2. another. —n. 3. one that is second. 4. person who aids another. 5. (pl.) imperfect goods. 6. sixtieth part of minute of time or degree. —v. 7. support; further. —adj. 8. in second place. —**sec'ond•ly,** adv.

sec'ond•ar'y, adj. 1. next after first. 2. of second rank or stage. 3. less important. —**sec'ond•ar'i•ly,** adv.

sec'ond-hand', adj. 1. not new. 2. not original.

second nature, deeply ingrained habit or tendency.

sec'ond-rate', adj. of lesser or minor quality or importance.

se'cret, adj. 1. kept from knowledge of others. —n. 2. something secret or hidden. —**se'cre•cy,** n. —**se'cret•ly,** adv.

sec're•tar'i•at, n. group of administrative officials.

sec're•tar'y, n., pl. **-taries.** 1. office assistant. 2. head of department of government. 3. tall writing desk. —**sec're•tar'i•al,** adj.

se•crete', v., **-creted, -creting.** 1. hide. 2. discharge or release by secretion.

se•cre'tion, n. 1. glandular function of secreting, as bile or milk. 2. product secreted. —**se•cre'to•ry,** adj.

se•cre'tive, adj. 1. disposed to keep things secret. 2. secretory. —**se•cre'tive•ly,** adv. —**se•cre'tive•ness,** n.

sect, n. group with common religious faith. —**sec•tar'i•an,** adj.

sec'tion, n. 1. separate or distinct

part. —v. 2. divide into sections.
—sec'tion•al, adj.

sec'tor, n. 1. plane figure bounded by
two radii and an arc. 2. part of combat area.

sec'u•lar, adj. worldly; not religious.
—sec'u•lar•ize', v.

se•cure', adj., v., -cured, -curing.
—adj. 1. safe. 2. firmly in place. 3.
certain. —v. 4. get. 5. make secure.
—se•cure'ly, adv.

se•cu'ri•ty, n., pl. -ties. 1. safety. 2.
protection. 3. pledge given on loan. 4.
certificate of stock, etc.

se•dan', n. closed automobile for four
or more.

se•date', adj. 1. quiet; sober. —v. 2.
give sedative to. —se•date'ly, adv.
—se•date'ness, n.

sed'a•tive, adj. 1. soothing. 2. relieving pain or excitement. —n. 3. sedative medicine.

sed'en•tar•y, adj. characterized by
sitting.

Se'der (sā'dər), n. ceremonial dinner
at Passover.

sedge, n. grasslike marsh plant.

sed'i•ment, n. matter settling to bottom of liquid. —sed'i•men'ta•ry,
adj.

se•di'tion, n. incitement to rebellion.
—se•di'tious, adj.

se•duce', v., -duced, -ducing. 1. corrupt; tempt. 2. induce to surrender
chastity. 3. induce to have sexual intercourse. —se•duc'tion, n. —se•
duc'tive, adj.

sed'u•lous, adj. diligent.

see, v., saw, seen, seeing. —v. 1.
perceive with the eyes. 2. find out. 3.
make sure. 4. escort. —n. 5. office or
jurisdiction of bishop.

seed, n. 1. propagating part of plant.
2. offspring. —v. 3. sow seed. 4. remove seed from. —seed'less, adj.

seed'ling, n. plant grown from seed.

seed'y, adj., seedier, seediest. 1. having many seeds. 2. shabby. —seed'i•
ness, n.

see'ing, conj. inasmuch as.

seek, v., sought, seeking. 1. search
for. 2. try. —seek'er, n.

seem, v. appear (to be or do).

seem'ing, adj. apparent. —seem'•
ing•ly, adv.

seem'ly, adj., -lier, -liest. decorous.
—seem'li•ness, n.

seep, v. ooze; pass gradually. —seep'•
age, n.

seer, n. 1. person who sees. 2. prophet.
—seer'ess, n. fem.

seer'suck•er, n. crinkled cotton fabric.

see'saw', n. 1. children's sport played

on balancing plank. —v. 2. alternate,
waver, etc., as on seesaw.

seethe, v., seethed, seething. boil;
foam.

seg'ment, n. 1. part; section. —v. 2.
divide into segments. —seg'men•
ta'tion, n. —seg•men'tal, seg•
men'ta•ry, adj.

seg're•gate', v., -gated, -gating. separate from others. —seg're•ga'tion,
n.

se'gue (sā'gwā, seg'wā), v., segued,
seguing. —v. 1. continue at once
with the next section, as in piece of
music. 2. make smooth transition.
—n. 3. smooth transition.

seine (sān), n., v., seined, seining.
—n. 1. kind of fishing net. —v. 2. fish
with seine.

seis'mic (sīz'-), adj. of or caused by
earthquakes.

seis'mo•graph', n. instrument for recording earthquakes.

seize, v., seized, seizing. 1. take by
force or authority. 2. understand.

seiz'ure (sē'zhər), n. 1. act of seizing.
2. attack of illness.

sel'dom, adv. not often.

se•lect', v. 1. choose. —adj. 2. selected. 3. choice. —se•lec'tion, n.
—se•lec'tive, adj.

se•lect'man, n., pl. -men. town officer
in New England.

self, n., pl. selves, adj. —n. 1. person's
own nature. 2. personal advantage or
interests. —adj. 3. identical.

self'-as•sur'ance, n. confidence in
one's ability or rightness. —self'as•
sured', adj.

self'-cen'tered, adj. interested only in
oneself.

self'-con'fi•dence, n. faith in one's
own judgment, ability, etc. —self'-
con'fi•dent, adj.

self'-con'scious, adj. excessively
aware of being observed by others;
embarrassed or uneasy.

self'-con•tained', adj. 1. containing
within itself all that is necessary. 2. reserved in behavior.

self'-de•ter'mi•na'tion, n. right or
ability to choose government or actions.

self'-ev'i•dent, adj. obvious.

self'-im'age, n. conception or evaluation of oneself.

self'-im•por'tant, adj. having or
showing exaggerated sense of one's
own importance.

self'-in'ter•est, n. consideration of
things to one's benefit.

self'ish, adj. caring only for oneself.
—self'ish•ly, adv. —self'ish•ness,
n.

self'less, *adj.* having little concern for oneself; unselfish.

self'-made', *adj.* owing success entirely to one's own efforts.

self'-pos·sessed', *adj.* calm; poised. —**self'-pos·ses'sion**, *n.*

self'-re·spect', *n.* proper esteem for oneself. —**self'-re·spect'ing**, *adj.*

self'-right'eous (-rī'chas), *adj.* convinced one is morally right. —**self'-right'eous·ness**, *n.*

self'same', *adj.* identical.

self'-seek'ing, *n.* 1. selfish seeking of one's own interests or ends. —*adj.* 2. given to or characterized by self-seeking.

self'-serv'ice, *adj.* 1. of a commercial establishment in which customers serve themselves. 2. designed to be used without the aid of an attendant.

self'-serv'ing, *adj.* serving to further one's own selfish interests.

self'-styled', *adj.* so called only by oneself.

self'-willed', *adj.* stubborn; obstinate.

sell, *v.*, **sold, selling.** 1. part with for payment. 2. betray. 3. be for sale. —**sell'er**, *n.*

selt'zer, *n.* effervescent mineral water.

sel'vage, *n.* finished edge on fabric.

se·man'tics, *n.* study of meanings of words.

sem'a·phore', *n.* apparatus for signaling.

sem'blance, *n.* 1. appearance. 2. copy.

se'men, *n.* male reproductive fluid.

se·mes'ter, *n.* half school year.

sem'i·an'nu·al, *adj.* occurring every half-year. —**sem'i·an'nu·al·ly**, *adv.*

sem'i·cir'cle, *n.* half circle. —**sem'i·cir'cu·lar**, *adj.*

sem'i·co'lon, *n.* mark of punctuation (;) between parts of sentence.

sem'i·fi'nal, *adj.* 1. of the next to last round in a tournament. 2. semifinal round or bout.

sem'i·nal, *adj.* 1. of or consisting of semen. 2. influencing future development; original and creative.

sem'i·nar', *n.* class of advanced students.

sem'i·nar'y, *n., pl.* -naries. school, esp. for young women or for divinity students.

sem'i·pre'cious, *adj.* of moderate value.

Se·mit'ic, *n.* 1. language family of Africa and Asia, including Hebrew and Arabic. —*adj.* 2. of Semitic languages or their speakers.

sen'ate, *n.* legislative body, esp. (*cap.*) upper house of legislatures of United States, Canada, etc. —**sen'a·tor**, *n.* —**sen'a·to'ri·al**, *adj.*

send, *v.*, **sent, sending.** 1. cause to go. 2. have conveyed. 3. emit. —**send'er**, *n.*

se·nile (sē'nīl), *adj.* feeble, esp. because of old age. —**se·nil'i·ty**, *n.*

sen'ior, *adj.* 1. older. 2. of higher rank. 3. denoting last year in school. —*n.* 4. senior person. —**sen·ior'i·ty**, *n.*

senior citizen, person 65 years of age or more.

se·ñor' (se nyōr'), *n., pl.* -ñores. *Spanish.* 1. gentleman. 2. Mr. or sir. —**se·ño'ra**, *n. fem.*

se·ño·ri'ta (se'nyō rē'tä), *n. Spanish.* 1. Miss. 2. young lady.

sen·sa'tion, *n.* 1. operation of senses. 2. mental condition from such operation. 3. cause of excited interest.

sen·sa'tion·al, *adj.* 1. startling; exciting. 2. of senses or sensation. —**sen·sa'tion·al·ly**, *adv.*

sense, *n., v.*, **sensed, sensing.** —*n.* 1. faculty for perceiving physical things (sight, hearing, smell, etc.). 2. feeling so produced. 3. (*pl.*) consciousness. 4. (*often pl.*) rationality; prudence. 5. meaning. —*v.* 6. perceive by senses. —**sense'less**, *adj.*

sen·si·bil'i·ty, *n., pl.* -ties. 1. capacity for sensation. 2. (*often pl.*) sensitive feeling.

sen'si·ble, *adj.* 1. wise or practical. 2. aware. —**sen'si·bly**, *adv.*

sen'si·tive, *adj.* 1. having sensation. 2. easily affected. —**sen'si·tiv'i·ty**, *n.*

sen'si·tize', *v.*, -tized, -tizing. make sensitive.

sen'sor, *n.* device sensitive to light, temperature, or radiation level that transmits signal to another instrument.

sen'so·ry, *adj.* of sensation or senses.

sen'su·al, *adj.* inclined to pleasures of the senses. 2. lewd. —**sen'su·al·ist**, *n.* —**sen'su·al·ism**, *n.* —**sen'su·al·i·ty**, *n.*

sen'su·ous, *adj.* 1. of or affected by senses. 2. giving or seeking enjoyment through senses. —**sen'su·ous·ly**, *adv.* —**sen'su·ous·ness**, *n.*

sen'tence, *n., v.*, -tenced, -tencing. —*n.* 1. group of words expressing complete thought. 2. judgment; opinion. 3. assignment of punishment. —*v.* 4. pronounce sentence on.

sen·ten'tious, *adj.* 1. using maxims. 2. affectedly judicious. 3. pithy.

sen'tient (-shant), *adj.* having feeling. —**sen'tience**, *n.*

sen'ti·ment, *n.* 1. opinion. 2. emotion. 3. expression of belief or emotion.

sen'ti•men'tal, *adj.* expressing or showing tender emotion. **—sen'ti•men'tal•ist,** *n.* **—sen'ti•men'tal•ism,** *n.* **—sen'ti•men•tal'i•ty,** *n.* **—sen'ti•men'tal•ly,** *adv.*

sen'ti•nel, *n.* guard.

sen'try, *n., pl.* **-tries.** soldier on watch.

se'pal (sē'pəl), *n.* leaflike part of flower.

sep'a•rate', *v.,* **-rated, -rating,** *adj.* *—v.* (-rāt') 1. keep, put, or come apart. **—adj.** (-rit). 2. not connected; being apart. **—sep'a•ra'tion,** *n.* **—sep'a•ra•ble,** *adj.* **—sep'a•rate•ly,** *adv.*

sep'a•ra'tor, *n.* apparatus for separating ingredients.

se•pi'a, *n.* 1. brown pigment. 2. dark brown.

sep'sis, *n.* infection in blood. **—sep'tic,** *adj.*

Sep•tem'ber, *n.* ninth month of year.

sep•tet', *n.* group of seven. Also, **sep•tette'.**

septic tank, tank for decomposition of sewage.

sep'tu•a•ge•nar'i•an (sep'chŏŏ ə-), *n.* person 70 to 79 years old.

sep'ul•cher (-kər), *n.* burial place. Also, **sep'ul•chre.** **—se•pul'chral,** *adj.*

se'quel, *n.* 1. subsequent event; result. 2. literary work, film, etc., continuing earlier one.

se'quence, *n.* 1. succession; series. 2. result.

se•ques'ter, *v.* 1. seclude. 2. seize and hold. **—se'ques•tra'tion,** *n.*

se'quin, *n.* small spangle.

se•quoi'a, *n.* very large tree of northwest U.S.

se•ra'pe (sə rä'pē), *n.* blanketlike wrap used in Mexico.

ser'aph, *n., pl.* **-aphs, -aphim.** angel of highest order. **—se•raph'ic,** *adj.*

sere, *adj.* withered.

ser'e•nade', *n., v.,* **-naded, -nading.** *—n.* 1. music performed as compliment outside at night. *—v.* 2. compliment with serenade.

ser'en•dip'i•ty, *n.* luck in making discoveries.

se•rene', *adj.* 1. calm. 2. fair. **—se•ren'i•ty,** *n.* **—se•rene'ly,** *adv.*

serf, *n.* 1. person in feudal servitude. 2. slave. **—serf'dom,** *n.*

serge, *n.* stout twilled fabric.

ser'geant, *n.* noncommissioned officer above corporal.

se'ri•al, *n.* 1. story, etc., appearing in installments. **—adj.** 2. of serial. 3. of or in series. **—se'ri•al•ly,** *adv.*

se'ries, *n.* things in succession.

se'ri•ous, *adj.* 1. solemn. 2. important.

ser'mon, *n.* religious discourse.

ser'pent, *n.* snake. **—ser'pen•tine'** (-tēn'), *adj.*

ser•rat'ed (ser'ā tid), *adj.* toothed; notched. Also, **ser'rate** (ser'it).

se'rum, *n., pl.* **-rums, -ra.** 1. pale-yellow liquid in blood. 2. such liquid from animal immune to certain disease.

serv'ant, *n.* 1. person employed at domestic work.

serve, *v.,* **served, serving.** 1. act as servant. 2. help. 3. do official duty. 4. suffice. 5. undergo (imprisonment, etc.). 6. deliver.

serv'ice, *n., v.,* **-iced, -icing.** *—n.* 1. helpful activity. 2. domestic employment. 3. armed forces. 4. act of public worship. 5. set of dishes, etc. *—v.* 6. keep in repair.

serv'ice•a•ble, *adj.* usable.

serv'ice•man', *n., pl.* **-men.** 1. person in armed forces. 2. gasoline station attendant.

ser'vile (-vil), *adj.* slavishly obsequious. **—ser•vil'i•ty,** *n.*

ser'vi•tor, *n.* servant.

ser'vi•tude', *n.* bondage.

ses'a•me, *n.* small edible seed of tropical plant.

ses'qui•cen•ten'ni•al, *n.* 150th anniversary. **—ses'qui•cen•ten'ni•al,** *adj.*

ses'sion, *n.* sitting, as of a court or class.

set, *v.,* **set, setting,** *n., adj.* *—v.* 1. put or place. 2. put (broken bone) in position. 3. arrange (printing type). 4. pass below horizon. 5. become firm. *—n.* 6. group; complete collection. 7. radio or television receiver. 8. represented setting of action in drama. **—adj.** 9. prearranged. 10. fixed. 11. resolved.

set'back', *n.* return to worse condition.

set•tee', *n.* small sofa.

set'ter, *n.* kind of hunting dog.

set'ting, *n.* 1. surroundings. 2. music for certain words.

set'tle, *v.,* **-tled, -tling.** 1. agree. 2. pay. 3. take up residence. 4. colonize. 5. quiet. 6. come to rest. 7. deposit dregs. **—set'tle•ment,** *n.* **—set'tler,** *n.*

set'up', *n.* Informal. situation in detail.

sev'en, *n., adj.* six plus one. **—sev'enth,** *adj., n.*

sev'en•teen', *n., adj.* sixteen plus one. **—sev'en•teenth',** *adj., n.*

sev·en·ty, n., adj. ten times seven. **—sev'en·ti'eth,** adj., n.

sev·er, v. separate; break off. **—sev'er·ance,** n.

sev·er·al, adj. 1. some, but not many. 2. respective. 3. various. —n. 4. some.

se·vere', adj. -verer, -verest. 1. harsh. 2. serious. 3. plain. 4. violent or hard. **—se·ver'i·ty,** n. **—se·vere'ly,** adv.

sew (sō), v., sewed, sewed or sewn, sewing. join or make with thread and needle. **—sew'er,** n.

sew·age (soo'-), n. wastes carried by sewers.

sew'er, n. conduit for refuse, etc.

sex, n. 1. character of being male or female. 2. sexual intercourse. **—sex'u·al,** adj. **—sex'u·al·ly,** adv.

sex'ism, n. bias because of sex, esp. against women. **—sex'ist,** n., adj.

sex'tant, n. astronomical instrument for finding position.

sex·tet', n. group of six. Also, **sex·tette'.**

sex'ton, n. church caretaker.

sex'tu·ple, adj. sixfold.

sex'y, adj. sexier, sexiest. sexually interesting or exciting; erotic.

shab'by, adj. -bier, -biest. 1. worn; wearing worn clothes. 2. mean. **—shab'bi·ly,** adv. **—shab'bi·ness,** n.

shack, n. rough cabin.

shack'le, n., v., -led, -ling. —n. 1. iron bond for wrist, ankle, etc. 2. U-shaped bolt of padlock. —v. 3. put shackle on; restrain.

shad, n. kind of herring.

shade, n., v., shaded, shading. —n. 1. slightly dark, cool place. 2. ghost. 3. degree of color. 4. slight amount. —v. 5. protect from light.

shad'ow, n. 1. dark image made by body intercepting light. 2. shade. 3. trace. —v. 4. shade. 5. follow secretly. **—shad'ow·y,** adj.

shad'ow·box', v. go through motions of boxing without an opponent, as in training.

shad'y, adj., shadier, shadiest. 1. in shade. 2. arousing suspicion. **—shad'i·ness,** n.

shaft, n. 1. long slender rod. 2. beam. 3. revolving bar in engine. 4. vertical space.

shag, n. matted wool, hair, etc. 2. napped cloth. **—shag'gy,** adj.

shah, n. (formerly) ruler of Persia (now Iran).

shake, v., shook, shaken, shaking, n. —v. 1. move with quick irregular motions. 2. tremble. 3. agitate. —n. 4. act of shaking. 5. tremor. **—shak'er,** n.

shake'down', n. 1. extortion, as by blackmail. 2. thorough search.

shake'up', n. Informal. organizational reform.

shak'y, adj., shakier, shakiest. 1. not firm; insecure. 2. quavering. 3. affected by fright. **—shak'i·ly,** adv. **—shak'i·ness,** n.

shale, n. kind of layered rock.

shall, v. 1. am (is, are) going to. 2. am (is, are) obliged or commanded to.

shal·lot', n. small onionlike plant.

shal'low, adj. not deep.

sham, n., v. 1. pretense or imitation. —adj. 2. pretended.

sham'ble, v., -bled, -bling, n. —v. 1. walk awkwardly. —n. 2. shambling gait. 3. (pl.) scene of confusion.

shame, n., v., shamed, shaming. —n. 1. painful feeling from wrong or foolish act or circumstance. 2. disgrace. —v. 3. cause to feel shame. **—shame'ful,** adj. **—shame'less,** adj.

shame'faced', adj. 1. bashful. 2. showing shame.

sham·poo', v. 1. wash (hair, rugs, or upholstery). —n. 2. act of shampooing. 3. soap, etc., for shampooing.

sham'rock, n. plant with three-part leaf.

shang·hai', v., -haied, -haiing. (formerly) abduct for service as sailor.

shank, n. part of leg between knee and ankle.

shan'ty, n., pl. -ties. rough hut.

shape, n., v., shaped, shaping. —n. 1. form. 2. nature. —v. 3. give form to; take form. 4. adapt. **—shape'less,** adj.

shape'ly, adj., -lier, -liest. handsome in shape. **—shape'li·ness,** n.

shard, n. fragment, esp. of broken earthenware.

share, n., v., shared, sharing. —n. 1. due individual portion. 2. portion of corporate stock. —v. 3. distribute. 4. use, enjoy, etc., jointly. **—shar'er,** n.

share'crop'per, n. tenant farmer who pays as rent part of the crop.

shark, n. 1. marine fish, often ferocious. 2. person who victimizes.

shark'skin', n. smooth, silky fabric with dull surface.

sharp, adj. 1. having thin cutting edge or fine point. 2. abrupt. 3. keen. 4. shrewd. 5. raised in musical pitch. —adv. 6. punctually. —n. 7. musical tone one half step above given tone. **—sharp'en,** v. **—sharp'en·er,** n. **—sharp'ly,** adv. **—sharp'ness,** n.

sharp'er, n. swindler.

sharp'shoot'er, n. skilled shooter.

shat'ter, v. break in pieces.

shave, v., **shaved, shaved** or **shaven, shaving,** n. —v. 1. remove hair with razor. 2. cut thin slices. —n. 3. act of shaving.

shav'ings, n.pl. thin slices of wood.

shawl, n. long covering for head and shoulders.

she, pron. female last mentioned.

sheaf, n., pl. **sheaves.** bundle.

shear, v., **sheared, sheared** or **shorn, shearing.** clip, as wool.

shears, n.pl. large scissors.

sheath, n. 1. case for sword blade. 2. any similar covering.

sheathe, v., **sheathed, sheathing.** put into or enclose in sheath.

shed, v., **shed, shedding,** n. —v. 1. pour forth. 2. cast (light). 3. throw off. —n. 4. simple enclosed shelter.

sheen, n. brightness.

sheep, n., pl. **sheep.** mammal valued for fleece and flesh.

sheep'ish, adj. embarrassed or timid.

sheer, adj. 1. very thin. 2. complete. 3. steep. —v., n. 4. swerve.

sheet, n. 1. large piece of cloth used as bedding. 2. broad thin mass or piece. 3. rope or chain to control sail.

sheik, n. (Arab) chief.

shek'el (shek'əl), n. ancient Hebrew and modern Israeli monetary unit.

shelf, n., pl. **shelves.** 1. horizontal slab on wall, etc., for holding objects. 2. ledge.

shell, n. 1. hard outer covering. 2. shotgun cartridge. 3. explosive missile from cannon. 4. light racing boat. —v. 5. remove shell from. 6. take from shell. 7. bombard with shells.

shel·lac', n., v., **-lacked, -lacking.** —n. 1. substance used in varnish. 2. varnish. —v. 3. coat with shellac.

shell'fish', n. aquatic animal having shell.

shel'ter, n. 1. place of protection. —v. 2. protect.

shelve, v., **shelved, shelving.** 1. put on shelf. 2. lay aside. 3. furnish with shelves. 4. slope.

she·nan'i·gans, n.pl. Informal. mischief.

shep'herd, n. 1. person who tends sheep. —v. 2. guide while guarding. —**shep'herd·ess,** n.fem.

sher'bet, n. frozen fruit-flavored dessert.

sher'iff, n. county law-enforcement officer.

sher'ry, n., pl. **-ries.** strong wine served as cocktail.

shib'bo·leth (shib'ə lith, -leth'), n. 1. peculiarity of pronunciation or usage that distinguishes a group. 2. slogan; catchword.

shield, n. 1. plate of armor carried on arm. —v. 2. protect.

shift, v. 1. move about. 2. interchange positions. —n. 3. act of shifting. 4. period of work.

shift'less, adj. resourceless or lazy.

shift'y, adj., **shiftier, shiftiest.** tricky; devious. —**shift'i·ly,** adv. —**shift'i·ness,** n.

shill, n. person who poses as a customer to lure others.

shil·le'lagh (shə lā'lē), n. rough Irish walking stick or cudgel.

shil'ling, n. former British coin, 20th part of pound.

shil'ly-shal'ly, v., **-lied, -lying.** be irresolute.

shim'mer, v. 1. glow faintly; flicker. —n. 2. faint glow. —**shim'mer·y,** adj.

shim'my, n., pl. **-mies,** v., **-mied, -mying.** Informal. —n. 1. vibration. —v. 2. vibrate.

shin, n. front of leg from knee to ankle.

shin'dig', n. Informal. elaborate and usu. large party.

shine, v., **shone** or (for 4) **shined, shining,** n. —v. 1. give forth light. 2. sparkle. 3. excel. 4. polish. —n. 5. radiance. 6. polish. —**shin'y,** adj.

shin'gle, n., v., **-gled, -gling.** —n. 1. thin slab used in overlapping rows as covering. 2. close haircut. 3. (pl.) viral skin disease marked by blisters. —v. 4. cover with shingles. 5. cut (hair) short.

shin'ny, n. form of hockey.

shin splints, painful condition of shins associated with strenuous activity.

ship, n., v., **shipped, shipping.** —n. 1. vessel for use on water. —v. 2. send as freight. 3. engage to serve on ship. —**ship'board',** n. —**ship'mate',** n. —**ship'ment,** n. —**ship'per,** n. —**ship'ping,** n.

ship'shape', adj., adv. in good order.

ship'wreck', n. destruction of ship.

ship'wright', n. carpenter in ship repair or construction.

ship'yard', n. place where ships are built or repaired.

shire, n. Brit. county.

shirk, v. 1. evade (obligation). —n. 2. Also, **shirk'er.** person who shirks.

shirr, v. 1. gather (cloth) on parallel threads. 2. bake (eggs).

shirt, n. garment for upper body.

shiv'er, v. 1. tremble as with cold. 2. splinter. —n. 3. quiver. 4. splinter. —**shiv'er·y,** adj.

shoal, n. 1. shallow part of stream. 2. large number, esp. of fish.

shoat, n. young pig.

shock, n. 1. violent blow, impact, etc. 2. anything emotionally upsetting. 3. state of nervous collapse. 4. group of sheaves of grain. 5. bushy mass of hair, etc. —v. 6. strike with force, horror, etc.

shod'dy, adj., **-di•er**, **-di•est**. of poor quality. —**shod'di•ly**, adv. —**shod'di•ness**, n.

shoe, n., v., **shod**, **shoeing**. —n. 1. external covering for foot. 2. shoelike machine part. —v. 3. provide with shoes. —**shoe'string**, n.

shoe'horn, n. shaped object to assist in slipping into shoe.

shoe'mak'er, n. person who makes or mends shoes.

shoe'string', n. 1. lace or string for tying shoes. 2. very small amount of money.

shoo, v., **shooed**, **shooing**. drive away by shouting "shoo."

shoot, v. 1. hit or kill with bullet, etc. 2. discharge (firearm, bow, etc.). 3. pass or send rapidly along. 4. emit. 5. grow; come forth. —n. 6. shooting contest. 7. young twig, etc. —**shoot'er**, n.

shop, n., v., **shopped**, **shopping**. —n. 1. store. 2. workshop. —v. 3. inspect or purchase goods. —**shop'per**, n.

shop'lift'er, n. person who steals from shops while posing as customer.

shop'talk', n. conversation about one's work or occupation.

shore, n., v., **shored**, **shoring**. —n. 1. prop. —n. 2. prop. 3. land beside water. 4. land or country.

shorn, v. pp. of shear.

short, adj. 1. not long or tall. 2. rudely brief. 3. scanty. 4. inferior. 5. crumbly, as pastry. 6. abruptly. —n. 7. anything short. 8. (pl.) short, loose trousers. 9. short circuit. —**short'en**, v. —**short'ness**, n.

short'age, n. scarcity.

short'change', v., **-changed**, **-changing**. 1. give less than the correct change to. 2. cheat; defraud.

short circuit, Elect. abnormal connection between two points in circuit.

short'com'ing, n. defect.

short'cut', n. shorter way to goal.

short'en•ing, n. 1. butter or other fat used to make pastry short. 2. act of making or becoming short.

short'hand', n. system of swift handwriting.

short'-hand'ed, adj. not having enough workers.

short'-lived' (-līvd', -livd'), adj. lasting but short time.

short'ly, adv. in short time.

short shrift, little attention or consideration.

short'•sight'ed, adj. lacking foresight.

short'stop', n. Baseball player or position between second and third base.

short'wave', n. radio frequencies used for long-distance, as intercontinental, transmission.

shot, n., pl. **shots** or (for 3) **shot**. 1. discharge of firearm, bow, etc. 2. range of fire. 3. (often pl.) lead pellets. 4. act or instance of shooting. 5. person who shoots. 6. heavy metal ball.

shot'gun', n. kind of smoothbore gun.

shot put, competition in which heavy metal ball is thrown for distance. —**shot'-put'ter**, n.

should, v. pt. of shall.

shoul'der, n. 1. part of body from neck to upper joint of arm or foreleg. 2. unpaved edge of road. —v. 3. push as with shoulder. 4. take up, as burden.

shout, v. 1. call or speak loudly. —n. 2. loud cry. —**shout'er**, n.

shove, v., **shoved**, **shoving**, n. —v. 1. push hard. —n. 2. hard push.

shov'el, n., v., **-eled**, **-eling**. —n. 1. implement with broad scoop and handle. —v. 2. dig or clear with shovel. —**shov'el•er**, n.

show, v., **showed**, **shown** or **showed**, **showing**, n. —v. 1. display. 2. guide. 3. explain. 4. prove. 5. be visible. —n. 6. exhibition. 7. acted entertainment. 8. appearance.

show'down', n. decisive confrontation.

show'er, n. 1. short fall of rain. 2. any similar fall. 3. bath in which water falls from above. —v. 4. rain briefly. 5. give liberally. —**show'er•y**, adj.

show'-off', n. person who seeks attention by ostentatious behavior.

show'y, adj., **showier**, **showiest**. conspicuous; ostentatious.

shrap'nel, n. shell filled with missiles.

shred, n., v., **shredded** or **shred**, **shredding**. —n. 1. torn piece or strip. 2. bit. —v. 3. reduce to shreds.

shrew, n. 1. quarrelsome woman. 2. small mouselike mammal. —**shrew'ish**, adj.

shrewd, adj. astute. —**shrewd•ly**, adv. —**shrewd'ness**, n.

shriek, n. 1. loud shrill cry. —v. 2. utter shrieks.

shrike, n. predatory bird.

shrill, adj. 1. high-pitched; sharp. —v. 2. cry shrilly. —**shril'ly**, adv. —**shrill'ness**, n.

shrimp, n. small long-tailed edible shellfish.

shrine, n. place for sacred relics.

shrink, v., **shrank** or **shrunk** or **shrunken, shrinking. 1.** draw back. **2.** become smaller.

shrink'age, n. **1.** act of shrinking. **2.** amount of shrinking.

shriv'el, v., **-eled, -eling.** wrinkle in drying.

shroud, n. **1.** burial gown or cloth. **2.** (pl.) set of ropes supporting masts of vessel. —v. **3.** wrap; cover.

shrub, n. woody perennial plant. —**shrub'ber•y,** n.

shrug, v., **shrugged, shrugging.** —v. **1.** move shoulders to show ignorance, indifference, etc. —n. **2.** this movement.

shtick, n. Slang. **1.** show-business routine. **2.** special interest, talent, etc. Also, **shtik.**

shuck, n. **1.** husk. **2.** shell. —v. **3.** remove shucks from.

shud'der, v. **1.** tremble, as from horror. —n. **2.** this movement.

shuf'fle, v., **-fled, -fling.** —v. **1.** drag feet in walking. **2.** mix (playing cards). **3.** shift. —n. **4.** shuffling gait. **5.** act of shuffling of cards.

shuf'fle•board', n. game played on marked floor surface.

shun, v., **shunned, shunning.** avoid.

shunt, v. divert; sidetrack.

shut, v., **shut, shutting,** adj. —v. **1.** close. **2.** confine. **3.** exclude. —adj. **4.** closed.

shut'-in', n. person confined, as by illness, to the house, a hospital, etc.

shut'out', n. game in which one side does not score.

shut'ter, n. **1.** cover for window. **2.** device for opening and closing camera lens.

shut'tle, n., v., **-tled, -tling.** —n. **1.** device for moving thread back and forth in weaving. **2.** bus, plane, etc., moving between two destinations. —v. **3.** move quickly back and forth.

shut'tle•cock', n. feathered object hit back and forth in badminton.

shy, adj., **shyer** or **shier, shyest** or **shi•est,** v., **shied, shying,** n., pl. **shies.** —adj. **1.** bashful. **2.** wary. **3.** short. —v. **4.** start aside, as in fear. **5.** throw suddenly. —n. **6.** shying movement. **7.** sudden throw. —**shy'ly,** adv. —**shy'ness,** n.

shy'ster, n. Informal. unscrupulous lawyer.

Si•a•mese' twins, twins joined together by some body part.

sib'i•lant, adj. **1.** hissing. —n. **2.** hissing sound. —**sib'i•lance,** n.

sib'ling, n. brother or sister.

sib'yl (sib'əl), n. female prophet. —**sib'yl•line,** adj.

sic, v., **sicked, sicking,** adv. —v. **1.** urge to attack. —adv. **2.** Latin. so (it reads).

sick, adj. **1.** ill; not well. **2.** of sickness. **3.** nauseated. —n.pl. **4.** sick people. —**sick'ness,** n. —**sick'en,** v.

sick'le, n. reaping implement with curved blade.

sick'ly, adj., **-lier, -liest,** adv. **1.** ailing. **2.** faint; weak. —adv. **3.** in sick manner.

side, n., adj., v., **sided, siding.** —n. **1.** edge. **2.** surface. **3.** part other than front, back, top, or bottom. **4.** aspect. **5.** region. **6.** faction. —adj. **7.** at, from, or toward side. **8.** subordinate. —v. **9.** align oneself.

side'board', n. dining-room cupboard.

side'burns', n.pl. short whiskers in front of ears.

side'kick', n. **1.** close friend. **2.** confederate or assistant.

side'line', n., v., **-lined, -lining.** —n. **1.** business or activity in addition to one's primary business. **2.** additional line of goods. **3.** line defining the side of an athletic field. —v. **4.** remove from action.

side'long', adj., adv. to or toward the side.

si•de're•al, adj. of or determined by stars.

side'sad'dle, adv. with both legs on one side of a saddle.

side'show', n. **1.** minor show connected with principal one, as at circus. **2.** subordinate event or spectacle.

side'-step', v., **-stepped, -stepping.** avoid, as by stepping aside.

side'swipe', v., **-swiped, -swiping.** strike along side.

side'track', v. divert.

side'walk', n. paved walk along street.

side'ward, adj. toward one side. —**side'ward, side'wards,** adv.

side'ways', adj., adv. **1.** with side foremost. **2.** toward or from a side. Also, **side'wise'.**

sid'ing, n. short railroad track for halted cars.

si'dle, v., **-dled, -dling.** move sideways or furtively.

SIDS, sudden infant death syndrome.

siege, n. surrounding of place to force surrender.

si•en'na, n. yellowish- or reddish-brown pigment.

si•er'ra, n. chain of hills or mountains whose peaks suggest the teeth of a saw.

si·es'ta, *n.* midday nap or rest.

sieve (siv), *n.*, *v.*, **sieved, sieving.** —*n.* 1. meshed implement for separating coarse and fine loose matter. —*v.* 2. sift.

sift, *v.* separate with sieve. —**sift'er,** *n.*

sigh, *v.* 1. exhale audibly in grief, weariness, etc. 2. yearn. —*n.* 3. act or sound of sighing.

sight, *n.* 1. power of seeing. 2. glimpse; view. 3. range of vision. 4. device for guiding aim. 5. interesting place. —*v.* 6. get sight of. 7. aim by sights. —**sight'less,** *adj.*

sight'ly, *adj.*, **-lier, -liest.** pleasing to sight. —**sight'li·ness,** *n.*

sight'see'ing, *n.* visiting new places of interest. —**sight'se'er,** *n.* —**sight'see',** *v.*

sign, *n.* 1. indication. 2. conventional mark, figure, etc. 3. advertising board. —*v.* 4. put signature to. —**sign'er,** *n.*

sig'nal, *n.*, *adj.*, *v.*, **-naled, -naling.** —*n.* 1. symbolic communication. —*adj.* 2. serving as signal. 3. notable. —*v.* 4. communicate by symbols. —**sig'nal·er,** *n.*

sig'nal·ize', *v.*, **-ized, -izing.** make notable.

sig'nal·ly, *adv.* notably.

sig'na·to'ry, *n.*, *pl.* **-ries.** signer.

sig'na·ture, *n.* 1. person's name in own handwriting. 2. *Music.* sign indicating key or time of piece.

sig'net, *n.* small seal.

sig·nif'i·cance, *n.* 1. importance. 2. meaning. —**sig·nif'i·cant,** *adj.*

sig'ni·fy', *v.*, **-fied, -fying.** 1. make known. 2. mean. —**sig'ni·fi·ca'tion,** *n.*

Sikh (sēk), *n.* member of religion of India that rejects Hindu caste system. —**Sikh'ism,** *n.*

si'lage (sī'lij), *n.* fodder preserved in silo.

si'lence, *n.*, *v.*, **-lenced, -lencing.** —*n.* 1. absence of sound. 2. muteness. —*v.* 3. bring to silence. —**si'lent,** *adj.*

sil'hou·ette' (sil'oo et'), *n.*, *v.*, **-etted, -etting.** —*n.* 1. filled-in outline. —*v.* 2. show in silhouette.

sil'i·ca, *n.* silicon dioxide, appearing as quartz, sand, flint, etc.

sil'i·con', *n.* abundant nonmetallic element.

sil'i·cone', *n.* polymer with silicon and oxygen atoms, used in adhesives, lubricants, etc.

silk, *n.* 1. fine soft fiber produced by silkworms. 2. thread or cloth made of

it. —*adj.* 3. Also, **silk'en, silk'y.** of silk.

silk'worm', *n.* caterpillar that spins silk to make its cocoon.

sill, *n.* horizontal piece beneath window, door, or wall.

sil'ly, *adj.*, **-lier, -liest.** 1. stupid. 2. absurd. —**sil'li·ness,** *n.*

si'lo, *n.*, *pl.* **-los.** airtight structure to hold green fodder.

silt, *n.* 1. earth, etc., carried and deposited by a stream. —*v.* 2. fill with silt.

sil'ver, *n.* 1. valuable white metallic element. 2. coins, utensils, etc., of silver. 3. whitish gray. —*adj.* 4. of or plated with silver. 5. eloquent. 6. indicating 25th anniversary. —**sil'ver·y,** *adj.*

sil'ver·fish', *n.* 1. wingless, silvery-gray insect that damages books, wallpaper, etc.

sil'ver·ware', *n.* eating and serving utensils of silver or other metal.

sim'i·an, *n.* 1. ape or monkey. —*adj.* 2. of apes or monkeys.

sim'i·lar, *adj.* with general likeness. —**sim'i·lar'i·ty,** *n.* —**sim'i·lar·ly,** *adv.*

sim'i·le', *n.* phrase expressing resemblance.

si·mil'i·tude', *n.* 1. likeness. 2. comparison.

sim'mer, *v.* remain or keep near boiling.

sim'per, *v.* 1. smile affectedly. —*n.* 2. affected smile.

sim'ple, *adj.*, **-pler, -plest.** 1. easy to grasp, use, etc. 2. plain. 3. mentally weak. —**sim·plic'i·ty,** *n.* —**sim'ply,** *adv.*

sim'ple·ton, *n.* fool.

sim'pli·fy', *v.*, **-fied, -fying.** make simpler. —**sim'pli·fi·ca'tion,** *n.*

sim·plis'tic, *adj.* foolishly or naïvely simple. —**sim·plis'ti·cal·ly,** *adv.*

sim'u·late', *v.*, **-lated, -lating.** feign; imitate. —**sim'u·la'tion,** *n.* —**sim'u·la·tive,** *adj.*

si'mul·ta'ne·ous, *adj.* occurring at the same time. —**si'mul·ta'ne·ous·ly,** *adv.* —**si'mul·ta·ne'i·ty,** *n.*; **si'mul·ta'ne·ous·ness,** *n.*

sin, *n.*, *v.*, **sinned, sinning.** —*n.* 1. offense, esp. against divine law. —*v.* 2. commit sin. —**sin'ful,** *adj.* —**sin'ful·ly,** *adv.* —**sin'ful·ness,** *n.*

since, *adv.* 1. from then till now. 2. subsequently. —*conj.* 3. from time when. 4. because.

sin·cere', *adj.*, **-cerer, -cerest.** honest; genuine. —**sin·cer'i·ty,** *n.* —**sin·cere'ly,** *adv.*

si′ne•cure′ (sī′ni kyŏŏr′), n. job without real responsibilities.

si′ne qua non′ (sin′ə kwä nōn′, non′, kwä), indispensable condition or element.

sin′ew, n. 1. tendon. 2. strength. —**sin′ew•y**, adj.

sing, v., **sang** or **sung**, **sung**, **singing**. 1. utter words to music. 2. acclaim. —**sing′er**, n.

singe, v., **singed**, **singeing**, n. scorch.

sin′gle, adj., v., **-gled**, **-gling**, n —adj. 1. one only. 2. unmarried. —v. 3. select. —n. 4. something single. 5. unmarried person. —**sin′gly**, adv.

single file, line of persons or things one behind the other.

sin′gle-hand′ed, adj. 1. accomplished by one person. 2. by one's own effort; unaided. —adv. 3. by one person alone. —**sin′gle-hand′ed•ly**, adv.

sin′gle-mind′ed, adj. having or showing a single aim or purpose.

sing′song′, adj. monotonous in rhythm.

sin′gu•lar, adj. 1. extraordinary. 2. separate. 3. denoting one person or thing. —n. 4. singular number or form. —**sin′gu•lar′i•ty**, n. —**sin′gu•lar•ly**, adv.

sin′is•ter, adj. threatening evil.

sink, v., **sank** or **sunk**, **sunk** or **sunken**, **sinking**, n. —v. 1. descend or drop. 2. deteriorate gradually. 3. submerge. 4. dig (a hole, etc.). 5. bury (pipe, etc.). —n. 6. basin connected with drain. —**sink′er**, n.

sin′ner, n. person who sins.

sin′u•ous, adj. winding.

si′nus, n. cavity or passage, esp. one in the skull connecting with the nasal cavities.

sip, v., **sipped**, **sipping**, n. —v. 1. drink little at a time. —n. 2. act of sipping. 3. amount taken in sip.

si′phon, n. 1. tube for drawing liquids by gravity and suction to another container. —v. 2. move by siphon.

sir, n. 1. formal term of address to man. 2. title of knight or baronet.

sire, n., v., **sired**, **siring**. —n. 1. male parent. —v. 2. beget.

si′ren, n. 1. mythical, alluring sea nymph. 2. noise-making device used on emergency vehicles.

sir′up, n. syrup.

si′sal, n. fiber used in ropes.

sis′sy, n., pl. **-sies**. 1. effeminate boy or man. 2. timid or cowardly person.

sis′ter, n. 1. daughter of one's parents. 2. nun. —**sis′ter•hood**, n. —**sis′ter•ly**, adj.

sis′ter-in-law′, n., pl. **sisters-in-law**.

1. sister of one's spouse. 2. wife of one's brother.

sit, v., **sat**, **sitting**. 1. rest on lower part of trunk of body. 2. be situated. 3. pose. 4. be in session. 5. seat. —**sit′ter**, n.

site, n. position; location.

sit′-in′, n. protest by demonstrators who occupy premises or seats refused to them.

sit′u•ate′, v., **-ated**, **-ating**. settle; locate.

sit′u•a′tion, n. 1. location. 2. condition. 3. job.

six, n., adj. five plus one. —**sixth**, adj., n.

six′teen′, n., adj. ten plus six. —**six•teenth′**, adj., n.

six′ty, n., adj. ten times six. —**six′ti•eth**, adj., n.

siz′a•ble, adj. fairly large. Also, **size′-a•ble**.

size, n., v., **sized**, **sizing**. —n. 1. dimensions or extent. 2. great magnitude. 3. Also, **sizing**. coating for paper, cloth, etc. —v. 4. sort according to size. 5. treat with sizing.

siz′zle, v., **-zled**, **-zling**, n. —v. 1. make hissing sound, as in frying. —n. 2. sizzling sound.

skate, n., pl. **skates** or (for 3) **skate**, v., **skated**, **skating**. —n. 1. steel runner fitted to shoe for gliding on ice. 2. roller skate. 3. flat-bodied marine fish; ray. —v. 4. glide on skates. —**skat′er**, n.

skate′board′, n. oblong board on roller-skate wheels.

skeet, n. sport of shooting at clay targets hurled to simulate flight of game birds. Also, **skeet shooting**.

skein (skān), n. coil of yarn or thread.

skel′e•ton, n. bony framework of human or animal. —**skel′e•tal**, adj.

skep′tic, n. person who doubts or questions. —**skep′ti•cal•ly**, adv. —**skep′ti•cal**, adj. —**skep′ti•cism**, n.

sketch, n. 1. simple hasty drawing. 2. rough plan. —v. 3. make sketch (of).

sketch′y, adj., **sketchier**, **sketchiest**. vague; approximate. —**sketch′i•ly**, adv.

skew (skyōō). v. turn aside; swerve or slant.

skew′er, n. 1. pin for holding meat, etc., while cooking. —v. 2. fasten with skewer.

ski, n. 1. slender board fastened to shoe for traveling over snow. —v. 2. travel by skis. —**ski′er**, n.

skid, v., **skidded**, **skidding**. —n. 1. surface on which to support or slide heavy object. 2. act of skidding. —v. 3. slide on skids. 4. slip.

skiff, n. small boat.

skill, n. expertness; dexterity. —**skilled,** adj. —**skill′ful,** adj. —**skill′ful·ly,** adv.

skil′let, n. frying pan.

skim, v. **skimmed, skimming.** 1. remove from surface of liquid. 2. move lightly on surface.

skim milk, milk from which cream has been removed. Also, **skimmed milk.**

skimp, v. scrimp.

skimp′y, adj., **skimpier, skimpiest.** scant. —**skimp′i·ness,** n.

skin, n., v. **skinned, skinning.** —n. 1. outer covering, as of body. —v. 2. strip of skin. —**skin′ner,** n.

skin diving, underwater swimming with flippers and face mask, sometimes with scuba gear. —**skin diver,** n.

skin′flint′, n. stingy person.

skin′ny, adj., **-nier, -niest.** very thin.

skip, v., **skipped, skipping,** n. —v. 1. spring; leap. 2. omit; disregard. —n. 3. light jump.

skip′per, n. 1. master of ship. —v. 2. act as skipper of.

skir′mish, n. 1. brief fight between small forces. —v. 2. engage in skirmish. —**skir′mish·er,** n.

skirt, n. 1. part of gown, etc., below waist. 2. woman's garment extending down from waist. 3. (pl.) outskirts. —v. 4. pass around edge of. 5. border.

skit, n. short comedy.

skit′tish, adj. apt to shy; restless.

skul·dug′ger·y, n., pl. **-geries.** trickery.

skulk, v. sneak about; lie hidden. —**skulk′er,** n.

skull, n. bony framework around brain.

skunk, n. 1. small, striped, fur-bearing mammal that sprays acrid fluid to defend itself. 2. contemptible person.

sky, n., pl. **skies.** region high above earth. —**sky′ward,** adv., adj.

sky′dive′, v., **-dived, -diving.** make parachute jump with longest free fall possible. —**sky′div′er,** n.

sky′jack′, v. Informal. seize (aircraft) while in flight. —**sky′jack′er,** n.

sky′light′, n. window in roof, ceiling, etc.

sky′line′, n. 1. outline against sky. 2. apparent horizon.

sky′rock′et, n. firework that rises into air before exploding.

sky′scrap′er, n. building with many stories.

slab, n. broad flat piece of material.

slack, adj. 1. loose. 2. inactive. —adv.

3. slackly. —n. 4. slack part. 5. inactive period. —v. 6. slacken. —**slack′ly,** adv. —**slack′ness,** n.

slack′en, v. 1. make or become slack. 2. weaken.

slacks, n.pl. loose trousers.

slag, n. refuse matter from smelting metal from ore.

slake, v., **slaked, slaking.** 1. allay (thirst, etc.). 2. treat (lime) with water.

sla′lom (slä′ləm -lôm), n. downhill ski race over winding course, around numerous barriers.

slam, v., **slammed, slamming.** —v. 1. shut noisily. —n. 2. this sound.

slan′der, n. 1. false, defamatory spoken statement. —v. 2. utter slander against. —**slan′der·ous,** adj.

slang, n. markedly informal language. —**slang′y,** adj.

slant, v. 1. slope. —n. 2. slope. 3. opinion. —**slant′ing·ly,** adv.

slap, n., v. **slapped, slapping.** —n. 1. strike, esp. with open hand. —n. 2. such blow.

slap′dash′, adj. hasty and careless.

slap′stick′, n. boisterous comedy with broad farce and horseplay.

slash, v. 1. cut, esp. violently and at random. —n. 2. such cut.

slat, n., v. **slatted, slatting.** —n. 1. thin narrow strip. —v. 2. furnish with slats.

slate, n., v., **slated, slating.** —n. 1. kind of layered rock. 2. dark bluish gray. 3. list of nominees. —v. 4. put in line for appointment.

slat′tern, n. untidy woman. —**slat′tern·ly,** adj.

slaugh′ter, n. 1. killing of animals, esp. for food. 2. brutal killing of people, esp. in great numbers. —v. 3. kill for food. 4. massacre. —**slaugh′ter·house′,** n.

slave, n., v., **slaved, slaving.** —n. 1. person owned by another. —v. 2. drudge. —**slav′er·y,** n.

slav′er, v. 1. let saliva run from mouth. —n. 2. saliva coming from mouth.

Slav′ic, n. 1. language family that includes Russian, Polish, Czech, etc. —adj. 2. of these languages or their speakers.

slav′ish (slāv′-), adj. 1. without originality. 2. servile. —**slav′ish·ly,** adv.

slaw, n. chopped seasoned raw cabbage.

slay, v., **slew, slain, slaying.** kill. —**slay′er,** n.

slea′zy (slē′zē), adj., **-zier, -ziest.** shoddy. —**slea′zi·ness,** n.

sled, n., v., **sledded, sledding.** —n. 1.

vehicle traveling on snow. —v. 2. ride on sled.

sledge, n., v., **sledged, sledging.** —n. 1. heavy sledlike vehicle. 2. Also, **sledge'ham'mer.** large heavy hammer. —v. 3. travel by sledge.

sleek, adj. 1. smooth; glossy. —v. 2. smooth. —**sleek'ly,** adv. —**sleek'-ness,** n.

sleep, v., **slept, sleeping,** n. —v. 1. rest during natural suspension of consciousness. —n. 2. state or period of sleeping. —**sleep'less,** adj. —**sleep'y,** adj. —**sleep'i·ly,** adv.

sleep'er, n. 1. person who sleeps. 2. railroad car equipped for sleeping. 3. raillike foundation member. 4. unexpected success.

sleet, n. hard frozen rain.

sleeve, n. part of garment covering arm.

sleigh, n. light sled.

sleight of hand, (slīt), skill in conjuring or juggling.

slen'der, adj. 1. small in circumference. 2. scanty or weak. —**slen'der·ize',** v. —**slen'der·ness,** n.

sleuth, n. detective.

slew, pt. of **slay.**

slice, n., v., **sliced, slicing.** —n. 1. broad flat piece. —v. 2. cut into slices. —**slic'er,** n.

slick, adj. 1. sleek. 2. sly. 3. slippery. —n. 4. oil-covered area. —v. 5. smooth.

slick'er, n. raincoat.

slide, v., **slid, sliding,** n. —v. 1. move easily; glide. —n. 2. act of sliding. 3. area for sliding. 4. landslide. 5. glass plate used in microscope. 6. transparent picture.

sliding scale, scale, as of prices, that varies with such conditions as the ability of individuals to pay.

slight, adj. 1. trifling; small. 2. slim. —v. 3. treat as unimportant. —n. 4. such treatment; snub. —**slight'ness,** n.

slight'ly, adv. barely; partly.

sli'ly, adv. slyly.

slim, adj., **slimmer, slimmest.** 1. slender. 2. poor. —v. 3. make or become slim. —**slim'ly,** adv. —**slim'ness,** n.

slime, n. 1. thin sticky mud. 2. sticky secretion of plants or animals. —**slim'y,** adj.

sling, n., v., **slung, slinging.** —n. 1. straplike device for hurling stones. 2. looped rope, bandage, etc., as support. —v. 3. hurl. 4. hang loosely.

sling'shot', n. Y-shaped stick with elastic strip between prongs, for shooting small missiles.

slink, v., **slunk, slinking.** go furtively. —**slink'y,** adj.

slip, v., **slipped, slipping,** n. —v. 1. move or go easily. 2. slide accidentally. 3. escape. 4. make mistake. —n. 5. act of slipping. 6. mistake. 7. undergarment. 8. space between piers for vessel. 9. twig for propagating. —**slip'page,** n.

slip'per, n. light shoe.

slip'per·y, adj. 1. causing slipping. 2. tending to slip.

slip'shod', adj. careless.

slit, v., **slit, slitting.** —v. 1. cut apart or in strips. —n. 2. narrow opening.

slith'er, v. slide.

sliv'er, n. splinter.

slob, n. slovenly or boorish person.

slob'ber, v. slaver.

sloe, n. small sour fruit of blackthorn.

slog, v., **slogged, slogging.** plod heavily. —**slog'ger,** n.

slo'gan, n. motto.

sloop, n. kind of sailing vessel.

slop, v., **slopped, slopping,** n. —v. 1. spill liquid. —n. 2. spilled liquid. 3. swill.

slope, v., **sloped, sloping,** n. —v. 1. incline; slant. —n. 2. amount of inclination. 3. sloping surface.

slop'py, adj. **-pier, -piest.** 1. untidy. 2. careless. —**slop'pi·ly,** adv. —**slop'-pi·ness,** n.

slosh, v. splash.

slot, n. narrow opening.

sloth, (slōth), n. 1. laziness. 2. tree-living South American mammal. —**sloth'ful,** adj.

slouch, v. 1. move or rest droopingly. —n. 2. drooping posture. —**slouch'y,** adj.

slough, n. 1. (slou). muddy area. 2. (slōō). marshy pond or inlet. 3. (sluf). cast-off skin or dead tissue. —v. (sluf). 4. be shed. 5. cast off.

slov'en, (sluv'an), n. untidy or careless person. —**slov'en·ly,** adj.

slow, adj. 1. not fast. 2. not intelligent or perceptive. 3. running behind time. —adv. 4. slowly. —v. 5. make or become slow. —**slow'ly,** adv. —**slow'ness,** n.

slow'down', n. slackening of pace or speed.

slow motion, process of projecting or replaying film or television sequence so that action appears to be slowed down.

slow'poke', n. Informal. person who moves, works, or acts very slowly.

sludge, n. mud.

slue, v., **slued, sluing.** turn round.

slug, v., **slugged, slugging,** n. —v. 1.

hit with fists. —*n.* 2. slimy, crawling mollusk having no shell. 3. billet. 4. counterfeit coin. —**slug'ger**, *n.*

slug'gard, *n.* lazy person.

slug'gish, *adj.* inactive; slow. —**slug'gish·ly,** *adv.* —**slug'gish·ness,** *n.*

sluice (sloos), *n.* channel with gate to control flow.

slum, *n.* squalid, overcrowded residence or neighborhood.

slum'ber, *v., n.* sleep.

slump, *v.* 1. drop heavily or suddenly. —*n.* 2. act of slumping.

slur, *v.* **slurred, slurring,** *n.* —*v.* 1. say indistinctly. 2. disparage. —*n.* 3. slurred sound. 4. disparaging remark.

slurp, *v.* eat or drink with loud sucking noises.

slush, *n.* partly melted snow. —**slush'y,** *adj.*

slut, *n.* slatternly or dissolute woman.

sly, *adj.* **slyer, slyest** or **slier, sliest.** 1. cunning. 2. stealthy. —**sly'ly,** *adv.* —**sly'ness,** *n.*

smack, *v.* 1. separate (lips) noisily. 2. slap. 3. have taste or trace. —*n.* 4. smacking of lips. 5. loud kiss. 6. slap. 7. taste. 8. trace. 9. small fishing boat. 10. *Slang.* heroin.

small, *adj.* 1. not big; little. 2. not great in importance, value, etc. 3. ungenerous. —*adv.* 4. in small pieces. —*n.* 5. small part, as of back. —**small'ness,** *n.*

small'pox', *n.* contagious disease marked by fever and pustules.

smart, *v.* 1. cause or feel sharp superficial pain. —*adj.* 2. sharp; severe. 3. clever. 4. stylish. —*n.* 5. sharp local pain. —**smart'ly,** *adv.* —**smart'ness,** *n.*

smart al'eck, *Informal.* obnoxiously conceited and impertinent person. Also, **smart al'ec.**

smart'en, *v.* improve in appearance.

smash, *v.* 1. break to pieces. —*n.* 2. act of smashing; destruction.

smat'ter·ing, *n.* slight knowledge.

smear, *v.* 1. rub with dirt, grease, etc. 2. sully. —*n.* 3. smeared spot. 4. slanderous attack.

smell, *v.* 1. perceive with nose. 2. have odor. —*n.* 3. faculty of smelling. 4. odor.

smelt, *n., pl.* **smelts, smelt,** *v.* —*n.* 1. small edible fish. —*v.* 2. melt (ore or metal). —**smelt'er,** *n.*

smid'gen (smij'ən), *n.* very small amount. Also, **smid'gin, smid'geon.**

smi'lax, *n.* delicate twining plant.

smile, *v.* **smiled, smiling,** *v.* 1. assume look of pleasure, etc. 2. look favorably. —*n.* 3. smiling look.

smirch, *v.* 1. soil or sully. —*n.* 2. stain.

smirk, *v.* 1. smile smugly or affectedly. —*n.* 2. such a smile.

smite, *v.* **smote, smitten** or **smit, smiting,** 1. strike. 2. charm.

smith, *n.* worker in metal.

smith·er·eens', *n.pl.* fragments.

smith'y, *n., pl.* **smithies.** blacksmith's shop.

smock, *n.* long, loose overgarment.

smog, *n.* smoke and fog.

smoke, *n., v.* **smoked, smoking.** —*n.* 1. visible vapor from burning. —*v.* 2. emit smoke. 3. draw into mouth and puff out tobacco smoke. 4. treat with smoke. —**smok'er,** *n.* —**smok'y,** *adj.*

smoke'stack', *n.* 1. pipe for escape of smoke, combustion gases, etc. —*adj.* 2. engaged in heavy industry, as steelmaking.

smol'der, *v.* 1. burn without flame. 2. exist suppressed. Also, **smoul'der.**

smooch, *v.* *Informal.* kiss.

smooth, *adj.* 1. even in surface. 2. easy; tranquil. —*v.* 3. make smooth. —*n.* 4. smooth place. —**smooth'ly,** *adv.* —**smooth'ness,** *n.*

smooth'bore', *adj.* (of gun) not rifled.

smor'gas·bord', *n.* table of assorted foods.

smoth'er, *v.* suffocate.

smudge, *n., v.* **smudged, smudging.** —*n.* 1. dirty smear. 2. smoky fire. —*v.* 3. soil.

smug, *adj.* 1. self-satisfied. 2. trim. —**smug'ly,** *adv.* —**smug'ness,** *n.*

smug'gle, *v.,* **-gled, -gling.** 1. import or export secretly and illegally. 2. bring or take secretly. —**smug'gler,** *n.*

smut, *n.* 1. soot. 2. smudge. 3. obscenity. 4. plant disease. —**smut'ty,** *adj.*

snack, *n.* light meal.

snaf'fle, *n.* kind of bit used on bridle.

snag, *n., v.,* **snagged, snagging.** —*n.* 1. sharp projection. 2. obstacle. —*v.* 3. catch on snag.

snail, *n.* crawling, single-shelled mollusk.

snake, *n., v.,* **snaked, snaking.** —*n.* 1. scaly limbless reptile. —*v.* 2. move like snake. 3. drag. —**snak'y,** *adj.*

snap, *v.,* **snapped, snapping,** *n., adj.* —*v.* 1. make sudden sharp sound. 2. break abruptly. 3. bite (at). 4. photograph. —*n.* 5. snapping sound. 6. kind of fastener. 7. *Informal.* easy thing. —*adj.* 8. unconsidered.

snap'drag'on, *n.* plant with spikes of flowers.

snap'pish, *adj.* cross.

snap'py, *adj.* **-pier, -piest.** 1. quick. 2. smart; stylish.

snap'shot', *n.* unposed photograph.

snare, *n., v.,* **snared, snaring.** —*n.* 1.

kind of trap. 2. strand across skin of small drum. —v. 3. entrap.

snarl, v., n. 1. growl. 2. tangle.

snatch, v. 1. grab. —n. 2. grabbing motion. 3. snatch of melody, etc. —**snatch'er,** n.

sneak, v. 1. go or act furtively. —n. 2. person who sneaks. —**sneak'y,** adj.

sneak'er, n. rubber-soled shoe.

sneer, v. 1. show contempt. —n. 2. contemptuous look or remark.

sneeze, v., sneezed, sneezing, n. —v. 1. emit breath suddenly and forcibly from nose. —n. 2. act of sneezing.

snick'er, n. derisive, stifled laugh. —**snick'er,** v. Also, **snig'ger.**

snide, adj., snider, snidest. derogatory in nasty, insinuating way.

sniff, v. 1. inhale quickly and audibly. —n. 2. such an inhalation. Also, **snif'fle.**

snip, v., snipped, snipping, n. —v. 1. cut with small, quick strokes. —n. 2. small piece cut off. 3. cut. 4. (pl.) large scissors.

snipe, n., v., sniped, sniping. —n. 1. shore bird. —v. 2. shoot from concealment. —**snip'er,** n.

snip'pet, n. small bit, scrap, or fragment.

snip'py, adj., -pier, -piest. sharp or curt, esp. in haughty or contemptuous way.

snit, n. agitated or irritated state.

snitch, Informal. —v. 1. steal; pilfer. 2. turn informer; tattle. —n. 3. informer.

sniv'el, v. 1. weep weakly. 2. run at nose.

snob, n. person overconcerned with position, wealth, etc. —**snob'bish,** adj. —**snob'ber·y,** n.

snood, n. band or net for hair.

snoop, Informal. —v. 1. prowl or pry. —n. 2. Also, **snoop'er.** person who snoops.

snoot'y, adj., snootier, snootiest. Informal. snobbish; condescending. —**snoot'i·ness,** n.

snooze, v., snoozed, snoozing, n. Informal. nap.

snore, v., snored, snoring, n. —v. 1. breathe audibly in sleep. —n. 2. sound of snoring. Also, **snor'er,** n.

snor'kel, n. 1. tube through which swimmer can breathe while underwater. 2. ventilating device for submarines.

snort, v. 1. exhale loudly and harshly. —n. 2. sound of snorting.

snot, n. Informal. nasal mucus.

snout, n. projecting nose and jaw.

snow, n. 1. white crystalline flakes that fall to earth. —v. 2. fall as snow.

snow'drift, n. —**snow'fall,** n. —**snow'flake,** n. —**snow'storm,** n. —**snow'y,** adj.

snow'ball, n. 1. ball of snow. 2. flowering shrub. —v. 3. grow rapidly.

snow'mo·bile, n. motor vehicle built to travel on snow.

snow'shoe, n. racketlike shoe for walking on snow.

snub, v., snubbed, snubbing, n., adj. —v. 1. treat with scorn. 2. check or stop. —n. 3. rebuke or slight. —adj. 4. (of nose) short and turned up.

snuff, v. 1. inhale. 2. smell. 3. extinguish. —n. 4. powdered tobacco.

snuf'fle, v. —fled, -fling, n. sniff.

snug, adj., snugger, snuggest. 1. cozy. 2. trim; neat. —**snug'ly,** adv.

snug'gle, v., -gled, -gling. nestle.

so, adv. 1. in this or that way. 2. to such degree. 3. as stated. —conj. 4. consequently. 5. in order that.

soak, v. 1. wet thoroughly. 2. absorb. —**soak'er,** n.

soap, n. 1. substance used for washing. —v. 2. rub with soap. —**soap'y,** adj.

soar, v. fly upward.

sob, v., sobbed, sobbing, n. —v. 1. weep convulsively. —n. 2. convulsive breath.

so'ber, adj. 1. not drunk. 2. quiet; grave. —v. 3. make or become sober. —**so·bri'e·ty, so'ber·ness,** n. —**so'ber·ly,** adv.

so'bri·quet' (sō'bri kā´, -ket´), n. nickname.

so'-called', adj. called thus.

soc'cer, n. game resembling football.

so'cia·ble, adj. friendly. —**so'cia·bly,** adv. —**so'cia·bil'i·ty,** n.

so'cial, adj. 1. devoted to companionship. 2. of human society. —**so'cial·ly,** adv.

so'cial·ism, n. theory advocating community ownership of means of production, etc. —**so'cial·ist,** n. —**so'cial·is'tic,** adj.

so'cial·ite, n. socially prominent person.

so'cial·ize, v., -ized, -izing. 1. associate with others. 2. put on socialist basis.

social security, (often caps.) federal program of old age, unemployment, health, disability, and survivors' insurance.

social work, services or activities designed to improve social conditions among poor, sick, or troubled persons.

so·ci'e·ty, n., pl. -ties. 1. group of persons with common interests. 2. human beings generally. 3. fashionable people.

Society of Friends, sect founded 1650; Quakers.

so'ci·ol'o·gy, n. science of social relations and institutions. —**so'ci·o·log'i·cal,** adj. —**so'ci·ol'o·gist,** n.

sock, n. Informal. short stocking.

sock'et, n. holelike part for holding another part.

sod, n. grass with its roots.

so'da, n. 1. drink made with soda water. 2. preparation containing sodium.

soda water, water charged with carbon dioxide.

sod'den, adj. 1. soaked. 2. stupid. —**sod'den·ness,** n.

so'di·um, n. soft whitish metallic element.

sod'o·my (sod'-), n. anal or oral copulation.

so'fa (sō'fa), n. couch with back and arms.

soft, adj. 1. yielding readily. 2. gentle; pleasant. 3. not strong. 4. (of water) free from mineral salts. 5. without alcohol. —**soft'en,** v. —**soft'ly,** adv. —**soft'ness,** n.

soft'ball', n. 1. form of baseball played with larger, softer ball. 2. the ball used.

soft drink, nonalcoholic drink, often carbonated.

soft'ware', n. programs, charts, etc., for use with a computer.

sog'gy, adj., **-gier, -giest.** 1. soaked. 2. damp and heavy. —**sog'gi·ness,** n.

soil, v. 1. dirty; smudge. —n. 2. spot or stain. 3. sewage. 4. earth; ground.

soi·rée' (swä rā'), n. evening party.

so'journ, v. 1. dwell briefly. —n. 2. short stay.

sol'ace (sol'is), n., v. comfort in grief.

so'lar, adj. of the sun.

so·lar'i·um (-lâr'-), n., pl. **-iums, -ia.** glass-enclosed room for enjoying sunlight.

solar system, sun and all the celestial bodies revolving around it.

sol'der (sod'ər), n. 1. fusible alloy for joining metal. —v. 2. join with solder.

sol'dier, n. 1. member of army. —v. 2. serve as soldier. —**sol'dier·ly,** adj. —**sol'dier·y,** n.

sole, n., v., **soled, soling,** adj. —n. 1. bottom of foot or shoe. 2. edible flatfish. —v. 3. put sole on. —adj. 4. only. —**sole'ly,** adv.

sol'emn, adj. 1. grave; serious. 2. sacred. —**so·lem'ni·ty,** n. —**sol'emn·ly,** adv.

sol'em·nize', v., **-nized, -nizing.** observe with ceremonies. —**sol'em·ni·za'tion,** n.

so·lic'it (-lis'-), v. 1. entreat; request. 2. lure; entice, as to a prostitute. —**so·lic'i·ta'tion,** n.

so·lic'i·tor, n. 1. person who solicits. 2. Brit. lawyer.

so·lic'it·ous, adj. anxious; concerned. —**so·lic'it·ous·ly,** adv. —**so·lic'i·tude',** n.

sol'id, adj. 1. having length, breadth, and thickness. 2. not hollow. 3. dense. 4. substantial. 5. entire. —n. 6. solid body. —**so·lid'i·fy',** v. —**so·lid'i·ty,** n.

sol'i·dar'i·ty, n., pl. **-ties.** unanimity of attitude or purpose.

sol'id·ly, adv. 1. so as to be solid. 2. whole-heartedly; fully.

so·lil'o·quy (-kwē), n., pl. **-quies.** speech when alone. —**so·lil'o·quize',** v.

sol'i·taire' (-târ'), n. 1. card game for one person. 2. gem set alone.

sol'i·tar'y, adj. 1. alone. 2. single. 3. secluded. —**sol'i·tude',** n.

so'lo, n., pl. **-los.** performance by one person. —**so'lo·ist,** n.

sol'stice, n. time in summer (June 21) or winter (Dec. 21) when sun is at its farthest from equator.

sol'u·ble, adj. able to be dissolved. —**sol'u·bil'i·ty,** n. —**sol'u·bly,** adv.

so·lu'tion, n. 1. explanation or answer. 2. dispersion of one substance in another. 3. resulting substance.

solve, v., **solved, solving.** find explanation of. —**solv'a·ble,** adj. —**solv'er,** n.

sol'vent, adj. 1. able to pay one's debts. 2. causing dissolving. —n. 3. agent that dissolves. —**sol'ven·cy,** n.

som'ber, adj. gloomy; dark. Also, **som'bre.** —**som'ber·ly,** adv.

som·bre'ro (-brâr'ō), n., pl. **-ros.** tall, broad-brimmed hat.

some, adj. 1. being an unspecified one or number. 2. certain. —pron. 3. unspecified number or amount.

some'bod'y, pron. some person. Also, **some'one'.**

some'day', adv. at some distant time.

some'how', adv. in some way.

som'er·sault', n. heels-over-head turn of body.

some'thing, n. unspecified thing.

some'time', adv. 1. at indefinite time. —adj. 2. former.

some'times', adv. at times.

some'what', adv. to some extent.

some'where', adv. in, at, or to unspecified place.

som·nam'bu·lism, n. sleep-walking. —**som·nam'bu·list,** n.

som'no•lent, *adj.* sleepy. **—som'no•lence,** *n.*

son, *n.* male offspring.

so'nar, *n.* method or apparatus for detecting objects in water by means of sound waves.

so•na'ta, *n.* instrumental composition.

song, *n.* music or verse for singing. **—song'ster,** *n.* **—song'stress,** *n.fem.*

son'ic, *adj.* of sound.

son'-in-law', *n., pl.* **sons-in-law.** husband of one's daughter.

son'net, *n.* fourteen-line poem in fixed form.

so•no'rous, *adj.* 1. resonant. 2. grandiose in expression. **—so•nor'i•ty,** *n.* **—so•no'rous•ly,** *adv.*

soon, *adv.* in short time.

soot, *n.* black substance in smoke. **—soot'y,** *adj.*

soothe, *v.* **soothed, soothing.** calm; allay.

sooth'say•er, *n.* person who predicts.

sop, *n., v.* **sopped, sopping.** **—n.** 1. food dipped in liquid. 2. something given to pacify. **—v.** 3. soak (food). 4. absorb.

so•phis'ti•cat•ed, *adj.* worldly; not simple. **—so•phis'ti•cate** (-kit), *n.* **—so•phis'ti•ca'tion,** *n.*

soph'ist•ry, *n., pl.* **-ries.** clever but unsound reasoning. **—soph'ist,** *n.*

soph'o•more', *n.* second-year high school or college student.

soph'o•mor'ic, *adj.* intellectually immature.

so•po•rif'ic, *adj.* 1. causing sleep. **—n.** 2. soporific agent.

so•pra'no, *n., pl.* **-pranos.** 1. highest singing voice. 2. singer with such voice.

sor'cer•er, *n.* magician. Also, *fem.* **sor'cer•ess.** **—sor'cer•y,** *n.*

sor'did, *adj.* 1. dirty. 2. ignoble.

sore, *adj.,* **sorer, sorest,** *n.* **—adj.** 1. painful or tender. 2. grieved. 3. causing misery. 4. *Informal.* annoyed. **—n.** 5. sore spot. **—sore'ly,** *adv.* **—sore'ness,** *n.*

sor'ghum (-gəm), *n.* cereal used in making syrup, etc.

so•ror'i•ty, *n., pl.* **-ties.** club of women or girls.

sor'rel, *n.* 1. reddish brown. 2. sorrel horse. 3. salad plant.

sor'row, *n.* 1. grief; regret; misfortune. **—v.** 2. feel sorrow. **—sor'row•ful,** *adj.* **—sor'row•ful•ly,** *adv.* **—sor'row•ful•ness,** *n.*

sor'ry, *adj.* 1. feeling regret or pity. 2. wretched.

sort, *n.* 1. kind or class. 2. character. 3.

manner. **—v.** 4. separate; classify. **—sort'er,** *n.*

sor'tie (sôr'tē), *n.* 1. attack by defending troops. 2. combat mission.

SOS, call for help.

so'-so', *adj.* 1. neither good nor bad. **—adv.** 2. tolerably.

sot, *n.* drunkard. **—sot'tish,** *adj.*

sot'to vo'ce (sot'ō vō'chē), in a low voice; softly.

souf•flé' (soo flā') *n.* fluffy baked dish.

sough (sou), *v.* 1. rustle or murmur, as wind. **—n.** 2. act of soughing.

sought, pt. and pp. of **seek.**

soul, *n.* 1. human spiritual quality. 2. essential quality. 3. person. 4. Also, **soul music.** black popular music drawing on church influences. **—adj.** 5. of black customs and culture. **—soul'ful,** *adj.* **—soul'less,** *adj.*

sound, *n.* 1. sensation affecting organs of hearing, produced by vibrations (**sound waves**). 2. special tone. 3. noise. 4. inlet or passage of sea. **—v.** 5. make sound. 6. say. 7. give certain impression. 8. measure depth of. 9. examine; question. **—adj.** 10. healthy; strong. 11. reliable. 12. valid. **—sound'proof',** *adj.* **—sound'ly,** *adv.* **—sound'ness,** *n.*

sound bite, brief, memorable statement excerpted, as from an interview, for broadcast news.

sound'track', *n.* band on motion-picture film on which sound is recorded.

soup, *n.* liquid food of meat, vegetables, etc.

sour, *adj.* 1. acid in taste; tart. 2. spoiled. 3. disagreeable. **—v.** 4. turn sour. **—sour'ly,** *adv.* **—sour'ness,** *n.*

source, *n.* origin.

souse, *v.,* **soused, sousing,** *n.* **—v.** 1. immerse; drench. 2. pickle. **—n.** 3. act of sousing. 4. pickled food. 5. *Slang.* drunkard.

south, *n.* 1. point of compass opposite north. 2. this direction. 3. territory in this direction. **—adj.,** *adv.* 4. toward, in, or from south. **—south'er•ly,** *adj., adv.* **—south'ern,** *adj.* **—south'ern•er,** *n.* **—south'ward,** *adj., adv.*

south'east', *n.* point or direction midway between south and east. **—south'east',** *adj., adv.*

south'paw', *n. Informal.* left-handed person, esp. baseball pitcher.

south'west', *n.* point or direction midway between south and west. **—south'west',** *adj., adv.*

sou've•nir' (soo'və nēr'), *n.* memento.

sov'er•eign (sov'rin), *n.* 1. monarch. 2. (formerly) British gold coin worth one pound. —*adj.* 3. of a sovereign; supreme. —**sov'er·eign·ty,** *n.*

so'vi·et', *n.* 1. (in USSR) governing body. —*adj.* 2. (*cap.*) of USSR.

sow, *v.* 1. (sō). plant seed. —*n.* 2. (sou). female hog. —**sow'er,** *n.*

soy'bean', *n.* nutritious seed of leguminous plant.

soy sauce, salty sauce made from soybeans.

spa, *n.* resort at mineral spring.

space, *n., v.,* **spaced, spacing.** —*n.* 1. unlimited expanse. 2. particular part of this. 3. linear distance. 4. interval of time. —*v.* 5. divide into space. 6. set at intervals.

space'craft', *n., pl.* **-craft.** vehicle for traveling in outer space.

space'ship', *n.* rocket vehicle for travel between planets.

spa'cious, *adj.* large; vast. —**spa'cious·ly,** *adv.* —**spa'cious·ness,** *n.*

Spack'le, *n. Trademark.* brand of plasterlike material for patching cracks.

spade, *n., v.,* **spaded, spading.** —*n.* 1. tool with blade for digging. 2. (*pl.*) suit of playing cards. —*v.* 3. dig with spade.

spa·ghet'ti, *n.* pasta in form of long strings.

span, *n., v.,* **spanned, spanning.** —*n.* 1. distance between extended thumb and little finger. 2. space between two supports. 3. full extent. 4. team of animals. —*v.* 5. extend over.

span'gle, *n., v.,* **-gled, -gling.** —*n.* 1. small bright ornament. —*v.* 2. decorate with spangles.

span'iel, *n.* kind of dog.

Span'ish, *n.* language or people of Spain. —**Spanish,** *adj.*

spank, *v.* 1. strike on buttocks. —*n.* 2. such a blow.

spank'ing, *adj.* brisk; vigorous.

spar, *v.,* **sparred, sparring,** *n.* —*v.* 1. box. 2. bandy words. —*n.* 3. *Naut.* mast, yard, etc. 4. bright crystalline mineral.

spare, *v.,* **spared, sparing,** *adj.,* **sparer, sparest.** —*v.* 1. deal gently with. 2. part with easily. —*adj.* 3. kept in reserve. 4. extra. 5. lean.

spare'rib', *n.* cut of pork ribs.

spark, *n.* 1. burning particle. 2. flash of electricity. 3. trace.

spar'kle, *v.,* **-kled, -kling,** *n.* —*v.* 1. emit sparks. 2. glitter. 3. produce little bubbles. —*n.* 4. little spark. 5. brightness.

spark plug, device in internal-combustion engine that ignites fuel.

spar'row, *n.* small, common, hardy bird.

sparse, *adj.,* **sparser, sparsest.** thinly distributed. —**spar'si·ty, sparse'ness,** *n.* —**sparse'ly,** *adv.*

Spar'tan, *adj.* austere.

spasm, *n.* sudden involuntary muscular contraction.

spas·mod'ic, *adj.* 1. of spasms. 2. intermittent. —**spas·mod'i·cal·ly,** *adv.*

spas'tic, *adj.* of or marked by spasms.

spat, *n.* petty quarrel.

spate, *n.* sudden outpouring.

spa'tial, *adj.* of or in space.

spat'ter, *v.* 1. sprinkle in many fine drops.

spat'u·la (spach'-). *n.* broad-bladed implement.

spav'in (spav'an), *n.* disease of hock joint in horses.

spawn, *n.* 1. eggs of fish, mollusks, etc. —*v.* 2. produce spawn.

spay, *v.* neuter or castrate (dog, cat, etc.).

speak, *v.,* **spoke, spoken, speaking.** 1. talk; say. 2. deliver speech.

speak'er, *n.* 1. person who speaks. 2. presiding officer.

spear, *n.* 1. long staff bearing sharp head. —*v.* 2. pierce with spear.

spear'head', *n.* 1. head of spear. 2. leader. —*v.* 3. lead.

spear'mint', *n.* aromatic herb.

spe'cial, *adj.* 1. particular in nature or purpose. 2. unusual. —*n.* 3. special thing or person. —**spe'cial·ly,** *adv.*

spe'cial·ize', *v.,* **-ized, -izing.** study of work in special field. —**spe'cial·ist,** *n.* —**spe'cial·i·za'tion,** *n.*

spe'cial·ty, *n., pl.* **-ties.** field of special interest or competence.

spe'cie (spē'shē), *n.* coined money.

spe'cies, *n.* class of related individuals.

spe·cif'ic, *adj.* definite. —**spe·cif'i·cal·ly,** *adv.*

spec'i·fi·ca'tion, *n.* 1. act of specifying. 2. detailed requirement.

spec'i·fy', *v.,* **-fied, -fying.** mention or require specifically.

spec'i·men, *n.* anything typical of its kind.

spe'cious (spē'shəs), *adj.* plausible but deceptive. —**spe'cious·ly,** *adv.* —**spe'cious·ness,** *n.*

speck, *n.* 1. spot or particle. —*v.* 2. spot.

speck'le, *n., v.,* **-led, -ling.** —*n.* 1. small spot. —*v.* 2. mark with speckles.

specs, *n.pl. Informal.* 1. spectacles; eyeglasses. 2. specifications (def. 2).

spec'ta·cle, *n.* 1. anything presented to sight. 2. public display. 3. (*pl.*) eyeglasses.

spec·tac·u·lar, *adj.* dramatic; thrilling.

spec·ta·tor, *n.* observer.

spec·ter, *n.* ghost. Also, **spec·tre.** —**spec′tral**, *adj.*

spec·tro·scope, *n.* instrument for producing and examining spectra. —**spell′er**, *n.*

spec′trum, *n.*, *pl.* **-tra** (-tra), **-trums.** band of colors formed when light ray is dispersed.

spec·u·late, *v.*, **-lated, -lating.** 1. think; conjecture. 2. invest at some risk. —**spec·u·la′tion**, *n.* —**spec′u·la·tive**, *adj.* —**spec′u·la·tor**, *n.*

speech, *n.* 1. power of speaking. 2. utterance. 3. talk before audience. 4. language. —**speech′less**, *adj.*

speed, *n.*, *v.*, **sped** or **speeded, speeding.** —*n.* 1. swiftness. 2. rate of motion —*v.* 3. increase speed of. 4. move swiftly. —**speed′er**, *n.* —**speed′y**, *adj.* —**speed′i·ly**, *adv.*

speed·om·e·ter, *n.* device for indicating speed.

spell, *v.*, **spelled** or **spelt, spelling**, *n.* —*v.* 1. give letters of in order. 2. (of letters) form. 3. signify. 4. relieve at work. —*n.* 5. enchantment. 6. brief period. —**spell′er**, *n.*

spell′bound, *adj.* fascinated.

spe·lunk′er (spi lung′kər), *n.* person who explores caves. —**spe·lunk′ing**, *n.*

spend, *v.*, **spent, spending.** 1. pay out. 2. pass (time). 3. use up. —**spend′er**, *n.*

spend′thrift, *n.* extravagant spender.

sperm, *n.* male reproductive fluid or cell. —**sper·mat′ic**, *adj.*

sper·ma·cet′i (-sēt′ē), *n.* waxy substance from large square-headed whale (**sperm whale**).

spew, *v.* 1. vomit. 2. gush or pour out. —*n.* 3. something spewed.

sphere, *n.* 1. round ball. 2. particular field of influence or competence. —**spher′i·cal**, *adj.*

sphe·roid, *n.* body approximately spherical.

sphinc·ter, *n.* muscle closing anus or other body opening. —**sphinc′ter·al**, *adj.*

sphinx, *n.* figure of creature with man's head and lion's body.

spice, *n.*, *v.*, **spiced, spicing.** —*n.* 1. aromatic plant substance used as seasoning. —*v.* 2. season with spice. —**spic′y**, *adj.*

spick′-and-span, *adj.* 1. spotlessly clean. 2. perfectly new.

spi·der, *n.* wingless, web-spinning insectlike animal. —**spi′der·y**, *adj.*

spiel, *n. Slang.* high-pressure sales talk.

spig′ot, *n.* faucet.

spike, *n.*, *v.*, **spiked, spiking.** —*n.* 1. large stiff nail. 2. stiff, pointed part. 3. ear of grain. 4. stalk of flowers. —*v.* 5. fasten or pierce with spikes. 6. frustrate or stop.

spill, *v.*, **spilled** or **spilt, spilling.** 1. run or let run over. 2. shed (blood). —**spill′age**, *n.*

spill′way, *n.* overflow passage.

spin, *v.*, **spun, spinning**, *n.* —*v.* 1. make yarn or thread from fiber. 2. secrete filament. 3. whirl. —*n.* 4. spinning motion. 5. short ride. 6. *Slang.* particular viewpoint or bias. —**spin′ner**, *n.*

spin·ach (-ich), *n.* plant with edible leaves.

spin control, *Slang.* attempt to give a bias to news coverage.

spin·dle, *n.* 1. tapered rod. 2. any shaft or axis.

spin′dling, *adj.* tall and thin. Also, **spin′dly.**

spin doctor, *Slang.* press agent or spokesperson skilled in spin control.

spine, *n.* 1. Also, **spinal column.** connected series of bones down back. 2. any spinelike part. 3. stiff bristle or thorn. —**spi′nal**, *adj.* —**spin′y**, *adj.*

spine′less, *adj.* weak in character.

spin′et, *n.* small piano.

spin′-off, *n.* by-product or secondary development from primary effort or product. Also, **spin′off.**

spin′ster, *n.* unmarried woman, esp. elderly.

spi′ral, *n.*, *adj.*, *v.*, **-raled, -raling.** —*n.* 1. curve made by circling a point while approaching or receding from it. —*adj.* 2. like or of spiral. —*v.* 3. move spirally. —**spi′ral·ly**, *adv.*

spire, *n.* tall tapering structure, esp. on tower or roof.

spi·re′a (spī rē′ə), *n.* common garden shrub. Also, **spiraea.**

spir·it, *n.* 1. vital principle in humanity; soul. 2. supernatural being. 3. feelings. 4. vigor. 5. intent. 6. (*pl.*) alcoholic liquor. 7. (*cap.*) Holy Ghost. —*v.* 8. carry off secretly. —**spir′it·ed**, *adj.* —**spir′it·less**, *adj.*

spir·it·u·al, *adj.* 1. of or in spirit; ethereal. 2. religious. —*n.* 3. religious song. —**spir′it·u·al·ly**, *adv.* —**spir′it·u·al′i·ty**, *n.*

spir·it·u·al·ism, *n.* belief that spirits of dead communicate with living. —**spir′it·u·al·ist**, *n.*, *adj.*

spir′it·u·ous, *adj.* 1. alcoholic. 2. distilled.

spit, *v.*, **spat** or **spit** (for 2 **spitted**), **spitting.** —*v.* 1. eject from mouth. 2. pierce. —*n.* 3. saliva. 4. *Informal.*

image. 5. rod for roasting meat. 6. projecting point of land.

spite, *n.*, *v.*, **spited, spiting.** —*n.* 1. malice; grudge. —*v.* 2. annoy out of spite. —**spite'ful,** *adj.* —**spite'ful·ly,** *adv.* —**spite'ful·ness,** *n.*

spit'tle, *n.* saliva.

spit·toon', *n.* cuspidor.

splash, *v.* 1. dash water, mud, etc. —*n.* 2. act or sound of splashing. 3. spot. —**splash'y,** *adj.*

splat'ter, *v.* splash widely.

splay, *v.*, *adj.* spread out.

spleen, *n.* 1. ductless organ near stomach. 2. ill humor. —**sple·net'ic,** *adj.*

splen'did, *adj.* gorgeous; superb; fine. —**splen'did·ly,** *adv.* —**splen'dor,** *n.*

splice, *v.*, **spliced, splicing.** *n.* —*v.* 1. join, as ropes or boards. —*n.* 2. union made by splicing.

splint, *n.* 1. brace for broken part of body. 2. strip of wood for weaving. —*v.* 3. brace with splints.

splin'ter, *n.* 1. thin sharp fragment. —*v.* 2. break into splinters.

split, *v.*, **split, splitting.** *n.*, *adj.* —*v.* 1. separate; divide. 2. burst. —*n.* 3. crack or breach. —*adj.* 4. cleft; divided.

split'-lev'el, *adj.* 1. having rooms on levels a half story apart. —*n.* 2. split-level house.

splotch, *n.*, *v.*, blot; stain. —**splotch'y,** *adj.*

splurge, *n.*, *v.*, **splurged, splurging.** —*n.* 1. big display or expenditure. —*v.* 2. make splurge; be extravagant.

splut'ter, *v.* 1. talk vehemently and incoherently. —*n.* 2. spluttering talk.

spoil, *v.*, **spoiled** or **spoilt, spoiling.** —*v.* 1. damage; ruin. 2. become tainted. —*n.* 3. (*pl.*) booty. 4. waste material. —**spoil'age,** *n.* —**spoil'er,** *n.*

spoil'sport', *n.* person whose conduct spoils the pleasure of others.

spoke, *n.* bar between hub and rim of wheel.

spokes'man, *n.*, *pl.* **-men.** person speaking for others.

sponge, *n.*, *v.*, **sponged, sponging.** —*n.* 1. marine animal. 2. its light skeleton or an imitation, used to absorb liquids. —*v.* 3. clean with sponge. 4. impose or live on another. —**spong'er,** *n.* —**spon'gy,** *adj.*

spon'sor, *n.* 1. one that recommends or supports. 2. godparent. 3. advertiser on radio or television. —*v.* 4. act as sponsor for.

spon·ta'ne·ous, *adj.* 1. arising without outside cause. 2. impulsive. —**spon·ta'ne·ous·ly,** *adv.* —**spon·**

ta·ne'i·ty, **spon·ta'ne·ous·ness,** *n.*

spook, *Informal.* —*n.* 1. ghost. —*v.* 2. frighten. —**spook'y,** *adj.*

spool, *n.* cylinder on which something is wound.

spoon, *n.* 1. utensil for stirring or taking up food. —*v.* 2. lift in spoon. —**spoon'ful,** *n.*

spoor (spoor), *n.* trail of wild animal.

spo·rad'ic, *adj.* occasional; scattered. —**spo·rad'i·cal·ly,** *adv.*

spore, *n.* seed, as of ferns.

sport, *n.* 1. athletic pastime. 2. diversion. 3. abnormally formed plant or animal. —*adj.* 4. of or for sport. —*v.* 5. play. —**sports'man,** *n.* —**sports'man·ly,** *adj.* —**sports'man·ship,** *n.* —**sports'wear',** *n.*

spor'tive, *adj.* playful. —**spor'tive·ly,** *adv.* —**spor'tive·ness,** *n.*

spot, *n.*, *v.*, **spotted, spotting.** *adj.* —*n.* 1. blot; speck. 2. locality. —*v.* 3. stain with spots. 4. notice. —*adj.* 5. made, done, etc., at once. —**spot'less,** *adj.* —**spot'ter,** *n.* —**spot'ty,** *adj.*

spot check, random sampling or investigation. —**spot'-check',** *v.*

spot'light', *n.* 1. intense light focused on person or thing, as on stage. 2. intense public attention.

spouse, *n.* husband or wife.

spout, *v.* 1. discharge (liquid, etc.) with force. 2. utter insincerely. —*n.* 3. pipe or lip on container.

sprain, *v.* 1. injure by wrenching. —*n.* 2. such injury.

sprat, *n.* herringlike fish.

sprawl, *v.* 1. stretch out ungracefully. —*n.* 2. sprawling position.

spray, *n.* 1. liquid in fine particles. 2. appliance for producing spray. 3. branch of flowers, etc. —*v.* 4. scatter as spray. 5. apply spray to. —**spray'er,** *n.*

spread, *v.*, **spread, spreading.** *n.* —*v.* 1. stretch out. 2. extend. 3. scatter. —*n.* 4. extent. 5. diffusion. 6. cloth cover. 7. preparation for eating on bread. —**spread'er,** *n.*

spread'sheet', *n.* 1. outsize ledger sheet used by accountants. 2. such a sheet simulated electronically by computer software.

spree, *n.* frolic.

sprig, *n.* twig or shoot.

spright'ly, *adj.*, **-lier, -liest.** lively. —**spright'li·ness,** *n.*

spring, *v.*, **sprang** or **sprung, sprung, springing.** *n.*, *adj.* —*v.* 1. leap. 2. grow or proceed. 3. disclose. —*n.* 4. leap; jump. 5. natural fountain. 6. season after winter. 7. elastic device.

—*adj.* **8.** of or for spring (def. 6).
—**spring'time',** *n.* —**spring'y,** *adj.*

sprin'kle, *v.,* **-kled, -kling,** *n.* —*v.* **1.** scatter in drops. **2.** rain slightly. —*n.* **3.** instance of sprinkling. **4.** something sprinkled. —**sprin'kler,** *n.*

sprint, *v.* **1.** run fast. —*n.* **2.** short fast run. —**sprint'er,** *n.*

sprite, *n.* elf; fairy.

sprock'et, *n.* tooth on wheel for engaging with chain.

sprout, *v.* **1.** begin to grow; bud. —*n.* **2.** plant shoot.

spruce, *adj.,* **sprucer, sprucest,** *v.,* *n.* —*adj.* **1.** trim; neat. —*v.* **2.** make spruce. —*n.* **3.** cone-bearing evergreen tree.

spry, *adj.,* **spryer** or **sprier, spryest** or **spriest.** nimble. —**spry'ly,** *adv.* —**spry'ness,** *n.*

spud, *n.* **1.** spadelike tool. **2.** *Informal.* potato.

spume, *n.* foam.

spunk, *n. Informal.* courage; spirit. —**spunk'y,** *adj.*

spur, *n., v.,* **spurred, spurring.** —*n.* **1.** sharp device worn on heel to goad horse. **2.** spurlike part. —*v.* **3.** prick with spur. **4.** urge.

spu'ri·ous (spyŏr'-), *adj.* not genuine. —**spu'ri·ous·ly,** *adv.* —**spu'ri·ous·ness,** *n.*

spurn, *v.* scorn; reject.

spurt, *v.* **1.** gush or eject in jet. **2.** speed up briefly. —*n.* **3.** forceful gush. **4.** brief increase of effort.

sput'nik, *n.* first earth-orbiting satellite, launched by USSR in 1957.

sput'ter, *v.* **1.** emit violently in drops. **2.** splutter. —*n.* **3.** act or sound of sputtering.

spu'tum (spyōō'-), *n.* spittle, esp. mixed with mucus.

spy, *n., pl.* **spies,** *v.,* **spied, spying.** —*n.* **1.** secret observer, esp. one employed by government. **2.** watch secretly. **3.** sight.

squab, *n.* young pigeon.

squab'ble, *n., v.,* **-bled, -bling.** —*n.* **1.** petty quarrel. —*v.* **2.** have squabble.

squad, *n.* small group.

squad'ron, *n.* unit in Navy, Air Force, etc.

squal'id (skwol'id), *adj.* dirty or wretched. —**squal'id·ly,** *adv.* —**squal'id·ness,** *n.*

squall, *n.* **1.** strong gust of wind, etc. **2.** loud cry. —*v.* **3.** cry loudly. —**squall'y,** *adj.*

squal'or (skwol'ər), *n.* squalid state.

squan'der, *v.* use or spend wastefully.

square, *n., v.,* **squared, squaring,** *adj.* —*n.* **1.** plane figure with four equal sides and four

right angles. **2.** anything square. **3.** tool for checking right angles. **4.** product of number multiplied by itself. **5.** *Slang.* conventional, conservative, unimaginative person. —*v.* **6.** make square. **7.** adjust; agree. **8.** multiply by itself. —*adj.* **9.** being a square. **10.** level. **11.** honest. —*adv.* **12.** directly. —**square'ly,** *adv.* —**square'ness,** *n.*

square dance, dance by sets of four couples arranged in squares.

squash, *v.* **1.** crush; suppress. —*n.* **2.** game resembling tennis. **3.** fruit of vinelike plant.

squat, *v.,* **squatted** or **squat, squatting,** *adj., n.* —*v.* **1.** sit with legs close under body. **2.** settle on land illegally or to acquire title. —*adj.* **3.** Also, **squat'ty.** stocky. —*n.* **4.** squatting position. —**squat'ter,** *n.*

squaw, *n.* American Indian woman.

squawk, *n.* **1.** loud harsh cry. —*v.* **2.** utter squawks. —**squawk'er,** *n.*

squeak, *n.* **1.** small shrill sound. —*v.* **2.** emit squeaks. —**squeak'y,** *adj.* —**squeak'er,** *n.*

squeal, *n.* **1.** long shrill cry. —*v.* **2.** utter squeals. —**squeal'er,** *n.*

squeam'ish, *adj.* **1.** prudish. **2.** overfastidious. —**squeam'ish·ly,** *adv.* —**squeam'ish·ness,** *n.*

squee'gee, *n.* implement for cleaning glass surfaces.

squeeze, *v.,* **squeezed, squeezing,** *n.* —*v.* **1.** press together. **2.** cram. —*n.* **3.** act of squeezing. **4.** hug.

squelch, *v.* **1.** crush. **2.** silence. —*n.* **3.** crushing retort. —**squelch'er,** *n.*

squib, *n.* **1.** short witty item or paragraph. **2.** hissing firecracker.

squid, *n.* marine mollusk.

squig'gle, *n.* short, irregular curve or twist. —**squig'gly,** *adj.*

squint, *v.* **1.** look with eyes partly closed. **2.** be cross-eyed. —*n.* **3.** squinting look. **4.** cross-eyed condition.

squire, *n., v.,* **squired, squiring.** —*n.* **1.** country gentleman. **2.** escort. —*v.* **3.** escort.

squirm, *v., n.* wriggle.

squir'rel, *n.* bushy-tailed, tree-living rodent.

squirt, *v.* **1.** gush; cause to gush. —*n.* **2.** jet of liquid.

SST, supersonic transport.

stab, *v.,* **stabbed, stabbing,** *n.* —*v.* **1.** pierce with pointed weapon. —*n.* **2.** thrust with or wound from pointed weapon.

sta'bi·lize', *v.,* **-lized, -lizing.** make or keep stable. —**sta·bi·li·za'tion,** *n.* —**sta'bi·liz'er,** *n.*

sta'ble, *n., v.,* **-bled, -bling,** *adj.* —*n.*
1. building for horses, etc. —*v.*
2. keep in stable. —*adj.* 3. steady; steadfast. —**stab'ly,** *adv.* —**sta·bil'i·ty,** *n.*

stac·ca'to (stə kä'tō) *adj. Music.* disconnected; detached.

stack, *n.* 1. orderly heap. 2. (*often pl.*) book storage area. 3. funnel for smoke. —*v.* 4. pile in stack. 5. arrange unfairly.

sta'di·um, *n., pl.* **-diums, -dia** (-ə). large open structure for games.

staff, *n., pl.* **staves** (stāvz) *or* **staffs** (for 1, 3); **staffs** (for 2); *v.* —*n.* 1. stick carried as support, weapon, etc. 2. body of assistants or administrators. 3. set of five lines on which music is written. —*v.* 4. provide with staff.

stag, *n.* 1. adult male deer. —*adj.* 2. for men only. —*adv.* 3. without a date.

stage, *n., v.,* **staged, staging.** —*n.* 1. single step or degree. 2. raised platform. 3. theater. —*v.* 4. exhibit on stage.

stag'ger, *v.* 1. move unsteadily. 2. cause to reel. 3. arrange at intervals. —*n.* 4. staggering movement. 5. (*pl.*) disease of horses, etc.

stag'ing, *n.* scaffolding.

stag'nant, *adj.* 1. not flowing; foul. 2. inactive. —**stag'nate,** *v.* —**stag·na'tion,** *n.*

staid, *adj.* sedate. —**staid'ly,** *adv.* —**staid'ness,** *n.*

stain, *n.* 1. discolored patch. 2. kind of dye. —*v.* 3. mark with stains. 4. color with stain.

stain'less, *adj.* 1. unstained. 2. not liable to rusting.

stair, *n.* series of steps between levels. —**stair'case', stair'way',** *n.*

stair'well', *n.* vertical shaft containing stairs.

stake, *n., v.,* **staked, staking.** —*n.* 1. pointed post. 2. something wagered. 3. (*pl.*) prize. 4. hazard. —*v.* 5. mark off with stakes. 6. wager.

sta·lac'tite, *n.* icicle-shaped formation hanging from cave roof.

sta·lag'mite, *n.* cone-shaped deposit on cave floor.

stale, *adj.,* **staler, stalest,** *v.,* **staled, staling.** —*adj.* 1. not fresh. —*v.* 2. make or become stale. —**stale'ness,** *n.*

stale'mate', *n., v.,* **-mated, -mating.** —*n.* 1. deadlocked position, orig. in chess. —*v.* 2. bring to stalemate.

stalk, *v.* 1. pursue stealthily. 2. walk in haughty or menacing way. —*n.* 3. plant stem.

stall, *n.* 1. compartment for one animal. 2. sales booth. 3. (of airplane)
loss of air speed necessary for control. 4. *Slang.* pretext for delay. —*v.* 5. keep in stall. 6. stop; become stopped. 7. lose necessary air speed. 8. *Slang.* delay.

stal'lion (stal'yən) *n.* male horse.

stal'wart (stôl'wərt), *adj.* 1. robust. 2. brave. 3. steadfast. —*n.* 4. stalwart person.

sta'men, *n.* pollen-bearing organ of flower.

stam'i·na, *n.* vigor; endurance.

stam'mer, *v.* 1. speak with involuntary breaks or repetitions. —*n.* 2. such speech.

stamp, *v.* 1. trample. 2. mark. 3. put paper stamp on. —*n.* 4. act of stamping. 5. marking device. 6. adhesive paper affixed to show payment of fees.

stam·pede', *n., v.,* **-peded, -peding.** —*n.* 1. panicky flight. —*v.* 2. flee in stampede.

stance, *n.* position of feet.

stanch (stônch), *adj.* 1. staunch. —*v.* 2. stop flow. esp. of blood. —**stanch'ly,** *adv.* —**stanch'ness,** *n.*

stan'chion (-shən), *n.* upright post.

stand, *v.,* **stood, standing,** *n.* —*v.* 1. rise or be upright. 2. remain firm. 3. be located. 4. be candidate. 5. endure. —*n.* 6. firm attitude. 7. place of standing. 8. platform. 9. support for small articles. 10. outdoor salesplace. 11. area of trees. 12. stop.

stand'ard, *n.* 1. approved model or rule. 2. flag. 3. upright support. —*adj.* 4. being model or basis for comparison.

stand'ard·ize', *v.,* **-ized, -izing.** make standard. —**stand'ard·i·za'tion,** *n.*

stand'by', *n., pl.* **-bys,** *adj.* —*n.* 1. chief support. —*adj.* 2. substitute.

stand'-in', *n.* substitute.

stand'ing, *n.* 1. status or reputation. 2. duration. —*adj.* 3. upright. 4. stagnant. 5. lasting; fixed.

stand'off', *n.* tie or draw; situation in which neither side has advantage.

stand'off'ish, *adj.* tending to be aloof.

stand'point', *n.* point of view.

stand'still', *n.* complete halt.

stan'za, *n.* division of poem.

staph'y·lo·coc'cus (staf'ə lə kok'əs), *n., pl.* **-ci** (-sī, -sē). any of several spherical bacteria occurring in clusters, sometimes pathogenic.

sta'ple, *n., v.,* **-pled, -pling,** *adj.* —*n.* 1. bent wire fastener. 2. chief commodity. 3. textile fiber. —*v.* 4. fasten with staple. —*adj.* 5. chief. —**sta'pler,** *n.*

star, *n., adj., v.,* **starred, starring.** —*n.*

1. heavenly body luminous at night. 2. figure with five or six points. 3. asterisk. 4. principal performer. 5. famous performer. —*adj.* 6. principal. —*v.* 7. mark with star. 8. have leading part. —**star'ry,** *adj.* —**star'dom,** *n.*

star'board, *n.* right-hand side of vessel, facing forward. —**star'board,** *adj., adv.*

starch, *n.* 1. white tasteless substance used as food and as a stiffening agent. 2. preparation from starch. —*v.* 3. stiffen with starch. —**starch'y,** *adj.*

stare, *v.,* **stared, staring,** *n.* —*v.* 1. gaze fixedly. —*n.* 2. fixed look.

star'fish', *n.* star-shaped marine animal.

stark, *adj.* 1. utter; sheer. 2. stiff. —*adv.* 3. utterly.

star'ling, *n.* small bird.

start, *v.* 1. begin. 2. move or issue suddenly. —*n.* 3. beginning. 4. startled movement. 5. lead. —**start'er,** *n.*

star'tle, *v.,* **-tled, -tling.** disturb suddenly.

starve, *v.,* **starved, starving.** 1. die or suffer severely from hunger. 2. kill or weaken by hunger. —**star·va'tion,** *n.*

state, *n., adj., v.* —*n.* 1. condition. 2. pomp. 3. nation. 4. commonwealth of a federal union. 5. civil government. —*adj.* 6. ceremonious. —*v.* 7. declare. —**state'hood,** *n.* —**state'house,** *n.*

state'ly, *adj.* **-lier, -liest.** dignified. —**state'li·ness,** *n.*

state'ment, *n.* 1. declaration. 2. report on business account.

state'room', *n.* quarters on ship, etc.

states'man, *n.* leader in government. —**states'man·ship',** *n.*

stat'ic, *adj.* 1. fixed; at rest. —*n.* 2. atmospheric electricity. 3. interference caused by it.

sta'tion, *n.* 1. place of duty. 2. depot for trains, buses, etc. 3. status. 4. place for sending or receiving radio or television broadcasts. —*v.* 5. assign place to.

sta·tion·ar·y, *adj.* not moving; not movable; fixed.

sta'tion·er, *n.* dealer in stationery.

sta'tion·er·y, *n.* writing materials.

sta·tis'tics, *n.* science of collecting, classifying, and using numerical facts. —**sta·tis'ti·cal,** *adj.* —**sta·tis'ti·cal·ly,** *adv.* —**stat'is·ti'cian,** *n.*

stat'u·ar·y, *n.* statues.

stat'ue, *n.* carved, molded, or cast figure.

stat·u·esque', *adj.* like statue; of imposing figure.

stat'u·ette', *n.* little statue.

stat'ure, *n.* 1. height. 2. achievement.

sta'tus (stā'-, sta'-), *n.* 1. social standing. 2. present condition.

status quo, *Latin.* existing state.

stat'ute, *n.* law enacted by legislature. —**stat'u·to'ry,** *adj.*

staunch (stônch), *adj.* 1. firm; steadfast; strong. —*v.* 2. stanch. —**staunch'ly,** *adv.* —**staunch'ness,** *n.*

stave, *n., v.,* **staved** or (for 3) **stove, staving.** —*n.* 1. one of curved vertical strips of barrel, etc. 2. *Music.* staff. —*v.* 3. break hole in. 4. ward (off).

stay, *v.* 1. remain; continue. 2. stop or restrain. 3. support. —*n.* 4. period at one place. 5. stop; pause. 6. support; prop. 7. rope supporting mast.

stead, *n.* 1. place taken by another. 2. advantage.

stead'fast', *adj.* 1. fixed. 2. firm or loyal. —**stead'fast·ly,** *adv.* —**stead'fast·ness,** *n.*

stead'y, *adj.,* **steadier, steadiest,** *v.,* **steadied, steadying.** —*adj.* 1. firmly fixed. 2. uniform; regular. 3. steadfast. —*v.* 4. make or become steady. —**stead'i·ly,** *adv.* —**stead'i·ness,** *n.*

steak, *n.* slice of meat or fish.

steal, *v.,* **stole, stolen, stealing.** 1. take wrongfully. 2. move very quietly.

stealth, *n.* secret procedure. —**stealth'y,** *adj.* —**stealth'i·ly,** *adv.*

steam, *n.* 1. water in form of gas or vapor. —*v.* 2. pass off as or give off steam. 3. treat with steam, as in cooking. 4. operated by steam. 5. conducting steam. —**steam'boat, steam'ship',** *n.*

steam'er, *n.* 1. vessel moved by steam. 2. device for cooking, treating, etc., with steam.

steam·roll'er, *n.* 1. heavy vehicle with roller used for paving roads. —*v.* 2. crush, flatten, or overwhelm as if with steamroller.

steed, *n.* horse, esp. for riding.

steel, *n.* 1. iron modified with carbon. —*adj.* 2. of or like steel. —*v.* 3. make resolute. —**steel'y,** *adj.*

steel wool, mass of stringlike woven steel, used esp. for scouring and smoothing.

steel'yard', *n.* kind of scale.

steep, *adj.* 1. sloping sharply. —*v.* 2. soak. 3. absorb. —**steep'ly,** *adv.* —**steep'ness,** *n.*

stee'ple, *n.* 1. lofty tower on church, etc. 2. spire.

stee'ple·chase', *n.* horse or foot race over obstacle course.

steer, *v.* 1. guide; direct. —*n.* 2. ox.

steer'age, n. part of ship for passengers paying cheapest rate.

stein, n. mug, esp. for beer.

stel'lar, adj. of or like stars.

stem, n., v., **stemmed, stemming.** —n. 1. supporting stalk of plant or of leaf, flower, or fruit. 2. ancestry. 3. part of word not changed by inflection. 4. Naut. bow. —v. 5. remove stem of 6. originate. 7. stop or check. 8. make headway against.

stench, n. bad odor.

sten'cil, n., v., **-ciled, -ciling.** —n. 1. sheet cut to pass design through when colored over. —v. 2. print with stencil.

ste·nog'ra·pher, n. person skilled in shorthand and typing.

ste·nog'ra·phy, n. writing in shorthand. **—sten'o·graph'ic,** adj. **—sten'o·graph'i·cal·ly,** adv.

sten·to'ri·an, adj. very loud.

step, n., v., **stepped, stepping.** —n. 1. movement of foot in walking. 2. distance of such movement. 3. gait or pace. 4. footprint. 5. stage in process. 6. level on stair or ladder. —v. 7. move by steps. 8. press with foot.

step-, prefix showing relation by remarriage of parent. **—step'child,** n. **—step'son',** n. **—step'daugh'ter,** n. **—step'par'ent,** n. **—step'fa'ther,** n. **—step'moth'er,** n.

step'lad'der, n. ladder with flat treads.

steppe, n. vast plain.

ster'e·o, n., pl. **-eos.** stereophonic sound or equipment.

ster'e·o·phon'ic, adj. (of recorded sound) played through two or more speakers.

ster'e·op'ti·con, n. projector for slides, etc.

ster'e·o·scope', n. device for viewing two pictures at once to give impression of depth.

ster'e·o·type', n., v., **-typed, -typing.** —n. 1. process of making printing plates from mold taken from composed type. 2. idea, etc., without originality. 3. simplified image of person, group, etc. —v. 4. make stereotype of. 5. give fixed, trite form to.

ster'ile, adj. 1. free from living germs. 2. unable to produce offspring; barren. **—ste·ril'i·ty,** n.

ster'i·lize', v., **-lized, -lizing.** make sterile. **—ster'i·li·za'tion,** n. **—ster'i·liz'er,** n.

ster'ling, adj. 1. containing 92.5% silver. 2. of British money. 3. excellent.

stern, adj. 1. strict; harsh; grim. —n. 2. hind part of vessel. **—stern'ly,** adv. **—stern'ness,** n.

ster'num, n., pl. **-na, -nums.** flat bone in chest connecting with clavicle and ribs.

steth'o·scope', n. medical instrument for listening to sounds in body.

ste've·dore', n. person who loads and unloads ships.

stew, v. 1. cook by simmering. —n. 2. food so cooked.

stew'ard, n. 1. person who manages another's affairs, property, etc. 2. person in charge of food, supplies, etc., for ship, club, etc. 3. domestic employee on ship or airplane. **—stew'ard·ess,** n.fem. **—stew'ard·ship',** n.

stick, v., **stuck, sticking,** n. —v. 1. pierce; stab. 2. thrust. 3. cause to adhere. 4. adhere; cling. 5. persist. 6. extend. —n. 7. small length of wood, etc.

stick'er, n. 1. one that sticks. 2. adhesive label. 3. thorn.

stick'le, v., **-led, -ling.** 1. argue over trifles. 2. insist on correctness. **—stick'ler,** n.

stick'y, adj., **stickier, stickiest.** 1. adhering. 2. humid. **—stick'i·ness,** n.

stiff, adj. 1. rigid. 2. not moving easily. 3. formal. **—stiff'en,** v. **—stiff'ly,** adv. **—stiff'ness,** n.

sti'fle, v., **-fled, -fling.** 1. smother. 2. repress.

stig'ma, n., pl. **-mata, -mas.** 1. mark of disgrace. 2. pollen-receiving part of pistil. **—stig'ma·tize',** v.

stile, n. set of steps over fence, etc.

sti·let'to, n., pl. **-tos, -toes.** dagger.

still, adj. 1. motionless. 2. silent. 3. tranquil. —adv. 4. as previously. 5. until now. 6. yet. —conj. 7. nevertheless. —v. 8. make or become still. —n. 9. distilling apparatus. **—still'y,** adj. **—still'ness,** n.

still'born', adj. born dead.

stilt, n. one of two poles enabling user to walk above the ground.

stilt'ed, adj. stiffly dignified.

stim'u·lant, n. food, medicine, etc., that stimulates briefly.

stim'u·late', v., **-lated, -lating.** rouse to action. **—stim'u·la'tion,** n. **—stim'u·la'tive,** adj. **—stim'u·la'tor, stim'u·la'ter,** n.

stim'u·lus, n., pl. **-li.** something that stimulates.

sting, v., **stung, stinging,** n. —v. 1. wound with pointed organ, as bees do. 2. pain sharply. 3. goad. —n. 4. wound caused by stinging. 5. sharp-pointed organ. **—sting'er,** n.

stin'gy (stin'jē), adj., **-gier, -giest.** 1. miserly. 2. scanty. **—stin'gi·ness,** n.

stink, v., **stank** or **stunk, stunk, stink-**

ing, n. —v. **1.** emit bad odor. —n. **2.** bad odor.

stint, v. **1.** limit. **2.** limit oneself. —n. **3.** limitation. **4.** allotted task.

sti'pend (stī'pend), n. regular pay.

stip'ple, v., **-pled, -pling,** n. —v. **1.** paint or cover with tiny dots. —n. **2.** such painting.

stip'u·late, v., **-lated, -lating.** require as condition of agreement. —**stip'u·la'tion,** n.

stir, v., **stirred, stirring,** n. —v. **1.** mix or agitate (liquid, etc.), esp. with circular motion. **2.** move. **3.** rouse; excite. —n. **4.** movement; commotion. **5.** Slang. prison.

stir·cra'zy, adj. Slang. restless or frantic from close confinement.

stir'-fry', v., **-fried, -frying.** fry quickly while stirring constantly over high heat.

stir'rup, n. looplike support for foot, suspended from saddle.

stitch, n. **1.** complete movement of needle in sewing, knitting, etc. **2.** sudden pain. —v. **3.** sew.

stock, n. **1.** goods on hand. **2.** livestock. **3.** stem or trunk. **4.** line of descent. **5.** meat broth. **6.** part of gun supporting barrel. **7.** (pl.) framework in which prisoners were publicly confined. **8.** capital or shares of company. —adj. **9.** standard; common. **10.** of stock. —v. **11.** supply. **12.** store. —**stock'brok'er,** n. —**stock'hold'er,** n.

stock·ade', n., v., **-aded, -ading.** —n. **1.** barrier of upright posts. —v. **2.** protect with stockade.

stock exchange, place where securities are bought and sold. Also, **stock market.**

stock'ing, n. close-fitting covering for foot and leg.

stock'pile', n., v., **-piled, -piling.** —n. **1.** stock of things. —v. **2.** accumulate for eventual use.

stock'y, adj. **stockier, stockiest.** sturdily built. —**stock'i·ly,** adv. —**stock'i·ness,** n.

stock'yard', n. enclosure for livestock about to be slaughtered.

stodg'y, adj., **stodgier, stodgiest.** pompous and uninteresting. —**stodg'i·ness,** n.

sto'gy (stō'gē), n., pl. **-gies.** long, slender, cheap cigar.

sto'ic, adj. **1.** Also, **sto'i·cal.** not reacting to pain. —n. **2.** person who represses emotion. —**sto'i·cal·ly,** adv. —**sto'i·cism',** n.

stoke, v., **stoked, stoking.** tend (fire). —**stok'er,** n.

stole, n. scarf or narrow strip worn over shoulders.

stol'id, adj. unemotional; not easily moved. —**sto·lid'i·ty,** n. —**stol'id·ly,** adv.

stom'ach, n. **1.** organ of food storage and digestion. **2.** appetite; desire. —v. **3.** take into stomach. **4.** tolerate. —**sto·mach'ic,** adj.

stomp, v. tread or tromp on heavily.

stone, n., adj., pl. **stones** or (for 4) **stone,** adj., v., **stoned, stoning,** adv. —n. **1.** hard, nonmetallic mineral substance. **2.** small rock. **3.** gem. **4.** Brit. unit of weight = 14 pounds. **5.** stonelike seed. **6.** concretion formed in body. —adj. **7.** of stone. —v. **8.** throw stones at. **9.** remove stones from. —adv. **10.** entirely. —**ston'y,** adj. —**ston'i·ly,** adv.

Stone Age, prehistoric period before use of metals.

stooge, n. **1.** assistant to comedian. **2.** person acting in obsequious obedience.

stool, n. seat without arms or back.

stoop, v. **1.** bend forward. **2.** condescend. —n. **3.** stooping posture. **4.** small doorway or porch.

stop, v., **stopped, stopping,** n. —v. **1.** cease; halt. **2.** prevent. **3.** close up. **4.** stay. —n. **5.** act, instance, or place of stopping. **6.** hindrance. **7.** device on musical instrument to control tone. —**stop'page,** n.

stop'gap', n., adj. makeshift.

stop'o'ver, n. temporary stop on journey.

stop'per, n. **1.** plug. —v. **2.** close with stopper. Also, **stop'ple.**

stop'watch', n. watch with hand that can be stopped or started instantly, for precise timing.

stor'age, n. **1.** place for storing. **2.** act of storing. **3.** state of being stored. **4.** fee for storing.

store, n., v., **stored, storing.** —n. **1.** place where goods are kept for sale. **2.** supply. —v. **3.** lay up; accumulate. **4.** put in secure place. —**store'keep'er,** n.

store'front', n. small, street-level store.

store'house', n. building for storage. —**store'room',** n.

sto'ried, adj. famed in history or story.

stork, n. wading bird with long legs and bill.

storm, n. **1.** heavy rain, snow, etc., with strong winds. **2.** violent assault. —v. **3.** blow, rain, etc., strongly. **4.** rage. **5.** attack. —**storm'y,** adj. —**storm'i·ly,** adv.

sto'ry, *n., pl.* **-ries. 1.** fictitious tale. **2.** plot. **3.** newspaper report. **4.** *Informal.* lie. **5.** horizontal section of building.

stoup (stoop), *n.* basin for holy water.

stout, *adj.* **1.** solidly built; fat. **2.** bold or strong. **3.** firm. *—n.* **4.** dark, sweet ale. **—stout'ly,** *adv.* **—stout'ness,** *n.*

stove, *n.* apparatus for giving heat.

stow, *v.* **1.** put away, as cargo. **2.** stow away, hide on ship, etc., to get free trip. **—stow'age,** *n.* **—stow'a•way,** *n.*

stra•bis'mus, *n.* visual defect; crosseye.

strad'dle, *v.,* **-dled, -dling,** *n.* —*v.* **1.** have one leg on either side of. *—n.* **2.** straddling stance.

strafe, *v.,* **strafed, strafing.** shoot from airplanes.

strag'gle, *v.,* **-gled, -gling.** stray from course; ramble. **—strag'gler,** *n.*

straight, *adj.* **1.** direct. **2.** even. **3.** honest. **4.** right. **5.** *Informal.* heterosexual. *—adv.* **6.** directly. **7.** in straight line. **8.** honestly. *—n.* **9.** five-card consecutive sequence in poker. **—straight'en,** *v.* **—straight'ness,** *n.*

straight'a•way, *adv.* at once. Also, **straight'way'.**

straight face, expression that conceals feelings, as when keeping a secret.

straight'for'ward, *adj.* direct; frank.

strain, *v.* **1.** exert to utmost. **2.** injure by stretching. **3.** sieve; filter. **4.** constrain. *—n.* **5.** great effort. **6.** injury from straining. **7.** severe pressure. **8.** melody. **9.** descendants. **10.** ancestry. **11.** hereditary trait. **—strain'er,** *n.*

strait, *n.* **1.** narrow waterway. **2.** (*pl.*) distress.

strait'en, *v.* **1.** put into financial troubles. **2.** restrict.

strait'jack'et, *n.* **1.** garment of strong material designed to bind arms and restrain violent person. **2.** anything that severely confines or hinders.

strait'-laced', *adj.* excessively strict in conduct or morality.

strand, *v.* **1.** run aground. *—n.* **2.** shore. **3.** twisted component of rope. **4.** tress. **5.** string, as of beads.

strange, *adj.,* **stranger, strangest. 1.** unusual; odd. **2.** unfamiliar. **—strange'ly,** *adv.* **—strange'ness,** *n.*

stran'ger, *n.* person not known or acquainted.

stran'gle, *v.,* **-gled, -gling. 1.** kill by choking. **2.** choke. **—stran'gler,** *n.* **—stran'gu•la'tion,** *n.*

strap, *n., v.,* **strapped, strapping.** —*n.*

1. narrow strip or band. —*v.* **2.** fasten with strap.

strapped, *adj.* needing money; broke.

strat'a•gem (-jam), *n.* plan; trick.

strat'e•gy, *n., pl.* **-gies. 1.** planning and direction of military operations. **2.** plan for achieving goal. **—stra•te'gic,** *adj.* **—stra•te'gi•cal•ly,** *adv.* **—strat'e•gist,** *n.*

strat'i•fy', *v.,* **-fied, -fying.** form in layers. **—strat'i•fi•ca'tion,** *n.*

strat'o•sphere, *n.* upper region of atmosphere.

stra'tum (strā'tam, strat'am), *n., pl.* **-ta, -tums.** layer of material.

straw, *n.* **1.** stalk of cereal grass. **2.** mass of dried stalks.

straw'ber'ry, *n., pl.* **-ries.** fleshy fruit of stemless herb.

straw vote, unofficial vote taken to determine general trend of opinion.

stray, *v.* **1.** ramble; go from one's course or rightful place. *—adj.* **2.** straying. *—n.* **3.** stray creature.

streak, *n.* **1.** long mark or smear. **2.** vein; stratum. *—v.* **3.** mark with streaks. **4.** flash rapidly.

stream, *n.* **1.** flowing body of water. **2.** steady flow. *—v.* **3.** flow or move in stream. **4.** wave.

stream'er, *n.* long narrow flag.

stream'line', *adj., n., v.,* **-lined, -lining.** *—adj.* **1.** having shape past which fluids move easily. *—n.* **2.** streamline shape. *—v.* **3.** shape with streamline. **4.** reorganize efficiently.

street, *n.* public city road.

street'car', *n.* public conveyance running on rails.

street'walk'er, *n.* prostitute who solicits on the streets.

strength, *n.* **1.** power of body, mind, position, etc. **2.** intensity.

strength'en, *v.* make or grow stronger.

stren'u•ous, *adj.* vigorous; active. **—stren'u•ous•ly,** *adv.*

strep'to•coc'cus, *n., pl.* **-ci.** one of group of disease-causing bacteria.

stress, *v.* **1.** emphasize. *—n.* **2.** emphasis. **3.** physical pressure. **4.** mental or emotional strain.

stretch, *v.* **1.** extend; spread. **2.** distend. **3.** draw tight. *—n.* **4.** act of stretching. **5.** extension; expansion. **6.** continuous length.

stretch'er, *n.* **1.** canvas-covered frame for carrying sick, etc. **2.** device for stretching.

strew, *v.,* **strewed, strewed** or **strewn, strewing.** scatter; sprinkle.

stri'at•ed, *adj.* furrowed; streaked. **—stri•a'tion,** *n.*

strick'en, *adj.* 1. wounded. 2. afflicted, as by disease or sorrow.

strict, *adj.* 1. exacting; severe. 2. precise. 3. careful. —**strict'ly,** *adv.* —**strict'ness,** *n.*

stric'ture, *n.* 1. adverse criticism. 2. morbid contraction of body passage.

stride, *v.,* **strode, stridden, striding,** *n.* —*v.* 1. walk with long steps. 2. straddle. —*n.* 3. long step. 4. steady pace.

stri'dent, *adj.* harsh in sound. —**stri'dent·ly,** *adv.* —**stri'den·cy,** *n.*

strife, *n.* conflict or quarrel.

strike, *v.,* **struck, struck** or **stricken, striking,** *n.* —*v.* 1. deal a blow. 2. hit forcibly. 3. cause to ignite. 4. impress. 5. efface; mark out. 6. afflict or affect. 7. sound by percussion. 8. discover in ground. 9. encounter. 10. (of workers) stop work to compel agreement to demands. 11. **strike out,** *Baseball.* put or be put out on three strikes. —*n.* 12. act of striking. 13. *Baseball.* failure of batter to hit pitched ball; anything ruled equivalent. 14. *Bowling.* knocking-down of all pins with first bowl. —**strik'er,** *n.*

strik'ing, *adj.* 1. conspicuously attractive or impressive. 2. noticeable; conspicuous.

string, *n., v.,* **strung, stringing.** —*n.* 1. cord, thread, etc. 2. series or set. 3. cord on musical instrument. 4. plant fiber. —*v.* 5. furnish with strings. 6. arrange in row. 7. mount on string. —**stringed,** *adj.* —**string'y,** *adj.*

string bean, bean with edible pod.

strin'gent (strin'jənt), *adj.* 1. very strict. 2. urgent. —**strin'gen·cy,** *n.* —**strin'gent·ly,** *adv.*

strip, *v.,* **stripped, stripping,** *n.* —*v.* 1. remove covering or clothing. 2. rob. 3. cut into strips. —*n.* 4. long narrow piece.

stripe, *n., v.,* **striped, striping.** —*n.* 1. band of different color, material, etc. 2. welt from whipping. —*v.* 3. mark with stripes.

strip'ling, *n.* youth.

strip'tease', *n.* act, as in burlesque, in which performer gradually removes clothing. —**strip'per,** *n.*

strive, *v.,* **strove, striven, striving.** try hard; struggle.

strobe, *n.* electronic flash producing rapid bursts of light. Also, **strobe light.**

stroke, *n., v.,* **stroked, stroking.** —*v.* 1. rub gently. —*n.* 2. act of stroking. 3. blow. 4. blockage or hemorrhage of blood vessel leading to brain. 5. one complete movement. 6. piece of

luck, work, etc. 7. method of swimming.

stroll, *v.* 1. walk idly. 2. roam.

stroll'er, *n.* chairlike carriage in which young children are pushed.

strong, *adj.* 1. vigorous; powerful; able. 2. intense; distinct. —**strong'ly,** *adv.*

strong'hold', *n.* fortress.

strop, *n., v.,* **stropped, stropping.** —*n.* 1. flexible strap. —*v.* 2. sharpen on strop.

struc'ture, *n.* 1. form of building or arrangement. 2. something built. —**struc'tur·al,** *adj.* —**struc'tur·al·ly,** *adv.*

stru'del, *n.* fruit-filled pastry.

strug'gle, *v.,* **-gled, -gling,** *n.* —*v.* 1. contend; strive. —*n.* 2. strong effort. 3. combat. —**strug'gler,** *n.*

strum, *v.,* **strummed, strumming.** play carelessly on (stringed instrument).

strum'pet, *n.* prostitute.

strut, *v.,* **strutted, strutting,** *n.* —*v.* 1. walk in vain, pompous manner. —*n.* 2. strutting walk. 3. prop; truss.

strych'nine (strik'nin, -nīn), *n.* colorless poison.

stub, *n., v.,* **stubbed, stubbing.** —*n.* 1. short remaining piece. 2. stump. —*v.* 3. strike (one's toe) against something. —**stub'by,** *adj.*

stub'ble, *n.* 1. short stumps, as of grain stalks. 2. short growth of beard. —**stub'bly,** *adj.*

stub'born, *adj.* 1. unreasonably obstinate. 2. persistent. —**stub'born·ly,** *adv.* —**stub'born·ness,** *n.*

stuc'co, *n., pl.* **-coes, -cos,** *v.,* **-coed, -coing.** —*n.* 1. plaster for exteriors. —*v.* 2. cover with stucco.

stud, *n., v.,* **studded, studding.** —*n.* 1. projecting knob, pin, etc. 2. upright prop. 3. detachable button. 4. collection of horses or other animals for breeding. 5. stallion. —*v.* 6. set or scatter with studs.

stu'dent, *n.* person who studies.

stud'ied, *adj.* deliberate.

stu'di·o', *n., pl.* **-dios.** 1. artist's workroom. 2. place equipped for radio or television broadcasting.

stud'y, *n., pl.* **studies,** *v.,* **studied, studying.** —*n.* 1. effort to learn. 2. object of study. 3. deep thought. 4. room for studying, writing, etc. —*v.* 5. make study of —**stu'di·ous,** *adj.* —**stu'di·ous·ly,** *adv.* —**stu'di·ous·ness,** *n.*

stuff, *n.* 1. material. 2. worthless matter. —*v.* 3. cram full; pack.

stuffed shirt, pompous, self-satisfied, inflexible person.

stuff'ing, n. material stuffed in something.

stuff'y, adj., **stuffier, stuffiest. 1.** lacking fresh air. **2.** pompous; pedantic. —**stuff'i•ness,** n.

stul'ti•fy', v., **-fied, -fying. 1.** cause to look foolish. **2.** make futile.

stum'ble, v., **-bled, -bling. 1.** lose balance from striking foot. **2.** come unexpectedly upon.

stump, n. **1.** lower end of tree after top is gone. **2.** any short remaining part. —v. **3.** baffle. **4.** campaign politically. **5.** walk heavily.

stun, v., **stunned, stunning. 1.** render unconscious. **2.** amaze.

stun'ning, adj. strikingly attractive.

stunt, v. **1.** check growth. **2.** do showily. —n. **3.** performance to show skill, etc.

stu'pe•fy', v., **-fied, -fying. 1.** put into stupor. **2.** stun. —**stu'pe•fac'tion,** n.

stu•pen'dous, adj. **1.** amazing; marvelous. **2.** immense.

stu'pid, adj. having or showing little intelligence. —**stu•pid'i•ty,** n. —**stu'pid•ly,** adv.

stu'por, n. dazed or insensible state.

stur'dy, adj., **-dier, -diest. 1.** strongly built. **2.** firm. —**stur'di•ly,** adv. —**stur'di•ness,** n.

stur'geon, n. large fish of fresh and salt water.

stut'ter, v., n. stammer. —**stut'ter•er,** n.

sty, n., pl. **sties. 1.** pig pen. **2.** inflamed swelling on eyelid.

style, n., v., **styled, styling.** —n. **1.** particular kind. **2.** mode of fashion. **3.** elegance. **4.** distinct way of writing or speaking. **5.** pointed instrument. —v. **6.** name; give title to. —**sty•lis'tic,** adj.

styl'ish, adj. fashionable. —**styl'ish•ly,** adv.

sty'lus, n. pointed tool for writing, etc.

sty'mie, v., **-mied, -mying.** hinder or obstruct, as in golf.

styp'tic, adj. **1.** checking bleeding. —n. **2.** styptic substance.

Sty'ro•foam', n. Trademark. lightweight plastic.

suave (swäv), adj. smoothly agreeable. —**suave'ly,** adv. —**suav'i•ty, suave'ness,** n.

sub-, prefix. under; below; beneath; less than; secondary.

sub•al'tern (-ôl'-), n. Brit. low-ranking officer.

sub•a•tom'ic, adj. of particles within an atom.

sub•com•mit'tee, n. committee appointed out of main committee.

sub•con'scious, adj. **1.** existing beneath consciousness. —n. **2.** ideas, feelings, etc., of which one is unaware. —**sub•con'scious•ly,** adv.

sub•cul'ture, n. group with social, economic, or other traits distinguishing it from others within larger society.

sub•cu•ta'ne•ous, adj. beneath the skin.

sub•di•vide', v., **-vided, -viding.** divide into parts. —**sub•di•vi'sion,** n.

sub•due', v., **-dued, -duing. 1.** overcome. **2.** soften.

sub'ject, n. **1.** matter of thought, concern, etc. **2.** person under rule of government. **3.** Gram. noun or pronoun that performs action of predicate. **4.** one undergoing action, etc. —adj. **5.** being a subject. **6.** liable; exposed. —v. (səb jekt'). **7.** cause to experience. **8.** make liable. —**sub•jec'tion,** n.

sub•jec'tive, adj. **1.** personal. **2.** existing in mind. —**sub'jec•tiv'i•ty,** n. —**sub•jec'tive•ly,** adv.

sub•join', v. append.

sub•ju•gate', v., **-gated, -gating.** subdue; conquer. —**sub•ju•ga'tion,** n.

sub•junc'tive, adj. **1.** designating verb mode of condition, impression, etc. —n. **2.** subjunctive mode.

sub'lease', n., v., **-leased, -leasing. 1.** lease granted by tenant. —v. (sub lēs'). **2.** rent by sublease.

sub•let', v., **-let, -letting.** (of lessee) let to another person.

sub•li•mate', v., **-mated, -mating.** —v. **1.** deflect (biological energies) to other channels. **2.** sublime. —n. (-mit). **3.** substance obtained in subliming. —**sub•li•ma'tion,** n.

sub•lime', adj., n., v., **-limed, -liming.** —adj. **1.** lofty; noble. —n. **2.** that which is sublime. —v. **3.** heat (substance) to vapor that condenses to solid on cooling. —**sub•lim'i•ty,** n. —**sub•lime'ly,** adv.

sub•lim'i•nal, adj. below threshold of consciousness. —**sub•lim'i•nal•ly,** adv.

sub'ma•chine' gun, automatic weapon fired from shoulder or hip.

sub'ma•rine', n. **1.** vessel that can navigate under water. —adj. (sub'mə rēn') **2.** of submarines. **3.** being under sea.

sub•merge', v., **-merged, -merging.** plunge under water. —**sub•mer'gence,** n.

sub•merse', v., **-mersed, -mersing.** submerge. —**sub•mer'sion,** n. —**sub•mers'i•ble,** adj.

sub•mis'sive, adj. yielding or obeying

readily. —**sub·mis'sive·ly**, adv. —**sub·mis'sive·ness**, n.

sub·mit', v., **-mitted, -mitting. 1.** yield; surrender. **2.** offer for consideration. —**sub·mis'sion**, n.

sub·nor'mal, adj. of less than normal intelligence.

sub·or'di·nate, adj., n., v., **-nated, -nating.** —adj. (-nit). **1.** of lower rank or importance. —n. (-nit). **2.** subordinate person or thing. —v. (-nāt'). **3.** treat as subordinate. —**sub·or'di·na'tion**, n.

sub·orn', v. bribe or incite to crime, esp. to perjury.

sub·poe'na (sə pē'nə), n., v., **-naed, -naing. 1.** summons to appear in court. —v. **2.** serve with subpoena.

sub·scribe', v., **-scribed, -scribing. 1.** promise contribution. **2.** agree; sign in agreement. **3.** contract to receive periodical regularly. —**sub·scrib'er**, n. —**sub·scrip'tion**, n.

sub'se·quent, adj. later; following. —**sub'se·quent·ly**, adv.

sub·serve', v., **-served, -serving.** promote; assist.

sub·ser'vi·ent, adj. **1.** servile; submissive. **2.** useful. —**sub·ser'vi·ence**, v. —**sub·ser'vi·ent·ly**, adv.

sub·side', v., **-sided, -siding. 1.** sink; settle. **2.** abate. —**sub·sid'ence**, n.

sub·sid'i·ar·y, adj., n., pl. **-aries.** —adj. **1.** auxiliary. **2.** subordinate. —n. **3.** anything subsidiary.

sub'si·dy, n., pl. **-dies.** direct pecuniary aid, esp. by government. —**sub'si·dize'**, v.

sub·sist', v. **1.** exist. **2.** live (as on food). —**sub·sist'ence**, n.

sub·son'ic, adj. of or traveling at a speed below the speed of sound.

sub'stance, n. **1.** matter or material. **2.** density. **3.** meaning. **4.** likelihood.

sub·stand'ard, adj. below standard; not good enough.

sub·stan'tial, adj. **1.** actual. **2.** fairly large. **3.** strong. **4.** of substance. **5.** prosperous. —**sub·stan'tial·ly**, adv.

sub·stan'ti·ate', v., **-ated, -ating.** support with evidence. —**sub·stan'ti·a'tion**, n.

sub'stan·tive, n. **1.** noun, pronoun, or word used as noun. —adj. **2.** of or denoting substantive. **3.** independent. **4.** essential.

sub'sti·tute', v., **-tuted, -tuting.** —v. **1.** put or serve in place of another. —n. **2.** substitute person or thing. —**sub'sti·tu'tion**, n.

sub·sume', v., **-sumed, -suming.** consider or include as part of something larger.

sub'ter·fuge', n. means used to evade or conceal.

sub'ter·ra'ne·an, adj. underground.

sub'text, n. underlying or implicit meaning.

sub'tile, adj. subtle.

sub'ti·tle, n., v. **-tled, -tling.** —n. **1.** secondary or subordinate title, as of book. **2.** text of dialogue, etc., appearing at bottom of motion picture screen, etc. —v. **3.** give subtitles to.

sub'tle (sut'əl), adj., **-tler, -tlest. 1.** delicate; faint. **2.** discerning. **3.** crafty. —**sub'tle·ty**, n. —**sub'tly**, adv.

sub·tract', v. take from another; deduct. —**sub·trac'tion**, n.

sub·trop'i·cal, adj. bordering on tropics.

sub'urb, n. district just outside city. —**sub·ur'ban**, adj. —**sub·ur'ban·ite**, n.

sub·ur'bi·a, n. **1.** suburbs or suburbanites collectively. **2.** life in the suburbs.

sub·vert', v. overthrow; destroy. —**sub·ver'sion**, n. —**sub·ver'sive**, adj., n.

sub'way, n. underground electric railway.

suc·ceed', v. **1.** end or accomplish successfully. **2.** follow and replace.

suc·cess', n. **1.** favorable achievement. **2.** good fortune. **3.** successful thing or person. —**suc·cess'ful**, adj. —**suc·cess'ful·ly**, adv.

suc·ces'sion, n. **1.** act of following in sequence. **2.** sequence of persons or things. **3.** right or process of succeeding another. —**suc·ces'sive**, adj. —**suc·ces'sive·ly**, adv.

suc·ces'sor, n. one that succeeds another.

suc·cinct' (sək singkt'), adj. without useless words; concise. —**suc·cinct'ly**, adv. —**suc·cinct'ness**, n.

suc'cor, n., v. help; aid.

suc'co·tash', n. corn and beans cooked together.

suc'cu·lent, adj. juicy. —**suc'cu·lence**, n.

suc·cumb', v. **1.** yield. **2.** die.

such, adj. **1.** of that kind, extent, etc. —n. **2.** such person or thing.

suck, v. **1.** draw in by using lips and tongue. **2.** absorb. —n. **3.** act of sucking. **4.** nourishment, etc., gained by sucking.

suck'er, n. **1.** one that sucks. **2.** freshwater fish. **3.** Informal. lollipop. **4.** shoot from underground stem or root. **5.** Informal. gullible person.

suck'le, v., **-led, -ling.** nurse at breast.

suck'ling, n. **1.** infant. **2.** unweaned animal.

su'crose (sōō'krōs), *n.* sweet crystalline substance obtained esp. from sugar cane or sugar beet; sugar.

suc'tion, *n.* tendency to draw substance into vacuum.

sud'den, *adj.* abrupt; quick; unexpected. —**sud'den·ly,** *adv.* —**sud'den·ness,** *n.*

suds, *n.pl.* 1. lather. 2. soapy water. —**suds'y,** *adj.*

sue, *v.,* **sued, suing.** 1. take legal action. 2. appeal.

suede (swād), *n.* soft, napped leather.

su'et, *n.* hard fat about kidneys, etc., esp. of cattle.

suf'fer, *v.* 1. undergo (pain or unpleasantness). 2. tolerate. —**suf'fer·er,** *n.*

suf'fer·ance, *n.* 1. tolerance. 2. endurance.

suf·fice', *v.,* **-ficed, -ficing.** be enough.

suf·fi'cient, *adj.* enough. —**suf·fi'cien·cy,** *n.* —**suf·fi'cient·ly,** *adv.*

suf'fix, *n.* element added to end of word to form another word.

suf'fo·cate', *v.,* **-cated, -cating.** kill or choke by cutting off air to lungs. —**suf·fo·ca'tion,** *n.*

suf'frage, *n.* right to vote.

suf·fuse', *v.* overspread.

sug'ar, *n.* 1. sweet substance, esp. from sugar cane or sugar beet. —*v.* 2. sweeten with sugar. —**sug'ar·y,** *adj.*

sugar cane, tall grass that is the chief source of sugar.

sug'ar·coat', *v.* make more pleasant or acceptable.

sug·gest', *v.* 1. offer for consideration or action. 2. imply. —**sug·ges'tion,** *n.*

sug·gest'i·ble, *adj.* easily led or influenced. —**sug·gest'i·bil'i·ty,** *n.*

sug·ges'tive, *adj.* suggesting, esp. something improper. —**sug·ges'tive·ly,** *adv.* —**sug·ges'tive·ness,** *n.*

su'i·cide', *n.* 1. intentional killing of oneself. 2. person who commits suicide. —**su'i·cid'al,** *adj.*

suit, *n.* 1. set of clothes. 2. legal action. 3. division of playing cards. 4. petition. 5. wooing. —*v.* 6. clothe. 7. accommodate; adapt. 8. please.

suit'a·ble, *adj.* appropriate; fitting. —**suit'a·bly,** *adv.*

suit'case', *n.* oblong valise.

suite (swēt), *n.* 1. series or set, as of rooms. 2. retinue.

suit'or, *n.* wooer.

su·ki·ya'ki, *n.* Japanese dish of meat and vegetables cooked in soy sauce.

sul'fa drugs, group of antibacterial

substances used to treat diseases, wounds, etc.

sul'fate, *n.* salt of sulfuric acid.

sul'fide, *n.* compound of sulfur.

sul'fur, *n.* yellow nonmetallic element.

sul·fur'ic, *adj.* of or containing sulfur. Also, **sul'fur·ous.**

sulk, *v.* 1. hold sullenly aloof. —*n.* 2. fit of sulking.

sulk'y, *adj.,* **sulkier, sulkiest.** —*adj.* 1. sullen; ill-humored. —*n.* 2. two-wheeled racing carriage for one person. —**sulk'i·ly,** *adv.* —**sulk'i·ness,** *n.*

sul'len, *adj.* 1. silently ill-humored. 2. gloomy. —**sul'len·ly,** *adv.* —**sul'len·ness,** *n.*

sul'ly, *v.,* **-lied, -lying.** soil; defile.

sul'phur, *n.* sulfur.

sul'tan, *n.* ruler of Muslim country.

sul'try, *adj.,* **-trier, -triest.** hot and close. —**sul'tri·ness,** *n.*

sum, *n., v.,* **summed, summing.** —*n.* 1. aggregate of two or more numbers, etc. 2. total amount. 3. gist. —*v.* 4. total. 5. summarize.

su'mac (shōō'-), *n.* small tree with long pinnate leaves.

sum'ma·rize', *v.,* **-rized, -rizing.** make or be summary of.

sum'ma·ry, *n., pl.* **-ries,** *adj.* —*n.* 1. concise presentation of main points. —*adj.* 2. concise. 3. prompt. —**sum·mar'i·ly,** *adv.*

sum·ma'tion, *n.* 1. act of summing up. 2. total.

sum'mer, *n.* 1. season between spring and fall. —*adj.* 2. of, like, or for summer. —*v.* 3. pass summer. —**sum'mer·y,** *adj.*

sum'mit, *n.* highest point.

sum'mon, *v.* call or order to appear.

sum'mons, *n.* message that summons.

su'mo (shōō'-), *n.* Japanese form of wrestling featuring extremely heavy contestants.

sump, *n.* pit for collecting water, etc.

sump'tu·ous, *adj.* revealing great expense; luxurious. —**sump'tu·ous·ly,** *adv.* —**sump'tu·ous·ness,** *n.*

sun, *n., v.,* **sunned, sunning.** —*n.* 1. heat- and light-giving body of solar system. 2. sunshine. —*v.* 3. expose to sunshine. —**sun'beam',** *n.*

sun'bathe', *v.,* **-bathed, -bathing.** expose body to sunlight.

Sun'·belt', *n. Informal.* southern and southwestern U.S. Also, **Sun Belt.**

sun'block', *n.* substance, as a cream, to protect skin from sunburn. Also, **sun'screen'.**

sun'burn', *n., v.,* **-burned** or **-burnt, -burning.** —*n.* 1. superficial burn from sun's rays. —v. 2. affect with sunburn.

sun'dae, n. ice cream topped with fruit, etc.

Sun'day, n. first day of week.

sun'der, v. separate.

sun'di·al, n. outdoor instrument for telling time by shadow.

sun'dry (-drē), adj., n., pl. -dries. —adj. 1. various. —n. 2. (pl.) small items of merchandise.

sun'fish', n. fresh-water fish.

sun'flow'er, n. tall plant with yellow flowers.

sun'glass'es, n.pl. eyeglasses with tinted lenses to permit vision in bright sun.

sun'light', n. light from sun.

sun'lit', adj. lighted by the sun.

sun'ny, adj., -nier, -niest. 1. with much sunlight. 2. cheerful; jolly. —sun'ni·ness, n.

sun'rise', n. ascent of sun above horizon. Also, **sun'up'**.

sun'roof', n. section of automobile roof that can be opened.

sun'set', n. descent of sun below horizon. Also, **sun'down'**.

sun'shine', n. light of sun.

sun'spot', n. dark spot on face of sun.

sun'stroke', n. illness from overexposure to sun's rays.

sun'tan', n. darkening of skin caused by exposure to sun.

sup, v., **supped**, **supping**. eat supper.

su'per, n. 1. superintendent. —adj. 2. very good; first-rate.

su'per-, prefix. above or over; exceeding; larger or more.

su'per·an'nu·at'ed, adj. 1. retired. 2. too old for work or use. 3. antiquated; obsolete.

su·perb', adj. very fine. —su·perb'·ly, adv.

su'per·charge', v., -charged, -charging. 1. charge with abundant or excess energy, etc. 2. supply air to (engine) at high pressure. —su'per·charg'er, n.

su'per·cil'i·ous (-sil'-), adj. haughtily disdainful. —su'per·cil'i·ous·ly, adv. —su'per·cil'i·ous·ness, n.

su'per·con·duc·tiv'i·ty, n. disappearance of electrical resistance in certain metals at extremely low temperatures. —su'per·con·duc'tor, n.

su'per·fi'cial, adj. 1. of, on, or near surface. 2. shallow, obvious, or insignificant. —su'per·fi'ci·al'i·ty, n. —su'per·fi'cial·ly, adv.

su·per'flu·ous, adj. 1. being more than is necessary. 2. unnecessary. —su'per·flu'i·ty, n. —su·per'flu·ous·ly, adv.

su'per·high'way, n. highway for travel at high speeds.

su'per·hu'man, adj. 1. beyond what is human. 2. exceeding human strength.

su'per·im·pose', v., -posed, -posing. place over something else.

su'per·in·tend', v. oversee and direct. —su'per·in·tend'ence, su'per·in·tend'en·cy, n. —su'per·in·tend'ent, n., adj.

su·pe'ri·or, adj. 1. above average; better. 2. upper. 3. arrogant. —n. 4. superior person. 5. head of convent, etc. —su·pe'ri·or'i·ty, n.

su·per'la·tive, adj. 1. of highest kind; best. 2. highest in comparison. —n. 3. anything superlative. —su·per'la·tive·ly, adv.

su'per·man', n., pl. -men. person of extraordinary or superhuman powers.

su'per·mar'ket, n. self-service food store with large variety.

su'per·nat'u·ral, adj. 1. outside the laws of nature; ghostly. —n. 2. realm of supernatural beings or things.

su'per·nu'mer·ar'y, adj., n., pl. -aries. —adj. 1. extra. —n. 2. extra person or thing. 3. actor with no lines.

su'per·pow'er, n. large, powerful nation greatly influencing world affairs.

su'per·script', n. letter, number, or symbol written high on line of text.

su'per·sede', v., -seded, -seding. replace in power, use, etc.

su'per·son'ic, adj. faster than speed of sound.

su'per·star', n. entertainer or sports figure of world renown.

su'per·sti'tion, n. irrational belief in ominous significance of particular thing, occurrence, etc. —su'per·sti'tious, adj. —su'per·sti'tious·ly, adv.

su'per·struc'ture, n. upper part of building or vessel.

su'per·vene', v., -vened, -vening. 1. come as something extra. 2. ensue.

su'per·vise', v., -vised, -vising. direct and inspect. —su'per·vi'sion, n. —su'per·vi'sor, n. —su'per·vi'so·ry, adj.

su·pine' (sōō-), adj. 1. lying on back. 2. passive. —su·pine'ly, adv.

sup'per, n. evening meal.

sup·plant', v. supersede.

sup'ple, adj., -pler, -plest. flexible; limber. —sup'ple·ly, adv. —sup'ple·ness, n.

sup'ple·ment (-mant), n. 1. something added to complete or improve. —v. (-ment'). 2. add to or complete.

—**sup•ple•men'tal, sup•ple•men'ta•ry,** *adj.*

sup•pli•cate, *v.,* **-cated, -cating.** beg humbly. —**sup'pli•ant, sup'pli•cant,** *n., adj.* —**sup•pli•ca'tion,** *n.*

sup•ply', *v.,* **-plied, -plying,** *n., pl.* **-plies.** —*v.* 1. furnish; provide. 2. fill (a lack). —*n.* 3. act of supplying. 4. that supplied. 5. stock. —**sup•pli'er,** *n.*

supply'-side', *adj.* of economic theory that reduced taxes will stimulate investment and economic growth.

sup•port', *v.* 1. hold up; bear. 2. provide living for. 3. uphold; advocate. 4. corroborate. —*n.* 5. act of supporting. 6. maintenance; livelihood. 7. thing or person that supports. —**sup•port'a•ble,** *adj.* —**sup•port'ive,** *adj.*

support group, group of people who meet regularly to support each other by discussing shared problems.

sup•pose', *v.,* **-posed, -posing.** 1. assume; consider. 2. take for granted. —**sup•pos'ed•ly,** *adv.* —**sup•po•si'tion,** *n.* —**sup•po•si'tion•al,** *adj.*

sup•pos•i•to•ry, *n., pl.* **-ries.** solid mass of medicinal substance that melts on insertion into rectum or vagina.

sup•press', *v.* 1. end forcibly; subdue. 2. repress. 3. withhold from circulation. —**sup•pres'sion,** *n.* —**sup•pres'si•ble,** *adj.*

sup•pu•rate (sup'yə-), *v.,* **-rated, -rating.** form or discharge pus. —**sup•pu•ra'tion,** *n.* —**sup'pu•ra'tive,** *adj.*

su•preme', *adj.* chief; greatest. —**su•prem'a•cy,** *n.* —**su•preme'ly,** *adv.*

sur•cease', *n.* end.

sur'charge', *n., v.,* **-charged, -charging.** —*n.* 1. extra or excessive charge, load, etc. —*v.* (sŭr chärj'). 2. put surcharge on. 3. overburden.

sure, *adj.,* **surer, surest.** 1. certain; positive. 2. reliable. 3. firm. —**sure'ly,** *adv.* —**sure'ness,** *n.*

sure'fire', *adj. Informal.* certain to succeed.

sure'ty (shŏŏr'i tē), *n., pl.* **-ties.** 1. security against loss, etc. 2. person who accepts responsibility for another.

surf, *n.* waves breaking on shore or shoals.

sur'face, *n., adj., v.,* **-faced, -facing.** —*n.* 1. outer face; outside. —*adj.* 2. superficial. —*v.* 3. finish surface of. 4. come to surface.

sur'feit (-fit), *n.* 1. excess, esp. of food or drink. 2. disgust at excess. —*v.* 3. overeat; satiate.

surf'ing, *n.* sport of riding the surf, usu. on a **surf'board'.**

surge, *v.,* **surged, surging.** —*n.* 1. swelling or rolling movement or body. —*v.* 2. rise and fall.

sur'geon, *n.* person skilled in surgery.

sur'ger•y, *n., pl.* **-geries.** 1. treatment of disease, etc., by cutting and other manipulations. 2. room for surgical operations. —**sur'gi•cal,** *adj.* —**sur'gi•cal•ly,** *adv.*

sur•ly, *adj.,* **-lier, -liest.** rude; churlish. —**sur'li•ness,** *n.*

sur•mise', *v.,* **-mised, -mising.** guess.

sur•mount', *v.* 1. get over or on top of. 2. overcome. —**sur•mount'a•ble,** *adj.*

sur'name', *n.* family name.

sur•pass', *v.* 1. exceed; excel. 2. transcend.

sur'plice (-plis), *n.* white, loose-fitting robe worn over cassock.

sur'plus, *n.* 1. amount beyond that needed; excess. —*adj.* 2. being a surplus.

sur•prise', *v.,* **-prised, -prising,** *n.* —*v.* 1. come upon unexpectedly; astonish. —*n.* 2. act of surprising. 3. something that surprises. 4. feeling of being surprised.

sur•re'al•ism, *n.* art attempting to express the subconscious. —**sur•re'al•ist,** *n., adj.* —**sur•re•al•is'tic,** *adj.*

sur•ren'der, *v.* 1. yield. —*n.* 2. act of yielding.

sur•rep•ti'tious, *adj.* stealthy; secret. —**sur•rep•ti'tious•ly,** *adv.*

sur'rey, *n.* light carriage with two or more seats.

sur'ro•gate, *n.* 1. substitute. 2. judge concerned with wills, estates, etc.

sur•round', *v.* encircle; enclose.

sur•round'ings, *n.pl.* environment.

sur'tax', *n.* additional tax, esp. on high incomes.

sur•veil'lance (-vā'ləns), *n.* close watch.

sur•vey', *v.* (sər vā'). 1. view. 2. measure or determine dimensions or nature of. —*n.* (sŭr'vā). 3. methodical investigation. 4. description from surveying. —**sur•vey'or,** *n.*

sur•vive', *v.,* **-vived, -viving.** 1. remain alive. 2. outlive. —**sur•viv'al,** *n.* —**sur•vi'vor,** *n.*

sus•cep'ti•ble (sə sep'-), *adj.* apt to be affected; liable. —**sus•cep'ti•bil'i•ty,** *n.* —**sus•cep'ti•bly,** *adv.*

su'shi (sŏŏ'shē), *n.* Japanese dish of rice cakes with seaweed, raw fish, vegetables, etc.

sus•pect', *v.* 1. imagine to be guilty, false, etc. 2. surmise. —*n.* (sus'pekt).

3. one suspected. —*adj.* (sus'pekt). **4.** liable to doubt.

sus·pend', *v.* **1.** hang. **2.** keep temporarily inactive. **3.** refuse work to temporarily.

sus·pend'ers, *n.pl.* straps for holding up trousers.

sus·pense', *n.* uncertainty; anxiety. —**sus·pense'ful,** *adj.*

sus·pen'sion, *n.* **1.** act of suspending. **2.** temporary inactivity. **3.** state in which undissolved particles are dispersed in fluid.

sus·pi'cion, *n.* **1.** act or instance of suspecting. **2.** trace.

sus·pi'cious, *adj.* **1.** having suspicions. **2.** causing suspicion. —**sus·pi'cious·ly,** *adv.*

sus·tain', *v.* support; maintain. —**sus·tain'er,** *n.*

sus'te·nance, *n.* **1.** food. **2.** maintenance.

su'ture (sōō'chər), *n.,* *v.,* **-tured, -turing.** —*n.* **1.** closing of wound. **2.** stitch used to close wound. **3.** line joining two bones, esp. of the skull. —*v.* **4.** join by suture.

su'ze·rain·ty (sōō'zə rin tē), *n., pl.* **-ties.** sovereignty of one state over another.

svelte, *adj.* slender.

swab, *n., v.,* **swabbed, swabbing.** —*n.* **1.** bit of cloth, etc., esp. on stick. —*v.* **2.** clean with swab.

swad'dle, *v.,* **-died, -dling.** bind (infant) with strips of cloth.

swag'ger, *v.* **1.** walk with insolent air. —*n.* **2.** swaggering gait.

swain, *n.* **1.** country lad. **2.** male admirer or lover.

swal'low, *v.* **1.** take into stomach through throat. **2.** assimilate. **3.** suppress. —*n.* **4.** act of swallowing. **5.** small graceful migratory bird.

swa'mi, *n.* Hindu religious teacher.

swamp, *n.* **1.** marshy ground. —*v.* **2.** drench with water. **3.** overwhelm. —**swamp'y,** *adj.*

swan, *n.* large long-necked swimming bird.

swank, *adj.,* **swanker, swankest. 1.** stylish or elegant. **2.** pretentiously stylish. Also, **swank'y.**

swan song, final act or farewell appearance.

swap, *v.,* **swapped, swapping,** *n.* trade.

sward (swôrd), *n.* turf.

swarm, *n.* **1.** group of bees comprising colony. —*v.* **2.** fly off to start new colony. **3.** cluster; throng.

swarth'y, *adj.,* **swarthier, swarthiest.** (esp. of skin) dark. —**swarth'i·ness,** *n.*

swash'buck'ler, *n.* swaggering fellow. —**swash'buck'ling,** *adj., n.*

swas'ti·ka, *n.* **1.** kind of cross used as symbol and ornament. **2.** emblem of Nazi Party.

swat, *v.,* **swatted, swatting,** *n. Informal.* —*v.* **1.** strike. —*n.* **2.** sharp blow.

swatch, *n.* sample of material or finish.

swath (swoth), *n.* long cut made by scythe or mowing machine.

swathe (swoth), *v.,* **swathed, swathing,** *n.* —*v.* **1.** wrap closely. —*n.* **2.** bandage.

sway, *v.* **1.** swing to and fro. **2.** influence or incline. —*n.* **3.** act of swaying. **4.** rule.

swear, *v.,* **swore, sworn, swearing. 1.** affirm on oath; vow. **2.** use profane language. **3.** bind by oath.

sweat, *v.,* **sweat or sweated, sweating,** *n.* —*v.* **1.** excrete moisture through pores. **2.** gather moisture. —*n.* **3.** secretion of sweat glands. **4.** process of sweating. —**sweat'y,** *adj.*

sweat'er, *n.* knitted jacket.

sweat'shop', *n.* manufacturing establishment employing workers at low wages, for long hours, under poor conditions.

Swed'ish, *n.* language or people of Sweden. —**Swed'ish,** *adj.*

sweep, *v.,* **swept, sweeping,** *n.* —*v.* **1.** move or clear with broom, etc. **2.** clear or pass over with forceful, rapid movement. —*n.* **3.** act of sweeping. **4.** extent; range.

sweep'ing, *adj.* of wide range or scope.

sweep'stakes', *n.* **1.** race for stakes put up by competitors. **2.** lottery.

sweet, *adj.* **1.** having taste of sugar or honey. **2.** fragrant. **3.** fresh. **4.** pleasant in sound. **5.** amiable. —*n.* **6.** anything sweet. —**sweet'en,** *v.* —**sweet'ly,** *adv.* —**sweet'ness,** *n.*

sweet'bread', *n.* thymus or pancreas, esp. of calf or lamb, used for food.

sweet'bri'er, *n.* fragrant wild rose.

sweet'en·er, *n.* substance, esp. a substitute for sugar, to sweeten food or drink.

sweet'heart', *n.* beloved.

sweet'meat', *n.* confection.

sweet pea, annual vine with fragrant blooms.

sweet potato, plant with sweet edible root.

sweet'-talk', *v.* cajole; flatter.

sweet tooth, liking or craving for sweets.

sweet' wil'liam, low plant with dense flower clusters.

swell, *v.,* **swelled, swelled or swollen,**

swelling, n., adj. —v. 1. grow in degree, force, etc. —n. 2. act of swelling. 3. wave. —adj. 4. *Informal.* excellent.

swel'ter, v. perspire or suffer from heat.

swel'ter·ing, adj. 1. suffering from heat. 2. oppressively hot.

swerve, v., **swerved, swerving,** n. —v. 1. turn aside. —n. 2. act of swerving.

swift, adj. 1. moving with speed. 2. prompt or quick. —n. 3. small bird. —**swift'ly,** adv. —**swift'ness,** n.

swig, n., v., **swigged, swigging.** *Informal.* —n. 1. deep drink. —v. 2. drink heartily.

swill, n. 1. moist garbage fed to hogs. —v. 2. guzzle.

swim, v., **swam, swum, swimming,** n. —v. 1. move in water by action of limbs, etc. 2. be immersed. 3. be dizzy. —n. 4. period of swimming. —**swim'mer,** n.

swin'dle, v., **-dled, -dling,** n. —v. 1. cheat; defraud. —n. 2. act of swindling. —**swin'dler,** n.

swine, n. pl. **swine.** hog.

swing, v., **swung, swinging,** n. —v. 1. move to and fro around point. 2. brandish. —n. 3. act, way, or extent of swinging. 4. operation. 5. scope. 6. suspended seat for swinging. 7. style or quality in jazz marked by smooth beat and flowing phrasing.

swing'er, n. *Slang.* 1. person with modern attitudes. 2. sexually uninhibited person.

swipe, n., v., **swiped, swiping.** —n. 1. sweeping blow. —v. 2. deal such blow. 3. *Informal.* steal.

swirl, v., n. whirl; eddy.

swish, v. 1. rustle. —n. 2. swishing sound.

Swiss cheese, firm, pale yellow cheese with many holes.

switch, n. 1. flexible rod. 2. device for turning electric current on or off. 3. device for moving trains from one track to another. 4. change. —v. 5. whip with switch. 6. shift; divert. 7. turn (electric current) on or off.

switch'blade', n. pocketknife with blade released by spring.

switch'board', n. panel for controlling electric circuits.

swiv'el, n., v. **-eled, -eling.** —n. 1. device permitting rotation of thing mounted on it. —v. 2. rotate.

swol'len, pp. of **swell.**

swoon, v. 1. faint.

swoop, v. 1. sweep down upon. —n. 2. sweeping descent.

sword (sōrd), n. 1. weapon with blade fixed in hilt or handle. —**sword'play',** n. —**swords'man,** n.

sword'fish', n. marine fish with swordlike upper jaw.

syb'a·rite', n. person devoted to pleasure. —**syb'a·rit'ic,** adj.

syc'a·more', n. 1. plane tree. 2. *Brit.* maple tree.

syc'o·phant (sik'ə fant), n. flatterer; parasite. —**syc'o·phan·cy,** n.

syl·lab'i·cate', v., **-cated, -cating.** divide into syllables. Also, **syl·lab'i·fy'.** —**syl·lab'i·ca'tion,** n.

syl'la·ble, n. single unit of speech. —**syl·lab'ic,** adj.

syl'la·bus, n., pl. **-buses, -bi** (-bī'). outline or course of study.

syl'lo·gism, n. three-part chain of logical reasoning.

sylph, n. graceful woman.

syl'van, adj. 1. of forests. 2. wooded.

sym·bi·o'sis (sim'bē ō'sis, -bī-), n., pl. **-ses** (-sēz). living together of two dissimilar organisms. —**sym'bi·ot'ic,** adj.

sym'bol, n. 1. emblem; token; sign. 2. thing that represents something else. —**sym·bol'ic, sym·bol'i·cal,** adj. —**sym'bol·ize',** v.

sym'me·try, n., pl. **-tries.** pleasing balance or proportion. —**sym·met'ri·cal,** adj. —**sym·met'ri·cal·ly,** adv.

sym'pa·thize', v., **-thized, -thizing.** 1. be in sympathy. 2. feel or express sympathy. —**sym'pa·thiz'er,** n.

sym'pa·thy, n., pl. **-thies.** 1. agreement in feeling; accord. 2. compassion. —**sym'pa·thet'ic,** adj. —**sym'pa·thet'i·cal·ly,** adv.

sym'pho·ny, n., pl. **-nies.** 1. elaborate composition for orchestra. 2. harmonious combination. —**sym·phon'ic,** adj.

sym·po'si·um, n., pl. **-siums, -sia.** meeting to present essays on one subject.

symp'tom, n. sign or indication, esp. of disease. —**symp'to·mat'ic,** adj.

syn'a·gogue (-gog), n. 1. assembly of Jews for worship. 2. place of such assembly.

syn'chro·nize', v., **-nized, -nizing.** 1. occur at same time. 2. show or set to show same time. —**syn'chro·ni·za'tion,** n. —**syn'chro·nous,** adj.

syn'co·pate', v., **-pated, -pating.** 1. *Music.* play by accenting notes normally unaccented. 2. *Gram.* omit middle sound in (word). —**syn'co·pa'tion,** n.

syn'di·cate, n., v., **-cated, -cating.** —n. (sin'də kit). 1. combination of persons or companies for large joint enterprise. 2. agency dealing in news stories, etc. —v. (sin'di kāt'). 3. publish as syndicate. —**syn'di•ca'tion,** n.

syn'drome, n. characteristic group of symptoms.

syn'fu'el, n. synthetic fuel.

syn'od (sin'əd), n. meeting of church delegates.

syn'o•nym, n. word meaning same as another. —**syn•on'y•mous,** adj. —**syn•on'y•mous•ly,** adv.

syn•op'sis, n., pl. **-ses.** brief summary.

syn'tax, n. arrangement of words into sentences, phrases, etc.

syn'the•sis, n., pl. **-ses.** 1. combination of parts into whole. 2. such whole.

syn'the•size', v., **-sized, -sizing.** make by combining parts.

syn'the•siz'er, n. electronic, usu. computerized device for creating or modifying musical sounds.

syn•thet'ic, adj. 1. produced arti-

ficially rather than by nature. 2. of synthesis. —**syn•thet'i•cal•ly,** adv.

synthetic fuel, fuel manufactured esp. from coal or shale.

syph'i•lis, n. infectious venereal disease. —**syph•i•lit'ic,** adj., n.

sy•rin'ga (sə ring'gə), n. shrub with fragrant flowers, as lilac.

sy•ringe', n. device for drawing in and ejecting fluids.

syr'up, n. sweet thick liquid. —**syr'up•y,** adj.

sys'tem, n. 1. orderly assemblage of facts, parts, etc. 2. plan. 3. organization of one's body. —**sys•tem•at'ic,** adj. —**sys•tem•at'i•cal•ly,** adv. —**sys•tem'ic,** adj.

sys'tem•a•tize', v., **-tized, -tizing.** arrange in or by system.

sys'to•le' (sis'tə lē'), n. regular contraction of the heart. —**sys•tol'ic,** adj.

T

T, t, n. twentieth letter of English alphabet.

tab, n., v., **tabbed, tabbing.** —n. 1. small flap. 2. tag. —v. 3. furnish with tab.

Ta•bas'co, n. Trademark. pungent condiment sauce.

tab'by, n., pl. **-bies,** adj. —n. 1. striped or brindled cat. 2. silk fabric. —adj. 3. striped.

tab'er•nac'le, n. 1. temporary temple, esp. Jewish. 2. church for large congregation. 3. receptacle for reserved Eucharist.

ta'ble, n., v., **-bled, -bling.** —n. 1. piece of furniture consisting of level part on legs. 2. food. 3. company at table. 4. compact arrangement of information in parallel columns. —v. 5. place on or enter in table. 6. postpone deliberation on. —**ta'ble•cloth',** n.

ta'bleau' (tab lō'), n., pl. **-leaux.** picture.

ta'ble d'hôte' (tä'bəl dōt'), meal fixed in courses and price.

ta'ble•land', n. elevated, level region of considerable extent.

ta'ble•spoon', n. 1. large spoon in table service. 2. tablespoonful.

ta'ble•spoon•ful', n., pl. **-fuls.** quantity tablespoon holds, about ½ fluid ounce or 3 teaspoonfuls.

tab'let, n. 1. pad of writing paper. 2. small slab. 3. pill.

table tennis, game resembling tennis,

played on table with paddles and small hollow ball.

tab'loid, n. newspaper about half ordinary size.

ta•boo', adj., n., pl. **-boos,** v. —adj. 1. forbidden. —n. 2. prohibition. —v. 3. prohibit.

ta'bor (tā'bər), n. small drum.

tab'u•late', v., **-lated, -lating.** arrange in table. —**tab'u•lar,** adj. —**tab'u•la'tion,** n. —**tab'u•la'tor,** n.

ta•chom'e•ter (tə kom'ə tər), n. instrument for measuring velocity.

tac'it (tas'it), adj. 1. silent. 2. implied. 3. unspoken. —**tac'it•ly,** adv.

tac'i•turn, adj. inclined to silence. —**tac•i•tur'ni•ty,** n. —**tac'i•turn•ly,** adv.

tack, n. 1. short nail with flat head. 2. straight windward run of sailing ship. —v. 3. fasten by tack. 4. navigate by tacks.

tack'le, n., v., **-led, -ling.** —n. 1. fishing equipment. 2. hoisting apparatus. —v. 3. undertake to deal with. —**tack'ler,** n.

tack'y, adj., **tackier, tackiest.** 1. Informal. shabby; dowdy. 2. slightly sticky.

ta'co (tä'kō), n. fried tortilla folded and filled with chopped meat, cheese, lettuce, etc.

tact, n. skill in handling delicate situations. —**tact'ful,** adj. —**tact'less,** adj.

tac•ti'cian (tak tish'ən), *n.* person versed in tactics.

tac'tics, *n.* 1. maneuvering of armed forces. 2. methods for attaining success. —**tac'ti•cal,** *adj.* —**tac'ti•cal•ly,** *adv.*

tac'tile, *adj.* of sense of touch. —**tac•til'i•ty,** *n.*

tad, *n. Informal.* 1. small child. 2. small amount or degree.

tad'pole', *n.* immature form of frogs, toads, etc.

taf•fe'ta, *n.* lustrous silk or rayon fabric.

taf'fy, *n., pl.* **-fies.** molasses candy.

tag, *n., v.* **tagged, tagging.** —*n.* 1. small paper, etc., attached as mark or label. 2. game in which players chase and touch each other. —*v.* 3. furnish with tag. 4. touch in playing tag.

tail, *n.* 1. appendage at rear of animal's body. 2. something resembling this. 3. bottom or end part. —*v.* 4. follow.

tail'gate', *n., v.* **-gated, -gating.** —*n.* 1. hinged board at back of vehicle. —*v.* 2. drive too closely behind.

tail'light', *n.* light, usually red, at the rear of automobile, train, etc.

tai'lor, *n.* maker or mender of outer garments.

tail'piece', *n.* piece, design, etc., added at end; appendage.

tail'spin', *n.* descent of airplane in steep spiral course.

tail'wind', *n.* wind from directly behind.

taint, *n.* 1. unfavorable trace, as of dishonor. —*v.* 2. contaminate.

take, *v.,* **took, taken, taking.** 1. seize, catch, or embrace. 2. receive; obtain. 3. select. 4. remove. 5. deduct. 6. conduct. 7. travel by. 8. occupy. 9. assume. 10. require.

take'off', *n.* 1. leaving of ground in leaping or flying. 2. place at which one takes off. 3. *Informal.* piece of mimicry.

take'o'ver, *n.* 1. act of seizing authority or control. 2. acquisition of corporation through purchase or exchange of stock.

talc, *n.* soft mineral, used for lubricants, etc. Also, **tal'cum.**

tale, *n.* story or lie.

tale'bear'er, *n.* gossip.

tal'ent, *n.* natural ability. —**tal'ent•ed,** *adj.*

tal'is•man, *n.* amulet.

talk, *v.* 1. speak; converse. 2. gossip. —*n.* 3. speech; conversation. 4. conference. 5. gossip. —**talk'a•tive,** *adj.* —**talk'er,** *n.*

talk'y, *adj.* **talkier, talkiest.** 1. con-

taining too much talk, dialogue, etc. 2. talkative. —**talk'i•ness,** *n.*

tall, *adj.* high.

tal'low, *n.* 1. suet. 2. hardened fat for soap, etc.

tal'ly, *n., pl.* **-lies,** *v.,* **-lied, -lying.** —*n.* 1. notched stock indicating amount. 2. mark on tally. 3. record of amounts. —*v.* 4. register; record.

tal'ly•ho', *n., pl.* **-hos,** *interj.* —*n.* 1. *Chiefly Brit.* mail or pleasure coach. —*interj.* (tal'ē hō'). 2. cry in hunting on catching sight of fox.

Tal'mud (täl'mŏŏd), *n.* collection of Jewish laws. —**Tal•mud'ic,** *adj.*

tal'on, *n.* claw.

tam, *n.* tam-o'-shanter.

ta•ma'le (tə mä'lē), *n.* Mexican dish of corn meal, meat, red peppers, etc.

tam'a•rind, *n.* tropical fruit.

tam'bou•rine' (tam'bə rēn'), *n.* small drum with metal disks in frame.

tame, *adj.,* **tamer, tamest,** *v.,* **tamed, taming.** —*adj.* 1. not wild; domesticated. 2. uninterestingly conventional. —*v.* 3. domesticate. —**tam'a•ble, tame'a•ble,** *adj.* —**tame'ly,** *adv.* —**tame'ness,** *n.* —**tam'er,** *n.*

tam'-o'-shan'ter, *n.* cap with flat crown.

tamp, *v.* force down or in. —**tamp'er,** *n.*

tam'per, *v.* meddle.

tam'pon, *n.* plug of cotton or the like for insertion into wound or body cavity to absorb blood.

tan, *v.,* **tanned, tanning,** *n., adj.* —*v.* 1. convert into leather. 2. make or become brown by exposure to sun. —*n.* 3. light brown. 4. Also, **tan'bark'.** bark used in tanning hides. —*adj.* 5. light brown. —**tan'ner,** *n.* —**tan'ner•y,** *n.*

tan'a•ger, *n.* small, brightly colored bird.

tan'dem, *adv.* 1. one behind another. —*adj.* 2. having one following another. —*n.* 3. team of horses so harnessed.

tang, *n.* strong flavor.

tan'gent, *adj.* 1. touching. —*n.* 2. tangent line, etc. 3. sudden change of course, thought, etc. —**tan'gen•cy,** *n.*

tan•gen'tial, *adj.* 1. being tangent; touching. 2. not relevant. —**tan•gen'tial•ly,** *adv.*

tan•ge•rine' (tan'), *n.* loose-skinned fruit similar to orange.

tan'gi•ble, *adj.* 1. discernible by touch. 2. real. 3. definite. —**tan'gi•bil'i•ty,** *n.* —**tan'gi•bly,** *adv.*

tan'gle, *v.,* **-gled, -gling,** *n.* —*v.* 1. come or bring together in confused mass. 2. involve. 3. snare. 4. *Informal.* come into conflict. —*n.* 5. tangled state or mass.

tan'go, *n., pl.* **-gos.** —*goed, -going.** —*n.* 1. Spanish-American dance. —*v.* 2. dance the tango.

tank, *n.* 1. large receptacle. 2. armored combat vehicle on caterpillar treads.

tank'ard, *n.* large cup.

tank'er, *n.* ship, truck, or airplane for transporting liquid bulk cargo.

tan'ta•lize', *v.,* **-lized, -lizing.** torment by prospect of something desired. —**tan'ta•liz'ing•ly,** *adv.*

tan'ta•mount', *adj.* equivalent.

tan'trum, *n.* noisy outburst of ill-humor.

tap, *n., v.,* **tapped, tapping.** —*n.* 1. plug or faucet through which liquid is drawn. 2. light blow. —*v.* 3. draw liquid from. 4. reach or pierce to draw something off. 5. strike lightly.

tap dance, dance in which rhythm is audibly tapped out by toe or heel. —**tap'-dance',** *v.*

tape, *n., v.,* **taped, taping.** —*n.* 1. narrow strip of flexible material. —*v.* 2. furnish or tie with tape. 3. record on tape.

tape measure, tape marked for measuring. Also, **tape'line'.**

ta'per, *v.* 1. make or become narrower toward end. —*n.* 2. gradual decrease. 3. small candle.

tape recorder, electrical device for recording or playing back sound recorded on magnetic tape.

tap'es•try, *n., pl.* **-tries.** woven, figured fabric for wall hangings, etc.

tape'worm', *n.* parasitic worm in alimentary canal.

tap'i•o•ca, *n.* granular food from starch of tuberous plants.

ta'pir (tā'pər), *n.* tropical swinelike animal.

tap'root', *n.* main, central root pointing downward and giving off small lateral roots.

taps, *n.* bugle signal sounded at night as curfew to extinguish lights, and sometimes at military funerals.

tar, *n., v.,* **tarred, tarring.** —*n.* 1. dark viscid product made from coal, wood, etc. 2. sailor. —*v.* 3. cover with tar. —**tar'ry** (tär'ē), *adj.*

tar'an•tel'la (tar'ən tel'ə), *n.* rapid, whirling southern Italian dance.

ta•ran'tu•la (-chə lə), *n.* large hairy spider.

tar'dy, *adj.,* **-dier, -diest.** late. —**tar'-di•ly,** *adv.* —**tar'di•ness,** *n.*

tare (târ), *n.* 1. weed. 2. weight of a wrapping or receptacle.

tar'get, *n.* something aimed at.

tar'iff, *n.* 1. list of export or import duties. 2. one such duty.

tar'nish, *v.* 1. lose luster. 2. sully. —*n.* 3. tarnished coating on metal.

ta'ro, *n.* tropical plant cultivated for edible tuber.

tar'ot (tar'ō, ta rō'), *n.* any of set of 22 playing cards used for fortune-telling.

tar•pau'lin (tär pô'lin), *n.* waterproof covering of canvas, etc.

tar'pon, *n.* large game fish.

tar'ra•gon', *n.* plant with aromatic leaves used as seasoning.

tar'ry (tar'ē), *v.,* **-ried, -rying.** 1. stay. 2. linger.

tart, *adj.* 1. sour; acid. 2. caustic. —*n.* 3. pastry shell filled with fruit, etc. —**tart'ly,** *adv.* —**tart'ness,** *n.*

tar'tan, *n.* cloth worn by natives of N Scotland, having crisscross pattern.

tar'tar, *n.* 1. hard deposit on teeth. 2. savage, intractable person. —**tar•tar'ic,** *adj.*

task, *n.* 1. assigned piece of work. —*v.* 2. put strain on.

task force, 1. temporary group of armed units for carrying out specific mission. 2. temporary committee for solving specific problem.

task'mas'ter, *n.* assigner of tasks.

tas'sel, *n.* fringed ornament hanging from roundish knot.

taste, *n., v.,* **tasted, tasting.** —*v.* 1. try flavor by taking in mouth. 2. eat or drink a little of. 3. perceive flavor. 4. have particular flavor. —*n.* 5. act of tasting. 6. sense by which flavor is perceived. 7. flavor. 8. sense of fitness or beauty. —**taste'ful,** *adj.* —**taste'less,** *adj.* —**tast'er,** *n.*

tast'y, *adj.,* **tastier, tastiest.** 1. savory. 2. tasting good. —**tast'i•ness,** *n.*

tat, *v.,* **tatted, tatting.** to do, or make by, tatting.

tat'ter, *n.* 1. torn piece. 2. (*pl.*) ragged clothing.

tat'ting, *n.* 1. the making of a kind of knotted lace with a shuttle. 2. such lace.

tat'tle, *v.,* **-tled, -tling,** *n.* —*v.* 1. tell another's secrets. 2. chatter; gossip. —**tat'tler, tat'tle•tale',** *n.*

tat•too', *n.* 1. indelible marking on skin by puncturing and dyeing. 2. design so made. 3. military signal on drum, bugle, etc., to go to quarters. —*v.* 4. mark by tattoo.

taunt, *v.* 1. reproach insultingly or sarcastically. —*n.* 2. insulting or sarcastic gibe.

taupe (tōp), *n.* dark gray usually

tinged with brown, purple, yellow, or green.

taut, *adj.* tight; tense. —**taut'ly,** *adv.* —**taut'ness,** *n.*

tau·tol'o·gy, *n., pl.* **-gies.** needless repetition. —**tau'to·log'i·cal,** *adj.*

tav'ern, *n.* 1. saloon. 2. inn.

taw (tô), *n.* 1. choice playing marble with which to shoot. 2. game of marbles.

taw'dry, *adj.,* **-drier, -driest.** gaudy; cheap. —**taw'dri·ly,** *adv.* —**taw'dri·ness,** *n.*

taw'ny, *adj.,* **-nier, -niest,** —*adj.* 1. of a dark-yellow or yellow-brown color. —*n.* 2. tawny color.

tax, *n.* 1. money regularly paid to government. 2. burdensome duty, etc. —*v.* 3. impose tax. 4. burden. 5. accuse. —**tax'a·ble,** *adj.* —**tax·a'tion,** *n.* —**tax'pay'er,** *n.*

tax'i, *n., v.* taxied, taxiing. —*n.* 1. taxicab. —*v.* 2. go in taxicab. 3. (of airplane) move on ground or water under its own power.

tax'i·cab', *n.* automobile carrying paying passengers.

tax'i·der'my, *n.* art of preserving and mounting skins of animals. —**tax'i·der'mist,** *n.*

tax·on'o·my, *n., pl.* **-mies.** classification, esp. in relation to principles or laws.

TB, tuberculosis. Also, **T.B.**

T cell, cell involved in regulating the immune system's response to infected or malignant cells.

tea, *n.* 1. dried aromatic leaves of Oriental shrub. 2. beverage made by infusion of these leaves in hot water. 3. similar beverage made by steeping leaves or flowers of other plants. 4. afternoon meal or reception. —**tea'cup',** *n.* —**tea'ket'tle,** *n.* —**tea'pot',** *n.*

teach, *v.,* **taught, teaching.** impart knowledge to. —**teach'er,** *n.* —**teach'a·ble,** *adj.*

teak, *n.* East Indian tree with hard wood.

teal, *n., pl.* **teals, teal.** any of certain small fresh-water ducks.

team, *n.* 1. persons, etc., associated in joint action. —*v.* 2. join in team. —**team'mate',** *n.* —**team'work',** *n.*

team'ster, *n.* driver of team or truck.

tear, *v.,* **tore, torn, tearing.** —*v.* 1. pull apart by force. 2. distress. 3. divide. 4. lacerate. 5. rend. —*n.* 6. act of tearing. 7. torn place. 8. (tēr). Also, **tear'drop'.** drop of fluid secreted by eye duct. —**tear'ful,** *adj.*

tear gas (tēr), gas, used esp. in riots, that makes eyes smart and water.

tease, *v.,* **teased, teasing.** annoy by raillery. —**teas'er,** *n.*

tea'spoon', *n.* small spoon. —**tea'spoon·ful',** *n.*

teat, *n.* nipple.

tech'ni·cal, *adj.* 1. pertaining to skilled activity. 2. considered in strict sense. —**tech'ni·cal·ly,** *adv.*

tech'ni·cal'i·ty, *n., pl.* **-ties.** 1. technical point or detail. 2. technical character.

Tech'ni·col'or (tek'-), *n. Trademark.* system of making color motion pictures.

tech·nique' (-nēk'), *n.* skilled method. Also, **tech·nic'.**

tech·noc'ra·cy, *n., pl.* **-cies.** government by technological experts. —**tech'no·crat',** *n.*

tech·nol'o·gy, *n., pl.* **-gies.** 1. practical application of science. 2. technological invention or method. —**tech·no·log'i·cal,** *adj.*

tec·ton'ic, *adj.* 1. of building or construction. 2. of the structure and movements of the earth's crust.

Te De'um (tā dā'əm), hymn of praise and thanksgiving.

te'di·ous, *adj.* long and tiresome. —**te'di·um,** *n.* —**te'di·ous·ly,** *adv.* —**te'di·ous·ness,** *n.*

tee, *n., v.,* **teed, teeing.** *Golf.* —*n.* 1. hard mound of earth at beginning of play for each hole. 2. object from which ball is driven. —*v.* 3. place (ball) on tee. 4. strike (ball) from tee.

teem, *v.* abound; swarm.

teens, *n.pl.* years (13–19) of ages ending in *-teen.* —**teen'-ag'er, teen,** *n.* —**teen'age', teen'aged',** *adj.*

tee'ter, *Informal.* —*v.* 1. seesaw. 2. walk unsteadily. —*n.* 3. seesaw.

teethe, *v.,* **teethed, teething.** grow or cut teeth.

tee·to'tal·er, *n.* person who does not drink alcoholic beverages.

Tef'lon, *n. Trademark.* 1. polymer with nonsticking properties, used to coat cookware. —*adj.* 2. impervious to blame or criticisms.

tel'e·cast', *v.,* **-cast or -casted, -casting,** *n.* —*v.* 1. broadcast by television. —*n.* 2. television broadcast.

tel'e·com·mu'ni·ca'tions, *n.* science and technology of transmitting information in the form of electromagnetic signals.

tel'e·graph', *n.* 1. electrical apparatus or process for sending message (**tel'e·gram'**). —*v.* 2. send by telegraph. —**te·leg'ra·pher,** *n.* —**tel'e·graph'ic,** *adj.* —**te·leg'ra·phy,** *n.*

tel'e·mar'ket·ing, *n.* selling or advertising by telephone.

te·lep·a·thy, n. communication between minds without physical means. —**te·lep·a·thist,** n. —**tel·e·path·ic** (-path'ik), *adj.* —**tel·e·path·i·cal·ly,** *adv.*

tel·e·phone, n., v., **-phoned, -phon·ing.** —n. 1. electrical apparatus or process for transmitting sound or speech. —v. 2. speak to or transmit by telephone. —**tel·e·phon·ic** (-fon'-), *adj.* —**tel·e·phon·i·cal·ly,** *adv.* —**te·leph·o·ny,** n.

tel·e·pho'to, *adj.* of a lens producing large image of small or distant object.

tel·e·scope, n., v., **-scoped, -scop·ing.** —n. 1. optical instrument for enlarging image of distant objects. —v. 2. force or slide one object into another. —**tel·e·scop'ic,** *adj.*

Tel'e·type', n. Trademark. teletypewriter.

tel·e·type'writ·er, n. telegraphic apparatus with typewriter terminals.

tel'e·view, v. view with a television receiver. —**tel'e·view'er,** n.

tel'e·vise', v., **-vised, -vis·ing.** send or receive by television.

tel'e·vi'sion, n. radio or electrical transmission of images.

Tel'ex, n. Trademark. two-way teletypewriter system.

tell, v., **told, tell·ing.** 1. relate. 2. communicate. 3. say positively. 4. distinguish. 5. inform. 6. divulge. 7. order. 8. produce marked effect. —**tell'ing,** *adj.*

tell'er, n. bank cashier.

tell'tale', n. 1. divulger of secrets. —*adj.* 2. revealing.

te·mer'i·ty, n. rash boldness.

temp, n. temporary worker.

tem'per, n. 1. state or habit of mind. 2. heat or passion. 3. control of one's anger. 4. state of metal after tempering. —v. 5. moderate. 6. heat and cool metal to obtain proper hardness, etc.

tem'per·a, n. technique of painting using media containing egg.

tem'per·a·ment, n. mental disposition.

tem'per·a·men'tal, *adj.* 1. moody or sensitive. 2. of one's personality. —**tem'per·a·men'tal·ly,** *adv.*

tem'per·ance, n. 1. moderation. 2. total abstinence from alcoholic liquors.

tem'per·ate, *adj.* moderate. —**tem'per·ate·ly,** *adv.* —**tem'per·ate·ness,** n.

Temperate Zone, part of earth's surface lying between either tropic and nearest polar circle.

tem'per·a·ture, n. degree of warmth or coldness.

tem'pest, n. violent storm, commo-

tion, or disturbance. —**tem·pes'tu·ous,** *adj.*

tem'plate (tem'plit), n. pattern, mold, etc., serving as gauge or guide in mechanical work.

tem'ple, n. 1. place dedicated to worship. 2. flat region at side of forehead.

tem'po, n., pl. **-pos, -pi.** 1. rate of speed of musical work. 2. any characteristic rate or rhythm.

tem'po·ral, *adj.* 1. of time. 2. worldly. —**tem'po·ral·ly,** *adv.*

tem'po·rar'y, *adj.* not permanent. —**tem'po·rar'i·ly,** *adv.*

tem'po·rize', v., **-rized, -riz·ing.** 1. delay by evasion or indecision. 2. compromise. —**tem'po·ri·za'tion,** n. —**tem'po·riz'er,** n.

tempt, v. 1. entice. 2. appeal strongly. —**temp·ta'tion,** n. —**tempt'er,** n. —**tempt'ress,** n. fem.

tem·pu'ra (tem poor'ə), n. Japanese deep-fried dish of vegetables or seafood.

ten, n., *adj.* nine plus one.

ten'a·ble, *adj.* defensible in argument. —**ten'a·bly,** *adv.*

te·na'cious, *adj.* 1. holding fast. 2. retentive. 3. obstinate. 4. sticky. —**te·na'cious·ly,** *adv.* —**te·nac'i·ty, te·na'cious·ness,** n.

ten'an·cy, n., pl. **-cies.** holding; tenure.

ten'ant, n. 1. one renting from landlord. 2. occupant.

Ten Commandments, precepts spoken by God to Israel (Exodus 20, Deut. 10) or delivered to Moses (Exodus 24:12, 34) on Mount Sinai.

tend, v. 1. incline in action or effect. 2. lead. 3. take care of.

tend'en·cy, n., pl. **-cies.** 1. disposition to behave or act in certain way. 2. predisposition; preference.

ten·den'tious, *adj.* having or showing bias.

ten'der, *adj.* 1. soft; delicate; weak. 2. immature. 3. soft-hearted. 4. kind. 5. loving. 6. sensitive. —v. 7. present formally. 8. offer. —n. 9. something offered. 10. person who tends. 11. auxiliary vehicle or vessel. —**ten'der·er,** n. —**ten'der·ly,** *adv.* —**ten'der·ness,** n. —**ten'der·ize',** v.

ten'der·foot', n., pl. **-foots, -feet.** Informal. 1. inexperienced person; novice. 2. Western U.S. newcomer to ranching and mining regions.

ten'der·heart'ed, *adj.* soft-hearted; sympathetic. —**ten'der·heart'ed·ness,** n.

ten'der·loin', n. 1. tender meat on loin of beef, pork, etc. 2. brothel district of city.

ten'don, n. band of fibrous tissue connecting muscle to bone or part.

ten'dril, n. clinging threadlike organ of climbing plants.

ten·e·ment, n. 1. dwelling place. 2. Also, **tenement house.** cheap apartment house.

ten'et, n. principle, doctrine, dogma, etc.

ten'nis, n. game of ball played with rackets (**tennis rackets**) on rectangular court (**tennis court**).

ten'on, n. projection inserted into cavity (**mortise**) to form joint.

ten'or, n. 1. continuous course or progress. 2. perceived meaning or intention. 3. male voice between bass and alto. 4. singer with this voice.

ten'pins', n. bowling game played with ten pins.

tense, adj., **tenser, tensest,** v., **tensed, tensing,** n. —adj. 1. taut; rigid. 2. emotionally strained. —v. 3. make or become tense. —n. 4. verb inflection indicating time of action or state. —**tense'ly,** adv. —**tense'ness,** n.

ten'sile (-səl), adj. 1. of tension. 2. ductile.

ten'sion, n. 1. stretching or being stretched. 2. strain. 3. strained relations.

tent, n. portable shelter, usually canvas.

ten'ta·cle, n. slender, flexible organ for feeling, etc.

ten'ta·tive, adj. in trial; experimental. —**ten'ta·tive·ly,** adv.

ten'ter·hook', n. 1. hook to hold cloth stretched on frame. 2. **on tenterhooks,** in suspense.

tenth, adj., n. next after ninth.

ten'u·ous, adj. 1. unsubstantiated. 2. thin. 3. rarefied. —**ten·u·ous·ly,** adv. —**ten·u'i·ty, ten'u·ous·ness,** n.

ten'ure (-yər), n. 1. holding of something. 2. assurance of permanent work.

te'pee, n. American Indian tent.

tep'id, adj. lukewarm. —**te·pid'i·ty, tep'id·ness,** n. —**tep'id·ly,** adv.

te·quil'a (-kē'-), n. Mexican liquor.

ter·cen·ten'ni·al, n. 300th anniversary or its celebration. Also, **ter'cen·ten'a·ry.**

term, n. 1. name for something. 2. period, as of school instruction. 3. (pl.) conditions of agreement or bargain. —v. 4. name; designate.

ter'ma·gant, n. shrew (def. 1).

ter'mi·nal, adj. 1. at end; concluding. 2. leading to death. —n. 3. end or extremity. 4. terminating point for

trains, buses, etc. 5. point of electrical connection. 6. device for entering information into or receiving information from computer. —**ter'mi·nal·ly,** adv.

ter'mi·nate, v., **-nated, -nating.** 1. end or cease. 2. occur at end. —**ter'mi·na·ble,** adj. —**ter'mi·na·bly,** adv. —**ter'mi·na'tion,** n.

ter·mi·nol'o·gy, n., pl. **-gies.** terms of technical subject.

ter'mi·nus, n. 1. terminal. 2. goal. 3. limit.

ter'mite, n. destructive woodeating insect.

tern, n. gull-like aquatic bird.

terp·si·cho·re'an (tûrp'si kə rē'ən, -kôr'ē ən), adj. of dancing.

ter'race, n., v., **-raced, -racing.** —n. 1. raised level with abrupt drop at front. 2. flat roof. 3. open area connected with house. —v. 4. make or furnish as row with terrace.

ter'ra cot'ta, 1. hard, usually unglazed earthenware. 2. brownish red.

ter'ra fir'ma (ter'ə fûr'mə), solid land.

ter·rain', n. area of land of specified nature.

ter'ra·pin, n. edible North American turtle.

ter·rar'i·um, n., pl. **-iums, -ia.** glass tank for raising plants or land animals.

ter·raz'zo (tə rä'tsō, -raz'ō), n. mosaic flooring composed of stone chips and cement.

ter·res'tri·al, adj. of or living on earth.

ter'ri·ble, adj. 1. dreadful. 2. severe. —**ter'ri·ble·ness,** n. —**ter'ri·bly,** adv.

ter'ri·er, n. hunting dog.

ter·rif'ic, adj. 1. excellent. 2. terrifying.

ter'ri·fy, v., **-fied, -fying.** fill with terror. —**ter'ri·fy'ing·ly,** adv.

ter'ri·to·ry, n., pl. **-ries.** 1. region. 2. land and waters of state. 3. region not a state but having elected legislature and appointed officials. —**ter'ri·to'ri·al,** adj. —**ter'ri·to'ri·al·ly,** adv.

ter'ror, n. intense fear.

ter'ror·ism, n. use of violence and threats to obtain political demands. —**ter'ror·ist,** n.

ter'ror·ize', v., **-ized, -izing.** fill with terror. —**ter'ror·i·za'tion,** n.

ter'ry, n., pl. **-ries.** pile fabric with loops on both sides. Also, **terry cloth.**

terse, adj. 1. concise. 2. curt; brusque. —**terse'ly,** adv. —**terse'ness,** n.

ter·ti·ar·y (tûr′shē·), *adj.* of third rank or stage.

test, *n.* 1. trial of or substance used to try quality, content, etc. 2. examination to evaluate student or class. —*v.* 3. subject to test.

tes·ta·ment, *n.* legal will. —**tes·ta·men·ta·ry**, *adj.*

tes·tate, *adj.* having left a valid will.

tes·ti·cle, *n.* either of two male sex glands located in scrotum. Also, **tes·tis**.

tes·ti·fy, *v.*, **-fied, -fy·ing.** 1. give evidence. 2. give testimony.

tes·ti·mo·ni·al, *n.* writing certifying character, etc.

tes·ti·mo·ny, *n., pl.* **-nies.** 1. statement of witness under oath. 2. proof.

tes·tos·ter·one, *n.* male sex hormone.

test tube, *Chem.* small cylindrical glass container.

tes·ty, *adj.*, **-tier, -tiest.** irritable. —**tes·ti·ly**, *adv.* —**tes·ti·ness**, *n.*

tet·a·nus, *n.* infectious disease marked by muscular rigidity.

tête-à-tête (tāt′ə tāt′), *n.* private conversation.

teth·er, *n.* 1. rope, chain, etc., for fastening animal to stake. —*v.* 2. fasten with tether.

text, *n.* 1. main body of matter in book or manuscript. 2. quotation from Scripture, esp. as subject of sermon, etc. —**tex′tu·al**, *adj.* —**tex′tu·al·ly**, *adv.*

text′book′, *n.* student's book of study.

tex·tile (-tīl, -til), *n.* 1. woven material. —*adj.* 2. woven. 3. of weaving.

tex·ture, *n.* characteristic surface or composition. —**tex′tur·al**, *adj.*

than, *conj.* particle introducing second member of comparison.

than·a·top·sis, *n.* view or contemplation of death.

thane, *n. Early Eng. Hist.* person ranking between earl and ordinary freeman, holding lands of king or lord by military service.

thank, *v.* 1. express gratitude for. —*n.* 2. (*usually pl.*) expression of gratitude. —**thank′ful**, *adj.* —**thank′less**, *adj.* —**thanks′giv′ing**, *n.*

Thanksgiving Day, festival in acknowledgment of divine favor, celebrated in U.S. on fourth Thursday of November and in Canada on second Monday of October.

that, *pron.*, *pl.* **those**, *adj., adv., conj.* —*pron., adj.* 1. demonstrative word indicating **a.** the thing, thing, etc., more remote. **b.** one of two persons, etc., pointed out or mentioned before

(opposed to **this**). 2. relative pronoun used as: **a.** subject or object of relative clause. **b.** object of preposition. 3. to that extent. —*conj.* 4. word used to introduce dependent clause or one expressing reason, result, etc.

thatch, *n.* 1. rushes, leaves, etc., for covering roofs. —*v.* 2. cover with thatch.

thaw, *v.* 1. melt. 2. remove ice or frost from. —*n.* 3. act or instance of thawing.

the, *def. article.* 1. word used, esp. before nouns, with specifying effect. —*adv.* 2. word used to modify comparative or superlative form of adjective or adverb.

the′a·ter, *n.* 1. building for dramatic presentations, etc. 2. dramatic art. 3. place of action. Also, **the′a·tre**. —**the·at′ri·cal**, *adj.* —**the·at′ri·cal·ly**, *adv.*

thee, *pron. Archaic* you.

theft, *n.* act or instance of stealing.

their, *pron.* 1. possessive form of **they** used before noun. 2. (*pl.*) that which belongs to them.

the′ism, *n.* belief in one God. —**the′ist**, *n.*

them, *pron.* objective case of **they**.

theme, *n.* 1. subject of discourse, etc. 2. short essay. 3. melody. —**the·mat′ic**, *adj.*

them·selves′, *pron.* emphatic or reflexive form of **them**.

then, *adv.* 1. at that time. 2. soon afterward. 3. at another time. 4. besides. 5. in that case. —*adj.* 6. being such at that time.

thence, *adv.* 1. from that place or time. 2. therefore.

thence′forth′, *adv.* from that place or time on. Also, **thence′for′ward**.

the·oc·ra·cy, *n., pl.* **-cies.** 1. government in which authorities claim to carry out divine law. 2. government by priests.

the·ol·o·gy, *n.* study dealing with God and God's relations to universe. —**the·o·lo′gian**, *n.* —**the·o·log′i·cal**, *adj.* —**the·o·log′i·cal·ly**, *adv.*

the′o·rem (thē′ə rəm), *n.* 1. *Math.* statement embodying something to be proved. 2. rule or law, esp. one expressed by equation or formula.

the·o·ret′i·cal, *adj.* 1. in theory. 2. not practical. 3. speculative. —**the·o·ret′i·cal·ly**, *adv.*

the′o·ry, *n., pl.* **-ries.** 1. proposition used to explain class of phenomena. 2. proposed explanation. 3. principles. —**the′o·rist**, *n.* —**the′o·rize**, *v.*

the·os·o·phy, n. any of various forms of thought based on mystical insight into the divine nature.

ther·a·py, n., pl. -pies. 1. treatment of disease. 2. psychotherapy. —ther'a·pist, n. —ther·a·peu'tic (-pyoo'tik), adj. —ther·a·peu'ti·cal·ly, adv. —ther·a·peu'tics, n.

there, adv. 1. in or at that place, point, matter, respect, etc. 2. to that place. —there·a·bout', there·a·bouts', adv. —there·af'ter, adv. —there·by', adv. —there·for', adv. —there·from', adv. —there·in', adv. —there·in'to, adv. —there·to', adv. —there·un'der, adv.

there'fore', adv. consequently.

there·of', adv. of or from that.

there·on', adv. 1. on that. 2. immediately after that.

there·up·on', adv. 1. immediately after that. 2. because of that. 3. with reference to that.

there·with', adv. with or in addition to that.

ther'mal, adj. of heat.

ther·mo·dy·nam'ics, n. science concerned with relations between heat and mechanical energy or work.

ther·mom'e·ter, n. instrument for measuring temperature. —ther'mo·met'ric, adj.

ther·mo·nu'cle·ar, adj. of nuclear-fusion reactions at extremely high temperatures.

ther·mo·plas'tic, adj. 1. soft and pliable whenever heated, as some plastics, without change of inherent properties. —n. 2. such plastic.

Ther'mos, n. Trademark. container with vacuum between double walls for heat insulation.

ther'mo·stat', n. device regulating temperature of heating system, etc.

the·sau'rus, n., pl. -ruses, -ri. book of synonyms and antonyms.

these, pron. pl. of this.

the'sis, n., pl. -ses. 1. proposition to be proved. 2. essay based on research.

thes'pi·an, adj. 1. of dramatic art. —n. 2. actor or actress.

they, pron. nominative plural of he, she, and it.

thi'a·mine (thī'ə min), n. vitamin B₁. Also, thi'a·min.

thick, adj. 1. not thin. 2. in depth. 3. compact. 4. numerous. 5. dense. 6. husky. 7. slow-witted. —adv. 8. so as to be thick. —n. 9. something thick. —thick'en, v. —thick'ly, adv. —thick'ness, n.

thick'et, n. thick growth of shrubs, bushes, etc.

thick'set', adj. 1. set thickly; dense. 2. with heavy or solid body.

thick'-skinned', adj. 1. having thick skin. 2. not sensitive to criticism or contempt.

thief, n., pl. thieves. person who steals. —thieve, v. —thiev'er·y, n.

thigh, n. part of leg between hip and knee.

thim'ble, n. cap to protect finger while sewing.

thin, adj., thinner, thinnest. v., thinned, thinning. —adj. 1. having little extent between opposite sides; slender. 2. lean. 3. scanty. 4. rarefied; diluted. 5. flimsy. 6. weak. —v. 7. make or become thinner. —thin·ner, n. —thin'ly, adv. —thin'ness, n.

thing, n. 1. inanimate object. 2. entity. 3. matter. 4. item.

think, v., thought, thinking. 1. conceive in mind. 2. meditate. 3. believe. —think'er, n. —think'a·ble, adj.

think tank, research organization employed to analyze problems and plan future developments.

thin'-skinned', adj. 1. having thin skin. 2. sensitive to criticism or contempt.

third, adj. 1. next after second. —n. 2. next after the second. 3. any of three equal parts.

third degree, Chiefly U.S. use of brutal measures by police (or others) in extorting information or confession.

third party, 1. party to case or quarrel who is incidentally involved. 2. in two-party political system, usu. temporary party composed of independents.

third'-rate', adj. distinctly inferior.

Third World, developing countries of Asia, Africa, and Latin America.

thirst, n. 1. sensation caused by need of drink. —v. 2. be thirsty. —thirst'y, adj. —thirst'i·ly, adv. —thirst'i·ness, n.

thir·teen', n., adj. ten plus three. —thir·teenth', n., adj.

thir'ty, n., adj. ten times three. —thir'ti·eth, adj., n.

this, pron., pl. these, adj., adv. —pron., adj. 1. demonstrative word indicating something as just mentioned, present, near, etc. —adv. 2. to the indicated extent.

this'tle, n. prickly plant.

thith'er, adv. to that place, point, etc.

tho (thō), conj., adv. Informal. though.

thong, n. strip of hide or leather.

tho'rax, n., pl. -raxes, -races. part of trunk between neck and abdomen. —tho·rac'ic, adj.

thor•i•um, *n.* grayish-white radioactive metallic element.

thorn, *n.* sharp spine on plant. **—thorn'y,** *adj.*

thor•ough (thûr'-), *adj.* complete. **—thor'ough•ly,** *adv.* **—thor'ough•ness,** *n.*

thor'ough•bred, *adj.* **1.** of pure breed. **2.** well-bred. **—n. 3.** thoroughbred animal or person.

thor'ough•fare, *n.* road, street, etc., open at both ends.

thor'ough•go•ing, *adj.* doing things thoroughly.

those, *pron.; adj.* pl. of **that.**

thou, *pron.* you (now little used except provincially, archaically, in poetry or elevated prose, in addressing God, and by Friends).

though, *conj.* **1.** notwithstanding that. **2.** even if. **3.** nevertheless. **—adv. 4.** however.

thought, *n.* **1.** mental activity. **2.** idea. **3.** purpose. **4.** regard.

thought'ful, *adj.* **1.** meditative. **2.** heedful. **3.** considerate. **—thought'ful•ly,** *adv.* **—thought'ful•ness,** *n.*

thought'less, *adj.* **1.** showing lack of thought. **2.** careless; inconsiderate. **—thought'less•ly,** *adv.*

thou'sand, *n., adj.* ten times one hundred. **—thou'sandth,** *adj., n.*

thrall, *n.* **1.** person in bondage; slave. **2.** slavery; bondage. **—thrall'dom,** *n.*

thrash, *v.* **1.** beat thoroughly. **2.** toss wildly. **—thrash'er,** *n.*

thread, *n.* **1.** fine spun cord of flax, cotton, etc. **2.** filament. **3.** helical ridge of screw. **4.** connected sequence. **—v. 5.** pass end of thread through needle's eye. **6.** fix beads, etc., on thread.

thread'bare, *adj.* shabby.

threat, *n.* menace. **—threat'en,** *v.*

three, *n., adj.* two plus one.

three'-di•men'sion•al, *adj.* having or seeming to have depth as well as width and height.

thren'o•dy, *n., pl.* **-dies.** song of lamentation.

thresh, *v.* separate grain or seeds from a plant. **—thresh'er,** *n.*

thresh'old, *n.* **1.** doorway sill. **2.** entrance. **3.** beginning; border.

thrice, *adv.* three times.

thrift, *n.* frugality. **—thrift'less,** *adj.*

thrift'y, *adj.,* **thriftier, thriftiest.** saving; frugal. **—thrift'i•ly,** *adv.* **—thrift'i•ness,** *n.*

thrill, *v.* **1.** affect with sudden keen emotion. **2.** vibrate. **—n. 3.** sudden wave of keen emotion or excitement.

thrill'er, *n.* suspenseful play or story.

thrive, *v.,* **thrived, thriving.** flourish.

throat, *n.* passage from mouth to stomach or lungs.

throat'y, *adj.,* **throatier, throatiest.** (of sound) husky; hoarse.

throb, *v.,* **throbbed, throbbing,** *n.* **—v. 1.** beat violently or rapidly. **2.** vibrate. **—n. 3.** act of throbbing.

throe, *n.* **1.** spasm. **2.** (*pl.*) pangs.

throm•bo'sis, *n.* clotting of blood in circulatory system.

throne, *n.* official chair of sovereign, bishop, etc.

throng, *n.; v.* crowd.

throt'tle, *n., v.* **-tled, -tling. —n. 1.** device controlling flow of fuel. **—v. 2.** choke. **3.** check.

through, *prep.* **1.** in at one end and out at other. **2.** during all of. **3.** having finished. **4.** by means or reason of. **—adv. 5.** in at one end and out at other. **6.** all the way. **7.** to the end. **8.** finished. **—adj. 9.** passing through.

through•out', *prep.* **1.** in all parts of. **—adv. 2.** in every part, etc.

throw, *v.,* **threw, thrown, throwing,** *n.* **—v. 1.** propel or cast. **2.** fell in wrestling. **—n. 3.** act of throwing. **—throw'er,** *n.*

throw'a•way, *n.* **1.** to be discarded after use. **—n. 2.** circular or notice distributed free.

throw'back', *n.* **1.** setback or check. **2.** reversion to ancestral type.

thru, *prep., adv., adj.* Informal. through.

thrum, *v.,* **thrummed, thrumming,** *n.* **—v. 1.** to play on stringed instrument, as guitar, by plucking strings. **2.** to tap with fingers. **—n. 3.** act or sound of thrumming. **—thrum'mer,** *n.*

thrush, *n.* **1.** migratory singing bird. **2.** fungal disease of mouth.

thrust, *v.,* **thrust, thrusting,** *n.* **—v. 1.** push; shove. **2.** stab. **—n. 3.** push; lunge. **4.** stab.

thud, *n., v.,* **thudded, thudding. —n. 1.** dull striking sound. **—v. 2.** make thudding sound.

thug, *n.* violent criminal.

thumb, *n.* **1.** short, thick finger next to the forefinger. **—v. 2.** manipulate with thumb.

thumb'screw', *n.* **1.** instrument of torture that compresses thumbs. **2.** screw turned by thumb and finger.

thumb'tack', *n.* **1.** tack with large, flat head. **—v. 2.** secure with thumbtack.

thump, *n.* **1.** blow from something thick and heavy. **—v. 2.** pound.

thun'der, *n.* **1.** loud noise accompanying lightning. **2.** give forth thunder. **3.** speak loudly. **—thun'der•**

ous, *adj.* —**thun′der•storm′,** *n.* —**thun′der•show′er,** *n.*

thun′der•bolt′, *n.* flash of lightning with thunder.

thun′der•clap′, *n.* crash of thunder.

thun′der•cloud′, *n.* electrically charged cloud producing lightning and thunder.

thun′der•head′, *n.* mass of cumulus clouds warning of thunderstorms.

thun′der•struck′, *adj.* astonished.

Thurs′day′, *n.* fifth day of week.

thus, *adv.* **1.** in this way. **2.** consequently. **3.** to this extent.

thwack, *v.* **1.** strike hard with something flat. —*n.* **2.** thwacking blow.

thwart, *v.* **1.** frustrate; prevent. —*n.* **2.** seat across a boat.

thy, *adj. Archaic.* your.

thyme (tīm), *n.* plant of mint family.

thy′mus, *n.* gland at base of neck that aids in production of T cells.

thy′roid, *adj.* of thyroid gland.

thyroid gland, ductless gland near windpipe, involved in controlling metabolism and growth.

thy•self′, *pron.* **1.** emphatic appositive to **thou** or **thee.** **2.** substitute for reflexive thee.

ti•ar′a (tē är′ə), *n.* woman's ornamental coronet.

Ti•bet′an, *n.* native or language of Tibet. —**Tibetan,** *adj.*

tib′i•a, *n., pl.* **-iae, -ias.** bone from knee to ankle. —**tib′i•al,** *adj.*

tic, *n.* sudden twitch.

tick, *n.* **1.** soft, recurring click. **2.** bloodsucking mitelike animal. **3.** cloth case of mattress, pillow, etc. —*v.* **4.** produce tick (def. 1).

tick′er, *n.* **1.** one that ticks. **2.** telegraphic instrument that prints stock prices and market reports, etc., on tape (**ticker tape**). **3.** *Slang.* heart.

tick′et, *n.* **1.** slip indicating right to admission, transportation, etc. **2.** tag. **3.** summons for traffic or parking violation. —*v.* **4.** attach ticket to.

tick′ing, *n.* cotton fabric for ticks (def. 3).

tick′le, *v.*, **-led, -ling,** *n.* —*v.* **1.** touch lightly so as to make tingle or itch. **2.** gratify; amuse. —*n.* **4.** act of tickling. —**tick′lish,** *adj.* —**tick′lish•ly,** *adv.*

tidal wave, large, destructive ocean wave produced by earthquake or the like.

tid′bit′, *n.* choice bit.

tide, *n.*, *v.*, **tided, tiding.** —*n.* **1.** periodic rise and fall of ocean waters. **2.** stream. —*v.* **3.** help over difficulty. —**tid′al,** *adj.*

tide′land′, *n.* land alternately exposed and covered by tide.

tide′wa′ter, *n.* **1.** water affected by tide. —*adj.* **2.** of lowland near sea.

ti′dings, *n.pl.* news.

ti′dy, *adj.*, **-dier, -diest,** *v.*, **-died, -dying.** —*adj.* **1.** neat; orderly. **2.** make tidy. —**ti′di•ly,** *adv.* —**ti′di•ness,** *n.*

tie, *v.*, **tied, tying,** *n.* —*v.* **1.** bind with cord, etc. **2.** confine. **3.** equal or be equal. —*n.* **4.** something used to tie or join. **5.** necktie. **6.** equality in scores, votes, etc. **7.** contest in which this occurs. **8.** bond of kinship, affection, etc.

tie′-dye′ing, *n.* method of dyeing with sections of garment bound so as not to receive dye. —**tie′-dyed′,** *adj.*

tie′-in′, *n.* link, association, or relationship.

tier (tēr), *n.* row or rank.

tie′-up′, *n.* **1.** undesired stoppage of business, traffic, etc. **2.** connection.

tiff, *n.* petty quarrel.

ti′ger, *n.* large striped Asian feline. —**ti′gress,** *n.fem.*

tiger lily, lily with flowers of dull-orange color spotted with black.

tight, *adj.* **1.** firmly in place. **2.** stretched; taut. **3.** fitting closely. **4.** impervious to fluids. —**tight′en,** *v.* —**tight′ly,** *adv.* —**tight′ness,** *n.*

tight′-fist′ed, *adj.* stingy.

tight′-lipped′, *adj.* reluctant to speak.

tight′rope′, *n.* taut wire or cable on which acrobats perform.

tights, *n.pl.* close-fitting pants, worn esp. by acrobats, etc.

tight′wad′, *n. Slang.* stingy person.

til′de (til′də), *n.* diacritical mark (∼) placed over letter.

tile, *n.*, *v.*, **tiled, tiling.** —*n.* **1.** thin piece of baked clay, etc., used as covering. —*v.* **2.** cover with tiles.

til′ing, *n.* **1.** operation of covering with tiles. **2.** tiles collectively.

till, *prep.*, *conj.* **1.** until. —*v.* **2.** labor on to raise crops. **3.** plow. —*n.* **4.** drawer in back of counter for money. —**till′a•ble,** *adj.* —**till′age,** *n.*

till′er, *n.* **1.** one that tills. **2.** handle on head of rudder.

tilt, *v.* **1.** lean; slant. **2.** charge or engage in joust. —*n.* **3.** act of tilting. **4.** slant.

tim′bale (tim′bəl), *n.* **1.** a preparation of minced meat, etc., cooked in mold. **2.** this mold, usually of paste, and sometimes fried.

tim′ber, *n.* **1.** wood of growing trees. **2.** trees. **3.** wood for building. **4.** wooden beam, etc. —*v.* **5.** furnish or support with timber. —**tim′bered,** adj.

tim′ber•line′, n. altitude or latitude at which timber ceases to grow.

timber wolf, large brindled wolf of forested Canada and northern United States.

tim′bre, n. characteristic quality of a sound.

time, n., v., **timed, timing.** —n. 1. duration. 2. period of time. 3. occasion. 4. point in time. 5. appointed or proper time. 6. meter of music. 7. rate. —v. 8. determine or record time. —**tim′er,** n.

time′-hon′ored, adj. long valued or used; traditional.

time′keep′er, n. 1. person who keeps time. 2. timepiece, esp. as regards accuracy.

time′less, adj. 1. eternal. 2. referring to no particular time.

time′ly, adj., **-lier, -liest,** adv. —adj. 1. opportune. —adv. 2. opportunely.

time′-out′, n. brief suspension of activity, as in sports contest.

time′piece′, n. clock; watch.

times, prep. multiplied by.

time′ta′ble, n. schedule of times of departures, work completion, etc.

tim′id, adj. 1. easily alarmed. 2. shy. —**tim•id′i•ty,** adv. —**ti•mid′i•ty, tim′id•ness,** n.

tim′ing, n. control of speed or occasion of an action, event, etc., so that it occurs at the proper moment.

tim′or•ous, adj. 1. fearful. 2. timid. —**tim′or•ous•ly,** adv. —**tim′or•ous•ness,** n.

tim′o•thy, n., pl. **-thies.** coarse fodder grass.

tim′pa•ni′ (-nē′) n.pl. kettledrums. —**tim′pa•nist,** n.

tin, n., v., **tinned, tinning.** —n. 1. malleable metallic element. —v. 2. cover with tin. —**tin′ny,** adj.

tinc′ture, n. medicinal solution in alcohol.

tin′der, n. inflammable substance. —**tin′der•box′,** n.

tine, n. prong of fork.

tinge, v., **tinged, tingeing** or **tinging,** n. —v. 1. impart trace of color, taste, etc. —n. 2. slight trace.

tin′gle, v., **-gled, -gling,** n. —v. 1. feel or cause slight stings. —n. 2. tingling sensation.

tink′er, n. 1. mender of pots, kettles, pans, etc. —v. 2. do the work of a tinker. 3. work or repair unskillfully or clumsily.

tin′kle, v., **-kled, -kling,** n. —v. 1. make light ringing sounds. —n. 2. tinkling sound.

tin′sel, n. 1. glittering metal in strips, etc. 2. anything showy and worthless.

tint, n. 1. color or hue. —v. 2. apply tint to.

tin′tin•nab′u•la′tion, n. ringing or sound of bells.

ti′ny, adj. **-nier, -niest.** very small.

tip, v., n., **tipped, tipping.** —n. 1. small gift of money. 2. piece of private information. 3. useful hint. 4. tap. 5. slender or pointed end. 6. top. —v. 7. give tip to. 8. furnish with tip. 9. tilt. 10. overturn. 11. tap. —**tip′per,** n.

tip′-off′, n. Slang. hint or warning.

tip′pet, n. scarf.

tip′ple, v., **-pled, -pling.** drink alcoholic liquor. —**tip′pler,** n.

tip′sy, adj., **-sier, -siest.** slightly intoxicated. —**tip′si•ly,** adv. —**tip′si•ness,** n.

tip′toe′, n., v., **-toed, -toeing.** —n. 1. tip of toe. —v. 2. move on tiptoes.

tip′top′, n. 1. extreme top. —adj. 2. situated at very top. 3. Informal. of highest excellence.

ti′rade, n. long denunciation or speech.

tire, v., **tired, tiring,** n. —v. 1. exhaust strength, interest, patience, etc. —n. 2. hoop of metal, rubber, etc., around wheel. —**tire′less,** adj. —**tire′some,** adj.

tired, adj. 1. exhausted; fatigued. 2. weary. —**tired′ly,** adv. —**tired′ness,** n.

tis′sue, n. 1. substance composing organism. 2. light, gauzy fabric.

tissue paper, very thin paper.

ti′tan (tīt′n) n. person or thing of great size or power. —**ti•tan′ic,** adj.

ti•ta′ni•um (tī tā′nē əm), n. corrosion-resistant metallic element, used to toughen steel.

tit for tat, equivalent given in retaliation, repartee, etc.

tithe, n. tenth part.

ti′tian (tish′ən), adj. yellowish or golden brown.

tit′il•late′, v., **-lated, -lating.** 1. tickle. 2. excite agreeably. —**tit′il•la′tion,** n.

tit′i•vate′, v., **-vated, -vating.** make smart or spruce. —**tit′i•va′tion,** n.

ti′tle, n., v., **-tled, -tling.** —n. 1. name of book, picture, etc. 2. caption. 3. appellation, esp. of rank. 4. championship. 5. right to something. 6. document showing this. —v. 7. furnish with title.

tit′mouse′, n., pl. **-mice.** small bird having crest and conical bill.

tit′ter, n. 1. low, restrained laugh. —v. 2. laugh in this way.

tit'u·lar, *adj.* 1. of or having a title. 2. being so in title only. —**tit'u·lar·ly**, *adv.*

tiz'zy, *n., pl.* **-zies.** *Slang.* dither.

TNT, trinitrotoluene.

to, *prep.* 1. particle specifying point reached. 2. sign of the infinitive. —*adv.* 3. toward. 4. to and fro, and from place to thing.

toad, *n.* tailless, froglike amphibian.

toad'stool', *n.* fungus with umbrella-like cap.

toad'y, *n., pl.* **toadies**, *v.*, **toadied**, **toadying.** —*n.* 1. fawning flatterer. —*v.* 2. be toady.

toast, *n.* 1. person whose health is proposed and drunk. 2. the proposal. 3. sliced bread browned by heat. —*v.* 4. propose as toast. 5. make toast.

toast'er, *n.* appliance for toasting bread.

toast'mas'ter, *n.* person who introduces the after-dinner speakers or proposes toasts. —**toast'mis'tress**, *n.fem.*

to·bac'co, *n., pl.* **-cos, -coes.** 1. plant with leaves prepared for smoking or chewing. 2. the prepared leaves.

to·bac'co·nist, *n.* dealer in or manufacturer of tobacco.

to·bog'gan, *n.* 1. long, narrow, flat-bottomed sled. —*v.* 2. coast on toboggan.

toc·ca'ta (tə kä'tə), *n. Music.* keyboard composition in style of improvisation.

toc'sin, *n.* signal, esp. of alarm.

to·day', *n.* 1. this day, time, or period. —*adv.* 2. on this day. 3. at this period. Also, **to·day'.**

tod'dle, *v.*, **-dled, -dling.** go with short, unsteady steps. —**tod'dler**, *n.*

tod'dy, *n., pl.* **-dies.** drink made of alcoholic liquor and hot water, sweetened and sometimes spiced.

to-do' (tə dōō'), *n., pl.* **-dos.** *Informal.* fuss.

toe, *n.* 1. terminal digit of foot. 2. part covering toes. —**toe'nail'**, *n.*

tof'fee, *n.* taffy.

to'fu (tō'fōō), *n.* soft cheeselike food made from curdled soybean milk.

to'ga, *n.* ancient Roman outer garment.

to·geth'er, *adv.* 1. into or in proximity, association, or single mass. 2. at same time. 3. in cooperation.

togs, *n.pl. Informal.* clothes.

toil, *n.* 1. hard, exhausting work. —*v.* 2. work hard. —**toil'er**, *n.*

toi'let, *n.* 1. receptacle for excretion. 2. bathroom. 3. Also, **toi·lette'.** act or process of dressing.

toilet water, scented liquid used as light perfume.

toil'some, *adj.* laborious or fatiguing. —**toil'some·ly**, *adv.* —**toil'some·ness**, *n.*

to·kay' (tō kā'), *n.* 1. rich, sweet, aromatic wine. 2. the variety of grape from which it is made.

to'ken, *n.* 1. thing expressing or representing something else. 2. metal disk used as ticket, etc. —*adj.* 3. being merely a token; minimal.

to'ken·ism, *n.* minimal conformity to law or social pressure.

tol'er·a·ble, *adj.* 1. endurable. 2. fairly good. —**tol'er·a·bly**, *adv.*

tol'er·ance, *n.* fairness toward different opinions, etc. —**tol'er·ant**, *adj.* —**tol'er·ant·ly**, *adv.*

tol'er·ate', *v.*, **-ated, -ating.** 1. allow. 2. put up with. —**tol·er·a'tion**, *n.*

toll, *v.* 1. sound bell slowly and repeatedly. —*n.* 2. payment, as for right to travel. 3. payment for long-distance telephone call.

tom'a·hawk', *n.* light ax used by North American Indians, esp. in war.

Tom and Jerry, hot drink of rum, milk, and beaten eggs.

to·ma'to, *n., pl.* **-toes.** cultivated plant with pulpy, edible fruit.

tomb, *n.* burial place for dead body; grave. —**tomb'stone'**, *n.*

tom'boy', *n.* boisterous, romping girl. —**tom'boy·ish**, *adj.*

tom'cat', *n.* male cat.

Tom Col'lins, tall iced drink containing gin, lemon or lime juice, and carbonated water.

tome, *n.* large book.

tom'fool'er·y, *n., pl.* **-eries.** foolish or silly behavior.

Tommy gun, *Slang.* type of submachine gun.

tom'my·rot', *n. Slang.* nonsense.

to·mog'ra·phy, *n.* method of making x-rays of selected plane of the body.

to·mor'row, *n.* 1. day after this day. —*adv.* 2. on day after this day. Also, **to-mor'row.**

tom'-tom', *n.* primitive drum.

ton, *n.* 1. unit of weight, equal to 2000 pounds (**short ton**) in U.S. and 2240 pounds (**long ton**) in Great Britain. 2. *Naut.* unit of volume, equal to 100 cubic feet.

to·nal'i·ty, *n., pl.* **-ties.** relation between tones of musical scales. 2. the tones.

tone, *n., v.*, **toned, toning.** —*n.* 1. sound. 2. quality of sound. 3. quality, etc., of voice. 4. firmness. 5. expressive quality. 6. elegance; amenity.

—v. 7. give proper tone to. —**ton′al**, adj. —**ton′al•ly**, adv.

tongs, n.pl. two-armed implement for grasping.

tongue (tung), n. 1. organ on floor of mouth, used for tasting, etc. 2. language. 3. tonguelike thing.

tongue′-lash′ing, n. severe scolding.

tongue′-tied′, adj. unable to speak, as from shyness.

ton′ic, n. 1. invigorating medicine. —adj. 2. invigorating.

to•night′ (-nīt′), n. 1. this night. —adv. 2. on this night.

ton′nage, n. 1. carrying capacity or total volume of vessel. 2. duty on cargo or tonnage. 3. ships.

ton•neau′ (tu nō′), n., pl. **-neaus, -neaux** (-nōz′). rear compartment of automobile with seats for passengers.

ton′sil, n. oval mass of tissue in throat.

ton′sil•lec′to•my, n., pl. **-mies.** removal of tonsils.

ton′sil•li′tis, n. inflammation of tonsils.

ton•so′ri•al, adj. of barbers.

ton′sure, n. 1. shaving of head. 2. shaved part of cleric's head.

too, adv. 1. also. 2. excessively.

tool, n. 1. mechanical instrument, as hammer or saw. 2. exploited person; dupe. —v. 3. decorate with tool.

toot, v. sound horn.

tooth, n., pl. **teeth.** 1. hard body attached to jaw, used in chewing, etc. 2. projection. 3. taste, relish, etc. —**tooth′ache′**, n. —**tooth′brush′**, n. —**tooth′paste′**, n. —**tooth′pick′**, n.

tooth′some, adj. tasty.

tooth′y, adj., **toothier, toothiest.** having or displaying conspicuous teeth.

top, n., v., **topped, topping.** —n. 1. highest point, part, rank, etc. 2. lid. 3. child's spinning toy. 4. separable upper part of clothing. —v. 5. put top on. 6. be top of. 7. surpass.

to′paz, n. colored crystalline gem.

top′coat′, n. light overcoat.

top′er (tō′pər), n. drunkard.

top hat, man's tall silk hat.

top′-heav′y, adj. disproportionately heavy at top.

top′ic, n. subject of discussion or writing.

top′i•cal, adj. 1. of or dealing with matters of current interest. 2. of topics. 3. applied to local area. —**top′i•cal•ly**, adv.

top kick, Mil. Slang. first sergeant.

top′most, adj. highest.

top′notch′, adj. Informal. first-rate.

to•pog′ra•phy, n., pl. **-phies.** description of features of geographical area. —**to•pog′ra•pher**, n. —**top•o•graph′ic, top•o•graph′i•cal**, adj.

top′per, n. 1. one that tops. 2. Slang. top hat. 3. short coat worn by women.

top′ple, v., **-pled, -pling.** fall; tumble.

top′sail′ (top′sāl′; Naut. -səl), n. square sail next above lowest or chief sail.

top′-se′cret, adj. extremely secret.

top′soil′, n. fertile upper soil.

top′sy-tur′vy, adv., adj. 1. upside down. 2. in confusion.

toque (tōk), n. hat with little or no brim.

tor, n. hill.

To′rah (tōr′ə), n. 1. five books of Moses; Pentateuch. 2. (also l.c.) whole Jewish Scripture. Also, **To′ra.**

torch, n. light carried in hand.

tor′e•a•dor′, n. bullfighter.

tor•ment′, v. 1. afflict with great suffering. —n. (tôr′ment). 2. agony. —**tor•men′tor, tor•ment′er**, n.

tor•na′do, n., pl. **-does, -dos.** destructive storm.

tor•pe′do, n., pl. **-does**, v. **-doed, -doing.** —n. 1. self-propelled missile launched in water and exploding on impact. —v. 2. strike with torpedo.

torpedo boat, small fast warship used to launch torpedoes.

tor′pid, adj. 1. inactive; sluggish. 2. dull; apathetic; lethargic. —**tor•pid′i•ty**, n. —**tor′pid•ly**, adv.

tor′por, n. 1. suspension of physical activity. 2. apathy.

torque (tôrk), n. rotating force.

tor′rent, n. rapid, violent stream. —**tor•ren′tial**, adj. —**tor•ren′tial•ly**, adv.

tor′rid, adj. very hot.

Torrid Zone, part of earth's surface between tropics.

tor′sion, n. 1. act of twisting. 2. twisting by two opposite torques. —**tor′sion•al**, adj.

tor′so, n., pl. **-sos, -si.** trunk of body.

tort, n. Law. civil wrong (other than breach of contract or trust) for which law requires damages.

torte (tôrt), n., pl. **tortes.** rich cake, made with eggs, nuts, and usu. no flour.

tor•til′la (tôr tē′yä), n. flat, round bread of Mexico, made from cornmeal or wheat flour.

tor′toise, n. turtle.

tor′toise•shell′, n. 1. horny brown and yellow shell of certain turtles, used for making combs, etc. 2. synthetic tortoiseshell. —adj. 3. colored like tortoiseshell.

tor·tu·ous, *adj.* 1. twisting; winding. 2. indirect. —**tor'tu·ous·ly,** *adv.* —**tor'tu·ous·ness,** *n.*

tor·ture, *n., v.,* **-tured, -turing.** —*n.* 1. infliction of great pain. —*v.* 2. subject to torture. —**tor'tur·er,** *n.* —**tor'tur·ous,** *adj.*

To'ry, *n., pl.* **-ries.** 1. (*also l.c.*) conservative. 2. American supporter of Great Britain during Revolutionary period. —**To'ry·ism,** *n.*

toss, *v.* 1. throw or pitch. 2. pitch about. 3. throw upward. —*n.* 4. throw or pitch.

toss'up', *n.* 1. tossing of coin to decide something by its fall. 2. *Informal.* even chance.

tot, *n.* small child.

to'tal, *adj., n., v.,* **-taled, -taling.** —*adj.* 1. entire. 2. utter; outright. —*n.* 3. total amount. —*v.* 4. add up. —**to·tal'i·ty,** *n.* —**to'tal·ly,** *adv.*

to·tal·i·tar·i·an, *adj.* of centralized government under sole control of one party. —**to·tal·i·tar'i·an·ism,** *n.*

tote, *v.,* **toted, toting,** *n. Informal.* —*v.* 1. carry or bear, as burden. —*n.* 2. act or course of toting. 3. that which is toted. 4. tote bag.

tote bag, open handbag.

to'tem, *n.* object in nature, often an animal, assumed as emblem of clan, family, or related group. —**to·tem'ic,** *adj.*

totem pole, pole with totemic figures, erected by Indians of northwest coast of North America.

tot'ter, *v.* 1. falter. 2. sway as if about to fall.

tou·can (tōō'kan), *n.* large-beaked tropical American bird.

touch, *v.* 1. put hand, finger, etc., in contact with something. 2. come or be in contact. 3. reach. 4. affect with sympathy. 5. refer to. —*n.* 6. act or instance of touching. 7. perception of things through contact. 8. contact. —**touch'a·ble,** *adj.* —**touch'ing,** *adj.*

touch' and go', precarious condition.

touch'down', *n. Football.* act of player in touching ball down to ground behind opponent's goal line.

tou·ché (tōō shā'), *interj.* (used to acknowledge telling remark or rejoinder).

touched, *adj.* 1. moved; stirred. 2. slightly crazy; unbalanced.

touch'-me-not', *n.* yellow-flowered plant whose ripe seed vessels burst open when touched.

touch'stone', *n.* 1. stone used to test purity of gold and silver by color pro-

duced when it is rubbed with them. 2. any criterion.

touch'y, *adj.,* **touchier, touchiest.** 1. irritable. 2. requiring tact. —**touch'i·ness,** *n.*

tough, *adj.* 1. not easily broken. 2. difficult to chew. 3. sturdy. 4. pugnacious. 5. trying. —**tough'en,** *v.* —**tough'ly,** *adv.* —**tough'ness,** *n.*

tou·pee' (tōō pā'), *n.* wig or patch of false hair worn to cover bald spot.

tour, *v.* 1. travel or travel through, esp. for pleasure. —*n.* 2. trip. 3. period of duty. —**tour'ist,** *n.* —**tour'ism,** *n.*

tour·na·ment, *n.* 1. meeting for contests. 2. contest between mounted knights. 3. competition involving number of rounds. Also, **tour'ney.**

tour'ni·quet (tûr'no kit), *n.* bandlike device for arresting bleeding by compressing blood vessels.

tou'sle, *v.,* **-sled, -sling.** dishevel.

tout, *Informal. v.* 1. solicit (business, votes, etc.) importunately. 2. proclaim; advertise. 3. give tip on (race horse, etc.). —*n.* 4. person who touts. —**tout'er,** *n.*

tow, *v.* 1. drag by rope or chain. —*n.* 2. act of towing. 3. thing towed.

to·ward', *prep.* Also, **to·wards'.** 1. in direction of. 2. with respect to. 3. nearly.

tow'boat', *n.* boat for pushing barges.

tow'el, *n.* cloth or paper for wiping.

tow'el·ing, *n.* fabric of cotton or linen used for towels.

tow'er, *n.* 1. tall structure. —*v.* 2. rise high.

tow'er·ing, *adj.* 1. very high or great. 2. violent; furious.

tow'head' (tō'hed'), *n.* 1. head of light-colored hair. 2. person with such hair.

tow'line', *n.* cable for towing.

town, *n.* 1. small city. 2. center of city. —**towns'man,** *n.* —**towns'wom'an,** *n.fem.* —**towns'peo'ple, towns'folk',** *n.pl.*

town'ship, *n.* 1. division of county. 2. (in U.S. surveys) district 6 miles square.

tox·e'mi·a, *n.* blood poisoning resulting from presence of toxins in blood.

tox'ic, *adj.* 1. of toxin. 2. poisonous. —**tox·ic'i·ty,** *n.*

tox·i·col'o·gy, *n.* science of poisons. —**tox·i·col'o·gist,** *n.*

tox'in, *n.* poisonous product of microorganism, plant, or animal.

toy, *n.* 1. plaything. —*v.* 2. play.

trace, *n., v.,* **traced, tracing.** —*n.* 1. mark or track left by something. 2.

small amount. **3.** pulling part of harness. —*v.* **4.** follow trace of. **5.** find out. **6.** draw. —**trace′a·ble,** *adj.* —**trac′er,** *n.*

trac′er·y, *n., pl.* **-eries.** ornamental pattern of interlacing lines, etc.

tra′che·a (trā′kē ə), *n., pl.* **-cheae** (-kē ē′). air-conveying tube from larynx to bronchi.

tra′che·ot′o·my, *n., pl.* **-mies.** operation of cutting into trachea, usu. to relieve difficulty in breathing.

track, *n.* **1.** parallel rails for railroad. **2.** wheel rut. **3.** footprint or other mark left. **4.** path. **5.** course. —*v.* **6.** follow; pursue.

track record, record of achievements or performance.

tract, *n.* **1.** region. **2.** brief treatise.

trac′ta·ble, *adj.* easily managed. —**trac·ta·bil′i·ty,** *n.* —**trac′ta·bly,** *adv.*

trac′tion, *n.* **1.** act or instance of pulling. **2.** adhesive friction.

trac′tor, *n.* self-propelled vehicle for pulling farm machinery, etc.

trade, *n., v.,* **traded, trading.** —*n.* **1.** buying, selling, or exchange of commodities; commerce. **2.** exchange. **3.** occupation. —*v.* **4.** buy and sell. **5.** exchange. —**trad′er,** *n.* —**trades′man,** *n.*

trade′-in′, *n.* goods given in whole or part payment for purchase.

trade′mark′, *n.* name, symbol, etc., identifying brand or source of things for sale.

trade name, word or phrase whereby particular class of goods is designated.

trade union, labor union.

trade wind, sea wind blowing toward equator from latitudes up to 30° away.

tra·di′tion, *n.* **1.** handing down of beliefs, customs, etc., through generations. **2.** something so handed down. —**tra·di′tion·al,** *adj.* —**tra·di′tion·al·ly,** *adv.* —**tra·di′tion·al·ist,** *n., adj.* —**tra·di′tion·al·ism,** *n.*

tra·duce′, *v.,* **-duced, -ducing.** slander.

traf′fic, *n., v.,* **-ficked, -ficking.** —*n.* **1.** traveling persons and things. —*v.* **3.** trade. **3.** traffic. —**traf′fick·er,** *n.*

tra·ge′di·an, *n.* actor or writer of tragedy. —**tra·ge′di·enne′,** *n. fem.*

trag′e·dy, *n., pl.* **-dies. 1.** serious drama with unhappy ending. **2.** sad event. —**trag′ic, trag′i·cal,** *adj.* —**trag′i·cal·ly,** *adv.*

trail, *v.* **1.** draw or drag. **2.** be drawn or dragged. **3.** race. —*n.* **4.** path. **5.** track, scent, etc., left.

trail′er, *n.* **1.** van attached to truck for hauling freight, etc. **2.** vehicle attached to car or truck with commodations for living, working, etc.

train, *n.* **1.** railroad locomotive with cars. **2.** moving line of persons, vehicles, etc. **3.** series of events, ideas, etc. **4.** trailing part. **5.** retinue. —*v.* **6.** instruct or undergo instruction. **7.** make fit. **8.** aim; direct. —**train′a·ble,** *adj.* —**train·ee′,** *n.* —**train′er,** *n.*

train′man, *n., pl.* **-men.** member of crew of railroad train.

traipse (trāps), *v.,* **traipsed, traipsing.** *Informal.* walk aimlessly.

trait, *n.* characteristic.

trai′tor, *n.* **1.** betrayer of trust. **2.** person guilty of treason. —**trai′tor·ous,** *adj.* —**trai′tress,** *n. fem.*

tra·jec′to·ry, *n., pl.* **-ries.** curve described by projectile in flight.

tram, *n. Brit.* streetcar or trolley car.

tram′mel, *n., v.,* **-meled, -meling.** —*n.* **1.** impediment to action. —*v.* **2.** hamper.

tramp, *v.* **1.** tread or walk firmly. **2.** march. —*n.* **3.** firm, heavy tread. **4.** hike. **5.** vagabond.

tram′ple, *v.,* **-pled, -pling.** step roughly on.

tram′po·line′ (-lēn′), *n.* cloth springboard for tumblers.

trance, *n.* half-conscious or hypnotic state.

tran′quil, *adj.* peaceful; quiet. —**tran′quil·ly,** *adv.* —**tran·quil′li·ty,** *n.* —**tran′quil·ize′,** *v.*

tran′quil·iz′er, *n.* drug to reduce tension.

trans-, *prefix.* across; through; on the other side; changing thoroughly; beyond or surpassing.

trans·act′, *v.* carry on business. —**trans·ac′tion,** *n.* —**trans·ac′tor,** *n.*

trans′at·lan′tic, *adj.* **1.** passing across Atlantic. **2.** on other side of Atlantic.

tran·scend′ (-send′), *v.* **1.** go or be beyond. **2.** excel.

tran·scend′ent, *adj.* **1.** extraordinary. **2.** superior; supreme.

tran′scen·den′tal, *adj.* beyond ordinary human experience. —**tran′scen·den′tal·ly,** *adv.*

tran·scribe′, *v.,* **-scribed, -scribing. 1.** copy. **2.** make recording of. —**tran·scrip′tion, tran′script,** *n.* —**tran·scrib′er,** *n.*

tran′sept, *n.* transverse portion of cross-shaped church.

trans·fer′, *v.,* **-ferred, -ferring.** —*v.* (trans fûr′). **1.** convey, hand over, or transport. **2.** be transferred. —*n.* (trans′fər). **3.** means or act of transferring. —**trans·fer'a·ble**, *adj.* —**trans·fer'ence**, *n.*

trans·fig'ure, *v.*, **-ured, -uring. 1.** transform. **2.** glorify. —**trans·fig·u·ra'tion**, *n.*

trans·fix', *v.* **1.** pierce. **2.** paralyze with terror, etc.

trans·form', *v.* change in form, nature, etc. —**trans·for·ma'tion**, *n.*

trans·form'er, *n.* device for converting electrical currents.

trans·fuse', *v.*, **-fused, -fusing. 1.** transmit, as by pouring. **2.** transfer blood from one person to another. —**trans·fu'sion**, *n.*

trans·gress', *v.* **1.** go beyond limit. **2.** violate law, etc. —**trans·gres'sion**, *n.* —**trans·gres'sor**, *n.*

tran'sient, *adj.* **1.** transitory. —*n.* **2.** transient person. —**tran'sient·ly**, *adv.*

tran·sis'tor, *n.* small electronic device replacing vacuum tube.

trans'it, *n.* passage or conveyance.

tran·si'tion, *n.* passage from one condition, etc., to another. —**tran·si'tion·al**, *adj.* —**tran·si'tion·al·ly**, *adv.*

tran'si·tive, *adj.* (of verb) regularly accompanied by direct object. —**tran'si·tive·ly**, *adv.*

tran'si·to·ry, *adj.* **1.** not enduring. **2.** brief. —**tran'si·to·ri·ness**, *n.*

trans·late', *v.*, **-lated, -lating.** change from one language into another. —**trans·la'tion**, *n.* —**trans·lat'a·ble**, *adj.* —**trans·lat'or**, *n.*

trans·lit'er·ate', *v.*, **-ated, -ating.** change into corresponding characters of another alphabet or language. —**trans·lit·er·a'tion**, *n.*

trans·lu'cent (-loo'sənt), *adj.* transmitting light diffusely. —**trans·lu'cence, trans·lu'cen·cy**, *n.*

trans'mi·gra'tion, *n.* passage of soul into another body.

trans·mis'sion, *n.* **1.** act or process of transmitting. **2.** something transmitted. **3.** set of gears to transfer force between mechanisms, as in automobile. **4.** broadcast.

trans·mit', *v.*, **-mitted, -mitting. 1.** send over or along. **2.** communicate. **3.** hand down. **4.** cause or permit light, heat, etc., to pass through. **5.** emit radio waves. —**trans·mit'tal**, *n.* —**trans·mit'ter**, *n.*

trans·mog'ri·fy, *v.*, **-fied, -fying.** change in appearance or form; transform. —**trans·mog'ri·fi·ca'tion**, *n.*

trans·mute', *v.*, **-muted, -muting.** change from one nature or form to another. —**trans·mut'a·ble**, *adj.* —**trans·mu·ta'tion**, *n.*

trans'o·ce·an'ic, *adj.* across or beyond ocean.

tran'som, *n.* **1.** window above door. **2.** crosspiece separating door from window, etc.

tran·son'ic, *adj.* close to speed of sound; moving 700–780 miles per hour.

trans·pa·cif'ic, *adj.* **1.** passing across Pacific. **2.** on other side of Pacific.

trans·par'ent, *adj.* **1.** allowing objects to be seen clearly through it. **2.** frank. **3.** obvious. —**trans·par'en·cy**, *n.*

tran·spire', *v.*, **-spired, -spiring. 1.** occur. **2.** give off waste matter, etc., from surface.

trans·plant', *v.* **1.** remove and put or plant in another place. —*n.* **2.** (trans'plant'). act of transplanting. **3.** something transplanted. —**trans'plan·ta'tion**, *n.*

trans·port', *v.* **1.** convey from one place to another. **2.** enrapture. —*n.* (trans'pōrt). **3.** something that transports. —**trans'por·ta'tion**, *n.*

trans·pose', *v.*, **-posed, -posing.** alter relative position, order, musical key, etc. —**trans'po·si'tion**, *n.*

trans·sex'u·al, *n.* **1.** person with sex surgically altered. **2.** person feeling identity with opposite sex.

trans·verse', *adj.* **1.** lying across. —*n.* **2.** something transverse. —**trans·verse'ly**, *adv.*

trans·ves'tite, *n.* person who dresses like opposite sex.

trap, *n.*, *v.*, **trapped, trapping. 1.** device for catching animals. **2.** scheme for catching a person unawares. **3.** U-shaped section in pipe to prevent escape of air or gases. —*v.* **4.** catch in or set traps. —**trap'per**, *n.*

tra·peze', *n.* suspended bar used in gymnastics.

trap'e·zoid', *n.* four-sided figure with two parallel sides.

trap'pings, *n.pl.* equipment or dress.

trash, *n.* rubbish. —**trash'y**, *adj.*

trau'ma (trou'-), *n.* **1.** externally produced injury. **2.** experience causing permanent psychological harm. —**trau·mat'ic**, *adj.*

tra·vail' (trə vāl'), *n.* **1.** toil. **2.** labor pains.

trav'el, *v.*, **-eled, -eling,** *n.* —*v.* **1.** journey. **2.** move. —*n.* **3.** journeying. —**trav'el·er**, *n.*

trav'e·logue' (trav'ə lôg', -log'), *n.* lecture describing travel, usually illustrated. Also, **trav'e·log'.**

trav·erse', *v.*, **-ersed, -ersing.** —*v.* **1.** pass over or through. —*n.* **2.** act of traversing.

trav'es·ty, *n.*, *pl.* **-ties,** *v.*, **-tied,**

-tying. —n. 1. literary burlesque. 2. debased likeness. —v. 3. make travesty on.

trawl, n. 1. fishing net dragged on bottom of water. —v. 2. fish with trawl. —**trawl′er,** n.

tray, n. flat, shallow receptacle or container.

treach′er·y, n., pl. **-ies.** betrayal; treason. —**treach′er·ous,** adj.

tread, v., **trod, trodden** or **trod, treading,** n. —v. 1. step, walk, or trample. 2. crush. —n. 3. manner of walking. 4. surface meeting road or rail. 5. horizontal surface of step. —**tread′er,** n.

trea′dle, n. lever, etc., worked by foot to drive machine.

tread′mill′, n. apparatus worked by treading on moving steps, as for exercise.

trea′son, n. violation of allegiance to sovereign or state. —**trea′son·a·ble, trea′son·ous,** adj.

treas′ure, n., v., **-ured, -uring.** —n. 1. accumulated wealth. 2. thing greatly valued. —v. 3. prize. 4. put away for future use.

treas′ure-trove′, n. 1. anything valuable that one finds. 2. treasure of unknown ownership, found hidden.

treas′ur·y, n., pl. **-uries.** 1. place for keeping public or private funds. 2. the funds. 3. government department handling funds. —**treas′ur·er,** n.

treat, v. 1. behave toward. 2. deal with. 3. relieve or cure. 4. discuss. 5. entertain. —n. 6. entertainment. —**treat′ment,** n. —**treat′a·ble,** adj.

trea′tise, n. writing on particular subject.

trea′ty, n., pl. **-ties.** formal agreement between states.

tre′ble, adj., n., v., **-bled, -bling.** —adj. 1. triple. 2. of highest pitch or range. 3. shrill. —n. 4. treble part, singer, instrument, etc. —v. 5. triple. —**tre′bly,** adv.

tree, n., v., **treed, treeing.** —n. 1. plant with permanent, woody, usually branched trunk. —v. 2. drive up tree.

tre′foil, n. 1. herb with leaf divided in three parts. 2. ornament based on this leaf.

trek, v., **trekked, trekking,** n. journey.

trel′lis, n. lattice.

trem′ble, v., **-bled, -bling,** n. —v. 1. quiver. —n. 2. act or state of trembling.

tre·men′dous, adj. extraordinarily great. —**tre·men′dous·ly,** adv.

trem′o·lo, n., pl. **-los.** vibrating effect on instrument or in voice.

trem′or, n. 1. involuntary shaking. 2. vibration.

trem′u·lous, adj. 1. trembling. 2. fearful. —**trem′u·lous·ly,** adv.

trench, n. ditch or cut.

trench′ant, adj. 1. incisive. 2. vigorous. —**trench′ant·ly,** adv.

trench coat, belted raincoat with epaulets.

trend, n. 1. tendency. 2. increasingly popular fashion.

trend′y, adj., **trendier, trendiest.** Informal. following current fads. —**trend′i·ness,** n.

trep·i·da′tion, n. tremulous alarm.

tres′pass, v. 1. enter property illicitly. 2. sin. —n. 3. act of trespassing. —**tres′pass·er,** n.

tress, n. braid of hair.

tres′tle, n. supporting frame or framework.

trey, n. Cards or Dice. three.

tri′ad, n. group of three.

tri′al, n. 1. examination before judicial tribunal. 2. test. 3. attempt. 4. state of being tested. 5. source of suffering.

tri′an·gle, n. figure of three straight sides and three angles. —**tri·an′gu·lar,** adj.

tribe, n. people united by common descent, etc. —**trib′al,** adj.

tribes′man, n., pl. **-men.** man belonging to tribe. —**tribes′wom·an,** n.fem.

trib·u·la′tion, n. 1. trouble. 2. affliction.

tri·bu′nal, n. 1. court of justice. 2. place of judgment.

trib′une, n. 1. person who defends rights of the people. 2. rostrum.

trib′u·tar·y, n., pl. **-taries,** adj. —n. 1. stream flowing into larger body of water. 2. payer of tribute. —adj. 3. flowing as tributary.

trib′ute, n. 1. personal offering, etc. 2. sum paid for peace, etc.

trice, n. instant.

tri′ceps (trī′seps), n. muscle at back of upper arm.

trich·i·no′sis (trik′ə-), n. disease due to parasitic worm.

trick, n. 1. artifice or stratagem. 2. prank. 3. knack. 4. cards won in one round. —v. 5. deceive or cheat by tricks. —**trick′er·y,** n. —**trick′y,** adj.

trick′le, v., **-led, -ling,** n. —v. 1. flow in small amounts. —n. 2. trickling flow.

tri′col·or, adj. 1. of three colors. —n. 2. three-colored flag, esp. of France.

tri·cus′pid, adj. having three cusps or points, as tooth.

tri′cy·cle, n. child's vehicle with large front wheel and two smaller rear wheels.

tri'dent, n. three-pronged spear.

tried, adj. tested; proved.

tri•en'ni•al (trī-), adj. **1.** lasting three years. **2.** occurring every three years. —n. **3.** period of three years. **4.** third anniversary.

tri'fle, n., v. **-fled, -fling.** —n. **1.** article of small value. **2.** trivial matter or amount. —v. **3.** deal without due respect. **4.** act idly or frivolously. —**tri'fler,** n. —**tri'fling,** adj.

tri•fo'li•ate (trī-), adj. having three leaves or leaflike parts.

trig'ger, n. **1.** projecting tongue pressed to fire gun. **2.** device to release spring. —v. **3.** precipitate.

trig•o•nom'e•try, n. mathematical study of relations between sides and angles of triangles. —**trig•o•no•met'ric,** adj.

trill, v. **1.** sing or play with vibratory effect. —n. **2.** act or sound of trilling.

tril'lion, n., adj. **1** followed by 12 zeroes.

tril'o•gy, n., pl. **-gies.** group of three plays, operas, etc., on related theme.

trim, v., **trimmed, trimming,** adj., **trimmer, trimmest.** —v. **1.** make neat by clipping, paring, etc. **2.** adjust (sails or yards). **3.** dress or ornament. —n. **4.** proper condition. **5.** adjustment of sails, etc. **6.** dress or equipment. **7.** trimming. —adj. **8.** neat. **9.** in good condition. —**trim'ly,** adv. —**trim'mer,** n. —**trim'ness,** n.

tri'ma•ran, n. boat with three hulls.

trim'ming, n. something used to trim.

tri•ni'tro•tol'u•ene', n. high explosive, known as TNT.

Trin'i•ty, n. unity of Father, Son, and Holy Ghost.

trin'ket, n. bit of jewelry, etc. **2.** trifle.

tri'o, n., pl. **trios.** group of three.

trip, n., v., **tripped, tripping.** —n. **1.** journey. **2.** stumble. —v. **3.** stumble or cause to stumble. **4.** slip. **5.** tread quickly and lightly. —v.

tri•par'tite (trī-), adj. **1.** divided into or consisting of three parts. **2.** participated in by three parties.

tripe, n. **1.** ruminant's stomach, used as food. **2.** Slang. worthless statements or writing.

tri'ple, adj., n., v., **-pled, -pling.** —adj. **1.** of three parts. **2.** three times as great. —n. **3.** Baseball. hit allowing batter to reach third base. —v. **4.** make or become triple. —**tri'ply,** adv.

tri'plet, n. one of three children (**triplets**) born at a single birth.

trip'li•cate (-kit), adj. **1.** triple. —n. **2.** set of three copies.

tri'pod, n. three-legged stool, support, etc.

trip'tych (trip'tik), n. set of three panels side by side, with pictures or carvings.

trite, adj., **triter, tritest.** commonplace; hackneyed. —**trite'ly,** adv. —**trite'ness,** n.

trit'u•rate, v., **-rated, -rating,** n. —v. **1.** to reduce to fine particles or powder; pulverize. —n. **2.** triturated substance. —**trit•u•ra'tion,** n.

tri'umph, n. **1.** victory. **2.** joy over victory. —v. **3.** be victorious or successful. **4.** rejoice over this. —**tri•um'phal,** adj. —**tri•um'phant,** adj.

tri•um'vir (trī um'vər), n., pl. **-virs, -viri** (-və rī') Rom. Hist. any of three magistrates exercising same public function. —**tri•um'vi•ral,** adj.

tri•um'vi•rate (trī um'və rit), n. **1.** Rom. Hist. the office of triumvir. **2.** government of three joint magistrates. **3.** association of three, as in office.

triv'et, n. device protecting table top from hot objects.

triv'i•al, adj. trifling. —**triv•i•al'i•ty,** n. —**triv'i•al•ly,** adv.

tro'che (-kē), n. small tablet of medicinal substance.

tro'chee (-kē), n. verse foot of two syllables, long followed by short. —**tro•cha'ic,** adj.

trog'lo•dyte' (trog'lə dīt'), n. **1.** cave dweller. **2.** person living in seclusion. **3.** person unacquainted with affairs of the world.

troll, v. **1.** sing in rolling voice; sing as round. **2.** fish with moving line. —n. **4.** Music. round. **5.** underground monster.

trol'ley, n. **1.** trolley car. **2.** pulley on overhead track or wire.

trolley car, electric streetcar receiving current from a trolley.

trol'lop (trol'əp), n. **1.** untidy or slovenly woman; slattern. **2.** prostitute.

trom•bone', n. brass wind instrument with long bent tube. —**trom•bon'ist,** n.

troop, n. **1.** assemblage. **2.** cavalry unit. **3.** body of police, etc. —v. **4.** gather. **5.** go or come in numbers. —**troop'er,** n.

troop'ship', n. ship for conveyance of military troops; transport.

trope, n. figure of speech.

tro'phy, n., pl. **-phies. 1.** memento taken in hunting, war, etc. **2.** silver cup, etc., given as prize.

trop'ic, n. **1.** either of two latitudes (**tropic of Cancer** and **tropic of Capricorn**) bounding torrid zone. **2.** (pl.)

tro′pism, *n.* response of plant or animal, as in growth, to influence of external stimuli. —**tro·pis′tic,** *adj.*

trot, *v.,* **trotted, trotting.** —*v.* 1. go at gait between walk and run. 2. go briskly. 3. ride at trot. —*n.* 4. trotting gait. —**trot′ter,** *n.*

troth (trôth), *n.* 1. fidelity. 2. promise.

trou·ba·dour′ (trōō′bə dôr′), *n.* medieval lyric poet of W Mediterranean area who wrote on love and gallantry.

trou′ble, *v.,* **-bled, -bling,** —*v.* 1. distress. 2. put to or cause inconvenience. 3. bother. —*n.* 4. annoyance or difficulty. 5. disturbance. 6. inconvenience. —**trou′bler,** *n.* —**trou′ble·some,** *adj.*

trou′bled, *adj.* 1. emotionally or mentally distressed. 2. economically or socially distressed.

trou·ble·shoot′er, *n.* expert in eliminating causes of trouble.

trough (trôf), *n.* 1. open boxlike container. 2. long hollow or channel.

trounce, *v.,* **trounced, trouncing.** beat severely.

troupe (trōōp), *n.* company of performers. —**troup′er,** *n.*

trou′sers, *n.pl.* outer garment divided into two separate leg coverings.

trous′seau′ (trōō′sō), *n., pl.* **-seaux, -seaus** (-sōz), bride's outfit.

trout, *n.* fresh-water game fish.

trow′el, *n.* 1. tool for spreading or smoothing. 2. small digging tool.

troy weight, system of weights for precious metals and gems.

tru′ant, *n.* 1. student absent from school without leave. —*adj.* 2. absent from school without leave. —**tru′an·cy,** *n.*

truce, *n.* suspension of military hostilities.

truck, *n.* 1. hand or motor vehicle for carrying heavy loads. 2. vegetables raised for market. 3. miscellaneous articles. —*v.* 4. transport by or drive a truck. 5. trade. —**truck′er,** *n.*

truck′le, *v.,* **-led, -ling.** submit humbly.

truckle bed, trundle bed.

truc′u·lent, *adj.* fierce. —**truc′u·lence,** *n.* —**truc′u·lent·ly,** *adv.*

trudge, *v.,* **trudged, trudging.** walk, esp. wearily. —*n.*

true, *adj.,* **truer, truest.** 1. conforming to fact. 2. real. 3. sincere. 4. loyal. 5. correct. —**tru′ly,** *adv.* —**true′ness,** *n.*

true′-blue′, *adj.* staunch; true.

truf′fle, *n.* 1. edible fungus. 2. chocolate confection resembling truffle.

tru′ism, *n.* obvious truth.

trump, *n.* 1. playing card of suit outranking other cards. 2. the suit. —*v.* 3. take with or play trump. 4. fabricate.

trump′er·y, *n., pl.* **-eries.** 1. something without use or value. 2. nonsense; twaddle.

trum′pet, *n.* 1. brass wind instrument with powerful, penetrating tone. —*v.* 2. blow trumpet. 3. proclaim. —**trum′pet·er,** *n.*

trun′cate, *v.,* **-cated, -cating.** shorten by cutting. —**trun·ca′tion,** *n.*

trun′cheon, *n.* club.

trun′dle, *v.,* **-dled, -dling,** —*v.* 1. roll, as on wheels. —*n.* 2. small roller, wheel, etc.

trun′dle bed, low bed on casters, usually pushed under another bed when not in use. Also, **truckle bed.**

trunk, *n.* 1. main stem of tree. 2. box for clothes, etc. 3. body of person or animal, excepting head and limbs. 4. main body of anything. 5. elephant's long flexible nasal appendage.

truss, *v.* 1. bind or fasten. 2. furnish or support with a truss. —*n.* 3. rigid supporting framework. 4. apparatus for confining hernia. 5. bundle.

trust, *n.* 1. reliance on person's integrity, justice, etc. 2. confident hope. 3. credit. 4. responsibility. 5. care. 6. something entrusted. 7. holding of legal title for another's benefit. 8. combination of companies, often monopolistic, controlled by central board. —*v.* 9. place confidence in. 10. rely on. 11. hope. 12. believe. 13. give credit. —**trust′ful,** *adj.* —**trust′wor·thy,** *adj.*

trus·tee′, *n.* 1. administrator of company, etc. 2. holder of trust (def. 7).

trus·tee′ship, *n.* 1. office of trustee. 2. control of territory granted by United Nations. 3. the territory.

trust′y, *adj.,* **trustier, trustiest,** *n., pl.* **trusties.** —*adj.* 1. reliable. —*n.* 2. trusted one. 3. trustworthy convict given special privileges. —**trust′i·ly,** *adv.* —**trust′i·ness,** *n.*

truth, *n.* 1. true facts. 2. conformity with fact. 3. established fact, principle, etc. —**truth′ful,** *adj.*

try, *v.,* **tried, trying.** 1. attempt. 2. test. 3. examine judicially. 4. strain endurance, patience, etc., of.

try′ing, *adj.* annoying; irksome.

try′out′, *n. Informal.* trial or test to ascertain fitness for some purpose.

tryst (trist), *n.* 1. appointment, as of lovers, to meet. 2. the meeting. 3. place of meeting. —*v.* 4. meet.

tsar (zär), *n.* czar.

tset'se fly (tset'sē), African fly transmitting disease.

T'-shirt', *n.* short-sleeved knitted undershirt. Also, **tee'-shirt'.**

T square, T-shaped ruler used in mechanical drawing.

tsu•na'•mi (tsoo nä'mē), *n.* huge wave caused by undersea earthquake or volcano.

tub, *n.* 1. bathtub. 2. deep, open-topped container.

tu'ba, *n.* low-pitched brass wind instrument.

tube, *n.* 1. hollow pipe for fluids, etc. 2. compressible container for toothpaste, etc. 3. railroad or vehicular tunnel. —**tu'bu•lar,** *adj.* —**tub'ing,** *n.*

tu'ber, *n.* fleshy thickening of underground stem or shoot. —**tu'ber•ous,** *adj.*

tu'ber•cle, *n.* small roundish projection, nodule, or swelling.

tu•ber•cu•lo'sis, *n.* infectious disease marked by formation of tubercles. —**tu•ber'cu•lar,** or **tu•ber'cu•lous,** *adj.*

tube'rose', *n.* cultivated flowering plant.

tuck, *v.* 1. thrust into narrow space or retainer. 2. cover snugly. 3. draw up in folds. —*n.* 4. tucked piece of cloth.

tuck'er, *n.* 1. piece of cloth formerly worn by women about neck and shoulders. —*v.* 2. *Informal.* tire; exhaust.

Tues'day, *n.* third day of week.

tuft, *n.* 1. bunch of feathers, hairs, etc., fixed at base. 2. clump of bushes, etc. —*v.* 3. arrange in or form tufts. —**tuft'ed,** *adj.*

tug, *v.* **tugged, tugging.** —*v.* 1. drag; haul. —*n.* 2. act of tugging. 3. tugboat.

tug'boat', *n.* powerful vessel used for towing.

tug of war, 1. contest between teams pulling opposite ends of rope. 2. struggle for supremacy.

tu•i'tion, *n.* charge for instruction.

tu'lip, *n.* plant bearing showy, cup-shaped flowers.

tulle (tool), *n.* thin silk or rayon net.

tum'ble, *v.,* **-bled, -bling.** —*v.* 1. fall over or down. 2. perform gymnastic feats. 3. roll about; toss. —*n.* 4. act of tumbling.

tum'ble-down', *adj.* dilapidated; run-down.

tum'bler, *n.* 1. drinking glass. 2. performer of tumbling feats. 3. lock part engaging bolt.

tum'ble•weed', *n.* plant whose upper

part becomes detached and is driven about by wind.

tu'mid, *adj.* 1. swollen. 2. turgid; bombastic. —**tu•mid'i•ty,** *n.* —**tu•mes'cent,** *adj.*

tu'mor, *n.* abnormal swelling of cells in part of body. —**tu'mor•ous,** *adj.*

tu'mult, *n.* disturbance, commotion, or uproar. —**tu•mul'tu•ous,** *adj.*

tun, *n.* large cask.

tu'na, *n.* 1. large oceanic fish. 2. tunny. Also, **tuna fish.**

tun'dra, *n.* vast, treeless, arctic plain.

tune, *n., v.,* **tuned, tuning.** —*n.* 1. melody. 2. state of proper pitch, frequency, or condition. 3. harmony. —*v.* 4. adjust to correct pitch. 5. adjust to receive radio or television signals. —**tune'ful,** *adj.* —**tune'a•ble,** *adj.* —**tune'less,** *adj.* —**tun'er,** *n.*

tung'sten, *n.* metallic element used for electric-lamp filaments, etc.

tu'nic, *n.* 1. coat of uniform. 2. ancient Greek and Roman garment. 3. woman's upper garment.

tun'ing fork, steel instrument struck to produce pure tone of constant pitch.

tun'nel, *n., v.,* **-neled, -neling.** —*n.* 1. underground passage. —*v.* 2. make tunnel.

tun'ny, *n., pl.* **-ny, -nies.** large mackerel-like fish.

tur'ban, *n.* head covering made of scarf wound round head.

tur'bid, *adj.* 1. muddy. 2. dense. 3. confused. —**tur•bid'i•ty,** *n.*

tur'bine, *n.* motor producing torque by pressure of fluid.

tur'bo•jet', *n.* 1. jet engine that compresses air by turbine. 2. airplane with such engines.

tur'bo•prop', *n.* 1. turbojet with turbo-driven propeller. 2. airplane with such engines.

tur'bu•lent, *adj.* 1. disorderly. 2. tumultuous. —**tur'bu•lence,** *n.* —**tur'bu•lent•ly,** *adv.*

tu•reen' (tŏŏ rēn'), *n.* large covered dish for soup, etc.

turf, *n.* 1. covering of grass and roots. 2. familiar area, as of residence or expertise. —**turf'y,** *adj.*

tur'gid (tûr'jid), *adj.* 1. swollen. 2. pompous or bombastic. —**tur•gid'i•ty, tur'gid•ness,** *n.* —**tur'gid•ly,** *adv.*

tur'key, *n.* large, edible American bird.

tur'moil, *n.* tumult.

turn, *v.* 1. rotate. 2. reverse. 3. divert; deflect. 4. depend. 5. sour; ferment. 6. nauseate. 7. alter. 8. become. 9. use.

10. pass. 11. direct. 12. curve. —n. 13. rotation. 14. change or point of change. 15. one's due time or opportunity. 16. trend. 17. short walk, ride, etc. 18. inclination or aptitude. 19. service or disservice.

turn'buck'le, n. link used to couple or tighten two parts.

turn'coat', n. renegade.

tur'nip, n. 1. fleshy, edible root of cabbagelike plant. 2. the plant.

turn'key, n. keeper of prison keys.

turn'out', n. 1. attendance at meeting, show, etc. 2. output.

turn'o'ver, n. 1. rate of replacement, investment, trade, etc. 2. small pastry with filling.

turn'pike', n. 1. barrier across road (**turnpike road**) where toll is paid. 2. turnpike road.

turn'stile', n. horizontal crossed bars in gateway.

turn'ta'ble, n. rotating platform.

tur'pen·tine', n. 1. type of resin from coniferous trees. 2. oil yielded by this.

tur'pi·tude', n. depravity.

tur'quoise (-koiz), n. 1. greenish-blue mineral used in jewelry. 2. bluish green.

tur'ret, n. 1. small tower. 2. towerlike gun shelter.

tur'tle, n. marine reptile with shell-encased body.

tur'tle·dove', n. small Old World dove.

tur'tle·neck', n. 1. high, close-fitting collar. 2. garment with turtleneck.

tusk, n. very long tooth, as of elephant or walrus.

tus'sle, v., **-sled, -sling.** fight; scuffle.

tu'te·lage, n. 1. guardianship. 2. instruction. —**tu'te·lar'y, tu'te·lar,** adj.

tu'tor, n. 1. private instructor. 2. college teacher (below instructor). —v. 3. teach. —**tu·to'ri·al,** adj.

tut'ti-frut'ti (tōō'tē frōō'tē), n. confection, esp. ice cream, flavored with variety of fruits.

tu'tu' (tōō'tōō'), n. short, full skirt worn by ballerina.

tux·e'do, n., pl. **-dos.** semiformal jacket or suit for men.

TV, television.

twad'dle, n. nonsense.

twain, n., adj. Archaic. two.

twang, v. 1. sound sharply and ringingly. 2. have nasal tone. —n. 3. twanging sound.

tweak, v. 1. seize and pull or twist. —n. 2. sharp pull and twist.

tweed, n. coarse, colored wool cloth.

tweet'er, n. small loudspeaker reproducing high-frequency sounds.

tweez'ers, n.pl. small pincers.

twelve, n., adj. ten plus two. —**twelfth,** adj. n.

twen'ty, n., adj. ten times two. —**twen'ti·eth,** adj., n.

twerp, n. Slang. insignificant or despicable person.

twice, adv. 1. two times. 2. doubly.

twid'dle, v., **-dled, -dling.** 1. turn round and round, esp. with the fingers. 2. twirl (one's fingers) about each other.

twig, n. slender shoot on tree.

twi'light', n. light from sky when sun is down.

twill, n. 1. fabric woven in parallel diagonal lines. 2. the weave. —v. 3. weave in twill.

twin, n. either of two children born at single birth.

twine, n., v., **twined, twining.** —n. 1. strong thread of twisted strands. —v. 2. twist or become twisted together. 3. encircle.

twinge, n., v., **twinged, twinging.** —n. 1. sudden, sharp pain. —v. 2. give or have twinge.

twin'kle, v., **-kled, -kling,** n. —v. 1. shine with light, quick gleams. —n. 2. sly, humorous look. 3. act of twinkling.

twirl, v. 1. spin; whirl. —n. 2. a twirling.

twist, v. 1. combine by winding together. 2. distort. 3. combine in coil, etc. 4. wind about. 5. writhe. 6. turn. —n. 7. curve or turn. 8. spin. 9. wrench. 10. spiral.

twist'er, n. 1. person or thing that twists. 2. Informal. whirlwind or tornado.

twit, v., **twitted, twitting.** —v. 1. taunt; tease. —n. 2. Informal. insignificant or bothersome person.

twitch, v. 1. jerk; move with jerk. —n. 2. quick jerky movement, as of muscle.

twit'ter, v. 1. utter small, tremulous sounds, as bird. 2. tremble with excitement. —n. 3. twittering sound. 4. state of tremulous excitement.

two, n., adj. one plus one.

two'-bit', adj. Informal. inferior or unimportant.

two'-faced', adj. deceitful or hypocritical.

two'some (-səm), n. pair.

ty·coon', n. businessperson having great wealth and power.

tyke, n. small child.

tympanic membrane, membrane separating middle from external ear.

tym'pa·num (tim'pə nəm), n. 1. middle ear. 2. tympanic membrane. —**tym·pan'ic,** adj.

type, n., v., **typed, typing.** —n. 1. kind or class. 2. representative specimen. 3. piece bearing a letter in relief, used in printing. 4. such pieces collectively. —v. 5. typewrite. —**typ'ist,** n.

type'writ'er, n. machine for writing mechanically. —**type'write',** v.

ty'phoid, n. infectious disease marked by intestinal disorder. Also, **typhoid fever.**

ty·phoon', n. cyclone or hurricane of western Pacific.

ty'phus, n. infectious disease transmitted by lice and fleas.

typ'i·cal, adj. 1. serving as a representative specimen. 2. conforming to the characteristics of a particular group. —**typ'i·cal·ly,** adv.

typ'i·fy', v., **-fied, -fying.** serve as typical example of.

ty'po (tī'pō), n., pl. **-pos.** error in typography or typing.

ty·pog'ra·phy, n. 1. art or process of printing. 2. general character of printed matter. —**ty·pog'ra·pher,** n. —**ty'po·graph'i·cal,** adj.

tyr'an·ny, n., pl. **-nies.** 1. despotic abuse of authority. 2. government or rule by tyrant. —**ty·ran'ni·cal,** adj. —**tyr'an·nize',** v.

ty'rant, n. oppressive, unjust, or absolute ruler.

ty'ro, n., pl. **-ros.** novice.

tzar, n. czar.

U

U, u, n. twenty-first letter of English alphabet.

u·biq'ui·tous, adj. simultaneously present everywhere. —**u·biq'ui·ty,** n.

ud'der, n. mammary gland, esp. of cow.

UFO, unidentified flying object.

ug'ly, adj., **-lier, -liest.** 1. repulsive. 2. dangerous. —**ug'li·ness,** n.

u·kase' (yoo kās', -kāz'), n. order by absolute authority.

u·ku·le'le (yoo'kə lā'lē), n. small guitar.

ul'cer, n. open sore, as on stomach lining. —**ul'cer·ous,** adj. —**ul'cer·ate',** v.

ul'na, n. larger bone of forearm. —**ul'nar,** adj.

ul·te'ri·or, adj. 1. not acknowledged; concealed. 2. later.

ul'ti·mate, adj. 1. final; highest. 2. basic. —**ul'ti·mate·ly,** adv.

ul'ti·ma'tum (-mā'təm), n., pl. **-tums, -ta.** final demand.

ul·tra-, prefix. beyond; on the far side of; extremely.

ul'tra·ma·rine', n. deep blue.

ul'tra·sound', n. 1. sound above limit of human hearing. 2. application of ultrasound to medical diagnosis and therapy. —**ul'tra·son'ic,** adj.

ul'tra·vi'o·let, adj. of invisible rays beyond violet in spectrum.

um'ber, n. 1. reddish brown. —adj. 2. of or like umber.

umbilical cord, cordlike structure connecting fetus with placenta, conveying nourishment and removing wastes.

um·bil'i·cus, n., pl. **-ci.** navel. —**um·bil'i·cal,** adj.

um'brage, n. resentment.

um·brel'la, n. cloth-covered framework carried for protection from rain, etc.

um'pire, n., v., **-pired, -piring.** —n. 1. judge or arbitrator. —v. 2. be umpire in.

un-, prefix indicating negative or opposite sense, as in **unfair, unwanted,** and **unfasten.** See list below.

un·af·fect'ed, adj. 1. without affectation. 2. not concerned or involved.

u·nan'i·mous, adj. completely

---

un·a'ble	un·clean'
un·ack·now'ledged	un·cloak'
un·a·void'a·ble	un·clothe'
un·a·ware'	un·com'fort·a·ble
un·be·liev'a·ble	un·com'mon
un·born'	un·con'scious
un·bound'ed	un'con·trol'la·ble
un·bur'den	un·cork'
un·but'ton	un·cov'er
un·cer'tain	un'de·cid'ed
un·civ'il	un'de·clared'

agreed. —**u·nan'i·mous·ly**, adv.
—**u'a·nim'i·ty**, n.

un·as·sum'ing, adj. modest; without vanity.

un'a·vail'ing, adj. not effective; futile.

un'a·wares', adv. not knowingly.

un·bal'anced, adj. 1. out of balance. 2. irrational; deranged.

un·bend', v., -bent, -bending. 1. straighten. 2. act in genial, relaxed manner.

un·bend'ing, adj. rigidly formal or unyielding.

un·blush'ing, adj. showing no remorse; shameless.

un·bos'om, v. disclose (secrets, etc.).

un·bri'dled, adj. unrestrained.

un·called'-for', adj. not warranted.

un·can'ny, adj. unnaturally strange or good.

un·cer'e·mo'ni·ous, adj. 1. informal. 2. rudely abrupt.

un'cle, n. brother of one's father or mother.

Uncle Sam, United States government.

un·com'pro·mis'ing, adj. refusing to compromise; rigid.

un'con·cern', n. lack of concern; indifference.

un'con·di'tion·al, adj. absolute; without conditions or reservations. —**un'con·di'tion·al·ly**, adv.

un·con'scion·a·ble (-shan-), adj. not reasonable or honest.

un·con'scious, adj. 1. lacking awareness, sensation, or cognition. 2. not perceived at level of awareness. 3. done without intent. —n. 4. the unconscious, part of psyche rarely accessible to awareness but influencing behavior.

un·couth', adj. rude; boorish.

unc'tion, n. 1. anointment with oil. 2. soothing manner of speech.

unc'tu·ous (-choo əs), adj. 1. oily. 2. overly suave.

un·cut', adj. 1. not shortened; unabridged. 2. not given shape, as a gemstone.

un'der, prep., adj., adv. 1. beneath; below. 2. less than. 3. lower.

un'der·brush', n. low shrubs, etc., in forest.

un'der·clothes', n.pl. underwear. Also, **un'der·cloth'ing**.

un'der·cov'er, adj. secret.

un'der·cur'rent, n. 1. hidden tendency or feeling. 2. current below surface or beneath another current.

un'der·cut', v., -cut, -cutting. sell at lower price than.

un'der·de·vel'oped, adj. 1. insufficiently developed. 2. having relatively low living standards and industrial development.

un'der·dog', n. 1. weaker contestant, etc. 2. victim of injustice.

un'der·es'ti·mate', v., -mated, -mating. estimate too low.

un'der·gar'ment, n. item of underwear.

un'der·go', v., -went, -gone, -going. experience; endure.

un'der·grad'u·ate, n. college student before receiving first degree.

un'der·ground', adj., adv. 1. under the ground. 2. secret. —n. (un'dər ground') 3. secret resistance army.

un'der·growth', n. underbrush.

un'der·hand', adj. sly; secret. Also, **un'der·hand'ed**.

un'der·lie', v., -lay, -lain, -lying. 1. lie beneath. 2. be the cause or basis of.

un'der·line', v., -lined, -lining. 1. draw line under. 2. stress; emphasize.

un'der·ling', n. subordinate.

un'der·mine', v., -mined, -mining. weaken or destroy, esp. secretly.

un'der·neath', prep., adv. beneath.

un'der·pass', n. passage running underneath.

un'der·pin'ning, n. 1. system of supports. 2. foundation; basis.

un'der·priv'i·leged, adj. denied normal privileges of society, esp. because poor.

un'der·score', v., -scored, -scoring. underline; stress.

un'der·stand', v., -stood, -standing. 1. know meaning of. 2. accept as part

---

un'de·feat'ed
un'de·ni'a·ble
un·doubt'ed
un·dress'
un·due'
un·du'ly
un·e'qual
un·err'ing
un·e'ven
un'ex·pect'ed
un·fail'ing

un·fair'
un·faith'ful
un'fa·mil'iar
un·fas'ten
un·fit'
un·fold'
un'for·get'ta·ble
un'for·giv'a·ble
un·for'tu·nate
un·friend'ly
un·god'ly

of agreement. 3. sympathize. —**un′·der·stand′ing**, n.

un·der·state′, v., **-stated, -stating.** 1. state less strongly than facts warrant. 2. set forth in restrained terms. —**un′der·state′ment**, n.

un·der·stood′, adj. agreed or assumed.

un·der·stud·y, n., pl. **-studies.** substitute for performer.

un·der·take′, v., **-took, -taken, -taking.** 1. attempt. 2. promise. 3. arrange funerals, etc.

un·der·tak′er, n. funeral director; mortician.

un·der·tak′ing, n. enterprise; task.

un·der·tow′, n. strong subsurface current moving opposite surface current.

un·der·wear′, n. garments worn next to skin, under other clothing.

un·der·world′, n. 1. criminal element. 2. land of the dead.

un·der·write′, v., **-wrote, -written, -writing.** guarantee, esp. expense.

un·do′, v., **-did, -done, -doing.** 1. return to former state. 2. untie. 3. destroy.

un·du·late, v., **-lated, -lating.** have wavy motion or form. —**un′du·la′tion,** n.

un·dy′ing, adj. eternal; unending.

un·earth′, v. discover.

un·earth′ly, adj. 1. not of this world. 2. supernatural; weird. 3. unreasonable; absurd.

un·eas′y, adj., **-easier, -easiest.** anxious. —**un·eas′i·ly**, adv. —**un·eas′i·ness,** n.

un·feel′ing, adj. lacking sympathy. —**un·feel′ing·ly**, adv.

un·found′ed, adj. not supported by evidence.

un·gain′ly, adj. clumsy.

un·guent (ung′gwant), n. salve.

un·hand′, v. release from grasp.

un·hinge′, v., **-hinged, -hinging.** 1. take off hinges. 2. upset reason of; unbalance.

u′ni·corn′, n. mythical horselike animal with one horn.

u′ni·form′, adj. 1. exactly alike. 2. even. —n. 3. distinctive clothing of specific group. —v. 4. put in uniform. —**u′ni·form′i·ty,** n.

u′ni·fy′, v., **-fied, -fying.** make into one. —**u′ni·fi·ca′tion,** n.

u′ni·lat·er·al, adj. one-sided.

un·ion, n. 1. uniting; combination. 2. labor group for mutual aid on wages, etc. —**un′ion·ism′**, n. —**un′ion·ist**, n., adj. —**un′ion·ize′**, v.

Union Jack, British flag.

u·nique′, adj. 1. only. 2. most unusual or rare. —**u·nique′ly**, adv.

u′ni·sex′, adj. of type or style used by both sexes.

u′ni·son, n. agreement.

u′nit, n. one of number of identical or similar things.

U·ni·tar′i·an, n. 1. member of Christian denomination asserting unity of God. —adj. 2. concerning Unitarians or their beliefs.

u·nite′, v., **united, uniting.** join, make, etc., into one.

United Nations, organization of nations to preserve peace and promote human welfare.

u′ni·ty, n., pl. **-ties.** 1. state of being one. 2. agreement. 3. uniformity.

u′ni·ver′sal, adj. 1. of all; general. 2. of universe. 3. having many skills, much learning, etc. —**u′ni·ver′sal·ly**, adv. —**u′ni·ver·sal′i·ty,** n.

u′ni·verse′, n. all things that exist, including heavenly bodies.

u′ni·ver′si·ty, n., pl. **-ties.** institution composed of various specialized colleges.

un·kempt′, adj. untidy.

un·lead′ed (-led′id), adj. (of gasoline) free of pollution-causing lead.

un·less′, conj., prep. except that.

un·let′tered, adj. illiterate.

un·nerve′, v., **-nerved, -nerving.** deprive of courage, strength, or determination.

un·prin′ci·pled, adj. without principles or ethics.

un·print′a·ble, adj. unfit for print, esp. because obscene.

un·gra′cious
un·guard′ed
un·hap′py
un·heard′-of′
un·ho′ly
un′in·tel′li·gi·ble
un′in·ter·est′ed
un′in·ter·rupt′ed
un·kind′
un·known′
un·lace′

un·law′ful
un·like′
un·like′ly
un·load′
un·lock′
un·mask′
un′mis·tak′a·ble
un·mor′al
un·nat′u·ral
un·nec′es·sar′y
un·pack′

un•rav'el, v., **-eled, -eling. 1.** disentangle. **2.** solve.

un're•mit'ting, adj. not abating; incessant.

un•rest', n. **1.** restless state. **2.** strong, almost rebellious, dissatisfaction.

un•ru'ly, adj., **-lier, -liest.** lawless.

un•sa'vo•ry, adj. **1.** tasteless; insipid. **2.** unpleasant in taste or smell. **3.** morally objectionable.

un•seat', v. **1.** dislodge from seat. **2.** remove from political office.

un•set'tle, v., **-tled, -tling. 1.** cause to be unstable; disturb. **2.** agitate mind or emotions of.

un•speak'a•ble, adj. too disgusting to speak of. —**un•speak'a•bly,** adv.

un•strung', adj. nervously upset; unnerved.

un•sung', adj. not celebrated, as in song; unappreciated.

un•ten'a•ble, adj. not defensible as true.

un•think'a•ble, adj. not to be imagined; impossible.

un•ti'dy, adj., **-dier, -diest.** not tidy or neat. —**un•tid'i•ly,** adv.

un•tie', v., **-tied, -tying.** loosen or open (something tied).

un•til', conj., prep. **1.** up to time when. **2.** before.

un'to, prep. Archaic to.

un•told', adj. countless.

un•touch'a•ble, adj. **1.** beyond control or criticism. **2.** too vile to touch. —**un•touch'a•ble,** n.

un•to•ward', adj. unfavorable or unfortunate.

un•well', adj. ill or ailing.

un•wield'y, adj., **-wieldier, -wieldiest.** awkward to handle.

un•wit'ting, adj. not aware. —**un•wit'ting•ly,** adv.

un•wont'ed, adj. not habitual or usual.

up, adv., prep., n., v., **upped, upping.** —adv. **1.** to higher place, etc. **2.** erectly. **3.** out of bed. **4.** at bat. —prep. **5.** up higher place, etc., on or in. —n. **6.** rise. —v. **7.** increase.

up'-and-com'ing, adj. likely to succeed; promising.

up'beat', adj. optimistic; happy.

up•braid', v. chide.

up•bring'ing, n. care and training of children.

up•com'ing, adj. about to take place or appear.

up•date', v., **-dated, -dating.** modernize, esp. in details.

up•end', v. set on end.

up'-front', adj. **1.** invested or paid in advance. **2.** honest; candid.

up•grade', n., v., **-graded, -grading.** —n. **1.** upward incline. **2.** increase, rise, or improvement. —v. **3.** raise in rank, position, quality, or value.

up•heav'al, n. sudden and great movement or change.

up•hill', adv. up a slope or incline. —**up'hill'.**

up•hold', v., **-held, -holding.** support. —**up•hold'er,** n.

up•hol'ster, v. provide (furniture) with coverings, etc. —**up•hol'ster•er,** n.

up'keep', n. maintenance.

up'land (up'land), n. elevated region.

up•lift', v. **1.** improve; exalt. —n. **2.** (up'lift'). improvement. **3.** inspiration.

up•on', prep. on.

up'per, adj. higher. —**up'per•most',** adj.

upper hand, controlling position; advantage.

up•pi'ty, adj. Informal. haughty, snobbish, or arrogant.

up•right', adj. **1.** erect. **2.** righteous. —**up'right'ness,** n.

up•ris'ing, n. revolt.

up•roar', n. tumult; noise; din. —**up•roar'i•ous,** adj.

up•root', v. tear up by roots.

up'scale', adj. of or for people at upper end of economic scale.

up•set', v., **-set, -setting,** n., adj. —v. **1.** turn over. **2.** distress emotionally. **3.** defeat. —n. (up'set'). **4.** overturn. **5.** defeat. —adj. **6.** disorderly. **7.** distressed.

---

un•pop'u•lar
un•rea'son•a•ble
un•roll'
un•screw'
un•set'tle
un•shack'le
un•sight'ly
un•skilled'
un•tan'gle
un•true'
un•truth'

un•twist'
un•typ'i•cal
un•used'
un•u'su•al
un•veil'
un•wind'
un•wise'
un•worn'
un•wor'thy
un•wrap'
un•yoke'

up'shot', *n.* final result.

up'side down', 1. with upper part undermost. **2.** in or into complete disorder. —**up'side-down'**, *adj.*

up'stage', *adv.*, *v.*, **-staged, -staging.** —*adv.* **1.** at or toward back of stage. —*v.* **2.** draw attention away from by moving upstage. **3.** outdo professionally or socially.

up'stairs', *adv., adj.* on or to upper floor.

up'start', *n.* person newly risen to wealth or importance.

up'-to-date', *adj.* **1.** until now. **2.** modern; latest.

up'ward, *adv.* to higher place. Also, **up'wards.** —**up'ward**, *adj.*

u•ra'ni•um, *n.* white, radioactive metallic element, important in development of atomic energy.

ur'ban, *adj.* of or like a city.

ur•bane', *adj.* polite or suave. —**ur•ban'i•ty**, *n.*

ur'chin, *n.* ragged child.

u•re'a (yŏŏ rē'ə, yŏŏr'ē ə), *n.* compound occurring in body fluids, esp. urine.

u•re'thra (yŏŏ thra'), *n., pl.* **-thrae** (-thrē), **-thras.** duct that conveys urine and, in most male animals, semen.

urge, *v.*, **urged, urging**, *n.* —*v.* **1.** force, incite, or advocate. **2.** entreat. —*n.* **3.** desire; impulse.

ur'gent, *adj.* vital; pressing. —**ur'gent•ly**, *adv.* —**ur'gen•cy**, *n.*

u•ri'nal, *n.* wall fixture used by men for urinating.

u•ri•nal'y•sis, *n., pl.* **-ses.** diagnostic analysis of urine.

u'ri•nar'y, *adj.* **1.** of urine. **2.** of organs that secrete and discharge urine.

u'ri•nate', *v.*, **-nated, -nating.** pass urine. —**u'ri•na'tion**, *n.*

u'rine, *n.* secretion of kidneys. —**u'ric**, *adj.*

urn, *n.* vase or pot.

us, *pron.* objective case of **we**.

us'age, *n.* **1.** custom. **2.** treatment.

use, *v.*, **used, using**, *n.* —*v.* (yŏōz). **1.** do something with aid of. **2.** expend. **3.** make practice of. **4.** treat. **5.** accustom. —*n.* (yŏōs). **6.** act or way of using. **7.** service or value. —**us'a•ble**, *adj.* —**use'ful**, *adj.* —**use'less**, *adj.* —**us'er**, *n.*

us•er-friend'ly, *adj.* easy to operate or understand.

ush'er, *n.* person who escorts people to seats, as in theater.

u'su•al, *adj.* **1.** customary. **2.** common. —**u'su•al•ly**, *adv.*

u•surp' (yŏŏ zûrp'), *v.* seize without right. —**u•surp'er**, *n.*

u'su•ry (yŏō'zhə rē), *n.* lending money at exorbitant rates of interest. —**u'sur•er**, *n.*

u•ten'sil, *n.* device, container, etc., esp. for kitchen.

u'ter•us, *n., pl.* **-teri.** part of woman's body in which fertilized ovum develops. —**u'ter•ine**, *adj.*

u•til•i•tar'i•an, *adj.* of practical use.

u•til'i•ty, *n., pl.* **-ties. 1.** usefulness. **2.** public service.

u'ti•lize', *v.*, **-lized, -lizing.** use. —**u'ti•li•za'tion**, *n.*

ut'most', *adj.* **1.** greatest. **2.** furthest.

U•to'pi•an, *adj.* impossibly perfect.

ut'ter, *v.* **1.** speak; say. —*adj.* **2.** complete; total. —**ut'ter•ance**, *n.*

ut'ter•ly, *adv.* completely; absolutely.

u'vu•la (yŏŏ'vyə lə), *n., pl.* **-las, -lae.** small, fleshy part on soft palate.

ux•o'ri•ous (uk sôr'ē əs), *adj.* foolishly or excessively fond of one's wife.

V

V, v, *n.* twenty-second letter of English alphabet.

va'can•cy, *n., pl.* **-cies. 1.** state of being vacant. **2.** vacant space.

va'cant, *adj.* **1.** empty. **2.** devoid. **3.** unintelligent. —**va'cant•ly**, *adv.*

va'cate', *v.*, **-cated, -cating. 1.** empty. **2.** quit. **3.** annul.

va•ca'tion, *n.* **1.** freedom from duty, business, etc. **2.** holiday. —*v.* **3.** take a vacation. —**va•ca'tion•ist**, *n.*

vac'ci•nate', *v.*, **-nated, -nating.** inoculate against smallpox, etc. —**vac'ci•na'tion**, *n.*

vac•cine' (vak sēn'), *n.* substance injected into bloodstream to give immunity. —**vac'ci•nal**, *adj.*

vac'il•late' (vas'ə-), *v.*, **-lated, -lating. 1.** waver; fluctuate. **2.** be irresolute. —**vac'il•la'tion**, *n.*

va•cu'i•ty, *n., pl.* **-ties. 1.** emptiness. **2.** lack of intelligence. —**vac'u•ous**, *adj.* —**vac'u•ous•ly**, *adv.*

vac'u•um, *n.* space from which all matter has been removed.

vacuum cleaner, apparatus for cleaning by suction.

vacuum tube, sealed bulb, formerly used in radio and electronics.

vag•a•bond', adj. **1.** wandering; homeless. —n. **2.** vagrant.

va•gar'y (va gâr'ē), n., pl. **-garies.** capricious act or idea.

va•gi'na (va ji'na), n., pl. **-nas, -nae.** passage from uterus to vulva. —**vag'i•nal,** adj.

va'grant, n. **1.** idle wanderer. —adj. **2.** wandering. —**va'gran•cy,** n.

vague, adj., **vaguer, vaguest. 1.** not definite. **2.** indistinct. —**vague'ly,** adv. —**vague'ness,** n.

vain, adj. **1.** futile. **2.** conceited. —**vain'ly,** adv. —**vain'ness,** n.

val'ance (val'ans, vā'lans), n. drapery across top of window.

vale, n. valley.

val•e•dic•to'ri•an, n. graduating student who delivers valedictory.

val•e•dic'to•ry, n., pl. **-ries.** farewell address, esp. one delivered at commencement.

va'lence (vā'lans), n. combining capacity of atom or radical.

val'en•tine', n. **1.** affectionate card or gift sent on February 14 (**Saint Valentine's Day**). **2.** sweetheart chosen on that day.

val'et (val'it, val'ā), n. personal manservant.

val'iant, adj. **1.** brave. —**val'iance,** n. —**val'iant•ly,** adv.

val'id, adj. **1.** sound; logical. **2.** legally binding. —**val'i•date',** v. —**va•lid'i•ty,** n. —**val'id•ly,** adv.

va•lise' (-lēs'), n. traveling bag.

val'ley, n. long depression between uplands or mountains.

val'or, n. bravery, esp. in battle. —**val'or•ous,** adj. —**val'or•ous•ly,** adv.

val'u•a•ble, adj. **1.** of much worth, importance, etc. —n. **2.** (usually pl.) valuable articles. —**val'u•a•bly,** adv.

val'u•a'tion, n. estimation or estimated value.

val'ue, n., v. **-ued, -uing.** —n. **1.** worth or importance. **2.** equivalent or estimated worth. **3.** conception of what is good. —v. **4.** estimate worth of. **5.** esteem. —**val'ue•less,** adj.

valve, n. device controlling flow of liquids, etc. —**val'vu•lar,** adj.

va•moose', v., **-moosed, -moosing.** Slang. leave hurriedly.

vamp, n. **1.** upper front part of shoe or boot. **2.** Slang. seductive woman. —v. **3.** improvise (as music).

vam'pire, n. **1.** corpse supposed to be reanimated and to suck blood of living persons. **2.** extortionist. **3.** Also, **vampire bat.** South and Central American bat.

van, n. **1.** vanguard. **2.** covered truck for moving furniture, etc. **3.** small closed trucklike vehicle.

va•na'di•um (va nā'-), n. rare silvery metallic element, used esp. to toughen steel.

van'dal, n. person who damages or destroys wantonly. —**van'dal•ism,** n. —**van'dal•ize',** v.

Van•dyke', n. short, pointed beard.

vane, n. **1.** weathervane. **2.** one of set of blades set diagonally on a rotor to move or be moved by fluid.

van'guard', n. **1.** foremost part. **2.** leaders of a movement.

va•nil'la, n. **1.** tropical orchid, whose fruit (**vanilla bean**) yields flavoring extract. **2.** the extract.

van'ish, v. disappear. —**van'ish•er,** n.

van'i•ty, n., pl. **-ties. 1.** vainness. **2.** makeup table. **3.** compact (def. 4).

van'quish, v. conquer; defeat. —**van'quish•er,** n.

van'tage, n. superior position or situation.

vap'id, adj. **1.** insipid. **2.** dull. —**va•pid'i•ty,** n. —**vap'id•ly,** adv.

va'por, n. **1.** exhalation, as fog or mist. **2.** gas. —**va'por•ous,** adj.

va'por•ize', v., **-ized, -izing.** change into vapor. —**va'por•i•za'tion,** n. —**va'por•iz'er,** n.

va'ri•a•ble, adj. **1.** changeable. **2.** inconstant. —n. **3.** something variable. —**var'i•a•bil'i•ty,** n. —**var'i•a•bly,** adv.

va'ri•ance, n. **1.** divergence or discrepancy. **2.** disagreement.

va'ri•ant, adj. **1.** varying. **2.** altered in form. —n. **3.** variant form, etc.

va'ri•a'tion, n. **1.** change. **2.** amount of change. **3.** variant. **4.** transformation of melody with changes in harmony, etc. —**var'i•a'tion•al,** adj.

va'ri•cose', adj. abnormally swollen, as veins.

va'ri•e•gate', v., **-gated, -gating. 1.** mark with different colors, etc. **2.** vary. —**va'ri•e•gat'ed,** adj.

va•ri'e•ty, n., pl. **-ties. 1.** diversity. **2.** number of different things. **3.** kind; category. **4.** variant. —**va•ri'e•tal,** adj.

va•ri'o•la, n. smallpox.

va'ri•ous, adj. **1.** of different sorts. **2.** several. —**va'ri•ous•ly,** adv.

var'mint, n. **1.** undesirable, usu. verminous animal. **2.** obnoxious person.

var'nish, n. **1.** resinous solution drying in hard, glossy coat. **2.** gloss. —v. **3.** lay varnish on.

var'y, v., **varied, varying. 1.** change; differ. **2.** cause to be different. **3.** deviate; diverge.

vas'cu·lar, *adj.* of vessels that convey fluids, as blood or sap.

vase, *n.* tall container, esp. for flowers.

vas·ec'to·my, *n., pl.* **-mies.** surgery for male sterilization.

vas'sal, *n.* 1. feudal holder of land who renders service to superior. 2. subject, follower, or slave. —**vas'sal·age**, *n.*

vast, *adj.* immense; huge. —**vast'ly**, *adv.* —**vast'ness**, *n.*

vat, *n.* large container for liquids.

vaude'ville (vôd'vil), *n.* theatrical entertainment made up of separate acts.

vault, *n.* 1. arched ceiling or roof. 2. arched space, chamber, etc. 3. room for safekeeping of valuables. —*v.* 4. build or cover with vault. —*n.* 5. leap.

vaunt, *v.* 1. boast of. —*n.* 2. boast.

VCR, videocassette recorder.

VDT, video display terminal.

veal, *n.* flesh of calf as used for food.

veep, *n. Informal.* Vice President, esp. of U.S.

veer, *v.* change direction.

veg'e·ta·ble, *n.* 1. plant used for food. 2. any plant. —**veg'e·ta·ble**, **veg'e·tal**, *adj.*

veg'e·tar'i·an, *n.* 1. person who eats only vegetable food on principle (**vegetarianism**). —*adj.* 2. of or advocating vegetarianism. 3. suitable for vegetarians.

veg'e·tate', *v.,* **-tated, -tating.** 1. grow as plants do. 2. live dull, inactive life. —**veg'e·ta'tive**, *adj.*

veg'e·ta'tion, *n.* 1. plants collectively. 2. act or process of vegetating.

ve'he·ment, (vē'ə mənt), *adj.* 1. impetuous or impassioned. 2. violent. —**ve'he·mence**, **ve'he·men'cy**, *n.* —**ve'he·ment·ly**, *adv.*

ve'hi·cle, *n.* means of transport, etc. —**ve·hic'u·lar**, *adj.*

veil, *n.* 1. material concealing face. 2. part of headdress, as of nun or bride. 3. cover; screen. 4. pretense. —*v.* 5. cover with veil.

vein, *n.* 1. vessel conveying blood from body to heart. 2. tubular riblike thickening, as in leaf or insect wing. 3. stratum of ore, coal, etc. 4. mood. —*v.* 5. furnish or mark with veins.

Vel'cro, *n. Trademark.* fastening tape with opposing pieces of nylon that interlock.

vel'lum, *n.* parchment.

ve·loc'i·ty, *n., pl.* **-ties.** speed.

ve·lour' (və lŏŏr'), *n.* velvetlike fabric used for clothing and upholstery. Also, **ve·lours'**.

vel'vet, *n.* fabric with thick, soft pile. —**vel'vet·y**, *adj.*

vel'vet·een', *n.* cotton fabric resembling velvet.

ve'nal, *adj.* corrupt; mercenary. —**ve'nal·ly**, *adv.* —**ve·nal'i·ty**, *n.*

vend, *v.* sell. —**ven'dor**, *n.*

ven·det'ta, *n.* long, bitter feud.

ve·neer', *v.* 1. overlay with thin sheets of fine wood, etc. —*n.* 2. veneered layer of wood. 3. superficial appearance.

ven'er·a·ble, *adj.* worthy of reverence. —**ven'er·a·bil'i·ty**, *n.*

ven'er·ate', *v.,* **-ated, -ating.** revere. —**ven'er·a'tion**, *n.*

ve·ne're·al (və nēr'ē əl), *adj.* relating to or caused by sexual intercourse.

ve·ne'tian blind, window blind with horizontal slats.

venge'ance, *n.* revenge.

venge'ful, *adj.* seeking vengeance. —**venge'ful·ly**, *adv.*

ve'ni·al, *adj.* pardonable.

ven'i·son, *n.* flesh of deer as used for food.

ven'om, *n.* 1. poisonous fluid secreted by some snakes, spiders, etc. 2. spite; malice. —**ven'om·ous**, *adj.* —**ven'om·ous·ly**, *adv.*

vent, *n.* 1. outlet, as for fluid. 2. expression. —*v.* 3. express freely.

ven'ti·late', *v.,* **-lated, -lating.** 1. provide with fresh air. 2. submit to discussion. —**ven'ti·la'tion**, *n.* —**ven'ti·la'tor**, *n.*

ven'tral, *adj.* 1. of or near belly; abdominal. 2. on lower, abdominal plane of animal's body.

ven'tri·cle, *n.* either of two lower cavities of heart. —**ven·tric'u·lar**, *adj.*

ven·tril'o·quism', *n.* art of speaking so that voice seems to come from another source. —**ven·tril'o·quist**, *n.*

ven'ture, *n., v.,* **-tured, -turing.** —*n.* 1. hazardous undertaking. —*v.* 2. risk; dare. 3. enter daringly. —**ven'ture·some**, **ven'tur·ous**, *adj.*

ven'ue, *n.* 1. place of crime or cause of action. 2. place where jury is gathered and case tried. 3. scene or locale of action or event.

Ve'nus, *n.* 1. Roman goddess of love. 2. second planet from sun.

ve·ra'cious, *adj.* truthful. —**ve·rac'i·ty** (və ras'ə tē), *n.*

ve·ran'da, *n.* open porch. Also, **ve·ran'dah**.

verb, *n.* part of speech expressing action, occurrence, existence, etc., as "saw" in the sentence "I saw Tom."

ver'bal, *adj.* 1. of or in form of words. 2. oral. 3. word for word. 4. of verbs. —*n.* 5. word, as noun, derived from verb. —**ver'bal·ly**, *adv.*

ver·bal·ize, v., -ized, -izing. express in words. —**ver·bal·i·za'tion**, n.

ver·ba'tim, adv. word for word.

ver·be'na, n. plant with long spikes of flowers.

ver'bi·age, n. 1. wordiness. 2. manner of verbal expression.

ver·bose', adj. wordy. —**ver·bose'ness**, **ver·bos'i·ty**, n.

ver'dant, adj. 1. green. 2. inexperienced. —**ver'dan·cy**, n.

ver'dict, n. decision.

ver'di·gris' (vûr'də grēs'), n. green or bluish patina.

ver'dure (vûr'jər), n. 1. greenness. 2. green vegetation.

verge, n., v., verged, verging. —n. 1. edge or margin. —v. 2. border. 3. incline; tend.

ver'i·fy', v., -fied, -fying. 1. prove to be true. 2. ascertain correctness of. —**ver'i·fi'a·ble**, adj. —**ver'i·fi·ca'tion**, n. —**ver'i·fi'er**, n.

ver'i·ly, adv. Archaic. truly.

ver'i·si·mil'i·tude, n. 1. appearance of truth.

ver'i·ta·ble, adj. genuine. —**ver'i·ta·bly**, adv.

ver'i·ty, n., pl. -ties. truth.

ver·mi·cel'li (-chel'ē, -sel'ē), n. pasta in long threads.

ver·mil'lion, n. 1. bright red. —adj. 2. of or like vermilion.

ver'min, n.pl. or sing. troublesome animals collectively. —**ver'min·ous**, adj.

ver·mouth' (vər mōōth'), n. white wine flavored with herbs.

ver·nac'u·lar, adj. 1. (of language) used locally or in everyday speech. —n. 2. native speech. 3. language of particular group.

ver'nal, adj. of spring. —**ver'nal·ly**, adv.

ver'sa·tile, adj. doing variety of things well. —**ver'sa·til'i·ty**, n.

verse, n. 1. line of poem. 2. type of metrical line, etc. 3. poem. 4. poetry. 5. division of Biblical chapter.

versed, adj. expert; skilled.

ver'si·fy', v., -fied, -fying. 1. treat in or turn into verse. 2. compose verses. —**ver'si·fi'er**, n. —**ver'si·fi·ca'tion**, n.

ver'sion, n. 1. translation. 2. account.

ver'sus, prep. in opposition or contrast to.

ver'te·bra, n., pl. -brae, -bras. bone or segment of spinal column. —**ver'te·bral**, adj.

ver'te·brate, adj. 1. having vertebrae. —n. 2. vertebrate animal.

ver'tex, n., pl. -texes, -tices (-tə sēz'). highest point.

ver'ti·cal, adj. 1. perpendicular to plane of horizon. —n. 2. something vertical. —**ver'ti·cal·ly**, adv.

ver·ti'go, n., pl. -goes. dizziness.

verve, n. 1. vivaciousness, energy, or enthusiasm.

ver'y, adv., adj., verier, veriest. —adv. 1. extremely. —adj. 2. identical. 3. mere. 4. actual. 5. true.

ves'i·cle, n. small sac in body.

ves'per, n. 1. Archaic. evening. 2. (pl.) evening prayer, service, etc.

ves'sel, n. 1. ship or boat. 2. hollow or concave container, as dish or glass. 3. tube or duct, as for blood.

vest, n. 1. sleeveless garment worn under jacket. —v. 2. clothe or robe. 3. put in someone's possession or control. 4. endow with powers, etc.

ves'ti·bule, n. small room between entrance and main room. —**ves·tib'u·lar**, adj.

ves'tige, n. 1. trace of something extinct. 2. slight trace of something. —**ves·tig'i·al**, adj.

vest'ment, n. ceremonial garment.

vest'-pock'et, adj. conveniently small.

ves'try, n., pl. -tries. 1. room in church for vestments or for meetings, etc. 2. church committee managing temporal affairs. —**ves'try·man**, n.

vetch, n. plant used for forage and soil improvement.

vet'er·an, n. 1. person who has seen service, esp. in armed forces. —adj. 2. experienced.

vet'er·i·nar'i·an, n. veterinary practitioner.

vet'er·i·nar'y, n., pl. -naries. 1. veterinarian. —adj. 2. of medical and surgical treatment of animals.

ve'to, n., pl. -toes, v., -toed, -toing. —n. 1. power or right to reject or prohibit. 2. prohibition. —v. 3. reject by veto.

vex, v. 1. irritate. 2. worry. 3. discuss vigorously. —**vex·a'tion**, n. —**vex·a'tious**, adj. —**vexed**, adj. —**vex'ed·ly**, adv.

vi'a (vī'ə), prep. by way of.

vi'a·ble, adj. 1. capable of living. 2. practicable; workable.

vi'a·duct', n. long highway or railroad bridge.

vi'al, n. small glass container.

vi'and, n. 1. article of food. 2. (pl.) dishes of food.

vibes, n.pl. Slang. something, esp. an emotional aura, emitted as if by vibration. 2. vibraphone.

vi'brant, adj. 1. resonant. 2. energetic; vital. —**vi'bran·cy**, n.

vi'bra•phone (vī'brə fōn'), n. instrument like metal xylophone, with electrically enhanced resonance.

vi'brate, v., **-brated, -brating.** 1. move very rapidly to and fro; oscillate. 2. tremble. 3. resound. 4. thrill. —**vi•bra'tion,** n. —**vi'bra•tor,** n. —**vi'bra•to•ry,** adj. —**vi•bra'tion•al,** adj.

vic'ar, n. 1. parish priest. 2. representative of bishop. 3. deputy. —**vic'ar•ship',** n. —**vi•car'i•al,** adj.

vic'ar•age, n. residence or position of vicar.

vi•car'i•ous, adj. 1. done or suffered in place of another. 2. substitute. —**vi•car'i•ous•ly,** adv.

vice, n. 1. evil habit or fault. 2. immoral conduct. 3. vise. —prep. 4. instead of.

vice' pres'i•dent, n. officer next in rank to president. —**vice' pres'i•den•cy,** n.

vice'roy, n. ruler of country or province as deputy of sovereign. —**vice-re'gal,** adj.

vi'ce ver'sa, in opposite way.

vi•cin'i•ty, n., pl. **-ties.** neighborhood; nearby area.

vi'cious, adj. 1. immoral; depraved. 2. evil. 3. malicious. —**vi'cious•ly,** adv. —**vi'cious•ness,** n.

vi•cis'si•tude' (vi sis'ə tyōōd'), n. change, esp. in condition.

vic'tim, n. 1. sufferer from action or event. 2. dupe. 3. sacrifice. —**vic'tim•ize',** v.

vic'tor, n. conqueror or winner. —**vic•to'ri•ous,** adj. —**vic•to'ri•ous•ly,** adv.

vic'to•ry, n., pl. **-ries.** success in contest.

vict'ual (vit'al), n. 1. (pl.) food. —v. 2. supply with victuals. —**vict'ual•er,** n.

vid'e•o', adj. 1. of television. —n. 2. television. 3. the visual elements of a telecast. 4. videotape or videocassette.

vid'e•o•cas•sette', n. cassette containing videotape.

vid'e•o•disc', n. disc on which pictures and sound are recorded for playback on TV set.

vid'e•o•tape', n., v., **-taped, -taping.** —n. 1. magnetic tape on which TV program, motion picture, etc., can be recorded. —v. 2. record on this.

vie, v., **vied, vying.** contend for superiority.

view, n. 1. seeing or beholding. 2. range of vision. 3. sight, esp. within one's sight. 4. aspect. 5. mental survey. 6. purpose. 7. notion, opinion, etc. —v. 8. see; look at. 9. regard. —**view'er,** n. —**view'less,** adj.

view'point', n. 1. place from which view is seen. 2. attitude toward something.

vig'il, n. period of staying awake, esp. as watch.

vig'i•lant, adj. 1. wary. 2. alert. —**vig'i•lance,** n. —**vig'i•lant•ly,** adv.

vig'i•lan'te (-lan'tē), n. person who takes law into own hands.

vi•gnette' (vin yet'), n., v., **-gnetted, -gnetting.** —n. 1. small decorative design. 2. photograph, etc., shading off at edges. 3. literary sketch. —v. 4. make vignette of.

vig'or, n. 1. active strength. 2. energy. —**vig'or•ous,** adj. —**vig'or•ous•ly,** adv.

Vik'ing, n. medieval Scandinavian raider.

vile, adj., **viler, vilest.** 1. very bad. 2. offensive. 3. evil. —**vile'ly,** adv. —**vile'ness,** n.

vil'i•fy', v., **-fied, -fying.** defame. —**vil'i•fi•ca'tion,** n. —**vil'i•fi•er,** n.

vil'la, n. luxurious country residence.

vil'lage, n. small town. —**vil'lag•er,** n.

vil'lain, n. wicked person. —**vil'lain•ous,** adj. —**vil'lain•y,** n.

vim, n. vigor.

vin'ai•grette' (vin'ə gret'), n. dressing, esp. for salad, of oil and vinegar, usu. with herbs.

vin'di•cate', v., **-cated, -cating.** 1. clear, as from suspicion. 2. uphold or justify. —**vin'di•ca'tion,** n. —**vin'di•ca'tor,** n.

vin•dic'tive, adj. holding grudge; vengeful. —**vin•dic'tive•ly,** adv. —**vin•dic'tive•ness,** n.

vine, n. creeping or climbing plant with slender stem.

vin'e•gar, n. sour liquid obtained by fermentation. —**vin'e•gar•y,** adj.

vine'yard (vin'-), n. plantation of grapevines.

vin'tage, n. 1. wine from one harvest. 2. grape harvest.

vi'nyl (vī'nəl), n. type of plastic.

Vi'nyl•ite (vī'nə līt', vin'ə-), n. Trademark. vinyl.

vi•o'la, n. Music. instrument resembling violin but slightly larger.

vi'o•late', v., **-lated, -lating.** 1. break or transgress. 2. break into or into. 3. desecrate. 4. rape. —**vi'o•la'tion,** n. —**vi'o•la'tor,** n.

vi'o•lent, adj. 1. uncontrolled, strong, or rough. 2. of destructive force. 3. intense; severe. —**vi'o•lence,** n. —**vi'o•lent•ly,** adv.

vi•o•let, n. 1. low herb bearing flowers, usually purple or blue. 2. bluish purple.

vi•o•lin′, n. Music. stringed instrument played with bow. —**vi′o•lin′ist**, n.

vi•o•lon•cel′lo (vē′ə lən chel′ō), n., pl. **-los**. cello. —**vi′o•lon•cel′list**, n.

VIP, Informal. very important person.

vi′per, n. 1. Old World venomous snake. 2. malicious or treacherous person. —**vi′per•ous**, adj.

vi•ra′go (vi rä′gō, -rā′-), n., pl. **-goes, -gos**. shrewish woman.

vi′ral, adj. of or caused by virus.

vir′gin, n. 1. person, esp. woman, who has not had sexual intercourse. —adj. 2. being or like virgin. 3. untried; unused. —**vir•gin•al**, adj. —**vir•gin′i•ty**, n.

vir′ile (vir′al), adj. 1. manly. 2. vigorous. 3. capable of procreation. —**vi•ril′i•ty**, n.

vir′tu•al, adj. 1. such in effect, though not actually. 2. simulated by computer. —**vir′tu•al•ly**, adv.

virtual reality, realistic simulation by computer system.

vir′tue, n. 1. moral excellence. 2. chastity. 3. merit. —**vir′tu•ous**, adj. —**vir′tu•ous•ly**, adv. —**vir′tu•ous•ness**, n.

vir•tu•o′so, n., pl. **-sos, -si**. person of special skill, esp. in music. —**vir•tu•os′i•ty**, n.

vir′u•lent (vir′ya-), adj. 1. poisonous; malignant. 2. hostile. —**vir′u•lence, vir′u•len•cy**, n. —**vir′u•lent•ly**, adv.

vi′rus, n. 1. infective agent. 2. corrupting influence. 3. segment of self-replicating code planted illegally in computer program.

vi′sa (vē′zə), n. 1. passport endorsement permitting foreign entry or immigration.

vis′age, n. 1. face. 2. aspect.

vis′-à-vis′ (vē′zə vē′), prep. 1. in relation to; compared with. 2. opposite.

vis′cer•a (vis′ər ə), n.pl. 1. soft interior organs of body. 2. intestines. —**vis′cer•al**, adj.

vis′cid (vis′id), adj. sticky; gluelike. Also, **vis′cous** (vis′kəs). —**vis•cos′i•ty**, n.

vis′count (vī′-), n. nobleman ranking below earl or count. —**vis′count•ess**, n.fem.

vise, n. device, usually with two jaws, for holding object firmly.

vis′i•ble, adj. 1. capable of being seen. 2. perceptible. 3. manifest. —**vis′i•bil′i•ty**, n. —**vis′i•bly**, adv.

vi′sion, n. 1. power or sense of sight. 2. imagination or unusually keen perception. 3. mental image of something supernatural or imaginary. —**vi′sion•al**, adj.

vi′sion•ar′y, adj., n., pl. **-aries**. —adj. 1. fanciful. 2. seen in vision. 3. unreal. —n. 4. seer or visions. 5. bold or impractical schemer.

vis′it, v. 1. go to for purposes of talking, staying, etc. 2. afflict. —n. 3. act of visiting. 4. stay as guest. —**vis′i•tor**, vis′i•tant, n.

vis′it•a′tion, n. 1. visit. 2. bringing of good or evil, as by supernatural force.

vi′sor, n. front piece, as of helmet or cap.

vis′ta, n. extended view in one direction.

vis′u•al, adj. 1. of or by means of sight. 2. visible. —**vis′u•al•ly**, adv.

vis′u•al•ize′, v., **-ized, -izing**. 1. make visual. 2. form mental image of. —**vis′u•al•i•za′tion**, n.

vi′tal, adj. 1. of life. 2. living; energetic; vivid. 3. giving or necessary to life. 4. essential. —**vi′tal•ly**, adv.

vi•tal′i•ty, n., pl. **-ties**. 1. vital force. 2. physical or mental vigor. 3. power of continued existence.

vi′ta•min, n. food element essential in small quantities to maintain life. —**vi′ta•min′ic**, adj.

vi′ti•ate′ (vish′ē āt′), v., **-ated, -ating**. 1. impair. 2. corrupt. 3. invalidate. —**vi′ti•a′tion**, n.

vit′re•ous, adj. of or like glass.

vit′ri•fy′, v., **-fied, -fying**. change to glass.

vit′ri•ol, n. 1. glassy metallic compound. 2. sulfuric acid. 3. caustic criticism, etc. —**vit′ri•ol′ic**, adj.

vi•tu′per•ate′ (vī tyoo′-), v., **-ated, -ating**. 1. criticize abusively. 2. revile. —**vi•tu′per•a′tion**, n. —**vi•tu′per•a′tive** (-pə rā′tiv), adj.

vi•va′cious, adj. lively; animated. —**vi•va′cious•ly**, adv. —**vi•va′cious•ness, vi•vac′i•ty**, n.

viv′id, adj. 1. bright, as color or light. 2. full of life. 3. intense; striking. —**viv′id•ly**, adv. —**viv′id•ness**, n.

vi•vip′a•rous (vī vip′ər əs, vi-) adj. bringing forth living young rather than eggs.

viv′i•sec′tion, n. dissection of live animal. —**viv′i•sec′tion•ist**, n.

vix′en, n. 1. female fox. 2. ill-tempered woman.

vo•cab′u•lar′y, n., pl. **-aries**. 1. words used by people, class, or person. 2. collection of defined words, usually in alphabetical order.

vo′cal, adj. 1. of the voice. 2. of or for

singing. 3. articulate or talkative. —*n.* 4. vocal composition or performance. —**vo′cal•ize**, *v.* —**vo′cal•i•za′tion**, *n.* —**vo′cal•ly**, *adv.*

vocal cords, membranes in larynx producing sound by vibration.

vo′cal•ist, *n.* singer.

vo•ca′tion, *n.* occupation, business, or profession. —**vo•ca′tion•al**, *adj.*

vo•cif′er•ate′ (-sif′ə-), *v.*, **-ated, -ating.** cry noisily; shout. —**vo•cif′er•a′tion**, *n.* —**vo•cif′er•ous**, *adj.* —**vo•cif′er•ous•ly**, *adv.*

vod′ka, *n.* colorless distilled liquor.

vogue, *n.* 1. fashion. 2. popular favor.

voice, *n.*, *v.*, **voiced, voicing.** —*n.* 1. sound uttered through mouth. 2. speaking or singing voice. 3. expression. 4. choice. 5. right to express opinion. 6. verb inflection indicating whether subject is acting or acted upon. —*v.* 7. express or declare. —**voice′less**, *adj.*

voice mail, electronic system that routes voice messages to appropriate recipients.

voice′-o′ver, *n.* voice of off-screen narrator or announcer, as on television.

void, *adj.* 1. without legal force. 2. useless. 3. empty. —*n.* 4. empty space. —*v.* 5. invalidate. 6. empty out. —**void′a•ble**, *adj.* —**void′ance**, *n.*

voile (voil), *n.* lightweight, semisheer fabric.

vol′a•tile, *adj.* 1. evaporating rapidly. 2. rapidly changeable in emotion. —**vol′a•til′i•ty**, *n.*

vol•ca′no, *n.*, *pl.* **-noes, -nos.** 1. vent in earth from which lava, steam, etc., are expelled. 2. mountain with such vent. —**vol•can′ic**, *adj.*

vo•li′tion, *n.* act or power of willing. —**vo•li′tion•al**, *adj.*

vol′ley, *n.* 1. discharge of many missiles together. 2. returning of ball before it hits ground. —*v.* 3. hit or fire volley.

vol′ley•ball′, *n.* 1. game in which large ball is volleyed back and forth over net. 2. ball used in this game.

volt, *n.* unit of electromotive force. —**volt′age**, *n.* —**volt′me′ter**, *n.*

vol′u•ble, *adj.* glibly fluent. —**vol′u•bil′i•ty**, *n.* —**vol′u•bly**, *adv.*

vol′ume, *n.* 1. book. 2. size in three dimensions. 3. mass or quantity. 4. loudness or fullness of sound.

vo•lu′mi•nous, *adj.* 1. filling many volumes. 2. ample. —**vo•lu′mi•nous•ly**, *adv.*

vol′un•tar′y, *adj.* 1. done, made, etc.,

by free choice. 2. controlled by will. —**vol′un•tar′i•ly**, *adv.*

vol′un•teer′, *n.* 1. person who offers self, as for military duty. 2. worker forgoing pay. —*v.* 3. offer for some duty or purpose.

vo•lup′tu•ous, *adj.* luxurious; sensuous. —**vo•lup′tu•ous•ly**, *adv.* —**vo•lup′tu•ous•ness**, *n.*

vom′it, *v.* 1. eject from stomach through mouth. 2. eject with force. —*n.* 3. vomited matter.

voo′doo, *n.* polytheistic religion deriving chiefly from African cults.

vo•ra′cious, *adj.* greedy; ravenous. —**vo•ra′cious•ly**, *adv.* —**vo•rac′i•ty**, *n.*

vor′tex, *n.*, *pl.* **-texes, -tices.** whirling movement or mass.

vote, *n.*, *v.*, **voted, voting.** —*n.* 1. formal expression of wish or choice, as by ballot. 2. right to this. 3. votes collectively. —*v.* 4. cast one's vote. 5. cause to go or occur by vote. —**vot′er**, *n.*

vouch, *v.* 1. answer for. 2. give assurance, as surety or sponsor.

vouch′er, *n.* 1. one that vouches. 2. document, receipt, etc., proving expenditure.

vouch•safe′, *v.*, **-safed, -safing.** grant or permit.

vow, *n.* 1. solemn promise, pledge, or personal engagement. —*v.* 2. make vow.

vow′el, *n.* 1. speech sound made with clear channel through middle of mouth. 2. letter representing vowel.

voy′age, *n.*, *v.*, **-aged, -aging.** —*n.* 1. journey, esp. by water. —*v.* 2. make voyage. —**voy′ag•er**, *n.*

vo•yeur′ (vwä yûr′, voi ûr′), *n.* person who obtains sexual gratification by looking at sexual objects or acts. —**vo•yeur′ism**, *n.* —**voy•eur•is′tic**, *adj.*

vul′can•ize′, *v.*, **-ized, -izing.** treat rubber with sulfur and heat. —**vul′can•i•za′tion**, *n.* —**vul′can•iz′er**, *n.*

vul′gar, *adj.* 1. lacking good breeding or taste; unrefined. 2. indecent; obscene. 3. plebeian. 4. vernacular. —**vul•gar′i•ty**, *n.* —**vul′gar•ly**, *adv.*

vul′ner•a•ble, *adj.* 1. liable to physical or emotional hurt. 2. open to attack. —**vul′ner•a•bil′i•ty**, *n.* —**vul′ner•a•bil′i•ty**, *n.*

vul′ture, *n.* large, carrion-eating bird.

vul′va, *n.*, *pl.* **-vae, -vas.** external female genitals.

vy′ing, *adj.* competing.

W

W, w, *n.* twenty-third letter of English alphabet.

wad, *n., v.,* **wadded, wadding.** —*n.* 1. small soft mass. —*v.* 2. form into wad. 3. stuff.

wad'dle, *v.,* **-dled, -dling.** —*v.* 1. sway in walking, as duck. —*n.* 2. waddling gait.

wade, *v.,* **waded, wading.** —*v.* 1. walk through water, sand, etc. —*n.* 2. act of wading. —**wad'er,** *n.*

wa'fer, *n.* 1. thin crisp biscuit. 2. small disk of bread used in Eucharist.

waf'fle, *n., v.,* **-fled, -fling.** —*n.* 1. batter cake baked in a double griddle (**waffle iron**). —*v.* 2. speak or write equivocally.

waft, *v.* 1. float through air or over water. —*n.* 2. sound, odor, etc., wafted.

wag, *v.,* **wagged, wagging,** *n.* —*v.* 1. move rapidly back and forth. —*n.* 2. act of wagging. 3. joker. —**wag'gish,** *adj.*

wage, *n., v.,* **waged, waging.** —*n.* 1. pay; salary. 2. recompense. —*v.* 3. carry on (war, etc.)

wa'ger, *n., v.* bet.

wag'gle, *v.,* **-gled, -gling,** *n.* wag.

wag'on, *n.* four-wheeled vehicle for drawing heavy loads. Also, *Brit.,* **wag'gon.**

waif, *n.* homeless child.

wail, *n.* 1. long mournful cry. —*v.* 2. utter wails. —**wail'er,** *n.*

wain'scot, *n., v.,* **-scoted, -scoting.** —*n.* 1. woodwork lining wall. —*v.* 2. line with wainscot.

waist, *n.* 1. part of body between ribs and hips. 2. garment or part of garment for upper part of body. —**waist'band',** *n.* —**waist'line',** *n.*

waist'coat' (wes'kət), *n. Brit.* vest.

wait, *v.* 1. stay in expectation. 2. be ready. 3. await. 4. wait on; serve. —*n.* 5. act of waiting. 6. delay. 7. ambush.

wait'er, *n.* man who waits on table. —**wait'ress,** *n.fem.*

waiting list, list of persons waiting, as for reservations or admission.

waive, *v.,* **waived, waiving.** give up; forgo.

waiv'er, *n.* statement of relinquishment.

wake, *v.,* **waked** or **woke, waked, waking.** —*v.* 1. stop sleeping; rouse from sleep. —*n.* 2. vigil, esp. beside corpse. 3. track or path, esp. of vessel.

wake'ful, *adj.* alert. —**wake'ful·ly,** *adv.* —**wake'ful·ness,** *n.*

wak'en, *v.* wake.

wale, *n., v.,* **waled, waling.** —*n.* 1. mark left on skin by rod or whip. 2. vertical rib or cord in fabric. —*v.* 3. mark with wales.

walk, *v.* 1. go or traverse on foot. 2. cause to walk. —*n.* 3. act, course, or manner of walking. 4. branch of activity. 5. sidewalk or path. —**walk'er,** *n.*

walk'ie-talk'ie, *n.* portable radio transmitter and receiver.

walk'out', *n.* strike in which workers leave place of work.

wall, *n.* 1. upright structure that divides, encloses, etc. —*v.* 2. enclose, divide, etc., with wall.

wall'board', *n.* artificial material used to make or cover walls, etc.

wal'let, *n.* small flat case for paper money, etc.

wall'flow'er, *n.* 1. person who, because of shyness, remains at side of party. 2. perennial plant with fragrant flowers.

wal'lop, *Informal.* —*v.* 1. thrash or defeat. —*n.* 2. blow.

wal'low, *v.* 1. lie or roll in mud, etc. —*n.* 2. place where animals wallow.

wall'pa'per, *n.* decorative paper for covering walls and ceilings.

wal'nut', *n.* northern tree valued for wood and edible nut.

wal'rus, *n.* large tusked mammal of Arctic seas.

waltz, *n.* 1. dance in triple rhythm. —*v.* 2. dance a waltz. —**waltz'er,** *n.*

wam'pum, *n.* shell beads, formerly used by North American Indians as money and ornament.

wan, *adj.,* **wanner, wannest.** pale; worn-looking. —**wan'ly,** *adv.*

wand, *n.* slender rod or shoot.

wan'der, *v.* move aimlessly; stray. —**wan'der·er,** *n.*

wan'der·lust', *n.* desire to travel.

wane, *v.,* **waned, waning.** —*v.* 1. (of moon) decrease periodically. 2. decline or decrease. —*n.* 3. decline or decrease.

wan'gle, *v.,* **-gled, -gling.** bring out or obtain by scheming or underhand methods.

wan'na·be' (won'a bē', wô'na-), *n. Informal.* one who aspires, often vainly, to emulate another's success or status.

want, *v.* 1. feel need or desire for. 2. lack; be deficient in. —*n.* 3. desire or need. 4. lack. 5. poverty.

want'ing, *adj., prep.* lacking.

wan'ton, *adj.* 1. malicious; unjustifia-

ble. 2. lewd. —*n.* 3. lascivious person.
—*v.* 4. act in wanton manner. —**wan'ton•ly,** *adv.* —**wan'ton•ness,** *n.*

war, *n., v.,* **warred, warring,** *adj.* —*n.* 1. armed conflict. —*v.* 2. carry on war. —*adj.* 3. of, for, due to war.

war'ble, *v.,* **-bled, -bling,** *n.* —*v.* 1. sing with trills, etc., as birds. —*n.* 2. warbled song.

war'bler, *n.* small songbird.

ward, *n.* 1. division of city. 2. division of hospital. 3. person under legal care of guardian or court. 4. custody. —*v.* 5. ward off, repel or avert.

ward'en, *n.* 1. keeper. 2. administrative head of prison.

ward'er, *n.* guard.

ward'robe, *n.* 1. stock of clothes. 2. clothes closet.

ward'room, *n.* living quarters for ship's officers other than captain.

ware, *n.* 1. (*pl.*) goods. 2. pottery. 3. vessels for domestic use.

ware'house, *n., v.,* **-housed, -housing.** —*n.* 1. (wâr'hous'). storehouse for goods. —*v.* (-houz'). 2. store in warehouse.

war'fare, *n.* waging of war.

war'head, *n.* section of missile containing explosive or payload.

war'like, *adj.* waging or prepared for war.

war'lock, *n.* male witch.

warm, *adj.* 1. having, giving, or feeling moderate heat. 2. cordial. 3. lively. 4. kind; affectionate. —*v.* 5. make or become warm. —**warm'er,** *n.* —**warm'ly,** *adv.* —**warm'ness, warmth,** *n.*

war'mon•ger, *n.* person who advocates or incites war.

warn, *v.* 1. give notice of danger, evil, etc. 2. caution. —**warn'ing,** *n.* —**warn'ing•ly,** *adv.*

warp, *v.* 1. bend out of shape; distort. 2. guide by ropes. —*n.* 3. bend or twist. 4. lengthwise threads in loom.

war'rant, *n.* 1. justification. 2. guarantee. 3. document certifying or authorizing something. —*v.* 4. authorize or justify. 5. guarantee. —**war'rant•a•ble,** *adj.*

warrant officer, military officer between enlisted and commissioned grades.

war'ran•ty, *n., pl.* **-ties.** guarantee.

war'ren, *n.* place where rabbits live.

war'ri•or, *n.* soldier.

war'ship, *n.* ship for combat.

wart, *n.* small hard elevation on skin. —**wart'y,** *adj.*

war'y (wâr'ē), *adj.,* **warier, wariest.**

watchful; careful. —**war'i•ly,** *adv.* —**war'i•ness,** *n.*

was, *v.* first and third pers. sing., past indicative of **be.**

wash, *v.* 1. cleanse in or with water. 2. flow over. 3. carry in flowing. 4. cover thinly. —*n.* 5. act of washing. 6. Also, **wash'ing.** clothes, etc., to be washed. 7. liquid covering. 8. rough water or air behind moving ship or plane. —**wash'a•ble,** *adj.* —**wash'board',** *n.* —**wash'bowl',** *n.* —**wash'cloth',** *n.* —**wash'stand',** *n.* —**wash'room',** *n.*

washed'-out', *adj.* 1. faded. 2. *Informal.* weary or tired-looking.

washed'-up', *adj. Informal.* done for; having failed.

wash'er, *n.* 1. machine for washing. 2. flat ring of rubber, metal, etc., to give tightness.

wash'out', *n.* 1. destruction from action of water. 2. *Slang.* failure.

wasn't, contraction of **was not.**

wasp, *n.* 1. stinging insect. 2. *Slang.* (*cap. or caps.*) white Anglo-Saxon Protestant.

wasp'ish, *adj.* irritable; snappish.

was'sail (wos'al), *n.* 1. drinking party. 2. toast (def. 2).

waste, *v.,* **wasted, wasting,** *n., adj.* —*v.* 1. squander. 2. fail to use. 3. destroy gradually. 4. become wasted. —*n.* 5. useless expenditure. 6. neglect. 7. gradual decay. 8. devastation. 9. anything left over. —*adj.* 10. not used. 11. left over or worthless. —**waste'ful,** *adj.* —**waste'bas'ket,** *n.* —**waste'pa'per,** *n.*

wast'rel (wās'tral), *n.* 1. spendthrift. 2. idler.

watch, *v.* 1. look attentively. 2. be careful. 3. guard. —*n.* 4. close, constant observation. 5. guard. 6. period of watching. 7. *Naut.* period of duty. 8. small timepiece. —**watch'er,** *n.* —**watch'ful,** *adj.* —**watch'man,** *n.*

watch'dog', *n.* 1. dog that guards property. 2. guardian, as against illegal conduct.

watch'word', *n.* 1. password. 2. slogan.

wa'ter, *n.* 1. transparent liquid forming rivers, seas, lakes, rain, etc. 2. surface of water. 3. liquid solution. 4. liquid organic secretion. —*v.* 5. moisten or supply with water. 6. dilute. 7. discharge water. —*adj.* 8. of, for, or powered by water.

wa'ter•bed', *n.* water-filled plastic bag used as bed.

water closet, room containing flush toilet.

wa'ter•col'or, *n.* 1. pigment mixed

with water. **2.** painting using such pigments.

wa·ter·fall, *n.* steep fall of water.

wa·ter·front, *n.* part of city or town on edge of body of water.

water glass, **1.** vessel for drinking. **2.** sodium silicate.

wa·ter·ing place, resort by water or having mineral springs.

water lily, aquatic plant with showy flowers.

wa·ter·logged, *adj.* filled or soaked with water.

wa·ter·mark, *n.* **1.** mark showing height reached by river, etc. **2.** manufacturer's design impressed in paper. —*v.* **3.** put watermark in (paper).

wa·ter·mel·on, *n.* large sweet juicy fruit of a vine.

water moccasin, cottonmouth.

wa·ter·proof, *adj.* **1.** impervious to water. —*v.* **2.** make waterproof.

wa·ter·shed, *n.* **1.** area drained by river, etc. **2.** high land dividing such areas. **3.** important point of division or transition.

water ski, short, broad ski for gliding over water while being towed by boat. —**wa·ter·ski′**, *v.* —**skied**, **-skiing.** —**wa·ter·ski′er**, *n.*

wa·ter·spout′, *n.* tornadolike storm over lake or ocean.

water table, underground level beneath which soil and rock are saturated with water.

wa·ter·tight, *adj.* **1.** constructed or fitted to be impervious to water. **2.** incapable of being nullified or discredited.

wa·ter·way, *n.* body of water as route of travel.

water wheel, wheel turned by water to provide power.

wa·ter·works, *n.pl.* apparatus for collecting and distributing water, as for city.

wa·ter·y, *adj.* of, like, or full of water. —**wa′ter·i·ness**, *n.*

watt, *n.* unit of electric power. —**watt′age**, *n.*

wat·tle, *n.* **1.** flesh hanging from throat or chin. **2.** interwoven rods and twigs.

wave, *n.*, *v.*, **waved, waving.** —*n.* **1.** ridge on surface of liquid. **2.** surge; rush. **3.** curve. **4.** vibration, as in transmission of sound, etc. **5.** sign with moving hand, flag, etc. —*v.* **6.** move with waves. **7.** curve. **8.** signal by wave. —**wav′y**, *adj.*

wa·ver, *v.* **1.** sway. **2.** hesitate. **3.** fluctuate.

wax, *n.* **1.** yellowish substance secreted by bees. **2.** any similar substance. —*v.*

3. rub with wax. **4.** (esp. of moon) increase. **5.** become. —**wax′en**, *adj.* —**wax′er**, *n.* —**wax′y**, *adj.*

wax′wing, *n.* small crested bird.

way, *n.* **1.** manner; fashion. **2.** plan; means. **3.** direction. **4.** road or route. **5.** custom. **6.** (*pl.*) timbers on which ship is built.

way·far′er, *n.* list of goods with shipping directions.

way·far′er, *n.* rover.

way·lay′, *v.* ambush.

way′side′, *n.* **1.** side of road. —*adj.* **2.** beside road.

way′ward, *adj.* capricious. —**way′ward·ness**, *n.*

we, *pron.* nominative plural of **I.**

weak, *adj.* **1.** not strong; fragile; frail. **2.** deficient. —**weak′en**, *v.* —**weak′ness**, *n.*

weak′-kneed′, *adj.* yielding readily to opposition, pressure, or intimidation.

weak′ling, *n.* weak creature.

weak′ly, *adj.*, **-lier**, **-liest**, *adv.* —*adj.* **1.** sickly. —*adv.* **2.** in weak manner.

weal, *n. Archaic.* well-being.

wealth, *n.* **1.** great possessions or riches. **2.** profusion. —**wealth′y**, *adj.*

wean, *v.* **1.** accustom to food other than mother's milk. **2.** detach from obsession or vice.

weap′on, *n.* instrument for use in fighting.

weap′on·ry, *n.* weapons collectively.

wear, *v.*, **wore, worn, wearing.** —*v.* **1.** have on body for covering or ornament. **2.** impair or diminish gradually. **3.** weary. **4.** undergo wear. **5.** last under use. —*n.* **6.** use of garment. **7.** clothing. **8.** gradual impairment or diminution. —**wear′a·ble**, *adj.* —**wear′er**, *n.*

wea′ri·some, *adj.* **1.** tiring. **2.** tedious.

wea′ry, *adj.*, **-rier**, **-riest**, *v.*, **-ried**, **-rying.** —*adj.* **1.** tired. **2.** tedious. —*v.* **3.** tire. —**wea′ri·ly**, *adv.* —**wea′ri·ness**, *n.*

wea′sel, *n.* small carnivorous animal.

weath′er, *n.* **1.** state of atmosphere as to moisture, temperature, etc. —*v.* **2.** expose to weather. **3.** withstand. —*adj.* **4.** of or on windward side.

weath′er·beat′en, *adj.* worn or marked by weather.

weath′er·ize, *v.*, **-ized**, **-izing.** make secure against cold weather.

weath′er·proof, *adj.* **1.** able to withstand all kinds of weather. —*v.* **2.** make weatherproof.

weath′er·vane′, *n.* device to show direction of wind.

weave, *v.*, **wove, woven** or **wove, weaving**, *n.* —*v.* **1.** interlace, as to form cloth. **2.** take winding course.

—n. 3. manner of weaving. —weav'er, n.

web, n., v., webbed, webbing. —n. 1. something woven. 2. fabric spun by spiders. 3. membrane between toes in ducks, etc. —v. 4. cover with web. —webbed', adj. —web'bing, n.

web'foot', n. foot with webbed toes. —web'foot'ed, adj.

wed, v., wedded, wedded or wed, wedding. 1. bind or join in marriage. 2. attach firmly.

wed'ding, n. marriage ceremony.

wedge, n. v., wedged, wedging. —n. 1. angled object for splitting. —v. 2. split with wedge. 3. thrust or force like wedge.

wed'lock, n. matrimony.

Wednes'day, n. fourth day of week.

wee, adj. tiny.

weed, n. 1. useless plant growing in cultivated ground. 2. (pl.) mourning garments. —v. 3. free from weeds. 4. remove as undesirable. —weed'er, n. —weed'y, adj.

week, n. 1. seven successive days. 2. working part of week.

week'day', n. any day except Sunday, or, often, Saturday and Sunday. —week'day', adj.

week'end', n. 1. Saturday and Sunday. —v. 2. of or for weekend.

week'ly, adj., adv., n., pl. -lies. —adj. 1. happening, appearing, etc., once a week. 2. lasting a week. —adv. 3. once a week. 4. by the week. —n. 5. weekly periodical.

weep, v., wept, weeping. 1. shed tears. 2. mourn. —weep'er, n.

wee'vil, n. beetle destructive to grain, fruit, etc. —wee'vil·y, adj.

weft, n. threads interlacing with warp.

weigh, v. 1. measure heaviness of. 2. burden. 3. consider. 4. lift. 5. have heaviness. —weigh'er, n.

weight, n. 1. amount of heaviness. 2. system of units for expressing weight. 3. heavy mass. 4. pressure. 5. burden. 6. importance. —v. 7. add weight to. —weight'y, adj. —weight'i·ly, adv. —weight'less, adj.

weir (wēr), n. 1. dam in a stream. 2. fence set in stream to catch fish.

weird, adj. uncannily strange. —weird'ly, adv. —weird'ness, n.

weird'o, n. Slang. odd, eccentric, or abnormal person.

wel'come, n., v., -comed, -coming. adj. —n. 1. friendly reception. —v. 2. receive or greet with pleasure. —adj. 3. gladly received. 4. given permission or consent.

weld, v. 1. unite, esp. by heating and

pressing. —n. 2. welded joint. —weld'er, n.

wel'fare', n. 1. well-being. 2. provision of benefits to poor.

well, adv., compar. better, superl. best, adj., n., v. —adv. 1. excellently; properly. 2. thoroughly. —adj. 3. in good health. 4. good; proper. —n. 5. hole made in earth to reach water, oil, etc. 6. source. 7. vertical shaft. —v. 8. rise or gush.

well'-be'ing, n. good or prosperous condition.

well'born', adj. of good family.

well'-bred', adj. showing good manners.

well'-dis·posed', adj. feeling favorable, sympathetic, or kind.

well'-done', adj. 1. performed accurately and skillfully. 2. thoroughly cooked.

well'-found'ed, adj. having or based on good reasons, sound information, etc.

well'-heeled', adj. prosperous; well-off.

well'-mean'ing, adj. intending good. —well'-meant', adj.

well'-nigh', adv. nearly.

well'-off', adj. 1. in good or favorable condition. 2. prosperous.

well'spring', n. source.

well'-to-do', adj. prosperous.

Welsh (welsh, welch), n. people or language of Wales.

welt, n. 1. wale from lash. 2. strip around edge of shoe. 3. narrow border along seam. —v. 4. put welt on.

wel'ter, v. 1. roll, as waves. 2. wallow. —n. 3. confused mass.

wen, n. small cyst.

wench, n. girl or young woman.

wend, v., wended, wending. Archaic. go.

went, v. pt. of go.

were, v. past plural and pres. subjunctive of be.

weren't, contraction of were not.

were'wolf' (wēr'-), n., pl. -wolves. (in folklore) human turned into wolf.

west, n. 1. point of compass opposite east. 2. direction of this point. 3. area in this direction. —adv. 4. toward, from, or in west. —adv. 5. toward or from west. —west'er·ly, adj., adv. —west'ern, adj. —west'ern·er, n.

west'ward, adj. 1. moving or facing west. —adv. 2. Also, west'wards. toward west. —n. 3. westward part. —west'ward·ly, adj., adv.

wet, adj., wetter, wettest, n., v. wet or wetted, wetting. —adj. 1. covered or soaked with water. 2. rainy. —n. 3. moisture. —v. 4. make or become wet. —wet'ness, n.

wet'land, *n.* low land with usu. wet soil.

wet suit, close-fitting rubber suit worn for body warmth, as by scuba divers.

whack, *Informal. v.* 1. strike sharply. —*n.* 2. smart blow.

whale, *n., pl.* **whales** or **whale**, *v.*, **whaled, whal•ing.** —*n.* 1. large fishlike marine mammal. —*v.* 2. kill and render whales. —**whal'er**, *n.*

whale'bone, *n.* elastic horny substance in upper jaw of some whales.

wharf, *n., pl.* **wharves.** structure for mooring vessels.

wharf'age, *n.* 1. use of wharf. 2. charge for such use.

what, *pron., pl.* **what**, *adj.* —*pron.* 1. which one? 2. that which. 3. such. —*adv.* 4. how much. 5. partly.

what•ev'er, *pron.* 1. anything that. 2. no matter what. —*adj.* 3. no matter what.

what'not', *n.* small open cupboard, esp. for knickknacks.

what'so•ev'er, *pron., adj.* whatever.

wheal, *n.* swelling, as from mosquito bite.

wheat, *n.* grain of common cereal grass, used esp. for flour.

whee'dle, *v.*, **-dled, -dling.** influence by artful persuasion.

wheel, *n.* 1. round object turning on axis. —*v.* 2. turn on axis. 3. move on wheels. 4. turn.

wheel'bar•row, *n.* one-wheeled vehicle lifted at one end.

wheel'base', *n. Auto.* distance between centers of front and rear wheel hubs.

wheel'chair', *n.* chair mounted on wheels for use by persons who cannot walk.

wheeze, *v.*, **wheezed, wheezing**, *n.* —*v.* 1. whistle in breathing. —*n.* 2. wheezing breath. 3. trite saying.

whelm, *v.* 1. engulf. 2. overwhelm.

whelp, *n.* 1. young of dog, wolf, bear, etc. —*v.* 2. bring forth whelps.

when, *adv.* 1. at what time. —*conj.* 2. at time that. 3. and then.

whence, *adv., conj.* from what place.

when•ev'er, *adv.* at whatever time.

where, *adv.* 1. in, at, or to what place? 2. in what respect? —*conj.* 3. in, at, or to what place. 4. and there.

where'a•bouts', *adv.* 1. where. —*n.* 2. location.

where•as', *conj.* 1. while on the contrary. 2. considering that.

where•by', *conj.* by what or which; under the terms of which.

where•fore', *adv., conj.* 1. why; for what. —*n.* 2. reason.

where•in', *conj.* 1. in what or in

which. —*adv.* 2. in what way or respect?

where•of', *adv., conj.* of what.

where•up•on', *conj.* 1. upon which. 2. at or after which.

wher•ev'er, *conj.* at or to whatever place.

where•with•al', *n.* means.

whet, *v.*, **whetted, whetting.** sharpen. —**whet'stone'**, *n.*

wheth'er, *conj.* (word introducing alternative.)

whey (hwā), *n.* watery part that separates out when milk curdles.

which, *pron.* 1. what one? 2. the one that. —*adj.* 3. what one of (those mentioned).

which•ev'er, *pron.* any that.

whiff, *n.* 1. slight puff or blast. —*v.* 2. blow in whiffs.

while, *n., conj., v.*, **whiled, whiling.** —*n.* 1. time. —*conj.* 2. in time that. —*v.* 3. pass (time) pleasantly.

whim, *n.* irrational or fanciful decision or idea.

whim'per, *v.* 1. cry softly and plaintively. —*n.* 2. whimpering cry. —**whim'per•er**, *n.*

whim'sy, *n., pl.* **-sies.** fanciful idea; whim. —**whim'si•cal**, *adj.* —**whim'si•cal'i•ty**, *n.* —**whim'si•cal•ly**, *adv.*

whine, *n., v.*, **whined, whining.** —*n.* 1. low complaining sound. —*v.* 2. utter whines. —**whin'er**, *n.* —**whin'ing•ly**, *adv.*

whin'ny, *n., v.*, **-nied, -nying**, *n., pl.* **-nies.** neigh.

whip, *v.*, **whipped, whipping**, *n.* —*v.* 1. strike repeatedly; flog. 2. jerk; seize. 3. cover with thread; overcast. 4. beat (cream, etc.). 5. move quickly; dash about. —*n.* 6. instrument with lash and handle for striking. 7. party manager in legislature. —**whip'per**, *n.*

whip'cord', *n.* fabric with diagonal ribs.

whip'lash', *n.* 1. lash of whip. 2. neck injury caused by sudden jerking of the head.

whip'per•snap'per, *n.* insignificant, presumptuous person, esp. young one.

whip'pet, *n.* small swift dog.

whip'poor•will', *n.* nocturnal American bird.

whir, *v.*, **whirred, whirring.** —*v.* 1. move with buzzing sound. —*n.* 2. such sound. Also, **whirr.**

whirl, *v.* 1. spin or turn rapidly. 2. move quickly. —*n.* 3. whirling movement. 4. round of events, etc. —**whirl'er**, *n.*

whirl'i•gig', *n.* toy revolving in wind.

whirl'pool', n. whirling current in water.

whirl'wind', n. whirling mass of air.

whisk, v. 1. sweep up. 2. move or carry lightly. —n. 3. act of whisking.

whisk'er, n. 1. (pl.) hair on man's face. 2. bristle on face of cat, etc.

whis'key, n. distilled alcoholic liquor made from grain or corn. Also, **whis'ky.**

whis'per, v. 1. speak very softly. —n. 2. sound of whispering. 3. something whispered. —**whis'per•er**, n.

whist, n. card game.

whis'tle, v., -tled, -tling, n. —v. 1. make clear shrill sound with breath, air, or steam. —n. 2. device for making such sounds. 3. sound of whistling. —**whis'tler**, n.

whis'tle-blow'er, n. person who publicly discloses corruption or wrongdoing.

whit, n. particle; bit.

white, adj. 1. of color of snow. 2. having light skin. 3. pale. —n. 4. color without hue, opposite to black. 5. Caucasian. 6. white or light part. —**whit'en**, v. —**white'ness**, n. —**whit'ish**, adj.

white'cap', n. wave with foaming white crest.

white'-col'lar, adj. of professional or office workers whose jobs usu. do not involve manual labor.

white elephant, useless, expensive possession.

white'fish', n. small food fish.

white flag, all-white flag used to signal surrender or truce.

white lie, harmless lie; fib.

white'wash', n. 1. substance for whitening walls, etc. —v. 2. cover with whitewash. 3. cover up faults or errors of.

whith'er, adv., conj. Archaic. where; to what (which) place.

whit'ing, n. 1. small Atlantic food fish. 2. ground chalk used to whiten.

whit'low, n. inflammation on finger or toe.

Whit'sun•day, n. seventh Sunday after Easter.

whit'tle, v., -tled, -tling. 1. cut bit by bit with knife. 2. reduce. —**whit'tler**, n.

whiz, v., whizzed, whizzing, n. —v. 1. move with hum or hiss. —n. 2. whizzing sound. 3. person who is very good at something. Also, **whizz.**

who, pron. 1. what person? 2. the person that.

whoa, interj. stop!

who•dun'it, n. detective story.

who•ev'er, pron. anyone that.

whole, adj. 1. entire; undivided. 2. undamaged. 3. Math. not fractional. —n. 4. entire amount or extent. 5. complete thing. —**whol'ly**, adv. —**whole'ness**, n.

whole'-heart'ed, adj. sincere.

whole'sale', n., adj., v., -saled, -saling. —n. 1. sale of goods in quantity, as to retailers. —adj. 2. of or engaged in wholesale. —v. 3. sell by wholesale. —**whole'sal'er**, n.

whole'some, adj. beneficial; healthful. —**whole'some•ly**, adv. —**whole'some•ness**, n.

whom, pron. objective case of who.

whoop, n. 1. loud shout or cry. 2. gasping sound characteristic of whooping cough. —v. 3. utter whoops.

whoop'ing cough, infectious disease characterized by short, convulsive coughs followed by whoops.

whop'per (hwop'ar, wop'-), n. Informal. 1. something uncommonly large. 2. big lie.

whore (hōr), n., v., whored, whoring. —n. 1. prostitute. —v. 2. consort with whores.

whorl, n. 1. circular arrangement, as of leaves. 2. any spiral part.

whose, pron. possessive case of who.

who•so•ev'er, pron. whoever.

why, adv., n., pl. whys. —adv. 1. for what reason. —n. 2. cause or reason.

wick, n. soft threads that absorb fuel to be burned in candle, etc.

wick'ed, adj. 1. evil; sinful. 2. naughty. —**wick'ed•ly**, adv. —**wick'ed•ness**, n.

wick'er, n. 1. slender pliant twig. —adj. 2. made of wicker. —**wick'er•work'**, n.

wick'et, n. 1. small gate or opening. 2. framework in cricket and croquet.

wide, adj., wider, widest, adv. —adj. 1. broad. 2. extensive. 3. expanded. 4. far. —adv. 5. far. 6. to farthest extent. —**wide'ly**, adv. —**wid'en**, v. —**wide'ness**, n.

wide'-eyed', adj. having eyes open wide, as in amazement or innocence.

wide'spread', adj. occurring widely.

widg'eon, n. fresh-water duck.

wid'ow, n. 1. woman whose husband has died. —v. 2. make widow of. —**wid'ow•er**, n.masc. —**wid'ow•hood**, n.

width, n. 1. breadth. 2. piece of full wideness.

wield, v. 1. exercise (power, etc.). 2. brandish. —**wield'er**, n. —**wield'y**, adj.

wie'ner, n. small sausage; frankfurter.

wife, *n., pl.* **wives.** married woman. **—wife′ly,** *adj.*

wig, *n.* artificial covering of hair for head.

wig′gle, *v.,* **-gled, -gling,** *n.* —*v.* 1. twist to and fro; wriggle. —*n.* 2. wiggling movement. **—wig′gly,** *adj.* **—wig′gler,** *n.*

wig′wag′, *v.,* **-wagged, -wagging,** *n.* —*v.* 1. signal in code with flags, etc. —*n.* 2. such signaling. 3. message so sent.

wig′wam (-wom), *n.* American Indian dwelling.

wild, *adj.* 1. not cultivated. 2. uncivilized. 3. violent. 4. uninhabited. 5. disorderly. —*adv.* 6. wildly. —*n.* 7. uncultivated or desolate tract. **—wild′ly,** *adv.* **—wild′ness,** *n.*

wild′cat′, *n.,* **-catted, -catting.** —*n.* 1. large North American feline. —*v.* 2. prospect independently. —*adj.* not called or sanctioned by labor union.

wil′der•ness, *n.* wild or desolate region.

wild′-eyed′, *adj.* 1. having a wild expression in the eyes. 2. extreme or radical.

wild′fire′, *n.* outdoor fire that spreads rapidly and is hard to extinguish.

wild′life′, *n.* animals living in nature.

wile, *n.* cunning; artifice.

will, *n.* 1. power of conscious action or choice. 2. wish; pleasure. 3. attitude, either hostile or friendly. 4. declaration of wishes for disposition of property after death. —*v.* 5. decide to influence by act of will. 6. consent to. 7. give by will. **—auxiliary verb.** 8. am (is, are) about to. 9. am (is, are) willing to.

will′ful, *adj.* 1. intentional. 2. headstrong. Also, **wil′ful. —will′ful•ly,** *adv.* **—will′ful•ness,** *n.*

will′ing, *adj.* 1. consenting. 2. cheerfully done, given, etc. **—will′ing•ly,** *adv.* **—will′ing•ness,** *n.*

will′-o′-the-wisp′, *n.* 1. flitting, elusive light. 2. something that fascinates and deludes.

wil′low, *n.* slender tree or shrub with tough, pliant branches.

wil•low•y, *adj.,* **-lower, -lowest.** tall and slender. **—wil′low•i•ness,** *n.*

will•y-nil′ly, *adv.* willingly or unwillingly.

wilt, *v.* 1. wither or droop. —*n.* 2. wilted state.

wil′y, *adj.,* **wilier, wiliest.** crafty; cunning. **—wil′i•ness,** *n.*

wimp, *n. Informal.* weak, ineffectual person. **—wimp′y,** *adj.*

win, *v.,* **won, winning,** *n.* —*v.* 1. suc-ceed or get by effort. 2. gain (victory). 3. persuade. —*n.* 4. victory.

wince, *v.,* **winced, wincing,** *n.* —*v.* 1. shrink, as from pain or blow. —*n.* 2. wincing movement.

winch, *n.* 1. windlass. 2. crank.

wind, *n.* (wind for 1–7; wind for 8–11), *n., v.,* **winded** (for 5–7) or **wound** (wound) (for 8–11), **winding.** —*n.* 1. air in motion. 2. gas in stomach or bowels. 3. animal odor. 4. breath. —*v.* 5. make short of breath. 6. let re-cover breath. 7. expose to wind. 8. change direction. 9. encircle. 10. roll into cylinder or ball. 11. turn (handle, etc.). **—wind′y,** *adj.* **—wind′er,** *n.*

wind′break′, *n.* shelter from wind.

wind′ed, *adj.* 1. having wind. 2. out of breath.

wind′fall′, *n.* 1. something blown down. 2. unexpected luck.

wind instrument, musical instrument sounded by breath or air.

wind′lass (-ləs), *n.* drum mechanism for hoisting.

wind′mill′, *n.* mill operated by wind.

win′dow, *n.* opening for air and light, usually fitted with glass in frame.

window dressing, 1. art, act, or tech-nique of decorating store display win-dows. 2. something done solely to create favorable impression.

wind′pipe′, *n.* trachea.

wind′shield′, *n.* glass shield above au-tomobile; dashboard.

wind′surf′ing, *n.* sport of riding on surfboard mounted with a sail. **—wind′surf′,** *v.* **—wind′surf′er,** *n.*

wind′up′ (wīnd′-), *n.* close; end.

wind′ward, *n.* 1. quarter from which wind blows. 2. of, in, or to windward. —*adv.* 3. against wind.

wine, *n., v.,* **wined, wining.** —*n.* 1. fer-mented juice, esp. of grape. 2. dark purplish red. —*v.* 3. entertain with wine. **—win′y,** *adj.*

win′er•y, *n., pl.* **-eries.** place for mak-ing wine.

wing, *n.* 1. organ of flight in birds, in-sects, and bats. 2. winglike or project-ing structure. 3. flight. 4. supporting surface of airplane. —*v.* 5. travel on wings. 6. wound in wing or arm. **—wing′ed,** *adj.*

wink, *v.* 1. close and open (eye) quickly. 2. signal by winking. 3. twin-kle. —*n.* 4. winking movement.

win′ner, *n.* one that wins.

win′ning, *n.* 1. (*pl.*) that which is won. —*adj.* 2. charming. **—win′ning•ly,** *adv.*

win′now, *v.* 1. free from chaff by wind. 2. separate.

win′some, *adj.* sweetly or innocently

charming. **—win'some·ly,** adv. **—win'some·ness,** n.

win'ter, n. **1.** last season of year. **—adj. 2.** of, like, or for winter. **—v. 3.** pass winter. **4.** keep during winter. **—win'try, win'ter·y,** adj.

win'ter·green', n. **1.** creeping aromatic shrub.

win'ter·ize', v., **-ized, -izing.** prepare to withstand cold weather.

wipe, v., **wiped, wiping.** —v. **1.** rub lightly. **2.** remove or blot. —n. **3.** act of wiping. **—wip'er,** n.

wire, n., adj., v., **wired, wiring.** —n. **1.** slender, flexible piece of metal. **2.** telegram or telegraph. —adj. **3.** made of wires. —v. **4.** bind with wires. **5.** Elect. install system of wires in. **6.** telegraph.

wire'less, adj. activated by electromagnetic waves rather than wires. —n. **2.** Brit. radio.

wire'tap', v., **-tapped, -tapping.** —v. **1.** connect secretly into telephone. —n. **2.** act of wiretapping.

wir'y, adj., **wirier, wiriest.** like wire; lean and strong. **—wir'i·ness,** n.

wis'dom, n. **1.** knowledge and judgment. **2.** wise sayings.

wisdom tooth, molar apt to erupt.

wise, adj. **1.** having knowledge and judgment. **2.** prudent. **3.** informed. —n. **4.** way; respect. **—wise'ly,** adv.

wise'a·cre (-'ā'kər), n. conceited, often insolent person.

wise'crack', n. **1.** smart or facetious remark —v. **2.** make or say as a wisecrack.

wish, v. **1.** want; desire. **2.** bid. —n. **3.** desire. **4.** that desired. **—wish'er,** n. **—wish'ful,** adj. **—wish'ful·ly,** adv. **—wish'ful·ness,** n.

wish'y-wash'y, adj. thin or weak.

wisp, n. small tuft. **—wisp'y,** adj.

wis·te'ri·a, n. climbing shrub with purple flowers. Also, **wis·tar'i·a.**

wist'ful, adj. **1.** pensive. **2.** longing. **—wist'ful·ly,** adv. **—wist'ful·ness,** n.

wit, n. **1.** power of combining perception with clever expression. **2.** person having this. **3.** (pl.) intelligence. —v. **4.** Archaic. know. **5. to wit,** namely.

witch, n. **1.** woman thought to practice magic. **2.** ugly or mean old woman. **—witch'craft',** n.

witch doctor, person in some cultures who uses magic esp. to cure illness.

witch'er·y, n., pl. **-eries. 1.** magic. **2.** charm.

witch hazel, preparation for bruises, etc.

witch'ing, adj. suitable for sorcery.

with, prep. **1.** accompanied by. **2.** using. **3.** against.

with·draw', v. **-drew, -drawn, -drawing. 1.** draw back. **2.** retract. **—with·draw'al,** n.

with'er, v. **1.** shrivel; fade. **—with'er·ing·ly,** adv.

with'ers, n.pl. part of animal's back just behind neck.

with·hold', v., **-held, -holding.** hold or keep back.

with·in', adv. **1.** inside; inwardly. **—prep. 2.** in; inside of. **3.** at point not beyond.

with·out', prep. **1.** lacking. **2.** beyond. **—adv. 3.** outside. **4.** outwardly. **5.** lacking.

with·stand', v., **-stood, -standing.** resist.

wit'less, adj. stupid. **—wit'less·ly,** adv. **—wit'less·ness,** n.

wit'ness, v. **1.** see. **2.** testify. **3.** attest by signature. —n. **4.** person who witnesses. **5.** testimony.

wit'ti·cism', n. witty remark.

wit'ting, adj. knowing; aware. **—wit'ting·ly,** adv.

wit'ty, adj., **-tier, -tiest.** showing wit. **—wit'ti·ly,** adv. **—wit'ti·ness,** n.

wive, v., **wived, wiving.** marry.

wiz'ard, n. magician. **—wiz'ard·ry,** n.

wiz'ened (wiz'-), adj. shriveled.

wob'ble, v., **-bled, -bling.** move unsteadily from side to side. **—wob'bly,** adj.

woe, n. grief or affliction. **—woe'ful,** adj. **—woe'ful·ly,** adv. **—woe'ful·ness,** n.

woe'be·gone', adj. showing woe.

wok, n. Chinese cooking pan.

wolf, n., pl. **wolves,** v. —n. **1.** wild carnivorous animal of dog family. —v. **2.** Informal. eat ravenously. **—wolf'ish,** adj. **—wolf'ish·ly,** adv.

wolf'hound', n. kind of hound.

wolfs'bane', n. poisonous plant.

wol'ver·ine', n. North American mammal of weasel family.

wom'an, n., pl. **women.** adult female human being. **—wom'an·hood',** n. **—wom'an·ish,** adj. **—wom'an·ly,** adj. **—wom'an·li·ness,** n.

womb (woom), n. uterus.

won'der, v. **1.** be curious about. **2.** marvel. —n. **3.** something strange. **4.** Also, **won'der·ment.** amazement. **—won'der·ing·ly,** adv.

won'der·ful, adj. **1.** exciting wonder. **2.** excellent. **—won'der·ful·ly,** adv.

won'drous, adj. **1.** wonderful. —adv. **2.** remarkably. **—won'drous·ly,** adv.

wont (wunt, wōnt), adj. **1.** accustomed. —n. **2.** habit. **—wont'ed,** adj.

won't, contraction of **will not.**

woo, v. seek to win, esp. in marriage. —**woo'er**, n.

wood, n. 1. hard substance under bark of trees and shrubs. 2. timber or firewood. 3. (often pl.) forest. —adj. 4. made of wood. 5. living in woods. —v. 6. plant with trees. —**wood'craft'**, n. —**woods'man**, n. —**wood'y**, adj. —**wood'ed**, adj.

wood'bine', n. any of various vines, as the honeysuckle.

wood'chuck', n. bushy-tailed burrowing rodent. Also called **ground'hog'**.

wood'cut', n. print made from a carved block of wood.

wood'en, adj. 1. made of wood. 2. without feeling or expression. —**wood'en•ly**, adv. —**wood'en•ness**, n.

wood'peck'er, n. bird with hard bill for boring.

woods'y, adj., **woodsier, woodsiest.** of or resembling woods.

wood'wind', n. musical instrument of group including flute, clarinet, oboe, and bassoon.

wood'work', n. wooden fittings inside building. —**wood'work'er**, n. —**wood'work'ing**, n., adj.

woof, n. 1. yarns from side to side in loom. 2. texture or fabric. —v. 3. bark like a dog.

woof'er, n. loudspeaker to reproduce low-frequency sounds.

wool, n. 1. soft curly hair, esp. of sheep. 2. garments, yarn, etc., of wool. 3. curly, fine-stranded substance. —**wool'en** or (esp. Brit.) **wool'len**, adj. n. —**wool'ly**, adj. —**wool'li•ness**, n.

wool'gath•er•ing, n. daydreaming.

word, n. 1. group of letters or sounds that represents concept. 2. talk or conversation. 3. promise. 4. tidings. 5. (pl.) angry speech. —v. 6. express in words. —**word'less**, adj.

word'ing, n. way of expressing.

word processing, production of letters, reports, etc., using computers.

word processor, computer program or system for word processing.

word'y, adj., **wordier, wordiest.** using too many words. —**word'i•ness**, n.

work, n. 1. exertion; labor. 2. task. 3. employment. 4. materials on which one works. 5. result of work. 6. (pl.) industrial plant. —adj. 7. of or for work. —v. 8. do work. 9. operate successfully. 10. move or give. 11. solve. 12. excite. 13. ferment. —**work'a•ble**, adj. —**work'er**, n.

work'a•day', adj. commonplace; uneventful.

work'a•hol'ic, n. person who works compulsively.

work'horse', n. 1. horse used for heavy labor. 2. person who works tirelessly.

work'house', n. penal institution for minor offenders.

working class, n. 1. persons working for wages, esp. in manual labor. 2. social or economic class composed of these workers.

work'man, n., pl. -men. worker; laborer. Also, **work'ing•man'**, fem. **work'ing•wom'an**. —**work'man•like'**, adj. —**work'man•ship'**, n.

work'out', n. 1. practice or test to maintain or determine physical ability or endurance. 2. structured regime of physical exercise.

work'shop', n. place where work is done.

work sta'tion, n. 1. work area for one person, as in office, usu. with electronic equipment. 2. powerful small computer used for graphics-intensive processing.

world, n. 1. earth; globe. 2. particular part of earth. 3. things common to profession, etc.; milieu. 4. humanity. 5. universe. 6. great quantity.

world'ling, n. worldly person.

world'ly, adj., -lier, -liest. 1. secular or earthly. 2. devoted to affairs of this world; sophisticated; shrewd. 3. of this world. —**world'li•ness**, n.

worm, n. 1. small slender creeping animal. 2. something suggesting worm, as screw thread. 3. (pl.) intestinal disorder. —v. 4. move like worm. 5. extract (secret) craftily. 6. free from worms. —**worm'y**, adj.

worm'wood', n. bitter aromatic herb.

worn'-out', adj. 1. exhausted. 2. destroyed by wear.

wor'ry, v., -ried, -rying, n., pl. -ries. —v. 1. make or feel anxious. 2. seize with teeth and shake. —n. 3. anxiety. 4. cause of anxiety. —**wor'ri•er**, n. —**wor'ri•some**, adj.

worse, adj. 1. less good; less favorable. —n. 2. that which is worse. —adv. 3. in worse way. —**wors'en**, v.

wor'ship, n., v., -shiped, -shiping or -shipped, -shipping. —n. 1. homage paid to God. 2. rendering of such homage. —v. 3. render religious reverence to. —**wor'ship•er**, n. —**wor'ship•ful**, adj.

worst, adj. 1. least satisfactory; least well. —n. 2. that which is worst. —adv. 3. in the worst way. —v. 4. defeat.

wor'sted (wŏŏs'tid), n. 1. firmly

twisted wool yarn or thread. **2.** fabric made of it.

wort (wûrt), *n.* malt infusion before fermentation.

worth, *adj.* **1.** good enough to justify. **2.** having value of. —*n.* **3.** excellence; importance. **4.** quantity of specified value. —**worth′less,** *adj.* —**worth′less•ness,** *n.*

worth′while′, *adj.* repaying time and effort spent.

wor′thy, *adj.,* **-thier, -thiest,** *n., pl.* **-thies.** —*adj.* **1.** of adequate worth. **2.** deserving. —*n.* **3.** person of merit. —**wor′thi•ly,** *adv.* —**wor′thi•ness,** *n.*

would, *v.* past of **will** (defs. 8, 9).

would′-be′, *adj.* wishing, pretending, or intended to be.

wound (wōōnd), *n.* **1.** puncture from external violence. —*v.* **2.** inflict wound. **3.** grieve with insult or reproach.

wrack, *n.* ruin.

wraith, *n.* ghost.

wran′gle, *v.,* **-gled, -gling,** *n.* dispute. —**wran′gler,** *n.*

wrap, *v.,* **wrapped** or **wrapt, wrapping,** *n.* —*v.* **1.** enclose; envelop. **2.** wind or fold about. —*n.* **3.** (*often pl.*) outdoor clothes.

wrap′per, *n.* **1.** one that wraps. **2.** Also, **wrapping.** outer cover. **3.** long loose garment.

wrath, *n.* **1.** stern or fierce anger. **2.** vengeance. —**wrath′ful,** *adj.* —**wrath′ful•ly,** *adv.* —**wrath′y,** *adj.*

wreak, *v.* inflict.

wreath, *n.* circular band of leaves, etc.

wreathe, *v.,* **wreathed, wreathing.** encircle with wreath.

wreck, *n.* **1.** anything reduced to ruins. **2.** destruction. —*v.* **3.** cause or suffer wreck. —**wreck′age,** *n.* —**wreck′er,** *n.*

wren, *n.* small active bird.

wrench, *v.* **1.** twist forcibly. **2.** injure by wrenching. —*n.* **3.** wrenching

movement. **4.** tool for turning bolts, etc.

wrest, *v.* **1.** twist violently. **2.** get by effort. —*n.* **3.** twist; wrench.

wres′tle, *v.,* **-tled, -tling,** —*v.* **1.** contend with by trying to force other person down. —*n.* **2.** this sport. **3.** struggle. —**wres′tler,** *n.*

wretch, *n.* **1.** pitiable person. **2.** scoundrel.

wretch′ed, *adj.* **1.** pitiable. **2.** despicable. **3.** pitiful. —**wretch′ed•ly,** *adv.* —**wretch′ed•ness,** *n.*

wrig′gle, *v.,* **-gled, -gling,** *n.* wiggle; squirm. —**wrig′gler,** *n.* —**wrig′gly,** *adj.*

wright, *n.* worker who builds.

wring, *v.,* **wrung, wringing,** *n.* —*v.* **1.** twist or compress. **2.** expel by wringing. —*n.* **3.** twist or squeeze. —**wring′er,** *n.*

wrin′kle, *v.,* **-kled, -kling.** —*n.* **1.** ridge or furrow. —*v.* **2.** form wrinkles in. —**wrin′kly,** *adj.*

wrist, *n.* joint between hand and arm.

writ, *n.* **1.** formal legal order. **2.** writing.

write, *v.,* **wrote, written, writing. 1.** form (letters, etc.) by hand. **2.** express in writing. **3.** produce as author or composer. —**writ′er,** *n.*

writhe, *v.,* **writhed, writhing,** —*v.* **1.** twist, as in pain. —*n.* **2.** writhing movement. —**writh′er,** *n.*

wrong, *adj.* **1.** not right or good. **2.** deviating from truth or fact. **3.** not suitable. **4.** under or inner (side). —*n.* **5.** evil; injury; error. —*v.* **6.** do wrong to. **7.** misjudge. —**wrong′do′er,** *n.* —**wrong′do′ing,** *n.* —**wrong′ful,** *adj.* —**wrong′ly,** *adv.*

wroth (rôth), *adj.* angry.

wrought, *adj.* **1.** worked. **2.** shaped by beating.

wrought′-up′, *adj.* perturbed.

wry, *adj.,* **wrier, wriest. 1.** twisted; distorted. **2.** ironic. —**wry′ly,** *adv.* —**wry′ness,** *n.*

XYZ

X, x, *n.* **1.** twenty-fourth letter of English alphabet. **2.** those less than 17 years old not admitted: motion-picture classification.

xan′thic (zan′thik), *adj.* yellow.

xen•o•pho′bi•a (zen′ə fō′bē ə, zē′nə-), *n.* fear or hatred of foreigners or strangers or of anything foreign or strange. —**xen′o•pho′bic,** *adj.*

xe•rog′ra•phy (zi rog′rə fē), *n.* copying process in which resins are fused

to paper electrically. —**xe′ro•graph′ic,** *adj.*

Xe′rox (zēr′oks), *n.* **1.** *Trademark.* brand name for copying machine using xerography. **2.** (*l.c.*) copy made on Xerox. —*v.* **3.** (*l.c.*) print or reproduce by Xerox.

Xmas, *n.* Christmas.

x′-ray′, *n.* **1.** highly penetrating type of electromagnetic ray, used esp. in medicine. —v. 2. photograph or treat with x-rays.

xy′lem (zī′lem), n. woody tissue of plants.

xy′lo·phone′, n. musical instrument of wooden bars, played with small hammers. —**xy′lo·phon′ist**, n.

Y, y, n. twenty-fifth letter of English alphabet.

yacht, n. pleasure ship. —**yacht′ing**, n. —**yachts′man**, n.

ya′hoo, n. coarse stupid person.

yak, n., v. **yakked, yakking.** —n. 1. long-haired Tibetan ox. 2. Slang. incessant idle or gossipy talk. —v. 3. Slang. gab; chatter.

yam, n. edible potatolike root.

yam′mer, v. Informal. whine or chatter.

yank, v. 1. pull suddenly; jerk. —n. 2. sudden pull; jerk.

Yan′kee, n. native or inhabitant of the United States, northern U.S., or New England.

yap, v., **yapped, yapping,** n. yelp.

yard, n. 1. linear unit (3 feet). 2. long spar. 3. enclosed outdoor area, used as a lawn, etc.

yard′age, n. amount in yards.

yard′stick′, n. 1. measuring stick one yard long. 2. criterion.

yar′mul·ke (yär′mäl kə, -mə-, yä′-), n. cap worn by Jewish males, esp. during prayer.

yarn, n. 1. many-stranded thread. 2. story.

yaw, v. 1. deviate. —n. 2. deviation.

yawl, n. small sailboat.

yawn, v. 1. open mouth wide involuntarily, as from sleepiness or boredom. —n. 2. act of yawning.

yawp, v., n. Informal. bawl.

yaws (yôz), n. infectious tropical disease characterized by raspberrylike eruptions of skin.

ye, pron. Archaic. 1. you. 2. the.

yea, adv., n. yes.

year, n. period of 365 or 366 days. —**year′ly,** adv., adj.

year′book′, n. 1. book published annually with information on past year. 2. commemorative book published as by graduating class.

year′ling, n. animal in its second year.

yearn, v. desire strongly. —**yearn′ing,** adj.

year′-round′, adj. 1. continuing, available, or used throughout the year. —adv. 2. throughout the year.

yeast, n. yellowish substance, used to leaven bread, ferment liquor, etc.

yell, v. shout loudly.

yel′low, n. 1. color of butter, lemons, etc. —adj. 2. of like yellow. 3. Slang. cowardly. —**yel′low·ish,** adj.

yellow fever, infectious tropical disease transmitted by certain mosquitoes. Also, **yellow jack.**

yellow jacket, yellow and black wasp.

yelp, v. 1. give sharp, shrill cry. —n. 2. such cry.

yen, n. Informal. desire.

yeo′man, n. 1. petty officer in navy. 2. independent farmer.

yes, adv., n. expression of affirmation or assent.

yes·ter·day, adv., n. day before today.

yet, adv. 1. so far; up to this (or that) time. 2. moreover. 3. still. 4. nevertheless. —conj. 5. but.

yew, n. evergreen coniferous tree.

Yid′dish, n. German-based Jewish language.

yield, v. 1. produce; give. 2. surrender. —n. 3. that which is yielded; product. —**yield′er,** n.

yip, v., **yipped, yipping.** Informal. bark sharply.

yo′del, v., **-eled, -eling.** 1. sing with quick changes to and from falsetto. 2. song yodeled.

yo′gi (-gē), n. Hindu practicing asceticism (**yo′ga**).

yo′gurt (-gərt), n. curdled milk product. Also, **yo′ghurt.**

yoke, n., v. **yoked, yoking.** —n. 1. piece put across necks of oxen pulling cart, etc. 2. pair. —v. 3. couple with, or place in, yoke.

yo′kel, n. rustic.

yolk (yōk), n. yellow part of egg.

yon′der, adj., adv. Archaic. over there. Also, **yon.**

yore, n. time past.

you, pron. person or persons addressed.

young, adj. 1. in early stages of life, operation, etc. 2. of youth. —n. 3. young persons. 4. young offspring. —**young′ish,** adj.

young′ster, n. child.

your, pron., adj. possessive of **you;** (without noun following) **yours.**

you′re, contraction of **you are.**

your·self′, pron. emphatic or reflexive form of **you.**

youth, n. 1. young state. 2. early life. 3. young person or persons. —**youth′-ful,** adj. —**youth′ful·ly,** adv. —**youth′ful·ness,** n.

yowl, v., n. howl.

yo′-yo, n., pl. **-yos,** v., **-yoed, -yoing.** —n. 1. spoollike toy spun out and reeled in by string looped on finger. —v. 2. move up and down or back and forth; fluctuate.

yu•an' (yōō än'), *n.* Taiwanese dollar.

yuc'ca, *n.* tropical American plant.

yuck, *interj. Slang.* (exclamation of disgust or repugnance). **—yuck'y,** *adj.*

yule, *n.* Christmas.

yule'tide', *n.* Christmas season.

yum'my, *adj.,* **-mier, -miest.** very pleasing, esp. to taste.

yup'pie, *n.* young, ambitious, and affluent professional who lives in or near a city. Also, **yup'py.**

Z, z, *n.* twenty-sixth letter of English alphabet.

za'ny, *n., pl.* **-nies,** *adj.* **-nier, -niest.** **—1.** clown. **—adj. 2.** silly. **—za'ni•ness,** *n.*

zap, *v.,* **zapped, zapping.** *Slang.* kill or defeat.

zeal, *n.* intense ardor or eagerness. **—zeal'ous** (zel'-), *adj.* **—zeal'ous•ly,** *adv.* **—zeal'ous•ness,** *n.*

zeal'ot (zel'-), *n.* excessively zealous person. **—zeal'ot•ry,** *n.*

ze'bra, *n.* wild, striped horselike animal.

Zen, *n.* Buddhist movement emphasizing enlightenment by meditation and direct, intuitive insight. Also, **Zen Buddhism.**

ze'nith, *n.* **1.** celestial point directly overhead. **2.** highest point or state.

zeph'yr, *n.* mild breeze.

zep'pe•lin, *n.* large dirigible of early 20th century.

ze'ro, *n., pl.* **-ros, -roes. 1.** symbol (0) indicating nonquantity. **2.** nothing. **3.** starting point of a scale.

zero hour, starting time.

zest, *n.* something adding flavor, interest, etc. **—zest'ful,** *adj.* **—zest'ful•ly,** *adv.* **—zest'ful•ness,** *n.* **—zest'less,** *adj.*

zig'zag', *n., adj., adv., v.,* **-zagged, -zagging.** **—n. 1.** line going sharply from side to side. **—adj., adv. 2.** with sharp turns back and forth. **—v. 3.** go in zigzag.

zilch, *n. Slang.* zero; nothing.

zinc, *n.* bluish metallic element. **—zinc'ous,** *adj.*

zinc oxide, salve made of zinc and oxygen.

zing, *n.* **1.** sharp singing sound. **—v. 2.** make such sound. **—interj. 3.** (descriptive of such sound.)

zin'ni•a, *n.* bright, full-flowered plant.

Zi'on•ism', *n.* advocacy of Jewish establishment of state of Israel. **—Zi'on•ist,** *n., adj.*

zip, *v.,* **zipped, zipping.** *Informal.* **—v. 1.** go very speedily. **—n. 2.** energy.

Zip code, code numbers used with address to expedite mail.

zip'per, *n.* fastener with interlocking edges.

zip'py, *adj.,* **-pier, -piest.** *Informal.* lively; smart.

zir'con, *n.* mineral used as gem when transparent.

zit, *n. Slang.* pimple.

zith'er, *n.* stringed musical instrument. Also, **zith'ern.**

zi'ti (zē'tē), *n.* short, tubular pasta.

zo'di•ac', *n.* imaginary belt of heavens containing paths of all major planets, divided into twelve constellations. **—zo•di'a•cal** (-dī'ə kəl), *adj.*

zom'bie, *n.* reanimated corpse.

zone, *n., v.,* **zoned, zoning.** **—n. 1.** special area, strip, etc. **—v. 2.** mark or divide into zones. **—zon'al,** *adj.*

zoo, *n.* place where live animals are exhibited. Also, **zoological garden.**

zo•ol'o•gy, *n.* scientific study of animals. **—zo'o•log'i•cal,** *adj.* **—zo•ol'o•gist,** *n.*

zoom, *v.* speed sharply.

zoom lens, camera lens allowing continual change of magnification without loss of focus.

zo'o•pho'bi•a (zō'ə-), *n.* fear of animals.

zo'o•phyte' (-fīt'), *n.* plantlike animal, as coral.

zuc•chi'ni (zōō kē'nē), *n.* cucumber-shaped squash.

zwie'back' (swē'bak'), *n.* kind of dried, twice-baked bread.

zy'gote (zī'gōt), *n.* cell produced by union of two gametes. **—zy•got'ic,** *adj.*

Nations of the World

Nation	Population	Area (sq. mi.)	Capital
Afghanistan	15,810,000	252,000	Kabul
Albania	3,080,000	10,632	Tirana
Algeria	23,850,000	919,352	Algiers
Angola	9,390,000	481,226	Luanda
Argentina	31,060,000	1,084,120	Buenos Aires
Armenia	3,283,000	11,490	Yerevan
Australia	16,250,000	2,974,581	Canberra
Austria	7,555,000	32,381	Vienna
Azerbaijan	7,029,000	33,430	Baku
Bahamas	236,000	5,353	Nassau
Bahrain	486,000	266	Manama
Bangladesh	104,100,000	54,501	Dhaka
Barbados	254,000	166	Bridgetown
Belarus	10,200,000	80,154	Minsk
Belgium	9,813,000	11,800	Brussels
Belize	193,000	8,866	Belmopan
Benin	4,440,000	44,290	Porto Novo
Bhutan	1,400,000	19,300	Thimphu
Bolivia	7,000,000	404,388	La Paz
Bosnia and Herzegovina	4,360,000	19,741	Sarajevo
Botswana	1,210,000	275,000	Gaborone
Brazil	155,560,000	3,286,170	Brasilia
Brunei	241,400	2,226	Bandar Seri Begawa
Bulgaria	8,761,000	42,800	Sofia
Burkina Faso	8,530,000	106,111	Ouagadougou
Burundi	5,130,000	10,747	Bujumbura
Cambodia	6,230,000	69,866	Phnom Penh
Cameroon	11,000,000	179,558	Yaoundé
Canada	25,354,000	3,690,410	Ottawa
Cape Verde	360,000	1,557	Praia
Central African Republic	2,759,000	238,000	Bangui
Chad	5,400,000	501,000	N'Djamena
Chile	12,680,000	286,396	Santiago
China	1,133,683,000	3,691,502	Beijing
Colombia	27,900,000	439,828	Bogotá
Comoros	434,166	719	Moroni

Nation	Population	Area (sq. mi.)	Capital
Congo	2,270,000	132,000	Brazzaville
Costa Rica	2,810,000	19,238	San José
Croatia	4,660,000	21,835	Zagreb
Cuba	10,240,000	44,200	Havana
Cyprus	680,000	3,572	Nicosia
Czech Republic	10,343,000	30,449	Prague
Denmark	5,130,000	16,576	Copenhagen
Djibouti	484,000	8,960	Djibouti
Dominica	94,000	290	Roseau
Dominican Republic	6,700,000	19,129	Santo Domingo
Ecuador	9,640,000	109,483	Quito
Egypt	49,280,000	386,198	Cairo
El Salvador	5,480,000	13,176	San Salvador
Equatorial Guinea	400,000	10,824	Malabo
Eritrea	3,200,000	47,076	Asmara
Estonia	1,573,000	17,413	Tallinn
Ethiopia	42,800,000	424,724	Addis Ababa
Fiji	715,000	7,078	Suva
Finland	4,940,000	130,119	Helsinki
France	56,560,000	212,736	Paris
Gabon	1,220,000	102,290	Libreville
Gambia	788,000	4,003	Banjul
Georgia	5,449,000	26,872	Tbilisi
Germany	78,420,000	137,852	Berlin
Ghana	13,800,000	91,843	Accra
Greece	9,990,000	50,147	Athens
Grenada	108,000	133	St. George's
Guatemala	8,990,000	42,042	Guatemala City
Guinea	6,530,000	96,900	Conakry
Guinea-Bissau	932,000	13,948	Bissau
Guyana	812,000	82,978	Georgetown
Haiti	5,300,000	10,714	Port-au-Prince
Honduras	4,300,000	43,277	Tegucigalpa
Hungary	10,604,000	35,926	Budapest
Iceland	247,357	39,709	Reykjavik
India	844,000,000	1,246,880	New Delhi
Indonesia	172,000,000	741,100	Jakarta

Nation	Population	Area (sq. mi.)	Capital
Iran	53,920,000	635,000	Tehran
Iraq	17,060,000	172,000	Baghdad
Ireland	3,540,000	27,136	Dublin
Israel	4,440,000	7,984	Jerusalem
Italy	57,400,000	116,294	Rome
Ivory Coast	11,630,000	127,520	Abidjan
Jamaica	2,300,000	4,413	Kingston
Japan	122,260,000	141,529	Tokyo
Jordan	2,970,000	37,264	Amman
Kazakhstan	16,538,000	1,049,155	Alma-Ata
Kenya	22,800,000	223,478	Nairobi
Kuwait	1,960,000	8,000	Kuwait
Kyrgyzstan	4,291,000	76,460	Bishkek
Laos	3,830,000	91,500	Vientiane
Latvia	2,681,000	25,395	Riga
Lebanon	3,500,000	3,927	Beirut
Lesotho	1,670,000	11,716	Maseru
Liberia	2,440,000	43,000	Monrovia
Libya	3,960,000	679,400	Tripoli
Liechtenstein	27,700	65	Vaduz
Lithuania	3,690,000	25,174	Vilnius
Luxembourg	377,100	999	Luxembourg
Macedonia	2,040,000	9,928	Skopje
Madagascar	10,919,000	226,657	Antananarivo
Malawi	7,059,000	49,177	Lilongwe
Malaysia	16,968,000	127,317	Kuala Lumpur
Maldives	214,139	115	Malé
Mali	9,092,000	478,841	Bamako
Malta	354,900	122	Valletta
Marshall Islands	50,000	70	Majuro
Mauritania	1,894,000	398,000	Nouakchott
Mauritius	1,075,000	788	Port Louis
Mexico	82,700,000	756,198	Mexico City
Micronesia	108,600	271	Kolonia
Moldova	4,341,000	13,100	Kishinev
Monaco	29,900	½	Monaco
Mongolia	2,001,000	600,000	Ulan Bator
Morocco	23,000,000	172,104	Rabat

Nation	Population	Area (sq. mi.)	Capital
Mozambique	14,900,000	297,731	Maputo
Myanmar (Burma)	42,600,000	261,789	Yangon
Nepal	16,630,000	54,000	Katmandu
Netherlands	14,715,000	16,163	Amsterdam
New Zealand	3,307,084	103,416	Wellington
Nicaragua	3,500,000	57,143	Managua
Niger	7,190,000	458,976	Niamey
Nigeria	88,500,000	356,669	Abuja
North Korea	21,890,000	50,000	Pyongyang
Norway	4,200,000	124,555	Oslo
Oman	1,200,000	82,800	Muscat
Pakistan	102,200,000	310,403	Islamabad
Panama	2,320,000	28,575	Panama City
Papua New Guinea	3,400,000	178,260	Port Moresby
Paraguay	4,010,000	157,047	Asunción
Peru	21,300,000	496,222	Lima
Philippines	60,477,000	114,830	Manila
Poland	37,800,000	121,000	Warsaw
Portugal	10,290,000	35,414	Lisbon
Qatar	371,863	8,500	Doha
Romania	22,823,000	91,654	Bucharest
Russian Federation	147,386,000	6,593,000	Moscow
Rwanda	6,710,000	10,169	Kigali
St. Kitts-Nevis	44,400	104	Basseterre
St. Lucia	146,000	238	Castries
St. Vincent and the Grenadines	112,614	150	Kingstown
San Marino	22,750	24	San Marino
São Tomé and Principe	115,600	387	São Tomé
Saudi Arabia	12,566,000	830,000	Riyadh
Senegal	6,980,000	76,084	Dakar
Seychelles	67,000	175	Victoria
Sierra Leone	3,880,000	27,925	Freetown
Singapore	2,610,000	240	Singapore
Slovakia	5,297,000	18,932	Bratislava

Nations of the World (Continued)

Nation	Population	Area (sq. mi.)	Capital
Slovenia	1,930,000	7,819	Ljubljana
Solomon Islands	285,796	11,458	Honiara
Somalia	6,260,000	246,198	Mogadishu
South Africa	29,600,000	472,000	Pretoria & Cape Town
South Korea	42,082,000	38,232	Seoul
Spain	39,000,000	194,988	Madrid
Sri Lanka	16,600,000	25,332	Colombo
Sudan	25,560,000	967,500	Khartoum
Suriname	415,000	63,251	Paramaribo
Swaziland	676,000	6,704	Mbabane
Sweden	8,414,000	173,394	Stockholm
Switzerland	6,620,000	15,944	Bern
Syria	11,400,000	71,227	Damascus
Tajikistan	5,112,000	55,240	Dushanbe
Tanzania	23,200,000	363,950	Dodoma
Thailand	53,900,000	198,242	Bangkok
Togo	3,246,000	21,830	Lomé
Trinidad and Tobago	1,243,000	1,980	Port-of-Spain
Tunisia	7,320,000	48,330	Tunis
Turkey	50,664,000	300,948	Ankara
Turkmenistan	3,534,000	188,417	Ashkhabad
Uganda	15,500,000	91,343	Kampala
Ukraine	51,704,000	233,090	Kiev
United Arab Emirates	1,600,000	32,300	Abu Dhabi
United Kingdom	53,917,000	94,242	London
United States	248,710,000	3,615,122	Washington, D.C.
Uruguay	3,080,000	172,172	Montevideo
Uzbekistan	19,906,000	172,741	Tashkent
Vanuatu	149,400	5,700	Vila
Venezuela	18,770,000	352,143	Caracas
Vietnam	64,000,000	126,104	Hanoi
Western Samoa	163,000	1,133	Apia
Yemen	12,000,000	207,000	Sanaa
Yugoslavia	10,392,000	39,449	Belgrade
Zaire	32,560,000	905,063	Kinshasa

Nation	Population	Area (sq. mi.)	Capital
Zambia	7,384,000	290,585	Lusaka
Zimbabwe	9,174,000	150,804	Harare

Great Oceans and Seas of the World

Ocean or Sea	Area		Location
	sq. mi.	sq. km	
Pacific Ocean	70,000,000	181,300,000	Bounded by N and S America, Asia, and Australia
Atlantic Ocean	31,530,000	81,663,000	Bounded by N and S America, Europe, and Africa
Indian Ocean	28,357,000	73,444,630	S of Asia, E of Africa, and W of Australia
Arctic Ocean	5,540,000	14,350,000	N of North America, Asia, and the Arctic Circle
Mediterranean Sea	1,145,000	2,965,550	Between Europe, Africa, and Asia
South China Sea	895,000	2,318,050	Part of N Pacific, off coast of SE Asia
Bering Sea	878,000	2,274,000	Part of N Pacific, between N America and N Asia
Caribbean Sea	750,000	1,943,000	Between Central America, West Indies, and S America
Gulf of Mexico	700,000	1,813,000	Arm of N Atlantic, off SE coast of North America
Sea of Okhotsk	582,000	1,507,380	Arm of N Pacific, off E coast of Asia

Great Oceans and Seas of the World (Continued)

Ocean or Sea	Area sq. mi.	Area sq. km	Location
East China Sea	480,000	1,243,200	Part of N Pacific, off E coast of Asia
Yellow Sea	480,000	1,243,200	Part of N Pacific, off E coast of Asia
Sea of Japan	405,000	1,048,950	Arm of N Pacific, between Asia mainland and Japanese Isles
Hudson Bay	400,000	1,036,000	N North America
Andaman Sea	300,000	777,000	Part of Bay of Bengal (Indian Ocean), off S coast of Asia
North Sea	201,000	520,600	Arm of N Atlantic, off coast of NW Europe
Red Sea	170,000	440,300	Arm of Indian Ocean, between N Africa and Arabian Peninsula
Black Sea	164,000	424,760	SE Europe-SW Asia
Baltic Sea	160,000	414,000	N Europe
Persian Gulf	92,200	238,800	Between Iran and Arabian Peninsula
Gulf of St. Lawrence	92,000	238,280	Arm of N Atlantic, between mainland of SE Canada and Newfoundland
Gulf of California	62,600	162,100	Arm of N Pacific, between W coast of Mexico and peninsula of Lower California

Continents

Name	Area in Sq. Mi.	Population
Asia	17,000,000	2,405,000,000
Africa	11,700,000	455,000,000
North America	9,400,000	370,000,000
South America	6,900,000	238,000,000
Antarctica	5,100,000	—
Europe	4,063,000	650,600,000
Australia	2,966,000	14,289,000

Notable Mountain Peaks of the World

		Altitude	
Name	Country or Region	ft.	m
Mt. Everest	Nepal-Tibet	29,028	8848
K2	Kashmir	28,250	8611
Kanchenjunga	Nepal-Sikkim	28,146	8579
Makalu	Nepal-Tibet	27,790	8470
Dhaulagiri	Nepal	26,826	8180
Nanga Parbat	Kashmir	26,660	8125
Annapurna	Nepal	26,503	8078
Gasherbrum	Kashmir	26,470	8068
Gosainthan	Tibet	26,291	8013
Nanda Devi	India	25,661	7820
Tirich Mir	Pakistan	25,230	7690
Muztagh Ata	China	24,757	7546
Communism Peak	Tajikistan	24,590	7495
Pobeda Peak	Kyrgyzstan-China	24,406	7439
Lenin Peak	Kyrgyzstan-Tajikistan	23,382	7127
Aconcagua	Argentina	22,834	6960
Huascarán	Peru	22,205	6768
Illimani	Bolivia	21,188	6458
Chimborazo	Ecuador	20,702	6310
Mt. McKinley	United States (Alaska)	20,320	6194
Mt. Logan	Canada (Yukon)	19,850	6050
Cotopaxi	Ecuador	19,498	5943
Kilimanjaro	Tanzania	19,321	5889
El Misti	Peru	19,200	5880
Demavend	Iran	18,606	5671

Notable Mountain Peaks of the World *(Continued)*

Name	Country or Region	Altitude ft.	m
Orizaba (Citlaltepetl)	Mexico	18,546	5653
Mt. Elbrus	Russian Federation	18,465	5628
Popocatépetl	Mexico	17,887	5450
Ixtaccíhuatl	Mexico	17,342	5286
Mt. Kenya	Kenya	17,040	5194
Ararat	Turkey	16,945	5165
Mt. Ngaliema (Mt. Stanley)	Zaire-Uganda	16,790	5119
Mont Blanc	France	15,781	4810
Mt. Wilhelm	Papua New Guinea	15,400	4694
Monte Rosa	Italy-Switzerland	15,217	4638
Mt. Kirkpatrick	Antarctica	14,855	4528
Weisshorn	Switzerland	14,804	4512
Matterhorn	Switzerland	14,780	4505
Mt. Whitney	United States (California)	14,495	4418
Mt. Elbert	United States (Colorado)	14,431	4399
Mt. Rainier	United States (Washington)	14,408	4392
Longs Peak	United States (Colorado)	14,255	4345
Mt. Shasta	United States (California)	14,161	4315
Pikes Peak	United States (Colorado)	14,108	4300
Mauna Kea	United States (Hawaii)	13,784	4201
Grand Teton	United States (Wyoming)	13,766	4196
Mauna Loa	United States (Hawaii)	13,680	4170
Jungfrau	Switzerland	13,668	4166
Mt. Victoria	Papua New Guinea	13,240	4036
Mt. Erebus	Antarctica	13,202	4024
Eiger	Switzerland	13,025	3970
Mt. Robson	Canada (B.C.)	12,972	3954
Mt. Fuji	Japan	12,395	3778
Mt. Cook	New Zealand	12,349	3764
Mt. Hood	United States (Oregon)	11,253	3430
Mt. Etna	Italy	10,758	3280

World Time Differences†

Amsterdam	6:00 P.M.	Manila	1:00 A.M.*
Athens	7:00 P.M.	Mexico City	11:00 A.M.
Bangkok	12:00 Mid.	Montreal	12:00 Noon
Berlin	6:00 P.M.	Moscow	8:00 P.M.
Bombay	10:30 P.M.	Paris	6:00 P.M.
Brussels	6:00 P.M.	Prague	6:00 P.M.
Buenos Aires	2:00 P.M.	Rio de Janeiro	2:00 P.M.
Cape Town	7:00 P.M.	Rome	6:00 P.M.
Dublin	5:00 P.M.	Shanghai	1:00 A.M.*
Havana	12:00 Noon	Stockholm	6:00 P.M.
Honolulu	7:00 A.M.	Sydney (N.S.W.)	3:00 A.M.*
Istanbul	7:00 P.M.	Tokyo	2:00 A.M.*
Lima	12:00 Noon	Vienna	6:00 P.M.
London	5:00 P.M.	Warsaw	6:00 P.M.
Madrid	6:00 P.M.	Zurich	6:00 P.M.

†at 12:00 noon Eastern Standard Time
*morning of the following day

U. S. Time Differences†

Atlanta	12:00 Noon	Memphis	11:00 A.M.
Baltimore	12:00 Noon	Miami	12:00 Noon
Boston	12:00 Noon	Milwaukee	11:00 A.M.
Buffalo	12:00 Noon	Minneapolis	11:00 A.M.
Chicago	11:00 A.M.	Nashville	11:00 A.M.
Cincinnati	12:00 Noon	New York	12:00 Noon
Cleveland	12:00 Noon	New Orleans	11:00 A.M.
Columbus	12:00 Noon	Omaha	11:00 A.M.
Dallas	11:00 A.M.	Philadelphia	12:00 Noon
Denver	10:00 A.M.	Phoenix	10:00 A.M.
Des moines	11:00 A.M.	Pittsburgh	12:00 Noon
Detroit	12:00 Noon	Salt Lake City	10:00 A.M.
El Paso	10:00 A.M.	San Diego	9:00 A.M.
Houston	11:00 A.M.	San Francisco	9:00 A.M.
Indianapolis	12:00 Noon	Seattle	9:00 A.M.
Kansas City	11:00 A.M.	St. Louis	11:00 A.M.
Los Angeles	9:00 A.M.	Washington, D.C.	12:00 Noon

†at 12:00 noon Eastern Standard Time

Facts About the United States

State	Population (1990)	Area (sq. mi.)	Capital
Alabama	4,040,587	51,609	Montgomery
Alaska	550,403	586,400	Juneau
Arizona	3,665,228	113,909	Phoenix
Arkansas	2,350,725	53,103	Little Rock
California	29,760,021	158,693	Sacramento
Colorado	3,294,394	104,247	Denver
Connecticut	3,287,116	5,009	Hartford
Delaware	666,168	2,057	Dover
Florida	12,937,926	58,560	Tallahassee
Georgia	6,478,216	58,876	Atlanta
Hawaii	1,108,229	6,424	Honolulu
Idaho	1,006,749	83,557	Boise
Illinois	11,430,602	56,400	Springfield
Indiana	5,544,159	36,291	Indianapolis
Iowa	2,776,755	56,290	Des Moines
Kansas	2,477,574	82,276	Topeka
Kentucky	3,685,296	40,395	Frankfort
Louisiana	4,219,973	48,522	Baton Rouge
Maine	1,227,928	33,215	Augusta
Maryland	4,781,468	10,577	Annapolis
Massachusetts	6,016,425	8,257	Boston
Michigan	9,295,297	58,216	Lansing
Minnesota	4,375,099	84,068	St. Paul
Mississippi	2,573,216	47,716	Jackson
Missouri	5,117,073	69,674	Jefferson City
Montana	799,065	147,138	Helena
Nebraska	1,578,385	77,237	Lincoln
Nevada	1,201,833	110,540	Carson City
New Hampshire	1,109,252	9,304	Concord
New Jersey	7,730,188	7,836	Trenton
New Mexico	1,515,069	121,666	Santa Fe
New York	17,990,455	49,576	Albany
North Carolina	6,628,637	52,586	Raleigh
North Dakota	638,800	70,665	Bismarck
Ohio	10,847,115	41,222	Columbus
Oklahoma	3,145,585	69,919	Oklahoma City

Facts About the United States *(Continued)*

State	Population (1990)	Area (sq. mi.)	Capital
Oregon	2,842,321	96,981	Salem
Pennsylvania	11,881,643	45,333	Harrisburg
Rhode Island	1,003,464	1,214	Providence
South Carolina	3,486,703	31,055	Columbia
South Dakota	696,004	77,047	Pierre
Tennessee	4,877,185	42,246	Nashville
Texas	16,986,510	267,339	Austin
Utah	1,722,850	84,916	Salt Lake City
Vermont	562,758	9,609	Montpelier
Virginia	6,187,358	40,815	Richmond
Washington	4,866,692	68,192	Olympia
West Virginia	1,793,477	24,181	Charleston
Wisconsin	4,891,769	56,154	Madison
Wyoming	453,588	97,914	Cheyenne
Washington, D.C.	606,900	63	—
Total U.S.	248,709,873		

Major Cities of the United States
(1990)

Rank	City, State	Population
1	New York, N.Y.	7,322,564
2	Los Angeles, Calif.	3,485,398
3	Chicago, Ill.	2,783,726
4	Houston, Tex.	1,630,553
5	Philadelphia, Pa.	1,585,577
6	San Diego, Calif.	1,110,549
7	Detroit, Mich.	1,027,974
8	Dallas, Tex.	1,006,877
9	Phoenix, Ariz.	983,403
10	San Antonio, Tex.	935,933
11	San Jose, Calif.	782,248
12	Baltimore, Md.	736,014
13	Indianapolis, Ind.	731,327
14	San Francisco, Calif.	723,959
15	Jacksonville, Fla.	635,230
16	Columbus, Ohio	632,910
17	Milwaukee, Wis.	628,088
18	Memphis, Tenn.	610,337
19	Washington, D.C.	606,900
20	Boston, Mass.	574,283
21	Seattle, Wash.	516,259
22	El Paso, Tex.	515,342
23	Cleveland, Ohio	505,616
24	New Orleans, La.	496,938
25	Nashville-Davidson, Tenn.	488,374
26	Denver, Colo.	467,610
27	Austin, Tex.	465,622
28	Fort Worth, Tex.	447,619
29	Oklahoma City, Okla.	444,719
30	Portland, Oreg.	437,319
31	Kansas City, Mo.	435,146
32	Long Beach, Calif.	429,433
33	Tucson, Ariz.	405,390
34	St. Louis, Mo.	396,685
35	Charlotte, N.C.	395,934
36	Atlanta, Ga.	394,017
37	Virginia Beach, Va.	393,069
38	Albuquerque, N. Mex.	384,736

Rank	City, State	Population
39	Oakland, Calif.	372,242
40	Pittsburgh, Pa.	369,879
41	Sacramento, Calif.	369,365
42	Minneapolis, Minn.	368,383
43	Tulsa, Okla.	367,302
44	Honolulu, Hawaii	365,272
45	Cincinnati, Ohio	364,040
46	Miami, Fla.	358,548
47	Fresno, Calif.	354,202
48	Omaha, Nebr.	335,795
49	Toledo, Ohio	332,943
50	Buffalo, N.Y.	328,123
51	Wichita, Kans.	304,011
52	Santa Ana, Calif.	293,742
53	Mesa, Ariz.	288,091
54	Colorado Springs, Colo.	281,140
55	Tampa, Fla.	280,015
56	Newark, N.J.	275,221
57	St. Paul, Minn.	272,235
58	Louisville, Ky.	269,063
59	Anaheim, Calif.	266,406
60	Birmingham, Ala.	265,968
61	Arlington, Tex.	261,721
62	Norfolk, Va.	261,229
63	Las Vegas, Nev.	258,295
64	Corpus Christi, Tex.	257,453
65	St. Petersburg, Fla.	238,629
66	Rochester, N.Y.	231,636
67	Jersey City, N.J.	228,537
68	Riverside, Calif.	226,505
69	Anchorage, Alaska	226,338
70	Lexington-Fayette, Ky.	225,366
71	Akron, Ohio	223,019
72	Aurora, Colo.	222,103
73	Baton Rouge, La.	219,531
74	Stockton, Calif.	210,943
75	Raleigh, N.C.	207,951
76	Richmond, Va.	203,056

Major Cities of the United States
(1990) *(Continued)*

Rank	City, State	Population
77	Shreveport, La.	198,525
78	Jackson, Miss.	196,637
79	Mobile, Ala.	196,278
80	Des Moines, Iowa	193,187
81	Lincoln, Nebr.	191,972
82	Madison, Wis.	191,262
83	Grand Rapids, Mich.	189,126
84	Yonkers, N.Y.	188,082
85	Hialeah, Fla.	188,004
86	Montgomery, Ala.	187,106
87	Lubbock, Tex.	186,206
88	Greensboro, N.C.	183,521
89	Dayton, Ohio	182,044
90	Huntington Beach, Calif.	181,519
91	Garland, Tex.	180,650
92	Glendale, Calif.	180,038
93	Columbus, Ga.	178,681
94	Spokane, Wash.	177,196
95	Tacoma, Wash.	176,664
96	Little Rock, Ark.	175,795
97	Bakersfield, Calif.	174,820
98	Fremont, Calif.	173,339
99	Fort Wayne, Ind.	173,072
100	Newport News, Va.	170,045
101	Worcester, Mass.	169,759
102	Knoxville, Tenn.	165,121
103	Modesto, Calif.	164,730
104	Orlando, Fla.	164,693
105	San Bernardino, Calif.	164,164
106	Syracuse, N.Y.	163,860
107	Providence, R.I.	160,728
108	Salt Lake City, Utah	159,936
109	Huntsville, Ala.	159,789
110	Amarillo, Tex.	157,615
111	Springfield, Mass.	156,983
112	Irving, Tex.	155,037
113	Chattanooga, Tenn.	152,466
114	Chesapeake, Va.	151,976

Major Cities of the United States
(1990) *(Continued)*

Rank	City, State	Population
115	Kansas City, Kans.	149,767
116	Fort Lauderdale, Fla.	149,377
117	Glendale, Ariz.	148,134
118	Warren, Mich.	144,864
119	Winston-Salem, N.C.	143,485
120	Garden Grove, Calif.	143,050
121	Oxnard, Calif.	142,216
122	Tempe, Ariz.	141,865
123	Bridgeport, Conn.	141,686
124	Paterson, N.J.	140,891
125	Flint, Mich.	140,761
126	Springfield, Mo.	140,494
127	Hartford, Conn.	139,739
128	Rockford, Ill.	139,426
129	Savannah, Ga.	137,560
130	Durham, N.C.	136,611
131	Chula Vista, Calif.	135,163
132	Reno, Nev.	133,850
133	Hampton, Va.	133,793
134	Ontario, Calif.	133,179
135	Torrance, Calif.	133,107
136	Pomona, Calif.	131,723
137	Pasadena, Calif.	131,591
138	New Haven, Conn.	130,474
139	Scottsdale, Ariz.	130,069
140	Plano, Tex.	128,713
141	Oceanside, Calif.	128,398
142	Lansing, Mich.	127,321
143	Lakewood, Colo.	126,481
144	Evansville, Ind.	126,272
145	Boise City, Idaho	125,738
146	Tallahassee, Fla.	124,773
147	Laredo, Tex.	122,899
148	Hollywood, Fla.	121,697
149	Topeka, Kans.	119,883
150	Pasadena, Tex.	119,363
151	Moreno Valley, Calif.	118,779
152	Sterling Heights, Mich.	117,810

Rank	City, State	Population
153	Sunnyvale, Calif.	117,229
154	Gary, Ind.	116,646
155	Beaumont, Tex.	114,323
156	Fullerton, Calif.	114,144
157	Peoria, Ill.	113,504
158	Santa Rosa, Calif.	113,313
159	Eugene, Oreg.	112,669
160	Independence, Mo.	112,301
161	Overland Park, Kans.	111,790
162	Hayward, Calif.	111,498
163	Concord, Calif.	111,348
164	Alexandria, Va.	111,183
165	Orange, Calif.	110,658
166	Santa Clarita, Calif.	110,642
167	Irvine, Calif.	110,330
168	Elizabeth, N.J.	110,002
169	Inglewood, Calif.	109,602
170	Ann Arbor, Mich.	109,592
171	Vallejo, Calif.	109,199
172	Waterbury, Conn.	108,961
173	Salinas, Calif.	108,777
174	Cedar Rapids, Iowa	108,751
175	Erie, Pa.	108,718
176	Escondido, Calif.	108,635
177	Stamford, Conn.	108,056
178	Salem, Oreg.	107,786
179	Abilene, Tex.	106,654
180	Macon, Ga.	106,612
181	El Monte, Calif.	106,209
182	South Bend, Ind.	105,511
183	Springfield, Ill.	105,227
184	Allentown, Pa.	105,090
185	Thousand Oaks, Calif.	104,352
186	Portsmouth, Va.	103,907
187	Waco, Tex.	103,590
188	Lowell, Mass.	103,439
189	Berkeley, Calif.	102,724
190	Mesquite, Tex.	101,484

Major Cities of the United States
(1990) *(Continued)*

Rank	City, State	Population
191	Rancho Cucamonga, Calif.	101,409
192	Albany, N.Y.	101,082
193	Livonia, Mich.	100,850
194	Sioux Falls, S. Dak.	100,814
195	Simi Valley, Calif.	100,217

Distances Between U.S. Cities

	Atlanta	Chicago	Dallas	Denver	Los Angeles	New York	St. Louis	Seattle
	—	592	738	1421	1981	762	516	2354
Boston	946	879	1565	1786	2739	184	1118	2831
Chicago	592	—	857	909	1860	724	251	1748
Cincinnati	377	255	870	1102	1910	613	550	2003
Cleveland	587	307	1080	1216	2054	458	558	2259
Dallas	738	857	—	683	1243	1391	547	2199
Denver	1421	909	683	—	838	1633	781	1074
Detroit	619	247	1045	1156	2052	486	463	1947
El Paso	1293	1249	543	554	702	1902	1033	1373
Kansas City	745	405	452	552	1360	1117	229	1626
Los Angeles	1981	1860	1243	838	—	2624	1589	956
Miami	614	1199	1405	1911	2611	1106	1123	2947
Minneapolis	942	350	860	840	1768	1020	492	1398
New Orleans	427	860	437	1120	1680	1186	609	2608
New York	762	724	1381	1633	2624	—	888	2418
Omaha	1016	424	617	485	1323	1148	394	1533
Philadelphia	667	671	1303	1578	2467	95	841	2647
Pittsburgh	536	461	1318	1349	2157	320	568	2168
St. Louis	516	251	547	781	1589	888	—	1890
San Francisco	2308	1856	1570	956	327	2580	1916	687
Seattle	2354	1748	2199	1074	956	2418	1890	—
Washington, D.C.	547	600	1183	1519	2426	215	719	2562

Presidents of the United States

Name (and party)	Birth State	Born	Term	Died
George Washington (F)	Va.	1732	1789–1797	1799
John Adams (F)	Mass.	1735	1797–1801	1826
Thomas Jefferson (D-R)	Va.	1743	1801–1809	1826
James Madison (D-R)	Va.	1751	1809–1817	1836
James Monroe (D-R)	Va.	1758	1817–1825	1831
John Quincy Adams (D-R)	Mass.	1767	1825–1829	1848
Andrew Jackson (D)	S.C.	1767	1829–1837	1845
Martin Van Buren (D)	N.Y.	1782	1837–1841	1862
William Henry Harrison (W)	Va.	1773	1841–1841	1841
John Tyler (W)	Va.	1790	1841–1845	1862
James Knox Polk (D)	N.C.	1795	1845–1849	1849
Zachary Taylor (W)	Va.	1784	1849–1850	1850
Millard Fillmore (W)	N.Y.	1800	1850–1853	1874
Franklin Pierce (D)	N.H.	1804	1853–1857	1869
James Buchanan (D)	Pa.	1791	1857–1861	1868
Abraham Lincoln (R)	Ky.	1809	1861–1865	1865
Andrew Johnson (R)	N.C.	1808	1865–1869	1875
Ulysses Simpson Grant (R)	Ohio	1822	1869–1877	1885
Rutherford Birchard Hayes (R)	Ohio	1822	1877–1881	1893
James Abram Garfield (R)	Ohio	1831	1881–1881	1881
Chester Alan Arthur (R)	Vt.	1830	1881–1885	1886
Grover Cleveland (D)	N.J.	1837	1885–1889	1908
Benjamin Harrison (R)	Ohio	1833	1889–1893	1901
Grover Cleveland (D)	N.J.	1837	1893–1897	1908
William McKinley (R)	Ohio	1843	1897–1901	1901
Theodore Roosevelt (R)	N.Y.	1858	1901–1909	1919
William Howard Taft (R)	Ohio	1857	1909–1913	1930
Woodrow Wilson (D)	Va.	1856	1913–1921	1924
Warren Gamaliel Harding (R)	Ohio	1865	1921–1923	1923
Calvin Coolidge (R)	Vt.	1872	1923–1929	1933
Herbert Clark Hoover (R)	Iowa	1874	1929–1933	1964
Franklin Delano Roosevelt (D)	N.Y.	1882	1933–1945	1945
Harry S. Truman (D)	Mo.	1884	1945–1953	1972
Dwight D. Eisenhower (R)	Tex.	1890	1953–1961	1969
John Fitzgerald Kennedy (D)	Mass.	1917	1961–1963	1963
Lyndon Baines Johnson (D)	Tex.	1908	1963–1969	1973

Presidents of the United States *(Continued)*

Name (and party)	Birth State	Born	Term	Died
Richard Milhous Nixon (R)	Cal.	1913	1969–1974	1994
Gerald R. Ford (R)	Neb.	1913	1974–1977	
James Earl Carter, Jr. (D)	Ga.	1924	1977–1981	
Ronald Wilson Reagan (R)	Ill.	1911	1981–1989	
George H. W. Bush (R)	Mass.	1924	1989–1993	
William J. Clinton (D)	Ark.	1946	1993–	

F–Federalist; D–Democrat; R–Republican; W–Whig.

Chief American Holidays

New Year's Day	January 1
Martin Luther King Day	January 15[1]
Inauguration Day	January 20
Lincoln's Birthday	February 12
Washington's Birthday	February 22[2]
Good Friday	Friday before Easter
Memorial Day	May 30[3]
Independence Day	July 4
Labor Day	First Monday in September
Columbus Day	October 12[4]
Veterans Day	November 11
Election Day	Tuesday after first Monday in November
Thanksgiving Day	Fourth Thursday in November
Christmas Day	December 25

[1]officially observed on 3rd Monday in January
[2]officially observed on 3rd Monday in February
[3]officially observed on last Monday in May
[4]officially observed on 2nd Monday in October

Planets of the Solar System

	Mean Distance from Sun in Miles	Diameter in Miles	Number of Satellites
Mercury	36,000,000	3,000	0
Venus	67,000,000	7,600	0
Earth	93,000,000	7,900	1
Mars	141,000,000	4,200	2
Jupiter	489,000,000	87,000	16
Saturn	886,000,000	72,000	15
Uranus	1,782,000,000	31,000	5
Neptune	2,793,000,000	33,000	2
Pluto	3,670,000,000	1,900	1

First-Magnitude Stars
(In Order of Brightness)

	Distance in Light-Years*		Distance in Light-Years*
Sirius	8.6	Altair	16
Canopus	700?	Betelgeuse	200
Alpha Centauri	4.3	Aldebaran	60
Vega	26	Spica	200
Capella	50	Pollux	32
Arcturus	40	Antares	400
Rigel	600?	Fomalhaut	24
Procyon	10.4	Deneb	700?
Achernar	70	Regulus	60
Beta Centauri	300	Alpha Crucis	200

*Light-year = 5,880,000,000,000 miles

Weights and Measures

Troy Weight

24 grains = 1 penny-weight

20 pennyweights = 1 ounce

12 ounces = 1 pound

Avoirdupois Weight

$27^{11}/_{32}$ grains = 1 dram

16 drams = 1 ounce

16 ounces = 1 pound

100 pounds = 1 short hundredweight

20 short hundredweight = 1 short ton

Apothecaries' Weight

20 grains = 1 scruple

3 scruples = 1 dram

8 drams = 1 ounce

12 ounces = 1 pound

Linear Measure

12 inches = 1 foot

3 feet = 1 yard

$5^{1}/_2$ yards = 1 rod

40 rods = 1 furlong

8 furlongs (5280 feet) = 1 statute mile

Mariners' Measure

6 feet = 1 fathom

1000 fathoms (approx.) = 1 nautical mile

3 nautical miles = 1 league

Apothecaries' Fluid Measure

60 minims = 1 fluid dram

8 fluid drams = 1 fluid ounce

16 fluid ounces = 1 pint

2 pints = 1 quart

4 quarts = 1 gallon

Square Measure

144 square inches = 1 square foot

9 square feet = 1 square yard

$30^{1}/_4$ square yards = 1 square rod

160 square rods = 1 acre

640 acres = 1 square mile

Cubic Measure

1728 cubic inches = 1 cubic foot

27 cubic feet = 1 cubic yard

Surveyors' Measure

7.92 inches = 1 link

100 links = 1 chain

Liquid Measure

4 gills = 1 pint

2 pints = 1 quart

4 quarts = 1 gallon

$31^{1}/_2$ gallons = 1 barrel

2 barrels = 1 hogshead

Dry Measure

2 pints = 1 quart

8 quarts = 1 peck

4 pecks = 1 bushel

Wood Measure

16 cubic feet = 1 cord foot

8 cord feet = 1 cord

Angular and Circular Measure

60 seconds = 1 minute

60 minutes = 1 degree

90 degrees = 1 right angle

180 degrees = 1 straight angle

360 degrees = 1 circle

Metric System

The metric system is a decimal system of weights and measures, adopted first in France, but now widespread over the world. It is universally used in science, mandatory for use for all purposes in a large number of countries, and permitted for use in most (as in U.S. and Great Britain).

The basic units are the *meter* (39.37 inches) for length, and the *gram* (15.432 grains) for mass or weight.

Derived units are the *liter* (0.908 U.S. dry quart, or 1.0567 U.S. liquid quart) for capacity, being the volume of 1000 grams of water under specified conditions, the *are* (119.6 square yards) for area, being the area of a square 10 meters on a side, and the *stere* (35.315 cubic feet) for volume, being the volume of a cube 1 meter on a side, the term stere being, however, usually restricted to measuring fire wood.

Names for units larger and smaller than the above are formed from the above names by the use of the following prefixes:

kilo	1000	deka	10	centi	0.01
hecto	100	deci	0.1	milli	0.001

To these are often added mega = 1,000,000, myria = 10,000, and micro = 0.000 001. Not all of the possible units are in common use.

In many countries names of old units are applied to roughly similar metric units.

Linear Measure

10 millimeters	= 1 centimeter
10 centimeters	= 1 decimeter
10 decimeters	= 1 meter
10 meters	= 1 dekameter
10 dekameters	= 1 hectometer
10 hectometers	= 1 kilometer

Square Measure

100 sq. millimeters	= 1 sq. centimeter
100 sq. centimeters	= 1 sq. decimeter
100 sq. decimeters	= 1 sq. meter
100 sq. meters	= 1 sq. dekameter
100 sq. dekameters	= 1 sq. hectometer
100 sq. hectometers	= 1 sq. kilometer

Cubic Measure

1000 cu. millimeters = 1 cu. centimeter
1000 cu. centimeters = 1 cu. decimeter
1000 cu. decimeters = 1 cu. meter

Liquid Measure

10 milliliters	= 1 centiliter
10 centiliters	= 1 deciliter
10 deciliters	= 1 liter
10 liters	= 1 dekaliter
10 dekaliters	= 1 hectoliter
10 hectoliters	= 1 kiloliter

Weights

10 milligrams	= 1 centigram
10 centigrams	= 1 decigram
10 decigrams	= 1 gram
10 grams	= 1 dekagram
10 dekagrams	= 1 hectogram
10 hectograms	= 1 kilogram
100 kilograms	= 1 quintal
10 quintals	= 1 ton